THE BIG SMOKE

New Zealand Cities
1840–1920

THE BIG SMOKE

New Zealand Cities
1840–1920

BEN SCHRADER

BRIDGET WILLIAMS BOOKS

First published in 2016 by Bridget Williams Books Ltd, PO Box 12474, Wellington 6144, New Zealand, www.bwb.co.nz

ISBN 9780947492434 (Paperback), ISBN 9780947492441 (EPUB)
ISBN 9780947492458 (KINDLE), ISBN 9780947492465 (PDF)
ISTC A0220160000000FE
DOI http://dx.doi.org/10.7810/9780947492434

Images

Acknowledgements
This book has been published with the support of the Bridget Williams Books Publishing Trust, the Stout Trust (with Friends of the Turnbull Library) and the New Zealand Centre for Sustainable Cities.

Title page image: The smoke of industry settles over the city on a still Wellington day in 1909. The two chimneys at left are part of the destructor, where the city's rubbish was burned. At right is the chimney from the tramway powerhouse. St Gerard's Church surmounts the foremost flank of Mt Victoria. *Walter Jefferson Leslie, Alexander Turnbull Library, C-009-018.*

A catalogue record for this book is available from the National Library of New Zealand.
Kei te pātengi raraunga o Te Puna Mātauranga o Aotearoa te whakarārangi o tēnei pukapuka.

Edited by Jane Parkin
Cover and internal design by Base Two
Typesetting by Tina Delceg
Printed in China through Colorcraft Limited, HK

Contents

Dedicated with much love to my partner Lis Cowey

Acknowledgements

I began this project in 2006 with the idea that it would be published in 2011: the official centenary of New Zealand moving from a rural to an urban society. This seemed like a fitting time to put out a book on New Zealand city life. But I was unable to secure sufficient funding to allow me to meet my goal, so the project was often pushed to the back burner while I earned a living. Things slowed down even further with several health setbacks. I am grateful to the staff at Wellington Hospital for their expert care. There has, however, been an advantage in the book coming out later. New Zealand might have officially become an urban society in 1911, but the census data confirming the change had excluded the (predominantly rural) Māori population. If these people are included in the count, the transition did not actually take place until 1916: 100 years ago. Although this book was too late for the official centenary, its publication marks the more accurate moment of change.

Dozens of people have helped bring *The Big Smoke* to completion. Initial supporters included the literary scholar Lydia Wevers and historians Richard Hill and Caroline Daley, all of whom gave helpful advice in the project's early stages. Two other historians, Jock Phillips and Malcolm McKinnon, have been supportive throughout. Having heard an early talk about the project, Jock suggested I tell a bigger story. I heeded his advice, and the book is better for it. Malcolm is a rare historian in that he is also a geographer. His help in teasing out ideas was invaluable, and he also provided wise counsel during a time of doubt. I was fortunate in the early stages of research to be appointed a co-editor, alongside Malcolm, for the City and Economy theme of *Te Ara: The Encylopedia of New Zealand* (of which Jock was the general editor). Because of a relative lack of New Zealand research on cities, much of what appeared in this theme was new. Some of the *Te Ara* entries originated in ideas I had been exploring; others generated new material that I subsequently developed for this book. So I am thankful to the former *Te Ara* staff and authors who provided new insights into New Zealand city life.

I have been greatly aided by the staff at various archives in the five cities considered in the book. There are too many people to thank individually, but I would like to single out archivists Jill Haley at Toitū Otago Settlers Museum, Ali Clarke at the Hocken Library, Zena Cooper at Christchurch City Archives and Adrian Humphris at Wellington City Archives for alerting me to rich material I would otherwise have missed. Numerous people have helped improve the work by

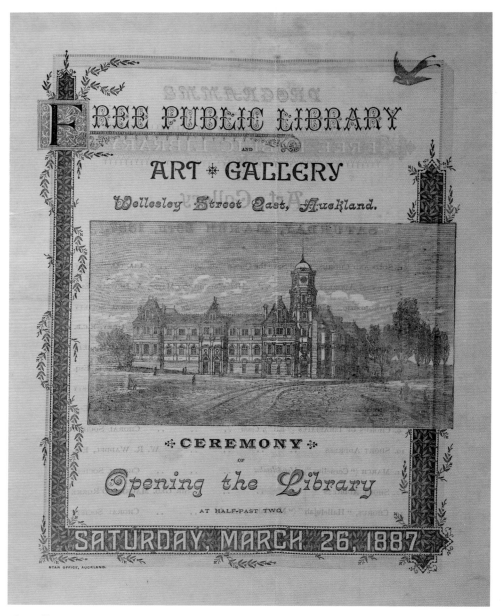

This silk-covered programme was issued to mark the 1887 opening of Auckland's new public library and art gallery in Wellesley Street. The building remains part of Auckland Art Gallery. Sir George Grey Special Collections, Auckland Libraries, Grey Ephemera 2883

reading draft chapters. These include epidemiologist Nick Wilson, who provided helpful comments on Chapter Seven, and members of the History Writers' Group (an informal circle of Wellington historians), who gave crucial feedback on Chapters Four, Six and Eight. I am also thankful to Charlotte Macdonald, Katie Pickles, Bruce Stirling and Melissa Matutina Williams for reading the manuscript and offering pertinent suggestions for final changes.

I am appreciative of two grants that helped me at the beginning and end of the project. In 2006 I was awarded a New Zealand History Trust Award from the Ministry for Culture and Heritage that enabled me to get things up and running; in 2015 I received a grant from the Centre for Sustainable Cities at the University of Otago that allowed me to work full time to finally finish the project. I am very grateful to Philippa Howden-Chapman, who oversees the Centre, for her longstanding interest in and support of this project. It was she who suggested I approach Bridget Williams Books (BWB) about publishing it. I was delighted when Bridget Williams and her editorial board responded positively to the idea. Since then the book has been in the capable hands of Tom Rennie. I have really appreciated his enthusiasm for the project and the way he has guided the manuscript through to publication. I would also like to thank Jane Parkin for her judicious editing and the rest of the publishing team that worked on the book: Neil Pardington, Alice Ferner, Melanie Lovell-Smith, Becky Masters-Ramsay, Kerryn Pollock, Nancy Swarbrick, Barbara Graham and Jane McRae.

Friends and family have provided great moral support. Within my local community of Northland, Wellington, I would like to thank Patrick Smellie, Ruth Nichol, Redmer Yska, Ruth Laugesen, Linley Boniface, Guy Somerset, Sarah Boyd, Graeme Speden, Matthew Everett and Dagmar Hempel for their interest and support. Redmer's expertise on Wellington's history provided some valuable leads and prompted some stimulating discussions. Matthew Grant, Michael Pringle and Bryan Patchett have provided much encouragement, as have Michael Baker, Jeremy Rose and Michael Kelly. My immediate and wider family have been pillars of strength, especially my partner Lis Cowey and our children Fred and Carlo. For a decade the book has been a constant presence in their lives as well as mine; it sometimes seemed a moot point as to whether I would finish before both boys left home. I did.

Of everyone involved in the process, Lis deserves my greatest thanks. Firmly believing in the story's worth, her confidence in the project never wavered despite the periodic setbacks. We share a fascination with cities and have had some great discussions about city life that have helped to shape my thinking on the project. She also made many incisive comments on the text, resulting in improvements. In heartfelt appreciation of her unceasing support, *The Big Smoke* is dedicated to her.

Introduction

The genesis of this book lies in my family. My great-great-grandfather, James Schrader, was born in 1834 to Francis and Esther in Bermondsey, a congested slum beside the Thames.[1] The area was known for its tanning and leather industries (Francis was a leather dresser), and much of London's food was unloaded at its bustling docks.[2] James would have grown up within sight of heaving merchant ships, from all ends of the earth, cutting through the river to and from the world's metropolis. He trained as a bookkeeper and in 1854 married Liverpudlian Mary Jane Povah. A son, Francis, was born in Liverpool in 1855, but two years later Mary Jane died. She was only 19. Perhaps suffering from a broken heart, in 1862 James left his son with Mary Jane's parents and went to London, where he boarded the ship *Bombay* for a new start in New Zealand.[3] After landing in Dunedin, he found work as a post office clerk and became a member of the volunteer fire brigade. By 1868 he had moved to Christchurch, where he continued as a clerk and joined the Canterbury Rifle Volunteers.[4] In 1870, aged 36, he married fellow Londoner Emily Paddy, aged 16, who was heavily pregnant with my great-grandfather, William.

The new family shifted to Wellington where James again worked as a post office clerk and Emily taught students the piano.[5] For unknown reasons James became indebted, and in 1874 he filed for bankruptcy. He was discharged a few months later and the family returned to Christchurch, settling in working-class Sydenham, where James set himself up as an accountant.[6] If he saw this as a step towards middle-class respectability, it was somewhat undone by convictions for public drunkenness and using obscene language.[7] Whether drink was the cause or result of James's troubles is uncertain. He became an alcoholic and died from liver disease in 1883.

This made Emily a widow at age 29, but she soon remarried. Her son William, after attending Christchurch West School, trained as a tailor – fittingly, Schrader means tailor in German. In 1896, he married Elizabeth White and the couple set

OPPOSITE Evelyn Page painted Wellington's Lambton Quay around 1950. This is what it would have looked like when my parents married and my father Warren began working as assistant minister at St Andrew's Church on The Terrace, one block over from Lambton Quay. Evelyn Page, *Lambton Quay* (detail), Museum of New Zealand Te Papa Tongarewa, 2003-0039-1

Four generations of the Jenkins family (including the Schraders) sit on the steps of Elizabeth Jenkins' Tīmaru home during a family gathering in the early 1950s. My parents and older sister (Warren, Nan and Jan) are seated at the front on the right. Private collection

up home in Sydenham too. Elizabeth bore five children, two of whom died as infants. My grandfather, Clarence, was born in 1900. By this time, William was a signalman at Christchurch railway station and Elizabeth a full-time mother and housewife. In 1909 the family moved to Tīmaru, where Clarence attended Timaru Boys' High School before landing a job as a clerk and meeting my grandmother, Mary Jenkins.

Born in Invercargill in 1904, Mary and her brother and two sisters had grown up in the nearby township of Browns, where her parents, Robert and Elizabeth, had run a grocery store. In the early 1920s, the Jenkins moved to Tīmaru, opening a grocery business at the bottom of Stafford Street. Mary worked in the shop and this might have been where she met Clarence. They married in 1925 and my father, Warren, the eldest of four children, was born the following year. By this time, the family had opened a delicatessen halfway down Stafford Street and taken over a tearoom at the top end. In 1938 these businesses were sold and the family built a new, larger tearoom and bakery opposite the deli. Called 'Jenkins', the venue employed about 30 staff, and was renowned for its three-course lunches, high teas and wedding breakfasts. Success enabled Clarence and Mary to buy their own home in nearby Sefton Street.

The passenger William Speer made this sketch of the ship *Bombay* on its 1862 voyage from London to Dunedin. Also on board was my great, great grandfather James Schrader. It seems likely that he came to New Zealand to start a new life following the death of his young wife. The *Bombay* also brought settlers to Auckland; a town to the city's south was subsequently named in the ship's honour. William Henry Speer, Alexander Turnbull Library, E-395-002-1

After finishing Timaru Boys' High School, Warren went to Otago University, where he trained for the Presbyterian ministry. At Otago he met my mother, Nan Thomson, who was finishing a Home Science degree. Her parents, Robert (a marine engineer) and Isabella (a pharmacist), had migrated from Greenock (near Glasgow) to Wellington in the late 1920s, buying a new bungalow in suburban Karori where they raised Nan and her two siblings. Warren married Nan in 1951. He began his career as an assistant minister at St Andrew's Church on The Terrace; moved to a new parish in Awapuni, Palmerston North, in 1958; and went on to become the chaplain at Christchurch's St Andrew's College in 1964. Defying the modern pattern of small families, the couple had eight children (of whom one was stillborn), of which I am the youngest. Nan died soon after I was born in 1964. Warren married Melburnian Margaret Stirling in 1966 and my half-brother was born in 1967. Three years later, the family moved back to Wellington after Warren was appointed to the Wadestown parish. I studied at Onslow College and then Victoria University of Wellington. There I met Lis Cowey, who had recently moved from Christchurch. We married in 1986. Since then we have lived in Auckland, Melbourne and London, but call Wellington home.

I've related this story about my family, my whakapapa, because it illustrates how my family's history has been an *urban* history. From the arrival of Londoner James Schrader in 1862, my forebears have, bar a stint in bucolic Southland, lived in large towns and cities. Their outlooks and sensibilities have been urban rather than rural. Most have pursued typically urban occupations: as clerks, tailors, grocers, restaurateurs and writers. Their businesses have been urban based and attracted an urban clientele, from fresh-faced piano students tickling the ivories to shopping-weary matrons sipping reviving tea. Their homes have not looked out upon pasture or bush but the street and their neighbour's fence. All have lived with the sights, sounds and smells of the people about them.

In piecing together these skeletal details in the early 1990s, I was surprised by my family's city-centric past. My recently completed university studies had stressed the rural character of colonial New Zealand society. The main story I learned was that Pākehā had been attracted to the colony by the opportunity to settle the land (countryside) and pursue what historians called the 'rural myth'. This ideal promoted New Zealand as a nation of farmers and smallholders; the typical settler would buy a parcel of forest or grassland, and then clear, fence and farm it. Alternatively, they could settle in villages and small towns, and provide services – grocery, blacksmithing, stock and station – to those on encircling farms. Within this model, the city's only function was as a market town and port. Real settlers lived on the land.

I found this a little unsettling. My own ties to the land are weak, as are my historical links to it. There is no grand homestead, rustic dairy cottage or even ruined miner's hut that I can return to and say: that's where my forebears worked the soil. I have sometimes thought this a blemish on my citizenship; it seems akin to being a white Australian and having no convict past. But it does not mean I am without a sense of place. In 1992, I went looking for my great-great-grandparents' cottage in Sydenham, only to discover a light-industrial workshop was on the site where it had stood. Yet in walking along the streets James and Emily and their children had once traversed, I felt a strong connection to them and the neighbourhood.

At this point I should acknowledge that the term 'land' has diverse meanings in New Zealand. Legislatively, land is generally treated as a commodity that is owned by an individual or a collective, or (if in the 'public domain') by government. 'Land' also often refers to ground used for farming or an expanse of country rather than the ground in towns and cities. The phrase: 'go onto the land', therefore means to settle in the countryside rather than a town. In Māori society, however, land was traditionally not 'owned', but tribal groups had well-established rights through ancestry (take tupuna), long-standing occupation (ahi kā), conquest (raupatu), or gift exchange (tuku whenua). Māori could therefore not sell their land in the

European sense, but could grant rights to newcomers to use it. Many Māori also see land in terms of its tribal associations rather than its current rural or urban use.

Whereas the historian Michael King and others have situated Pākehā social identities in the land, I have always had a much stronger affinity with towns and cities.[8] I like visiting the countryside and I enjoy tramping, but it is always in the knowledge I will return to the city. I can appreciate the beauty of the snow-clad Southern Alps glistening in the sun, but the vistas that enthral me are city ones: the gradual revealing of Wellington as the motorway leaves the Ngāūranga Gorge; Auckland's towering skyline from the undulating surface of the Waitematā Harbour, or the line of ornate Victorian buildings along Dunedin's Princes Street. In other words, my social identity is grounded more in the streets and lanes of the cities where my forebears and I have lived than in the forests and farms that surround them. I wondered if other Pākehā felt the same way. Of course I knew my family were not the only ones to prefer city life; the rapid growth of Auckland, Wellington, Christchurch and Dunedin underlines this. But it seemed to me that the rise of these cities and those who built them has been underplayed in New Zealand history writing. I wanted to find out what attracted settlers to live in cities; what did those cities look like and how did they change over time; and in what ways did townspeople experience daily city life and spaces? I wondered too whether Pākehā social identities were as much grounded in the city as in the land. Such questions were the catalyst for *The Big Smoke*.

New Zealand urban history: an overview

Unlike in Europe, North America, Australia and elsewhere, urban history has never been sustained as a distinct field of scholarship in New Zealand. This is surprising, considering that since the early twentieth century most New Zealanders have lived in towns and cities – 86 per cent were urban in 2014.[9] Yet we know surprisingly little about these urban dwellers and the spaces in which they lived. Aside from the Caversham Project (discussed further below), New Zealand lacks the substantial studies of urban social relations, suburbia and city cultures that are standard fare in national histories elsewhere. An exception is business history. Since the publication of University of Auckland historian Russell Stone's pioneering *Makers of Fortune* (1973), which examined Auckland's colonial commercial community, urban business histories have been staple fare in historiography.[10] However, those wanting to know about other aspects of urban life usually have to turn to general or survey New Zealand histories. Of these, Keith Sinclair and Wendy Harrex's photographic history *Looking Back* (1978) broke new ground, both in devoting a whole chapter to the topic and in recognising the importance of cities to developing organised culture.[11] Towns and cities are briefly considered in the 1981 and 1992 editions of *The Oxford History*

In the mid-1970s, Otago University historian Erik Olssen began a major historical study of south Dunedin between 1890 and 1940. Known as the Caversham Project, it considerably increased knowledge of townspeople's working and non-working lives in a particular place. This is south Dunedin, the site of the Caversham Project, in the 1880s. For reasons this photograph makes abundantly clear, the area was referred to by locals as 'the flat'.
Hocken Collections, Uare Taoka o Hākena, University of Otago Library, Box-03 Bub 0107, photograph by Burton Brothers

of New Zealand, but barely rate a mention in the new edition of 2007. Philippa Mein Smith's *Concise History of New Zealand* (2005) similarly gives city life scant regard.[12] Atholl Anderson, Judith Binney and Aroha Harris's Māori general history, *Tangata Whenua* (2014), has an understandable emphasis on rural life but also offers new insights into twentieth-century Māori urbanisation. Barbara Brookes's *A History of New Zealand Women* (2016) adeptly considers many aspects of city women's lives, although it arguably understates how cities framed and changed them.[13] The best overview is James Belich's two-volume history, *Making Peoples* (1996) and *Paradise Reforged* (2001). These stand out for the relatively fulsome attention given to towns and cities, and for showing some of the ways they shaped New Zealand life.[14]

Interestingly, it is the public history surveys that provide the broadest and most innovative treatment of the subject. Fifteen of the 100 plates in the *Bateman New Zealand Historical Atlas* (1997) concern cities and urban life.[15] The monograph

These men and women are toiling on the factory floor at Donaghy's Industries in south Dunedin. The lives of working people like these were studied as part of the Caversham Project. Hocken Collections, Uare Taoka o Hākena, University of Otago, AG-202/0424

Frontier of Dreams (2005) also has a strong urban focus, as does *Te Ara*, the New Zealand (online) encyclopedia, with one of its twelve themes examining many aspects of city life.[16] Yet as good as some of these works are, they can only ever provide an overview of the topics concerned, many of which cry out for more in-depth treatment.

It was overseas scholars who first drew attention to the deficit of New Zealand urban history research. In responding to the first edition of *The Oxford History of New Zealand*, the Canadian Graeme Wynn called for more studies on social relations in New Zealand, particularly in its cities, that could be used as a basis for comparative analyses with North American cities.[17] Visiting American historians Clyde and Sally Griffen repeated the call in a 1986 article. As they wrote: '[U]rban social history and urban history in any form has attracted relatively little attention from professional historians. No biographies of the four major cities have yet been attempted.'[18] They framed a research programme for New Zealand urban history that they suggested could form a basis for comparative overseas analysis.

If the Griffens thought their proposed agenda would generate a flurry of new city research, they were mistaken. In the intervening 30 years, little has changed. In the lead-up to the 150th anniversaries of Wellington and Christchurch, scholars produced collections of historical essays on each city, but the Wellington volume had to finish in 1914 due to the lack of twentieth-century research on the city.[19] These works have filled some gaps, but more substantial city biographies are needed, particularly of Auckland.[20] At a regional level there have been some very good town biographies, such as Caroline Daley's 1999 history of Taradale.[21] Other local histories and suburban biographies remain a publishing staple. This perhaps adds weight to Jim (W. J.) Gardner's point that New Zealanders lived their lives at the local level; but for all the merits of these local histories, many lack analytical depth and the authority of histories that consider national issues.[22] Further, local histories and town biographies often fail to address a core urban history concern of seeing towns and cities in comparative perspective. Even when studying a single place or community, urban historians seek to take into account its relations with a broader urban network: regional, national or trans-national.[23]

The Griffens noted that the exception to the lack of New Zealand urban history was the Caversham Project, established in the mid-1970s by University of Otago historian Erik Olssen. It began by examining the South Dunedin working-class suburb of Caversham, but the study area was later widened to surrounding suburbs. Informed by new methodologies of social science (quantitative) history and the 'new labour history', the project was the first major microanalysis of a New Zealand urban community, exploring such issues as spatial and social mobility, workplace social relations and culture, and gender relations between 1890 and 1940.[24] Like similar projects in Boston and elsewhere, the project was 'a way of looking at issues nationally', with Caversham serving as a model from which to make generalisations about the nation.[25]

With the late-twentieth-century cultural turn in scholarship, such approaches were criticised for being reductionist and ignoring difference. Olssen and his team subsequently became more aware of 'the extent to which the study area was distinctive rather than typical'.[26] The intellectual output from the project has been prolific and incisive, considerably enhancing our understanding of South Dunedin.[27] However, in reading this work the urban historian is struck by the way the city often recedes from view, becoming a backdrop for the study of abstract social relations like social class and gender rather than featuring as a protagonist itself. We learn much about social relations at particular sites but less about how the site's material fabric or form framed and mediated them.[28] This issue is not unique to New Zealand. American urban historians like Michael Katz made the distinction between cities as 'sites' for the study of social processes and institutions and cities as 'places' shaped by urban form. He argued that the former gave way to latter in the wake of the 1960s American urban crisis (when ethnic violence and civil disobedience erupted in numerous United States cities), generating studies on how ideas of race influenced spatial forms, for example.[29] However, Timothy Gilfoyle has noted that cities shaped by urban form never supplanted site studies, and new studies on city building often focus on both, 'weaving social and cultural history into the evolution of the built environment'.[30] *The Big Smoke* emulates this hybrid approach.

Erik Olssen joins Russell Stone as a pioneer in New Zealand urban history. Another was David Hamer of Victoria University of Wellington. During the 1970s, his work on the New Zealand Liberals ignited an interest in urban history. In 1979, he wrote an article on New Zealand's nineteenth-century towns that identified many of his subsequent research interests: urban growth and decline; boosterism (place promotion or marketing); and town and country social relations, among others.[31] Responding to Wynn's and the Griffens' call for comparative analyses, he focused on the nineteenth-century history of the Australasian and North American urban frontier. His most important and influential work, *New Towns in the New World* (1990), examined social representations of towns and cities, and the cultural milieu in which they developed.[32] Hamer created the first academic urban history programme at a New Zealand university – and I was a student of his. But when he died in 1999, the momentum he had generated in the sub-field was not sustained. The end of the Caversham Project in the early 2000s was a further blow. Since then, the sub-discipline has withered within academic history.[33] It retains a stronger presence in other disciplines, most notably in architecture and urban design programmes. In examining how architects and urban planners have helped to shape urban built environments, architectural historians like Julia Gatley, Paul Walker and Garth Falconer have pioneered New Zealand city building history.[34] It also persists in the public history realm, in my own work and that of others.[35]

So why hasn't urban history captured the imagination of New Zealand historians in the same way it has in comparable New World or settler societies like Australia, Canada and the United States? I am uncertain, but proffer three suggestions. The first is that New Zealand historians unconsciously absorbed the anti-city bias of mid-twentieth-century nationalist literary culture. As Chapter Eight shows, writers like Rex (A. R. D.) Fairburn endlessly celebrated the naturalness of country life over the artificiality of city life. *Real* New Zealanders, went the nationalist refrain, lived on the land (in the country). Historians have seemingly agreed. The two most influential late-twentieth-century histories of Pākehā society, Jock Phillips's *A Man's Country?* (1987) and Miles Fairburn's *The Ideal Society and its Enemies* (1989), are both rural-centric.[36] The bias has carried to the present, most notably in environmental history. Overseas the sub-field has a strong urban strain, exemplified by William Cronon's environmental history of Chicago and the Mid-West, but in New Zealand it is a surrogate for rural history.[37] This was underscored in a new edition of *Making a New Land: Environmental Histories of New Zealand* (2013), in which just two of the 18 essays consider city environments.[38] It is not the case that New Zealand cities want for subject matter – as Chapter Seven of this book shows, the environment was at the forefront of public-health concerns in cities from the 1850s onward – but rather that most environmental historians have been wedded to the land. Perhaps it's time more of them hung up their muddy gumboots and put on their city brogues.

A second possibility is that many historians have felt poorly equipped to engage in spatial analysis and so have veered away from examining the production and shaping of urban space – the Caversham Project being an obvious exception. It is perhaps not surprising that disciplines with a spatial bent, such as architecture/urban design and geography, have long been at the forefront of New Zealand scholarship on cities. Since the 1950s, university geographers like Kenneth Cumberland, Harvey Franklin, Mary Watson and, more recently, Eric Pawson have employed historical analysis to explain different aspects of New Zealand's urban spatial pattern.[39] In a seminal 2011 article, Tony Ballantyne called for a 'spatial turn' in scholarship, arguing that New Zealand historians needed to take more account of space and place in their research. He pointed out that settler society was anything but settled: as the movements of my own family show, colonists remained mobile after arriving in New Zealand and 'the circulation of people, money, goods, and news was the lifeblood of colonial life'. He urged historians to consider more intensively the role of transport and communications in framing the colonial economy and shaping specific social relations and cultural life in towns and their hinterlands.[40] Historical geographers pioneered such research in the 1960s, and these may be the people with whom historians could best pursue this and related urban history research.[41]

The third, and possibly most compelling, reason is that in a small professional historical community like New Zealand's, there is less room for the diversity of sub-fields that characterises the profession overseas. In recent times, the research interests of most New Zealand historians have simply lain elsewhere. But if Pākehā historians have lost interest in cities and city life, Māori historians like Melissa Matutina Williams have moved in the other direction. Her book *Panguru and the City: Kāinga Tahi, Kāinga Rua* (2014) uses mātauranga Māori (Māori epistemologies) to provide new and fascinating understandings of twentieth-century Māori urban migration experience. Emerging Māori scholars like Erin Keenan are adding to this innovative body of work.[42]

Scope and approach

There were five towns that became cities in colonial New Zealand: Auckland, Wellington, Nelson, Christchurch and Dunedin, all of which were port cities whose economic lifeblood was trade. Nelson might appear as the odd one out, but it was proclaimed a city by letters patent in 1858 because it was a Bishop's seat, and looked set to become a centre of national importance. However, due to a deficient natural harbour, small hinterland and poor access to national communication lines, it never realised this initial promise. In the late 1860s, it went into relative decline and developed as a large town rather than a city. As James Belich writes: 'The Big Five [cities] of the 1860s became the Big Four thereafter.'[43] Thus, while Nelson features at the beginning of this story, it drops out as the narrative enters the late nineteenth century. Nelson's experience illustrates the economic reality that urban growth was heavily reliant on a centre's ability to access and control a fertile and productive hinterland. During our period, the Big Four cities were best able to do this, carving up New Zealand into four spheres of influence and repelling all rivals.[44] That said, the focus of this book is on the cultural and social life of cities and less on their economic development. This was done to contain the project. An economic history of the five cities would be a rewarding exercise, but it was something I felt unable to give due weight to here.

Similarly, my decision to focus on towns that became cities and largely to overlook those that didn't was not to claim a special place for the cities but, again, to keep the project manageable. An urban history of colonial New Zealand is strongly warranted, but it's a herculean task.[45] Although this book makes little reference to settlements outside city limits, it must be acknowledged that the five cities did not exist in a vacuum. They sat at the apex of New Zealand's urban system, beneath which were a regional network of large towns, and a district network of small towns and townships. There were strong economic, social and cultural ties between each tier.[46] For example, the port town of Wanganui (Whanganui) was founded as an offshoot of Wellington in 1840, fostering, in turn, the creation of townships like Turakina and Brunswick. Similarly, Tīmaru began in 1853 as a service hub for South Canterbury and then became a secondary port town to Christchurch. Other towns like Hokitika and Thames were founded during the 1860s gold rushes to service thousands of miners and became relatively large settlements before declining when the boom times ended. These regional or secondary towns experienced many of the same modernising forces and changes that cities experienced. Places like Napier, New Plymouth, Inglewood, Ōamaru and Invercargill built libraries and performance venues; they were visited by Māori and itinerant traders, and attracted crowds to their streets to celebrate and protest events. I hope future historians will examine the place of secondary and tertiary towns within New Zealand's urban network, even if it has not been possible to do so here.

The book covers the period from 1840, when New Zealand's first planned town (Wellington) was founded, to 1920 when, following the end of the First World War, New Zealand emerged as a post-colonial society separate from Britain.[47] It was also the beginning of a decade in which Whanganui, Invercargill and Palmerston North became cities, suburbanisation took off and town-planning legislation came into effect, all signalling a new phase in New Zealand's modernity and hence a good place to stop. Primary sources have been garnered from dozens of manuscripts – letters, diaries and images – held by archives in each of the five cities. Immigration, booster and travel writing, and official reports are also important sources. Newspaper articles from the online Papers Past website have supplemented this material. I have aimed for balanced coverage of each of the cities, but owing to the closure of many Canterbury archives after the 2011 earthquake, Christchurch does not feature as highly as it might.

The Big Smoke is a survey of colonial city life rather than a thorough examination of one aspect of it. A reason for taking this approach is first to provide a stronger sense of the diversity and complexity of city life than can be realised in a micro-study of a particular aspect of it, and, secondly, to open up research. Each chapter concerns a different theme that could readily be a subject of inquiry in its own right. However, the book is not intended to be master-narrative (authoritative) history. There are some areas of city life that are only briefly considered, and a number not at all. Among these is the labour market. The world of paid work was a large component of many townspeople's lives, but this book focuses on the lived experience of their non-working lives. This was done both to contain the project and because the subject has attracted relatively strong attention from labour historians.[48] Religion is another area that framed social relations in cities but is not explored in depth here. Although consideration is given to Māori engagement with city life, other non-European ethnic city groups like the Chinese, Lebanese and Indian communities receive only passing reference. City sub-cultures like the homosexual community, the criminal underworld, and the poor and marginalised are also largely missing from view.[49] Their absence underscores the multifaceted character of colonial city life. As Timothy Gilfoyle reminds us: 'Cities are always in motion, pluralistic, rarely calm, resistant to efforts to logically comprehend their total meaning.'[50] This is what makes studying them so fascinating.

Following overseas trends, recent New Zealand history scholarship has moved away from nationalist approaches to history writing – with its focus on the nation state and nation-building narratives – and stressed the importance of locating New Zealand experience within a trans-national frame. This approach shows how the social, cultural and economic forces operating in New Zealand were part of a wider network that stretched around the globe. Whereas nationalist history writing identifies what was distinctive and even exceptional about a society or nation, trans-national history considers 'shared ties and common features' among different societies, and places them within a global matrix.[51] While this book draws on overseas evidence at appropriate points to illuminate local experience, it is not a trans-national history.[52] In focusing on the five New Zealand cities, however, it might be termed an intra-national (or trans-local) history. This method shares the trans-national aim of uncovering horizontal social connections and patterns between places and spaces, and of challenging notions of exceptionalism. In this way it also follows the urban history approach of situating cities within urban networks to provide a comparative perspective.

As with national histories, city biographies and regional histories often emphasise their subject's distinctiveness. Auckland is most often singled out as being exceptional, initially because it was the only non-New Zealand Company settlement and then because poor national communication networks kept it isolated from the other cities.[53] Dunedin has also been seen as a city apart, for a time more orientated to Melbourne than to its immediate neighbours. The strength of regional identities was highlighted during the 1860s when both Auckland and Otago provinces had strong political separation movements.[54] Regional cultures and other differences between New Zealand cities certainly existed, and this book considers some of these, but by looking through an intra-national lens we can also identify shared ties and common features.[55] Situating New Zealand cities within a colonial network (linked to an imperial one) brings greater clarity to what they held in common *and* what kept them apart.

Modernity and cities

Within the field of urban history the concept of modernity has been an important lens for analysing urban change. A central premise of this scholarship is that during the nineteenth and early twentieth centuries, the city was the both the location and embodiment of Western modernity.[56] The city and modernity were a collocation. The term modernity has a multiplicity of meanings that are understood and used differently across academic disciplines and even within historiography.[57] Urban historians and historical geographers have usually subscribed to the definition formulated by Marshall Berman and David Harvey in the early 1980s. This defines modernity as the intersection of political, socio-economic and scientific modernisation with the emergence of modern social identities: the discovery of self and the construction of otherness.[58] The historical geographer Richard Dennis has used this to develop an approach that examines 'the relationship between the modernisation of environment and society, the introduction of new ways of making sense of a changing world, and the development of new forms of

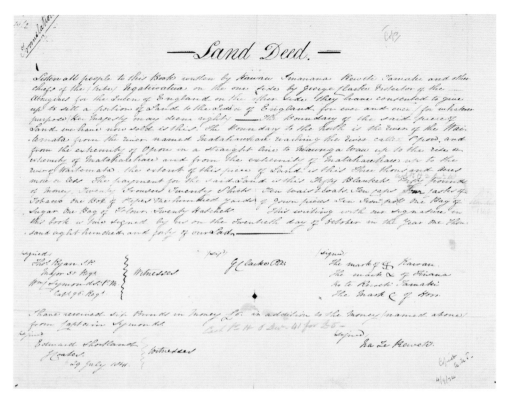

On 20 October 1840 the first sale of land at Tāmaki (Auckland) took place. This deed, made between Ngāti Whātua and the Crown, records that sale. The iwi received £50 and an assortment of goods including blankets, clothing, tobacco, hatchets and foodstuffs in exchange for 3,000 acres of land, which became the new city of Auckland. Archives New Zealand, Te Rua Mahara o te Kāwanatanga, ABWN 8102 W5279/154 AUC 83

self- and group-consciousness through the experience of modernisation'.[59] For Dennis, modernity is experiential: new ideas, modes of production and ways of living become significant by the way they reshape power structures, identities and social relations in urban space.[60]

Since the 1991 English translation of Henri Lefebvre's *The Production of Space*, urban historians have sought to 'spatialise' these modernising social processes. Lefebvre proposed a model for the production of urban space in which there is an association between modes of production and the spaces they created. He suggested the evolution of capitalism was accompanied by increasing abstraction of urban space, less focused on its unique geography and more on its quantifiable attributes: space as a commodity and an article of regulation. Lefebvre distinguished between 'representations of space' (plans, elevations and models) made by politicians, planners, reformers and the powerful, and 'representational spaces',

The site of the new town of Wellington included a number of existing Māori settlements. Among them was Te Aro pā. It was founded in the 1820s and when European settlers arrived in 1840 it was divided in two, with Taranaki people residing in the western end and Ngāti Ruanui people residing at the eastern end. This sketch shows the pā in the early 1840s. In 2005 archaeologists unearthed the remains of three whare (huts) and these are now on public display. John Alexander Gilfillan/Edmund Norman, Alexander Turnbull Library, A-049-001

the spaces of imagination, carnival, resistance, subversion and appropriation made by the powerless. A bridging third element was 'spatial practices'. These comprise spaces as used and experienced in everyday material life, such as the building of streets, the management of traffic and the journey to work. The first two are concerned with what things mean, and the third with how they work and what people do in them.[61] Within this frame, place is a location which we map, and space is how we actualise or experience place. Place is what Michel de Certeau calls 'practised space'.[62]

This study uses modernity as a frame to explore the production of space in New Zealand's five cities. Informed by Lefebvre's ideas about representations of space, representational spaces and spatial practices, it follows Dennis's experiential approach by examining the relationship between the modernisation of cities' physical and social fabric, the introduction of new ideas and ways of living, and the emergence of new forms of self and group consciousness through the experience of modernisation. *The Big Smoke* seeks to show not only how modernity transformed the five cities between 1840 and 1920 but also how townspeople shaped and experienced these changes in everyday life.

Tribal histories

While this story begins with the settler founding of the five cities, it is important to acknowledge those who preceded them. The sites on which the five cities arose were Māori cultural landscapes long before their streets, buildings and pipes marked them out as European spaces. Over centuries, different Māori social groups had either established their own pā (fortified villages) and/or kāinga (settlements) on these sites, or saw themselves as mana whenua (having tribal authority over land). When European settlers arrived, they saw only a barren wilderness that was ripe for commodification. These lands, however, were filled with histories and cultural meanings.

It was Tainui tribes that first settled Tāmaki (Auckland): Ngāi Tai at Maraetai, Te Kawerau-a-Maki in the Waitākere Ranges, and Ngāti Te Ata at Waiuku. A Hauraki tribe, Ngāti Pāoa, occupied the Whangaparāoa coast. The dominant presence on the isthmus was Wai-o-Hua, a federation of tribes linked to Ngā Oho of Te Arawa. Between 1600 and 1750, the Tāmaki tribes built pā and other settlements, and planted more than 2,000 hectares of kūmara; by 1750, the area was prosperous and its population numbered tens of thousands. About this time, Ngāti Whātua-o-Kaipara invaded Tāmaki, killing the paramount Wai-o-Hua chief Kiwi Tamaki and occupying his Māngere pā. Through intermarriage with Ngā Oho, Ngāti Whātua came to dominate the isthmus. In 1821, the Ngāpuhi chief Hongi Hika attacked the region using muskets, destroying the Ngāti Pāoa and then the Te Kawerau-a-Maki settlements, and forcing Ngāti Whātua chief Apihai Te Kawau and his people into exile. By 1827, the isthmus was largely abandoned. In 1836, Ngāti Whātua tentatively returned to Manukau. Te Kawau's fear of further Ngāpuhi aggression was one reason he invited Governor William Hobson to site New Zealand's capital at Tāmaki in 1840. Several months later, the tribe negotiated the first of several deals with the Crown that saw most of their Tāmaki lands alienated.[63]

Te Whanganui-a-Tara (Wellington) is named for the chief Tara, who first settled the area, his descendants becoming the Ngāi Tara tribe. During the seventeenth century, Ngāti Ira people from Heretaunga (Hawke's Bay) arrived and the two groups intermarried. Other tribes like Ngāi Tahu and Ngāti Māmoe also settled for a time. In 1819, the Ngāti Toa chief Te Rauparaha, armed with muskets, led a military campaign from Kāwhia to the Kapiti district. Recognising the area's potential, he settled his people there in 1821–22. Allies from Taranaki came too: Te Āti Awa, Ngāti Tama and Ngāti Mutunga. In 1824, the latter two moved to Te Whanganui-a-Tara, occupying its western shores from Te Aro to Pitone (Petone). Ngāti Ira stayed on the harbour's eastern side, but Ngāti Tama drove them away in the late 1820s. In 1831, another contingent of Te Āti Awa people migrated from Taranaki to Waikanae and Te Whanganui-a-Tara. Deteriorating relations with Ngāti Toa led Ngāti Mutunga and some Ngāti Tama to leave for the Chatham Islands in 1835, Ngāti Mutunga transferring mana whenua to Te Āti Awa and other Taranaki chiefs. Historians suggest that the controversial 1839 sale of Te Whanganui-a-Tara to the New Zealand Company by Te Āti Awa chiefs Te Wharepouri and Te Puni was designed to cement their mana whenua over the district.[64]

The Waimea plains, where the settlement Nelson was established in 1842, had been occupied by different Māori groups over the centuries. Ngāi Tara was there in the 1550s, but displaced by Ngāti Tūmatakōkiri in the following century. During the 1790s, neighbouring tribes Ngāi Tahu, Ngāti Kuia, Rangitāne and Ngāti Apa ousted them in turn. In the following century, the Ngāti Toa chief Te Rauparaha led a confederation of tribes – Te Āti Awa, Ngāti Tama, Ngāti Koata and Ngāti Rārua – through the area and gained control of Waimea and surrounding districts. It was with these groups that Arthur Wakefield negotiated the sale of land at Whakatū that became the city of Nelson.[65]

Both Ōtautahi (Christchurch) and Ōtepoti (Dunedin) fall within the mana whenua of Ngāi Tahu. The tribe initially lived on the East Cape, but internal disputes saw them migrate to Te Whanganui-a-Tara and then to Te Wai Pounamu (South Island), where they intermarried with Ngāti Māmoe. From the 1730s, Ngāi Tahu sub-tribes occupied Kaikōura and then Kaiapoi, formerly a stronghold of the Waitaha people. Other settlements developed at Rāpaki, Koukourarata (Port Levy) and Akaroa. Cooperation with Waitaha and Ngāti Māmoe saw Ngāi Tahu settling in Murihiku (southern South Island) too, building settlements at places like Ōtākou and Waikouaiti. During 1827–28, Te Rauparaha-led forces attacked Ngāi Tahu at Kaikōura, killing many. The invaders then attacked Kaiapoi pā, but were repulsed by its defenders, who killed many Ngāti Toa leaders. Te Rauparaha avenged this in 1831–32 by capturing Kaiapoi and taking Ōnawe pā near Akaroa. Counter-attacks by Murihiku Ngāi Tahu between 1832 and 1834 pushed Ngāti Toa back to Wairau. A stalemate led the two tribes to settle for peace in 1839.[66] In 1844, the Ngāi Tahu chief Hone Tuhawaiki and others sold the Otago block – including the western side of the Otago Peninsula and the Taieri – to the New Zealand Company for the Otago settlement. In 1848, the Crown bought, on the New Zealand Company's behalf, Canterbury, North Otago and much of Westland from Ngāi Tahu for the Canterbury settlement. In both cases a paltry sum was paid, and Crown pledges of reserves and other promises were never fully honoured.[67]

As we will see, settler capitalism necessitated the alienation of Māori land before the five cities could be founded. Historians have shown that this process was both unfair and flawed, creating longstanding Māori grievances, some of which are considered in the following pages. Recent Waitangi Treaty settlements with mana whenua in these cities have tried to redress the injustices. In some cases, Treaty settlements have prescribed the restoration of Māori names to landscape features. Where I live in Wellington, the landmark Tinakori Hill (a settler designation) was renamed Te Ahumairangi (appropriately meaning whirlwind).[68] Changes such as these allow townspeople to become more aware of the Māori history that surrounds them.

The Big Smoke: an outline

This book comprises eight chapters that are thematic but also broadly chronological. Chapter One resuscitates the dormant idea that town founding and colonisation was a capitalist venture. It argues that if the chance to make windfall profits attracted the first European settlers, the opportunity to pursue city life in a new land was to attract many more. The chapter also examines how townspeople went about making economic, social and cultural spaces that showcased their metropolitan ambitions both to themselves and to those back in Britain.

Chapter Two focuses on the production of material space in cities. From the planting of the grid plan and the erection of raupō (reed) and prefabricated buildings in the 1840s to their replacement with wooden, stone and masonry structures by the 1870s, it highlights how capitalist social relations transformed frontier towns into modern cities and shaped New Zealand's sprawling urbanism.

Chapter Three explores spaces of sociability and culture in the cities, and the ways they shaped identities and social relations. It shows how the production of new spaces, including theatres, libraries and sports grounds, both enriched city life and further integrated New Zealand's cities into wider urban networks.

Chapter Four examines the position of Māori in city life. It demonstrates how settlers' social relations with Māori were framed by European racial theory and the social construction of otherness. Settlers attempted to marginalise Māori in city life, but Māori subtly resisted these efforts and continued to claim urban spaces in novel ways.

Chapter Five considers the street as a site of sociability, theatre and conflict. It focuses on the urban crowd, distinguishing two main types: social and protest. It also shows how crowds created new modes of behaviour and facilitated fluid group identities.

Chapter Six explores how the colonial street was a democratic and pluralistic space, characterised by street traders, street people and ever-changing crowds. It charts how city streets underwent a fundamental social transformation as new ideas about organising city space and new technologies like motorcars removed people from them.

Chapter Seven examines how city environments became degraded by filth that caused deadly infectious diseases. It then follows public reformers' attempts to improve the public health of cities by building sanitary infrastructure and promoting new modes of living to make townspeople more robust.

Lastly, Chapter Eight charts New Zealand's transition from a rural to an urban society. It asks why urbanisation created widespread societal alarm and generated attempts to check it, attributing the reaction to prevailing anti-urban sentiment and deep unease over modernity's links with the city.

Finally, something should be said about the expression 'the Big Smoke'. In modern New Zealand it is a colloquial and generally affectionate term for a large town or city. It also carries emotional meanings. The term 'going to the Big Smoke' evokes the sense of anticipation and excitement of journeying to, and experiencing, the 'bright lights' of cities and city life. I used it as a working title for this project from the beginning, thinking a better one would emerge in due course. It didn't. The term originated in the 1860s to describe London's immense size and smoky pall.[69] As New Zealand's diminutive cities grew to better resemble the imperial metropolis, it began to be applied to them too, although this was surely aspirational – or ironical.[70] Still, transferring the term from metropolis to colony can be seen as emblematic of the wider imperial and colonising forces that shaped New Zealand's cities. Retaining *The Big Smoke* as the book's title seems apt.

Chapter One

Building Towns, Selling Cities

In 1903, Edward Seager of Christchurch recalled the period leading up to his decision to leave Britain a half-century before:

> I was a lad of nineteen, strong, healthy and adventurous when I made my mind to leave London and come to New Zealand. Born, bred and brought up in the heart of the great metropolis, I felt, at an early age, that there was a better life than that which was afforded in its teeming thoroughfares, and a midst the throngs of struggling humanity that passed to and from in endless procession.[1]

The passage captures the restless spirit of the emigrant who, dissatisfied with his or her life at home, dreams of leaving it behind for greener pastures elsewhere. With his reference to London's heaving and mechanical crowd, we might suppose Edward had imagined himself literally amid green pasture, perhaps as a pastoralist running thousands of sheep on a back-country station or as a smallholder farming a herd of cows on land cut from primeval forest. Certainly many immigrants came to New Zealand with this prospect in mind. But not everyone did.

Having arrived at the port of Lyttelton in 1851, Edward clambered up the Port Hills bridal path, pausing at the top to take in the breathtaking expanse of the Canterbury Plains, before coming down the other side towards the fledgling city of Christchurch. Rather than continuing his trek on to the land, he stopped in the town and took up a position as a government official.[2] He may have thought London too large a place to make his mark, but he was a townsperson at heart

OPPOSITE From the 1860s some cities began to erect memorials to their founders. Dunedin led the way with this 1864 monument to William Cargill, who had died in 1860. Designed by Charles Swyer in the flamboyant Neo-Gothic style it had a secondary function as a water fountain. It was originally sited in the Octagon, but was moved to its present site in Princes Street in 1873. Charles R. Swyer, Toitū Otago Settlers Museum, CS/1220

and felt no call to settle in the country. Some 50 years later, he marvelled at how a 'miniature London' had risen about him. '[N]ow here, too, there are endless processions of people passing along the well-paved streets, and I see the same men and women that I saw in my youth, with the same stamp and bearing of an Imperial race.'[3]

His sense of wonder at the rapidity of Christchurch's development into a miniature London and approval of the deportment of those filling its teeming streets underscores his urban sensibility and enthusiasm for modern city life. He was not alone. Thousands of other settlers who came to New Zealand had no intention of settling on the land, coming instead to exploit the urban opportunities, from speculating in town land, to opening a shop, to pursuing a profession or a multitude of other economic pursuits. Equally important to these settlers was the social and cultural milieu of cities. This was a group who wanted to live in a place where it was possible to meet friends at a local bar or coffee house; attend a play, lecture or concert; or seek like minds and interests in a club or fraternity. Their decision to leave the likes of London, Edinburgh or Dublin was therefore not a repudiation of city life as such, but rather sprang from a desire to help shape and profit from the creation of new cities in virgin territory.

Origin myths

Most writing on the founding and growth of New Zealand first cities – Wellington (1840), Auckland (1840), Nelson (1842), Dunedin (1848) and Christchurch (1850) – falls within the city biography genre: a history of a single place. Many of these works were published to celebrate a significant anniversary, such as a jubilee,

Early immigrants to Canterbury landed in Lyttelton and then had to walk the bridle path over the Port Hills to Christchurch. Among them was former Londoner Edward Seager, who paused at the path's crest to take in the view. It would have been similar to that seen in this 1850s painting, which shows the meander of Ōpāwaho (Heathcote River), its estuary, and the sweep of Pegasus Bay. Christchurch was sited in the top-left side of the image. Edmund Norman, Alexander Turnbull Library, D-001-032

centenary or sesqui-centenary. Until the late twentieth century, their emphasis was on charting the social, cultural and material progress of a place: from crude village to sophisticated city. They also served to create and perpetuate myths about their founders. As Jeffrey Alexander has pointed out, 'Myths of origins not only give to these founders pride of place, but they attribute their accomplishment to the primordial characteristics [unique qualities] of this founding group.'[4] Accordingly, the early chapters in these works were typically given over to showing how the first settlers, through inherent foresight and British pluck, overcame numerous hurdles and privations to establish their settlement on a secure footing.[5] Other myths fostered urban social identities and a unique sense of place. Auckland histories, for example, often related the story of John Logan Campbell, a budding merchant who in 1840 set up a shop in a tent on the town's foreshore. It was the genesis of a commercial empire that made Campbell very rich and helped foster the city's reputation for enterprise.[6] In Christchurch, the arrival of the first four settler ships in 1850 assumed a quasi-religious significance in the city's history, akin to the American Pilgrim narrative. As one historian has recently written, to 'be descended from one of these first "Pilgrims" still carries a certain social cachet in some Christchurch circles'.[7]

The dominance of the town and city biography genre, a function of a strong parochial sentiment in New Zealand, left little room for comparative history. For four of the five cities considered here (Auckland being the exception), a common bond was the figure of Edward Gibbon Wakefield, who became the centrepiece of another origin myth. This view lauded Wakefield for devising a scheme (systematic colonisation) to ship vertical slices of English and Scottish society halfway round the world to found idealised bucolic societies free from the urban ills of modern Britain. The perceived success of settlers in realising this aim made Wakefield and his New Zealand Company agents heroic figures in Pākehā society. By the 1880s, monuments to William Wakefield, William Cargill and John Robert Godley occupied prominent sites in Wellington, Dunedin and Christchurch respectively. Edward Gibbon lacked an equivalent memorial, but then as Auckland lawyer H. Dean Bamford proclaimed in 1903, 'The colonies of South Australia and New Zealand stand as monuments to his genius and unconquerable energy.' (A memorial to him was later erected on the eve of New Zealand's centenary at the crest of Wellington's Mt Victoria.)[8] Although some historians expressed reservations about Wakefield and the New Zealand Company settlements, most agreed the positive elements of systematic colonisation had outweighed any perceived negatives.[9]

Following the centenaries of the Wakefield settlements, this reverent view-point was challenged by a new generation of historians. In 1958, John Miller called the New Zealand Company's alleged purchase of Māori land a farce that had divided Māori and settlers and obstructed settlement. The Company's ignorance of Māori society, propensity to promise too many things, and insufficient attention to detail created problems that more caution and insight could have avoided.[10] The following year, Michael Turnbull argued the Wakefield settlements were above all capitalist speculations.[11] The point had been well understood in colonial society. For instance, in 1892 the local historian Lowther Broad wrote: 'The nature of the [New Zealand] Company was exclusively commercial; its avowed object was to employ capital in the purchase and resale of land, and to promote emigration – or, as the Directors put it, "the purpose of the Company as a body of shareholders is profit by the means of the sale of land."'[12] (The Company was dominated by shipowners, merchants and bankers, who were part of a wider group of British capitalists seeking to expand imperial commerce.)[13] However, from the early twentieth century, the economic imperatives underpinning New

OPPOSITE This colourful New Zealand Company recruitment poster of 1842 aimed to entice Irish people to Nelson by offering free passage. Hocken Collections, Uare Taoka o Hākena, University of Otago, Hocken Poster Collection

F. M. Hocken.

FREE EMIGRATION
TO
NEW ZEALAND.

NEW ZEALAND COMPANY,
INCORPORATED BY ROYAL CHARTER.
JOSEPH SOMES, Esq., GOVERNOR, HON F. BARING, M.P., DEPUTY GOVERNOR.

IT IS INTENDED THAT SO SOON AS A CERTAIN NUMBER OF SECTIONS OF LAND ARE DISPOSED OF, AN

EXPEDITION FROM DUBLIN

Will be despatched to the Second Settlement of Nelson ; and all persons desirous of joining this Expedition, are requested to enrol themselves immediately, so that adequate preparations be made for the Voyage.

A First Class Ship will be immediately chartered; and as it is intended that DUBLIN shall be made the Principal Shipping Port of Ireland for New Zealand, Emigrants may rely on everything being done, and the strictest regulations enforced to ensure their protection, safety, and comfort, on the Voyage, a Local Committee of highly influential persons being formed at Dublin to superintend their Embarkation.

PURCHASERS of LAND joining in this Expedition, will be entitled to have a sum, not exceeding 25 per cent. on the Purchase Money, applied in providing

A FREE CABIN PASSAGE

For themselves and Families ; and they may also nominate as many Labourers as they choose ; and provided such Labourers come within the Company's Regulations, and there be room for them, they shall have a FREE PASSAGE.
  A limited number of Agricultural Labourers, Shepherds, Mechanics, and Female Domestics and Farm Servants will receive

A FREE PASSAGE

including Provisions and Medical Attendance, on producing satisfactory Testimonials, as to character, health, &c., provided they are not less than 14, nor, generally speaking, more than 35 years of age, and married.
  Applications for Land Orders and for Free Passages, and every other requisite information, to be made (if by letter, Post-paid) to *N. ARMSTRONG, Esq., Agent for Ireland,* 72, *Dame-street, Dublin ;* or,

THOMAS H. KELLY, Esq.,
New Zealand Land and Emigration Office,
No. 1, LOWER HENRY-STREET, LIMERICK.

N B.—Mr. KELLY having but a short time since returned to this Country, after several years' residence in New Zealand, is enabled, from personal knowledge, to supply the most authentic information on every subject connected with that rapidly progressing Colony.

*Though the N. Z. Company in 184.
set up an influential committee in
Dublin including the Lord Mayor,
Archbishop Whately, & the Provost of
Trinity College but little interest
? ton left for new zealand - the slow*

PRINTED AT THE *REPORTER* OFFICE, 13, FRANCIS-STREET, LIMERICK.

Zealand's colonisation were submerged by the romanticised, settled landscape narrative referred to above. Turnbull resurrected the argument by asserting the primary rationale in Wakefield's ventures was not to shape ideal societies but to make money. As Broad identified, the fundamental commodity was land: buying it cheaply from its Māori owners and selling it at an inflated price to investors and colonists, with the difference used to fund settlements and deliver a dividend. In common with other British colonising ventures since the seventeenth century, land was sold as a package comprising a small town allotment and a large country allotment. The scheme's 'bait', as Turnbull idiomatically put it, was the town plot.[14] Urban land was more valuable than rural land because it was more densely settled and so commanded higher prices; early buyers could therefore expect to make substantial capital gains on selling or sub-dividing their property as towns grew into cities.

The speculative basis of Wakefield's model was further underscored by the lottery system he chose for distributing the land packages. Those who won an early draw would be able to choose the most prized town sections near to wharfage and main streets.[15] As Turnbull and others have shown, this stimulated huge interest in the scheme. The even odds of securing such prime property meant that when the land packages for the New Zealand Company's principal settlement reached the London market in mid-1839, they were quickly snapped up.[16] Investors were evidently more than willing to gamble on plots of land that were both unseen and unbought on the basis of potential huge returns from an imaginary city that had still to be built. Conversely, the Company came away with a very tangible £100,000 return. Some six months later, the principal settlement was founded at Te Whanganui-a-Tara, soon renamed Wellington after the great Duke. Wakefield's model unravelled when faced with the realities of colonial life, as historians like Miller and Patricia Burns, as well as a phalanx of Waitangi Tribunal researchers, have shown. But this did not stop the Company or its offshoots from using the same business model in its other settlements.

Turnbull also emphasised Auckland's speculative beginnings. The New Zealand Company had expected that Governor William Hobson would choose to fix his capital in the geographically central Wellington. To the Company's chagrin, Hobson chose Tāmaki instead. This was ostensibly because it was the demographic centre of New Zealand – most Māori lived in the upper North Island – but financial imperatives were equally important. The Colonial Office had told him he could not rely on imperial largesse to run his government, and he would have to source funds from land sales and customs duties.[17] As Turnbull identified, 'how was Hobson to raise a revenue if he planted his capital at Wellington, a place where land was already sold, instead of founding a new settlement where he could sell land himself'.[18] The method of land sales in Auckland was different from that of the Company settlements: land was sold on-site rather than in Britain, and at auction rather than for a fixed price. Neither was land sold as a package of urban and rural plots. Instead, the sales process followed the pattern commonly used in Australia, where town and country lands were sold separately to limit supply and inflate prices. The first 116 town allotments were sold in April 1841, attracting buyers from around the country and across the Tasman. The expectation had been that land would sell for £120–£250 per acre, but this proved well short of the mark, with one quarter-acre section selling for a frenzied £444.19. According to one eyewitness, Charles Terry, the extraordinary prices 'seemed to paralyse with astonishment the majority of persons assembled'.[20] In the end, the sales total reached £24,275 17 s 9 d, or an average of £595 per acre, putting Auckland's land prices on par with those in London and Liverpool. Hobson was delighted.[21]

Turnbull's essay was important in highlighting to a new audience how the colonisation of early New Zealand had been driven by capitalist imperatives. His and related accounts of the Wakefield settlements and Auckland were influential during the 1960s through to the 1980s, but they fell from view as historians became engaged in new areas of inquiry. This was underscored in Miles Fairburn's history of colonial Pākehā society, *The Ideal Society and its Enemies* (1989). He believed historians had given the Wakefield settlements (and presumably Auckland) undue attention and so left them out of his study, arguing they were untypical of colonial society and any influence they might have had was short-lived.[22] It is uncertain on what basis he made this claim, but it seems probable that it was because 1840s colonial society was predominantly urban, after which it became increasingly rural and continued to be so until the twentieth century. In discounting the urban origins of colonial society, Miles Fairburn's rural-centric story could begin and largely remain on the land.[23]

While historians vehemently contested Fairburn's main argument that colonial society was characterised by weak social bonds (considered further in Chapter Three), the exclusion of the 1840s from his periodisation was not. It could be that most historians agreed with him that the 1840s settlements had received too much attention and new research was better directed elsewhere. This might have been given further stimulus by the rise of the 1980s Māori protest movement. In highlighting the detrimental legacies of colonisation and the failure of the state to honour the principles of the Treaty of Waitangi, the 1840s became a politically charged area of study, encouraging many Pākehā historians to turn their attention elsewhere.[24] The upshot has been that in recent historical writing, the 1840s settlements have a diminished presence.[25] Consideration is still given to systematic colonisation, but this tends to emphasise its grounding in 'the romantic fantasies of English rural life', not the temporal realities of modern capitalism.[26]

An aim of this book is to take the 1840s settlements out of the historiographical shadows and place them back into the limelight. In recalling Turnbull's argument, we are reminded that the birth of colonial New Zealand was urban. There is little doubt that land speculation underpinned both the New Zealand Company and Auckland ventures. Without the opportunity to make windfall gains from the buying and selling of property, the Company settlements would have struggled to get off the ground. Without the profits from the sale of the Auckland lands, Hobson would have struggled to run a government. In short, without towns and their embedded promise of riches, settler society would have run a different course.

The lure of civilisation

If town land was the bait for investors and colonists, the lure for many others was the pursuit of city life. Historians have usually taken the line that it was the opportunity to escape the ills of an industrialising Britain and to live on the land that drew New Zealand immigrants. But this was clearly not the case for all settlers, such as Edward Seager and the hundreds, and then thousands, who lived in New Zealand's first cities. These people were the inheritors of a tradition of urban living in Britain that extended back to Roman times and the founding of London. It is worth briefly examining this tradition to gain a sense of its appeal.

Most British cities began as market towns: farmers went there to sell livestock and produce to town dwellers, and in return bought wares, clothing and foodstuffs made by urban craftspeople. Towns also became administrative centres for church and government, with their buildings becoming expressions of urban identity and power.[27] As towns grew, they became more multi-functional and specialised, offering a greater range of industries, occupations and services. By the late Middle Ages, brewing, construction and textiles were core urban industries.[28] With the founding of universities and the growth of municipal and private schooling, towns also increased their role as education and information centres.[29] At the same time, the institutionalisation of government increased the demand for officials to manage urban space and lawyers to settle disputes. Banking expanded as rulers and governments sought loans to fight wars and undertake other projects. Medical services also increased in response to fears about plague and to townspeople's greater spending power. Such specialisation helped to frame individual and collective identities, encouraging the creation of craft and professional guilds. Prostitution also became a more organised service trade, with some towns opening official brothels to lower sexual crime and boost urban income.[30] Retailing was another part of the service sector to expand, particularly specialist shops selling expensive and/or imported wares like silk and gold. The most successful of all retail outlets were drinking houses, which provided refreshments, entertainment and other services like prostitution.[31]

These trends continued into the early modern period and the Enlightenment as urbanisation increased – London's population grew from 600,000 in 1700 to about 750,000 in 1750.[32] Urban-based professions grew in size and influence. Education became more secularised, and book, periodical and newspaper reading soared. Shops became glitzier to better display and sell the latest goods to increasingly sophisticated consumers. The cultural life of cities also blossomed, notably in the performing arts. The first commercial music concerts were held in drinking houses in the 1670s (opera was invented in Vienna in the 1630s), and by the 1730s such events were flourishing. New capacious theatres were built to create modern social space.[33] As Peter Clark points out, such structures became 'worlds in which the latest fashions in dress, language, morals, and manners were displayed (and debated) not just on stage but in the amphitheatre, where spectators came as much to be seen as to see, and where wider political and social networking and discourse could take place'.[34] Meanwhile, fashionable coffee houses, restaurants and hotels expanded the service sector of cities. Associational culture became more urban, secular and diverse. A multitude of clubs and societies – from sporting, musical and theatrical to literary, scientific and social – served as sites for new forms of urban sociability and cultural activity.[35]

These qualities or attributes gave cities a modern vivacity the countryside lacked, leading some eighteenth-century critics to belittle rural life as backward by comparison. It was a view given weight by Adam Smith's theory of history (sometimes called stadial theory), which argued humankind evolved through stages from primitivism to civilisation: hunting and gathering (savagery), pastoralism (barbarism), agriculture (feudalism) and commerce (urbanism).[36] Smith valued the way city life encouraged intellectual ferment, cultivated refinement and sensibility, improved morals and manners, and strengthened the economic threads between social classes.[37] It was the incessant stimulus and intercourse of city life that fostered modernity and furthered civilisation. And although the rise of the nineteenth-century industrial city and modern capitalism – with its bourgeois employer class, machine-led production processes and wage-labour system – provided new challenges to the pursuit of urban life, it did not stem the flow of people seeking that experience.[38] The greater population in cities, and their functional specialisation, complex social and political structures, and diverse cultural production made urban life ever more appealing to ever more people.

Amidst all the talk about the ruralism of Wakefield's model, it is sometimes forgotten that towns were at the scheme's centre.[39] Since the 1820s, he had argued that settler colonies like New South Wales were faltering because cheap land had enabled too many workers to become landowners. This had encouraged extensive farming like pastoralism because the labour pool was too shallow to support intensive activities like cropping. This in turn had created a dispersed settlement

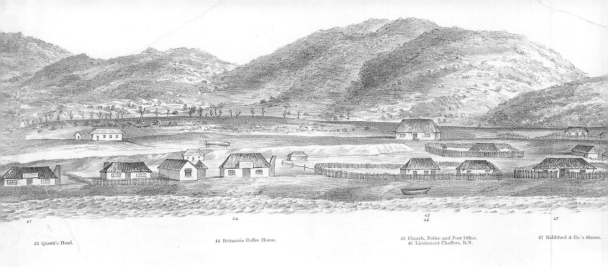

43 Queen's Head.   44 Britannia Coffee House.   45 Church, Police and Post Office.   47 Riddiford & Co.'s Stores.
                                                   46 Lieutenant Chaffers, R.N.

pattern that obstructed the growth of civilised society. For Wakefield, the growth
of pastoralism in Australia showed an alarming regression towards barbarism and
pre-modern social relations. The only way to turn this around, he argued, was to
promote market towns and increase population densities: 'CONCENTRATION
would produce what never did and never can exist without it – CIVILIZATION.'[40]
Towns were therefore at the forefront of Wakefield's colonising scheme, as
bulwarks of civilisation and bases for shaping a settled landscape. To encourage
closer settlement, he proposed a 'sufficient price' for colonial land: low enough
to attract capitalists, but high enough to prevent workers from gaining land too
soon. This meant the focus was on attracting those who could provide work and
cultivate the land: settler capitalists. Many in this target class either lived in cities
or appreciated the pleasures of city life; it formed part of their social identities
as modern Britons. The critical place of towns in Wakefield's model provided
reassurance to this group that if they settled the land they would still have access
to the amenities of civilisation.[41] To ensure balanced growth, town and country
would be developed in tandem. As the political economist John Stuart Mill wrote
in 1848, each needed the other: Wakefield's 'system consists of arrangements for
securing that every colony shall have from the first a town population, bearing
due proportion to its agricultural, and that the cultivators of the soil shall not
be so widely scattered as to be deprived, by distance, of the benefit of that town
population as a market for their produce'.[42]

   The New Zealand Company's emphasis was therefore on shaping an economic
infrastructure that could sustain their settlements, and a cultural and social
infrastructure that would facilitate civil society and encourage immigration.[43]

An economic base

Economically, the key was to develop an agricultural or mining hinterland.
Commodities grown or extracted from it would then be taken to the town's
ports and shipped to London and other nodes of imperial trade in exchange for

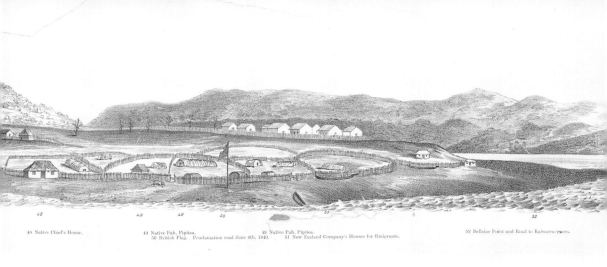

48 Native Chief's House.   49 Native Pah, Pipitea.   49 Native Pah, Pipitea.   52 Bellsize Point and Road to Kaiwarra-warra.
50 British Flag. Proclamation read June 4th, 1840.   51 New Zealand Company's Houses for Emigrants.

In 1841 Luke Nattrass sketched an extensive panorama of Wellington from the ship *London*. These two sections show the northern end of Lambton Quay. It reinforces the importance settlers placed on replicating the type of associational culture they had experienced in Britain. Barrett's and Queens Head hotels, Britannia coffee house, Wakefield Club, Mechanics' Institute and Library, and a church are all highlighted in the image. Pipitea pā is also visible on the right hand side of the image. Luke Nattrass, Alexander Turnbull Library, C-029-004

manufactured goods and investment capital. This was the economic blueprint of all settler colonies. As the imperial historian John Darwin writes:

> The hope in new settlements was to produce foodstuffs for export, or to support a colonial workforce producing saleable exports like timber and wool. Such export commodities, sometimes called 'staples', were vital to escape from stagnation or worse. They would attract investment from home … and suck in more migrants, to clear more land and produce more crops … A virtuous circle of ever-increasing prosperity would be the reward.[44]

New Zealand already had a thriving timber and whale-oil exporting trade before colonisation, and it was extractive industries like these as well as flax milling and agriculture that urban boosters and entrepreneurs promoted as an economic base for towns. Initially, though, the economies of the settler towns were import and consumption led. Retailing dominated economic activity. Settlers craved the sort of products they had enjoyed back home and merchants moved quickly to develop a consumption culture.[45] Among them was David Nathan. He emigrated from London to Kororāreka in early 1840, and there opened a store filled with wares he had brought with him. When it became apparent the capital would shift from the Bay of Islands to Auckland, he moved too and opened a shop in a tent on the foreshore. In 1841, he built a wooden store on the bustling Shortland Crescent and High Street intersection – a venture that, like Logan Campbell's, was the beginning of a commercial empire.[46]

The early newspapers of the 1840s settlements were filled with advertisements announcing the opening of shops like Nathan's or the arrival of consignments of goods from Britain and across the globe. Townspeople certainly did not want for much if they could afford it. Within a few months of Wellington's start, countless goods were on sale in the town: Westphalia and York hams; French brandy, Jamaica rums, Madeira port and pale ales; ironmongery and cutlery; dress coats, waistcoats and trousers; pit, cross-cut, hand and tenon saws. Some merchants specialised in particular products. This was true of 'skilled mechanics' such as bakers, butchers and tailors. For example, in April 1840, the baker Andrew Duncan announced the opening of his Wellington bakery, and sought orders for regular supplies of bread and biscuit. To meet his patrons' metropolitan tastebuds he promised all his dishes would be 'baked on the same principles as London'.[47] Others concentrated on general trade to cover as wide a market as possible. John Telford sold high-end ladies' and gentlemen's dress shoes from his Lambton Quay premises, but also ran an evening market twice a week at his warehouse, from where working people could buy supplies such as flour, oatmeal, sugar, tea, butter, cheese, candles and soap in small amounts at affordable prices.[48] By 1842, the town's commercial centre, Lambton Quay, was lined with shops and warehouses. Enterprises included fishmongers, a greengrocer, general stores, butchers, a pork butcher, bakers, shoemakers, tailors, a stay-maker, a hairdresser, carpenters, a painter, public houses, lodging houses, coffee houses and a solicitor.[49]

Christchurch too developed quickly. One commentator thought that the crowded classified pages of the *Lyttelton Times* conveyed the impression of a settlement of old standing rather than one founded only five months before. 'There are notices of vessels to sail and charter; land and houses to sell and let; money to borrow; confectionary and all other luxuries to be supplied; livery and bait stables opened; engineers, upholsterers, builders, and all classes of mechanics ready to execute orders.'[50]

In both Wellington and Christchurch we see the beginning of the specialist shops, services and occupations that characterised European cities. Missing from the list was prostitution. Prostitutes certainly existed in early Auckland and Wellington, as periodic court appearances of people charged with keeping brothels confirmed, but the profession attracted little public attention.[51] This was either because there were too few women involved to provoke moral indignation – the settler towns did not have the deficit of women experienced in places like 1830s Kororāreka (infamous for its sex trade) – or, as in Britain, it was blithely accepted as a facet of urban life.

So long as there was a constant flow of cashed-up new settlers eager to spend, a consumption-based economy was fine, but an over-reliance on imports was no way to operate a trading economy long term. In 1842, the Wellingtonian William

Dew conceded 'we have a great deal imported, but nothing exported, which robs us all of the ready money [cash]'. He advocated the cultivation of more of the town's hinterland and a stronger settler work ethic. 'Very many of the young gentlemen which come out, walk the beach and smoke their cigars, and spend their money in the grog shops which are very plentiful. *If every one was to try a little, the colony would very soon support itself.*'[52] Another settler took the view that a lack of roads was holding the town back: 'It has obliged too many people to remain in town, and turned many a good farmer into a bad storekeeper.'[53]

There were myriad other reasons for the slowness in shaping export-led economies. In Wellington and Nelson, land title disputes with Māori delayed settlement of hinterlands. Absentee investors also held on tightly to much of the best and most accessible lands, scattering settlement and leaving some colonists without close neighbours and mutual support. Still others found their land was too poor for cropping or too expensive to clear and cultivate.[54] Colonists therefore looked for an alternative economic base. As early as 1840, Wellingtonian Samuel Revans had reported that sheep grazing on Mana Island produced fleeces that were twice the weight of those in New South Wales. If such a result could be achieved on a windswept isle, what might be achieved in more favourable sites?[55] The New Zealand Company was never going to support pastoralism, but by 1843 many Wellingtonians could see that wool was their only viable export staple. This led to the famous 1844 drive by four colonists of 850 sheep around the Wellington coast to the grasslands of Wairarapa, where they negotiated with Ngāti Kahungunu leaders pastoral leases for about £12 per annum. It was a first step to securing Wellington's economic future.

Pastoralism also became a linchpin of Nelson, Otago and Canterbury's economies. By the mid-1850s, wool was the leading export staple of all these settlements.[56] Due to the policy of Crown pre-emption (whereby Māori land had to be sold to the Crown), Auckland avoided the land title disputes of Wellington and Nelson, enabling settlers to gain faster access to its hinterland.[57] It also had a more immediate export base. The discovery of large stands of kauri timber in the Waitākere Ranges and Kaipara district, as well as the success of early grain harvests in suburban Epsom, were welcomed as promising export staples. By the mid-1850s, wheat and timber led Auckland's list of exports.[58] It too had found an economic base.

The irony of pastoralism becoming the economic mainstay of the Wakefield settlements has long been recognised. The closer rural settlement pattern envisaged in Wakefield's model did not come to pass. But then neither did the feared regression to barbarism. This was because towns remained at the centre of settler society. Whereas in Australia pastoralists (or squatters) could be many days away from the nearest town and civilisation, the distances in New Zealand were

Modelled on gentlemen's clubs in back in Britain, the Christchurch Club was founded in 1856 as a retreat for the town's social elite. This group included many pastoralists who stayed there during their regular visits to town. The club moved into this Benjamin Mountfort-designed building in Worcester Street in 1862 – the photo shows it nearing completion. The Italianate-styled structure was damaged in the 2011 Christchurch earthquake, but was saved from demolition and restored. Alfred Charles Barker, Canterbury Museum, 1944.78.195

considerably shorter. As one commentator noted in 1852, this meant pastoralists could experience 'the forms and fashions of civilized life at a reasonable distance from their squatters' homes'.[59] That is, most pastoralists (and other country dwellers) were close enough to the civilising influences of a town to stave off barbarising tendencies. In fact, many pastoralists forged strong business and social ties with their local town, with some joining other leading colonists – merchants, lawyers, bankers, clergy and other professionals – in forming an urban elite. An important aim of this group was to replicate as far as possible the cultural and social life of urban Britain: to create civil society.[60]

Community formation

We have seen that clubs and societies emerged in Europe during the Enlightenment, but 'it was during the nineteenth century that they became one of the essential elements of urban cultural life'.[61] Planning for the production of social and cultural space in New Zealand therefore began before the first settler ships left Britain.[62] As an early Wellington immigrant recorded, settlers had been mindful of 'the elements of knowledge and civilization':

The need for towns to move from consumption-based to export-led economies saw the four southern towns turn to wool as their main export staple. Auckland focused instead on timber and wheat. This 1864 William Eastwood painting of Mears Farm in Mt Eden shows some of wheat fields that then ran across the Auckland isthmus. William Eastwood, Auckland Art Gallery Toi o Tāmaki, gift of Mr J Eastwood, 1900

They carried with them a collection of books, as the foundation of a Public Library; have formed a Literary and Scientific Institution; have made preparation for the early publication in the colony of a 'New Zealand Gazette;' and effected arrangements for the immediate opening of an Infant School, to which children of natives, as well as Europeans, were to be admitted without distinction.[63]

On arrival in Wellington, settlers became fully occupied providing housing and other necessities, including the printing of the *Gazette*, so it was not until the end of 1840 that a committee was created to form the Port Nicholson Exchange and Public Library. It wanted to promote economic and intellectual life by providing a place where professional gentlemen, merchants and general traders could transact business and peruse the latest overseas papers and periodicals. The purpose of the library was to diffuse knowledge throughout the colony by collecting scientific and other useful books as well as standard works of British and foreign literature. It soon had its own premises on Lambton Quay.[64] The antecedent of the Exchange was the eighteenth-century London coffee house, where a socially diverse mix of people conducted business, shared knowledge and debated public issues – something the presence of newspapers encouraged.[65] But the Wellington institution's high membership and subscription fees effectively ruled out workers becoming members, so it better resembled a gentlemen's club, joining the Pickford and Wakefield clubs as semi-public spaces of sociability from which non-members were excluded.[66]

The proprietor of the Britannia coffee house, Samuel Woodward, thought it unfair that mechanics and labourers were unable to access the print culture that had been brought out to benefit all settlers, and decided workers needed their own society. At a public meeting in the Queen's Head tavern in January 1841, it was agreed to create a Working Men's Association and Mechanics' Institute, open to workers of good character for a modest 2s 6d monthly subscription.[67] Mechanics' institutes had emerged in British cities during the 1820s as working-class versions of the literary and philosophical societies that had germinated in coffee houses; they combined an emphasis on mutual improvement with a mission for social respectability through self-improvement.[68] As Woodward explained, living in a new land away from family and friends, and with no soil of his own, the only capital the colonial worker held was his labour. The proposed association would allow him to 'advance his position in society through the purchase and establishment of a library of useful works on arts, sciences, history, and agriculture, daily and weekly papers, periodicals, magazines &c, to furnish him with knowledge, the real source of power'.[69] The Working Men's Association was duly formed, and by February was operating a labour exchange from the Hope and Britannia coffee houses.[70]

The proposed mechanics' institute failed to materialise and by early 1842 the Working Men's Association had fallen away. But others picked up the cause. In May 1842, the Port Nicholson Mechanics' Institute, Public School and Library was founded, with Colonel William Wakefield as president and 100 enrolled members. It had two main objectives: 'the education of the child and the improvement of the man'.[71] Ironically, the institution moved into the raupō building formerly occupied by the now defunct exchange and inherited its contentious library.[72] By December, the Mechanics' Institute was reported to be doing well. Various gentlemen had delivered well-attended lectures on education, political economy, physiology and geology. These events were as much about sociability and entertainment as education and mutual improvement. Meanwhile, the Institute's school was teaching 70 boys and girls at low charges, and its museum and library had received many donations.[73]

A society that pitched to all social classes and both genders was the town's Horticultural Society and Botanical Society. It was inspired by London's Royal Horticultural Society, and was founded in November 1841 to encourage and improve the urban cultivation of vegetables, fruits and flowers. It shared with the mechanics' institutes a mutual improvement aim. By offering annual prizes for

WELLINGTON ATHENÆUM
AND
Mechanics' Institute.

PUBLIC CONFERENCE
ON EVENING CLASSES.

The Committee of the Institute earnestly invite the Young Men of Wellington and others, to meet in the Hall on MONDAY, the 18th instant, at 8 o'clock P. M. precisely; to confer, generally, on the advantages to be derived from EVENING CLASSES, and as to the subjects best suited to form a course of Instruction for the present season.

JOHN PEARSE,
Hon. Sec.

Wellington, June 14, 1855.   [Printed at the " Independent " Office.

The purpose of athenaeums (libraries) and mechanics' institutes was to foster learning among working people so they could improve their position in life. An attempt to form such an institution in Wellington in 1842 was short-lived, but the idea was revived in 1848 and this time it gained a secure footing. The flyer advertises a meeting to discuss the creation of evening classes at the institute in June 1855. Alexander Turnbull Library, E-455-f-046

the best and neatest cottage garden, it hoped to 'encourage among the labouring classes industrious habits and a right employment of their leisure hours'.[74] The annual five-shilling subscription for workers was purposely small to encourage their membership. 'To the fair sex we are sure any appeal is unnecessary; this is peculiarly their province – at their presence the asperities of nature begin to disappear, and the wilderness to blossom with rose.'[75] But if it was women's province to domesticate nature, the society itself was the province of men. All its office holders were men, as were practically all the Exhibition prize-winners – an exception occurred in April 1843 when Emily Wakefield (William's daughter) won two minor prizes in the flower section.[76] Nonetheless, it is probable that many women became involved in the society, either as members themselves or as supporters of their menfolk who were.[77]

Wellington's cultural life received a significant boost in July 1843 when John Fuller built the Royal Victoria Theatre behind his Ship Inn in Manners Street. In laying the foundation stone on 31 July 1843, William Lyon welcomed the new amenity, considering 'a theatre a necessary concomitant of an advanced state of civilization'. He further praised it as a democratic space: a place where gentlemen and labourers 'meet upon equality to enjoy a banquet offered to them by the highest intellects that ever adorned our language'.[78] The theatre opened on 12 September with a performance of *Rover of the Seas*, to popular acclaim. Wellington's theatre-going public now had all the attractions of Hobart and Sydney, boasted the *Gazette*.[79] A second theatre called the Britannia Saloon opened in 1845.[80]

These were only some of the myriad societies and institutions founded to foster associational culture and civil society in 1840s Wellington. Others included lodges (Freemasons, Oddfellows, Rechabites), pubs, the aforementioned gentlemen's clubs, and the church (Anglican, Methodist, Baptist, Presbyterian and Catholic denominations). All were modelled on similar institutions in Britain, and comprised a mixture of public and semi-public spaces of urban sociability. They point to the emergence of a lively urban society that was beginning to resemble that of home.

This was a view supported by the scientist Ernst Dieffenbach, who in 1843 praised the town's rapid progress. Whereas three years before there had been 'a few hundred natives … [living] in rude villages … there is now a town, with warehouses, wharfs, club-houses, horticultural and scientific societies, racecourses, – in short, with all the mechanism of a civilized and commercial community'.[81] Yet it appears to have been one with a great deal of institutional instability. The Exchange closed after 16 months. The Mechanics' Institute, in its second half-yearly report, advised subscribers and friends that 'unlike many of the societies and schemes started in this Settlement, yours has progressed, and is enabled to celebrate its first anniversary'.[82] But declining membership thereafter, the defection of the teacher to found his own school, and the return home of its active secretary saw the institute fold before reaching its third year.[83] Churches too could want for members. During his twelve-month stay in Wellington from August 1841, John Wood attended the Revd John McFarlane's Scots church. The congregation often numbered in the tens, reported Wood; on fine Sundays sporting parties would pass by heading for the bush, in deliberate defiance of the Sabbath.[84]

It is possible that the relatively high failure rate of many societies and institutions was indicative of a society with weak social bonds – in the manner of Fairburn's atomised society. The Wellington experience suggests a more likely explanation lies in the inherent flux of a new society, where in the effort to build civic society some groups gain strong backing and put down deep foundations, while others fall before the fickle winds of public support or else crumble from within. Internal conflict and the random odds of success did not, however, stop new groups from forming or rising on the ashes of others.[85] For instance, reports that the books and periodicals from the dormant mechanics' institute were being

Major Baker's Cottage – Wellington May 1st 1841

Wellington's Horticultural and Botanical Society was founded in 1841 to encourage and improve the cultivation of produce among settlers. This view of Major Richard Baker's home shows some rose to the challenge; most of the property is planted out in vegetables, fruits and flowers. In 1842 his efforts were rewarded when he won prizes for his flowers and turnips in the Society's January show. Richard Baker, Alexander Turnbull Library, A-357-001

destroyed by damp and rats led to a new initiative to revive the institution. In August 1848, the Port Nicholson Mechanics' Institute (soon renamed Wellington Athenaeum and Mechanics' Institute) was formed with 135 members. Some 20 months later, workers mixed with the town's elite at the opening of the institute's new hall, erected on the same Lambton Quay site as its predecessor's raupō building. This time support for the institution was maintained, and it rose to become prominent in the city's intellectual and social life.[86]

The other towns went through a similar process to Wellington. Auckland's Albert Theatre opened in the back room of Watson's Hotel in December 1841; its Mechanics' Institute was founded in 1842, and an Agricultural and Horticultural Society in 1843. It also boasted numerous coffee houses, hotels, clubs and churches.[87] The Nelson Institute was founded at sea in January 1842 by a group of colonists travelling to the settlement; by the end of 1843, the town also had three churches, five schools and an Agricultural and Horticultural Society.[88]

This 1844 view of Auckland shows prominent buildings in the town, including several early places of sociability and associational culture. These include a theatre, mechanics' institute, post office, churches, and hotels. The main street was then Shortland Crescent (later Street), which linked the commercial hub to the government precinct on Rangipuke. A beached waka and Māori encampment are sited at the foot of Queen Street. John Adams, Alexander Turnbull Library, B-176-003

This notwithstanding, the fulcrum between civilisation and barbarism could be finely balanced. In May 1842, several Scots-Presbyterians petitioned the General Assembly of the Church of Scotland to send a resident minister to attend to Nelson's 300-odd Scots. The absence of such a figure had, they said, made people indifferent to religion, resulting in profanation of the Sabbath, 'drunkenness in its most obnoxious form', and couples living in sin. The petitioners feared immorality would worsen unless a minister was despatched forthwith; civilisation was assured when the Revd Thomas Nicholson arrived some time later.[89] The zealous and severe Revd Thomas Burns ensured there few such qualms in Dunedin, where the First (Presbyterian) Church and school was among the first public buildings. Many other societies and institutions followed. Erik Olssen has characterised these as spontaneous organisations that briefly bloomed under the energy of particular individuals but then withered once enthusiasm was spent.[90] We saw this in Wellington, but as was the case there some organisations, including Dunedin's Mechanics' Institute, were well supported and far from fleeting.[91] Within months of Christchurch's founding, a grammar school and evening classes had been established and 'instruction on the piano and in music proffered'.[92]

The experience of the five towns shows the high emphasis settlers placed on constructing civil society – an objective designed to benefit existing residents and attract new ones. Representations of towns and future cities and of urban life therefore featured strongly in 1840s and 1850s promotional or place-marketing culture.

Selling New Zealand

In exploring the correlation between writing and colonialism, Tony Ballantyne has identified four distinct modes of writing. His model (which can be applied to pictorial representations as well) is a useful basis for examining the place of marketing of New Zealand towns to prospective migrants. The first mode was 'imperial potentiality', where the potential of the colony's land and resources to generate wealth was placed within a context of an imagined imperial future: for example, Samuel Revans's vision for Wellington pastoralism. The second mode was 'colonial promotion'. This emphasised the colony's existing virtues and its ability to offer instant returns. The historiographical tradition has been to dismiss this type of literature as boosterism, unreliable propaganda that exaggerated the colony's prospects. Ballantyne argues this is too narrow a reading of the material, which included letters and reports sent through private networks and empirical data in reputable publications. In enticing colonists to emigrate, promotional literature was also an important instrument for extending British territorial reach and imperial networks, facilitating the displacement of indigenous peoples.

The third mode was 'ethnographic assessment', which 'produced understandings of cultural difference that enabled and authorised colonialism'. The last mode was 'improvement writing'. Ballantyne argues that self-improvement 'was an abiding concern within colonial culture'. It was thought to be best realised within a mutual context, as we saw with the mechanics' institutes and horticultural societies. Programmes for environmental improvement and the improvement/civilisation of Māori were also important in constructing colonial authority and rationalising colonisation: 'the colonists were improving the quality of the landscape, eliminating the practices that were holding Māori back, and, in both cases, making New Zealand modern'.[93] Improvement writing is considered further in later chapters; it is the first two modes that have direct relevance here. The New Zealand Company was a master in place marketing, employing both imperial potentiality – most famously, its claim that Wellington's soils were perfect for olives, grapes and wheat – and colonial promotion writing to sell its settlements to prospective migrants.[94] It invested heavily in books, pamphlets, magazine articles and editorials for this purpose. Much of this writing gave lustrous account of each settlement's potential, and falls into the genre of boosterism. Nonetheless, the Company was aware that unbridled puffery could be counter-productive, and so took care to publish critical opinion too. It also published quantitative data on population, climate and soil fertility to add rigour to its claims.[95] John Wood was one of those persuaded to immigrate to Wellington by the Company's publicity, only to discover the promise and reality of colonial life were miles apart. Among his complaints were the selling of inaccessible land, the infertility of the soil and the 'boisterous' climate.[96] In 1843 he condemned the Company's duplicity and 'insidious productions', declaring it 'must be held morally responsible for leading many families into error'.[97]

For Wood and many others, the Company's propaganda was misleading and unethical. But within the context of the nineteenth century, it was nothing out of the ordinary. In urban history, boosting is inextricably linked to the development of the American Mid-West from the 1840s, where fierce competition for settlers among new towns led to an outpouring of print culture from businessmen, newspaper editors and others extolling the virtues of their own town and hinterland while ridiculing parallel claims of rivals.[98] The New Zealand Company's efforts showed boosting was equally vigorous outside the Mid-West and that Wakefield and his associates were in fact pioneers of the craft. Their main competition was much less neighbouring towns than other settler societies in North America and Australia. Because New Zealand was the farthest from Britain, they had to convince prospective settlers to go the extra distance.

As Felicity Barnes has shown, the Company's strategy included reconfiguring the relationship between the centre (Britain) and colony. 'Usually colonies appeared as wilderness that confirmed the centre's more civilised status. But settler colonies worked differently. New Zealand was given the attributes of the centre, making it appear civilised.'[99] Towns were central to this revised understanding. Unlike New Zealand's landscape, which was unfamiliar and often foreboding, its towns were evocative of home. John Wood acknowledged this point in his account of arriving in Wellington in August 1841. The passage has often been used to show how the settlement failed to meet immigrants' expectations.[100] It begins with Wood's ship coming through the narrow harbour entrance, from the edges of which rose steep scrub- and bush-clad hills. 'The passengers on the deck were all straining their eyes to catch a glimpse of civilization. Little was said, though disappointment was visible on the countenance of every one.' Historians have left it there, with the despondent settlers, but Wood continues:

> As the vessel shot up the harbour, a few cattle browsing on the lower slopes of a fern-clad hill, were hailed as a favourable omen, and our hearts gladdened as we counted them over to each other. At length on rounding Port Halswell the settlement came into view, and its picturesque appearance prolonged the cheerful impression which the last sight imparted. A canvas cantonment was

what most of us had anticipated; but here the beach was lined with wooden buildings, while along the sides of the hills were dotted neat cottages, the smoke from which, rising among the trees, sent many a heart back to the happy firesides of similar structures in our own country.[101]

Anguish about Wellington's rugged and intimidating topography turned to eager anticipation and good cheer as the settlement (civilisation) itself came to view. Far from being disappointed by what they saw, the passengers were agreeably surprised and relieved at how closely the town evoked Britain. The scene lessened the psychological, if not the physical, space between metropolitan and colonial society.

The importance of mental imprints of home is further highlighted in Samuel Cobham's proposed plan for the City of Wellington, drawn up in London in 1840 to entice prospective colonists. The plan comprised a substantial grid of 7.8 square kilometres and was centred on the Hutt River, mirroring London's position on the Thames. In line with great European cities, land use was functionally defined, with districts set aside for government, commerce, the professions, education, the arts, defence and other purposes. Many of these areas adopted London nomenclature (Billingsgate Fish Market, Covent Garden Theatre, Russell Square), further contributing to a sense of the familiar.[102] The plan bore no resemblance to the site it purported to show – for one thing, the Hutt River was a shallow waterway and navigable only for a short distance – but then depicting reality had little to do with it. Cobham's plan was about presenting a city of the future that would in the fullness of time resemble the metropolis on which it was based. The prospect of being involved in the making of a great city would, immigration agents hoped, fuel settlers' imagination and lead them to it.

David Hamer has shown that future-orientation (or imperial potentiality) was a defining attribute of New World settler towns. He identified two main reasons for this. The first was the prevalence of speculation in urban lands and the expectation of great riches as towns grew into cities. The second was psychological: conditions in towns during their early years were often harsh; townspeople's preoccupation with a glorious future was therefore important to their sense of wellbeing.[103] Many early topographical images of New Zealand's towns are titled as cities, but incongruously depict settlements barely more than villages. However, if we place these images within the frame of imperial potentiality, the titles makes more sense. By carrying the moniker 'city', the viewer is encouraged to see past what the settlement is now and imagine what it will become. For example, the lithograph of Auckland by an unknown artist, published in London in 1843, shows the tiny settlement strung out along the foreshore of Commercial, Official and Mechanics' bays. A number of buildings of church and state – Government House,

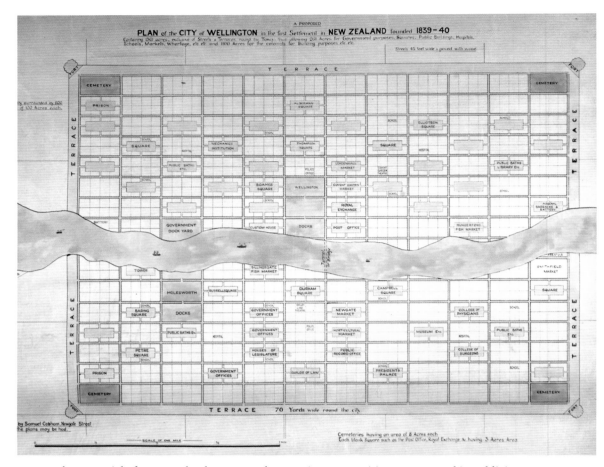

The potential of New Zealand's towns to become important cities was stressed in publicity aimed at luring settlers; the inference was that those who settled in them could expect to profit from their growth. The Cobham plan of Wellington was drawn up in London in 1840 with this aim in mind. With its vast scale and use of London nomenclature, the idea was to imagine Wellington as a metropolis of the future. Archives New Zealand, Te Rua Mahara o te Kāwanatanga, AAOD W3273 Box 26 WDO 32042

St Paul's Church and Britomart Barracks – stand out as beacons of civilisation. The anchored ships suggest commerce and enterprise, while the two Māori waka (canoes) provide an exotic motif that firmly locates the image in New Zealand. It carries the title 'The City of Auckland'. Clearly it was not, but most viewers would have understood its future-orientation: the village was a city in waiting.

Pictorial images were also employed to convey a town's progress and modernity. This is evident in Edward Abbot's 1849 painting titled 'Dunedin from Little Paisley' (see page 57).[104] In the foreground a family and its hound stand in a

Lithographs like this one of Auckland in 1843 were widely used to promote immigration to New Zealand. Here the town's built environment provides a sense of (European) civilisation, while the large number of ships on the Waitematā Harbour suggests trade and prosperity. The image portrays little more than a village but its grand title implies it is a city in waiting. Hocken Collections, Uare Taoka o Hākena, University of Otago, 12,951

recently burned clearing that faces the rising town. The dirt track that is Princes Street rises from the water's edge up to Stafford Street, along which runs a line of workers' cottages. Behind these a few structures cling to the steep slope of Bell Hill, while others hug the harbour's edge, their rising smoke projecting a mood of industry and cosy domesticity. Again, the settlement is a mere village, but the ordered lines of the streets, cultivated landscape and buildings suggest convincing progress since its founding only twelve months before. Abbot's painting was published in London as a lithograph in 1853. As Robert Grant notes, lithographs 'were a medium *par excellence* for promoting ... distant landscapes to which ... [emigrating] companies wished to allure their customers'.[105] Interestingly, the lithographer made some subtle changes to the image so it would more strongly appeal to viewers' metropolitan sensibilities. He restored the foliage to the branches of the clearing's trees because the charred vegetation was too raw and compromised its picturesque qualities. He also dressed the family in more fashionable clothing to show they were not behind the times, even at the edge of Empire. For unknown reasons, the family dog was expunged.

Colonial panorama of New Zealand

How far such images were influential in settlers' decisions to immigrate to New Zealand is impossible to know, but the sheer volume of such material suggests that colonising companies and immigration agents believed they played a significant role. One such promoter was Samuel Brees. On 24 December 1849, he opened his 'Colonial Panorama of New Zealand' at 6 Leicester Square, London.[106] Brees had been the New Zealand Company's principal engineer and surveyor from 1841, but returned to England in 1844 when his financially embattled employer could no longer pay him. He had often painted the landscapes he had passed through for work. Many of these appeared in his 1847 book *Pictorial Illustrations of New Zealand* and then again in his panorama.[107]

The Edinburgh entrepreneur Robert Barker had invented the panorama in the 1780s as a new form of urban entertainment. It was a massive circular painting that gave spectators, perched on a special platform, a 360-degree view of a scene. In 1793, Barker built the first panorama rotunda in Leicester Square; it specialised in depicting cities and famous battles in spectacular detail.[108] The well-heeled and fashionable flocked to the new diversion, immersing themselves in fantastical voyages to exotic and strange places over space and time. This aspect was emphasised in Brees's publicity: one poster invited viewers to take a 'Trip from Leicester Square to New Zealand and back, in one hour and a half, with a peep at the Colonists and the Natives'.[109] Alongside these flights of fancy, Brees had a temporal objective. He was the first to recognise the medium's potential for colonial promotion, for fostering emigration to and investment in Britain's colonies. The panorama's West End location and two-shilling admission charge indicates his target audience were the urbane middle class who either had the means to invest in New Zealand or were plucky enough to go themselves. (Brees

OPPOSITE TOP A family group looks north from Little Paisley towards Dunedin in this 1849 painting by Edward Abbot. About them are burned foliage and tree stumps from the process of taming the land. The town and its pastoral setting highlights the significant material progress Dunedin had made since its founding the previous year. Edward Immyns Abbot, Hocken Collections, Uare Taoka o Hākena, University of Otago, 14,414

OPPOSITE BOTTOM Edward Abbot's 1849 painting was turned into a lithograph that was published in London in 1853 to promote the settlement. In the process the burned foliage was restored to improve the composition's picturesque qualities and the family group was dressed in more modern clothing to show Dunedin was up with the times. Edward Immyns Abbot, Alexander Turnbull Library, B-051-014-a

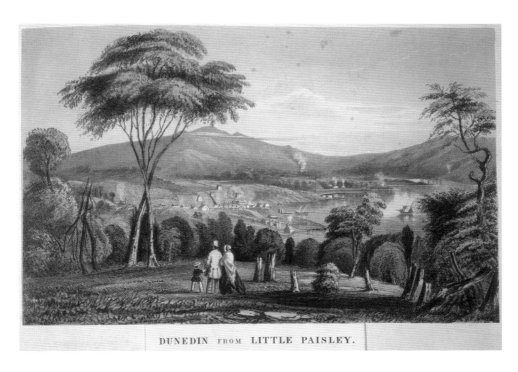

DUNEDIN FROM LITTLE PAISLEY.

actually had a trial run of the panorama at Brighton, a fashionable retreat for London's wealthy.) His publicity pointed out that the paintings were made 'from drawings taken on the spot', the eyewitness status providing a means of validating the show's content.[110]

Brees used a moving panorama rather than a circular painting. Audiences sat in an auditorium while a long strip of painted canvas, comprising multiple scenes, was unrolled from a spindle across the proscenium. This led him to boast that his panorama was the longest painting in the world, but it also enabled him to better control proceedings. As each new scene unfolded, Brees directed the spectators' gaze with a pointer and spouted his showman's patter. An accompanying text-based *Guide and Description* also provided fulsome accounts of each scene. A New Zealand Company pamphlet outlining rates of passage to, and land packages in, the colony was on hand.[111]

The panorama's programme of 33 paintings focused on the Wellington settlement or colony – so its New Zealand title was a misnomer. But Brees's task was to entice prospective immigrants by employing both imperial-potentiality and colonial-promotion modes of representation. The show began with a view high above the settlement. Titled *The Entrance to Port Nicholson in Cook's Straits*, it takes the viewer from the harbour entrance, over the Miramar peninsula and harbour, and up the forested and fertile Hutt Valley to the snow-capped peaks of the Tararua Range, a distance of some 40 kilometres. The landscape conveys both the region's expanse and its economic potential.[112] However, most of the scenes (18 of 33) focus on the town and its social, cultural and economic infrastructure. For instance, in *Te Aro Flat, Wellington*, Brees navigates viewers along Manners Street, past the 'mass of houses on the left … the Southern Star Hotel, the premises of the meat company, a billiard room, and Mr Edward Taylor's store' and towards Fuller's Hotel, the Theatre and the Wesleyan chapel.[113] This was followed by a series of views showing 'every building of importance' in the town, including the residences of the late Colonel Wakefield and other gentlemen; the Courts of Justice; the Presbyterian, Anglican and Catholic churches; the shops of leading merchants; and Barrett's Hotel – its new wing sporting a 'billiard room below and a Freemason's hall above'.[114] The aim of the sequence was to emphasise Wellington's civil society and show prospective settler capitalists it was no backwater. His appeal to this group was further emphasised by the under-representation of working people; their homes and work places are confined to general scenes, and none feature among the settlement's 'important buildings'. Those structures that do make the list are public buildings or belong to those of the same class as Brees's audience – reassurance that new arrivals would not want for social peers. Another aim was to highlight economic opportunities in the town for budding entrepreneurs. For instance, *Mt Victoria, Wellington* emphasises

LEFT Samuel Brees was a former New Zealand Company surveyor who had returned to London in 1844. In 1849 he opened the 'Colonial Panorama of New Zealand' at Leicester Square. The panorama usually featured painted scenes of historical battles or cities. Brees was the first to use the medium to promote emigration. His panorama depicted images of New Zealand towns, countryside and Māori; an accompanying lecture reinforced the colony as an immigration field. Brees is shown here during a performance, with a scene of Māori performing a haka. Their genitalia was covered for sensibility reasons. G.B. Black, Alexander Turnbull Library, B-031-034

RIGHT This flyer was used by Samuel Brees to promote his 'Colonial Panorama of New Zealand'. It has been estimated that he showed his panorama about 2,000 times to 40,000 people. A reviewer's declaration that his panorama 'will do more to promote emigration than a thousand speeches and resolutions' became a catchphrase for Brees. Alexander Turnbull Library, B-031-034-1

Simon and Hoggart's flourmill and the hill's flax-covered flanks. In his guide, Brees provides a lengthy biological description of the plant and its promising potential as an export staple.[115]

Brees then takes his audience from the familiar cultural landscape of a European-styled town into the foreign one composed of Māori and the bush. *Pipitea Point* shows the 'native town' of Pipitea pā, which he uses to describe a pōwhiri (welcoming ceremony).[116] Another image illustrates Te Puni's pā at Petone. It includes a whare (dwelling) used by the first settlers, and a native chapel, indicative of the success of Christian proselytisers. Brees acknowledges

A waka has landed on the beach at Petone, the site of Te Āti Awa chief Te Puni's pā. Behind the pā are a church and a European dwelling. Petone was initially the site of the New Zealand Company's new town of Wellington, but after the Hutt River flooded the area it was moved to Lambton Harbour. Samuel Charles Brees, Alexander Turnbull Library, PUBL-0020-20-1

previous friction between Māori and settlers, but emphasises that Māori living near Wellington are now a benign presence and settlers are in control of the colony.[117] From the Hutt Valley the panorama passes through forested Upper Hutt and carries over the Rimutaka Range to the settled landscape of Wairarapa. Brees waxes lyrical about life in the bush, his experiences working and camping in the district, and his contacts with local Māori. He concludes the show with a suitably salacious account of his guide, the Ngāti Tama chief Te Kaeaea, whom he describes as having a fierce (but historical) reputation in the region for slaughtering and eating his enemies.[118]

London reviews of the panorama were effusive. The *Morning Post* admired the modernity and spectacle of the event, declaring it 'the best thing of the kind that has yet been exhibited. The sense of accuracy is so great that we feel no disposition to question the largest object or the minutest detail ... We left the room delighted ... To the conclusion the entertainment never flags.' The *Patriot* was captivated by the juxtaposition of the sophisticated world of the settler and the primitive world of Māori: 'Sometimes the shore was seen; with dwellings, ships, stores, and

Samuel Brees wanted to dispel notions in Britain that New Zealand was a wilderness by showing that towns like Wellington had the trappings of civilisation. His scenes included images of the main public buildings in the town, such as this one of the Courts of Justice on Mulgrave Street in 1843. Next to the courthouse, by the water edge, is the first Thistle Inn – a later building of the same name still occupies the site. Samuel Charles Brees, Alexander Turnbull Library, B-031-009

warehouses – the elements of advanced civilization – at others the views were varied by the representation of Native Settlements, with blacks as large as life, in their original costume ... bearing the impress of Aboriginal simplicity.' *The Times* proclaimed, 'Mr Brees's panorama will do more to promote emigration than a thousand speeches and resolutions.'[119] That paper and others recommended that all intending colonists as well as those interested in New Zealand see the panorama.[120]

Following this success, Brees moved his panorama to the neighbouring Linwood Gallery, where he expanded the content to include scenes of Canterbury, Nelson, Otago, Taranaki, Auckland and the Bay of Islands. The show ran from May 1850 to January 1851. By then he had opened another panorama in the Strand, this one comprising scenes from India, Ceylon and New Zealand (December 1850 to August 1851). In May 1851, he placed an advertisement in *The Times* announcing he was returning to New Zealand and was seeking gentlemen with capital to join him: '£1,000 would go as far £10,000 under his management; £5,000 would be ample ... There would be no risk whatsoever.'[121] It seems he got no takers, for a few months later he immigrated to Australia.

Robin Skinner has calculated that Brees presented his shows approximately 2,000 times to an amassed audience of up to 40,000 people.[122] He argues this level of exposure about New Zealand was unmatched in print and other media in Britain, and that Brees's images continued to shape metropolitan understandings of the colony throughout the 1850s. Further research is required to substantiate this claim – newspaper reports also had a wide reach – but the success of Brees's book and panoramas shows his reading of New Zealand was certainly influential. How far his performances swayed intending colonists is difficult to gauge, but we know of at least one who was impressed: Edward Seager. He attended a Linwood Gallery performance in 1851, recalling Brees as a 'worthy gentleman' and 'capable showman' but acknowledging his pictures were misleading:

> There were magnificent views of Auckland, Wellington ... Lyttelton, and Christchurch. The last-named place was made to literally bloom as the rose, though at that time it bloomed with nothing but tussock and flax. Green hedges, bedecked with many varieties of bright flowers, bordered imaginary streets, on which there ran imaginary vehicles, carrying imaginary goods to imaginary people, who lived in imaginary houses ... The Christchurch depicted for our delectation, in short, was 'made in London,' and existed inside Mr Brees's panorama, but nowhere else.[123]

As with Cobham's plan of Wellington, Brees's representation of Christchurch was situated within the mode of imperial potentiality, an imaginary landscape of a future city. If Seager felt he was misled, it was surely a case of buyer beware; some quick homework would have revealed the settlement was barely established and its depiction premature. But as we have seen, Seager was already on the verge of emigrating. Brees's show provided him with a frame for visualising a new life, and it was the final push he needed. He wrote: 'the panorama, and my friend Mr Brees, fixed my determination to go to New Zealand, any indecision that I might have had vanishing before the pleasing prospects'. He embarked at London's East India Dock on 12 August 1851. All his relations and most of his friends were attending his brother's wedding, so his departure was unsentimental. At Gravesend he saw the wedding party pass by on the way to their honeymoon at Margate: 'there was a waving of handkerchiefs, and then they disappeared from sight, leaving me melancholy and dejected'. He drew strength by summoning up Brees's images: 'I was able to look courageously ahead and recall the panoramic hedges and roses in my Utopia over the seas.'[124]

Inter-urban migration

All immigrants would have held their own images of New Zealand to sustain them in times of doubt. What is evident about many public images of the colony during this time is their urban orientation. The New Zealand Company thought this was the best way to attract settler capitalists to the colony, but did it work? Historian Michael Turnbull has argued that 'the colonisation of the north and middle districts [Auckland to Nelson] in the early forties was predominantly a movement from towns in England and Australia to towns in New Zealand'. He claimed that the colonists who bought the Company's land orders were 'mainly merchants, speculators and professional men', and that 'practical, working [presumably tenant] famers' found Wakefield's model unattractive because it was premised on landowners employing wage workers and they relied on familial labour.[125] Recent research has indicated that there are strong kernels of truth in this analysis.

In a comprehensive study of British and Irish immigration to New Zealand, Jock Phillips and Terry Hearn identified the 1840s as a period of strong emigration from urban and peri-urban areas. Using a sample of nearly 6,000 English and Welsh settlers who arrived on New Zealand Company ships between 1840 and 1850, they identified that 25.9 per cent of them were born in London and a further 20.8 per cent in the peri-urban Home Counties of Kent, Sussex, Surrey and Hampshire (the South-east).[126] Similarly, a sample of 550 English and Welsh settlers to Auckland between 1840 and 1852 showed 20.1 per cent were born in London and 17.2 per cent in the South-east. In both cases only the south-west counties of Cornwall, Devon, Somerset, Dorset and Wiltshire had a higher proportion of settlers than London, and then only by a small margin.[127] Smaller samples of Scottish and Irish immigrants who arrived in New Zealand between 1840 and 1852 showed 18.8 per cent of Scots came from Lanark county (including Glasgow) and 16.9 per cent came from Mid-Lothian county (including Edinburgh), whereas 19.8 per cent of Irish came the county of Dublin.[128] The proportion of immigrants coming from cities and peri-urban counties fell thereafter, with the exception of Lanark county, which over the course of the nineteenth and early twentieth centuries increased its share of New Zealand immigrants.

Phillips and Hearn acknowledge the catchment bias is partly explained by recruiting agents being based in these areas, but then this made sense if the New Zealand Company wanted to attract settler capitalists.[129] Their research shows the Company's efforts met with a fair degree of success. In a sample of 604 British immigrants to New Zealand between 1840 and 1852, they found 19.6 per cent of them had white-collar (read urban) occupational backgrounds. This was a significantly higher proportion than in Britain itself (10.5 per cent). 'These were the troubled middle classes – the children of clerks and professionals who saw new opportunities in the New World.'[130] Further, if we add industrial occupations to this group (6.8 per cent compared to 16 per cent in Britain), then the total for urban-based occupations jumps to 26.5 per cent. By way of comparison, the combined figure falls to 18.1 per cent in the period 1853–70.[131]

Phillips and Hearn's study confirms that inter-urban migration from Britain and Ireland to New Zealand was greater between 1840 and 1852 than for the rest of the century. The importance of Australian towns in the process is less certain, because most immigrants from Sydney or Hobart were British or Irish in origin and would have been recorded as such. The Wakefield settlements actively discouraged Australian emigration owing to the colony's convict associations, but Auckland was less exclusive. By 1851, about half the town's population was from Australia, leading the former New Zealand Company agent William Fox to ridicule Auckland 'as a mere section of the town of Sydney transplanted to the shores of New Zealand'.[132]

A colonising agent

Phillips and Hearn's research underscores an urban orientation in early colonial society. Two essential reasons for this were that towns generated wealth through land sales and the creation of trading economies, and they promoted civil society by fostering cultural and associational life. Both were seen as crucial to attracting immigrants. Still, there was a third and arguably more important reason for the urban emphasis: towns were vital instruments of colonisation and racial dominance.[133]

The British had a long tradition of founding towns to impose control over new territories and their indigenous peoples. The Anglo-Norman monarchs established towns like Carlow, Kilkenny and New Ross in the east and south-east of Ireland for this purpose.[134] The planting of towns also underpinned British colonial expansion in North America, where governors in Maryland and Virginia were instructed to build towns to assert Crown authority over indigenous and settler populations.[135] Similar motivations underpinned Australia and New Zealand's colonisation.

Urban historians usually distinguish between two types of colonial cities: franchise colonial cities and settler colonial cities. The first were located in colonies that were already urbanised and where European colonists either seized existing cities or, in the case of New Delhi and Cairo, built their own cantonments within established ones. In these places, colonists were able to plug into existing socio-economic networks. Settler colonial cities were entirely new enterprises and were constructed in colonies such as North America, Australia and New Zealand that had little or no history of urbanism. Settlers therefore had the burden of building urban infrastructure and networks from nothing.[136] A third type of colony was the factory or fort, some of which grew into cities. These served as a trading nexus between European and indigenous merchants: places where commodities sourced from interior hinterlands were processed for export. For example, Bombay (Mumbai) began as an East India Company fort to organise the extraction of opium and cotton from its hinterland and its onward shipment to China and Britain.[137] Victoria in British Columbia is a North American example of a fort that became a city.

In 1837, Captain William Hobson of the Royal Navy spent some time in New Zealand on a reconnaissance mission. At the end of it, he wrote a report to the Colonial Office recommending a treaty be made with Māori to allow the establishment of factories in areas of European concentration like the Bay of Islands and Cloudy Bay. Others would be established elsewhere as the need arose. A chief factor (official) would act as a consul to Māori and be the conduit for communication with the British government. The factories would become dependencies of New South Wales, and be financed from shipping and other duties. Hobson foresaw factories as a means to introduce civil government to Māori and contain European incursion into New Zealand.[138] However, his proposal was overtaken by events. In 1839, the New Zealand Company despatched the *Tory* to New Zealand to identify a site where it could plant its principal settlement. It had no interest in factories; it wanted a settler colonial city. As Penelope Edmonds points out, the factory system was based on interdependent trade relationships between indigenous and European merchants. Aboriginal populations remained in control of their lands and allowed factories to exist for their own economic benefit. 'Settler colonialism, by contrast, sought to remove Indigenous peoples from their land and denied or extinguished Native title.'[139] Under the factory system, power was shared; under settler colonialism, settlers sought the upper hand.

Until the late 1840s, New Zealand's first towns resembled factories. Kororāreka, Auckland, Wellington, Whanganui, New Plymouth and Nelson were the only places where settlers exercised a degree of geo-political power. As the 1843 Wairau confrontation and the 1845 destruction of Kororāreka showed, settlers' grip on even these spaces was by no means certain, raising fears of a Māori invasion of Nelson and Wellington in the first instance and Auckland in the second.[140] Settlers responded to these threats by building stockades to shelter in during an attack. But in line with practice in other British colonies, settlers decided the more lasting solution was to subdue the threat.[141] This was realised both through

Towns were important agents in the colonising processes, providing a base from which to settle encircling lands. Growing Māori and settler disputes over land titles during the 1840s led to skirmishes between the groups and an increased military presence in towns. This Samuel Brees engraving shows a detachment of troops marching from their barracks (the middle building) and along Wellington's Willis Street in the mid-1840s. Samuel Charles Brees, Alexander Turnbull Library, A-109-034

military intervention, such as the deployment of imperial troops in the mid-1840s to defeat Te Rauparaha and Te Rangihaeata in Wellington, and the systematic alienation of Māori land in urban hinterlands. The colonists' control was further secured by the construction of communication lines that radiated from towns to the newly acquired and occupied territories. So by the time Brees was showing his panorama in London there was little doubt that New Zealand towns were European spaces and that their hinterlands were increasingly becoming so. The place of Māori in colonial city life and the role of cities in exerting European racial dominance are considered further in Chapter Four. What is important to register here is that towns were the vanguard of New Zealand's colonisation. It was from these seemingly inconsequential settlements that the European colonisation of Māori land was planned and then executed.[142] Without towns and their place as nodes within imperial trading and military networks, settlers would have found it much harder to gain authority over the land. To invoke pioneering American urban historian Richard Wade's famous phrase: 'Towns were the spearheads of the frontier.'[143]

Conclusion

The sale of urban land in the New Zealand Company settlements as well as Auckland underwrote the early colonisation of New Zealand. This reminds us that the founding of towns was primarily a commercial venture. While Michael Turnbull and others have convincingly shown that speculation was instrumental in drawing settler capitalists to New Zealand, it was the ability to access or pursue urban life that provided the more enduring attraction. This was because towns and cities offered multiple economic opportunities and the chance to engage in civil society. Towns also embodied ideas about European modernity and civilisation that supported the notion that Britons were a modern people. The first settlers therefore focused their efforts on building an economic, social and cultural infrastructure that would facilitate the pursuit of urban life and demonstrate that settler society was both modern and civilised.

The New Zealand Company and other boosters certainly emphasised this aspect in their publicity. They also were also at pains to represent the 1840s towns as progressive and future-oriented: as great cities in the making. Among the most entrepreneurial boosters was Samuel Brees. He adopted the fashionable medium of the panorama to create a spectacular piece of theatre that put New Zealand in the metropolitan gaze as nothing had before. His images of New Zealand towns gave prospective settlers a reassuring sense of the familiar in an otherwise exotic cultural and physical landscape. The success of these strategies was reflected in migration statistics, which recorded relatively high rates of emigration from the urban and peri-urban areas of Britain between 1840 and 1852. If Pākehā later saw themselves as rooted in the land, large numbers of them had been townspeople first. Finally, the creation of New Zealand's settler colonial cities had signalled a territorial claim not only over the space on which they were sited but also over their hinterlands. Within this frame, the cities were hubs from which a settled landscape would systematically advance over Māori-alienated land. Towns were colonising agents.

PLAN OF
THE TOWN OF
DUNEDIN
With additions to
1872

Chapter Two

Towns Becoming Cities

In exploring how settlers colonised and modified New Zealand landscapes, historians usually identify the felling or burning of millions of hectares of native forests and grasslands, the draining of wetlands, and the introduction of exotic flora and fauna as the most important measures. About the burned-out stumps of once-towering trees and in the peaty soils of former swamps, settlers sowed the European grasses that created New Zealand's grasslands economy.[1] These changes had not only an economic rationale but a psychological one too. The sight of sheep and cattle grazing in a fenced paddock, the song of a thrush or blackbird, or the scent of daphne and roses provided settlers with welcome senses of the familiar in landscapes that were often forbidding.[2] Usually left off the list of such changes are towns and cities. Their spatial impact was more concentrated than large-scale forest clearance, but they also modified landscapes in dramatic ways: hills were levelled or reshaped to accommodate linear streets; swamps and foreshores were reclaimed to create more land; streams were buried and carried through pipes. Along the streets, buildings of raupō, wood, brick, cob and stone, and of various types and designs, were erected, consuming ever more space, and producing a built environment of an entirely new scale and form. The hotels, churches, houses, shops and warehouses of the settlers were arguably more exotic than grasses, daffodils, sheep, cattle and sparrows. And as with the introduced flora and fauna, towns and cities both colonised the landscape and gave settlers a reassuring sense of home.

Studying the built environment

Among the fields of historical study, urban history particularly lends itself to a material focus. As Chris Otter has written, 'However the urban is understood,

OPPOSITE Charles Kettle's plan of Dunedin is an accomplished exercise in surveying. The traditional grid pattern takes account of the site's varied topography, with streets on the west running diagonally up hills to lessen their gradient. Those on the east run north-south, reflecting the low-lying nature of the land. The plan's centrepiece is the Octagon, an elegant set of rings connecting the city's two parts. F.W. Flanagan, Toitū Otago Settlers Museum, MP-0194 its physicality – in the forms of buildings streets and pipes – is seldom in doubt.'[3] Even so, urban historians have traditionally focused on the immaterial rather than the material dimensions of cities.[4] In this they followed the lead of early sociologists who saw the built environment as a backdrop within which social forces (like capital) work and social structures (like industrial society) are created.[5] Moving on from this approach, in the late twentieth century, some urban historians recognised that cities were not only 'sites' for studying abstract social relations but also 'places' shaped by material form. The British geographer David Harvey broke new ground in the 1980s by examining the link between capitalist over-accumulation and urban form. He argued that in times of over-production or under-selling, capitalists invest in the built environment. These speculations are in turn periodically destroyed by new waves of capitalist activity – a process known as 'creative destruction'.[6] In other words, the built environment is both a product and a channel for reproducing capitalist social relations: 'a tangible vector through which capitalism prolongs its existence'.[7]

With the 'cultural turn' in scholarship, historians began studying cities in terms of symbols, language and imagination – the latter referring to the culturally specific ways in which social groups defined themselves and others. The built environment was now viewed as the materialisation of cultural values, a text to be interpreted or a symbolic carrier of meaning.[8] For example, Mona Domosh's 1996 study of the rebuilding of nineteenth-century New York and Boston shows how divergent bourgeois value systems in the two cities saw New York embrace skyscraper urbanism and Boston spurn it.[9] But as Otter notes, by the early twenty-first century, the preoccupation with texts, symbols, mentalities and imaginings was threatening to dematerialise the city altogether. Since then, new studies have attempted to fuse the immaterial and material spaces (as sites *and* places) of cities. Gail Fenkse's 2008 history of New York's Woolworth Building addresses the social, economic and cultural meanings of the building while also considering its physical form and spatial relationships within the city.[10] In New Zealand, architectural historians, historical geographers and public historians working in the heritage sector have used this approach.[11] And it is the method adopted for this chapter in focusing on the built environments of the five cities and on how they changed from frontier to modern cultural landscapes between 1840 and 1880.

Town plans

The first element in this cultural landscape was the town plan. The early town planning of the five cities is relatively well known. Most city biographies include the laying out or planning of towns. These stories often became part of each city's origin myths – including the oft-repeated but false claim that Wellington's original plan was the London-like Cobham plan.[12] That such stories continue to resonate in the present is largely due to the fact the plans have changed little since they were put down, and continue to shape how townspeople navigate and travel through cities. (Although the built environment of central Christchurch was largely destroyed after the 2011 earthquake, the original colonial town plan survived and the city is being rebuilt along the same street grid.)[13] The main reason for covering familiar ground here is that town plans were central to the production of colonial urban space.

All the town plans were made up of grids, with space organised as rectangular or geometric plots. The grid has its roots in the ancient civilisations of Mesopotamia and Rome, and experienced resurgence in the British 'Grand Model', most famously in Savannah, Georgia.[14] It became the archetypal model for settler colonial cities thereafter. Many abstract attributes commended the grid to town founders: it was simple to survey and lay out; imposed a familiar and rational order over an unfamiliar and irrational wilderness (turning 'topography into geometry'); could be extended at a future date (had potential for unlimited growth); and enabled space to be easily commodified (a rectangular plot could be sub-divided exactly in two, and two again). Moreover, as Giselle Byrnes has pointed out, the grid 'was useful in translating the land into a blueprint for colonisation'. Once the land was geometrically configured, those living on it could be brought into line too.[15] The grid's emphasis on rational, ordered space has led scholars to call it 'a spatial signature of modernity'.[16] Within Lefebvrian spatial theory (discussed in the introduction), the town plans are representations of space made by New Zealand Company and colonial government officials, but as we will see their realisation departed in some significant ways from the conceived vision.

The first town to be laid out was Wellington. The New Zealand Company surveyor, William Mein Smith, had been told by William Wakefield to fix the settlement beside the deep-water Lambton Harbour, but Smith decided the more spacious Petone was a better bet. The gamble did not pay off. The flooding of the site by the Hutt River forced him to pack up his theodolite and start again at Lambton Harbour.[17] In creating the town plan, Smith had been told to:

> make ample reserves for all public purposes; such as a cemetery, a market-place, wharfage, and probable public buildings, a botanical garden, a park and extensive boulevards. It is, indeed, desirable that the whole outside of the town, inland, should be separated from the country sections by a broad belt of land which you will declare that the company intends to be public property, on condition that no buildings be ever erected upon it.[18]

The brief providing for public infrastructure like buildings, boulevards and parks was typical of the British Grand Model. More unusual was the inclusion of

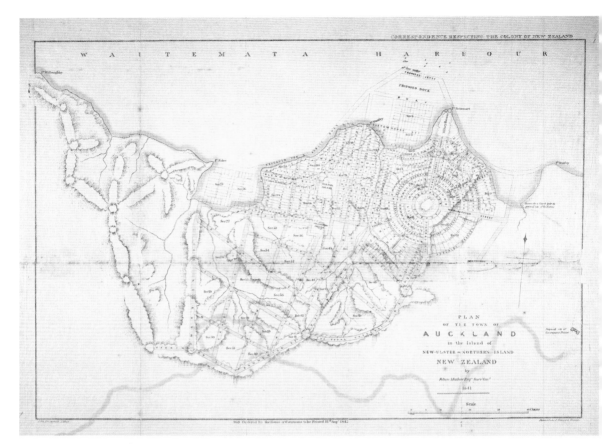

New Zealand's Surveyor General Felton Mathew drew up this town plan for Auckland in 1841. Its most striking feature was a circular element centred on Rangipuke (Albert Park). However, critics ridiculed it as a 'cobweb' that compromised the profit-making potential of the land. Accordingly, this aspect of the plan was largely dropped in favour of a traditional grid. Sir George Grey Special Collections, Auckland Libraries, NZ Map 245

a green or town belt.[19] Such space had first been implemented in Colonel William Light's 1837 plan for Adelaide, where parklands for public recreation encircled the town. In an age when modern cities lacked recreational space, and pollutants often cast a pall, the reserves were intended as places of healthy retreat and re-invigoration.[20] A further motivation was to maintain town land values by creating a barrier to sprawl. Smith's new plan comprised a matrix of small, interconnected grids so placed to maximise the use of level land.[21] The first two landholders (as determined in the London lottery) chose the valuable waterfront sections either side of the planned Taranaki Street wharf.[22] The only problem was that Te Aro pā occupied this prized site and its occupants were unwilling to give it up.

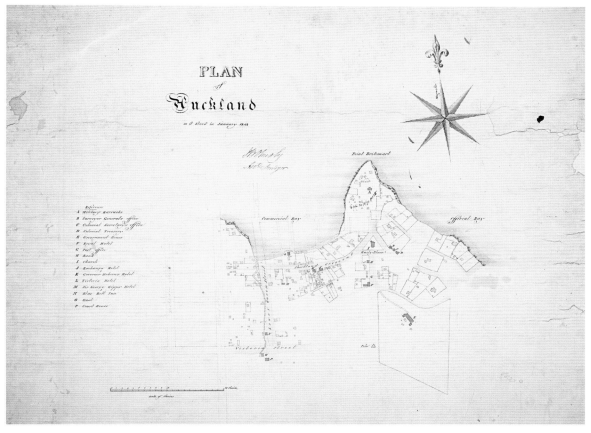

This map depicts Auckland and its buildings as they were in 1842. The main street, Shortland Crescent (later Street), runs along the centre. It connects the commercial and government (centred on Emily Place) sides of the town. The faint line of Felton Mathew's grid is discernable across the map and signals the future shape of the settlement. The headland is Britomart Point, the site of the military barracks. J.B. O'Mealy, Alexander Turnbull Library, MapColl-832.1291gbbd/1842/Acc.22934

Missing from Smith's plan was the promised public space. Like their counterparts in other settler societies, Wellington's settler capitalists thought giving prime urban land over to public use was a waste of a profit-making resource; the promised marketplace, park and extensive boulevards were never built.[23] One-tenth of the land had been put aside for Māori, and Smith chose the 110 'Native reserves'.[24] It was an early principle of Wakefield's colonising scheme that at least one-tenth of all land in New Zealand Company settlements would be set aside for the benefit of Māori chiefly families.[25] This was based on the European idea that Māori interaction with settlers would aid their 'civilisation' – of which more is said in Chapter Four. The Company argued that if chiefly families could 'be

made persons of consequence in the settlements established by a civilized race, they will be able to protect and improve the lower orders of their countrymen'.[26] Such stratification underscored the importance of social class as an organising principle in Wakefield's scheme. In choosing the Wellington reserves, Smith made some attempt to accommodate existing Māori settlements and cultivations, assigning reserves to Kumutoto and parts of Pipitea pā, but the land beneath Te Aro pā was far too valuable to be reserved.[27] Conflict erupted when settlers began moving onto land that Te Aro Māori (Taranaki and Ngāti Ruanui) still saw as their own. Peace was restored when Colonial Secretary Willoughby Shortland reached an agreement with the pā's leaders to sign over their land to the Crown on the promise that due compensation would be paid if official inquiries found it had been unfairly purchased.[28]

Surveyor General Felton Mathew was responsible for Auckland's plan. Rather than employing the standard grid, he made some attempt to accommodate the lie of the land by placing a circus (a street in the form of a circle) on the summit of Rangipuke (Albert Park), from which ran a series of quadrants and crescents. These elements had become fashionable in the eighteenth-century Neo-Renaissance town-planning tradition, of which John Wood the Elder's plan for Bath is an exemplar (Mathew came from Bath).[29] Their use also had economic advantages. As Mathew explained, grid plans necessitated 'cutting down hills and filling up hollows' to ensure streets maintained reasonable gradients. In following the contours of slopes, curvilinear streets were cheaper to build.[30] It is therefore curious that he applied a standard grid plan over the rest of the town, its uniformity relieved only by the provision of two public squares on Hobson

This John Saxton lithograph of Nelson shows the progress of the settlement nearly 12 months after its founding in early 1842. In the foreground a surveyor runs a line while builders work on erecting a house. A woman washes clothes in a tub, leaving it to dry on scrub. In the middle distance the town's plan is taking shape, with numerous buildings arising along tentative streets. John Waring Saxton, Alexander Turnbull Library, PUBL-0011-06-2 (left) and PUBL-0011-06-3 (right)

Street. This created a town of two halves: a curvilinear half east of the Queen Street axis and a strongly linear half west of it. It is an awkward arrangement that separates the government and commercial sides of the town. We can only surmise this was deliberate. In referencing the gracious circuses and crescents of Bath, the government side carried a cultural cachet that the other side lacked. It was probably Mathew's way of signalling the primacy of government over commerce in the settlement.

Reaction to the plan ranged from bemusement to outright hostility. Alexander Marjoribanks explained how it was 'designed apparently for a magnificent metropolis, one-fourth of it being covered with what appears at first to be a spider's web, consisting of circular streets, circuses, crescents, and an infinite number of radiations'.[31] Critics lambasted the plan for departing from the proven benefits of the grid. Samuel Martin complained: 'every street is made either to slant or curve in such a manner, that there is not a single allotment laid out at right angles with its street, nor a single street at right angles with a street – nor, as a consequence, a single house built upon a square'.[32] The implication was that the plan's irregular lines failed to maximise the profit-making potential of the land. In the end, Mathew's hope to make the government quarter ascendant in Auckland's townscape was undone by commercial imperatives which, as in Wellington, had no tolerance for amenities like public squares (the Hobson Street squares came to nought), let alone for artifices like circuses and crescents. When the navvies began their work, only a few threads of Mathew's cobweb were etched into the landscape. Surviving elements include Shortland Street (Crescent in the plan), Emily Place, Eden Crescent and perhaps the curve of Kitchener Street.

In Nelson, Frederick Tuckett laid out the town on a grid centred on a public reserve called Trafalgar Square. As in Wellington, the sections close to the proposed port and wharfage – principally, those opposite the harbour entrance and along Haven Road – were chosen first. Sections near the expected commercial hub – defined by Trafalgar, Bridge, Collingwood and Hardy streets – were also popular. Chosen by Police Magistrate Henry Thompson, 11 per cent of the total land was assigned as Native reserves to benefit Māori.[33]

Charles Kettle's plan of Dunedin comprised two main grids that met along the George and Princes streets axis. The western grid ran diagonally over hilly terrain in a south–west direction, an orientation that lessened some street gradients. The eastern grid ran in a north–south direction, over low-lying and swampy ground. The focal point was the Octagon, whose angles matched the grid. The Octagon was also one of the few garden reserves in the plan, a deficit that was compensated by an encircling and spacious town belt. Reserves were also set aside for churches, schools, public buildings, baths, wharfage and cemeteries.[34] Of the five towns considered here, Kettle's plan was the most accomplished. It provides a skilful resolution to the problem of adapting the grid plan to the specifics of an irregular site while also creating a total composition that has an elegant sense of proportion and unity.[35]

Joseph Thomas laid down Christchurch's grid. Its unrelenting geometry is relieved only by the meander of the Ōtākaro (Avon River) and two diagonal streets, which were to connect the town to Ferry Road and Papanui Bush respectively.[36] Still, the plan had generous provision for public reserves and squares. This included the 165-hectare Hagley Park, a large central square (Cathedral Square), two smaller squares (Cranmer and Latimer) and a spacious market place (Victoria Square). Collective sentiment was evidently stronger in Christchurch than in the other towns, because all its reserves were realised; its city builders were apparently willing to forgo short-term capital gain for long-term public benefit.[37] There was at least one unexpected element to the plan: it was half its promised 1,000-acre size. This was because land orders were under-subscribed and demand could be met within a reduced footprint.[38] To make up the difference, another 500 acres of town reserve land was laid out in a belt surrounding three sides of the settlement – the fourth side was Hagley Park. This became a land bank the Canterbury Association (the colonising company) could progressively sell, at urban prices, as Christchurch expanded and demand for new town sections increased.[39] Thomas still delivered the requisite 1,000 allotments by cutting their size from a half to a quarter-acre.[40] The quarter-acre section was to become the archetypal residential allotment in New Zealand towns and cities.

This overview underscores how town plans were central to the production of capitalist space in the five towns. While the representations made by the planners included ample provision for public squares and parks, when it came to spatial practices these were sacrificed to commercial imperatives. Only Christchurch succeeded in bucking the trend in a significant way. The legacy of this beginning was that Auckland and Wellington, in particular, lacked organised public space to foster public life. As we will see in Chapters Five and Six, streets came to serve this purpose instead.

The first buildings

The town plans provided the frame for the building of towns. But in the case of Wellington and Auckland, building had already begun before the plans were put down. Many of these first buildings were in fact homemade. In Britain a number of companies manufactured prefabricated cottages and other buildings that emigrants could take with them and assemble on site. The most prominent of these was Henry Manning of Holborn. In the late 1820s, he invented a prefabrication system whereby grooved wooden posts were slotted and bolted into a floor plate carried on bearers. The posts carried the wall plate with supporting triangulated trusses. Standardised wooden cladding panels slotted between the grooved posts. The roof, doors, glazed windows, locks and other components were all included, and each building was pre-painted, inside and out. Each component was numbered to aid assembly and a small compass was provided to orientate the structure. All that was needed was a wrench to put it together, and this could reportedly be done in a day.[41] As the immigration agent George Earp enthused, a prefabricated dwelling meant the settler had 'nothing to do but to get his location, and set up his house almost with the same ease with which he could have done a tent'.[42] The cottages were designed in a simple English cottage style and came in different sizes – a two-roomed cottage measured 7.3 by 3.7 metres. Prices began at a relatively modest £15.[43] Historians have identified Manning's cottages as the first (European) houses made for ease of transport and construction, the antecedent for the industrialised prefabricated housing that rebuilt cities in the twentieth century.[44]

Manning did not stop at cottages. His firm made New Zealand's first Govern-ment House, a capacious dwelling assembled in Auckland in 1841. He also made dressers, sofas, tables, chairs 'and a variety of economical Colonial Furniture made to pack into each other to save freight'.[45] His firm was part of a cluster of British companies specialising in 'colonial outfitting', provisioning emigrants with a

From the 1830s some London building firms – such as Manning of Holborn – began selling prefabricated houses that could be quickly assembled in the colonies to provide near-instant shelter. Many well-off settlers brought such dwellings with them to towns like Wellington and Nelson. John Pearse painted this view of his Wellington home in 1852; its size and style suggests it was a prefabricated cottage. John Pearse, Alexander Turnbull Library, E-455-f-039-4

diverse range of goods specifically designed for conditions in settler societies.[46] In promotional material, Manning gave the example of Perth, where in 1830 his cottages were found to be of the greatest service to settlers, protecting their families from the weather and their property from theft:

> Many persons who took only tents, suffered severely in both respects; their tents frequently blown down in the middle of a stormy night, and their goods being thus not only exposed to the weather, but to pilfering. Provided with a cottage of this description, an emigrant might land from a ship in the morning and sleep on his home on shore at night.[47]

Subsequent publicity emphasised testimonials from leading officials in Australian colonies who had lived in Manning cottages, including Charles La Trobe, Governor of Port Phillip (Melbourne), and James Stirling, Governor of Western Australia.[48]

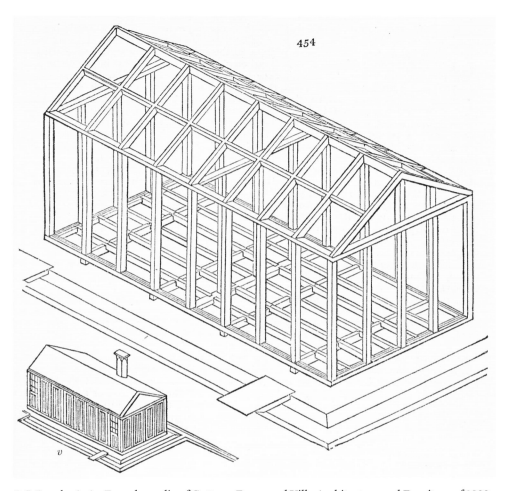

454

J. C. Loudon's *An Encyclopaedia of Cottage, Farm, and Villa Architecture and Furniture* of 1833 included a diagram of a Manning portable cottage before and after it was clad. All components were numbered to aid assembly and each package included a compass to orientate the structure. Some settlers complained their cottages were cold and flimsy, preferring locally built raupō or wooden dwellings instead. Alexander Turnbull Library, B-K-1240-255

Numerous settler capitalists in Wellington and Nelson – Francis Molesworth, George Evans, Henry Petre, Henry St Hill and Samuel Revans – brought Manning cottages with them. Such buildings are visible in early images of Wellington.[49] For example, a Robert Park painting of the Te Aro foreshore in the early 1840s includes of line of prefabricated dwellings joined together to form a terrace. In 1852, John Pearce painted his first lodgings at the northern end of The Terrace. The dwelling's low-hipped roof and fenestration suggest it was a prefabricated cottage. The city's most famous kitset structure was Barrett's Hotel. This was a

Manning building shipped out by the New Zealand Company to be used as school, but was subsequently gifted by its chairman George Evans to Richard Barrett for his help in securing the town.[50]

Although primarily designed to provide near-instant shelter, the prefabricated homes were also intended to facilitate colonisation. Constructed in groups, they would immediately create a townscape that would signal to Māori an explicit European claim over the landscape. Yet despite the glowing testimonials about their suitability for all colonial contexts, it seems their makers had not taken into account conditions in Wellington. Lieutenant John Wood purchased a prefabricated cottage in 1841 and had it erected near the top of The Terrace. The first night he and his family slept in the structure, it was hit by a violent southerly gale, forcing the occupants to ballast it with heavy trunks and boxes to stop it becoming airborne.[51] Another settler, Mary Swainson, complained the walls of her Manning cottage were too thin and the windows too large and as a result

ABOVE The arrival of hundreds of settlers in Wellington at once meant housing demand outstripped supply. Settlers commissioned Māori to build them raupō huts like these at Petone. Although built using Māori techniques and local materials, their steeply pitched gables and chimneys were evocative of the English cottage style, making them culturally hybrid structures. William Swainson, Alexander Turnbull Library, A-190-013

OPPOSITE This sketch presents an interior view of Dr Alfred Barker's ironically named Studdingsail Hall in Christchurch. It was a temporary dwelling he made for his family in 1851 out of packing cases and a studding sail from an immigrant ship. Barker recorded the place was tolerable in fine weather but miserable in the wet. Alfred Charles Barker, Canterbury Museum, 1949.29.6

In 1844 William Bambridge drew his wife Sophia and servant Emma shelling peas on the floor at their home in Judges Bay, Auckland, with the couple's two young children playing alongside. The Bambridge's house was prefabricated in England and William made a number of sketches of it, mainly the interior, in his diary. William Bambridge, Alexander Turnbull Library, MS-0130-214

her family 'felt the cold very much'.[52] In Nelson, Sarah Greenwood reported she could 'see the light through in most parts' of her prefabricated dwelling.[53] Their insubstantiality may explain why none has survived.

A raupō town

While such structures provided townscapes with an instant imprint of home, in Wellington, at least, the reality was that most settlers lived in Māori-built dwellings. These were constructed with raupō and flax over a tōtara wooden frame, or else were made using wattled hurdle walls (supplejack covered in clay).[54] The houses were distinguished from whare by their design and function. The walls were

Sarah and Felton Mathew arrived in Auckland in 1840 and lived in tents and a raupō hut before this house was built for them near St Paul's Church. It cost the couple £2,000, a considerable sum of money for a modest dwelling. The gardens were planted with native trees as well as exotic species like oak, chestnut and walnut. Felton Mathew, Sir George Grey Special Collections, Auckland Libraries, 7-A4046

higher, and featured external chimneys, small windows and hipped or gabled thatched roofs. These were hybrid dwellings, their design resembling a traditional English cottage but built using traditional Māori materials and techniques. They also cost about one-fifth the price of the imported cottages, and were warmer.[55] 'We all prefer them to the trumpery wooden houses built in England,' reported Wellingtonian George Evans.[56] In Auckland, Felton Mathew employed Māori to build him and his wife Sarah a two-roomed raupō cottage so they could move out of their draughty and leaky tent. The couple bought the doors and window frames from a local carpenter, and used oiled calico for glass; this provided ample light and kept out the rain but blocked the magnificent view.[57] In British culture, wooden buildings were perceived as temporary, even uncouth, so many settlers found the use of the material novel.[58] In April 1840, Wellington's Presbyterian minister, Revd John Macfarlane, reported: 'I am getting up my home, though you

would think it a rather strange one, for there is not a single stone in it. It is built of wood, thatched with reeds – 28 feet [8.5 metres] long, 18 [5.5 metres] feet wide, roof 8 [2.4 metres] feet high. It contains a good parlour, bedroom and kitchen.'[59] The different rooms and the multi-functional use of these dwellings – where occupants slept, cooked and socialised – set them apart from one-roomed whare, whose functions were more strongly defined by building type.[60]

The main problem with raupō buildings was their flammability. This was illustrated by a terrifying fire along Wellington's beach (Lambton Quay) during the night of 9–10 November 1842. Starting in Lloyd's bakehouse beside Kumutoto pā (Woodward Street), and fanned by a blustery northerly wind, the blaze consumed some structures and leapt over others. Sydney Wright was shipboard in Lambton Harbour and came up on deck at eleven o'clock to see 'a great fire on the beach running along with the gales in solid flames'.[61] One eyewitness reported: 'so rapidly was the fire communicated from one to another thatched roof, that it was almost impossible to proceed along the beach at an equal rate'.[62] 'Many were obliged to catch their children in their arms, and escape with nothing but their bed linen on,' recorded another.[63] Such was the heat that John Plimmer plunged into the sea to stop being burned.[64] The inferno was arrested only after people pulled down three dwellings at the north end of the beach (near Plimmer Lane)

Aucklanders saw raupō buildings as an intolerable fire hazard and in 1842 Auckland became the first town to ban their construction in favour of timber, brick and stone structures. This William Fox painting from 1849 shows the town's development, with buildings spreading south from Shortland Crescent and west into the foreground. Dominating the scene is St Paul's Church, an Auckland landmark until its 1885 demolition. William Fox, Hocken Collections, Uare Taoka o Hākena, University of Otago, 12,881

to starve it of fuel. In only 30 minutes, 57 buildings and a substantial £12,000 of property were destroyed, though no lives were lost.[65] Settlers and Māori quickly rallied to help the fire's victims, donating money, timber, food and clothes.[66]

Recognition that raupō structures had aided the spread of the fire led to calls for the Governor to apply New Zealand's first building regulation, the Raupo House Ordinance, to Wellington.[67] The measure levied a £20 annual rating on any urban building built wholly or partly of raupō, straw or thatch. New buildings of these materials were subject to a £100 tax.[68] The Legislative Council had passed the ordinance in March 1842 following lobbying by Auckland property owners worried that raupō houses were an intolerable fire hazard. Auckland was the first to adopt the measure but few thought it could be applied to Wellington. As one commentator noted: 'the town of Wellington consists so generally of Raupo houses ... that their removal would have the effect of unhousing *thousands*'.[69] The point was supported by an 1843 survey of Wellington's buildings that showed over half of all dwellings were of raupō construction.[70] However, the fire of November 1842 had exposed the danger of raupō structures, and the ordinance was applied to the town in October 1844.[71]

Why raupō buildings proliferated in Wellington, but not in Auckland, was a function of each town's initial size. With hundreds of settlers arriving at once, Wellington lacked the infrastructure and resources to accommodate everyone in wooden houses, so became reliant on Māori provision of raupō dwellings. With fewer people arriving in Auckland, the town was better able to fend for itself. Although raupō dwellings were initially common in Auckland, the situation changed after the April 1841 land sale, when wood became the dominant building material. By July, the settler Joseph Newman noted 'the sound of the hammering has hardly ceased to ring in our Ears, and Weather Board Buildings are being erected in every part of Town'.[72] Whereas Wellington began with a culturally hybrid built environment, comprising both settler- and Māori-built structures, Auckland moved promptly to create one that was overtly European. Nonetheless, Wellington's raupō fabric was also fleeting. The fire ordinance, the fact that raupō became brittle through weathering, and settlers' desire for more permanent buildings meant that by the late 1840s the town's raupō buildings had largely given way to wooden or brick ones.[73] Among these was the Athenaeum and Mechanics' Institute, which, as we saw in Chapter One, opened in April 1850. The Greek Revival-styled building comprised a Doric-columned portico and pediment, and two well-proportioned wings, one for a museum and the other a library. It was built of wood but plastered to resemble stone. The building was the first of architectural substance in Wellington and can be seen as a deliberate attempt to move past the utilitarian style of the first settlers and to build in a mode that put a sophisticated European stamp on the town. As one delighted aesthete proclaimed: at least they now had one public building that was 'creditable to the taste of the community'.[74]

Thanks to plentiful supplies and its ability to be easily fashioned, wood was the primary building material in the South Island towns too, although a few earth (cob, sod or pise) and brick buildings were built in Nelson, Dunedin and Christchurch. As elsewhere, many Christchurch settlers began life in temporary dwellings. A distinctive regional example of this type was the 'V-hut', a gabled wooden structure with a door and window at one end and a canvas or thatched roof.[75] Among those who lived in a V-hut were Dr Alfred Barker, his wife Emma and their three boys. Barker built the dwelling using packing cases for walls and one of the *Charlotte Jane*'s studding sails for the roof – he wryly named it Studdingsail Hall. Inside, the family sought to create a semblance of domesticity by filling it with some of their English furniture, including a table and chairs, chest

Until the 1850s most town buildings were utilitarian in style. This began to change that decade when a few buildings of architectural merit went up. This included the Neo-classical Wellington Athenaeum and Mechanics' Institute, which opened on Lambton Quay in 1850 and is shown here about 1860. In what became a Wellington tradition, it was a wooden building crafted to resemble stone. Alexander Turnbull Library, 1/2-008507-F

of drawers and a mantel clock.[76] The habitation was tolerable in fine weather but proved miserable in the wet. In south-west storms, Barker wrote:

> the strong rafters bent like osiers before the wind, while the rain squeezed through the painted sail-cloth as if it had been a sieve, wetting and drenching everything in the tent ... Frequently at times the fire would be put out, and we had nothing but to sit shivering in cold and hunger from morning till night.[77]

A further problem was caused by drunks from a neighbouring pub falling against the tent at all hours of the night.[78] Such experiences encouraged Barker to erect a more secure, permanent home. He chose pise construction (where slightly damp earth is rammed into a timber frame to make a sort of instant concrete). To better protect the dwelling from the elements, he was persuaded to cover it with tar and lime, an irremediable move that he thought made it 'hideously ugly'. His only consolation was 'that it is very snug inside'.[79]

The colonial cottage

Barker's dwelling was in the colonial cottage architectural style. This was the case for most urban housing until the villa style emerged in the 1860s.[80] As with the prefabricated and raupō cottages, this idiom was based on the English rural cottage – one architectural historian has traced its origins to the late eighteenth- and early-nineteenth-century weatherboard houses of Kent and East Sussex – and was widespread throughout New Zealand and Australia.[81] Cottages were graded according to size. The smallest houses were called 'cottages', the next step up were 'superior cottages' and the bigger still were 'houses', often further distinguished as 'substantial' or 'of more pretentions'.[82] At its simplest, the cottage was a rectangular box with a gabled or hipped roof, and a chimney at one end. The front comprised a central door with two windows placed symmetrically either side of it. The smallest cottage was a single room but most had three to five: a sitting room, kitchen (often combined in smaller dwellings) and two or more bedrooms. Extra rooms could be readily created through skillions (lean-tos) at the back. Some cottages had dormer windows and/or windows under the gable to make use of space in roof cavities.

Interiors were lined with plain boards.[83] Such linings gave little protection against heat loss, and this, alongside the fact that not all rooms had fireplaces, made houses cold and damp in winter. In 1850, Charlotte Godley wrote that the draughts coming under the doors and through the boards in a southerly wind made her Wellington home 'really quite cold'.[84] Similarly, in 1860 Annabel Owen bemoaned the lack of fireplaces in her Auckland home. She was pregnant and dreaded the prospect of a cold bedroom during the forthcoming winter. In a letter to her sister at Prince Edward Island she wrote: 'Just fancy yourself confined to your room in cold damp weather just like you have at home in November without a warm fire.'[85] Conditions were cooler still in Dunedin. In June 1888, Emma Thomson complained that she and her husband George 'could not sleep for the cold last night'.[86] Why houses were under-heated is uncertain. It could be that having lived in brick and stone dwellings in Britain, most settlers were unfamiliar with the lower thermal qualities of timber buildings. New Zealand's temperate climate might have also led them to underestimate the coolness of its winters. It can only be surmised that a settler proclivity towards stoicism – discomfort was an attribute of colonial life – meant they gave little thought to improving things. So it became a New Zealand custom to heat the kitchen, where the coal range was, and the sitting room, but not the other rooms.[87]

Dr Alfred Barker was an amateur photographer and in the early 1860s he took this image of Christchurch's Armagh Street looking west towards Riccarton Bush. A range of single and two-story wooden cottages lines the street, which at this time was little more than a dirt and grass track. Alfred Charles Barker, Alexander Turnbull Library, 1/2-022719-F

A final attribute of the colonial cottage was the veranda. It originated in the southern United States before spreading to the West Indies and Australia. While some Auckland houses sported the feature in the 1840s, it became ubiquitous in the rest of the colony only from the 1860s.[88] Verandas provided shelter from the elements and were a transitional zone between indoors and outdoors: a place to take off sodden coats or catch cooling summer breezes.[89]

Much of what we know about colonial urban housing comes from analysing the materiality and spatial arrangements of the dwellings that survive into the present. Settler accounts of their dwellings and their spatial organisation increase this understanding. For instance, in 1858 Revd John Crump recorded how the appearance of Auckland's 'wooden stable-like houses is surprising when you get inside'. They were 'splendidly carpeted and furnished & [had] clear indications of wealth almost everywhere'.[90] The following year, the Christchurch builder James Parr described the interior of his Kilmore Street home:

It is lined with totara – a red wood that planes very easy when it is dry. We have oiled it. The ceiling is calico. The floor is white pine. It is roofed with ... shingle ... In one corner of the kitchen we have 2 shelves to put our crocks on ... As for furniture we have a table, a camp stool, 1 black box with a back to it for a seat ... The window curtains are red with white leaves and flowers.

He made much of some of the chattels the siblings brought with them and that provided a mnemonic or psychological connection to their former home. 'We have the Sefton Church [St Helen's] picture over the chimneypiece. We framed and glazed the "Happy Homes of England" last night and hung it up opposite the fireplace.' To help locate themselves in their new land, the family had a map of New Zealand 'hung beside the window'. William also described their garden. It 'is fenced in with galvanised wire and a Cape broom hedge in the front. The back is a native hedge. We have some cabbages, beans & peas in our garden besides 2 walnuts, 2 cherry trees & a plum, abt [about] 100 gooseberry cuttings, besides other things too numerous to mention'.[91]

During the 1870s, the villa joined the cottage as an urban housing type. In eighteenth-century Britain, a villa referred to a country house of a wealthy person, but by the mid-nineteenth century it more commonly described a stand-alone, middle-class suburban dwelling. In New Zealand these were usually built in Gothic or (Neo-classical) Italianate architectural styles. A cottage was henceforth any smaller house of lesser pretension. Both cottages and villas usually comprised square or L-shaped plans, where rooms came off a central passage or hall. Bay windows also became a common feature, while machine moulding of wood provided for increased ornamentation. Later, some villas featured highly decorative fretwork and bargeboards – attributes that reflected the wealth and taste of their owners.[92]

The struggle for streets

While the buildings in towns were becoming more civilised, the same could not be said about the streets. In many cases, the grids of streets that surveyors had so mathematically configured on paper remained unformed. Viewing the state of Wellington in 1842, one observer reported 'there is no attempt at a street, save in two places, where a few houses are built in a straight line'.[93] At the same time, Auckland had only three streets to speak of: Princes Street, Shortland Crescent and Lower Queen Street. Often a track running through an open space signalled the intention of a street, but sometimes there was not even that. One famed Canterbury tale relates how a man battling his way through the high scrub in Cathedral Square ran into a prominent early settler and indignantly demanded to be shown the way to Christchurch.[94] Moreover, the dirt surface of streets could make travelling along them a trial. Summer winds whipped up blinding dust; winter rain created porridge-like bogs. In wet weather, Dunedin's streets became 'canals of liquid mud and clay', earning the settlement the moniker 'Mud-Edin'. Pedestrians were forced to cling to street edges to avoid the knee-deep sludge in the middle, or to throw bundles of flax over the mire before stepping out.[95] Horses, bullocks and drays often became stuck. In one incident, a wagon was trapped in the Rattray Street mud up to its axle and its horse up to it its belly. It took a man with eight bullocks to pull them out.[96]

The prevalence of open drains and sewers was another irritant. The most famous of these was Auckland's Ligar Canal (the stream Te Wai Horotiu) that ran down the middle of Queen Street. During rainstorms it was prone to flooding. In one 1848 event, '[e]very cut, every drain, became a brawling brook, dashing its fretful waters towards the Queen-street rivulet, which assumed the breadth, depth, and volume of an impatient mountain torrent "on mischief bent".' Moments later, the surge broke the canal's banks and inundated the cottages and buildings of lower Queen Street before flushing away the muck piles of Fort Street.[97] Drains and streams became even more hazardous at night; street lighting was limited to a few flickering candle lanterns hung over hotel entrances.[98] As Aucklander Joseph Blades recalled, these 'served the purpose of making the darkness visible, and very often deluded the unwary into the belief that he was treading on solid ground, when he would suddenly find himself … up to his knees in mud'.[99] While the colonial government undertook some street improvements, these were never enough to improve conditions overall.

In these early settlements, the infrastructure had to be built from scratch; this was the reality of the settler colonial city. But the provision of streets, pipes and lighting was hampered also by the speculative model on which these cities were founded. The tendency of absentee or long-term investors to sit on their land and wait for its value to rise meant the task of developing infrastructure fell on settler communities. As early as 1842, the unfairness of this burden led Wellington capitalists to call for absentee landowners to contribute to its cost.[100] 'You absentees', protested one landowner, 'are content to sit by the fire-side and speculate upon the advance which will take place … at our expense.'[101] The complainant suggested British absentees form a loan and trust company to help fund public infrastructure – as had happened in Adelaide – but the proposal failed to find a sponsor, leaving the settler community to continue to shoulder the expense. Settler capitalists in Nelson considered absenteeism 'the evil of new settlements'.[102] Essentially, the absentee landowners were sleeping investors who provided start-up capital but played no active role. Still, the alternative of a highly centralised town-founding model would have placed constraints on private property rights and hence individual wealth creation. Settlers might grumble about sacrifices they made that benefited others, but few doubted the capitalist model was the best way to deliver prosperity.

With the passing of the 1852 Constitution Act, responsibility for building and maintaining streets passed to provincial governments, which could levy rates or borrow to fund public works. Some governments passed this function on to locally elected municipal councils or town boards. Dunedin and Nelson went down this route in 1855 and 1856 respectively, and by 1862 the three other towns had followed suit.[103] An early funding model for street improvements was grants-in-aid: residents in a particular street, or part thereof, paid half the cost of a street improvement and the government the other half. Residents would form street committees and solicit funds from those affected before calling for tenders. In some cases, prison labour was used to reduce costs. Improvements included constructing footpaths, building kerbs and drains, bridging waterways and putting down macadam street surfaces – metal (gravel) mixed with clay cement. In Wellington, Abel Smith, Tory, Dixon, Manners and Molesworth streets were all improved using this model.[104] The downside was that some property owners refused to pay, meaning the financial burden fell on the more public-spirited. Improvements were also intermittent: a long street could be very good in one section but terrible in another. The model also favoured wealthier districts; poorer areas often missed out altogether.[105] The Australian writer Henry Lawson later satirised the New Zealand attribute of uncompleted footpaths:

> Another thing that strikes a new chum is the way the footpaths are half-paved. There are flags from the kerb to a line running along the centre of the path, and the rest is gravel. The stranger is told that the Council agreed to pave one half, if the ratepayers did the other. The city fathers fulfilled their part of the contract, but the respected citizens didn't come up to time: they declined to shell out. They walked on the paved half and chuckled.[106]

For these reasons, some boards relied on rates and loans to fund public works. Christchurch's board adopted this approach from its creation, concentrating its early energies on building and repairing streets in the town centre. By October 1862, 5 miles (8 kilometres) of streets had been formed, metalled and provided with footpaths: 'many places which three months ago were completely impassable, now have a good solid roadway'. The board also began employing men to water the streets to keep down the acrid summer dust.[107]

In the same month in Dunedin, some 500 men began work on levelling Bell Hill. While the town's grid had Princes Street running up and over the hill, it was in fact too steep for most vehicular traffic, meaning that Dunedin's commercial hub (centred on Jetty Street) was cut off from the Octagon. It was typical of the

The lack of flat land in all cities but Christchurch obstructed development. From 1872 authorities in Auckland began excavating Britomart Point, using the spill to reclaim land from Waitematā Harbour between Freemans and Mechanics bays. The sheer scale of the task is evident in this 1885 photograph, taken shortly before the demolition of St Paul's Church, which was in the way of the venture. Sir George Grey Special Collections, Auckland Libraries, 7-A4999

settlers' mindset that rather than adapting the grid to the lie of the land, they preferred to modify the land so it conformed to the grid. In 1858, a 6-metre-wide cutting was blasted through the hill to link the two sides of town. This was just the start. For a decade from 1862, both contract and prison labour were used to remove the hill to a depth of up to 25 metres, with the spoil being used to reclaim the foreshore and to create much-needed level land and form streets such as Cumberland Street.[108] It was a massive undertaking that was done without heavy machinery: the production of urban space could be every bit as 'heroic' as the felling of forests. While the doctrine of 'improvement' or 'progress' has often been used as an explanatory framework for settlers' taming of the land, projects like Bell Hill (or the later removal of Britomart Point in Auckland) show the doctrine was by no means exclusively a rural construct.[109] Urban lands were tamed too.

Colonial urbanism

Improved housing and streets gave the settlements a greater sense of urbanity. As one observer said of Christchurch, the 'whare and V hut stage of civilisation passed away and the capital began to look like a town'.[110] Alfred Barker was one of those who recorded the change, in his case through the modern medium of photography. Of particular value is a panorama of the town taken in about 1860

Rather than adapt the grid plan to conform to the lay of the land city builders more often adapted the land to conform to the grid. In Dunedin, the steepness of Bell Hill hindered the flow of traffic along lineal Princes Street. This image from the early 1860s shows workers using pick and shovel to lower the hill to provide an easier gradient. Toitū Otago Settlers Museum, 1986.69.1

from the tower of the newly built Provincial Council Buildings. It shows the extent of the ten-year-old town, and highlights the low-density and sprawling nature of early New Zealand urbanism, characterised by built-up areas with either empty space or small groups of buildings in between.[111] The pattern was a product of capitalist social relations. The unbuilt spaces were the result of long-term investors waiting for land values to rise before developing their properties. Conversely, intensively built-up areas were created by short-term speculators' sub-dividing their lands for quick capital gain. Observing this latter process in Auckland in 1842, one critic had warned: 'Miserable lanes will usurp the place of streets, blind alleys will be as common as Deptford ... and hovels will be packed as closely as in St Giles.'[112] He proved prophetic. By the 1870s, Chancery Lane and its neighbouring alleys had become the city's slum. Even so, such intensive development was unusual, and low-density urbanism remained the norm.

This is the view over the Chancery Lane district of Auckland towards Queens Wharf in the 1860s. The neighbourhood had been quickly subdivided after the 1840s land sales and became an area of intensive working-class housing, defying the low-density, sprawling pattern of the rest of the city. By the 1870s it was widely viewed as a slum. Sir George Grey Special Collections, Auckland Libraries, 4-8993

Some observers condemned the settlement pattern. In 1853, the travel writer Warren Adams described Christchurch's 'straggling and irregular' appearance as 'decidedly ugly' and proclaimed the more compact Lyttelton far prettier.[113] Others were more complimentary. William Parr told his brother that Christchurch was 'well laid out with good wide streets, some of them without any house in. But you must not think from that it is a small town. There are somewhere about 400 houses and some of them very nice ones too.'[114] Yet the straggling nature of towns raised logistical issues, not the least of which was their defence. A government official examining how towns might be secured against Māori attack concluded that the manner in which they had been built made their 'defence impossible'. He continued: 'Houses, generally of weatherboards, are as built as wide apart, and scattered over as great an extent of open land, as is compatible with their being considered collection of dwellings (in other words, a town or village) at all.'[115]

Unlike European towns that were tightly built up, and traditionally contained within defensive walls, the haphazard expanse of New Zealand urbanism defied traditional expectations of what constituted a town.

New Zealand's sprawling urbanism followed that of Australia's. In laying out Sydney in 1788, Governor Phillip promoted the stand-alone house on an individual section and a cultivated garden – an important element in many household economies, allowing families to self-provision with fresh vegetables and fruit, and so gain a degree of independence. Hobart too was characterised by single houses on their own plots with gardens. As one historian has observed, 'Australia's founders anticipated a sprawl of homes and gardens rather than a clumping of terraces and alleys.'[116] New Zealand was quick to follow the same path. In 1842, a Wellington printer recorded how '[e]very person seems to have an inclination to build houses and fence in their ground … Brick and wooden houses are springing up on ground that appeared deserted; gardens fenced in and cultivated'.[117] Similarly, fellow Wellingtonian Mary Petre 'much admired the many little cottages with a small patch of cultivated ground around them'.[118]

Historians have located the origins of this settlement pattern in the countryside. Erik Olssen has written: 'The ubiquity of the owner-occupied single-unit house on its own often quite large section transposed into an urban environment the possibilities for independence once assumed to be the exclusive preserve of yeoman farmers.'[119] Within this paradigm, the colonial town can be viewed as a web of small smallholdings and as an overt expression of anti-urban sentiment. It was certainly a refutation of the cheek-by-jowl urbanism that characterised large European towns and cities, where most buildings were packed together and sections or plots were either non-existent or small. It was also a rebuff to the class-defined housing typology of urban Britain: row and tenement housing for workers, terrace or semi-detached housing for the middle classes, and stand-alone villas on suburban plots for the capitalist elite.[120] By the time of New Zealand's colonisation, row and tenement housing was associated with the overcrowding and squalor of Old World industrial city slums – a taint that few wanted replicated in the New. Aside from a few examples of terrace housing in Christchurch and Dunedin, medium-density housing was virtually unknown in New Zealand.[121] This aspect was to differentiate New Zealand's cities from their Australian counterparts, whose larger populations and the need to be within walking distance of city workplaces generated higher inner-city housing densities, leading to streets of terrace housing in Sydney and Melbourne.[122] Yet opposition to aspects of metropolitan urbanism did not necessarily make colonial society anti-urban. Rather, it signalled an ambition to create more spacious and modern cities that would offer most settlers a better quality of life than in Britain. Understood this way, the single-unit house on its own section

The suburban nature of cities is highlighted in this view of Auckland's Parnell in 1914. It shows the prevalence of single detached houses on their own sections, many with gardens to grow home produce and keep chickens. The houses in the foreground are on Birdwood Crescent, with Knox Presbyterian Church in the centre. Robert Walrond, Museum of New Zealand Te Papa Tongarewa, A.018199

referenced the suburban villas and parkland settings of Manchester and London's capitalist elites.

The reality was that New Zealand developed a hybrid urbanism, incorporating both country and city elements – a 'middle landscape'. The large section with a fecund garden evoked the self-provisioning smallholder; the higher population density suggested the propinquity and sociability of metropolitan life. We would now refer to this morphology as suburban, but in New Zealand the term originally referred to smallholding-size allotments on town peripheries, as in Nelson and Dunedin. Urban was the town. Yet the sprawling and shapeless nature of colonial towns showed that 'urban' had different meanings in colonial New Zealand and Britain.[123]

This difference included home ownership. Official data on housing tenure was not collected in New Zealand until the 1916 Census, so it is difficult to ascertain

Mary Petre arrived in Wellington in 1843 with her husband Henry. Mary was a sociable woman and found life in the new city very convivial. Alexander Turnbull Library, 1/2-047261-F

the extent to which colonial city dwellers were homeowners. A comparison with Australia might provide an indicative measure: in 1890, 41 per cent of Melbourne households and 30 per cent of Sydney households owned their own homes. We can speculate that the rate for New Zealand fell within this range or may have been even higher – in 1916, the New Zealand home-ownership rate was 52 per cent.[124] In any event, it was certainly higher than in Britain, where before the First World War fewer than 10 per cent of homes were owner occupied.[125]

Within Victorian society, home ownership was equated with a greater level of independence and respectability than renting. Prior to universal male suffrage, property ownership conferred the right to vote, increasing the owner's social status and self-respect and lessening the obligation of deference. The prospect of home ownership was therefore a strong factor in the decision of working people to immigrate to the settler colonies. If British 'migrants were pushed out by economic hardship or worse, they were also pulled out by the lure of free or cheap land,' writes John Darwin.[126] Similarly, Graeme Davison has argued that 'the only real prospect of freehold ownership for most British working men was in the colonies'. He notes that in their letters home Australian immigrants often spoke

Many working people were attracted to colonies like New Zealand by the prospect of becoming property owners. Theodor Görmann and his wife (name unknown) personify the success of this ambition. In this circa 1870s photograph he poses in the doorway of his Nelson workshop while she stands on the hearth of their home. Theodor Bloch, Alexander Turnbull Library, PA1-q-035-28-1

of the desire for home ownership, its association with independence and their success in realising it.[127] This was true for many New Zealand immigrants too, among them Dunedin resident J. F. Blackwood, his wife Elizabeth and their four children. In a letter to his parents in 1861, the general hand spoke of his success in building his Maitland Street home:

> We have now got into our own new house. It has been a strugle [*sic*] to get it up but we are now into it at a cost of upwards of Seventy £. That is one of the great comforts of a Colonist that altho [*sic*] the life be a little rugged you have your own dwelling and piece of Ground a thing almost out of the power of any working man in the home country.[128]

That he and his family moved into his own home only four years after arriving in New Zealand highlights the importance some working-class settlers placed on becoming owner-occupiers. The travel writer Alexander Bathgate reinforced the

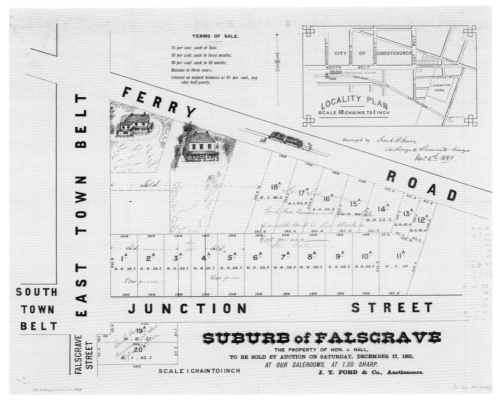

This plan advertises the 1881 sale of sections in the suburb of Falsgrave (now Waltham) in Christchurch. The drawings of single houses in spacious grounds underscore the subdivision's bucolic attributes, while the modern steam tram locates it close to the city. Such imagery reinforced the idea of suburbia as a 'middle landscape' between town and country. Alexander Turnbull Library, MapColl834.4492gbbd/1881/Acc.39358

point in 1874, reporting that some of Dunedin's 'suburbs are almost exclusively filled with neat little cottages owned by working men'.[129]

It was a feature of colonial urbanism that rich and poor often lived in the same streets. (Spatial segregation became more pronounced only in the twentieth century as suburbanisation increased.)[130] But if the pervasiveness of home ownership and the move to a common housing type and greater social mixing in New Zealand was a nod in the direction of New World egalitarianism, it did not negate the importance of social status. Working people might rightly luxuriate in the fact they lived in a stand-alone house on its own plot with a garden, but they also knew the larger house with the more spacious garden further up the street most likely belonged to people who were above them in the social hierarchy.[131]

The last defining feature of colonial urbanism was its eclecticism. Rather than streets of buildings of a similar design and/or scale, as was common in European cities, buildings in New Zealand's streets were a hotchpotch of different heights and designs. As early as 1842, Wellington was described as a scattered village of 1,100 town acres 'on which every one has built as suited his tastes and means'.[132] A decade later, George Earp observed of Auckland that '[u]niformity in the town has been set at defiance, every one building according to his means or fancy'.[133] William Swainson agreed, and asserted '[t]he only approach to uniformity is in the material: with a few exceptions, all are of wood'.[134] The eclecticism was a result of the laissez-faire political economy of New World societies which promoted individualism and the primacy of private property rights. Accordingly, property owners were largely free to construct what they liked, the size and style of buildings reflecting their wealth, power and aesthetic taste.[135] So in contrast to the standardised British row house or the common building style of cities like Bath that conveyed collective urban identities, the divergent sizes and designs of houses and buildings in urban New Zealand expressed the diverse identities of their owners.[136] Even in residential streets, houses of a common style were often distinguished by different architectural treatments or additions. Twentieth-century critics were to condemn this aspect of New Zealand's urbanism. For instance, in 1947 the Modernist architect Ernst Plischke characterised the New Zealand town as 'a haphazard collection of all sorts of buildings and most of the styles of the last two thousand years … strung along a road, without regard to the size or character of the neighbouring buildings or the appearance of the street'.[137] Such criticism eventually led to controls on the size and bulk of buildings but largely stopping short of regulating for style.[138] To restrict property owners from constructing a building of their own design would have gone against the cultural grain.

Becoming cities

By the early 1860s, the five towns were moving past their provisional and makeshift origins and cementing a more durable and distinguished image that underscored their transition from towns to cities. Christchurch had been the first to officially become a city, in 1856 by letters patent – a practice under British law whereby the monarch could designate a town a city if it became a bishop's seat. Nelson also became a city this way in 1858, even though its population was barely 3,000. Dunedin, Wellington and Auckland were each bestowed city status during the 1860s by their provincial governments, a standing ratified by the (central government) Municipal Corporations Act of 1867. Dunedin was the first to establish a city council in 1865, after the provincial government dissolved its ineffective Town Board. Christchurch made the move in 1868, followed by

Wellington, Auckland and Nelson in 1870, 1871 and 1874 respectively.[139] No other cities were proclaimed until Wanganui in 1924.

The most tangible marker of this change was the rebuilding of their Central Business Districts (CBDs) and the erection of buildings of permanent materials – brick, masonry and stone – to show material progress from frontier towns to modern cities. Auckland was the first to undergo substantial change. In the early 1860s, it benefited from strong immigration (its population doubled, from 6,300 to 12,400, between 1858 and 1864) and its being the base for the Crown invasion of Waikato.[140] The growth increased central-city land values, encouraging building owners to redevelop their properties to generate higher returns – the process of creative destruction. In 1864, a city newspaper observed how the business district was being transformed. 'Streets that less than three years ago were lined with wooden buildings and shanties of unsightly appearance and doubtful security, have been replaced by handsome buildings, which would be a credit to any city.'[141] Arriving in the mid-1860s, Lewis Haslam was surprised to find Auckland was 'a much larger place than I expected it would be ... shops are as large as in Cheapside and Bishopsgate St [London]'.[142]

The rebuilding of the city was supported by overseas investment capital. This included the New Zealand head office of the Union Bank of Australia, opened in May on the corner of Queen Street and Victoria Street West. Designed in the Greek Revival (Neo-classical) style by the Melbourne architect Leonard Terry, the two-storey building sat on a scoria block base and had masonry walls that were dressed to look like stone. The Queen Street elevation was an expansive 24 metres long and 15 metres high, and dominated by a four-columned Corinthian portico. Three flights of stone steps led to the main door and into a spacious and ornate 9-metre-high banking chamber. It was not long before the imposing pile was soon dubbed 'the chief architectural ornament in the city'.[143] In referencing the great civic architecture of both ancient Rome and modern London, the building evoked imperial ties and prestige and also suggested the emergence of a new cultural depth in Auckland. As Tristram Hunt has written in respect of nineteenth-century British city-building: 'Classical architecture became intimately associated not only with commercial and cultural ideals of the Greek city states, but also with a more philosophical celebration of the public sphere ... To build in the Greek style indicated a confidence in the value of urban living and the ethic of citizenship.'[144]

Such sentiments were alluded to in a commentary piece about the new building published in the *Daily Southern Cross*. The writer claimed the town's commercial class had previously been indifferent to their workplaces, but this building suggested a growing aesthetic awareness within the group that 'a handsome building is not necessarily an inconvenient or undesirable one for the conduct of business'. He continued: 'Everything connected with the new bank premises is

Auckland's first commercial building of architectural substance was the Union Bank, erected on the corner of Queen Street and Victoria Street West and opened in 1864. Melburnian Leonard Terry designed it in the fashionable Greek Revival style and it is shown here shortly after its completion. Also captured within the frame is a hawker's cart. Hocken Collections, Uare Taoka o Hākena, University of Otago, P1922-001 KIN055

got up with exceeding taste, and has the advantage, moreover, of being substantial. There is an air of permanence about it which must strike every one on entering the building.' He predicted rival institutions would soon erect similar edifices, making Auckland second to Melbourne in the elegance of its bank buildings.[145] He did not have to wait long. In 1867, the locally owned Bank of New Zealand head office opened further down Queen Street. This too was designed by Terry and built in the same well-mannered Greek Revival style. In deference to parochial pride, it was larger than the Union Bank, being three storeys high, with a longer street frontage and a more imposing banking chamber.[146]

The comparison to Melbourne underlines the importance such buildings had in place-promotion and civic boosterism – of the need to keep ahead or at least abreast of rival towns.[147] The air of permanence that such buildings were said to carry was of course ephemeral. The production of capitalist space

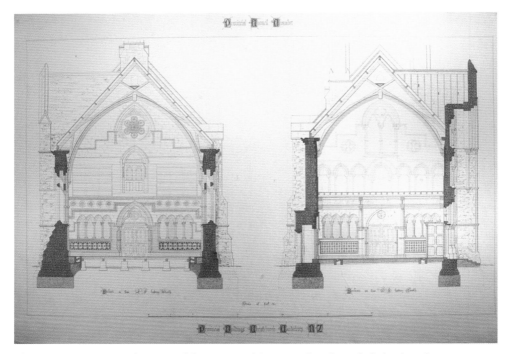

This is a cross-section drawing of the Neo-Gothic stone chamber of Christchurch's Canterbury Provincial Buildings. It was designed by Benjamin Mountfort and completed in 1865. The structure was New Zealand's best example of High Victorian Gothic architecture, but it collapsed in the 2011 Christchurch earthquake and in 2016 its future was uncertain. Benjamin Mountfort, Canterbury Museum, 19XX.2.347

required continual cycles of creative destruction, and both buildings fell victim to new waves of capitalist activity in the twentieth century. The Union Bank was replaced in 1972 by a glass and steel skyscraper, which although taller lacked the commanding presence of the former building. All but the Bank of New Zealand's street facade was demolished in 1986. It now stands as a tangible, if forlorn, link to Auckland's genesis as a city.[148]

Christchurch's first Neo-classical building of merit was another Terry-designed Bank of New Zealand building, a commanding one-storey structure completed in 1866 on the corner of Colombo and Hereford streets – and demolished in 1963.[149] Christchurch had in fact led the way in erecting buildings, initially in wood, that were redolent of a city rather than a town. Foremost among these was the two-storey Provincial Council Buildings in Durham Street. The local architect Benjamin Mountfort designed the complex in the Gothic Revival style. The Gothic style was associated with the soaring cathedrals and striking civic buildings of medieval Europe; nineteenth-century English architects like Augustus Pugin

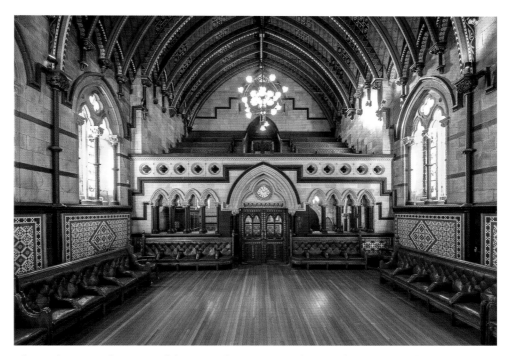

The Gothic Revival interior of the Canterbury Provincial Council's stone chamber was one of the complex's most striking features. The richly coloured room was accentuated by the stained glass windows on either side. Photograph by David Ford

believed the style was more vernacular and Christian than classicism, and so promoted its revival.[150] It was made fashionable by Sir Gilbert Scott's new Houses of Parliament at Westminster. As Ian Lochhead has pointed out, this made the Provincial Council Buildings 'right up to the minute architecturally speaking', highlighting how there was 'no cultural lag' between metropole and colony.[151] The ceremony marking the laying of their foundation stone in January 1858 was deemed so civically important that a public holiday was declared. The event drew a large crowd of all social classes and began with a procession, led by a brass band, of clergy, justices, politicians and others through city streets to the building site. There the footprint of the building had been marked out using a series of poles, each with a pennon (a long triangular streamer), placed 3 metres apart. Higher poles carrying two festoons of flowers and foliage signalled the entrance porch, and a 15-metre mast bearing the Union Jack and four 12-metre masts denoted the proposed clock tower. A temporary covered grandstand was erected for ladies to watch proceedings. With the flags fluttering and bouquets of flowers placed about the site, 'the arrangements were the most artistic that have ever been seen here', declared one delighted observer. Canterbury superintendent William

Arguably Dunedin's grandest 19th-century building was the Neo-classical Post Office designed by William Mason and opened in 1868 – seen here in 1890. For political reasons it never served its designated purpose. Instead, it became a museum, university, bank, and then the city's stock exchange. It was unceremoniously demolished in 1969. Hocken Collections, Uare Taoka o Hākena, University of Otago, Box-224-001

Moorhouse laid the stone using a special silver trowel, after which the band struck up 'Rule Britannia' and a nine-gun salute was fired. Following a speech by Moorhouse, the band played 'God Save the Queen', three cheers were given and the crowd departed.[152]

Mountfort-designed additions to the wooden buildings were made in stone in the mid-1860s in the same style, notably the magnificent Great Hall and Bellamy's. As these were being completed, work was beginning on what later became an emblem of the city: Gilbert Scott's Neo-Gothic Christchurch Cathedral.[153] Both buildings were severely damaged in the 2011 Christchurch earthquake, and in early 2016 their future was still uncertain.

The greatest material transition from town to city occurred in Dunedin, where the 1861 discovery of gold in Central Otago led to an influx of thousands of miners and new settlers, and made the province the most populous in New Zealand. The returns from gold also made it the wealthiest.[154] Some of this capital was invested in the built environment, triggering a process of creative destruction in the CBD. The change is evident in two photographs of Princes Street looking south-east from Dowling Street, one taken in 1861 and the other about a decade later. The first shows rudimentary wooden shops running down the street in a line broken only by a two-storey stone structure nearing completion in the middle distance. Further along is the Mechanics' Institute (the square structure with a hipped roof) and behind that stands the Town Board building. The image highlights the primitive condition of the street. It is unsealed and there are no footpaths. Less than a decade later, and it has been graded and widened. It also has a macadam surface. Footpaths have been formed and have a stable woodblock surface. Almost all the buildings have been replaced with two- and three-storey stone and masonry edifices in Classical Revival styles. These include three banks, the Bank of New South Wales, Bank of Otago and Bank of New Zealand, reinforcing the area's status as Dunedin's financial district.

The most impressive of the street's new buildings was the post office, built on the Town Board building site. Designed in a Neo-classical or (more strictly) Palladian style by former Aucklander William Mason, it is regarded by architectural historian John Stacpoole as Mason's 'finest achievement'.[155] The handsome two-storey building was built of Ōamaru limestone, a Dunedin first, and measured 46 metres long and 40 metres deep. Its main feature was a 37-metre illuminated clock tower facing Princes Street. (Its clock and bell had been ordered from Edinburgh by the Provincial Council back in 1864 on the expectation that a suitable public building would be found to house them in the city centre.)[156] The ground floor featured spacious colonnades, providing welcome shelter from the elements. The interior comprised offices and an ornately decorated central hall, 'intended as place where the townspeople might gather for the arrival of mail from the "Old Country"', and later used for official balls and other civic events.[157] As with Auckland's Colonial Bank, and Christchurch's Provincial Council Buildings, the post office was Dunedin's most prominent city-like building. As Stacpoole writes, the edifice 'was not noticeably colonial and would not have looked strange in a European setting'.[158] Shortly after it opened in 1868, an exuberant provincial politician called it 'a temple which every man who passed it must, or ought to, feel proud of having in New Zealand'.[159]

However, the building never fulfilled its designated purpose. As it was nearing completion, the colourful and parochial superintendent of Otago province, James Macandrew, declared a better use should be found for it. By the time it was completed, it would have cost the province between £20,000 and £30,000, he said. A perfectly good post office building could be erected for one-sixth of that. He proposed the central government hand the building over to the province and

This is Dunedin's Princes Street looking southeast from Dowling Street in 1861, the start of Otago's gold rush. Most of the buildings are a modest one-storey. Alexander Turnbull Library, 10x8-1662-G

in exchange it would erect a smaller post office elsewhere. More fitting functions could then be found for the building, such as a university, museum, town hall, free public library, or even a school of mines and agricultural chemistry. The two governments subsequently cut a deal along these lines.[160]

Why Macandrew thought a post office was a poor use for Mason's building is best explained by political gamesmanship.[161] Post offices, a vital node in local and global communications systems, were the most important public buildings in everyday city life – a status often expressed in their imposing scale and sophisticated architecture. Mason's grand design was therefore appropriate for such a significant edifice, and the previous provincial administration had supported it.[162] In showing no compunction to follow suit and honour the agreement made, Macandrew was exercising his newly won authority. His re-election in 1867 had been controversial because he had been dismissed from the same office in 1861 over a financial scandal. The Premier had expressed his disapproval of his re-

The same view of Dunedin's Princes Street a decade later shows how the gold rush completely altered the built environment of Dunedin's finance district. The low-rise buildings have been replaced by substantial masonry structures. Alexander Turnbull Library, 1/2-004505-F

election by withholding some superintendency powers. So Macandrew called, and won, a new plebiscite, forcing the central government to back down.[163] The acquisition of the post office can therefore be viewed as a muscular assertion of provincial power.[164]

Significantly, the building's first tenant was the Otago Museum, and it was soon to house the new University of Otago. As well as showcasing the city's wealth, material progress and modernity, the building spoke of regional identity and civic pride. In 1877, the Colonial Bank moved in.[165] In 1900, it was taken over by Dunedin's stock exchange and the area about it became known as 'The Exchange'. Sixty years later, the cultural meanings ascribed to the building had changed completely. Many now saw it as an archaic eyesore and raw reminder of the city's economic stasis. Local politicians and business leaders campaigned for a new building on the prominent site that expressed modern times and their aspirations for the city's renewal. In 1969, the now derelict structure was demolished and replaced with an unspectacular Modernist office tower and plaza – John Wickliffe House. In what might be interpreted as a belated collective sense of regret over the building's demise, locals continued to refer to the area in which it once stood as The Exchange.[166]

While Auckland, Christchurch and Dunedin were rebuilding in brick, masonry and stone, Wellington and Nelson continued to be largely wooden cities. In Wellington, this was a response to the 1848 and 1855 earthquakes. Many of the town's brick structures either collapsed or sustained significant damage, whereas most wooden buildings came through largely unscathed.[167] Accordingly, Wellington's city builders deemed it prudent to stick with wood as the settlement's main building material. Yet the European cultural bias against timber buildings meant many people saw the city's built environment as inherently inferior to its local counterparts'. Edward Hodder expressed a common sentiment in 1863, declaring Wellington's 'public buildings are not equal to those in some of the other provinces'.[168] Occasionally a different view was heard. Visiting in the early 1870s, David Kennedy was struck by the novelty of the city's buildings:

> Imagine a timber-built metropolis! Wellington, being subject to earthquakes, is constructed entirely of wood. It has, however, really a splendid appearance. Grand cornices, towers, steeples, balconies, verandahs, porches, shop-fronts, and pillars are seen at every turn – all wooden, but having a quite an imposing look … even when you are close to them. It is surprising the variety and elegance of form produced by means of wood.[169]

That a wooden building could be both imposing and elegant (adjectives usually reserved for masonry or stone structures) was obviously a surprise. But Wellington's city builders had long tried to temper the prejudice toward timber buildings by erecting structures that employed the language of stone. As we have seen, the wooden cladding of the Athenaeum and Mechanics' Institute had been plastered for this purpose. Its architectural treatments – quoins, window heads, columns, entablature and pediment – furthered the illusion. Many subsequent public and commercial buildings presented a similar front until 1881 when the city's first masonry structure was completed.

Wellington's rebuild was underpinned by its becoming the political capital in 1865. Initially the shift had little effect on the town because the scale of central government was relatively small. With the 1876 abolition of provincial governments, the role and importance of central government increased, necessitating more space for a growing civil service.[170] The Fox ministry had anticipated the need in the early 1870s by enlarging Parliament (the Legislature) and making plans for a new structure, Government Buildings, to accommodate the Executive (the cabinet and civil service). The four-storey edifice was constructed on a 1.2-hectare square of reclaimed land on Lambton Quay opposite Parliament. The Colonial Architect William Mason designed it in the Neo-classical style, with Doric-columned entrance porches, alternating window treatments and a projecting roof cornice. In the Wellington tradition it was built of timber fashioned to look like stone: wooden blocks were used as quoins and rusticated weatherboards imitated stone courses. But its most prominent attribute was its size and bulk. When it opened in 1876, it was New Zealand's biggest building and among the largest wooden office buildings in the world, a fact Wellingtonians incessantly impressed on visitors.[171] It was certainly a strong statement about the growing role of the state in New Zealand life and in the production of urban space.

With the Legislature and Executive now handsomely housed, attention turned to rehousing the third arm of government: the Judiciary. The existing courthouse was considered unworthy for a capital city, and a site for a new Supreme Court was secured in Stout Street, creating a symbolic triangle between Parliament, Government Buildings and the courthouse that embodied colonial authority.[172] The two-storey building was designed by Clayton's successor, Pierre Burrows, in an elegantly proportioned Neo-classical style. The first floor was rusticated and featured a colonnaded entrance portico; the second had Corinthian columns rising to an ornate entablature, cornice and three pediments. It was an elegant companion to the next-door Government Buildings but departed from it in being of masonry construction, the first public building in Wellington to be built in permanent materials since the 1855 earthquake.[173] A crowd of at least 4,000 watched the unveiling of its foundation stone in December 1879. As it was for Christchurch's Provincial Council Buildings, the event was observed as a public holiday. Unlike in Christchurch, it took the form of a Masonic ceremony. Some 150 Masons marched to the site to the tune of 'Onward Mason Brothers', with the Wellington battery of the New Zealand Artillery (Volunteers) and a naval brigade providing a guard of honour. By late morning 'the grand stand which had been erected for the lady ticket-holders was thronged with gaily-dressed ladies, whose varied toilets enhanced the brilliancy of the scene'.[174] Leading the spectacle was Right Worshipful Grand Master of the North Island and New Zealand Attorney General, Frederick Whitaker. Other prominent Masons in attendance were Justice Minister William Rolleston, the Governor, Sir Hercules Robinson, and Burrows. The stone was laid according to Masonic ritual – including the pouring of wine and oil over it – and was accompanied by the singing of Masonic anthems. A local newspaper proclaimed it the 'most imposing public ceremonial' New Zealand had witnessed, but the city's Catholic community condemned it as sacrilegious.[175] In the House of Representatives Walter Johnston asked the government why the Supreme Court's foundation stone had been laid by a

Foundation laying ceremonies for important public buildings could attract large crowds. Nearly 4,000 people turned out to see the laying of the foundation stone for Wellington's new Supreme Court in 1879. The event took the form of a masonic ritual, reflecting freemasonry's importance in colonial life. James Bragge, Museum of New Zealand Te Papa Tongarewa, D.000001

secret society. Rolleston replied the decision had been the contractor's rather than the government's. Johnston said this was regrettable and declared it 'hardly right' that contractors were able to call out the Volunteers.[176] Rolleston might have been technically correct in distancing the government from the event, but the attendance of government ministers and the military made it a quasi-state occasion nonetheless, so highlighting the extent to which Freemasonry had become a powerful influence in the public sphere.[177] The building itself opened in 1881, and in 2010 it was incorporated into a new Supreme Court complex necessitated by New Zealand's severing of its imperial ties to the Privy Council in London in 2003.

The Supreme Court helped to break Wellington's embargo on the use of permanent building materials, after which most of the city's larger buildings were constructed of concrete, brick or stone. Its time as a timber town was behind it.

This is an elevation drawing by architect William Clayton of Wellington's Neo-classical Government Buildings. Due to the danger posed by earthquakes, it was erected in wood (which was malleable) but fashioned to look like stone. It became an immediate landmark on its 1876 completion and an emblem of central government. William Henry Clayton, Alexander Turnbull Library, D-016-006

Not so in Nelson. Due to its lower population and slower development, it largely remained a wooden town until the twentieth century.[178] While it still erected buildings that spoke of big-city aspirations, including the elegant Provincial Council Building of 1862 (demolished in 1969) and the 1,000-seat Theatre Royal (1878), it was apparent that Nelson was a large provincial town and a city in name only.

The buildings considered here are only a few of the hundreds of new edifices that arose in the five cities' CBDs from the late 1850s to the early 1880s, replacing lesser structures from their formative period and illustrating the process of creative destruction. The rebuilt streetscapes acted as a gauge of each city's modernity and material progress. Cities that developed rapidly experienced the most change, and Dunedin stood out in this regard. Its gold-driven growth completely transformed its CBD. Conversely, Nelson's sluggish evolution meant its streets continued to express its frontier origins. Some new buildings communicated civic identities and a sense of place. The grand parochial statement that was Dunedin's Post Office Building was the most potent expression of this, but the likes of Auckland's Union Bank and Wellington's Government Buildings also generated civic pride among townspeople. The pomp of foundation-laying ceremonies similarly promoted civic identities and supported urban social hierarchies, with the city's elite leading proceedings or having ringside seats. Such rituals added colour and richness to the experience of city life.

Most new buildings were designed in the revivalist architectural styles that were in vogue in Britain and wider Europe, and were strongly imbued with cultural meanings. Classical Revival buildings celebrated the civic sphere and city life; Gothic Revival buildings evoked vernacularism and the divine. Both expressed the architecture of British colonialism. New Zealand's buildings referenced those of London, a pattern repeated in other British settler colonial cities: many buildings of downtown Bombay, Melbourne and Victoria bore the same imperial stamp. This is to say that New Zealand cities were situated within a wider aesthetic network, a common architecture providing a cultural bond between metropolis and colony, as well as across colonies. The practice supports Felicity Barnes's point that 'settler colonies were not only borrowing Britishness, but collaborating in its construction'.[179] In this way, the built environment of such cities came to symbolise the reach and perceived success of British colonialism.

Conclusion

The building and rebuilding of cities demonstrates how the built environment was a protagonist in colonial city life rather than a static backdrop to events. Buildings and streets defined the spatial arrangements of the five cities, and determined how townspeople traversed and conducted social relations within them: the material and immaterial were inextricably linked. This included the grid plan. Its simplicity and ability to impose abstract order on the landscape commended it to town founders, but settler capitalists valued it more as a mechanism for commodifying land. As a result, conceptions of public city space were often privatised in practice. Across the grid, settlers busied themselves creating material space imbued with immaterial meanings. Manning's prefabricated cottages provided not only instant shelter but also an instant imprint of home – a physical and symbolic claim over the landscape. When these structures proved ill-suited to local conditions, many town dwellers took to living in raupō dwellings, a brief recognition of Māori building knowledge and prowess. But the settler imperative to build towns in their own image meant a bicultural townscape was only ever going to be a short-term proposition, and by the 1850s the English-style colonial cottage had become the ubiquitous urban dwelling type. Meanwhile, living conditions in towns were increasingly marred by inadequate infrastructure, a situation that improved only with the creation of provincial governments and town boards.

In the following decades, New Zealand towns better resembled those of Britain, but there were also factors that set them apart. This included their sprawling form and the prevalence of the owner-occupied, stand-alone house on its own section – elements that contributed to the development of a hybrid urbanism that redefined 'urban' in the New Zealand context. At the same time, the erection of new and permanent public and commercial buildings in the latest architectural styles highlighted both the reproduction of capitalist social relations and the location of the five cities within imperial cultural networks. But these structures also carried specific local meanings that contributed to city dwellers' sense of place and collective social identities. Over time, these were over-written by new meanings that might lead to the building's complete removal from the cityscape, reminding us of the ephemeral nature of modernity.

Chapter Three

Social and Cultural Life

Soon after arriving in Wellington from London in June 1841, 15-year-old Mary Swainson wrote her English grandparents an animated account of her new life. Mary was a daughter of the distinguished naturalist William Swainson and his first wife Mary. William, having failed for a second time to secure a position in the British Museum, had given up on the metropolis, and with his children and second wife Anne had left for a fresh start in New Zealand.[1] In penning her first impressions, Mary was surprised by the vitality of Wellington society: 'What do you think of two balls having been given!!? – one on board the London [*sic*], and the other at Barret's [*sic*] hotel … And do you know there is a <u>club</u> called the Wakefield Club? Indeed, Wellington is much more advanced than anyone would suppose.'[2] Her most exciting news was the revelation 'that Papa has fixed on settling on Wellington!! I am very glad for many reasons. First, we shall have a much great [*sic*] facility of both receiving and sending letters to England, and we shall have another advantage, both in getting things and having society.'[3]

Mary's pleasure at the prospect of residing in a port city underscores the importance many settlers placed on maintaining their links with metropolitan society; correspondence with family and friends in Britain continued to be a pivotal aspect of their social world. She was equally pleased that being in the town provided more opportunities for shopping and sociability than country life. Familiar with the diversity and richness of London society, she was obviously relieved that Wellington offered something akin to what she had left behind. This chapter shows she was not alone in this sentiment. Settlers were drawn to urban life because it nourished and extended their social and cultural worlds.

OPPOSITE The Spackman family are relaxing in the back garden of their Newtown home 'Ben Venuto' around 1899. Sylvie sits on Daisy's lap while Herbert looks proudly on. Herbert and Daisy exemplified the modern companionate form of marriage, the couple spending much time in each other's company and sharing their emotional lives. Alexander Turnbull Library, PA1-o-465-24-2

Debating colonial society

The nature of Pākehā colonial society and sociability was the subject of stimulating historiographical debate in the 1990s as historians responded to Miles Fairburn's atomisation thesis, discussed soon. While the debate created a flurry of new research activity at the time, this fell away as social history lost ground to cultural history (the cultural turn) as a field of historical inquiry, historians 'becoming interested in questions of meaning rather than material experience.'[4] This has meant the historiography of colonial social space remains largely unchanged since the late 1990s and early 2000s.[5] A notable recent addition to this body of work is Tony Ballantyne's research on Gore, although this emphasises the production of intellectual and cultural space over social space.[6] The cultural approach has been a rewarding methodology, but it has its limits. We can learn much about the meanings settlers ascribed to particular social relations but less about how they materially experienced them. We need to know how city dwellers lived out their social lives: how people pursued and experienced social relations, and to what extent their social needs were met. Knowing this helps us to understand better how cultural meaning was made and remade. For this reason, Fairburn's ideas still provide a useful starting point to test ideas about Pākehā colonial society.

Fairburn developed his stimulating thesis in reaction to the orthodoxy that colonial Pākehā society was characterised by a multitude of insulated local communities. The European ideal of local community had traditionally been associated with a rural way of life. In the 1880s, the German sociologist Ferdinand Tönnies famously distinguished between *gemeinschaft* (community) and *gesellschaft* (society or association). The first described (pre-modern) village society, where social relations were spatially contained and characterised by group solidarity, mutual obligation and parochialism. The second described (modern) city society, where social relations were more mediated and characterised by disparate social groups based on common interest rather than place.[7] The ideal of community continued to be linked to a rural way of life until the 1960s when American social activists adopted the term to describe the urban poor. Other minority groups embraced the term, as in the 'African American community', to express a politics of social identity. Community took on a meaning closer to the *gesellshaft* definition, where place was not necessarily important to social group identification.[8] Community could now be understood not solely as a socio-spatial construct but also a socio-cultural one, describing a sub-culture or a community of interest.

The first meaning still had a strong rural connotation; the second tended to be associated with cities. This distinction was applicable to colonial New Zealand. Jim (W. J.) Gardner and others have argued that local community existed in villages and small towns. There, bonds of kinship and the similar occupational experience of settlers as well as membership of community institutions encouraged social integration, common values and shared identities.[9] Local community in cities, by contrast, wrote Gardner, 'seems to have been amorphous and often weak'.[10] However, as cities grew and work became more sectoral, horizontal (social class-based) common-interest groups formed.[11] As Erik Olssen wrote, 'By 1890 people in urban areas already thought of themselves as members of groups and took action through their group institutions. Voluntary associations proliferated.'[12]

Fairburn turned these assumptions on their head, arguing nineteenth-century Pākehā society was characterised by weak social bonds and by anomie.[13] He said that settlers generally emigrated alone or in nuclear-family units, and so lacked the type of extended kin network that would encourage people to settle in one place.[14] Moreover, the temporary nature of work meant individuals were continually moving in search of employment and betterment.[15] In this footloose society there was no time for people to put down roots in one place and forge the type of social relations and associational culture needed for local community to operate.[16] Cities too experienced high rates of residential mobility which, together with long working hours, precluded the type of horizontal (or class) bonds promoted by Olssen.[17] Accordingly, in both town and country individuals were not integrated into, but atomised from, society, and this led to boredom and chronic loneliness that manifested itself in high rates of drunkenness and interpersonal violence.[18]

Fairburn's thesis provoked a vigorous response from historians. Caroline Daley criticised its totalising sweep, arguing his model did not describe Pākehā society but a masculine sub-culture of it.[19] Women, who were more likely to marry and stay put, were largely overlooked by Fairburn. Daley questioned whether the low survival rate of voluntary associations was a signifier of social alienation. People did not have to belong to a church or lodge to establish social relations; urban women, for example, created informal social networks through visiting. Using evidence from the town of Taradale, she also showed that a high rate of residential mobility did not stop people from forging warm social ties, even fleeting ones.[20] Dean Wilson disputed the absence of horizontal social bonds in cities. His research into nineteenth-century Auckland identified a tightly bound working-class neighbourhood in the central city. He argued that the nature of community within it was defined by gender: women were bonded in tight networks centred on their immediate environs, while those of men were more socially and spatially diffuse.[21] Others criticised Fairburn's reliance on quantitative data to draw his conclusions; it was ill-suited to challenging concepts and ignored specific circumstances. As Jock Phillips wrote, 'What Fairburn's book lacks, for all its brilliance, is sense behind the cold statistics of human diversity and interaction – there is no sense of people with language, and rituals and traditions.'[22]

Historians have traditionally located the roots of Pākehā society in the small communities of rural New Zealand. These were places where settlers cleared and cultivated the land and formed close social relations with neighbours. The idea is exemplified in this 1890s image of two cottages and a family situated in recently burned bush – the location and family is unknown. From the 1980s Miles Fairburn disputed the notion settlers formed strong social ties, leading to a stimulating debate among historians. Alexander Turnbull Library, 1/2-066719-G

It is evident that colonial society was more diverse and interactive than Fairburn's model allowed for. This was particularly true for urban society, which he only partially considered. Fairburn's story is predominantly focused on backblock farms and isolated settlements. Cities are included, but the image of them is largely quantitatively constructed in terms of variables like rates of residential mobility, membership of voluntary associations, and incidents of interpersonal violence and litigation.[23] His main qualitative source on city life is the 1887 book '*Taken In*' by the pseudonymous and female 'Hopeful'. It is a caustic account of Christchurch society and provides support for Fairburn's contention of anomie. In a section detailing the city's drinking culture, Hopeful argues a temptation to drink was 'the want of social amusements and places to go. There is not the same amount of social intercourse in the Colonies as at home, where different families from the same locality visit each other.'[24] Fairburn seizes on the passage, first to buttress his point that visiting was not a widespread social practice, and secondly to support his contention that lonely single men turned to drink because of a dearth of associational culture.[25] Yet if we read further we

These people eked out a basic living in the Waikato bush in the early 1860s. The men are likely soldiers, part of the troop that constructed a military road through the Waikato in 1863. Getting the clothes washed and dried would have been an onerous task for the woman at right. Such living conditions were the reality of rural life in this period. William Temple, Alexander Turnbull Library, 1/2-004135-F

discover the forces of social isolation were not as strong in Christchurch as the passage suggests. In a chapter on social and intellectual space, Hopeful noted the popularity of the public library. Although the theatre was 'not well attended as a rule … it fills now and again for any special occasion'; it was also used as a lecture hall, and for bazaars and horticultural shows. Once a fortnight the workingmen's club hosted well-supported dramatic and other performances. 'I must say I passed two or three most agreeable evenings at these entertainments; they were done very well, and did great credit to those engaged – songs, recitations, violin and other instrumental performances made the programme.'[26] Then there were the public houses, where single men of all classes went to drink, socialise, and play billiards and other games. She also understood that 'there is a great deal of dancing by a certain class, such as servants, barmen, barmaids, loafers, shop-girls' in the back room of a local hotel. For the 'better class' there were 'well-patronised' quarterly balls.[27] Her observation underscores how urban sociability was group-based but not always organised by social class; single men from all classes found a common bond in pub culture.

Ironically, after describing a relatively rich urban social fabric, Hopeful concluded that Christchurch was 'about as dull a spot as anyone would wish to pass their days in – there is very little amusement; everything is horribly local.'[28] The ambiguity of her representation probably lies in her desire to appeal to her imagined readership. She employed acerbic humour to generally disparage colonial society, so reinforcing its wilderness image among metropolitan society. Even so, the level of sociability she described sits uneasily with Fairburn's view of widespread anomie.[29]

What follows is an attempt to paint a richer, more nuanced picture of urban social and cultural life than Fairburn's rural-centric model allowed for. In an effort to go beyond 'cold statistics', this is drawn mainly from qualitative sources like settlers' letters and diaries. Most of these are derived from middle-class correspondents, who tended to leave a heavier paper trail than their working-class neighbours.[30] While acknowledging that what is presented here is only a partial view of the panorama of colonial city life, it provides a counterbalance to existing research that has focused on working-class urban communities. For, as historians have long shown, the making of modern urban society was fundamentally a bourgeois project.[31]

Engagement in society

We saw in Chapter One that the first settlers exerted much effort in constructing a cultural and social infrastructure to facilitate sociability and associational life in towns. Certainly by the early 1840s, both Auckland and Wellington had the makings of an urban society that was resonant of that back home. The examples of three settlers show how individual temperament was an important factor in the way townspeople engaged with it. The first, Edmund Webber, arrived in Auckland in November 1841 after serving under General Edward Belcher on the West African Survey. The 24-year-old sought a job as an official in William Hobson's government, and accepted temporary work as a 'scribbler' (clerk) in the Colonial Secretary's office on the understanding a permanent position would be forthcoming. He initially resided at Wood's (Royal) Hotel in Princes Street – 'it's no very nice place, but I can't find a better,' he recorded – before moving to the Military (Britomart) Barracks Mess. Edmund found Auckland society dreary. 'In this hole nothing is new, it's a dull spot indeed.'[32] But rather than taking steps to enliven things by cultivating social relations, he adopted a detached attitude to those around him. He refused to mingle with his fellow hotel guests and dismissed Hobson's senior officials as 'lick-spittels'. The few people who passed his muster were Surveyor-General Felton Mathew's wife Sarah – 'a chatty amusing sort of heifer' – and several officers and soldiers in the barracks.[33]

In a revealing passage from his journal, Edmund outlined a typical day. He rose

LEFT Sarah Mathew was the first middle-class woman to settle in Auckland and was a central figure in fostering social relations and associational culture within the settlement. She was married to the Surveyor General Felton Mathew and is shown here in the 1860s after her return to England. Sir George Grey Special Collections, Auckland Libraries, 7-A11646

RIGHT Eliza Grey and her husband Governor George Grey arrived in Auckland in November 1845. She found Auckland society objectionable and had no social peers, which made for a lonely life in the new city. Sir George Grey Special Collections, Auckland Libraries, 7-A598

between the hours of eight and ten, had breakfast, smoked a pipe and then went to the Treasury, 'where if there is nothing to do, we [as in the majestic plural] read the newspaper or write letters'. About one, he went out for lunch and a glass of beer before returning to the Treasury. 'At four we either do a little gardening, walk a little or ride a little ... dinner at six, then a cigar and a cup of tea at Bennett's'. This was followed by a glass of grog, after which he went home to read or write until one or two in the morning. On Sundays he read or wrote, went out on a boat or paid visits; he was not a regular churchgoer.[34] While his description fuels the stereotype of the lackadaisical civil servant, the absence of other people in the account also suggests a self-contained person aloof from his social peers. As he admitted: 'We got not much into Society, for the reason that it's not good.'[35] Edmund had imagined his future in New Zealand, but in June 1842 he received a letter from Hobson saying there was no government position for him after all. Edmund was livid, and felt Hobson had unnecessarily led him on: 'I wish the son of a bitch had been in hell before I'd seen him.'[36] He does not reveal Hobson's reason for the retraction, but Edmund's reserve had left him with no one to argue his case.[37] Soon afterwards, he left the colony.

While Edmund Webber did not care for (official) Auckland society, his acquaintance Sarah Mathew was a pivotal figure within it.[38] She was the first middle-class woman to settle in Auckland and saw it as her role to foster social relations in the settlement. In early 1842, with new families arriving and Hobson and his family now in residence at Government House, her life was a flurry of visits to pay and receive, and parties and balls to attend. She was also active in building associational culture, helping to found an amateur philharmonic society. It initially met at people's houses before securing a large room used for public entertainments at Wood's Hotel. Meetings were held monthly and each normally ended with a dance. Although Sarah and her husband Felton, both in their forties, 'thought it right to take our part in these duties to Society, and aids to civilization', she disclosed they 'were never so happy as when alone, & at home reading or conversing'.[39]

In Wellington, Mary Petre (see page 98) led a similarly busy social life. She was the wife of the colonist Henry Petre, a member of the town's social elite. He had come out to Wellington in 1840 but returned to England in 1841 to find a spouse. Mary Walmsley was sent for from a convent school and, just shy of 16, she accepted Henry's hand in marriage. After their wedding and a spell living in London, the couple arrived in Wellington in January 1843. John Godley's wife, Charlotte, described her in 1850 as 'very young-looking and with wild spirits, and enjoys a ball, or a ride, or a scamper of any kind, and is sometimes very pretty'.[40] Mary soon struck up friendships with other women in her social class and age group, including Emily Wakefield and Mary Swainson. Their social lives were a succession of tea and dinner parties, amateur musical recitals and balls held in each other's homes – the informal social networks identified by Daley. There were also riding, walks and picnics in the encircling bush. Her friend Eliza Fitzgerald's home was an after-church rendezvous for Catholics, 'and not a little gossip and fun we do have', Mary wrote in her diary in March 1843.[41] Eliza was a regular visitor to Mary's home. On one visit she 'brought her guitar and spent the morning playing and singing with me we [sic] had a great deal of the usual laughing and fun.'[42] A few days after that, she, Sarah Fox (wife of William) and Emily Wakefield walked to Mount Cook to see Wellington's first public building: a prison. That night the Fitzgeralds and the Foxes dined at her house: 'we had a merry musical evening,' she wrote. Balls were eagerly anticipated within Mary's group.[43] When the French corvette *Le Rhin* visited Wellington in mid-May, Henry St Hill arranged for the ship's band to play at one such upcoming event. 'After Mrs St Hill left us Mrs Fitzgerald and I danced the room for joy.'[44]

Mary Petre was among the social elite of early Wellington and she socialised with others from this group. This included giving parties and performances in each other's homes as well as walks and rides through town. This 1843 painting shows her friend Sarah Fox's house in Thorndon, with her own house behind it – both appear to be prefabricated cottages. William Fox, Alexander Turnbull Library, A-195-004

On other occasions, Mary's socialising was more spontaneous. In mid-September she wrote:

After church [and] the usual kororo [kōrero/talk] at Mrs Fitzgerald's we all went out for a walk. Miss Wakefield and Miss Swainson soon joined and before we got home we were a party of twenty ... [We] thought it would be good fun to storm someone's house and accordingly Mrs Baker being the nearest, in we went, we had great fun.[45]

Charlotte Godley's view of Mary as vivacious seems apt; she was clearly someone who was a social livewire. Her experiences exemplify 'women's culture': 'that congeries of relationships that provided women with social networks, support

These Aucklanders are queuing to receive their mail while others are reading theirs outside the post office in 1867. For most settlers the arrival of the English mail was keenly anticipated, offering news of events back home and the goings-on of friends and relatives. But it could also reinforce a sense of social isolation for those who did not receive letters from loved ones.
L. B. Temple, Alexander Turnbull Library, B-079-009

and influence'. As the historian Margaret Marsh explains, women's culture was based 'on the idea of significant gender separation'.[46] Certainly Mary's diary showed that in 1843 she spent much more of her social life with women than with men. Nonetheless, she and Henry clearly did not lack for physical intimacy. The following year she gave birth to the first of her 16 children.[47]

In Edmund, Sarah and Mary's accounts we see different levels of engagement in urban society. Edmund found little compelling about Auckland's, thinking it dull and beneath him, so he kept largely to himself – a man alone. Sarah was strongly involved in society, seeing her role as necessary to progress civilisation. Yet her eagerness for the task was equivocal. While she felt duty-bound to play her part, she was happiest when alone with her husband. Of the three, Mary had the most fervour for sociability; she was someone who sought out the company of others. Individual temperament and purpose were clearly important factors in the production of urban colonial social space, with extroverts like Mary at the centre of their social circles and introverts like Edmund at the periphery of theirs.

Saturday 17th October Today arrived the "Favorite" with His Excellency the Governor on board, but the weather being Showery he did not land. The Frigate looked beautiful at anchor off the Flag Staff Point and with H. M. Brig Britomart which has been here some days, and a few Small craft the Harbour looked quite respectable —

Sunday 18th. We have the Church Service in our Tent and all who choose attend. The Governor landed in the Afternoon and walked about a little. He seems pleased with the place and quite Satisfied with what has been done —

Monday 26th October His Excellency has this morning gone over to Manukao, and the "Favorite" & Britomart have taken their departure to Sydney & Hobart Town: The Governor has made our Tent, his home, his Office and every thing else; only sleeping on board the Favorite he will now sleep in the Ranger Cutter, & in a few

Sarah Mathew's diary is a valuable and lively record of life in the fledgling city of Auckland. On 17 October 1844 she noted the arrival of Governor Fitzroy on board the ship *Favorite*. The ship anchored alongside the *Britomart* and other smaller craft, making the harbour look in her words 'quite respectable'. The following day she recorded the Governor looking 'pleased with the place and quite satisfied with what has been done'. Sir George Grey Special Collections, Auckland Libraries, NZMS 79, p.156

Loneliness

For those who found it hard to forge social relations, colonial urban life could be lonely and miserable. In 1841, the labourer Joseph Hudgell wrote to his parents in London, explaining how he was living in Auckland with 400 others but had 'no friend that I can speak to, for here they are all utter strangers to me'. He admitted, 'When I think of this place, and compare it to my home that I have left, it drives me to despair. I sit down for hours and am quite melancholy.'[48] He was not the only one to feel homesick. The Scots colonist Samuel Martin recounted how, after arriving in Wellington, he had visited the town's Scottish settlement, Kaiwharawhara. On the way, he met a woman from Paisley. 'The sound of my voice, it appears, reminded her of her native country, at the recollection of which she could not help weeping, and wishing she were ... back again in Paisley.'[49]

Those further up the social hierarchy could also experience social alienation.[50] After retiring from military service in India, Captain John Wilson bought a land package in Nelson, leaving his wife Charlotte and children in London while he became established. He arrived in April 1842. Like many other petty capitalists, he soon found he had insufficient funds to develop his speculation and so decided to sell. He lived in town while waiting for a buyer, but found society and the cost of living taxing. His status as a gentleman proved burdensome, for he was expected to help foster associational life which, as he explained to Charlotte, 'means [I am] nailed for a subscription to this and that institution, when God and yourself, know, how little my purse is able to stand such attacks upon it'.[51] He had acquaintances but no friends: 'I often feel lonely, and miserable, but this I would readily endure, if solid advantage could arise from it.'[52] This was not forthcoming, and in July 1843 he packed things in and returned to London.

Eliza Grey, wife of Governor George Grey, was also socially isolated. In an 1846 letter to an Adelaide friend she revealed she was 'growing graver and gloomier than ever'. This was partly because her marriage was unhappy, but also because she had no social peers.[53] Eliza found Auckland society distasteful, proclaiming 'there is scarcely a lady here'; and without the strong military presence, 'there would scarcely be a Gentleman'. She complained the town's colonists were land jobbers (speculators) who could think of nothing else.[54]

Fairburn convincingly argued that loneliness was an attribute of backblocks life, in part because neighbours could be beyond the reach of regular contact. The experience of people like Joseph Hudgell, the woman from Paisley, John Wilson and Eliza Grey showed proximity to others was no guard against homesickness or loneliness, and highlights the mental dimension of city life. The sociologist Georg Simmel pioneered the idea of the city as a state of mind in the early twentieth century. Making a distinction between village and city, he argued that city dwellers developed an intellectualised and reserved (or blasé) mentality that contrasted with the emotional and genial psyche of rural dwellers. Such reserve made cities sites of anonymity in which neighbours might never meet. While this environment freed city dwellers from the close social policing of village life, it also made them more susceptible to social isolation: to feel alone in a crowd. Simmel reiterated previous sociological observation that kinship bonds weakened in cities, resulting in a tendency for city dwellers to form small and close-knit common-interest groups.[55] We can therefore suppose that Joseph, John and Eliza's loneliness was a function of not only the absence of kin support but also a lack of interest or peer groups that could meet their social needs – Eliza's complaint suggests this. It might be too that settlers from cities carried their metropolitan reserve to New Zealand, making it harder for them to make friends among complete strangers. Rose Hall, wife of the politician John Hall, found as much. Six months after arriving in Christchurch in 1861, she revealed that 'though I have a very large circle of calling acquaintances I do not yet possess any friends'.[56] In such situations, letters to and from kith and kin formed a pivotal aspect of settlers' social lives.

A virtual society

The coming of the English mail sent a buzz of anticipation through settler communities and created a rush to the post office. In 1843, Mary Petre recorded how the arrival in Wellington of two English ships at once led to impatient settlers breaking two of the postmaster's windows because he could not sort the mail fast enough.[57] In 1850, Charlotte Godley saw the ship *Poictiers* coming into Wellington harbour one breakfast time. 'I did little all the morning, as you can imagine, but stand at the window to watch her, and then go and poke the fire, and back to watch again. We could not get our letters till late in the afternoon, but then they were indeed worth waiting so long for.'[58] A lithograph of Auckland's post office in the 1860s shows a crowd queuing to receive mail, while those who had picked theirs up stand about, sit on the kerb, or attentively read their letters as they walk away (see page 126).

The 23-year-old Nelson settler Edwin Hodder recalled how the mail's arrival became a social event within his peer group, with neighbours coming together at evening gatherings to share their news from home. He felt that when reading letters from family and friends 'the written words spoke so plainly that I fancied I was again in the old country, surrounded with the companionships of home'.[59] Charlotte Godley, now living in Lyttelton, had a similar response:

> when I have read a good many together, it seems at last as if New Zealand was all a dream, and it is not till I look out at the bare hills, and the bridle path, and the town of wooden houses, and above all 'the Office' door at the bottom of our little green slope, that the dull reality comes back to me.[60]

This is a view from Wellington Harbour of Thorndon Quay and Mulgrave Street in 1866. On Thorndon Quay at left is a paint and paperhanging shop and a bootmaker's. The Thistle Inn pub and St Paul's Church in Mulgrave Street catered for the social and spiritual needs of Thorndon's residents. Alexander Turnbull Library, 10x8-2087-G

Edwin Hodder observed that most people started replying to their letters almost immediately, even though it might be another fortnight before the mail left on the return journey: 'It was such a pleasure to feel something like a conversational relationship still to friends far away – to be able at once to answer a question – to write while the feelings kindled by words of love from home were yet warm, and while these words had voice and sound.'[61]

Those who came away from the post office empty handed sorely missed such intimacy. In 1861, the Aucklander Samuel Harris wrote:

My Dear Father and Mother I feel very disappointed that I have not heard from home for so long in time. It is now six months since I heard from you. Every mail that arrives I go groping for Relations at the Post Office. With eager impatience we push to the window through masses of People and are repulsed by the answer no.[62]

Similarly, in the four years since arriving in Auckland in 1863, Mary Anne Hunter had received only one letter from her old Yorkshire friends. In the hope of maintaining contact she began one letter to a past acquaintance with the line: 'in despair of getting a letter from anyone else I now write to you', and ended with the plea for her address to be given to 'any one who will be friendly enough to write'.[63] Just as the receiving and reading of letters could seem to annihilate space, the lack thereof could make the distance between old and new worlds seem ever

Men of all classes socialised in pubs. The Palace Hotel pub (at left) on Christchurch's Gloucester Street was next to the Theatre Royal, both of which were owned by George Beatty. These men are gathered outside the buildings around 1877. Image courtesy of Steven McLachlan/Canterbury Heritage

more vast. Eliza Collier, for one, wished the gap were narrower. She confessed, '[w]e often look at your portraits & say how we would like to see you all. I think to myself sometimes, how I should like a walk down Tottenham C R [Court Road, London] but I give up knowing it is too <u>far</u> away.'[64]

Fairburn has argued the great importance placed on receiving letters, newspapers and periodicals from Britain suggested that settlers were driven to counteract loneliness and the lack of social relations in the new country by maintaining those with the old.[65] Print culture enabled settlers to live vicariously in metropolitan society, acting out in their imaginations the social exchanges and practices of everyday life that their new de-socialised environment denied them.[66] There is no doubt that, especially for those in distant and isolated rural areas, letter writing provided a surrogate society.[67] Plainly, Joseph Hudgell, John Wilson and Eliza Grey experienced a high degree of anomie (at least at the time of their writing), and found succour in their situation by corresponding with distant friends and family. Yet for Mary Swainson, Edwin Hodder, Eliza Collier and many others, letter writing was not about living in a surrogate society but extending the reach of their present one. Letters from home brought metropolitan society into their social world. And the reverse was also true. Settlers' letters carried colonial society into the social orbit of kith and kin in Britain. This two-way traffic helped to maintain familial and wider imperial networks.

Dull and boring?

As the five towns began to transition into cities from the late 1850s, it might be expected that colonial urban sociability became more sophisticated and metropolitan. Yet settlers and visitors held divergent and sometimes ambiguous views on the vitality and diversity of early colonial urban society. In 1857, the travel writer John Askew observed, 'Auckland's ladies appeared to be almost overwhelmed with *ennui*. There are no places of amusement; no theatres, nor exhibitions of any kind.'[68] In 1862, the newly arrived drapery salesman John Kirkwood repeated the refrain. He lodged with six of his workmates in accommodation above the shop in which they all worked, and the group socialised and ate together at the next-door restaurant. While he thought Auckland was thriving economically, he found it 'very dull after Business as there is no place for a stranger to go to for amusement, no theatre or anything'.[69] Interestingly, he did not mention the public house as a site of sociability.

Fellow Aucklander Lewis Haslam told his sister in London in 1865 that these were the principal places of entertainment in the town, and in his view there were far too many of them: 'There were 41 public houses and hotels opened last Sunday and there are a tremendous lot of drunkards, so the steady ones have a good chance to get on.'[70] We can presume that Kirkwood, in avoiding pub culture, was among the steady ones; his complaint, therefore, was less about the absence of sociability in public spaces and more about its lack of diversity and urbanity. As a self-identified stranger in the town, his social world was also restricted to public spaces; he was still to foster social relations that could provide entry into people's homes and other semi-public and private spaces of sociability. Sometimes one's social status could help in this respect. The Wesleyan minister, Revd John Crump, had barely got off the ship in Auckland in 1858 before he was invited to tea with 20 others at the home of Provincial Superintendent John Williamson. The 'smoking tea and the smiling women and the good humour' made the event 'thoroughly English', he wrote, before concluding, '[s]ociety generally far exceeds my expectation'.[71]

Edwin Hodder's view of Nelson society was equally positive. Acknowledging the metropolitan view that colonial society was coarse, he offered a counter-view that talked up its sophistication. The manners and customs of colonial urban society, he said, were the same as at home but carried out with less pretence and formality: the shared privations and struggles of emigration 'tend to knit people together; sympathies are shared in common'.[72] Tea parties were frequent and 'generally far more interesting than in England' because everyone knew each other, making them more sociable and familial.[73] Although Nelson's amusements could not match those of London, Hodder claimed it offered some convincing surrogates. There was no Regent Street, but ladies could shop at some 'very creditable stores'; there was no Rotten Row (in Hyde Park), but there were some 'good sound roads to ride or drive upon'; there was no 'Coldstream Band in the Park in the afternoon, but there is a capital substitute in the Nelson Amateur and Volunteer Bands which play once or twice a week'.[74] Numerous sporting pursuits were available, including racing, cricket and shooting. Evening pleasure seekers could attend balls, concerts or dinner parties, public or private. Circulating libraries and two bi-weekly newspapers fostered intellectual life, and religious needs were served by places of worship of all the leading denominations.[75] In short, Hodder argued Nelson society was a credible microcosm of London's, but was less formal and more fraternal.

Visiting for a week in 1861, he found Wellington similarly vital. One day he went to the Mechanics' Institute and was surprised to find such a large and well-run association. There, concerts, balls, lectures, meetings, evening classes were all held. Its library was well stocked with carefully selected and useful books, and the reading room was furnished with all the main English and colonial periodicals. That evening he attended a meeting there. He had no sense of local politics, but wrote:

> to judge from the excitement of the speakers, the heart-and-soul ecstasies of some of the audience when the men of their side of the question spoke, and the obstinate perseverance in hissing and groaning which prevailed on the opposite side, I imagined it must be some very weighty and important matter, in which the vital interests of the colony were affected. But I was informed by the friend who accompanied me that it was not a political meeting at all, only one regarding some new wharf, or jetty, which it was proposed should be built [Queens Wharf]; but political excitement was so necessary to the very existence of Wellingtonians, that that element was invariably introduced to all their meetings, to keep them in practice and 'up to the mark,' especially in dull seasons, when their zeal might wax cold.

Hodder went on to say that 'never was there another such place in the world for hot politics, strong party-ships, and intense officialism'. It would be another four years before Wellington was made the political capital, in 1865.[76]

A large crowd is listening to a speech by the Bishop of Nelson Charles Mules at the construction site of the Bishop Suter Art Gallery in Nelson. The gallery, which opened in 1899, commemorates the previous bishop Andrew Suter, who left money and art in his will for this purpose. Nelson Provincial Museum, C101

Reference points

Even accepting that Hodder was exaggerating for effect, his images of Nelson and Wellington show a degree of liveliness missing in Askew's, Kirkwood's and Haslam's portraits of Auckland. In comparing Nelson to London, he also highlights the importance of reference points in settlers' appraisals of colonial urban society. For instance, Daniel Campbell and his wife Agnes emigrated from Edinburgh to Dunedin in 1851. Daniel worked as a printer on a weekly newspaper (almost certainly the *Otago Witness*). He enjoyed his work, and spent much of his leisure time in his home orchard and vegetable garden. Even so, he missed the vitality of the big city and for this reason conceded in a letter home in 1852 that he was thinking of moving to Sydney: 'for this place is so small, and so very dull, just like a Scottish country village; so unlike what we have accustomed to – the din, life bustle, amusement, and entertainment, which are always to be seen in a large time the beautiful town of Edinbro'.[77]

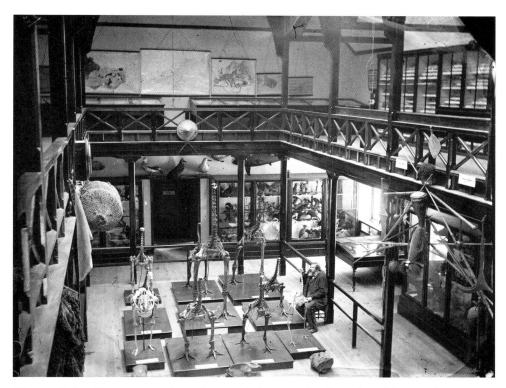

Director Julius Haast contemplates the moa skeletons at the Canterbury Museum in 1872. The institution was very popular right from its opening in 1870, with about 40,000 visitors (three times Christchurch's population) in the first year. Alfred Charles Barker, Canterbury Museum, 1944.78.66

If Hodder thought Nelson stood up well in relation to London, Agnes Hall (niece of Rose Hall) found Christchurch wanting in the same regard. Although she had spent her first years in the town, she went to London for her secondary schooling. On her return in 1868, the 17-year-old found the city a 'horribly slow dull place'. Writing to her London aunt, she related how she had recently attended two balls, at Cashmere and the town hall, but lamented that 'they are almost the <u>only</u> balls out here'.[78] Eliza Collier also continued to miss the metropolis. She said she liked Auckland, but 'I sometimes think I should like to be in London for 2 days & then come back again.'[79] Occasionally the settlement itself provided a reference, but at a point located in its past. Mary Anne Hunter thought Auckland 'quite a city' when she landed in 1863, but the departure of imperial troops (from the New Zealand wars) had made it 'very dull and miserable'. The situation had been made still worse by the removal of the 'seat of Government to Wellington'.[80]

In pining for the bustle, diversity and sheer energy of large cities like London and Edinburgh, New Zealand city dwellers were starkly reminded that their cities were really only the size of large British provincial towns and so were unable to offer the same social and cultural amenities of metropolitan life. While this might have gone unnoticed by emigrants from rural Britain, those who came from urban areas felt the loss keenly. The settler belief was, of course, that with continued immigration and natural population increase, it was only a matter of time before their cities became metropolises in their own right. Certainly the demographic evidence pointed in this direction for Auckland, Wellington, Christchurch and Dunedin, less so for Nelson.

Figure 3.1 shows the official population growth of the five colonial cities for the 25-year period 1861–1886 – exclusive of Māori. Auckland began the period as the largest town but by 1864 had been surpassed by Dunedin, whose rapid population increase was attributable to the Otago gold rush. From 1871, Christchurch grew sharply on the back of its prosperous pastoral hinterland; Wellington's boost from becoming the political capital also dated from that time. By 1886, Auckland's booming timber industry and buoyant commercial sector had helped it regain its mantle as the colony's most populous city. Whereas in 1861 the population of the four biggest cities was counted in the thousands, in 1886 it was in the tens of thousands. Meanwhile, Nelson, held back by a poor port and small hinterland, grew by only a few thousand. Over nearly the same period, the settler population of the whole colony grew from 106,200 to 578,300.[81] Conversely, the Māori population fell from 56,000 in 1856 to 44,000 in 1886.[82] Interestingly, the proportion of the total settler population in the five cities remained at a consistent 25 per cent.

New cultural space

As New Zealand's cities grew, their ability to provide for the type of cultural and social spaces that settlers had missed from modern metropolitan society also developed. As Peter Clark has shown, nineteenth-century European cities 'saw an efflorescence of secular entertainments, notably music performances, the theatre, museums and art galleries, and libraries and associations … Shedding their earlier identification with Courts and elites, these were often run on a commercial basis and were heavily targeted at bourgeois clientele.'[83] Urban historians have convincingly argued the middle classes adopted elite culture as a way of buttressing their power in urban society; investment in cultural capital was a way for them to counter the notion that they cared only for wealth creation and lacked a finer sensibility.[84] And historians of gender have argued the provision of new cultural capital was a major 'civic project' of the nineteenth century because it provided more public space for women.[85] The production of these new gender-inclusive spaces was instrumental in the creation of modern society, a point not

Figure 3.1 Population of the five colonial cities, 1861–1886

Note: Population figures exclude Māori. The populations of Auckland, Wellington, Christchurch and Dunedin exhibited strong overall growth between 1861 and 1886. By contrast Nelson, with its poor port and small hinterland, grew very little.

Source: New Zealand Census, 1861–1886

lost on New Zealand's middle class, who rallied to erect the same institutions in their own cities.[86]

The first public museum was Auckland Museum. It started in a Grafton Road cottage in 1852 and was housed in a number of premises, including the old post office, before gaining a purpose-built structure in Princes Street in 1876.[87] Wellington's Colonial Museum was built in 1865 and had as its director the notable scientist James Hector. The Otago Museum in Dunedin opened in Mason's post office building in 1868, before moving into an elegant Classical Revival structure in Great King Street in 1877. The impressive Gothic Revival Canterbury Museum in Christchurch opened in 1870 under the directorship of another eminent scientist, Julius Von Haast. The early emphasis of the museums was on natural history – the first gift to Auckland Museum was five glass cases of stuffed native birds – but over time ethnography and cultural history gained a stronger presence.[88] The institutions proved popular, and buildings were soon extended to better accommodate both exhibits and visitors. In its first year, the Canterbury Museum estimated 40,000 visitors (about three times the city's population) had passed through its doors. By 1883, the number had risen to more than 84,000. The rise was partly due to an initiative to open on Sunday afternoons: 37 per cent of all weekly visits occurred during this time.[89] Sabbatarian sanctions made the change contentious, but some communities accepted it on moral-improvement grounds. A key aim of the museum movement was to educate and civilise the lower social orders by communicating knowledge, culture and technology.[90] As an Auckland advocate of Sunday opening pointed out, weekday opening did not suit business and working people. They might steal half an hour on a lightning lunchtime visit, but this was insufficient time to gain 'instruction or improvement'. Sunday opening overcame this issue.[91]

New public libraries and art galleries had a similar aim. Under the 1869 Public Library Act, local governments were able to form free public libraries to make knowledge more available to citizens. Libraries had till then been mainly the preserve of mechanics' institutes, but by the 1870s their subscription-based service was struggling to retain support. In 1873, the Christchurch institute's library passed to the provincial council and, from 1876, Canterbury College. Similarly, the Auckland and Wellington mechanic institutes' libraries came under municipal control in 1879 and 1892 respectively.[92] The origin of the city art galleries was local art societies. The first was founded in Auckland in 1869. The Otago society was formed in 1876, followed by Christchurch (1880), Wellington (1882) and Nelson (1889). The societies held regular exhibitions for the public to view and buy works, while also creating their own collections. In 1884, the Otago society placed its collection in the Otago Museum, a measure the Otago Public Art Gallery takes as its birth – in 1907 it moved into a purpose-built structure. Wellington's art society (the New Zealand Academy of Fine Arts) opened the city's first public art gallery in 1892.[93]

Sometimes gifts from wealthy benefactors pushed things along. For instance, in 1882 James Mackelvie donated several European paintings to form the nucleus of an Auckland city art gallery (see page 8).[94] Mackelvie had made a fortune as a partner in the local mercantile firm, Brown and Campbell. He retained links to Auckland after returning to Britain, and became a leading benefactor to the city. In 1884, the Auckland City Council agreed to erect a new public library and art gallery, as the former Mechanics' Institute library was dilapidated and poorly sited. Sir George Grey, who intimated that he would gift his extensive library to a new institution, provided further stimulus. An architectural competition was held in 1884 and this was won by the Melbourne firm Grainger & D'Ebro, which had submitted a proposal for a building in an imposing French Renaissance style. In June 1885, some 5,000 people turned out to see Grey, Sir Maurice O'Rorke, Sir Frederick Whitaker and other luminaries lay the foundation stone, a local newspaper proclaiming it 'an epoch in the city's progress commercially, financially and intellectually'.[95] The library opened first in March 1887 and the art gallery followed in February 1888. Grey bequeathed it a collection of old master paintings that, alongside the Mackelvie gift, made the institution the most important in the colony.[96] Other art galleries also came about as a result of bequests. When Nelson's second Anglican bishop, Andrew Suter, died in 1895, he and his wife Amelia left land, money and art works for a public art gallery in the city. The Bishop Suter Art Gallery opened in 1899. Christchurch did not get a public art gallery until 1932, when city businessman Robert McDougall provided for one behind the museum.[97]

The performing arts began to loom larger in colonial city life too. Public music-making such as amateur choral societies had formed in the main towns from the 1850s, and these were followed by liedertafels (male voice choirs) and operatic societies. During the early 1860s, overseas opera and musical-theatre companies began touring the colony – the first substantial tour was by William Saurin Lyster's Royal Italian and English Opera Company in 1864–65 – and by the early 1870s such visits had become a near-annual event. Comic opera and musicals were also brought to the colonial stage. From the early 1880s, J. C. (James Cassius) Williamson's Royal Comic Opera Company regularly toured with the latest Gilbert and Sullivan works, sometimes within twelve months of their London openings.[98] New music halls went up in city streetscapes to accommodate the growing demand for such amusements. In 1868, the prodigious Auckland Choral Society (it boasted 200 singers and a 60-strong orchestra) erected a choral hall in Symonds Street, the first of three on the site.[99] During the 1870s, cultural entrepreneurs built new Theatres Royal (named for the famous London institution) in Wellington (1873), Auckland (1876), Christchurch (1876) and Nelson (1878), as well as a new Princess Theatre in Dunedin (1876). Opera houses were also erected in Auckland (1882), Christchurch (1882) and Wellington (1886).[100] They shared a common Classical Revival style, with auditoriums ranging from 600 to 1,600 seats, and were a source of civic pride. Their interiors featured fantastical proscenium arches and domed ceilings, designed to create a sense of occasion and promote sociability.

Taking their cue from metropolitan society, the buildings also expressed the social-class dimension of theatre-going: the high-end dress circle and the lower-end stalls and pit had separate entrances, and some theatres had proscenium boxes for the elite. These spatial arrangements were designed for audience members to look at each other as much as the stage. The dress circle usually had its own foyer for promenading. As Leif Jerram explains: 'within the new music halls, the promenading structure meant that they were used as much for flirting, getting together with friends, meeting prospective partners, or prostitution, as for seeking out entertainment'.[101] These were multi-functional venues. As well as hosting opera and musical performances, they were also used for meetings, lectures, concerts and vaudeville.[102] Many city dwellers took great pride in their city's growing cultural depth. In 1883, the 20-year-old Christchurch clerk William

Derry counted off the city's cultural institutions in a letter to his English cousin Harry. These included four colleges (including Canterbury College), a museum, the public library (which he had a subscription to), four theatres and four public halls, 'so you see we are well up for places of amusement'. His one regret was that there was no public art gallery.[103]

The growing importance of middle-class cultural production and consumption in city life was exemplified in the week-long Wellington Musical Festival held in the Opera House at the beginning of October 1894. A previous music festival had been held in the city in 1888 – a New Zealand's first – but it had run at a loss and so discouraged a repeat performance until now.[104] Musical director Robert Parker attracted both local and overseas soloists to the event, among them the baritones

OPPOSITE In 1888 the popular French operetta *Les Cloches de Corneville* (*The Chimes of Normandy*) was staged at Dunedin's Princess Theatre. These occasions were entertaining both on and off the stage, with theatregoers promenading and socialising with each other before, during and after performances. Alexander Turnbull Library, Eph-B-OPERA-1888-01

ABOVE The popularity of musical productions in Wellington led to a week-long musical festival in the city in October 1894, featuring works by the likes of Haydn, Dvořák and Sullivan. This is the festival's orchestra and choir. The event's success led to many hoping it would become a regular fixture. Louisa M. Herrmann, Alexander Turnbull Library, PAColl-3351-1

A. H. Gee (Auckland) and John Prouse (Wellington), the tenor Charles Saunders (Melbourne) and the soprano Fanny Bristowe (Melbourne), all backed by a 237-voice choir and a 60-strong orchestra.[105] The programme included Dvořák's *The Spectre's Bride*, Sullivan's *The Golden Legend* and Haydn's *The Creation*. The festival's patron was the Governor Lord Glasgow, who also opened the festival. According to Wellingtonian Herbert Spackman, 'The Governor ascended the platform after the national anthem and tried to make a speech, opening the Festival, but failed utterly; he had a bad attack of stage fright and couldn't express himself at all; it was rather painful.'[106]

The musical performances were much more successful. The festival drew people from throughout New Zealand and each night the auditorium was full to overflowing. Critical reaction was effusive, with one reviewer claiming it 'marked an era in the history of art in this colony. Never before has anything been attempted on such a large scale, and never before has it been possible for a performance of music of the highest class to draw audience night after night.' He further suggested that the performance of Haydn's work 'would not have disgraced a large English city; that such music can be produced in our thinly-populated colony is a veritable triumph'.[107] The festival's popularity and success (it made a small profit) led to claims that it would become a periodic fixture in the city, which in turn led to pleas for a proper choral hall to be built to host it. This was realised a decade later with the opening of the town hall and concert chamber.[108]

Sporting infrastructure

Also of growing importance was a city-based sporting infrastructure. The first organised sporting events had been those held on anniversary (of settlement) days in the 1840s. The programme typically included activities like horse and boat races (sometimes against Māori crews in waka), shooting, sack and wheelbarrow races, and folk events like climbing a greasy pole. These occasions were important in fostering sociability, attracting both participants and spectators, both settlers and Māori, and often concluding with dances or balls.[109] The emergence of racing and cricket clubs in the same decade was a first step towards the institutionalisation of sport. As Charlotte Macdonald notes, the first four decades of New Zealand settlement coincided with the codification of British sport (where games were given consistent rules and regular competitions introduced), 'meaning the sports that came to flourish here were modern from the outset'.[110]

Football is a good example. Organised football games were played in New Zealand from the 1860s, with Christchurch forming the first football club in 1863. At the same time, the diverse football codes in Britain were whittled down to rugby and football (soccer) and managed by national associations.[111] New Zealand's first rugby game played according to the new rules was in Nelson in 1870, after which the game quickly spread to the other cities and then the countryside.[112] New sportsgrounds were built to host games and accommodate paying spectators, paving the way for sport as an entertainment business.[113] These included Wellington's Basin Reserve (1868), Dunedin's Carisbrook (1880), Christchurch's Lancaster Park (1880) and Nelson's Trafalgar Park (1888) – Auckland's Eden Park did not open until 1902.[114] Meanwhile, sports days or carnivals continued to occupy city dwellers. In 1887, the Auckland Amateur Athletic Club ran 15 events in athletics and the relatively new sport of cycling, with a military band playing musical numbers in between.[115] The 8 Hours demonstration and Art Union picnic in 1896 at Auckland's Domain included both an adult and children's programme. Among the children's events were a 100-yards handicap (running) race for boys, a 75-yards race for girls, a sack race (boys), skipping races (girls) and a tug-of-war (boys versus girls).[116]

Although New Zealand sporting prowess has been located in the physicality of rural life, the reality is most sporting clubs and competitions originated in cities and large towns. With their greater populations and resources, cities were better able than rural areas to attract participants and maintain inter-club competitions.[117] Historians have also argued the competitive spirit that was endemic in (capitalist) cities also increased the magnetism of sport: 'events one attended or in which one took part that produced winners and losers appealed greatly to all sorts of city dwellers'.[118] Such competitions also encouraged the formation of geographically based social identities, with spectators usually barracking for teams that represented their own neighbourhoods or province. Even so, urban sporting participation rates in New Zealand were surprisingly low. This was largely because until the weekly half-day holiday (Saturday afternoon in most areas) came into force in 1894, few workers had the leisure time to pursue sport and Sabbatarian prescriptions ruled out Sunday sport.[119]

Until participation rates increased from the early twentieth century, most city dwellers' connection with organised sport was as spectators. Certainly, inter-provincial rugby matches were big events in cities and attracted large, socially diverse crowds. For example, when Otago played Wellington on 19 August 1891, Dunedin's mayor proclaimed a half-holiday and some 6,000 fans (13 per cent of the city's population) turned up to Carisbrook to watch Otago triumph 6 points to 3.[120] The touring of overseas sporting teams also generated much interest and emphasised imperial links. When James Lillywhite's 'All England Eleven' cricket team played at Christchurch's Hagley Oval in February 1877, up to 15,000 spectators watched the tourists defeat the local side by 23 runs.[121] By the 1890s, cycle track racing drew thousands to venues like Wellington's Athletic and Christchurch's Lancaster parks; night meets under modern electric lighting furthered the spectacle.[122]

These spectators are watching a game of cricket in Auckland's Domain during the late 1890s. The rise of organised sport in cities created a new form of popular entertainment. Spectators were encouraged to barrack for sports people and teams that represented their neighbourhoods or wider communities, fostering collective social identities. James Douglas Richardson, Auckland War Memorial Museum Tāmaki Paenga Hira, PH-ALB-1-p30-1

The provision of new cultural and sporting amenities like museums, art galleries, theatres and sportsgrounds showed the success of the middle-class project to enhance its position in urban society. This cultural capital increased the importance of cities in colonial life and, alongside their growing populations, made them more diverse, vital and fascinating places to live in. The change is reflected in the experiences of two middle-class city dwellers who lived in late-nineteenth-century Dunedin and Wellington respectively. The first was Emma Thomson, a suburban housewife, and the second was Herbert Spackman, a government clerk. And the diaries these two people kept highlight aspects of the debate about transience in colonial society.

Both the Thomsons and the Spackmans, for example, were 'persisters' (to use the term of the historiographical debate); they put down roots in their respective communities rather than moving on elsewhere after a short period of time. Also distinctive is their sense of ease with city life. John Webber had thought colonial urban society beneath him; Sarah Mathew had found fostering civilisation a (necessary) burden; John Wilson had experienced severe loneliness and anomie; John Kirkwood had felt urban society one-dimensional and dull; and Eliza Collier

These women were members of the Richmond Amateur Swimming Club in Christchurch. They are enjoying a dip on a summer's day, not long before the turn of the new century in 1900. *New Zealand Illustrated Magazine*, 1 January 1900, p.30

had missed the cultural diversity and vitality of London. Emma Thomson and Herbert Spackman seem much more at home in their New Zealand cities.

The Thomsons

Emma Thomson's diary begins in February 1887, by which time she was aged 35 and had been married to George Malcolm Thomson, aged 39, for eleven years.[123] The couple had three of their own children: Malcolm (9), Allan (6) and Stuart (5). A daughter, Florence, had died as an infant in 1885 and a further daughter, Annie, was born in September 1887. Maggie (11) and Jack (9), the children of George's older brother John, also lived with them – John resided in Calcutta. Another Maggie, Maggie Jackson, was their domestic servant. In 1892, Emma gave birth to a fourth son, Henry.[124] George was the science master at Otago Boys' High School, and had taught science and music at Otago Girls' High School. It was there he met Emma, a pupil; they married at Hopehill, Taieri. George was also an elder and Bible School teacher at Knox Church in George Street. This was a favoured church of the city's Presbyterian middle class, and many of Emma's and

George's friends also went there.[125] (Church attendance underlined class identity and provided opportunities for sociability at a local level.)[126] The family lived in nearby Newington, part of the middle-class suburb of Maori Hill.[127]

The Thomsons personified the middle-class nuclear family and the 'cult of domesticity' that spread through Anglo societies from the 1850s. The American Catharine Beecher was a leading exponent of the ideology, urging women to take command of the suburban family home and become its spiritual guardian. As Delores Hayden explains, Beecher's 'vision of domesticity was explicitly gendered: women were to create a peaceful domestic world, removed from the stresses of the city'.[128] In this revered environment, their breadwinner men could find daily redemption from the defiling effects of city workplaces. If the arrangement

OPPOSITE Emma Thomson and her husband George and their children lived in the Dunedin suburb of Maori Hill. The Thomsons personified the middle-class nuclear family. George was the family breadwinner while Emma undertook unpaid work at home. She is photographed here with her eldest son, Malcolm, in 1879. Courtesy of Sheila Irwin

ABOVE LEFT George Thomson was science master at Otago Boys' High School when this photograph was taken in the 1870s. He also taught at the nearby girls' high school, where he met Emma, who was a student there. After she finished her schooling the two courted and married in 1876. Courtesy of Sheila Irwin

ABOVE RIGHT The four Thomson children pose for a portrait in 1890: Malcolm (age 11), Annie (2), Stuart (7) and Allan (8). Courtesy of Sheila Irwin excluded women from the economic and political activities of public life, they would be rewarded in heaven for their self-sacrifice. Beecher's model gave rise to the notion that nineteenth-century urban space was gendered into 'separate spheres', with women dominant in domestic space and men in public space.[129]

There is much evidence to support this contention – many city clubs and associations were male-only institutions – but it is also true the boundaries between the spheres were more fluid than this, and women had greater agency in the public sphere than is sometimes supposed. The issue is considered in greater depth in Chapter Five, but in the meantime this fluidity or permissiveness is highlighted in the lives of George and Emma.

Both of them sought out sites of sociability and associational culture in Dunedin. George was a member of the gender-inclusive Dunedin Choral Society, but other social groups to which he belonged were male-only, including the Savage Club and the Knox Church Young Men's Society. Similarly, much of Emma's socialising was with other women. With fewer city public spaces available to women than for men, much of this continued to be carried on in the domestic sphere. On 16 November 1888, Emma recorded:

> Went out calling with Agnes [her sister] in the afternoon – we went to Mrs. Grant's and saw Katie for a time, then to Mrs. Whitson's, to Mrs. Hislop's, Mrs. Goyen's who was out and Mrs. Maitland's. In the evening went over to see Mrs. Thomson. George was out at the Dunlops to tea and for the evening.[130]

Not all of Emma's days were as socially active, but nor was this one unusual. Evening gatherings could involve music recitals, card playing (cribbage was a favourite) and charades. Some soirees involved twelve or more guests and the preparation of elaborate suppers. When Emma hosted such events, she usually spent the day baking cakes and arranging flowers.[131] She hosted one such occasion in February 1887 that 'passed off pleasantly with music and chatting'.[132] Another she felt was less successful: 'We had a rather quiet evening – I felt as I too often do as if I have nothing to say.'[133] Emma also joined a number of common-interest groups, including the 'Ladies Meeting', which was held monthly in members' homes to discuss a particular topic. Following the Presbyterian tenet to nourish the mind, the group was unafraid to tackle some big ideas. The 1887 meeting programme included the life of British theologian Frederick W. Robertson; Socialism; Carlyle's *Frederick the Great*; Goethe; Calvin's life and creed; and Bacon's essays.[134]

Shopping at the city's department stores and draperies was another activity she did with other women or her children, but not with her husband. This was almost certainly because department stores were imagined as feminised public spaces in which men were strangers – even though men worked in them. Unlike the streets, they were places where middle-class women could be without men and not compromise respectability. As historians have shown, the feminine association was deliberate. They trace the origin of the department store to the development of a consumer society that followed the increased production of manufactured goods in the mid-nineteenth century. The first stores were in Paris and London, but they soon spread around the globe. Their aim was to promote consumption beyond the bare necessities of life and turn shopping into a leisure activity.[135] Women were encouraged to see shopping as an extension of their spiritual domestic role, buying clothes, upholstery and furnishings that would improve their family and home. Popular terms such as 'cathedrals of consumption' provided a religious dimension. Store-owners represented shopping as a moral act and linked religious festivals like Christmas and Easter with consumption.[136] The stores' spectacular interiors and facilities were particularly aimed at women's sensibilities and needs: interiors were domestic-like; customers were free to browse and not buy; and ancillary services like teashops provided spaces where women could meet friends unchaperoned. Accordingly, 'shopping became a major form of female pleasure'.[137] Whether this was true of Emma is uncertain. Her diary provides numerous accounts of shopping expeditions into town, but in a perfunctory way that does not reveal her feelings about the activity. On some occasions she mentions going on for lunch or tea with her female companions at a restaurant or tearoom before catching the tram home, suggesting she enjoyed the opportunity for sociability that shopping presented.[138]

There were, however, many public city spaces where the sexes met on common ground. Knox Church was one such site. Alongside Sunday services (where people sat together), the church put on regular mixed-sex socials.[139] Emma also often accompanied George to the Otago Institute and other public meetings at the Choral Hall and museum.[140] A talk by Dr Thomas Hocken on the early history of Canterbury drew hundreds: 'There was a good attendance of ladies specially,' wrote Emma.[141] Another titled 'Light, Sound, Heat and Electricity' was by Dr Edwards. 'He had a battery and good apparatus and shewed a number of beautiful "lights" etc, but we did not care for his style.'[142] The two also heard Mrs Belcher speak on the higher education of women at St Paul's schoolroom. Belcher charted the institutional and cultural barriers to women's entry into university and demanded their removal – an appeal interrupted by 'frequent applause', said one reviewer.[143] Emma commented on the hall being crowded, 'mostly with ladies', but said nothing about Belcher's plea.[144] This reflected her conservative world view and suggests she was a disciple of the American Catharine Beecher. As Delores Hayden reminds us, Beecher had called 'for women's authority in the domestic sphere, but she had in mind a conservative version of women's lives, one

NEW ZEALAND AND SOUTH SEAS EXHIBITION.

DUNEDIN, 1889-90.   BURTON BROS., Photo.

The Thomsons took full advantage of Dunedin's social, cultural and recreational amenities. These included attending public meetings and talks, going to church, and taking excursions to the seaside. The New Zealand and South Seas Exhibition at Anderson's Bay was another attraction, the amusement zone (beside the steel tower) being popular with the children. Hocken Collections, Uare Taoka o Hākena, University of Otago, Misc-MS-0978

that specified women's competence at home but surrendered it in public life. Hers was a "domestic feminism" in contrast to the "social feminism" of temperance advocates.'[145] Emma was clearly a domestic feminist. She makes no reference to current social reform debates, such as the Women's Christian Temperance Union's campaigns to ban liquor, promote the female franchise and stop the sweated labour of working women in Dunedin's clothing industry.[146] This is not to say she was apolitical. In September 1890, she recorded how she was 'greatly interested in the labour movements – strikes and rumours of strikes, boycotts etc.' (The 1890 Maritime Strike was just beginning.) Emma then declared she had 'no sympathy with the action of the unionists'.[147] Apart from mentioning a church collection for the poor, this was her only reference to other city dwellers outside her own social class.[148]

Family life was another key site of sociability. When Emma wasn't out of the house or receiving visitors, her day was occupied with childcare and housework: cooking, cleaning, ironing, sewing and even brewing beer. In line with the cult of domesticity's gendered division of labour, this was largely carried out by Emma, Maggie and the maid; the boys would help if Emma was sick. Irksome as housework

International exhibitions were not confined to Dunedin. All the major cities had turns at hosting these events. The New Zealand International Exhibition was held in Christchurch between 1906 and 1907. This is the model pā Te Āraiteuru. Leslie Hinge, Alexander Turnbull Library, 1/1-022026-G

was, it was also a social activity.[149] On one occasion Emma and Maggie cleaned the veranda windows together; another time they wallpapered the boys' bedroom.[150] Both sexes worked in the garden, usually on Saturdays. Typically the boys would help George weed and prune, while Emma harvested produce, re-potted plants or grafted trees.[151] In the evening, all the family gathered in the living room for music recitals, book reading and card playing. Sometimes, extended family members or friends dropped by. One particularly cold winter evening, the children practised the polka to warm themselves up before going to bed.[152] Curiously, Emma, not George, was the family disciplinarian. One evening in 1888 she noted that she '[f]elt very angry with Jack and Malcolm tonight for deliberate disobedience and gave them both a whipping and sent them to bed earlier than usual'.[153]

Beyond the front gate, the city provided myriad opportunities for family excursions. Taking the children into town to shop for clothes and other items was a regular activity.[154] The museum and art gallery was also a popular destination; Emma recording several visits there with family members.[155] Some excursions were seasonal. These included winter rugby games at the Carisbrook sportsground, where in August 1891, George, Maggie and some of the boys attended the inter-provincial rugby match between Wellington and Otago. A couple of weeks later, Emma and George joined 4,000 others at the same ground to see Otago trounce Southland 17 to nil.[156] The sea was a focus of summer familial recreation; a 'bath in the breakers' at St Clair beach was a regular pursuit.[157] Periodically the family would go on boating and other trips with others, or by train to visit Emma's parents at Hopehill, near Mosgiel.[158] Fishing down at the harbour jetty was an activity the boys pursued by themselves. On one occasion Emma recorded:

> All our boys and Teddy [a family friend] went out fishing today and remained all day – I was getting anxious about them but they turned up all right about 6:30 P.M. Stuart fell into a pool and was very much wet but the boys did not think of bringing him home – they were more or less sunburnt, Malcolm especially and brought home two or three little fish.[159]

Then there were fantastical events that only cities could offer. In April 1887, George took Malcolm and Jack to the packed opening night of Fryer's Circus and Japanese Village. The village comprised a series of booths where spectators could watch Japanese artisans create items such as carvings, fans and embroidery for sale. The circus was a mixture of acrobatics and animal tricks, including goats riding on ponies; an invitation for audience members to perform the same feat sent the spectators 'into fits of laughter', reported a reviewer.[160] In a cultural milieu that was strongly British and ethnocentric, this was a rare glimpse into another culture. Emma recorded the 'boys came home quite delighted with it'.[161]

Between December 1889 and April 1890, the family were regular visitors at the New Zealand and South Seas Exhibition on Anderson's Bay Road. Held to commemorate the colony's jubilee, it was the latest in a number of international exhibitions, modelled on London's Great Exhibition of 1851, held in New Zealand cities since 1865.[162] These spectacles showcased new scientific knowledge and technology; exhibited local and overseas commodities; and provided a forum for cultural production and consumption.[163] The Dunedin event included a concert hall, where George and Emma attended several recitals, and George sang in the choir at a performance of *The Messiah*. The boys preferred the exhibition galleries and amusement zone, with Malcolm particularly enthusiastic about the switchback (rollercoaster).[164] The whole family attended the closing ceremony in the concert hall that was followed by a large fireworks display in the gardens.[165]

There is a gap in Emma's diary from the end of 1891 until she contracted tuberculosis in January 1894. In facing imminent death, she found comfort in her faith. In May she wrote to her son Jack, telling him she would have liked to see him grow up under her care 'but this does not seem to be God's will'. She told him that she and George were proud of him and were sure he would become a 'good useful man'. She concluded by saying: '[N]ow dear Son, may God bless you all your life. I leave you my love, and trust we shall all meet again in Heaven.' She died two months later, aged 41.[166] The sadness of Emma's death reminds us that diseases like tuberculosis were an everyday hazard of daily life, an issue we will return to in Chapter Seven.

The Spackmans

Herbert Spackman was a violinist, conductor and baritone singer. He emigrated from Bristol in 1891, aged 27, and settled in Wellington with the aim of establishing himself before sending for his fiancée Daisy (age and family name unknown). He was unable to secure a living from his profession, so took up a position as a clerk in the Government Life Insurance office in town.[167] In October 1892, he bought a villa in a new part of Rintoul Street in suburban Newtown.[168] Herbert became an important figure in the Wellington performing arts community, playing in amateur orchestras as the lead violinist and singing in choral events. After a performance at the Opera House in December 1892 he wrote: 'large attendance … and my solo was a great success; I was encored, and bowed, and afterwards many shook my hands.'[169] He also attended a diverse range of city performances. In May 1893, for instance, he saw the 90-strong London Gaiety Burlesque Company perform two different shows, *Faust up to Date* and *Miss Esmeralda*, at the Opera House. He enjoyed the spectacle 'very much, fine looking lot of girls in the chorus; splendid physique. Good orchestra.'[170] The troupe played to packed houses and was even given a vice-regal party at Government House.[171] As we have seen, he attended several performances at the Wellington Musical Festival in 1894.

Herbert also went to public lectures. Perhaps eager to learn more about the opposite sex before Daisy arrived, he attended French humourist Max O'Rell's lecture, 'Her Royal Highness Women'.[172] Referring to current calls for the greater public empowerment of women, O'Rell argued this was unnecessary because women already ruled men at home. As one historian has noted, he ridiculed social feminists as 'unloved spinsters who threw themselves into social reform movements because they had no family to look after'.[173] Herbert declared it 'one of the most enjoyable lectures I have ever heard. A very full house.' (Ironically, he supported social feminism.)[174] Two weeks later, he saw American physician Anna Potts speak on 'Hearts and Homes, or is Marriage a Failure'.[175] According to a reviewer, '[S]he warned young men against marrying the tight-laced and conceited girl of the period and urged them if they valued happiness never to marry a girl whose waist they could span with both hands. On the other hand, she urged greater tenderness and consideration upon the part of the husband to the wife.'[176] In her experience, two in three marriages were unhappy, and she blamed this on a lack of mutual respect between spouses. Potts was among a growing number of social reformers calling for a more modern, companionate form of marriage, where couples shared interests and strove for domestic parity.[177] Herbert went away pleased to have gained such practical advice.[178]

Daisy finally arrived in Wellington at the end of November 1893, and Archdeacon Stock married them a few days later. The couple personified the companionate marriage model, spending much of their free time together and sharing common interests, including membership of the St Thomas Church choir and the Newtown Tennis Club. Herbert described one summer Sunday at home: 'Lovely day. Busy in the garden weeding and helping Daisy make jam; enjoyed reading together on the veranda. In the evening Minnie Dugdale [a neighbour] came in and we played through the Lachner trios again, Daisy playing piano.'[179] The following evening they attended a dancing class and walked home together in the moonlight. They picnicked at places like Day's Bay, sometimes with neighbours, and went to demonstrations of new technology like the kinematograph: 'in spite of drawbacks (constant movement and jerkiness of the affair) it is really very wonderful'.[180]

Herbert and Daisy did not attend urban spectator sports like rugby; their cultural consumption was mainly confined to the performing arts. This included the Wellington Musical Festival, where they saw *The Spectre's Bride*.[181] A few months later, they saw Sydney Grundy's comedy *Sowing the Wind*, recommended by their Aunt Clara at home: 'It was very good indeed.'[182] The following year they went to Arthur Law's farcical comedy *The New Boy*. As Herbert explained, it was 'about a married man of small stature passed off by his wife as her son in order to secure a legacy, and then he is sent to a boys' school and made to fag and

OPPOSITE TOP Daisy Spackman stands holding her daughter Sylvie on the veranda of 'Ben Venuto', their Rintoul Street villa in the Wellington suburb of Newtown in 1898. As was typical of suburbs at this time, Newtown housed both working and middle-class residents. The size and decoration of Ben Venuto marked it out as a middle-class dwelling. Alexander Turnbull Library, PA1-q-222-30-1

OPPOSITE BOTTOM Baby Sylvie is sleeping in a cot next to her parents' bed in the Spackman home. The image provides a rare view of the interior of a middle-class dwelling. The room shows the Victorian aesthetic for floral wallpapers and bric-a-brac. Alexander Turnbull Library, PA1-o-465-11

play football etc.; very amusing.'[183] The show's promoters, (J. C.) Williamson and Musgrove, had travelled to London to secure the rights, returning with an all-English cast for an Australasian tour. Its publicity made much of the fact that it was playing concurrently in London and New Zealand, effectively eliminating the cultural lag between metropolis and colony.[184] This annihilation of distance was further emphasised by lecture tours of prominent overseas intellectuals, writers and reformers. Following in the wake of visits by Max O'Rell and Anna Potts in 1894, Herbert heard General William Booth and Mark Twain speak in 1895.[185] Such visits confirmed New Zealand's integration into a global network of modern cultural exchange and interaction.

We have seen that the city spaces Herbert and Daisy negotiated in their daily lives were gender inclusive. But, like George Thomson, Herbert frequented some male-only sites of associational culture and sociability. In February 1893, he was initiated into the Southern Cross Lodge of the Independent Order of Odd Fellows: 'it was a most mysterious ceremony', he noted.[186] In 1897, he recorded a visit to the Turkish baths with a male family friend. After a hot shower they went into the hot rooms – 'the perspiration ran off us' – then entered the cooling rooms for their shampoo. While waiting, they played draughts, with Sir Robert Stout looking on.[187]

Herbert's diary ignores Daisy's female social networks, but she appears to have had some close women friends. On one occasion she left Herbert alone for a few days to care for a sick friend in Crofton (present-day Ngaio). He wrote: 'It seems funny in the house without my darling. She left little notes for her Herbo. On the kitchen table there was a piece of paper on which was "'My poor lonely darling, I love you", and on the pillow at night another piece, "Good night my darling boy x x x x".'[188] The passage underscores their mutual affection and emotional intimacy; indeed, the degree to which Herbert recorded his feelings and emotional life defies the stereotype of the stoic and aloof colonial male considered further in Chapter Eight.

Daisy was also grounded in her Newtown neighbourhood, giving piano lessons to local children and socialising with the neighbours. One day in January 1897, she took a large party of the neighbour's children to Newtown Park for an excursion.[189] Two months later, she and Herbert visited a Dr Chappell about having children of their own.[190] Chappell gave Daisy a physical examination which she found painful and upsetting.[191] He told Herbert two days later that Daisy had a congenital barrier to conception (possibly a microperforate hymen) but an operation would solve the problem. The patriarchal culture of Victorian society meant it was Herbert's task to decide: 'My darling wife received my decision with resignation.' Chappell carried out the procedure at home the following day. Herbert lit a fire in the bedroom and got things ready – 'striving hard to keep cheerful but feeling miserable' – and then waited anxiously in the kitchen.

[After] a quarter of an hour I heard my darling's voice, very weak, saying the operation was over. The effects of the ether had made her very talkative and her brain seemed remarkably clear. I went to see her and kissed her; the doctors told me she had gone through it capitally ... I felt very thankful that the operation had passed off successfully and she was spared to me.[192]

Daisy fell pregnant soon after and gave birth to a daughter, Sylvia, on 2 February 1898. Herbert heard the news by telephone at work:

[a] thousand conflicting emotions passed through me at the news, and I hastened home to see my darling and kiss the little one. Nurse told me all about it; it was a very narrow squeak for the baby; instruments had to be used and after it was born the nurse and doctor had to work hard to save it. My darling is picking up nicely, bless her.[193]

Daisy's recuperation was helped by the employment of a nurse.

Herbert thrived in his new role as a father, declaring Sylvia to be the 'delight and admiration of her Dada and Mother' and the many visitors who came by.[194] He recorded Sylvia's development in his diary and in photographs. His interest in photography grew, and in June 1899 he exhibited his work at a Camera Club exhibition: 'my little exhibition doesn't look at all bad on the walls', he confessed. It was the start of a new career as a professional photographer that was to be pursued elsewhere: the Spackmans returned to England the following year for family reasons.

In a period better known and celebrated for the rugged smallholder and his helpmeet wife (discussed in Chapter Eight), what is striking about the Thomson and Spackman families is the extent to which their lives are city-centric. There is little reference (none in Herbert's case) to the rural space that encircles them, and neither family expresses any qualms about living in the city. So why were they so enamoured of city life? In examining their daily lives, three main attributes stand out: first, it provided them with multiple spaces of sociability, from church socials, to domestic living rooms, sports clubs, Masonic lodges and even Turkish baths. The second was that it offered cultural diversity and stimulus, from public talks that introduced new ideas, to the latest London musicals and comedies, through to barracking for the local team at an inter-provincial rugby game. The third was that the city was a key site of modernity, offering not only new cultural and technological production – burlesque, electric lighting, the kinematograph – but new social practices as well. The Thomsons and the Spackmans personified the modern companionate marriage and suburban nuclear family. An implicit fourth attribute was that city life offered broader work opportunities than rural life. While Herbert could not find a job as a professional musician in the city, he was soon able to find alternative work as a government clerk. Without further inquiry we cannot know how far the Thomsons and Spackmans typified middle-class colonial city life, but it is evident their experiences closely accord with those described in overseas urban research. In time, the city functionary and his domiciled wife may stand alongside their rural counterparts as emblematic figures of late-colonial Pākehā society. In their own ways, they were pioneers too.

Conclusion

It is apparent in the townspeople considered here that sociability in colonial cities was centred more in horizontal communities of common interest than in local or spatial communities. It was in the likes of churches, clubs and societies, as well as familial and informal social networks, that they mostly pursued social relations and created distinct cultures of sociability. This is not to say propinquity was unimportant: Wellingtonian Mary Petre's women's-based social network was composed of people who all lived in close proximity. Yet its exclusion of those in the neighbourhood who were not of her social class precluded it from being a local community. And while the Spackmans often socialised with their immediate neighbours, this was only one among a number of social networks they were involved in.

The lives of these townspeople do not support Fairburn's assertion of wide-spread anomie, but they do confirm that some experienced social dislocation and periods of deep loneliness. Writing letters to kith and kin back home could help fill the void and act as a surrogate or virtual society, but for many others this social practice was a simply a way of staying in touch and expanding their social world beyond their own environs. The extent to which individuals engaged with urban society was often a function of their temperament. Some townspeople were better able to forge social relations and create or penetrate social networks than others were. A few preferred to remain aloof from it altogether; the 'man alone' was not purely a rural phenomenon.

There is little doubt that despite settlers' initial efforts to create a social and cultural infrastructure akin to that at home, early colonial society lacked the vitality and diversity of metropolitan society. Those who had emigrated from London and other large cities felt this loss keenly. However, as New Zealand cities became larger, their capacity to provide for a more dynamic social and cultural environment also increased. From the 1870s, all cities experienced a boom in the production of new cultural space and sites of sociability: museums, public libraries, art galleries, theatres and sportsgrounds. These provided forums for overseas troupes and other entertainers to present the latest fashions and ideas, enabling local audiences to feel more connected to the modern world and less on its edge. Meanwhile, visits from sports teams offered local sides rare international or inter-provincial competition, as well as a public spectacle. Such developments increased the complexity and vivacity of colonial cities, making them more appealing places in which to live. The change was evident in the experiences of the Thomsons and Spackmans. Emma, George, Herbert and Daisy were fully enmeshed in city life, negotiating its myriad spaces with ease, and thriving in its social diversity, cultural vitality and sheer modernity. They were all at home in the Big Smoke.

This well-to-do Māori family group photographed about 1908 are Tureiti Te Heuheu Tukino, the fifth paramount chief of Ngāti Tūwharetoa, and two of his children, Hoani (left) and Te Wira. Political and tribal business took Māori leaders from their tribal areas into cities, where they maintained homes. Tureiti and his family lived predominately in Wellington from 1894. William Anderson Taylor, Hocken Collections, Uare Taoka o Hākena, University of Otago Library, Box-304-005

Chapter Four

Māori and the City

For centuries, European cities were contained within defensive walls or included a citadel to which citizens could escape in times of threat. The walls were an overt statement of a city's power to resist invasion and control its hinterland. Sometimes defences were taken down when the city's leaders felt themselves to be so powerful they must be immune to attack.[1] Yet even when cities were defenceless, the idea that they were an assertion of power remained embedded in European thought and was carried into colonial contexts. As we saw in Chapter One, settler colonial cities began as European toeholds in indigenous-controlled territories. From here settlers were expected to spread out and shape a productive hinterland that would enrich the town and make it powerful. The success of this goal relied on the cooperation or submission of indigenous populations. Both approaches had characterised Britain's first North American colony at Jamestown in 1607. Settlers and the local Powhatan people had initially co-existed peacefully, but cooperation later broke down over trade and land-title disputes. In 1622, the Powhatan chief Opechancanough moved to reclaim authority over his lands, leading a force that swept through Jamestown's hinterland and massacring a quarter of the 1,200-strong settler population. The settlers' revenge was clinical. Through intermittent killings and burning of crops, they extinguished the Powhatan threat and made Jamestown's hinterland their own.

The experience led the British to largely exclude indigenous populations from settler colonies – a policy followed in New South Wales and the other Australian colonies.[2] By the 1830s, reports of brutal settler treatment of Aboriginal people had sullied this strategy among humanists, who warned any colonisation of New Zealand would be as detrimental to Māori as it had been to Aboriginals.[3] In responding to these anxieties, promoters of New Zealand colonisation returned to the cooperative model. A crucial factor here was British recognition that Māori were land occupiers and owners with whom the British would need to negotiate for the purchase of land for settlers. This distinguished New Zealand from Australia, where the British had declared land *terra nullius* or unoccupied,

A group of Māori sit on a grassy verge alongside Wellington's Lambton Quay in the early 1840s. On the other side of the road is Barrett's Hotel, a well-known watering hole. Samuel Brees, Alexander Turnbull Library, A-109-027

meaning there was no need to buy land from Aboriginals. It was there for the taking.[4] Racial amalgamation was thus a foundation of Wakefield's systematic colonisation. Māori would be welcomed into settler society and, through such measures as the provision of Native reserves, have a stake in it.[5] With Māori as partners in the colonising project, there would be no military threat to consider: New Zealand cities would rise without walls. This proved a premature assertion.

Indigenous peoples in settler colonial cities

A common story in (Anglo) New World settler societies is that indigenous peoples were instrumental in founding and sustaining cities, but that as settlers became more numerous and powerful, indigenous people were marginalised in city space or expelled altogether. William Cronon describes pre-1830 Chicago (Fort Dearborn) as 'a polygot world of Indian, French, British and American cultures tied to a vast trading network that was no less Indian than European'. Marriages between the local Potawatomi people and European traders produced offspring who facilitated trade relationships and created a 'hybrid cultural universe' in

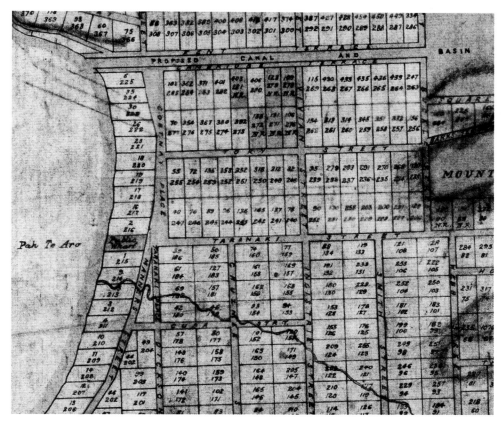

Wellington's founding was based on the mistaken European premise that Māori would assimilate into settler society. To aid this process Māori would be given one-tenth of all land in the new city. These were called native reserves (or tenths) and are shown here in this 1841 plan in green. Some of the tenths still remain in local Māori ownership. Archives New Zealand, Te Rua Mahara o te Kāwanatanga, AATE W4920 Box 79 (R2431150)

the region.[6] In 1832, groups of Iowan Indians crossed the Mississippi River to forcefully reclaim alienated lands, but they were defeated by an American force twice their number. Yankee soldiers sent glowing reports of the fertility of the Illinois prairies, spurring a wave of immigration to the Chicago region. Before too long, Yankee townspeople outnumbered the French and Potawatomi inhabitants. As settlers continued to arrive, the United States government acted to gain control of Chicago's hinterland. In 1833, the Potawatomi people were forced to sign two treaties that saw them removed to reservations west of the Mississippi. Many wanted to stay in Chicago to be close to where their ancestors were buried, but Yankee settlers were unwelcoming, and in 1835 most Potowatomi people left the city to join their clans.[7]

In a comparative study of Melbourne's Kulin people and the Lekwammen Nation people of Victoria, British Columbia, Penelope Edmonds showed that initial cooperation between European settlers and indigenous populations broke down as settlers gained control of urban space. The private Port Phillip Association was founded in Melbourne in 1835. After negotiating a dubious treaty with Kulin chiefs, the Association's leader, John Batman, chose a site beside the Yarra River for a town. Initially settlers and Aboriginal people lived in close proximity. However, following reports of an imminent attack on settlers, the Aboriginal population was expelled to a camp across the river and their canoes destroyed.[8] Kulin people continued to venture into Melbourne to barter, buy munitions, exchange their labour, and sell skins and feathers. By the late 1830s, settlers were complaining about the vagrant-like behaviours of Aboriginal people in Melbourne's streets, and their lack of clothing. The Kulin were increasingly represented as a public nuisance and an impediment to the production of urban space. Unprovoked settler attacks on Aboriginal people became common, yet a latent settler fear of attack led Governor La Trobe to engage in shows of force at peri-urban Kulin camps and to deploy police to remove Aboriginal people from city space.[9] As more settlers arrived, the need for indigenous labour diminished, making it easier to exclude Aboriginals from town. Edmonds says Kulin camps continued to exist around Melbourne until the 1850s, when these spaces too were colonised and the Kulin people moved to reservations.[10]

Meanwhile, the Hudson Bay Company founded Victoria on Aboriginal land at the southern tip of Vancouver Island in 1843 as a fort and trading centre. As Edmonds writes: 'Unlike Kulin peoples in Melbourne, who were quickly removed to the other side of the river, the Lekwammen established themselves as crucial middlemen who brokered trade between Europeans and other Aboriginal groups.'[11] The Lekwammen formed a settlement beside the fort, which they helped to build. They also cleared land, made shingles and shore sheep. However, conflict arose as settlers began cultivating and grazing livestock on the camas-bulb fields on which the Lekwammen people subsisted. They resented the appropriation of their land and retaliated by harvesting cattle. In 1844, they were accused of killing an ox; a dispute ensued and the Lekwammen threatened to attack the fort. The Company subdued the threat by firing a cannonball into a chief's (empty) house. Following a fire near the fort, the Lekwammen residents were pushed to a Native reserve on the other side of the harbour. It was the first of many settler ploys to segregate European and indigenous residents of the town and eventually marginalise Lekwammen people in city space.[12]

In many respects, New Zealand townspeople's social relations with Māori followed the same lamentable path. As in other settler colonies, New Zealand's indigenous people helped to found and sustain towns and cities, but as the settler population increased Pākehā represented Māori as outsiders in city space and encouraged them to stay away. The success of this strategy was reflected in official Census data that showed a diminishing number of Māori domiciled in cities from the 1870s. The decline created the impression among historians that Māori disengaged from city life and largely remained in rural homelands until the great wave of Māori urbanisation in the mid-twentieth century. Erin Keenan expresses the general view when she says, 'through processes of colonisation, sometimes immediate and sometimes gradual, Māori became marginalised from the growing towns and cities of Europeans – marginalisation that was physical and geographical, but also social and cultural'.[13] While it is true that settlers attempted to exclude Māori from city life, the contention that Māori disengaged from cities is not.

This chapter charts the marginalisation of Māori in New Zealand's cities, but also considers some of the ways Māori continued to exert their agency in city spaces and even manipulate them.[14] It follows American scholarship that has shown that, far from being eradicated from the Chicago landscape after 1835, the Potawatomi and other indigenous people continued to live in the city and contribute to its life.[15]

European racial theory

As the previous discussion suggests, settlers' social relations with indigenous peoples was framed by European racial theory.[16] This held as its fundamental premise that Europeans were superior to all other races, the European 'Self' being socially constructed in opposition to the non-European 'Other'.[17] During the nineteenth century, European racial discourse (or ethnographic assessment) was constantly redefined in response to new racial encounters and changing social, cultural and political power relationships in both metropolitan and colonial contexts.[18] In the first half of the century, racial and cultural differences were attributed to environmental factors like climate and geography rather than inherent biological difference. Aligned with this was the monogenetic belief that all humans were descended from a common ancestor, but that over space and time 'savage' (non-European) races had degenerated to varying degrees. However, the theory also asserted it was possible for savage races to 'improve' and become 'civilised' because there was no innate difference in humankind. A counter-view was the polygenetic belief that every race was biologically distinct and evolved from different ancestors. Using physiological 'evidence', it argued that dark races were intellectually inferior to white races and incapable of civilisation.[19]

In New Zealand monogenetic ideas prevailed. Few suggested that Māori were a different biological species from Europeans, so polygenetic thought gained few advocates. What was often contested was how long it would take Māori to

William Fox painted the Māori settlement of Rakawakaputa near Kaiapoi in 1848, the same year vast swathes of land in Canterbury were purchased by the Crown. The area was peaceful at the time, negating the need for defences around the settlement. The people would have used the land in the area seasonally to gather food, including the future site of Christchurch. William Fox, Hocken Collections, Uare Taoka o Hākena, University of Otago Library, A432

civilise. Early optimism that they would readily amalgamate with settler society dissipated in the 1860s as Māori continued to resist settler advances to assimilate. This coincided with a hardening of Pākehā attitudes toward Māori: the 'soft' racism of the 1840s 'civilising project' gave way to the 'hard' racism of policies demanding Māori submission to Crown authority.[20] This saw Pākehā emphasise Māori as 'Other' and outside civil society. Towards the end of the nineteenth century, with Māori no longer a threat to the Crown, a new social construct emerged: the Aryan Māori. It hypothesised that Māori were Aryans and therefore shared deep cultural bonds with Pākehā. As James Belich sardonically put it, 'the British colonisation of New Zealand was therefore a family reunion'.[21] These shifting sands of European racial theory are evident in social relations between Māori and Pākehā in New Zealand's cities.

The belief that Māori would quickly civilise and amalgamate with the settler population was at the forefront of the New Zealand Company's propaganda.

The people of Pipitea pā on shores of Wellington harbour are going about their daily business in 1842. The pā, established almost 20 years earlier by Ngāti Mutunga, was in the centre of the new town of Wellington and the people were pressured to sell the land by the Crown. William Mein Smith, Alexander Turnbull Library, PUBL-0011-04-1

Whereas others had used the notion of civilising savages as a pretext to oppress and even extinguish them, the Company claimed its plans were the first to use colonisation as a means to improve a savage people, asserting that because Māori were superior to most savage people they had greater capacity for improvement.[22] While missionaries promoted Christianity as the agent for civilisation, the Company believed Māori participation in urban life or civil society would hasten the process. As pointed out in Chapter Two, the Native reserves of Wellington and Nelson were therefore interspersed among settlers' allotments to encourage inter-racial mixing and amalgamation.

Māori were a ubiquitous presence in towns from the beginning of colonial settlement. In this 1845 view of Auckland's Princes Street – the town's government quarter – four Māori figures are visible in the middle of the thoroughfare. Cuthbert Clarke, National Library of Australia, nla.obj-134551139

By the mid-twentieth century, historians were criticising the ethnocentric basis of the Company's project: in 1958, for example, John Miller lampooned the image of 'brown John Bulls' smoking cigars and sipping 'claret like true Christian gentlemen'.[23] That such a policy was doomed to failure is manifest now, but in the context of its time its modernity was striking. As Erik Olssen reminds us: 'We tend to forget now, or dismiss if we remember, that the decision to reject American-style reservations and reserve one-tenth of all land bought, pepper-potted within the new communities, helped to define relations between Maori and European in what then was a most distinctive manner.'[24] Olssen suggests that the Miller-led perspective was overly cynical of Company aims, noting how the Company's plan of racial amalgamation gained widespread support among settlers. While Chicago Yankees and Melbourne settlers moved relatively quickly to discourage indigenous people in urban space, New Zealand townspeople sought to foster social relations with Māori and encourage their participation in civil society.

First encounters

Māori have traditionally identified themselves as tangata whenua or people of the land. Although some Māori had lived in large settlements of up to 1,000 people

These waka are racing each other on Auckland Harbour during a regatta in January 1862. The sleek, low vessels contrast with the upright forms of the European ships. Frederick Stack, Auckland Art Gallery Toi o Tāmaki, purchased 1989

before 1840, as they did around Maungakiekie (One Tree Hill, Auckland) in the eighteenth century, it was more usual for them to live in kāinga or villages of up to 250 people.[25] In European terms they were a rural rather than an urban people. So when settlers began building their towns, the sheer scale of the enterprise unsettled some Māori. A local Te Āti Awa leader, Te Wharepouri, famously expressed this at Wellington. Having watched settlers disembark from the first two immigrant ships, he went to Colonel William Wakefield's hut to report that he and his people were leaving Te Whanganui-a-Tara. According to Edward Jerningham Wakefield, he told William he had not expected so many settlers:

> I thought you would have nine or ten ... I thought that I could get one placed at each *pa*, as a white man to barter with the people and keep us well supplied with arms and clothing; and that I should be able to keep these white men under my hand and regulate their trade myself. But I see that each ship holds two hundred, and I believe, now, that you have more coming. They are well armed ... They will be too strong for us; my heart is dark. Remain here with your people; I will go with mine to Taranaki.[26]

His position made sense. With the exception of the town of Kororāreka, the pattern of European settlement in New Zealand had been much as he described,

Trade dominated social relations between townspeople and Māori. From the 1840s Māori would arrive in waka laden with fresh produce to sell to grateful settlers and leave with goods bought from Pākehā shops. The level of town trade declined from the 1850s, but continued in Auckland for decades. This image shows an unknown Māori man hawking produce near the city's Queens Wharf about 1890. Auckland War Memorial Museum Tāmaki Paenga Hira, PH-ALB-1-p66-4

with small numbers of Pākehā attaching themselves to particular Māori communities and becoming conduits for trade. Under these arrangements, Māori held the balance of power. Te Wharepouri would therefore have seen the arrival of so many Europeans at one time as a challenge to his authority. Rather than confront such overwhelming odds, he thought it wiser to return to his tribe's Taranaki homelands. Jerningham Wakefield said that Te Wharepouri's people, who saw the settlers more as an opportunity than a threat, dissuaded him from going.

The New Zealand Company was just as eager to foster cooperation between the two groups, not least because it knew reports of conflict with Māori would deter immigration. Accordingly, its promotional literature was careful to show Māori as benign and welcoming. For instance, Company stalwart Henry Petre's 1841 account of the first months in Wellington included an admission of early settler apprehension over Māori hostility:

Patrick Hogan's 1852 painting of the wharf at the foot of Auckland's Queen Street includes three waka, two moored and empty and a third being pulled up by one of its crew. Groups of Māori are sitting at the street edges. Patrick Joseph Hogan, Alexander Turnbull Library, C-010-020

Most of us had made anxious enquiries on this subject before we embarked, and our conviction was, that we should be received as friends of the natives, if our conduct towards them was just and friendly. Our most sanguine expectations were completely realized ... they received us in the most friendly manner.[27]

Equally important was finding evidence in support of the monogenetic view that Māori were capable of civilisation. In providing a sketch of Māori society to his Glaswegian parents, Wellington settler James Campbell explained: 'They are all in tribes, under different chiefs, something like the ancient tribes of Scotland, making war and peace with each other.' The inference was that if the Scots were capable of civilisation, then Māori were too. 'The men are a fine, working, intelligent race, tattooed over the face and other parts of the body, but that custom is about to be done away with by the influence of the missionaries.'[28] An unnamed mechanic was also certain Māori 'will civilise very fast, for they imitate everything we do ... They make capital traders, and know how to bargain for their pigs and potatoes as well as any European.'[29] Petre similarly praised Māori business acumen. He and his fellow capitalists employed Māori for hunting, fishing, chopping firewood and house-building. When the settlers had first arrived, the bartering system of trade had prevailed, but within months this was superseded by the money economy.[30] For Petre, the shift signalled an encouraging aptitude for commerce that would ease Māori amalgamation into civil society. Fellow colonist Job Murray hyperbolically predicted that in being lifted from heathenism Māori would 'take their places amongst the princes of the earth; then village *pahs* will become cities, and their country a kingdom rivalling in all things civil and religious'.[31]

The cultural transfer was not all one-way, with settlers adopting some Māori social practices, not the least of which was their language. In 1841, the colonist Donald Gollan found few Māori about Wellington spoke English but many settlers spoke Māori.[32] The diary of Petre's wife Mary is peppered with Māori words, with 'kai' and 'kororo' (kōrero) often supplanting their English equivalents (food and talking) in her entries.[33] Another colonist, Dr George Evans, also spoke Māori and enjoyed socialising with the local chiefs, whom he considered his social peers. 'They indulge in a quiet humour that is highly diverting, at the expense of the ignorant bullying Cocknies [*sic*], who are physically and morally their inferiors,' recorded Evans.[34] Many other settlers spoke of positive encounters with Māori. A surveying officer wrote of playing draughts with one while on a work break:

> We had no draftsman, so he made his out of wood, and I cut mine out of some potatoes; and on the flat of a paddle we made a draft-board. While we were engaged in our game, a little pig made off with one of my men, at which we had a hearty laugh. I find them always kind and obliging.[35]

Finally, Gollan also observed that quite a few Wellington settlers had Māori wives.[36]

Friendship and intimacy between settlers and Māori characterised other settlements as well.[37] We saw in the previous chapter how the Auckland government official Edmund Webber had remained aloof from his peers. But this did not mean he was socially isolated. Edmund spent some evenings at his friend Mari's house; she was the Māori wife of a soldier called Lockhart from the Britomart barracks.[38] It was there that Edmund 'lost his heart' to a Māori woman named Etoi. She had quarrelled with her Pākehā husband – Auckland businessman John Montefiore – and was returning to her Bay of Islands family.[39] Edmund described her as 'a young, good-looking girl with an exceedingly fine figure; her temper is good, and she has one of the kindest hearts, tho' at the same time she is wild, as wild as the wild Gazelle.' (Within European racial theory it was possible for Māori to exhibit both civilised and savage behaviours simultaneously.)[40] As someone who saw himself as a member of a superior race and society, he was astonished to be besotted with another who was not his social equal: 'I, an English gentleman, of somewhat refined feelings, having a fair education, and moving in good society, absolutely felt much pleasure in the company of this wild Maori girl, for which read savage.' He imagined keeping her himself, but he had insufficient income and no house, and 'it would not do for a Government officer to live with a Maori girl'.[41] He looked forward to evenings and to spending a few hours with her, and though he does not say as much, the intimacy of their relationship suggests they were lovers. He describes lying in her lap while she stroked his hair and furtively plucked some strands, which she fashioned into a lock and placed in her bosom as a keepsake.[42] Before she left, she gave him a lock of her own hair 'which I religiously guard', he confessed.[43] In short, Edmund found social fulfilment not among his own peers but with women from a so-called primitive society.

Trade and employment

Most settlers' daily relations with Māori revolved around trade. During the 1840s, Māori dominated the fresh produce trade, and without it townspeople would have gone hungry.[44] Within months of Nelson's founding, Bishop Selwyn observed that its residents were almost totally reliant on Māori-supplied vegetables, pork and firewood.[45] In Wellington, Māori cleared hundreds of acres of Hutt Valley land to grow cash crops for the town and export markets.[46] Auckland too was greatly dependent on Māori for food, some of which was grown at the nearby settlement of Ōkahu.[47] By 1847, Māori were being described as the 'very lifeblood' of the town.[48] William Swainson recorded that the biannual visit of the Coromandel chief Taraia Ngakuti Te Tumuhuia with a waka fleet laden with foodstuffs was eagerly anticipated in the town. For several days the party camped on the Mechanics' Bay beachfront, from where an abundance of pigs, potatoes, wheat, maize, melons, grapes, pumpkins, onions, flax, turkeys, geese, ducks, chickens and firewood were sold in a festive atmosphere. The traders then spent their earnings at the town's shops, buying items like spades, blankets, ironware and clothing; one observer noted that red and blue blankets and red handkerchiefs were the big sellers – red being a symbol of mana (prestige).[49] A Wellington draper had 100 Māori clients on his books and reported how they were 'fond of being dressed like the British' and quickly honoured their debts.[50]

In 1848, the New Zealand Company agent William Fox advanced the environmentalist argument that trade had encouraged Māori to embrace peaceful and industrious habits. Having lived amidst the settler communities, they had observed and learned from the Europeans' commercial practices, and now used that knowledge to successfully compete with them.[51] By the early 1850s, George

Early land title disputes between Māori and settlers came to a head in the 1843 Wairau confrontation, where people on both sides were killed. This raised fears within the settler community of a Māori attack and led to the building of stockades in Wellington and Nelson. This is a detail from an 1843 sketch of Nelson's Church Hill stockade. John Wallis Barnicoat, Hocken Collections, Uare Taoka o Hākena, University of Otago, 94/260

Earp reported Māori around Wellington had become important agriculturalists, livestock owners and ship owners. Some of them had become relatively rich, their bills being accepted by the town's bankers.[52] Māori engaged in the Auckland market also had their own fleet of ships, and William Swainson proclaimed that Māori trade had made 'Auckland the great emporium of New Zealand'.[53] We saw in Chapter Two how Māori were sought after as house builders. They also found work as general labourers, from cutting up kauri logs on the Auckland waterfront to building the Porirua and Wairarapa roads from Wellington.[54] These were designed to improve access to the town's hinterland and so further European settlement. The New Zealand Company began the Porirua road in 1843, but the need to expedite imperial troop movements during the mid-1840s skirmishes with Ngāti Toa leader Te Rangihaeata led the Crown to finish it in 1847.[55] The Wairarapa road was finally completed in 1856, just as the district was being carved up into freehold small farms and stations for settlers.[56]

The beginning of the 1863 Waikato campaign of the New Zealand wars raised fears of a Māori attack on Auckland. The city's Albert Barracks had been built in the mid-1840s as place of settler refuge in case of such an assault. In this 1848 depiction of the barracks, a group of Māori watch a regimental drill. John Johnson, Auckland War Memorial Museum Tāmaki Paenga Hira, PD-1963-8-10

Signs of dissent

It was in the road-building sector that settler unease over Māori labour-market penetration first emerged. In September 1847, the government announced that the pay rate of Pākehā navvies in Wellington would be cut from three to two shillings per day, the same as the Māori rate. The 50 affected Pākehā workers promptly petitioned Lieutenant Governor Edward Eyre to be reinstated to the job at their former wage. They argued Māori living costs were cheaper than their own, and that with little other regular work available in the district they would struggle to make ends meet.[57] Eyre dismissed their concerns. He said wages needed to come down because the high cost of labour was hindering economic growth. Continuing with the higher rate would exhaust the Crown's coffers and the roads would remain uncompleted. Only by finishing them would new tracts of land be opened for farming, so 'affording to the labouring classes that very work which you are now seeking'.[58] A spokesman for the group asserted it was insulting to price the labour of Britons 'at the same rate as that of individuals still in a state of semi-barbarism'. Further, it was well known Māori worked more slowly and to a lower standard than whites did; the idea of using Māori labour to save money was therefore 'very questionable'.[59] Others made the same point. The following year, an Auckland newspaper reported that about 30 Māori repairing Princes Street had made little headway: 'it is rare to see above one third of the party at work at the same time; some may be seen smoking – others folded in their blankets, or squatting on their hams; while some pass away the monotony of the hour in spinning yarns for each others amusement.' Meanwhile, two Pākehā labourers excavating soil for a nearby house were said to have completed more work in one day than the whole Māori road gang.[60]

The displacement of one group of workers by another group on lower wages is a theme in urban history. In settler societies like the United States, it usually involved a new immigrant group dislodging the existing workforce of a particular industry – the nineteenth-century Irish takeover of New York's construction and transport sectors is a famous example.[61] But in 1840s New Zealand the process was reversed: the existing or native population outcompeted the immigrant group. In being passed over for work, the Pākehā labourers feared being economically marginalised and so resorted to soft racism to discredit their competition. If George Evans and Māori chiefs had viewed Wellington's labouring population as their social inferiors, they in turn saw themselves as superior to Māori by the very fact they were white and British.

It was not only navvies who were feeling threatened by Māori economic power. As historian Hazel Petrie has shown, by the mid-1850s many European traders had come to see Māori commerce as detrimental to their own prospects: 'despite considerable public recognition of the value of Māori enterprise – by way of supplying cheap foodstuffs, as customers for imported goods, and as contributors to colonial revenue – there was also a more quietly expressed resentment that their success represented unwelcome competition for Pākehā.'[62] Further, as Māori increased their cultivations to meet the rising market demand, they became less willing to sell prime agricultural land, blocking settlers' ambitions to become farmers. Historians have identified a number of factors that turned things to the settlers' advantage. The first was the tipping of the Māori and European populations in favour of Europeans in 1856; as the settler population continued to increase, so did their ability to exert power and control space.[63] Another was the collapse of the Australian wheat and flour market in 1855–56 following the end of the Victorian gold rush. Having invested in infrastructure like flourmills and small ships, many Māori enterprises had to sell productive assets when loans were called in.[64] The final factor was the 1860s New Zealand wars, principally fought to satiate settler desire for Māori land.

Skirmishes and war

The conflicts of the 1860s were not the first time Māori and Pākehā had fought over land. The issue had resulted in the Wairau confrontation of June 1843, which raised alarm that Māori would attack Nelson and Wellington.[65] Suddenly the practice of building towns without walls seemed premature, and both these settlements quickly built defensive stockades and raised militias.[66] In Nelson, Sarah Greenwood recorded how the perceived danger divided the town. Some settlers fled, fearing for their lives; others ridiculed the threat and dismissed the stockade as folly. The 'diversity of opinion tends to greatly split our little society into parties, and destroy that feeling of unity and good-fellowship,' lamented Sarah.[67] In Wellington, Mary Petre recorded that Māori at Petone 'have been dancing their war dance for victory gained over the white people at Cloudy Bay'.[68] She became a warmonger. Seeing the militia marching along the beach from Te Aro to Thorndon, she wrote:

> [I] wish we could have some fighting [as] they look today such a brave lot with their bayonets glistening in the sun … [and] their English colours carried in the center … the natives who have only seen a handful exercise at a time on the flat … saw this muster of about 8 hundred men retired some distance and sitting down watched the English with grave faces. We will give the rebels a warm reception if they will only attack the town.[69]

The fighting she so desired came in 1846 when, following clashes between Māori and settlers in the Hutt Valley and Porirua, Governor George Grey boldly arrested Te Rauparaha and imperial troops drove Te Rangihaeata from the region.[70]

Auckland's status as capital meant that it had been home to a contingent of British troops at Fort Britomart since December 1840.[71] The Northern war (1845–1846) and the destruction of Kororāreka increased fears of a Māori invasion of Auckland – although local Māori were active in assuring Aucklanders this would not happen – and led to the erection of the larger Albert Barracks as a place of a refuge.[72] The 9-hectare, octagonal-shaped fortification was enclosed by a loop-holed basalt wall, largely constructed using 'friendly' Māori labour, and included buildings for the 900-strong garrison.[73] The only time Albert Barracks looked like it might be needed as a sanctuary was at the beginning of the Waikato campaign of the 1860s New Zealand wars.

The New Zealand wars arose following the 1858 creation of the Waikato-based Kīngitanga, or Māori King movement. Its aim was to unite Māori under a single sovereign to better exercise their political power and stem the sale of Māori land.[74] Settlers worried the new movement would impede Pākehā access to land and represented the Kīngitanga as a threat to Crown authority that should be subdued. A chance to do this arose when a minor Te Āti Awa chief, Te Teira Manuka, offered to sell land to the Crown at Waitara in Taranaki. A more senior tribal chief, Wiremu Kingi, strongly resisted the move. In March 1860 the Crown attacked a Te Āti Awa pā, resulting in the outbreak of the Taranaki war. A truce was brokered in 1861, but hostilities resumed in 1863, just before the Waikato invasion.[75]

Government planning for the Waikato campaign began in early 1862 with the construction of the Great South Road from Auckland into Waikato, and the building of redoubts at strategic points along it. The excuse for the impending invasion was the failure of the Kīngitanga movement to submit to Crown authority, Governor George Grey declaring in January 1863 that he would 'dig around' the Kīngitanga until they fell. In March, Grey stoked fears of an attack on Auckland.[76] The threat had arisen following the imprisonment in the town of the Ngāti Maniapoto leader Aporo Taratutu for his part in the theft of a government printing press and other goods from the Te Awamutu mission station in March 1863. It was rumoured that unless Aporo was freed, Ngāti Maniapoto would attack the settlement.[77] This was an unlikely prospect, not only given the strength of Auckland's defences but also because the leading Kīngitanga iwi, Waikato-Tainui and Ngāti Hauā, opposed any hostile action. Even so, Grey fostered the panic to justify his long-planned invasion of Waikato.

Among those drawn into events was Frederick Haslam, who had arrived in Auckland with his sister, Sarah Anne, from London's East End only months before. With rumours of an imminent Māori attack swirling through the town, Fred joined the Militia and Volunteers in aid of its defence.[78] By the beginning of July, the town was on a knife-edge. In a letter home, Fred described the atmosphere:

> The all absorbing topic is now what to do in case of an attack on the town. Anne and Mrs Pierce … will make at once for the Block house in the Fortifications [Albert Barracks] where all the women and children are to go. They expect a fire every night. Of course the utmost stretch and strain of excitement is kept constantly on the nerves … Tonight is the night of the rumoured attack on Auckland. Perhaps few will sleep tonight. We live in Queen Street, close to the Baracks [sic] or Fortifications, we have not far to run. I think Anne is rather frightened, Mrs Pierce is.[79]

The attack never came, but general unease remained, serving to increase settler belligerence toward the 'rebel' (Kīngitanga) Māori. Fred claimed there was no 'peace at any price' party in the town and that everyone wanted to clear the rebels from Waikato so the land could be sold to pay for the war.[80] The government's position toward Māori also hardened. On 9 July, Governor Grey ordered all Māori in Auckland and Waikato to swear an oath of allegiance to the Crown or face expulsion to Kīngitanga territory.[81] This was followed by the introduction of an overnight curfew for all Māori in the town. 'Loyal' Māori living in Auckland were encouraged to leave, but those remaining on their homelands were issued with badges to attach to their clothing to help identify them as 'friendly'.[82] The measure caused 'quite a commotion' among Māori, but authorities thought it prudent because 'treasonable natives' could set the place ablaze.[83]

Fred Haslam described how Auckland's defences were made up of a series of inlying (city) and outlying (suburban) military pickets. Serving overnight at an outlying picket with a dozen others, he explained that 'we did so want to catch some Maoris, we should have collared them or stuck them with our bayonets, we are all so exasperated with the cannibals, we would like to clear them all out'. He conceded Auckland was virtually in a state of siege, the sea being the only safe way in and out. A week later, his contingent was stationed to Ōtāhuhu, where they were bundled 26 into a hut designed to sleep 18. The next day, rain kept them inside with nothing to do: 'the noise and wickedness and swearing in the huts was dreadful'.[84] Watching women and children with furniture-laden carts heading to Auckland and bringing news of Māori attacking houses made him anxious. Moreover, the daily routine of soldiering was vexing. The Volunteers ate sour bread and boiled beef every day except Sunday, when it was boiled pork. Each night Fred and others would relieve the guard and watch over the Tāmaki River: if they saw any Māori, they were to fire on them and rouse the camp. 'Thus we stand in the long grass leaning on our rifles from one till daybreak, watching the river and the beautiful Moon and stars. It is very cold. We don't like the soldier life.'[85] By November, he had been re-stationed to the Commissariat Depot at Drury. He mentioned the Māori evacuation of Meremere pā and the occupants' escape further inland to drum up support. His mood was gloomy. He complained of constant rain, of clothes never being dry, of doing sentry duty in the mud. The 'awful effect of War' had seen his earlier bellicosity replaced by disillusionment:

> The once happy New Zealand, a land of homesteads and farms, cattle, and rosy children playing on the green meadows, is now the scene of ruin, desolation and bloodshed of the most barbarous character, and, worse than all, the destruction is <u>by our own defenders</u>, the lawless mob introduced from Australia.[86]

He claimed that while Māori had razed settlers' homes, the Waikato Militia had destroyed many more. 'What fearful scenes I have witnessed of late, years of toil demolished by Maoris & defenders while the inhabitants are out defending another part. Such is Auckland now.'[87] (Fred was neither the first nor the last soldier to observe how war barbarises both sides of a conflict.) He confessed to thinking often of his London home, and almost certainly regretted his decision to leave it.

Fred's war correspondence ends there at Drury. By this time, the British forces were moving further south into Waikato, diminishing the prospect of an attack on

Auckland. Although the city was to face other invasion threats – the 1885 Russian scare and during the Second World War – the Waikato war was the only time Aucklanders were drawn into hostilities on their own doorstep. With the end of the Waikato campaign in April 1864, Fred returned to Auckland but never really settled. The economic recession that followed the withdrawal of troops from the city and the shift of the capital to Wellington meant he was unable to find suitable work, and he returned to England in 1867.[88]

The New Zealand wars and subsequent Crown confiscation of hundreds of thousands of hectares of Māori land to pay for it removed Māori as an economic and military threat to colonial society.[89] With the balance of power now firmly in settlers' favour, the need for Albert Barracks passed. Demolition of its buildings and defensive wall (bar a small portion of the wall behind Government House) began in 1873, and the former space of refuge was given over to affluent housing and Albert Park.[90] But as this material wall was progressively dismantled, a metaphorical wall was already rising in its place, not only in Auckland but in the other cities as well.

White cities

Fred Haslam's experience shows how settlers' attitudes toward Māori hardened during the hostilities. The construction of difference between combatants is a common feature of war. Representing Māori as an inherently barbaric people made it easier for settlers to cast them as outside civil society and to rationalise using force against them. The perceived otherness of Māori led some to call for them to be excluded from civil society altogether. As Jeffrey Alexander explains, the civil sphere attaches status to primordial qualities – such as race, language, religion and social class – that identify individuals as members of a particular group. Those outside the group cannot obtain these qualities by definition:

> In different times and in different places, actors have become convinced that only those possessing certain versions of the qualities have what it takes to become members of the civil society. They have believed that individuals and groups who do not possess these qualities are uncivilized and cannot be included.[91]

The actors in this instance were hard racists who argued Māori did not have the requisite qualities to belong to civil society; they disparaged the belief that Māori would readily civilise and become like Europeans. Such thinking had been evident as early as 1858 when an editor of an immigrant handbook argued that the claim Māori had a 'greater aptitude for civilisation than any other race of savages ... [had] been unduly exaggerated'. He pointed to their continued devotion to traditional customs, housing and lifestyles as proof that Māori were still too primitive to become civilised.[92] Racial amalgamation was therefore a lost cause.

This view was underscored by a growing settler belief that city life was detrimental to Māori. In 1867, the scientist Ferdinand von Hochstetter claimed:

> the saddest proofs of the deterioration of the manners and the character of the natives in their intercourse with Europeans, are furnished in the cities by the class of 'town Maoris.' Too proud or too lazy to engage their services to Europeans, and by regular work to earn an honest living, they loaf and lounge about the streets and taverns, morally and physically bankrupt, a loathsome burden to the Europeans, and an abomination to their own countrymen.[93]

Within stadial theory, commerce or city life was the last stage and pinnacle of human progress and development. But observers like Hochstetter alleged that rather than lifting Māori to a higher (civilised) state, city life had enervated and degraded them. It was further evidence that their progress toward civilisation had stalled. Hard racists used this to argue that Māori, as an innately primitive people, were unable to cope with a higher level of social development.[94]

The belief that cities had a degenerative effect on indigenous people was already well established in other settler societies. As early as 1838, *The Australian* described Aboriginal townspeople as 'exhibiting symptoms of debasement and degradation … whilst they have lost the unadorned simplicity of nature they have gained nothing of the refinements of civilisation'.[95] David Hamer noted that most European observers described Aboriginal people in Melbourne as 'repulsive and degenerate and argued the town environment had caused a marked deterioration in their physique and style of living'.[96] Here we see Georg Simmel's theory of the stranger in operation: the stranger is perceived by civil society as not only lower or excluded but also different in more fundamental ways.[97] In asserting that city life made indigenous people debased and degenerate, settlers could claim these populations did not belong in colonial city space: they were strangers and outsiders. Within this discourse, settlers imagined and socially constructed colonial city space as white places – a muscular assertion of their growing political and spatial power in the colonial landscape.[98] As Hamer observed, this was a common strategy in Anglo settler societies. By the 1870s, indigenous populations in Australia and North America had only a marginal presence in towns and cities; when they did venture into them, they were regarded as strangers and trespassers.[99] The modern colonial settler city was a white city.[100]

Hard racists expected New Zealand to follow the same path. Visiting Auckland in the late 1870s, the Australian James Hingston was surprised to find so many Māori men, women and children on Queen Street. He noted that in Australian cities it was rare to see indigenous people; here, they were present in such

Waka laden with produce are coasting along the waters of Auckland Harbour in 1853. Māori brought fresh produce into Auckland from areas some distance from the city, including the Bay of Islands and Waikato. Patrick Joseph Hogan, Alexander Turnbull Library, A-004-005

numbers he felt as if he were a stranger, not they. 'The Maori is, however, quite out of place in a city of white people,' he declared.[101] The immigration agent Arthur Clayden agreed and even claimed Māori were holding cities back. Concerning Wellington, he wrote:

> An obstacle to the progress of the town is the large proportion of native population. It is all very fine to theorise about the noble savage, and I had read a strange lot of nonsense in England about the fine New Zealanders. Alas! for the nobility and the grandeur. A dirty, squalid, unimprovable, and intolerably ugly generation are they, and one felt tempted to think that the sooner they were translated to the happy hunting-grounds the better would it be for universal humanity.[102]

In expressing the view that Māori were a barrier to progress and modernity, Clayden offered an extreme solution informed by Social Darwinism.[103] The growing conviction that Māori had no place in cities led to increased Pākehā efforts to marginalise them and encourage them to leave – a process that led to

Auckland's Māori market was established at the foot of Queens Wharf in 1868. This engraving shows it bustling with life, with townspeople bartering with traders to buy melons, poultry and other fresh produce. *Illustrated New Zealand Herald*, 2 July 1873, p.1

the demise of Auckland's Māori street market in Queen Street and Wellington's Te Aro and Pipitea pā.

The Māori market

The Auckland provincial government created the Māori market, at the foot of Queens Wharf, in 1868 to complement a new Pākehā growers' market further up the street.[104] The Māori facility comprised a collection of tents and shanties surrounded by a low paling fence. Māori hawkers used it as base from which to journey into city and suburban streets to sell produce ranging from oysters to onions.[105] The place became as much a social as a commercial exchange as Māori and townspeople gathered there not just to trade but to meet friends and pass the time of day.[106] A contemporary engraving shows it teeming with settlers of different social classes, all of them intermingling and haggling with the traders holding kete (baskets) of produce. Traders performed haka daily, and 'every variety of costume' was to be found there.[107]

Accounts of police turning a blind eye to people gambling there at night, alongside reports of altercations and fighting, saw it develop a reputation as a liminal space. Such salacious and theatrical attributes furthered the market's attraction. A Hawke's Bay visitor lauded its vibrancy and colour. In a description that played up European racial stereotypes of Māori oscillating between savagery and civilisation, he wrote:

> hideous old wrinkled and withered hags, cowering beneath still older flax mats, swarming with vermin, sit cheek by jowl with pretty half-castes, who could scarce be distinguished from English ladies, but for the slight blue tracing on their tattooed chins. Faultless is the dress of some of these magnificent creatures; costly sky blue silks, black satins, feathers, high heeled boots, chignons, crystal earrings and bracelets, are the things the northern female half-caste loves.[108]

The writer found the pretty women alluring and went on to praise their affability. But realising that equating them to English ladies was untenable in colonial society, he described one who, after peeling off 'a perfect fitting beautiful little kid glove', dipped 'her fair hand into a dirty calabash full of rather strong-smelling grease' – possibly muttonbird grease. With fat running from both corners of her mouth, it was evident her modern attire could not hide her feral nature.[109]

Despite the market's valuable role in the city's commercial and wider life, by the early 1870s official opinion had conspired against it. The main complaint was its perceived insanitary state, one critic describing it as a pigsty of putrefying organic matter and other garbage.[110] It was further compromised in being above the city's main sewer outfall, the fetid stench of which pervaded the market at low tide.[111] One of the first actions of the new Auckland Harbour Board in 1871 was to pass a motion from its chair, Philip Philips, to close it. Ostensibly this was so new offices could be built on the site but a more plausible reason was that the board believed it was a blight that needed removing.[112] According to one detractor, the market, as the first place one encountered on stepping ashore, failed to 'convey very favorable impressions of the refinement of our civilization'.[113] Within weeks, however, Philips was having second thoughts and arguing that the market be rebuilt elsewhere. 'He said he was deeply sensible of the injustice he had done the native race, the more so as he now learned from Mrs. P. [his wife] that fish and other vegetables were much dearer than formerly.'[114]

OPPOSITE The palisades and buildings of Wellington's Te Aro pā can be made out in the centre-right of this 1850s photograph of Manners Street and Te Aro Flat. At this time the settlement accommodated about 150 people. The dirt track beyond the pā is Courtenay Place. Alexander Turnbull Library, PAColl-D-0008

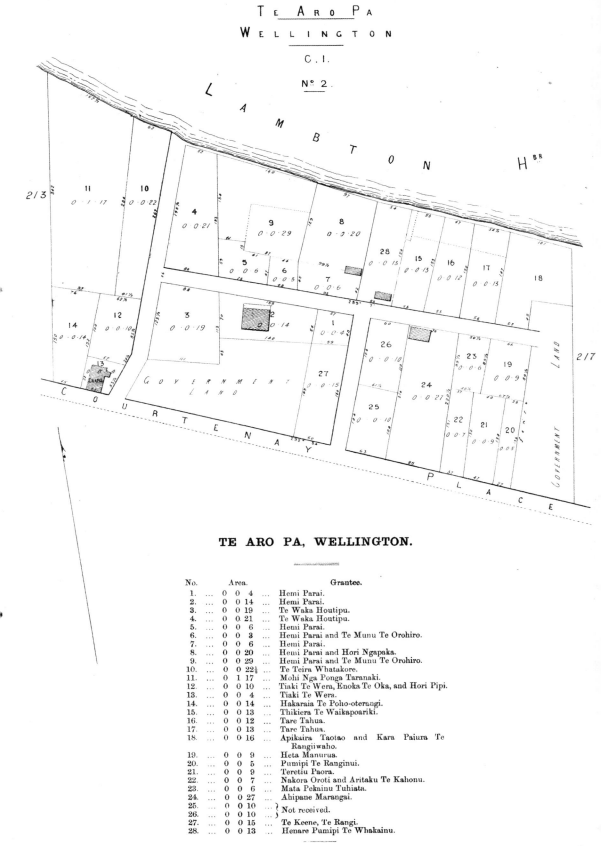

TE ARO PA, WELLINGTON.

No.	Area.	Grantee.
1.	0 0 4	Hemi Parai.
2.	0 0 14	Hemi Parai.
3.	0 0 19	Te Waka Houtipu.
4.	0 0 21	Te Waka Houtipu.
5.	0 0 6	Hemi Parai.
6.	0 0 3	Hemi Parai and Te Munu Te Orohiro.
7.	0 0 6	Hemi Parai.
8.	0 0 20	Hemi Parai and Hori Ngapaka.
9.	0 0 29	Hemi Parai and Te Munu Te Orohiro.
10.	0 0 22½	Te Teira Whatakore.
11.	0 1 17	Mohi Nga Ponga Taranaki.
12.	0 0 10	Tiaki Te Wera, Enoka Te Oka, and Hori Pipi.
13.	0 0 4	Tiaki Te Wera.
14.	0 0 14	Hakaraia Te Poho-oterangi.
15.	0 0 13	Thikiera Te Waikapoariki.
16.	0 0 12	Tare Tahua.
17.	0 0 13	Tare Tahua.
18.	0 0 16	Apikaira Taotao and Kara Paiura Te Rangiiwaho.
19.	0 0 9	Heta Manurua.
20.	0 0 5	Pumipi Te Ranginui.
21.	0 0 9	Teretiu Paora.
22.	0 0 7	Nakora Oroti and Aritaku Te Kahonu.
23.	0 0 6	Mata Pekainu Tuhiata.
24.	0 0 27	Ahipane Marangai.
25.	0 0 10	} Not received.
26.	0 0 10	
27.	0 0 15	Te Keene, Te Rangi.
28.	0 0 13	Henare Pumipi Te Whakainu.

NOTE.—Nos. 1, 2, and 5—in 1 grant = 24p.; Nos. 6 and 9 do. = 32r.
Nos. 16 and 17—in 1 grant = 25p.; Nos. 3 and 4 do. = 1p.

That Philips' initiative failed to gain wider support suggests another reason for the market's closure was to extinguish Māori competition.[115] This is given further weight by a simultaneous city council decision to erect a new market for Pākehā traders. This was built on site long set aside as a Market Reserve (now Aotea Square) and opened in October 1872. The possibility Māori might be given space in the new facility was never considered, presumably because Pākehā stallholders would have resisted the propinquity and competition. Māori continued to sell produce near Queens Wharf and hawk along streets into the 1880s, but by the end of the century this was a thing of the past.[116] As one newspaper commented in 1898: 'Town-dwelling Aucklanders do not see as much of the Maori as in days gone by, when the natives from the Thames, Coromandel, and Waiheke were

OPPOSITE By the 1860s settler sentiment was turning against the continued existence of pā and kāinga in city space. That decade Māori land titles in these settlements were individualised to make it easier to sell the land and change ownership. Te Aro pā in Wellington (in the centre of this image) was divided up between 1866 and 1868 and each plot was granted to only one or two owners. *Plans of Native Reserves in the Several Provinces of New Zealand*, Government Printer, Wellington, 1871

ABOVE Hana Te Awhitu and her husband Tamati Te Wera are believed to have been the last residents of Te Aro pā, probably leaving some time in the 1890s. This is the couple on the front porch of their home in the Wellington suburb of Brooklyn about 1900. Wellington City Archives, 00138:0:13849 wont to throng to the Horotiu (the present Queen-street) with their fruit and vegetables and other produce for sale.'[117] The departure of Māori created a gap that Chinese entrepreneurs moved to fill. Whereas Māori had focused on street trade, the Chinese progressed from hawking to opening greengrocer shops, which made them less vulnerable to public-nuisance charges. From the late nineteenth century, they established market gardens at Epsom and Mt Albert and, as Māori had before them, became pivotal players in Auckland's food-supply chain.[118]

Te Aro and Pipitea pā

Māori also had a diminishing presence in Wellington. We saw in Chapter Two how in 1840 Colonial Secretary Willoughby Shortland had stepped into a dispute over the ownership of Te Aro pā. The issue was resolved in 1847 when William McCleverty, charged with determining the final tenths and other Native reserves, confirmed Te Aro and Pipitea pā as Māori land.[119] In an 1850 report on Māori settlements in and about Wellington, the Native Secretary Henry Tacy Kemp counted 96 residents at the (Ngāti Awa) Pipitea pā. While noting some European wooden cottages had been built and leased to settlers, the 'Pa itself and the huts are much out of repair' and mortality rates were high. Similarly, the dwellings in Te Aro pā were 'in a state of dilapidation', and Kemp described the 186 residents as 'far from being healthy'. In an attempt to improve conditions, a government surveyor had proposed building a modern village with regular streets and houses on the site, but the scheme was stillborn. Kemp attributed this outcome to the fact the pā was a place of transience, with many visitors but few permanent residents.[120] Even so, the pā experienced a degree of modernisation. A photograph from 1857 identifies numerous whare-like huts within its palisade as well as several European-style buildings, including a chapel. In 1865, the resident (Taranaki) chief Hemi Parai built a new dwelling for the accommodation of visiting chiefs, one observer declaring it 'a rather imposing building' and 'a handsome addition to the pa'.[121]

Between 1866 and 1868, land titles in both pā were individualised under the Native Lands Act 1865. This was the beginning of the end of the settlements, as individual owners began to lease and then sell their allotments. They were encouraged to do so by the Commissioner of Native Reserves Charles Heaphy, who believed the pā were anti-modern and Māori ill-suited to city life. He proclaimed the communal living arrangements and material conditions within the pā immoral and insanitary, and asserted it was best for all concerned that Māori leave town and let their land pass to settlers.[122] Rather than encourage owners to lease their allotments, and so retain a stake in the land, Heaphy pushed them hard to sell.[123] Some longstanding residents heeded his call, including Hemi Parai, who left with eight others for Taranaki in 1871.[124] Two years later, the *Wellington Independent* reported: 'Te Aro pa, that last relic of the early days, and the last to change owners of any considerable piece of Maori property, in the city, is slowly but surely falling into the hands of the pakeha.' The provincial government and private interests now owned over half the land, and it was '[i]n the very nature of things, the rest must soon follow'. The lack of improvements on the site, the newspaper implied, had stood in the way of the city's progress: 'In the hands of the original owners, the land was comparatively useless; in the hands of the Government, it must become valuable property, with the existing demand for land with harbour frontage.'[125] The change showed the process of capitalist social relations, where city land is deemed valuable only when it is commodified. It has to be said, however, the charge that Māori were a barrier to progress was rich, considering the number of empty Te Aro Flat sections in the city still held by absentee speculators.[126] By 1881, Pipitea pā had only nine residents and Te Aro pā had 28.[127] After this time the communities went into terminal decline and it is likely that they ceased to exist as pā during the 1890s.[128]

It is striking to see the same modernising discourse came into play in respect of the Lekwammen reserve or settlement in the burgeoning city of Victoria, British Columbia. By the 1860s, Victoria's white community began proclaiming the reserve was an impediment to the city's progress and a threat to property values. As Penelope Edmonds writes, the city's 'Aboriginal spaces were viewed by European observers as dirty, disease-ridden places of vice and disorder, as the antithesis of the ordered, rational civil space of the gridded city'.[129] She shows how speculators lobbied local politicians to purchase and commodify the reserve; they responded by overturning the communal ownership of the land and allowing for individual title and sale. Many Lekwammen people fought to keep their land, but in 1911 the Native title was extinguished and the land transferred to the provincial government.[130] Like the pā and kāinga of Wellington Māori, the Lekwammen settlement vanished from the cityscape.

The end of Auckland's Māori market and of Te Aro and Pipitea pā can be seen as critical steps in the building of a metaphorical wall that would both enclose and create white colonial settler cities. The problem for the wall builders was that it was never completed and, as we will see later, Māori continued to enter through its gaps. One reason for this was that the forced removal of Māori from cities was never going to be politically acceptable in New Zealand. Despite the rise of hard racism among some settlers, humanist thought mainly continued to frame European representations of Māori; New Zealand largely avoided the chilling dehumanisation of indigenous people that occurred in the Australian and North American settler colonies.[131] Even so, soft racism was a constant component in Pākehā social relations with Māori. This was particularly evident in public debate over the provision of Māori accommodation in cities.

Nelson was the first city to provide accommodation for visiting Māori. These cottages were built on reserve land at Matangi Āwhio (Auckland Point) at the behest of Bishop George Selwyn after he visited Nelson in 1842. They were used by Māori for decades and later became an unofficial Māori hospital. Nelson Provincial Museum, AC838

Native hostelries

From the founding of the settler colonial cities, Māori had trouble finding places to stay overnight because hotels and boarding houses largely refused to accept them.[132] One explanation for the practice almost certainly lies in settlers' anxiety that having Māori and Pākehā sleeping under the same roof would compromise notions of European racial superiority and appropriate social intercourse – notwithstanding the reality that Māori and Pākehā couples had been sharing beds for decades.[133] Ideas about social class provide a further rationale. Accommodation in towns and cities was socially stratified by type: from comfortable hotels for the middle classes down to basic lodging houses for workers.[134] Within this framework, hoteliers and boarding-/lodging-house keepers could have viewed most Māori as being too socially inferior or poor to be accepted as guests.[135] The outcome of these conventions was that Māori wishing to stay overnight in towns were usually forced to camp on the outskirts or seek shelter wherever they could. Wellington was unique in having centrally situated pā and kāinga, so visiting Māori often stayed in one or other of these settlements.

Nelson led the way in providing somewhere for Māori to stay on short-term visits. In 1842, Bishop Selwyn (a trustee of Nelson's Native reserves) ordered a hostelry be built on reserve land at Matangi Āwhio (Auckland Point). Up to three European-styled cottages were erected to accommodate different tribal groups, and a low boulder wall was constructed to display fresh produce for sale to settlers. In the early 1860s, Nelsonian Edwin Hodder described Matangi Āwhio as 'two brick houses of very unarchitectural appearance, surrounded by a motley group of natives, some busily employed in dressing flax, others sitting listlessly on the ground smoking, and all dressed in a curious combination of European costume'.[136] The complex remained a Nelson base for visiting Māori and also served as a de facto Māori hospital.[137]

Progress towards building similar structures in the other towns was slower. In 1845, one troubled Auckland resident noted:

> They (the Natives) arrive here with their produce, perhaps in rainy weather, and are often detained by contrary winds for days and even weeks, and during that time (unless indeed in some solitary instance of favouritism when a few may find shelter in the out-houses of some kind person) they are obliged to swarm together in hordes upon the beach during the wet stormy nights, and sleep in the same blankets that have absorbed the rain during the day.[138]

Such conditions made the visitors particularly liable to the type of respiratory ailments that had contributed so much to their decline, suggested the writer. Surely a large house could be erected so that visiting Māori could be sheltered from Auckland's inclement weather?[139] By 1848, nothing had changed. A local newspaper condemned government inertia, asserting it was inhumane to deny Māori visitors decent accommodation. It was also a matter of fairness: 'Considering the large amount of taxation which is so unfairly wrung from the natives … it is the very least humanity can do, to employ a small portion of such revenue for the protection of the very lives which create the same.'[140] The following year the government finally agreed to erect a hostelry on Native reserve land at Beach Road, Mechanics Bay, where Māori and other needy visitors could temporarily stay free of charge.[141] (That it was for the use of poor Pākehā as well as Māori supports the class dimension referred to earlier.) The European-styled, U-shaped, wooden building was opened in February 1850. Sleeping quarters formed the sides of the U,

TOP Māori visitors to Auckland were obliged to sleep on the beaches until 1850, when a hostel at Mechanics Bay opened. As well as providing basic accommodation, the hostel was a marketplace, with moorings for waka on the beach in front, as shown in this photograph taken about 1860. It soon became the city's major fresh produce market. Sir George Grey Special Collections, Auckland Libraries, 4-2730

BOTTOM These 1903 residents of Auckland's native hostel are likely waiting for a tram to take them into the city. They are fashionably dressed for their city excursion. Sir George Grey Special Collections, Auckland Libraries, 1-W1540

Auckland's native hostel was rebuilt on the original Mechanics Bay site in 1903. This building was bigger than the first and had 10 bedrooms and a large internal kitchen. It continued to be used by Māori visiting and passing through Auckland for decades. Reginald Silvester Lediard, Auckland War Memorial Museum Tāmaki Paenga Hira, PH-NEG-A1734

with bundles of flax serving as bedding. The U's base was a living space. To reduce the fire hazard there were no fireplaces and all cooking was done outside. The U's middle comprised a courtyard and shelter. This was designed as a marketplace: traders could moor their waka on the beach and easily carry over their goods and wares.[142] A live-in custodian managed the place. Guests had to abide by a code of regulations ranging from keeping spaces tidy, clean and free of damage, to a ban on fighting, quarrelling and general disorder. As well as maintaining public health, the regulations had an improvement objective. As one supporter noted, the rules and the 'habits of order and carefulness' they promoted 'cannot fail to have a good *educational* influence on a people in a transition state from barbarism to civilization'.[143] In 1851, the government secured the institution's future by setting aside reserve lands as an endowment for its benefit.[144] Māori called the place after the bay in which it was located: Waipapa.[145]

By the mid-1850s, Waipapa was Auckland's main fresh produce market.[146] The bustle and animation of settlers and Māori buying and selling made it one of the 'most interesting places near Auckland', wrote John Askew. He had seen 50 large

To the Minister — Council of the Superintendent. [4] 13 Dec 1860

This is our word to you, about a house at Christchurch. For we have no resting place there. The evil of this is manifest. When we have to to pass through, some are obliged to sleep under the hedges by the roadside, others go the public houses and spend their money in spirits, to their hurt. The word of our maori meeting is this that the promise, that we should be treated as brethren, as one people be fulfilled.

We have lately shewn that it is our wish to assist our European friends as far as we can. Let the same spirit be manifested by you towards us, in this matter. Follow the example of Auckland, Wellington, Nelson and Otago, where houses have long been erected for the maoris. This is the only town without a resting place.

These are the persons who wrote these words,

Ihaia Taihewa
Hoani Paratene.
Pita te Hori. Ape
Rakapa Te Ata o Tu Apet.
Hamuora Tohueanuku
&c Signatures follow.

Kaiapoi
Dec. 12th 1860.

Despite being petitioned in 1860 by more than 100 Māori from Kaiapoi, Rāpaki and Port Levy, the Canterbury Provincial Council did not provide a hostel in Christchurch, making it the only city never to have such an institution. Archives New Zealand, Te Rua Mahara o te Kāwanatanga, CAAR 20410 CH287 CP 598/k PPC 4 (R20592329) canoes, heaving with potatoes, corn, pigs, fish and firewood, pulled up on the beach. Attending them were 200 to 300 Māori of both sexes.[147] Askew described the scene as picturesque during the day, but after dark the view became more primordial. Walking down from Parnell, he wrote:

> a most enchanting night-scene was unfolded before me. The darkness of the night, lit up by the lurid fires of the trading Maoris reflected in the waters of the bay – the fantastic forms of their numerous canoes – the dark outlines of their curious tents – and the weird look of their sombre figures, as they moved to and fro, or sat singing round the fires – all conspired to produce an impressive spectacle of the wildest grandeur.[148]

Askew noted that most traders stayed in tents, and used the hostelry only to store their produce. One factor was that it was too small to accommodate everyone. Poor living arrangements were another reason. Within two years of its opening, the Native Secretary Charles Nugent was receiving complaints about the building: the dirt floor was impossible to keep clean; it was cold in winter due to the fire ban; it was rife with vermin; and the lack of partitions (promised in the original plan) meant tribes could not be kept apart. Nugent told his superiors that Māori had requested that a wooden floor, fireplaces and a cooking area be installed.[149] The renovations, including the provision of internal partitions, were subsequently carried out.

The colonial government also built a Native hostelry in Wellington. Erected in 1856 on what had been Tenths reserve land on the corner of Molesworth and Murphy streets, the H-plan wooden building was larger and more striking than its Auckland counterpart.[150] Its most notable feature was a capacious veranda. One account tells of Māori sitting under it in groups, 'weaving mats, making kits, or polishing taiahas, while a pot of savoury kai was simmering nearby'.[151] Unlike the Nelson and Auckland hostelries (and the Dunedin one discussed below), it did not appear to have a marketplace, probably because of its distance from harbourside landing places.

Not everyone welcomed the new amenity. Among the most vehement critics was the politician William Fox. Having once praised the potential of cities to civilise Māori, he now adopted the counter-view that city life degraded them. He told Parliament the hostelry would 'engender immorality, filth and pestilence in the centre of the city'. The Nelson hostelry was 'a beastly den of contamination, and the one at Mechanics' Bay a flea-depot, a filth engendering plague-nursery – in short, the greatest disgrace possible to a civilized community'. His colleague Frederick Clifford agreed, and predicted the hostelry would cheapen adjacent property values and 'drive all respectable people from its neighbourhood'.[152]

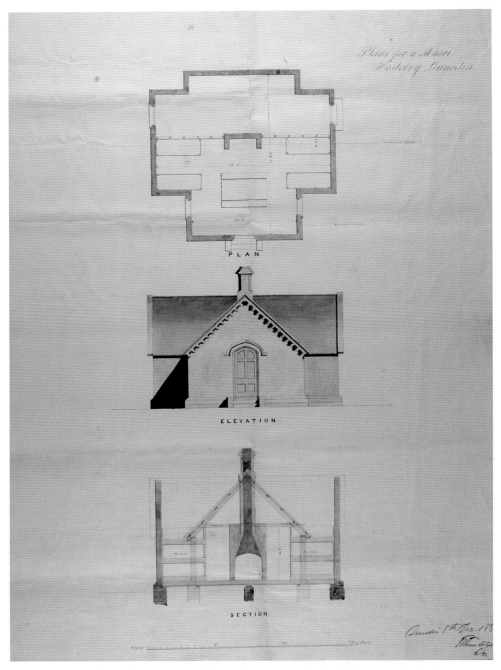

Dunedin's native hostel, which opened in 1860, was a modest building comprised of only two rooms, one for sleeping and one for storage. The sleeping area had four sets of bunks and three separate beds. Toitū Otago Settlers Museum, 1977.40.2

Nineteenth-century images of cities often depict Māori amongst the hustle and bustle of urban life; less common is the Dunedin scene painted by Walter Hatton in the early 1860s. Here Māori are outside the city, hovering above a scene of civility and order they are not a part of. However, they have been joined by a European man, suggesting their exclusion is not total. Hatton never visited New Zealand and none of the source material he used for this painting included Māori. Walter Scarlett Hatton, Alexander Turnbull Library, B-078-007

Despite the dire warnings, the exodus failed to eventuate, and the hostel and its neighbours were to happily coexist.[153]

It was Māori themselves who pushed for Native hostelries in the southern towns. In 1854, the Ngāi Tahu chief Potiki and 106 other Māori petitioned Otago Provincial Superintendent William Cargill to build a place of shelter for their use on the Dunedin foreshore out of funds set aside for Native purposes.[154] Cargill initiated plans for such a place, but these soon became stuck in bureaucratic mire. By 1857, the lack of progress prompted one newspaper to declare Dunedin's God-fearing reputation would ring hollow so long as Māori women continued to spend nights huddled and shivering in sub-zero temperatures on its beach. It noted Māori wanted a hostelry as much to keep them safe from Europeans as to give them shelter from the elements. Women sleeping on the beach were often woken by vagabonds 'and by them plied with intoxicating drink for the most debasing and foul purposes'. It was high time that something was 'done to show the native population that we regard them with more than good-hearted indifference'.[155]

In 1858, the colonial government stepped in and said it would build the hostel itself. Colonial Treasurer Christopher Richmond asked for Cargill to provide a beachfront site with a suitable landing place on Native reserve land between High

After European settlement, Auckland Māori lived outside the city in peri-urban areas like the Ngāti Whātua village of Ōrākei on the shores of Ōkahu Bay. Successive governments acquired land in this area for public works and residential development. In 1908 special legislation allowed for the laying of a sewer pipe (clearly visible in this photograph) along the beach, directly opposite the marae. The following decade the government started buying up the land for housing. By 1951 Ngāti Whātua had lost all tribal land in Ōrākei, aside from a cemetery. Alexander Turnbull Library, 1/2-010806-F

and Jetty streets; the chosen site was beside the Survey and Superintendent's office on Princes Street.[156] The building was completed in February 1860. It was not much bigger than a typical two-room settler cottage, with a communal living/sleeping area and a storehouse. It also had a gabled entrance porch with decorative bargeboards – an architectural embellishment in an otherwise plain design. Inside, there were four tiers of bunks with three bed places, a fireplace with a large hearth for cooking, and a central table and two benches. The structure was built of Caversham stone with a gabled corrugated-iron roof and wooden floors of Baltic pine.[157] The hostelry became a popular marketplace in the town, a place to buy barracouta, crayfish, eel and flounder. But almost as soon as it was up it was removed, in 1865, for the widening of Princes Street and not replaced.[158]

Māori hoped for a similar institution in Christchurch. In 1860, more than 100 Māori from Kaiapoi, Rāpaki and Port Levy petitioned Canterbury's provincial government to provide accommodation for their use in town. The petition explained that Māori visiting Christchurch were obliged to sleep under hedges and while away hours and money in pubs for the lack of somewhere to stay. But the provincial government narrowly voted down the proposal. This time the colonial

The people of Ōrākei marae, along with European visitors, were photographed in 1890 (above), probably on the day Ngāti Whātua leader Paora Tuhaere raced a waka taua (war canoe) in Ōkahu Bay (below). Alexander Turnbull Library, E-571-q-037-2 (above) and E-571-q-037-1 (below)

government did not intervene, leaving Christchurch as the only city without a Native hostelry.[159] Such an institution was subsequently built in Lyttelton in 1865, but like the Dunedin structure survived only a few years.[160]

The Wellington hostelry was still in use in the late 1880s, but was demolished in the 1890s, about the same time Pipitea and Te Aro pā disappeared. This did not mean the need for such an amenity had passed. Māori attending Native Land Court hearings in the capital in the early twentieth century complained of having to sleep in the railway station because they were refused lodgings.[161] Their calls for a new hostelry in Wellington continued to be made into the 1930s but went unheard.[162] Auckland fared better. In 1903, the Mechanics' Bay hostelry was rebuilt on the same site. The new brick building retained the internal courtyard, and featured ten large bedrooms, capacious kitchen, and bathrooms. In 1909, a tangi (funeral) for the parliamentarian Hone Heke Ngapua was held at Waipapa.[163] During the long trial of the prophet Rua Kenana in 1916, about 60 of his Tūhoe supporters resided at the hostelry.[164] With the 1920s rise of the Rātana movement, it became a stopping point for Māori travelling between Rātana and Northland. By the late 1930s, up to 3,000 Māori were staying there each year.[165] A 1944 report on the facility noted the hybrid quality of the space: 'Waipapa, with its communal kitchen and its courtyard, preserves for the Maori, amid the bustling scenes of the modern city, something of his ancient associations and enables him to meet others of his race in traditional manner.'[166] In providing space for the pursuit of Māori tikanga (social practice) within cities, Waipapa and its fellow Native hostelries were arguably antecedents to the urban marae of the 1950s. Yet Waipapa, too, eventually fell victim to modernising forces. It was summarily demolished in 1966 for an unbuilt motorway feeder route.[167]

Clearly there was a need for accommodation for Māori visiting cities, so why were authorities so reluctant to provide it? Victorian conventions about social mixing between races and classes provide convincing surface explanations, but a deeper rationale lies in conflicting views regarding the place of Māori in city life. Opposition to hostelries and the social practice of refusing Māori beds in traditional hotels and boarding houses echoed the hard racist conviction that Māori belonged outside civil society. Conversely, the erection of European-style hostel buildings and the rules over their use mirrored the soft racist premise that Māori could transition into it. Also important was the exercise of power.[168] In being sluggish to make room available within towns to accommodate Māori, settlers were signalling their power and control over city space. Yet when this assertion clashed with humanitarian notions of pastoral care, most townspeople recognised their obligation to provide Māori with shelter in cities was more important.

Māori congregated in central city spaces, often sitting in groups on street edges, talking together and observing their surroundings. In 1859 Bruno Hamel photographed one such group on Auckland's Shortland Street, then an uneven, rocky dirt track. Bruno Hamel, Auckland War Memorial Museum Tāmaki Paenga Hira, PH-ALB-84p3

Leaving town

As Pākehā endlessly debated whether Māori were welcome or unwelcome in cities, city-based Māori increasingly voted with their feet and returned to peri-urban areas or rural homelands. The trend was reflected in official statistics. The first official Māori Census of 1858 recorded 157 Māori living in Auckland and another 285 in its immediate environs. Two decades later and the 1878 Census showed the number had fallen to 28 in the city and 188 in its environs.[169] The 1858 figure for Wellington was 63 in the town and 623 in its environs, including 396 in the Hutt Valley. (An unofficial 1845 Wellington census had found 350 Māori living in the town and 640 in its environs.)[170] By 1878, there were 27 Māori living in the city and 91 in its environs.[171] Nelson's Māori population in 1858 was 33, falling to zero by 1878. Christchurch and Dunedin recorded no Māori city residents in either period, but did have significant populations in peri-urban areas.[172] In 1858, these were 292 and 195 respectively.[173] By 1878, the sum had fallen to 238 in Christchurch and risen to 270 in Dunedin. Looking at the total Māori population over the 20-year period, the proportion living in and about the five cities fell from 2.9 per cent to 1.9 per cent.[174]

The tiny proportion of city-based Māori in each census confirmed that nearly all Māori lived outside city limits. Rather than become townspeople and live in individual dwellings along lineal streets in settlements of thousands of people, most Māori continued to live communally in traditional whare and huts in rural or peri-urban village communities like Ōrākei, Waiwhetū and Ōtākou.[175] The example of Te Aro and Pipitea pā had shown settler unwillingness to accommodate different living arrangements in cities, and Māori, equally as unwilling to live like Europeans, stayed away. Another possible barrier to settling in cities was their location in particular rohe (tribal territory); under tikanga Māori those from another territory would have needed permission to reside there.[176] It was not until the 1920s that the notion of the city as a pan-tribal space where taura here (urban migrants) augment the mana whenua (those holding authority over land) gained currency. The prominent politician and Ngāti Porou leader Apirana Ngata alluded to the change in 1928. He noted that 30 years earlier:

> [Auckland's] Maori population was confined to small remnants of the descendants of the original occupiers at Orakei, Takapuna and Mangere. Now almost every tribe is represented in the Maori portion of the City populations. The Maori population of Wellington and its suburbs is said to number 300, most of it from tribes unconnected with the ownership of land in the district.[177]

This was a significant shift in the way Māori viewed territorial space, and fore-grounded the massive Māori urbanisation of the post-1945 era.

Visiting the Big Smoke

Even if Māori were not domiciled in cities, it did not stop them from engaging with city life. As with most Pākehā farmers and other country dwellers, many Māori periodically visited the Big Smoke for business and pleasure, refuting the idea that cities were white spaces only. As far back as 1859, William Swainson had observed that few Māori lived in Auckland, 'but numbers of them are constantly to be seen about the streets'.[178] In describing Christchurch to his English cousin in 1880, the clerk William Derry noted there were a high number of Māori on city streets, and that most went about barefoot, babies were carried on backs, and women smoked as well as men.[179] Locals accepted Māori on streets as a facet of city life, but many visitors and new arrivals found their presence both affronting and fascinating. One former Australian claimed: 'Nothing strikes a new chum in Auckland more forcibly than the haughty attitude assumed by the natives, or Maoris, towards Europeans.' He thought Māori acted as if they rather than the settlers owned the soil, and was mortified to see white bootblacks 'busily operating on the clumsy hoofs of Maori power'.[180] His compatriot James Hingston also took the view that Māori did not know their rightful place. He criticised how they sat 'about on the footpaths in little groups … dreadfully in the way, in the most prominent places'.[181]

The congregating of Māori on street edges was a longstanding social practice. In early topographical paintings of cities it is not unusual to see depictions of Māori gathered this way. For instance, Samuel Brees's 1847 painting of Wellington's Barrett's Hotel has several Māori sitting or standing engaged in conversation on the Lambton Quay verge (see page 162). Similarly, an 1852 Patrick Hogan lithograph of Auckland includes clusters of Māori gathered at the foot of Queen Street (see page 171); Aucklander Joseph Blades remembered the Queen and Shortland street corner as being 'a great rendezvous for the Maori' in the 1860s.[182] Photographers also recorded the practice. A Bruno Hamel image of Auckland in 1859 shows Māori sitting in a circle and conversing in Shortland Street. Their kōrero might have ranged over any number of topics – from the politics of the day, tribal affairs and trade to making whakapapa connections and confirming social events.

These early images show Māori social space being made in streets that were the heart of Wellington and Auckland public life. By contrast, concurrent pictorial images of Australian Aboriginal people usually show them at the edge of town, where they provide a standard against which settler material progress may be judged: from wilderness to civilisation. As Penelope Edmonds explains: 'In traditional artwork Aborigines inhabit the realm of the mythic; they look on from the margins at European progress and at the unveiling of the empire's ultimate destiny – the bustling settler-colonial city.'[183] This motif was less common in New Zealand.[184] Walter Hatton's 1861 topographical view of Dunedin comes close, depicting three Māori on a grassy hillock above Maclaggan Street (see page 197). It is possible to see the group as an allegory of settler progress, but this reading is made less certain by the inclusion of a European townsperson among them. Is the party inside or outside the city? In this sense, the hillock becomes a liminal space between wilderness and civilisation.

Māori continued to gather on city street edges until well into the twentieth century.[185] In 1911, Auckland's *Observer* newspaper declared Māori 'would appear to have successfully established a claim to form a properly-constituted pah on the Queen-street pavement'. The writer asserted that having taken up 'permanent board and lodging upon the pavement and in shop doorways', they remained 'placidly immovable to anything less than an earthquake or an eruption'. The newspaper claimed that Māori had 'always been treated with a certain amount of indulgence by their pakeha fellow-citizens, but it is certainly open to question whether that indulgence has not been pushed too far.' It said small groups of Pākehā were rarely allowed to stand conversing on the street before being moved on by an officious constable, but a crowd of Māori were permitted to monopolise the footpath for as long as they liked.[186] The newspaper's stance was part of a wider campaign to modernise city streets by clearing them of perceived nuisances (considered in Chapter Six), so it could be that it was exaggerating for

This incomplete watercolour depicts Māori engaged in a hongi in front of Isaac McEwan's bakery in Shortland Street, Auckland, in the early 1860s. A note on the back of the painting describes the bakery as a popular Māori meeting place, with many hongi exchanged outside its doors. Alexander Turnbull Library, A-439-010

effect. It certainly seems more likely the police were being pragmatic, rather than indulgent, in allowing Māori to gather in social groups on streets. The continuance of this longstanding social practice suggests Māori felt comfortable claiming some city public space as their own and city authorities felt no compunction to stop them.

If the *Observer* and the aforementioned Australians thought Māori a public nuisance, other visitors found their presence exotic and captivating. The travel writer G. L. Meredith toured New Zealand during the 1870s. Disembarking near Wellington's Lambton Quay, he wrote:

> I got a bit of a shock as I was walking the quay, carrying my modest belongings, at seeing a couple of Maori women strolling down the quay, smoking short black pipes. I am afraid I forgot my manners and stared at these native ladies,

Māori leaders involved in national politics spent much of their time in Wellington. Peter Buck (left, middle row), James Carroll (second from left, front row), Apirana Ngata (second from right) and Tame Parata (right) were photographed with other members of the Native Lands Committee in front of the General Assembly Library around 1905. Alexander Turnbull Library, 1/2-090445-F

whose attire consisted of a sort of dress-body and skirt … They evidently disdained any embellishment of their extremities, as their heads and feet were quite bare. No one else appeared to notice any incongruity about these ladies; and they themselves seemed to be quite at their ease despite my unintentional rudeness in staring at them.[187]

Meredith found it extraordinary not only that the women were defying European social convention by walking through a city 'underdressed' but also that nobody else thought it unusual.

Visiting Wellington around the same time was the Scottish vocalist David Kennedy. Commenting on Māori dress, he observed:

Maori girls in tartan dresses and Rob Roy shawls; others in light blue gowns; and, as we well remember, a Maori and his wife walking along the pavement in decent middle-class clothes, the husband carrying the baby very dutifully, and his spouse gazing at the ribbons in the drapers' windows. Both displayed high civilization![188]

God Save the King.

G. R.

GRAND OPERA HOUSE
WELLINGTON

LESSEES - - J. C. WILLIAMSON LTD.
DIRECTION THE MAORI OPERA CO.
BUSINESS MANAGER - - PATRICK J. O'BRIEN

Under the distinguished patronage and in the presence of Their
Excellencies the Governor and the Countess of Liverpool ; the Hon. W.
F. Massey ; Sir James Carroll ; His Worship the Mayor and Mayoress
of Wellington, Mr. and Mrs. J. P. Luke.

THURSDAY, 16th SEPTEMBER, 1915
(FOR SIX NIGHTS ONLY)

MR. F. BENNETT PRESENTS

THE MAORI OPERA COMPANY
— IN —

HINEMOA

A MAORI MUSICAL LYRICS AND MUSIC
PLAY IN 3 ACTS BY PERCY FLYNN

CAST OF CHARACTERS :

TUTANEKAI (Hinemoa's Lover) Mr. TIAWHI ROGERS—Tenor
TIKI (His Faithful Friend) Mr. T. MAHIMA—Baritone
NGARARANUI (Tutanekai's Rival) Mr. RUA TAWHAI—Heavy
TAWAKE (Ngararanui's Brother) Mr. HAMIORA—Bass
WHAKAUE (Maori Chief) Mr. ETIKA BUTT—Bass
HINEMARU (Hinemoa's Mother) Miss MORUNGA BUTT—Contralto
TUPA (Tutanekai's Sister) Miss MERE AMOHAU—Soprano
HINEMOA (Maori Puhi Maid forbidden to Marry)
Miss TIRITA BUTT—Soprano

ACT I. THE HOME OF WHAKAUE, ROTORUA.
ACT II. THE LAKE WITH MOKOIA IN THE DISTANCE.
ACT III. TUTANEKAI'S HOUSE.

Grand Full Chorus of Poi Girls, Warriors, Chiefs and Hunters.

ORCHESTRA UNDER THE BATON OF THE COMPOSER, MR. PERCY FLYNN.

PLAY PRODUCED BY MR. CHARLES ARCHER.

The First Night's Takings GILBERT H. WARREN-EMERY,
go to our Wounded Soldiers. Touring Manager.

He had expected to see Māori in their native costume, but learned they dressed as Pākehā when coming to town, then shed their city garb on returning to the country. Kennedy found Auckland more diverse: 'Everywhere about Auckland we saw Maories [sic] – not just a few here and there, but crowds of them.'[189] Many men donned European clothing, albeit with exotic flourishes, such as pheasants' feathers in black felt hats and gold ornaments.[190] The rest wore maro (kilts) and blankets thrown loosely over their shoulders.[191] Most women also sported European dress and 'were in many cases exceedingly showy'. On one occasion he described:

> a fashionable Maori lady with parasol, flowery bonnet, high heeled boots, and long train, sweeping her silks down Queen Street. On the opposite pavement sat a another Maori woman – squalid, wrapped in a shabby blanket, and looking in the depth of poverty; but, in a burst of friendliness, the Silk Dress hurriedly crossed the street and saluted the Blanket, shaking hands with her and rubbing noses in the most affectionate manner.[192]

Another time he watched a woman, whom he thought would be indistinguishable among the throng along Edinburgh's fashionable Princes Street save for her brown face, hail a cab with a parasol, step up into the compartment and sink back into its recess.[193] He 'was astonished at all this'. He may have been having trouble reconciling his image of Māori as savage with the sophisticated woman effortlessly negotiating city space. It might be too that he was startled to see her hail a cab; in Victorian society, an unaccompanied woman in a cab signalled she was a prostitute.[194]

These vignettes highlight how even in the face of some virulent opposition Māori continued to exert their agency in city space after the New Zealand wars. In entering cities, most Māori made some accommodation to Pākehā sensibilities, such as donning European dress, but this did not mean leaving their own culture at the city gates. In fact, in making street edges sites of sociability, in creating their own street fashion, and in subverting codes of street behaviour, Māori shaped a city sub-culture that was both modern and distinct.

During the 1890s, references to Māori in cities fall away in travel and other print culture. This was probably due to the rise of new tourist literature centred on the Rotorua thermal region and other wonderlands. New representations

OPPOSITE In July 1915 the newly formed Maori Opera Company performed Percy Flynn's *Hinemoa* throughout the North Island. The all-Māori cast received positive reviews, although critics thought the opera itself was less impressive. Alexander Turnbull Library, Eph-B-OPERA-1915-01 focused on Māori 'at home' in traditional and picturesque costume.[195] But there were also now fewer Māori on city streets. As opportunities for trade diminished, so did the rationale for regular visits.[196] When Māori did make the journey, they sometimes came en masse. For instance, in January 1895, some 200 Te Arawa people descended on Auckland. Their week-long stay coincided with the opening of the Auckland to Rotorua railway – partly built to facilitate thermal tourism; the government subsidised their fares to thank the tribe for supporting the line. As one Auckland newspaper noted, the line had compressed time and space: 'The iron road has made them much closer neighbours of ours … [and] its opening will prove a good augury of pleasant relations in future between the two people of Auckland and Rotorua.'[197] When the train arrived at Auckland station, its carriages were festooned with banners bearing the names of different Te Arawa hapū (sub-tribes). On stopping, the passengers performed a haka in the carriages and a waiata of greeting, after which Auckland mayor James Holland and a large crowd welcomed them. Accommodation was provided at the Agricultural Hall, and Holland offered to show the chiefs (such as Anaha Kepa Te Rahui) over the library and art gallery, as well as other places of interest.[198] Each of the hapū gave cultural performances to packed houses at different venues during their stay.[199]

Māori carnivals

Whether it was at organised visits such as these, or in encountering Māori attending Native Land Court hearings, playing in sporting fixtures, and participating in public events like royal tours and city anniversaries, townspeople crossed paths with Māori in city space. As the Te Arawa trip showed, some visits provided Pākehā with the opportunity to consume Māori culture. Among the most popular were (so-called) Māori carnivals, initially comprising performances of different haka and waiata. Possibly the first was held at the 1885 Wellington Exhibition, when a group of 30 Ngāti Raukawa from Ōtaki performed before thousands. Such was their success that the troupe went on a tour of South Island cities and towns.[200] The largest of its kind was the Māori carnival held in aid of the Boer War at Wellington's Basin Reserve on 28–29 March 1900. Many Māori had wanted to enlist in a New Zealand contingent, but imperial authorities ruled this out on the grounds it was a 'white man's' war.[201] Māori therefore looked to other ways of expressing their support. The Wellington couple Tare Parata (Charlie Pratt) and Katherine Te Rongokahira Parata suggested a carnival of Māori culture to fundraise for the More Men Fund.[202] Parata was a government official and well connected with lower North Island iwi, most of which sent groups to the carnival – about 500 people in all.[203] Many individuals and organisations contributed to the event. The Wairarapa runholder Edward Riddiford donated twelve sheep; the Gear Meat Company promised a bullock; and the Railways Department provided subsidised fares.[204] Two special trains brought the parties to town and trams took them to their Basin Reserve camp.[205]

On the opening morning the groups, led by the Pāpāwai and Ōtaki Māori brass bands, marched along streets filled with onlookers back to the Basin, where Native Minister James Carroll and Wellington's mayor John Aitken met them. The carnival began with a pōwhiri (welcome) led by Ngāti Kahungunu's Pene Te Uamairangi and supported by Ngāti Raukawa. The 100-strong Ngāti Kahungunu group then performed a tūtū ngārahu (haka with weapons). Following the pōwhiri, visitors could purchase hāngī-cooked food, see demonstrations of arts and crafts, and watch cultural performances, including a haka called 'Kiki te Poa' (Kick the Boer) that included a mock bayonet charge.[206] Another haka farewelling the New Zealand Fifth Contingent was given by 'East Coast wahine [women], in response to which members of the Fifth gave cheers for the Maoris and sang "Soldiers of the Queen"'.[207] Performances continued into the night under the blaze of modern electric lighting. Over the duration, some 20,000 people (two-fifths of Wellington's population) visited.[208] For Pākehā the carnival provided an opportunity to contribute to a good cause and experience an exotic culture – in a similar vein to Dunedin's Fryer's Circus and Japanese Village described in Chapter Three. As one newspaper recognised:

> Such interesting sights have seldom, if ever, been seen outside of the radius of the native pahs as those afforded city folks yesterday, and whether it was the operation of cooking, the manufacture of baskets, mats, etc., or the dancing, everything was followed with eager eyes unaccustomed to the ways of the Maori.[209]

The event raised £431 (the equivalent of $79,000 in today's currency) for the More Men Fund. Parata handed over a cheque for the sum to Carroll in April, but it was deposited in the general government account and the Fund saw none of it.[210]

The racial theory of Aryanism provides a lens through which to view the carnival. Tony Ballantyne has shown the genesis and diffusion of Aryanism across colonial space is complex, but it found local expression in Edward Tregear's 1885 book *The Aryan Maori*. The Aryan myth turned Māori into brown-skinned Britons, encouraged racial assimilation, and celebrated Māori prowess as warriors and sportsmen.[211] Parata identified as both Māori and a British subject. Although disappointed that Māori had been denied the chance to fight in South Africa, he proclaimed the carnival would 'testify our love to our Queen and the flag that gives justice to all people under the same'.[212] If the carnival enabled some Māori to pledge their support to the imperial project and showcase their warrior prowess, it also provided a means to refute the current Social Darwinian perception of

Organised events brought Māori into the city. Carnivals showcasing Māori culture were popular and drew large crowds. The largest was held at Wellington's Basin Reserve in 1900 in aid of New Zealand troops fighting in the Boer War. Māori were excluded from fighting in the war and the carnival, organised by Tare Parata and Katherine Te Rongokahira Parata, was an alternative way of showing support. Sir George Grey Special Collections, Auckland Libraries, NZG-19000414-692-1 (above and opposite) and Alexander Turnbull Library, 1/1-003754-G (below)

them as a dying race. Visitors saw not an enervated and diminished people, but one strong in body and spirit. It also showed Māori embracing the modernity of the age – trains, trams, electric lighting, and the city itself – to exhibit their culture and exercise their agency in city space.[213]

A further example of this was the Maori Opera Company. It was formed in 1915 by the Anglican minister Frederick Bennett and comprised a 40-strong all-Māori ensemble. In July the company began a North Island tour of Percy Flynn's opera *Hinemoa*, based on the well-known love story of Hinemoa and Tutanekai, as a fundraiser for the Wounded Soldiers' Relief Fund.[214] After a triumphant seven-night run at Auckland's His Majesty's Theatre, the company began a six-night season at Wellington's Grand Opera House; its gala opening was preceded by a parade of army reservists through city streets.[215] Critical reaction to the show was generally favourable.[216] One reviewer wrote: 'the singing and the acting of the Maoris are worthy of high praise ... Several of the leading wahines are gifted with fine voices which could be trained by a Marchesi into a possible marvellous Melba.' There was, however, 'room for improvement in Percy Flynn's composition; it lacks spirit, and resembles largely the simple tunes of the Sunday school.' It was the haka and poi songs that saved the 'show from slumber'.[217] The culturally hybrid performance raised £93 (some $13,000 in today's currency) for the relief fund, but it had other beneficial outcomes as well.[218] In relating the story of Hinemoa and Tutanekai through the exalted medium of opera, the Company disputed Pākehā notions that Māori culture was primitive, immutable and anti-modern; in performing it in theatres and opera houses – the cultural high temples of cities – it challenged the idea that Māori belonged outside civil society.

After the First World War, Māori continued to visit cities to stage cultural performances, but the period also saw increasing numbers of Māori settle in them as taura here. The 1926 Census identified 1,162 Māori living in Auckland city; 434 in Wellington city; 18 in Nelson city; 143 in Christchurch city; and 102 in Dunedin city.[219] The urban population continued to climb steadily before exploding with the wave of Māori urbanisation after the Second World War. Historians and demographers have viewed the rapid transition of Māori from a largely rural people to a largely urban one as radical and inexplicable.[220] Yet if we place it in the context of more than 100 years of Māori engaging with city life, it is less so. For many Māori, city space was not foreign territory. They already had a long history of making it their own.

Conclusion

Pākehā townspeople's social relations with Māori were mediated by European racial theory, which changed over this period largely in accordance with the shifting power balance between the two groups. At the beginning of colonisation

Māori were firmly in control, so persuasion rather than force drove settlers' racial amalgamation project. Settlers cited Māori commercial aptitude as evidence they would rapidly transition into civil society. However, when Māori began to threaten their prospects, settlers moved to marginalise the competition. As settler society gained greater power, Pākehā representations of Māori became less sympathetic and more antagonistic. This was exemplified during the New Zealand wars, when intense fighting and settler fears of an Auckland invasion popularised the view that Māori were innately barbaric – despite evidence of Pākehā barbarity too. Hard racism survived the war and encouraged the belief among some townspeople that Māori belonged outside civil society and cities should be white places. The demise of Auckland's Māori market and Wellington's Pipitea and Te Aro pā reinforced this conviction and underlined how modernity could be as much a regressive as a progressive force. Yet the view that indigenous people were unwelcome strangers in cities was never accepted to the same extent in New Zealand as it was in Australian and North American settler colonies. This was highlighted in the debate over the provision of native hostelries in cities. Soft racists saw hostelries as a way of improving Māori and easing their move into civil society; hard racists believed Māori degraded civil society and that providing hostelries would further pollute it. In short, townspeople's views on Māori and their place in city life was characterised by ambiguity and contradiction.

The reality was of course that Māori did not neatly fit the racialised social constructs of Pākehā. The environmentalist argument underpinning the racial theories was that civil society and the pursuit of city life could shape and modify Māori behaviours, both positively and negatively. It must therefore have been vexing for settlers that Māori did not always respond in the way the theories predicted. Māori adoption of some European social practices like the money economy might have excited those set on racial amalgamation, but in maintaining many of their own social practices Māori resisted being fully immersed in civil society. Another problem with the environmentalist premise was that the city was the subject and Māori the object: the city modified Māori. But the reverse was also true. Not only were Māori city-builders, constructing houses, roads and streets, they also shaped city social and cultural life. Māori traders and visitors introduced new modes of sociability and a distinctive street style; Māori cultural performance exhibited both an exotic and modern edge that illustrated the hybridising qualities of city life. The erection by some townspeople of walls – both literal and metaphorical – to block Māori entry to cities might have been intended as an assertion of their power, but the reality was that the walls, when they were only partially built, irrevocably weakened this power. In stepping through the breaches, Māori not only claimed city space but contributed to the production of new spaces as well.

The soaring Cargill monument, which commemorates Otago colonialist William Cargill, is one of a number of imposing structures in this lively 1885 sketch of central Dunedin. People fill the streets, some chatting with acquaintances and others going about their daily business. Alexander Turnbull Library, B-K-1243-649

Chapter Five

City Crowds

This sketch of central Dunedin on the opposite page shows the intersection of Princes and High streets in 1885. The magnificent colonial architecture is centre stage: the graceful tower of the Neo-classical Post Office counterbalancing the soaring lines of the Gothic Revival Cargill monument. But equally striking is the vitality of the street: men and women, boys and girls of different social classes converge at the monument; some stand about chatting; others amble or walk purposefully; and one sits on a step, observing the crowd. Contributing to the bustle are three wandering dogs and numerous horse-drawn carriages and trams. It is a daytime scene, but four modern gas street lamps suggest that this is also a place of nocturnal activity. Such rich depictions are relatively rare in New Zealand's colonial urban imagery. Few nineteenth-century artists painted street scenes, preferring the distant, topographical representations showcased in Chapter One.[1] Photography helped to fill the void. Yet early photographs of streetscapes were often taken when there were few people about (to minimise the 'ghosting' from long aperture times), creating the impression that streets were relatively lifeless. The 1885 sketch brings people back into the frame and highlights the importance of the street as a social space in colonial city life.

In Chapters One and Three we examined the production of social space and associational culture in New Zealand's cities, from the formation of social collectives like horticultural and other societies through to the provision of infrastructure like coffee houses, theatres and sports grounds. These were vital sites of sociability – but so was the street. In fact, the street was arguably the more important. As Peter Andersson has written: 'The life of the city is in the street, and in the little incidents that happen when people rub shoulders in a limited arena.'[2] Nonetheless, while street life has been the subject of overseas scholarship, comparatively little is known about it in New Zealand. As with other aspects of the built environment, streets are often implicit in accounts of city social relations and events such as street parades and protests, but few historians have considered them in their own right.[3] Robin Law's examination of street trade and play in South Dunedin between 1890 and 1940, and Alison Clarke's examination of Dunedin's jubilee street procession in 1898 and its role in strengthening Otago social identities, are exceptions.[4] This chapter and the next examine further ways in which townspeople rubbed shoulders on city streets. The focus in this chapter is on the social behaviour and experience of being in city crowds; the following chapter narrows in on street traders and other street people. Together they suggest that crowds and street people increased the diversity and vitality of street life, and in this way contributed to the growing appeal of city life in colonial society.

Street verve

If pictorial representations of street life are relatively rare, the same cannot be said of literary representations. New immigrants and visitors to the colony's cities were sometimes amazed by the verve of streets, and many committed their impressions to paper. Arriving in Auckland in 1869, 'New Chum' was struck by its energy and speed:

> I had lived so long in a quiet, easy going province ... where existence is merely a kind of vegetation, that when I stood in the busiest part of Queen-street on a Saturday, and witnessed its life, bustle and animation, I was fairly bewildered, and felt like a country bumpkin suddenly set down at a busy crossing somewhere in the neighbourhood of St. Paul's [Cathedral, London].[5]

He then gave an account of his first day in the city, beginning in the morning with merchants and stevedores at the bustling Queen's Wharf and ending with the heaving Saturday night crowd along Queen Street. A visitor from Otago in 1871 observed that Queen Street was 'pretty lively', with even more people and activity than Dunedin's Princes Street.[6] Another visitor, standing in lower Queen Street at lunchtime in 1885, was confronted with a 'wondrous scene of bustle and traffic'. Like New Chum, this visitor used London as a reference point: 'It reminds me a little of the enormous traffic about the Mansion House in the great English metropolis,' he mused.[7]

Other cities were similarly lively. In the same year, the columnist 'Touchstone' recorded the rhythm of Wellington's main streets over a working day. 'Shortly after 9 a.m. there descends from Upper Willis-street a crowd of smart, well-dressed men, young and old, hurrying along to that gigantic wooden building which shelters the great army of Government servants [Government Buildings].' From 10 to 11.30 Lambton Quay is subdued, but by late morning 'it is populated once more, this time by ladies bent on shopping excursions ... and the inevitable new chum gaping about in his usual helpless manner'. From four o'clock in the afternoon 'the fashionable loungers of the morning appear in tenfold numbers' to 'do the Beach' – promenade along Lambton Quay (formerly the beachfront)

– and at 5 p.m. 'there is a mighty exodus from the big buildings, and to all parts of the city hundreds of young people wend their way home'. The exceptions are the feckless, unmarried civil servants who stay in town and devote their time to 'billiards, barmaids, and beer'.[8] Touchstone's account captures the way crowds and gender shaped the everyday rhythm of street life.

The crowd

Crowds, defined here as temporary social collectives or groups who hold something in common for a transitory period, were an essential phenomenon of street life.[9] Urban sociologists from Georg Simmel to Richard Sennett have argued the crowd was the most powerful experience of nineteenth-century modernity, creating new ways of behaving and relating to others.[10] 'The Victorian crowd was a living thing,' says Peter Andersson. 'Crowds had gathered since time immemorial, but the industrial age offered conditions for crowds to be larger and more common than before.'[11] Their modernity and greater regularity led some to pathologise the crowd and to see it as a threat to public order.[12] Gustave Le Bon's 1895 book *The Crowd* popularised this view. He argued that in the anonymity of the crowd people lose their individual identity and therefore their capacity for reason and judgement. This leads to an unconscious or group mind that ensures crowd behaviours will be primitive and aggressive. Moreover, having lost their individual agency, crowd members can be directed at will by a charismatic leader to mindless violence: to become a mob.[13]

As psychologists Stephen Reicher and Clifford Stott explain, crowd psychology moved away from Le Bon's ideas, to be replaced by social identity theory. Rather than envisaging a singular social identity that is lost in groups, this argues people have multiple social identities that correspond with the different groups to which they identify. People's behaviour will therefore vary from context to context according to the shared values and beliefs of the group; in a crowd, the actions of the group will usually be consonant with their common understandings of their social identity. However, as Reicher and Stott point out, there are times 'when the indeterminacy of crowd events takes a more radical form, and where the response is not to elaborate social identity but redefine it'.[14] For instance, a protest crowd can be made up of multiple groups, each with different views of the police. But if the police see the crowd as a mob and move against it, the different groups can unite into a single group or community opposed to the police.[15] The psychologists also remind us that crowds can have an impact beyond their participants. They are a tangible expression of broader 'imagined communities', comprising all those who socially identify with crowd members – a union march in one place will usually be morally supported by unionists and sympathisers elsewhere.[16]

For Reicher and Stott, crowds are critical to understanding historical change and continuity. While some crowds disturb the social equilibrium, others strengthen existing identities and buttress the authority of the imagined community. In contrast to Le Bon, they argue human agency is not depleted in the crowd but enhanced by it:

> It both defines the norms, values, and moral sensibilities that shape what people want to do, and also provides the power that enables them to do it. In crowds people cease to be mere 'objects' whose fate is manipulated by others, and become subjects who, jointly, determine their own fate. Indeed, that sense of agency is one of the central joys of being in a crowd and does much to explain why people want to participate.[17]

This chapter adopts the social identity tradition of the crowd, accepting that crowd behaviour varies according to context and the composition of its members. It also accepts that crowds have human agency to shape events. Crowds can certainly form in other urban spaces, but the emphasis here is on the street. For our purpose, crowds are divided into two main types: social (where the object is to

DOING THE BLOCK

Mrs. Fazunplate   I have such an indulgent husband
Mrs. Sourgrapes   Yes, so George says. Sometimes indulges a little too much, doesn't he?

OPPOSITE These middle-class Melburnians are 'doing the block', the Australasian version of the Hyde Park promenade. Dressed in their finest, they make their leisurely way down Collins Street, seeing and being seen. P. Naumann, National Library of Australia, nla.pic-an8701388

LEFT This 1908 cartoon captures a waspish exchange between two women doing the block. The first figure, the showy-looking Mrs Fazunplate, complacently remarks on her husband's indulgence. Mrs Sourgrapes agrees all too readily, indicating distain for her companion's flamboyant appearance. National Library, Papers Past, *Free Lance*, 19 Dec 1908, p.4 (supplement)

promenade with fellow townspeople or congregate in public space to experience an event); and processional (where groups march along streets to emphasise their social identities or publicise a grievance, or both). Of course there is some inter-lap between the two. A procession can be a very social experience, and a promenade can strengthen participants' social identities. We might also see such crowds through the lens of Lefebvrian theory, as representational spaces: of carnival, imagination, resistance and appropriation by the powerless.

Gendered space

It needs to be stressed that street life was a gendered phenomenon, in which the movement of (particularly) middle-class women was circumscribed. It was based on the idea of separate spheres. The street was in the public sphere and was therefore imagined as a male space in which women had restricted entry. The exceptions were working-class women and prostitutes: 'public women' who lived outside the separate spheres paradigm.[18] Consequently, unaccompanied middle-class women venturing onto streets ran the risk of being understood as working class or prostitutes, or both.[19] As historian Jessica Ellen Sewell explains: 'Women in public were a source of cultural anxiety because of their discordance with the dominant linkage of women and domesticity.' The anxiety was an expression of the tension between an 'imagined landscape of gender and class segregation and people's experience of the built landscape, in which this separation was necessarily incomplete'.[20]

To attempt to bridge the two landscapes, contemporary etiquette books advised respectable middle-class women to be unobtrusive on streets: never to talk loudly, laugh boisterously or dress conspicuously. For them, the street was primarily a space to be moved through, not one to linger, gaze and socialise on.[21] Middle-class women's sociability instead occurred mainly at home. Conversely, working-class women's behaviour and dress did not emphasise discreetness in public space; for them, the street itself was an important a site of sociability.[22] There was, however, an exemption to the rule that middle-class women keep moving on city streets, and this was shopping. Window-shopping was permitted as part of the female gaze because it was seen as an extension of women's domestic role. Middle-class women were also permitted on streets for mission and philanthropic work.[23] Yet gender historians have argued that middle-class women's behaviour and social relations on streets were more open and fluid than the etiquette codes prescribed, and women took to the streets in ways other than as shoppers and philanthropists.[24] This chapter provides support for this idea. It shows that New Zealand middle-class women were not averse to challenging the gendered division of city space and manipulating streets for their own use.

Doing the block

Most social crowds were gender inclusive. Men and women, and often children, would come together to promenade along streets or gather to watch a street performance or event. Sometimes social class delineated them – as in the middle-class promenade mentioned by Touchstone. He called it 'to do the Beach', but it was more widely known in Australasia as 'doing the block', the Antipodean equivalent of the late-afternoon bourgeois promenade in London's Hyde Park, Paris's Bois de Boulogne or New York's Broadway.[25] We can see this daily event as an example of street theatre.

Drawing on sociological research, historians have shown how street and crowd behaviours have a performative aspect: 'Since we are being watched we cannot help but perform'.[26] That is, townspeople try to manage the impression they give to others – their projection of Self – through their manner and appearance, and by playing different roles in different contexts. To avoid everything becoming a performance, however, a distinction is usually made between formal rituals and the informal behaviours of everyday life.[27] 'Doing the block' was a formal ritual.

Doing the block involved traversing a section of a city's main street and seeing and being seen by one's peers. Beginning at one end, individuals, couples and groups would amble along the footpath, acknowledging friends and acquaintances, sometimes stopping to chat, and then, on reaching the end of the block, turn around and walk back to the start. The performance was as much a chance to flaunt one's finery as an opportunity for sociability, an occasion when exchanging looks was unceasing and pleasurable.[28] In 1873, 'Emily' gave an account of the ritual along Dunedin's Princes Street – the block that ran from Herbert Hayne's corner by the Octagon down the western side to Brown, Ewing's corner at Manse Street (about 500 metres). Starting at the 'most fashionable hour' beside Brown, Ewing's corner, she was soon among the throng. 'The streets were pretty full, and, as usual, every one was trying as much as possible to get into every one else's way.' She wondered why signs were not put up telling people to 'keep to the right' (then the convention) and offenders fined. She passed two children out with their nurse, one a thumb-sucking baby so tightly bound in swaddling clothes it could not move its limbs, and the other a toddler: 'a fat little thing, with tiny unsteady feet'. She was next struck by a 'Byronic looking individual' she had seen before on the street but did not know. She gave him the moniker 'Man with the Neck' owing to his turned-down collar 'that showed more of the neck than was at all necessary', and willed him to wear stick-up collars; she faulted him also for sporting his hat on the back of his head. Next she watched a gentleman coming down the street go crimson as he was 'cut' (ignored) by a lady going up:

> She was too much taken up with the lady she was talking to, however – a 'somebody,' by the way – to pay any attention to him. He didn't seem to know what to do, and it was only till he was fairly past, with his hand almost raised to his hat, that he seemed to realise that she had actually cut him. He looked very much hurt.[29]

Soon after, a group of ladies blocked Emily's passage along the footpath. 'They were all very demonstrative, very talkative, and seemingly much delighted to see each other.' It was as if they were meeting for the first time in years, but she had seen the same group 'congregated in exactly the same manner and talking in the same gushing style' three days before at Herbert Hayne's corner, and in George Street the day before that. The gathering transgressed the precept that middle-class women should not linger on streets, but Emily negotiated her way around the group and soon reached the end of the block.[30] Turning about, she met 'a real dandy' wearing a 'perfectly tight-fitting suit of iron grey', polished swell boots, 'the most dainty lavender kid gloves', a shiny bell-topper hat and the 'nattiest of sweet looking canes'. He also wore the 'most self-approving smile you can imagine'. On her way back, she observed a delivery boy staggering under a heavy load of parcels long after he should have been home; watched a gentleman

Gertie Tewsley (left) and Ethel Haggitt epitomise the New Woman in their dress and demeanour. Both are wearing 'rational' clothing (loose jackets and skirts teamed with a blouse and masculine accessories) and are corset-free. Gertie is smoking and Ethel is stuffing her pipe with tobacco. The scene is playful and the women may have been accentuating their masculine look to poke fun at male fears around the New Woman. James Reynolds Cameron, Alexander Turnbull Library, 1/2-024958-G flee through a shop doorway to avoid some approaching women; and overheard a young lady say to her male companion that last evening had been 'awfully jolly' but she'd felt 'horribly seedy this morning'.[31]

Emily's account is fascinating in that she adopts the position of the *flâneur*. As many urban theorists have argued, the flâneur was the quintessential figure of the modern nineteenth-century city, taking pleasure in roaming the streets alone and unobtrusively observing the crowd.[32] Though traditionally a male figure, women could become flâneurs too, primarily in their role as shoppers.[33] It may have been in this capacity that Emily traversed the block. She certainly had the flâneur's eye for detail and for capturing fleeting human encounters.

The formal and ritualised nature of doing the block made it a target for satire. For instance, a 1908 cartoon shows two women out promenading, one of whom is flamboyantly clothed. As they pass each other, the showy woman boasts how she has an indulgent husband, to which the other snidely suggests he indulges her a little too much (see page 219).[34] Historians have argued that the ridiculing of flamboyant or deviating appearance was a theme in Edwardian metropolitan popular culture, reflecting the way increasing conformity and restraint in dress was seen as an attribute of modern cities until the First World War.[35] In this vein, the showy woman in the cartoon was not only defying etiquette but was being unfashionable along with it.

At the same time, dress could be used as a tool to challenge convention and promote change. During the 1890s, New Women (social feminists) promoted 'rational' dress (a jacket, blouse and knickerbockers) instead of a corset and long skirt. They believed that dispensing with cumbersome garb would increase their freedom of movement and general independence.[36] In 1897, a group of Wellington New Women created their own street style by dispensing with gloves and carrying a (male) staff or cane. A visiting Cantabrian was appalled. This 'newest type of the New Woman' was a 'feminine larrikin', whose loud talking and laughing could be heard across the city, he protested. 'There are scores of her to be seen doing the block … any afternoon from four to five. She chooses that hour because it is then the Johnnies from the Government offices are let loose. She's trotted out for inspection like the fillies in Tattersall's [a British auctioneer of race horses] and everyday is market day for her.' The critic condemned the immodesty of the women's exposed hands, and ridiculed the notion that 'a large red, gloveless hand grasping a particularly masculine walking stick' had become the 'Wellington hall mark of fashion'. These 'rural red' hands were those of a dairy wench, he hissed. 'Were they dainty white hands, at the fingers tapering to filberts, one could forgive the feminine vanity of dispensing with gloves. But they are unhappily quite the other.' He applauded that the 'gloveless maiden, armed with a quarter staff' had not made it to Christchurch, and implored its citizens to resist her arrival there.[37]

We can locate the women's fleeting fashion statement within a wider campaign by 1890s social feminists to demand greater rights and freedoms as citizens. As Caroline Daley reminds us: 'The New Woman challenged ideas about everything from posture and dress to language and sexuality.'[38] The critic's misogynistic tone therefore suggests he was less worried about the women's perceived lack of decorum and more exercised by what it said about their empowerment in city space. In an age that championed respectable women's place in the domestic sphere and constrained their involvement in the public sphere, the women's boisterous behaviour and adoption of the masculine staff challenged feminine codes of respectable behaviour and male dominance in city public space. Equally, in a society where the public exposure of the body was tightly proscribed, the women's undressing of their hands showed their desire to more freely express their sexuality.

Body display was certainly a pivotal aspect of doing the block. In 1901, the *Press* newspaper lamented that Christchurch was alone among the main cities of Australasia in not having the institution of the block. As it wrote, this was 'not a rooted custom in Christchurch. The mere male often sighs for this pleasant institution. Christchurch women are as beautiful … as women anywhere. But they deny us the daily sight of their charms.' The writer of the piece relates his experience of doing the block on Melbourne's Collins Street, where 'pretty women, handsomely dressed, smile and bow to well-groomed men, with constant interchange of bright greetings'. In Sydney, too, a New Zealander 'finds unfailing delight an hour's lounge on the "block"'. Yet Christchurch ladies showed themselves only fleetingly, dashing to a draper's or lingering briefly in a teashop. After garden parties and civic functions they hurry home, 'and the poor men, who were not privileged to be among the guests, see no more of their pretty plumage'. He calls for the creation of a block in his city. 'Christchurch is robbed of much in missing an institution that – vanity of vanities, notwithstanding – is pretty, may give much pleasure, and is essentially humanising.'[39]

The plea highlights the extent to which doing the block was a sexualised activity. Like the elaborately presented displays of merchandise in the large plate-glass shop windows that lined their route, participants in the ritual dressed to draw the eye. For the *Press* writer, its central purpose was to serve the male gaze. He wanted the block to be instituted in the city so he and other men could observe beautiful women. In this context, women's bodies became objects of male desire. Yet it is amply evident that women returned the gaze. Wellington's New Women congregated outside Government Buildings at five o'clock so they could meet and flirt with men their own age in a socially sanctioned environment.[40] Similarly, in Dunedin, 'bewitching toilets may be seen in Princes Street about 5 o'clock, just when the young men come out'.[41] 'Emily' might have criticised the 'Man with the

Men and women are strolling about central Christchurch on a summer's day in 1913. The view is from Cathedral Square, looking towards the United Service Hotel on the corner. Both sexes wear hats in conformity with contemporary social expectations. Christchurch City Libraries, CCL KPCD05 IMG0063

Neck' for showing too much flesh, but in describing him as Byronic she indicates she also thought him desirable. These women's behaviour supports scholarship asserting that nineteenth-century women were not passive recipients of an avid male gaze. Instead, as Lynda Nead has argued, 'they can be imagined as women who enjoyed and participated in the "ocular economy" of the city: they were women who looked at and returned the gazes of passers-by'.[42] Such fleeting encounters provided a sexual charge or *frisson* to streets that increased the appeal of city life for many.

It seems likely the doing the block performance petered out in the 1910s. The onset of the First World War would have reduced the turnout of men, and the

Members of the Temperance Ladies Brass Band are pictured with their instruments in an Auckland park in the 1910s. William A. Price, Alexander Turnbull Library, 1/2-000336-G

1917 introduction of six o'clock closing almost certainly sealed its fate.[43] With only an hour between finishing work and the closure of bars, men headed for the pub rather than the block. In deciding between drinking industrial beer in smoke-filled rooms or meeting the gaze of women (or men) on city streets, New Zealand men chose beer. Women, prohibited from public bars, hung up their smart city threads and remained in their suburban aprons. The rush or swagger of men exiting pubs and piling onto homeward-bound trams became the new early-evening ritual in city life.

The Saturday night crowd

Doing the block was a middle-class social practice in which working people did not participate. One of the times when all townspeople came together was Saturday evening, the end of the working week for most, and when they got paid. It was also late shopping night.[44] New Chum related that as dusk turned to night on Queen Street 'the lamps seem to burn brighter, the people to throng more quickly, the shop-fronts to be gayer in their resplendent show, the ladies

Concert-goers hurry through a wet Wellington night for an evening of music at the town hall about 1905. The hall is ablaze with light, which spills out onto surrounding streets, adding richness to this night scene. Charles Nathaniel Worsley, Alexander Turnbull Library, A-166-001

to be prettier than ever'. He described the street as a 'motley crowd', comprising 'merchants, and clerks, and labourers, and loafers, and all the omnium gatherum of a goldfields city, passing to and fro in a continuous stream'.[45] The Saturday night crowd in Christchurch gathered in the Square: 'All the pathways are thronged, and impassioned street orators and evangelists hold forth,' observed Edith Searle Grossmann.[46] In Wellington, townspeople headed for Lambton Quay to promenade from Willis Street to Thorndon, and vice versa. On such occasions a stranger might think Wellington was 'ten times its actual size', suggested Touchstone.[47] By the beginning of the twentieth century, Cuba Street had supplanted Lambton Quay as Wellingtonians' chosen rendezvous.

In 1906, C. Allen Harris captured the scene in a montage of dynamic images:

Saturday night in Cuba Street! A stream of humanity on either side, the congested footpaths overflowed into and across the roadway; the clangour of approaching [tram] cars, the distance-muffled sound of those that have disappeared; garish and shadowy melting wells of electricity suspended in echoing mid-air. Underneath the dazzle all sorts and conditions of men, women, and children, sleek and happy, strolling casually, revelling in their 'night out.'[48]

A 'welter of noise' reverberated along the street. Adding to the clang and bells of the trams were the clip-clopping of horses' hooves, the 'shrill treble' of newsboys, the 'doleful melody' of a barrel organ, and myriad voices calling to others. In the manner of a flâneur, Harris observes men standing under shop verandas, their arms laden with parcels or babies, while their wives shop unencumbered inside. Single men loll about in groups along the kerb, chatting and soaking up the atmosphere. His gaze then falls on some working-class girls who were:

gorgeously upholstered and well groomed, boots and faces resplendent, with gay airs, and gayer flowers on the coat lapel … The long dragging hours in the clattering factory, the booming hum of wheels, the stifle of long tables, and the clicking of shears are dead as Nero to-night, and as faintly remembered. All the weary week has each looked forward to this Saturday night, with its street glamour.

He notes how people are wandering in and out of the 'humming stores' in an endless stream. 'Fresh feminine faces' crowd close to 'luring windows, resplendent with dainty headdress and lace "confections" that will temper the glare of the afternoon sun and provoke the criticism of envious dames in cool tea-rooms'. Harris fancies he sees some of the faces gain a 'resolve in [their] eyes' and enter the store to make their desired purchases 'on the altar of vanity'. As dusk approaches about eight o'clock, the street lamps flicker on, bathing the space in night-defying electric light. Alongside the brightly illuminated shop windows, they enhance the scene's modernity and vitality. By 9.30, the festive air of the street begins to dissipate. The trams, 'laden to the handrails', head home. A drunken man 'goes lurching and hiccoughing past, his legs amusingly disobedient, his language painfully incoherent'. The shops shut their doors 'as the three-quarter chimes', and their lamps and windows blacken. Not long after, the street is nearly empty, with only a few stragglers peppering the recently crammed thoroughfare.[49]

Harris's account emphasises a mass culture of consumption: the Saturday night focus was on shopping (for groceries and luxuries), body display and spectacle. For the factory girls and many others it was a chance to dress up and look glamorous, an unstructured, fun-filled interlude in otherwise regimented working lives. But while the sexes mixed in the street, the activity of shopping was reserved for women. They busied themselves in stores, or pored over elaborate and enticing window displays, while men remained on the kerb in clusters or alone, sometimes holding the baby. Yet it is evident the night was about more than shopping. A large part of its appeal was the crowd: the cacophony, vibrancy and sociability of being among hundreds of other animated people. Peter Andersson writes of the street being a 'frontstage of performances and as a place of togetherness, wherein the crowd assembled becomes a community rather than an anonymous mass'.[50] Touchstone's comment that on Saturday night Wellington felt much bigger than it actually was highlighted the modern sensibility of its citizens, and the extent to which they relished being amidst the crowd and belonging to an imagined community of fellow townspeople.

Women's expanding access to urban space – epitomised by the New Woman, working girl and female shopper – was a defining attribute of all modern cities in the late nineteenth century.[51] Harris's account, along with those of 'Emily' and Grossmann, suggest New Zealand cities shared this characteristic. Further research is needed to ascertain the extent to which (particularly) middle-class women's access to city space increased. But if we compare the experience of Mary Swainson and Emma Thomson (see Chapter Three), it seems that Emma had freer reign of Dunedin's streets in the 1880s than Mary had of Wellington's in the 1840s. It is true that Mary went riding and walking in Wellington's environs, but she made little mention of the town's street life or of activities as shopping. Her social and cultural world was centred in the private sphere. Emma's was more situated in the public sphere. She regularly went shopping in town, with her children or female companions, and often attended public events with her husband. Yet her social conservatism (and perhaps shyness) meant she did not walk streets alone or participate in the doing the block ritual.[52] Conversely, the experience of 'Emily' in the 1870s shows that respectable women could negotiate city streets alone, albeit not to the same extent as men. Such inequality provoked the Wellington New Women's protest to access streets on the same basis as men did; that males and females of all classes formed the Saturday night crowd shows some success in realising this aim.

Election night

The Saturday night crowd was a regular event. A less frequent but more dramatic social crowd formed on general election night. Before the completion of a national telegraph network in the early 1870s, general election results could take days to be confirmed; the telegraph meant results could be known within hours of the closing of polling booths. Metropolitan newspapers took advantage of the new technology to turn election night into a public spectacle. They erected large screens outside their central-city offices to project (using limelight lanterns) the latest election results as they came in by telegraph. Thousands of people flocked into town to watch events 'live' on the big screen.

A general election unlike any before it was the election of 28 November 1893, the first in which women voted. Wellingtonian Herbert Spackman recorded 'great excitement' in the city as the polls opened. Arriving at the polling booth, he was 'pestered by lady canvassers at the doorway and loaded with tickets of all kinds'. (Before the party system, candidates often ran as part of a ticket.)[53] As a teetotaller, he voted for the prohibitionist ticket: Sir Robert Stout, F. H. Fraser and John Duthie.[54] After his early-evening orchestral rehearsal he went to 'Evening Post Corner' (the corner of Willis Street and Lambton Quay) to watch the election unfold. Among the assembly were large numbers of women and many young children. The crowd had been building since the closing of polls at seven o'clock and reached over 10,000 when the pubs shut at eleven o'clock.[55] Spackman described it as 'tremendous'.[56]

Instead of the usual limelight lantern and screen, the *Post* had erected three hoardings on which the names of electorates and candidates were printed, with blank spaces for the posting of voting figures. The boards faced different directions so as to be visible from the contiguous streets, and were lit by 241 electric lights. The newspaper boasted the electrical display was the first of its kind in New Zealand and made the corner 'brighter than day'.[57] At 9.40 p.m. the results for Wellington City were put up on the boards. Stout (Liberal) topped the poll, followed by Harry Bell (independent Liberal) and Duthie (independent conservative).[58] This became 'the signal for a demonstration which lasted many minutes. Peal after peal of cheers reverberated up and down the streets, the cries being taken up from far and near, and echoed back to their source only to be sent forth again with equal vigour.'[59] Counter-demonstrations were drowned out by the prevailing sentiment. The conservative victor in the Wellington Suburbs seat, Dr Alfred Newman, was seen in the crowd and hoisted shoulder high by enthusiastic supporters; Duthie was also spotted, but his much bigger girth foiled the same stunt being pulled. Stout addressed a large gathering from the upstairs window of his committee rooms, crediting his win to the support of Wellington's women and pledging to work his hardest for the city.[60]

Similar scenes played out in the other cities. In Dunedin, 'a sea of faces' gathered outside the *Otago Daily Times* building in Dowling Street, and prolonged cheers rang out when at just after ten o'clock David Pinkerton (Liberal) topped the local poll.[61] When news of his success reached the Wellington crowd about an hour later, resounding cheers erupted there too.[62] The main venue in Christchurch was the *Lyttelton Times* office in Gloucester Street. A few larrikins caused annoyance by hurling rotten eggs at random, but this did not dampen the crowd's euphoric mood, each Liberal victory being greeted with a 'hearty cheer'. After midnight, William Pember Reeves, George Smith and William Collins (all Liberals) were declared the winners for Christchurch City; Reeves was lifted from his horse and carried aloft into the *Times* building, from where he addressed the assembled mass from a first-floor balcony.[63]

In Auckland, screens were erected on both the *New Zealand Herald* and *Auckland Star* buildings in Queen and Shortland streets respectively. In noting the novelty of the day, the *Star* recorded that many ladies who might have been expected to vote in the morning had waited until the afternoon, when 'they emerged in all the glory of their summer apparel, and perambulating the streets in numbers far exceeding the members of the coarser sex who were there, seemed to be enjoying their new power before they took the trouble exercising it'.[64] As in Wellington, the crowd thickened outside the *Star* building after polling closed, and Shortland Street was soon awash with people. As each result arrived in the *Star* office it was transferred to a glass slip and handed to the lantern operator. According to the paper, 'Some times deafening cheers rose as if from every throat in the crowd; sometimes prolonged howls and hisses were heard; sometimes the cheerers and the hooters were pretty evenly matched and the result was a discordant medley; and sometimes the news was greeted with silence almost.'[65] The crowd was kept amused between each result with cartoons of the politicians. At ten to twelve, the result for Auckland City was announced, with Sir George Grey (Liberal) topping the poll by a wide margin. Soon after, the crowd scattered.[66] Things were still in full swing in Wellington, with people waiting to hear results from Auckland and Christchurch. The overloading of the telegraph system meant it was two o'clock in the morning before the Christchurch return arrived, after which the electric lights were switched off and the now-enervated crowd dispersed.[67] The reforming Liberal government had been returned to office.

In the twenty-first century, most New Zealanders watch general election results on televisions in the privacy of their homes (if they watch at all), but the same night in late-colonial cities was a civic event. For an evening the streets outside metropolitan newspaper offices became agora-like as townspeople engaged with and debated the election, either as individuals discussing the latest results with those about them or through the multiple voices of the crowd.[68] There is no sense of Le Bon's anonymous mass devoid of human agency. Instead, the crowd comprised different groups firmly or loosely aligned to particular candidates or tickets. Each expressed their agency by cheering or hooting candidates' wins and so reinforced the social identity of their group. Periodically the multiple voices became a single voice: when a candidate with wide appeal topped a poll, the

OVERLEAF An enormous crowd in Christchurch's Cathedral Square is waiting for the results of the 1908 general election. The crowd is mostly comprised of men, but plenty of women are visible due to their large hats. This scene would have been repeated in the other cities.
Sir George Grey Special Collections, Auckland Libraries, AWNS-19081126-5-1

crowd's cry reverberated down streets and bounced off buildings to create an electrifying atmosphere. The attraction of the election-night spectacle therefore rested not only in following the election's progress in (near) real time but also on the exhilaration and fleeting fraternity of the crowd.

In a period known for its trenchant provincialism, general elections created a moment of national consciousness. Standing alongside thousands of others, watching the latest polling results from all corners of the country being projected or scribbled onto boards in each of the cities, few people would have been oblivious to being part of an (imagined) New Zealand body politic or community. The phenomenon adds weight to historians' claims that communications – road, rail and (in this instance) the telegraph – were instrumental in the production of national or nation space in colonial society.[69]

Public executions

The social crowds so far considered exhibited a high degree of bonhomie, but a few crowds can only be described as macabre – none more so than those that gathered for public executions. The first person to be executed by the Crown in New Zealand was 17-year-old Maketu Wharetotara in March 1842. The son of the Ngāpuhi chief Ruhe, Maketu lived in the Bay of Islands. In 1841 he found work on the farm of settler and widow Elizabeth Roberton. But following mistreatment by Roberton's servant, Thomas Bull, Maketu killed Thomas, then Elizabeth, her two children and the granddaughter of another Ngāpuhi chief, Rewa. Maketu sought refuge at his father's village, but the killing of Rewa's granddaughter was a cause for war, and Ruhe surrendered his son to avert this.[70] A meeting of Ngāpuhi leaders agreed to Maketu's being tried by the Crown for murder. This occurred in Auckland's newly completed Supreme Court before Chief Justice William Martin on Tuesday 1 March.[71]

Attending the jury trial was the Treasury clerk Edmund Webber (of Chapters Three and Four), who described Maketu as 'peculiarly prepossessing', noting that on entering the dock he 'leant his arms on the iron railings and never during the whole trial did he move from that position. His countenance at the same time showed the utmost determination.'[72] According to Edmund, he was tried only for Bull's murder, and proceedings lasted four hours. He expressed himself only twice: first to plead not guilty, and then to issue a grunt through clenched teeth on hearing the guilty verdict.[73] Edmund stated he found the trial 'most interesting' and 'would not have missed it for any money'. He was also present at the execution. This took place on Monday 7 March in front of the gaol on Victoria Street West, where carpenters constructed a black-draped gallows from early morning. As this was going on, the Revd John Churton attended to Maketu's request to be baptised before his death.[74] Edmund described his execution:

It was supposed he would be hung at eight, but the sentence was not put into execution till 12. Up to that hour, numbers of people gathered around, eager to witness the just end of this hardened villain, men, women, and children. At the hour appointed, the Troops formed in line before the gallows, the rope was taken behind the screen, and put round the unhappy wretche's [*sic*] neck. The bell was most mournfully tolling, he then came forward on the drop, stood about a minute, and awful spectacle, when the bolt was drawn, and he was dead almost instantly. The body hung for an hour, and was then burried [*sic*] underneath the drop.[75]

The writer George Earp also witnessed the execution. He says Auckland's 'lower orders' (working people) had declared that if any European acted as a hangman to a native chief then he would 'never see another sun rise'. As a result, Earp writes, Maketu assisted in hanging himself by tightening the noose that someone behind the screen had put around his neck and 'stepping boldly on the drop'.[76] This suggests a considerable unease within Auckland's settler community over Maketu's death sentence. Earp believed Governor Hobson should have either pardoned him or transported him to a penal colony, but Hobson had stated that if he pardoned him, 'no European life would be safe'.[77] A newspaper report estimated about 1,000 people watched the proceedings – half of Auckland's population.[78] There were few Māori among them. Edmund Webber said it had been Maketu's intention to address the crowd, but the size of it unnerved him and so he asked to be hung immediately.[79] Following his death, Maketu's family requested his body so it could be taken back to the Bay of Islands for burial. This was refused, but continued pleading by Ruhe eventuated in Maketu's exhumation ten months later and his reinterment at home.[80]

Maketu's execution was intended to uphold the idea of the civil sphere and public order. It was the first major application of British law to a Māori offender and helped to establish Crown jurisdiction over cases of inter-racial violence.[81] While few Māori had opposed the execution, many objected to the way it was carried out. Under Māori custom, Maketu would have been killed instantly by a blow to the head; Māori therefore saw the hanging as prolonged and cold-blooded.[82]

There were seven further public executions in Auckland and Wellington – none elsewhere – until the practice was banned in 1858.[83] The first Pākehā to be hanged was Aucklander Joseph Burns. In June 1848, he was convicted of murdering Robert Snow and his wife and daughter in their North Shore home in October 1847. His motive was theft: he stole £12 from Snow's house. The use of a tomahawk in the brutal killings and the burning of the house aroused suspicions that Māori had committed the crime, and this set the town on edge. But Burns confessed

to his de-facto wife, Margaret Reardon, who left him following the revelation. Fearful she would tell authorities, he coerced her to implicate two former shipmates, before eventually owning up to the deed himself.[84] On the morning of 17 June, Burns was transported in a cart through city streets, accompanied by a clergyman, prison officials and a military escort. One eyewitness recorded: 'The procession passed along Queen Street and up Shortland Crescent [now Street], crowds of people gazing with curious dread at the terrible show.'[85] At Official Bay, the party transferred to a boat to Devonport, where a scaffold had been erected on the site of the Snow killings. To encourage a large crowd, the 'unusual hour of midday' was chosen for the execution, which was carried out at the allotted time. (A plaque on the Devonport foreshore marks the site.)[86]

Public executions in Wellington also drew crowds. In April 1849, Maroro, of Ngāti Kahungunu descent, was convicted of the murder of John Branks and his three children in their Porirua Road home. He confessed to the crime and was hanged outside Wellington prison at Mount Cook before about 500 onlookers, many of whom were Māori.[87] The following year, William Good was executed at the same place in front of a similar-sized crowd for murdering John Ellis; before his death he converted to Catholicism and sought atonement for his actions.[88]

As Maketu's death highlighted, many reports of public executions gave graphic descriptions of the final moments of a condemned person's life, perhaps to satiate an appetite for the macabre. This reached a gruesome level with the 1856 execution in Auckland of Charles Marsden for murdering a Māori woman called Kerara the previous year.[89] On the morning of 12 February, lower Victoria Street West filled with expectant people; Marsden ascended the scaffold at twenty-five past eight, escorted by a clergyman, the sheriff and the executioner. The rope was placed about his neck:

the bolt was drawn, and the wretched man, in his dying agonies, exhibited to the indiscriminate gaze of the men, women and children who were

ABOVE This portrait of 17-year-old Maketu Wharetotara was made by Joseph Merrett just prior to Maketu's execution in 1842. Convicted of murder, he was the first person to be executed by the Crown in New Zealand. Joseph Jenner Merrett, Alexander Turnbull Library, E-216-f-141

OPPOSITE The execution by hanging of Maketu Wharetotara in 1842 attracted a sizeable crowd to the gallows outside the Auckland gaol, shown in this sketch from the 1850s. About 1,000 people witnessed the hanging, half of Auckland's population. Public executions ceased in New Zealand in 1858, putting an end to a ghoulish public spectacle. Sir George Grey Special Collections, Auckland Libraries, 4-2623

People line the streets of central Christchurch in 1901 to cheer on soldiers who had fought in the Boer War. Though the conflict was far away from New Zealand, the bonds of patriotism were strong and the government jumped to support Britain in its war with the Boer republics of South Africa. Most ordinary New Zealanders felt similarly and showed their support in the streets. Alexander Turnbull Library, PA1-q-1136-48-1

congregated in the immediate vicinity of the scaffold. The work of death was clumsily performed, and the struggles of the dying man were protracted to a period of, at least, fourteen minutes – his stertorious [*sic*] breathing, during this space and time, being audible for a considerable distance around.[90]

Six months later, John White met the same fate for murdering his de-facto wife, Ann Fay. Instead of the usual eight o'clock appointment, White was hanged at sunrise (seven o'clock), preventing the gathering of a large crowd. After White's execution, the *New Zealander* declared it regrettable that executions 'should still continue to be made a matter of public and disgusting exhibition'. It called for the colonial government to follow Australia's lead and 'render Executions Private'.[91]

Public executions were intended to be a deterrent to crime and a condemned prisoner's final humiliation. But critics charged they were only morbid and ghoulish spectacles. Following representations from the Auckland Provincial Council, the government passed the Execution of Criminals Act 1858. The measure ordained that death sentences now be carried out within prison walls or at another enclosed place.[92] Crowds at New Zealand executions were assigned to history.

Processions and marches

Processions and marches are organised and choreographed parades of social groups through streets and other public spaces. Their fundamental aim is to make a statement: from upholding the authority of power elites, to celebrating or commemorating an event, to publicising and seeking support for a grievance.[93] Most processions are therefore conducted through urban space rather than less-populated rural space.

Since medieval times, when the entourage of a king or priest would travel through London streets, processions have been an important aspect of metropolitan culture and society.[94] By the nineteenth century, many groups used processions to represent themselves in public space and bolster their social identities, viewing the symbolic power of their temporary mass occupation of city streets as a democratic and inalienable right.[95] Social identity and a group's agenda were also expressed through processional symbols and rituals, including flags, banners, songs, music and chants. Colour too could have significant symbolic meaning, indicating, for example, affiliation with a political movement (socialist red) or expressing emotions like grief (funereal black).[96]

Matthias Reiss has identified that processions share certain attributes: the involvement of crowds, the occupation of public space, movement through urban landscapes, and interaction with society.[97] Some processions and particularly protest ones also begin or end with rallies at public squares or parks. As he points out, '[a]t rallies there is usually little visible distinction between supporters and onlookers. Participation in a march, however, is quite deliberate and an open act of support, and the march, through its movement, creates a boundary between the static onlookers and the marching participants.'[98] Streets and other public space are clear protagonists in processions, but so are landmark buildings: parliaments, town halls, police stations, churches and memorials become focal points for processions so participants can emphasise their temporary occupation of elite urban space.[99] There were (and are) many types of processions, but most can be placed within the following four: military, civic, associational, and protest.

Military processions emphasise the power of the state. On hearing in April 1840 that Wellington settlers had set up a Council of Colonists to govern the

settlement, Governor Hobson dispatched a military contingent to assert his authority. The sight of heavily armed soldiers marching along Lambton Quay had the desired effect; settlers quickly disbanded the council and pledged their loyalty to the Crown.[100] Volunteers or Reservists led by a brass band also held periodic parades under arms through city streets to publicise their presence and encourage others to enlist.[101] Other processions stressed imperial links. The marriage of the Prince and Princess of Wales in July 1863 was celebrated with a parade of 700 troops and Volunteers through Auckland's principal streets.[102] News of the Relief of Mafeking (Boer War) in May 1900 ignited patriotic parades in all the cities and bigger towns. Watching the Wellington event was George Dutton:

> We had a great afternoon here yesterday. Military Bands playing, 500 or 600 Volunteers marching about as many thousands of citizens following, some in all the available vehicles but most of them on foot, flags flying, trumpets blowing, speechmaking etc and everybody in a state of pleasurable excitement.[103]

In Christchurch the 'wildest enthusiasm prevailed'. As well as the parade of Volunteers, a trades' procession was organised. Effigies of Paul Kruger, the Boer leader, were carried through the streets to Cathedral Square, where leading citizens delivered speeches to a sizeable crowd. In the evening bonfires were lit in Hagley Park and the Kruger effigies cremated.[104]

Imperial fervour peaked during Royal visits to the colony. The first visit was by the Duke of Edinburgh in 1869, followed by a 1901 tour by the Duke and Duchess of York. A pivotal feature each time was a civic procession of the Royal party and leading local dignitaries through principal streets to allow townspeople to see them. A photograph taken just before the Duke of Edinburgh's arrival in Auckland on 10 May shows a crowd at the foot of Queens Wharf. Railings strung along the footpath contain the throng, while some boys straddle a shed roof to get a better view. Bridging the wharf entrance is a tripartite floral arch with the slogan 'Peace and Plenty' emblazoned on it – a reference to the colony's natural abundance? A lithograph based on the photograph imagines the scene moments later, with the

OPPOSITE TOP In 1869 Albert, the Duke of Edinburgh, made the first Royal visit to New Zealand. He was greeted by a crowd of well-wishers when he docked at Queen's Wharf in Auckland. Sir George Grey Special Collections, Auckland Libraries, 4-420

OPPOSITE BOTTOM A Māori arch was built on Wellington's Molesworth Street for the Duke and Duchess of York's procession through the city in 1901. The message of welcome on the arch is given life by the party of men, women and children waiting to greet the royal couple. Alexander Turnbull Library, PA1-q-1003-08

Many provinces commemorated 50th anniversaries with jubilee processions in the main centres. A massive crowd of 100,000 people turned out for Dunedin's jubilee in 1898, double the city's population. This is the procession making its way through the Octagon. Toitū Otago Settlers Museum, 64_44

Duke's carriage setting off up Queen Street, the crowd cheering with hats upraised as the Royal party passes. The crowd is denser and livelier than in the previous image, and the removal of the railings presents the throng as uncontained and spontaneous. Also absent are the boys on the shed. The built environment became a protagonist in Royal visits. Streets were cleaned up, and dressed with floral arches, flags and bunting to promote a celebratory mood. Unsightly structures were removed from view, including, for the 1869 tour, Auckland's Māori market.[105]

Sometimes there was intense debate over procession routes. Before the Duke and Duchess of York's visit to Wellington, a business deputation met with Premier Richard Seddon to discuss the arrival procession route. Governor Ranfurly had declared it would leave Queens Wharf, go up Cuba Street, down Ingestre (now Vivian) Street, into Willis Street, and along Lambton Quay to Government House. However, Manners Street retailers felt miffed the procession would miss their street, arguing it 'was as much in the eyes of the general public as Cuba-Street'. Cuba Street promoters said their street was superior because it was 'perfectly straight', whereas Manners Street was crooked (it followed the former shoreline) and 'did no credit to the city'. Seddon declared the dispute unbecoming; the Royal party was not a circus parade. The Governor could have chosen the shortest route to Government House, but had agreed to a longer one because it would allow more people to see the Heir-Apparent. 'The procession could not go through every street,' said the Premier. 'It would be chaotic,' chipped in a businessman. Another participant suggested the party travel up Cuba Street to Ingestre Street and then double back to Manners Street. 'You can't take them up Cuba-street and then turn back,' blasted Seddon. He also rejected the option of going up Taranaki Street, along Vivian Street and then into Cuba Street on the grounds it went past foundries, backyards and humble dwellings. Eventually, a compromise was reached whereby the arrival route would go up Cuba Street and the following day's procession for the ceremonial laying of the town hall's foundation stone would go along Manners Street.[106]

The meeting bordered on farce but it underlined the importance Seddon and others placed on the built environment to convey a favourable first impression of the capital city to the Royal party. The axial-like Cuba Street, flanked by handsome and modern two- to four-storey masonry buildings, was deemed best suited to fulfil this purpose. Conversely, meandering Manners Street and its many wooden two-storey buildings failed to show Wellington's best side. To this degree the built environment was a gauge of the city's cultural worth; there was nervousness that if the Royal party went up one street and not another, New Zealand's 'Empire City' would not measure up.[107] This anxiety had its roots in the centre (Britain) and colony (New Zealand) paradigm discussed in Chapter One, where the centre saw the colony as wild and uncivilised. As we saw in Chapter Two, the building of cities in the image of the centre was meant dispel this image, but the fear remained that the centre (personified here by the Duke and Duchess) could still find the colony wanting. We would now see this defensiveness as cultural cringe, less about the centre evaluating the colony and more the colony evaluating itself.

A month later, on 18 June, the procession took place. Numerous triumphal arches – including two Māori, one Chinese – and other decorations created a festive atmosphere.[108] Cuba Street was decked out in ferns, nīkau fronds and other greenery, making it 'a veritable garden'. Despite the overcast skies, the crowd was jubilant. According to a reporter, the procession advanced 'amid a wave of enthusiasm such as Wellington, generally undemonstrative, has seldom seen'.

Nelson celebrated its 50th jubilee in 1892 with a week-long series of events, including a procession through the city centre. In this watercolor an impressive crowd lines Trafalgar Street, which sports celebratory flags. Edwin Harris, Nelson Provincial Museum, AC817

The Duke and Duchess smiled frequently, winning the gratitude of the crowd. There was no way of knowing what the couple thought of it all, but the reporter found surrogate-centre opinion in the guise of two British government officials he met in Cuba Street. They had been on the Melbourne and Sydney leg of the tour and told him Wellington was putting on a 'fine show' by comparison: 'During the conversation the cheers greeting the passage of the Royal party along Lower Cuba-street could be heard rolling in growing volume. "That's good cheering," observed one of the officials, "and compares well with Australian cheers."' The verdict would have been both a relief and fillip for Wellingtonians.[109]

Another occasion for civic pomp was the consecration of new buildings and other improvements. The order of these (and other) processions mirrored local power relations and social hierarchies, with the most important groups or individuals coming last. For instance, the 1858 procession through Christchurch streets for the laying of the Canterbury Provincial Council Buildings' foundation stone (Chapter Two) was ordered as follows: Police, Banner of New Zealand, Merton's Brass Band, Justices of the Peace, Banner of the Province, the Bishop of Christchurch and other clergy, the Architects, Provincial Council Officials, Provincial Council Members, the Executive Council and lastly the Superintendent. In surveying the list, the *Lyttelton Times* asked why there was no place for a local

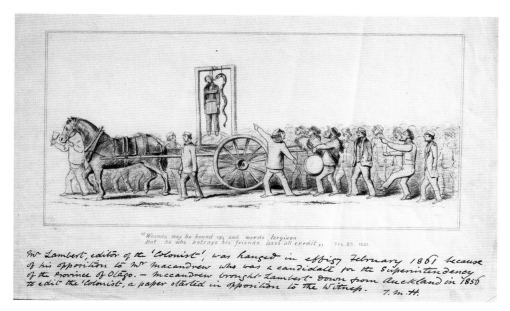

"Wounds may be bound up, and words forgiven
But he who betrays his friends loses all credit,, Feb. 23. 1861.

Mr Lambert, editor of the 'Colonist', was hanged in effigy February 1861 because of his opposition to Mr Macandrew who was a candidate for the Superintendency of the Province of Otago. – Macandrew brought Lambert down from Auckland in 1856 to edit the 'Colonist', a paper started in opposition to the Witness.
J. M. H.

Early protest marches often included effigies of hated figures. In 1861 a hanged effigy of William Lambert, editor of the *Otago Colonist*, was paraded through the streets of Dunedin. Lambert supported the removal from office of Superintendent James Macandrew, who had installed him as editor of the paper. The hanged snake signified betrayal. James Brown, Hocken Collections, Uare Taoka o Hākena, University of Otago Library, 7,331

Supreme Court judge, or Members of Parliament, or the Sheriff, or Customs and Post Office staff, or any other 'officer of the General Government'? Why 'are they to be cut out from seeing and being seen'?[110] The reason for the omissions was that the procession was to be a parochial statement. The building represented the emerging power of the province rather than the colony – hence the Canterbury banner followed the New Zealand one. Having central government officials in the procession would dilute the message.

Some processions were more democratic. In her study of Otago's jubilee procession through Dunedin's George and Princes streets in 1898, Alison Clarke identified the event had three main sections: societies, business and trade unions; historical groups; and dignitaries and the military. Organisers used the procession to promote an egalitarian ethos. While dignitaries like the Governor Lord Ranfurly, Premier Seddon and Minister of Lands John McKenzie brought up the rear, owners, foremen and workers marched together.[111] Some 2,500 people and eight bands were in the parade, which was watched by a crowd of about 100,000 – twice Dunedin's population. The largest contingent comprised 800 Friendly Society members, who presented tableaux of pastoral and other scenes on horse-drawn floats.[112] Some manufacturers created working models of their businesses on floats: metal workers fashioned ploughs and wheelwrights made wheels; bakers and confectioners made and handed out goods to appreciative onlookers.[113] As the first people of the province, Māori led the historical section. They were dressed in traditional costume and were cheered by the crowd. As Clarke notes, their role was to preface Pākehā settlement: 'they appeared as representative of their historical forebears rather than as currently active citizens'.[114] The biggest applause was reserved for the 500 to 600 early settlers, both men and women, who marched according to their date of arrival.[115] Clarke writes that aim of the procession organisers was 'to foster a united collective memory about the foundation and historical development of the province'.[116] But as she points out, this meant papering over some cracks. Sectarianism had long been a social divide in the province. The organisers tried to exclude religion from the procession to present the required united front, but Dunedin's Catholic Bishop Verdon and three of his priests joined the procession of their own accord, effectively subverting the Presbyterian claim to precedence in the province. Also missing from the procession were representatives of Otago's small but significant Chinese community, presumably because official hostility to their presence in the colony made it acceptable to leave them out.[117]

Associational processions, by contrast, were often annual events, and included the likes of Friendly Society and Sunday School parades. Among the largest of the type were Labour Day parades. These began on 28 October 1890, when thousands of working people and their supporters marched through the chief cities to celebrate the fiftieth anniversary of the eight-hour working day. The events strengthened the collective social identities of unionists, and their success led to annual processions to city parks for family-orientated picnics and sports events. Men, women and children marched behind brass bands, trade tableaux, flying banners and other emblems, and prizes were awarded for the best floats and athletes.[118] In 1899, Labour Day became a public holiday and the parades swelled. The 1905 Auckland procession was the largest seen in the city, taking over half an hour to progress up Queen Street.[119] By the 1920s, however, enthusiasm had waned and they were discontinued.

The purpose of protest marches was for a crowd to promote and gain public support for a grievance or cause. The first protest marches often included effigy burning, so combining protest with theatre. In 1843, a large crowd of Aucklanders marked the end of Willoughby Shortland's detested reign as Acting Governor with a large party and bonfire. After repeated cheering for the new Governor, Robert FitzRoy, 'three groans – most awful!' were proposed for Shortland, whose effigy was carried through the crowd and thrown on the fire.[120] FitzRoy's popularity was short-lived. His perceived bias toward Māori rather than settlers' interests

In 1911 members of the Labourers' Union went on strike after the Auckland Drainage Board contracted work out. The striking workers gathered in the street outside the Socialist Party hall. Sir George Grey Special Collections, Auckland Libraries, AWNS-19111102-9-1

soon alienated the settler community, and when he was recalled in 1845 his effigy was paraded through Wellington streets by three Māori and about 50 followers, and burned on a bonfire.[121] But if government officials and war enemies like Paul Kruger were targets for effigy burning, so too were people who were thought disloyal to local interests. A sketch shows the editor of the *Otago Colonist*, William Lambert, being hung in effigy alongside a snake (a symbol of betrayal) and paraded by a crowd through Dunedin streets on 23 February 1861 (see page 245). The marchers were protesting Lambert's support for the removal of James Macandrew, the Superintendent of Otago Province, over a financial scandal. Macandrew had brought Lambert down from Auckland in 1856 to edit the *Colonist*, so the protesters saw his stance as a betrayal.[122] Macandrew was subsequently forced to step down but, as shown in Chapter Two, was re-elected to the role in a landslide in 1867.

Most protest marches in the colonial period concerned labour grievances. Perhaps the first was a procession from the town to the port in January 1843 of striking Nelson labourers pressing their claim that the New Zealand Company honour its pledge to provide them with guaranteed work and decent rations. Under orders from London to reduce costs, the Company's representative Arthur

Wakefield declined to honour the promise, but he did provide some work building roads and allowed subsistence cultivations.[123] That governing authorities would provide work in times of shortage became a widespread expectation in colonial society. The seasonal and casual structure of much wage work, like harvesting or shearing, meant agricultural labourers often moved to cities during winter for work.

During economic slumps, rising unemployment led to calls for public work schemes. For instance, a downturn in the winter of 1877 left many hundreds of Christchurch workers unemployed. In early August, a crowd of between 300 and 400 of them rallied at Market Place (Victoria Square) and then marched along Colombo Street to the Customs House in Hereford Street with the aim of getting the Collector of Customs to petition the government to provide them with work and food. The official told a delegation from the group that only the Christchurch mayor could deal with the issue; the mayor subsequently arrived and pledged to spend £1,000 on council work schemes. The crowd left jubilant.[124] Similarly, in 1886 – in the midst of the 1880s Long Depression – 500 unemployed Aucklanders rallied at the Harbour Board offices and then marched to the city's Telegraph Office to send the following telegram to government: '750 unemployed, many of them on the verge of starvation. Want immediate relief and wait for an answer.' The procession then paraded through the city's main streets to publicise their plight. Premier Sir Robert Stout subsequently promised to consult the Minister for Public Works to see what could be done.[125]

In the same week of the Christchurch protest, about 1,500 of Dunedin's trade workers formed a torchlight procession through city streets to protest the government importation of railway rolling stock when building them locally would generate work.[126] Beginning at the Central Fire Station in High Street, and watched by thousands, the procession was led by the Caledonian Brass Band. Behind the band was a contingent of foundry men carrying a banner bearing the words 'Encourage local industry'. Fitters and smiths with sledgehammers and a model anvil followed. The boilermakers had a wagon with an operating boiler for heating rivets, the 'bright sparks flying at every blow of the hammer producing a capital effect'.[127] Other trades included patternmakers and millwrights, carpenters, bricklayers, labourers, bootmakers, curriers and tanners, with tailors and supporters bringing up the rear. Further banners carried slogans like 'Advance New Zealand! United we stand, divided we fall'. The procession comprised only men, but women were numerous among the throng of onlookers. The use of fire gave the procession a primeval quality. As one observer wrote:

> The lurid glare of the torches, combined with the brighter hues of the coloured fires, which lit up the whole place, and rendered every outline distinct, the

shrill shriek of the fife, the rumbling of the drums, waving of flags and banners produced a most animated yet earnest scene, such has never been witnessed before in Dunedin.[128]

The procession carried down George Street, turned into Frederick Street, along Great King Street, back up Hanover Street to George Street, and along to Guthrie and Larnach's Arcade in southern Princes Street. The arcade was part of a timber-processing and furniture factory and the only building in the city capable of holding the 3,000-strong crowd. For two hours the mixed-sex gathering heard speeches and resolutions calling on the government to promote the manufacture of railway rolling stock in New Zealand.[129] (This was realised a few years later.)[130]

If the purpose or statement of the procession and rally was to protest deficient government support for heavy industry, it was equally a powerful expression of solidarity among the city's building and manufacturing workers. Richard Dennis has noted that labour marches allow workers to lay claim to city centres both as symbolic acts of occupation and to advertise their cause. At the same time, these public performances often dramatise the workers' lack of power because they 'seldom persuade onlookers that they share a common cause, that their protests involve universal claims'.[131] The truth of this was highlighted by an 1879 *Star* editorial that condemned Cantabrians' indifference to the marching of unemployed in their midst.[132] On the other hand, the Dunedin demonstration showed how some labour grievances were able to engage a wider audience. The procession was a trades' event but it was supported by capital and the urban elite; Guthrie and Larnach provided the venue for the rally and Mayor Richard Leary chaired it. In this instance, labour and capital came together to foster economic growth in the city. The crowd of onlookers cheered them on.

Crowd or mob?

Occasionally, labour and capital came to blows, and no more so than during the 1913 Great Strike. The causes, actions and legacies of the strike have been well covered by labour historians, so only the barest details need concern us here.[133] The strike began on 18 October when Wellington shipwrights struck after their employers rejected a claim for improved conditions. Two days later, watersiders held a mass meeting to canvas the shipwrights' grievance. While this was being held, the employers put other men to work in their place and then refused to reinstate those who had been at the meeting on the grounds they were on strike; the watersiders counter-claimed the employers had locked them out. On 24 October, the strikers broke through wharf barriers and convinced the strikebreakers to stop work. Negotiations between the union and employers to settle the dispute collapsed and within days it had spread to other port cities.[134]

Laymen, mostly farmers and rural workers, were enlisted as special constables during the 1913 Great Strike. Called 'Massey's Cossacks' by unionists, the constables patrolled the streets on horseback with batons at the ready. These constables are swinging around the end of Wellington's Tasman Street, next to the Mount Cook Police Station. Alexander Turnbull Library, 1/2-049059-G

From the first days of the dispute Wellington's Post Office Square became a rallying point for unionists and their supporters. On 26 October they held a meeting there, before marching to the Basin Reserve (a city sports ground), where they broke down the gates and held another meeting. These gatherings and the watersiders' takeover of the wharves led the Commissioner of Police, John Cullen, to enrol laymen as special constables to help him maintain civil order. Many of them were farmers and their workers, fearful the dispute would curtail exports. Most of the 'specials' brought their horses with them; unionists soon dubbed them 'Massey's Cossacks' – after the Prime Minister. Historians have argued that their arrival in town, principally Auckland, Wellington and Christchurch, exacerbated an existing urban–rural societal divide. As Erik Olssen has written, 'there was no love lost between urban – especially unionizing urban – New Zealand and rural small-farm New Zealand. This had become one of the greatest tensions within New Zealand society, and the events of 1913 profoundly intensified that estrangement.'[135] But if the Great Strike pitted town against country, it also created a social-class divide among townspeople: working people broadly supported the

A crowd of working men, and the occasional woman, are listening to a speaker at a rally in Wellington's Post Office Square during the 1913 Great Strike. The square was opposite the wharves, where the strike began, and become a meeting place for unionists and their supporters. Alexander Turnbull Library, 1/2-048787

unionists and the middle classes favoured the employers. In Wellington about 500 local men enrolled as foot specials.[136]

Two Wellington children personified this fissure in city life. Marjorie Lees was the elder of two children of a prominent lawyer, and lived in a large house in salubrious Bolton Street; George Davies was one of five children of a solo mother, and lived in a small cottage in Myrtle Crescent in the 'slum' of Mount Cook. Marjorie's father, responding to Cullen's call for order, enrolled as a special constable. As she explained, he thought the 'waterside workers were less than dust. It was absolutely wicked for them to strike. They were damaging the country. I mean they had no case at all as far as he was concerned.'[137] On 29 October, the first specials arrived from the country and spent the night at warehouse near the railway station. In the morning hundreds of strikers attacked them, forcing the group to relocate to Alexandra Barracks on Mount Cook, not far from George's place. After being issued with batons, the contingent marched into town and soon clashed with strikers at Post Office Square. The melee spread to surrounding streets, and when two specials sheltered in Whitcombe & Tombs bookstore unionists smashed its windows. Some historians argue the specials charged the crowd in retribution for the earlier attack. Another explanation given by the army's Colonel Edward Heard was that the specials were a newly arrived contingent whom the police had inadvisably escorted past the strikers at Post Office Square, who turned on them.[138] Marjorie firmly believed it was the unionists who attacked the specials before rioting.[139] Her father came home 'in a frightful state and said this is the French Revolution all over again and you must be sent away, and so we were sent away into the country.'[140] When the perceived threat proved hollow, she was allowed to return home. She then helped her mother serve tea at the Star Boating Club to the specials patrolling the wharves, one of whom was Bernard Freyberg (later a war hero). Marjorie got an adolescent crush on him: 'I thought he was the most handsome and glorious man I'd ever seen.'[141] As for the strikers and their supporters, she considered them evil, recalling tales spread among her social class of strikers' wives emptying chamber pots over the specials 'and various things like that'.[142]

Meanwhile, George's mother had warned him to stay away from the strike. On 3 November, a crowd gathered at the intersection of Arthur, Taranaki and Buckle streets, and George and a few mates went to have a look. No other city space better represented the sharp demarcation between the strikers and their supporters on the one hand and the employers and forces of order on the other. Buckle Street was lined with the Garrison Hall and other military buildings. The Alexandra Barracks were located close by. Designed in a Classical Revival style and built of masonry, these edifices were unmistakable emblems of state power. On the other side of Taranaki Street, the thoroughfare continued as Arthur Street. It featured two-storey wooden shops and cottages of various sizes, and was a working-class stronghold. For several days, groups of working people had protested the state's role in the dispute and its deployment of special constables by occupying the end of Arthur Street.

The photographer Sydney Smith captured the scene in two photographs. The first shows a crowd of mainly men and boys blockading the entrance to Arthur Street. The second is taken from behind the crowd, looking across to Buckle Street. A military picket patrols the entrance to the street, beyond which soldiers and specials congregate along its length.[143]

Each day, as the specials left the Barracks for the port and later returned, they ran a gauntlet of abuse from the Arthur Street crowd. According to the (conservative) *Dominion* newspaper: 'A certain class of women have made themselves especially prominent in hurling insults at the mounted special constables, taunting and deriding them, and many of the men in the crowd have seconded their efforts with more violent measures in the form of stone-throwing.'[144] By the time George arrived at around seven o'clock on the evening of 3 November, the crowd had swelled to about 1,000 – men and women, boys and girls – most of whom, like George, had come out of curiosity. A noisy element within the crowd shouted abuse at the specials sheltering in the drill hall, and then began hurling stones and bottles into Buckle Street. Cullen directed two mounted constables to move the crowd back from the military picket, but two young women refused to budge and caught hold of the horses' bridles, encouraging the crowd to move forward again. Cullen then ordered a fire hose be directed on the crowd to disperse it, but it quickly reassembled when the hose was turned off. At this point a stone was lobbed from the crowd and hit Sergeant-Major Thompson on the head. He was seriously hurt and carted off to hospital. Soon after, two troops of mounted specials (comprising between 30 and 40 men) entered Buckle Street and charged the crowd, one heading down Taranaki Street and another along Arthur Street.[145]

George watched events unfold: 'Every so often the farmers would line up in Buckle Street, all abreast on their horses, and at a given signal they'd tear along Arthur Street like mad cavalries scattering all the strikers.' They would then regroup in Cuba Street and tear back again. The strikers 'provided themselves with a plentiful array of road metal and they used to let fly at these fellas'. He observed one chap banging the (macadam) street with a fence post, and George asked him what he was doing. The man said he was 'trying to get some rocks out to throw at these jokers'.

> Well, I said, I'll give you a hand. I'd taken sides straight away without knowing what it was all about. So I started bumping up these things and all of a sudden he sung out 'here they come' and I leapt over somebody's fence and then stood up to have a look, but unfortunately some fella from the other side had let fly at a striker; he'd missed him but he didn't miss me. I got a stone right on top of my head and I had to have three stitches in it.[146]

George had a week off school and received a hiding from his mother that he never forgot. He was not the only casualty of the day. During the melee, shots were fired and a worker and a boy received superficial bullet wounds in nearby Webb Street. *Dominion* journalist Pat Lawlor witnessed shooting from both sides in the darkness, but his editor censored his report to make out the gunfire came from the crowd only. Lawlor later wrote: 'the wonder was that nobody was killed'.[147] Things quietened down after Major Hume, clearly unarmed, went over to the crowd and convinced them to end the fracas.[148]

Throughout the melee the crowd had targeted the specials and not the regular police or the soldiers of the artillery regiment on the Buckle Street picket, the latter group having to stand passively between the crowd and specials and sometimes copping a special-directed missile. The crowd saw the latter group

These 1913 strike supporters are standing at the intersection of Taranaki and Arthur streets, directly across the road from the military complex centered on Buckle Street. It was a good spot from which to heckle the special constables, as they moved between their base at Alexandra Barracks and the port. Alexander Turnbull Library, 1/2-048788-G

as non-partisan and just doing their job, but viewed the specials as partisan and doing the bidding of an 'enemy' government. Colonel Heard recognised the point. 'It is a curious fact … that the rioters generally left the regular police alone and they openly said, "Leave the blue police alone, go for the specials."'[149] The crowd's respect for Hume as an independent agent was no doubt pivotal in his success in bringing the melee to a close.

The following day the *Dominion* reported the crowd as a 'mob' and the clash as a 'riot'. The language was situated in Le Bonian theory and the premise that in the crowd individuals surrender to a group mind that gives rise to senseless violence. Every time the specials had charged the mob, it scattered, only to collect again 'and resume its aggressiveness'. Conversely, the mounted specials had shown 'great forbearance' under the circumstances, a stance the newspaper attributed to the presence of women and children in the crowd. Their chivalrous behaviour had meant 'the rough element escaped a good deal of punishment they richly deserved'. It was intolerable that men who were attempting to uphold the law

Buckle Street in Wellington was populated with military buildings and overlooked by the forbidding Mt Cook Prison, all symbols of state power that gained a new significance during the 1913 Great Strike. The special constables were housed in the Alexandra Barracks close by. Soldiers patrolled the entrance to Buckle Street, preventing strike supporters from going any further. Alexander Turnbull Library, 1/2-049061-G

should have to endure such abuse while the perpetrators escaped punishment. Next time the Riot Act should be read, thundered the newspaper.[150]

The labour-aligned *Truth* gave a different perspective. It claimed the mounted specials had been drinking in a nearby hotel since the morning and were drunk when they charged the crowd:

> They seemed to entirely lose their heads, and forget, entirely, that the people in front of them were their fellow countrymen, women and children. The lust of blood was in their eyes, while, with madly careering horses and batons swinging, they cleared the roadway and footpath. Cries of rage, surprise and terror came from the crowd.[151]

Far from being gallant, they had mounted footpaths and bludgeoned people indiscriminately: 'Men, women and children were knocked down.' An old man too feeble to get out of the way was targeted and cut down by a baton. The bruised and bleeding were carried into houses for safety. One woman stood in her doorway, frozen by terror. The barbarity and brutality of the charge enraged the crowd and resulted in the barrage of missiles and some shots being fired at the Defence buildings. In return, the specials fired into the crowd. It was not the crowd that caused the riot but the 'mob of horsemen', asserted *Truth*.[152]

The divergent version of events was constructed to serve each paper's readerships: the establishment paper blamed the crowd; the labour paper blamed the horsemen. Fault lay on both sides. Clearly there was an element in the crowd who was intent on provoking the authorities. As the more measured *Evening Post* noted, the people who had been assembling at Arthur Street for the last few days 'were mostly of the class well known to the police and included a large number of women. Their language was most abusive, and there can be no doubt that a great deal of it arose not from sympathy with the strikers, but from the habitual enmity exhibited by these people to the forces of the law.'[153] The secretary of the Strike Committee of the Wellington Waterside Workers' Union, George Farland, was also eager to distance his members from this noisy element. He had visited the place and claimed those who were throwing missiles were intoxicated and not unionists. Well aware that any disorder would be blamed on the watersiders, he escorted them from the crowd with the help of his members.[154] Yet it is evident that by the time the charge took place, most of the crowd was made up of curious local residents like George Davies, who on hearing something was up at the intersection had come to have a look.

The subsequent turn of events can be attributed to Cullen's pugnacious character. According to one of the aforementioned young women, on arriving at the scene in his motorcar he crossed the street and poked the crowd back with his stick. He confronted her and told her to run away at once. She replied that she had as much right to be there as anyone else. He lifted his stick to hit her, but she reportedly shouted: 'Put down that stick. This is God's Own Country, and you have no right whatever to turn us off this earth.'[155] Probably unused to such assertiveness, least of all from a working-class woman, Cullen gave the order to clear the streets. A less bumptious leader would have sought to diffuse the situation by talking moderately with the crowd – as Major Hume later succeeded in doing – but Cullen clearly wanted to flex his power, and sent in the special constables with little regard for the consequences. When the resulting carnage became public, he emphatically denied his men had caused it despite all contrary evidence.[156] For Cullen, the end justified the means. Ignoring traditional civic rights of free assembly, he asserted: 'We cannot allow people to gather and block the thoroughfare, doing such damage as has been done. The roadway will have to be kept clear at all costs. Crowds are not going to take procession of the streets.'[157] Cullen's actions in ordering the charge served only to increase city workers' antagonism toward the specials. The next day, crowds attacked the nearby Royal Tiger Hotel (the specials' drinking hole) and McParland's Bakery (where specials bought bread), breaking windows and causing other wilful damage.[158] Unionists and sympathisers further vented their anger on 5 November by attacking a contingent of specials escorting horses destined for the New Zealand Cup meeting in Christchurch. The specials responded by again charging the crowd – the so-called 'Featherston Street riot'. During the fracas, the specials wrested control of the wharves from the strikers.[159] It was the beginning of the end of the Great Strike.

The Arthur Street and subsequent melees highlight how the street fighting was as much about the control of urban space in working-class Mount Cook and Te Aro as it was about the industrial dispute. Central-city workers had come to see the specials as an occupying force (a reviled 'Other') that needed to be pushed back to the middle-class suburbs and farming districts from where they had come. They were determined to reclaim *their* streets as their own. Such open 'warfare' between different social groups seeking control of New Zealand's city space was not seen again until the 1981 Springbok Tour.[160]

Cullen clearly saw the Arthur Street crowd as a Le Bonian-type mob. But the crowd is better understood using social identity theory. Rather than being an amorphous mass in which social identity was subsumed, the crowd comprised many groups of working people with multiple social identities: a small but noisy anti-authoritarian element; strikers; and a large collection of bystanders and the curious, as well as those passing through – one of those shot, Arthur Docherty, was in this last group.[161] The crowd was also delineated by gender and age, with notably large numbers of women and children. Apart from the noisy element, few in the crowd would have been expecting a violent confrontation with the authorities. When the charge came, the crowd became a single group or community that sought first to seek shelter from the rampage and then, as disbelief turned to anger, attack the column that was attacking them. George exemplified this process, arriving at the spot as a neutral onlooker but taking sides against the specials during the charge. In other words, people within the crowd were not objects being blindly manipulated by others, but subjects who collectively determined to resist the state-sanctioned force being used against them. In doing this, they clearly distinguished between regular forces of state policing (the army and police) and irregular ones (the specials). It was this sense of human agency – the ability to direct and shape events – that made being in a crowd empowering for many.

The Great Strike highlighted how the social equilibrium of cities was finely balanced, and that events could quickly tip the scales and turn townspeople against each other. It showed cities as places of intensity, tension and flux, where the course of modernity was hammered out, usually peacefully but sometimes violently. In this way it confirmed that modernity was Janus-faced: for better and worse, it had both light and dark sides. If the events of the strike exposed the darker side of city life, the gradual restoration of social equilibrium following its end shed new light.

Conclusion

The experience of the crowd, the spectacle and fleeting fraternity of being amongst hundreds if not thousands of other people in city streets, was a defining attribute of colonial city life. These were often representational spaces: of imagination, carnival and resistance. They fell into two main types: social and processional. Many social crowds embraced all townspeople: men, women and children. These included the Saturday night crowd made up of people from all walks of life who flocked into city centres to mingle, shop and promenade, and the crowd which gathered on general election night to watch voting results being beamed on large screens. These occasions enabled participants to feel part of imagined local and national communities. Other crowds were delineated by class, gender and ethnicity. 'Doing the block' was a performance that upheld the social identities of the white, urban middle class; participants faced social censure if they infringed dress and behavioural conventions. Also central to the promenade was body display, with both men and women free to gaze and return each other's looks. If such crowds highlighted a pleasurable side to city life, other crowds exposed a macabre side, no more so than at public executions.

As the nocturnal march of Dunedin tradesmen showed, processional crowds enabled groups to represent themselves in public space and bolster their individual and collective social identities. For military and civic processions, the main purpose was to uphold the authority of power elites or commemorate an important imperial or civic event, such as a Royal visit. On such occasions the processional order reflected urban social hierarchies, with those deemed the most important coming towards the end. The built environment also became a protagonist in processions, with routes wending their way through the best streets or past buildings of cultural importance.

Meanwhile, protest marches enabled participants to publicise and seek support for a grievance. In parading William Lambert's effigy through Dunedin's streets, marchers probably hoped he would refute his opposition to Macandrew – to no avail. Conversely, protest marches of the unemployed through Christchurch and Auckland streets eventuated in government pledges to find them work. Protest marches or rallies were rarely violent; the Great Strike of 1913 was a notable exception. Here, antagonism between urban working people and rural special constables generated waves of violence in city streets. An important flashpoint was at Wellington's Arthur Street, where a crowd was run down by mounted specials. The action unified a socially divergent crowd against the specials, highlighting how crowds enhance human agency by providing people with the power to shape events. This was particularly true of women. For the New Women who defied middle-class prescriptions to be inconspicuous in city space, the crowd provided the means to challenge and reframe the social identities of their class and make public space more gender inclusive. In standing up for the rights of free assembly at Arthur Street against state efforts to curtail it, two working-class women showed considerable courage and triggered events that led to the specials' charge. For these people and many others, the crowd provided a modern, dynamic and empowering edge that enhanced the appeal of city life.

Chapter Six

Street People

During the early 2010s, shared spaces were introduced into Auckland's CBD. These were streets on which there was no delineation between the footpath and carriageway and where pedestrians had the right of way. Fort and Elliot streets were early examples. In explaining the initiative in 2012, Auckland Council urban planner Ludo Campbell-Reid stated, 'We want to shift the balance of power from a city designed for private vehicles to a city designed for people.' In this, he said, Auckland was following the lead of cities like London, Copenhagen and New York, where shared spaces had increased the vitality of streets. 'What attracts people [to an area] is people … the joy and theatre of public life.' He reported that public feedback about the development had been overwhelmingly positive and further shared spaces were in the pipeline.[1] About the same time, Wellington introduced a shared space in lower Cuba Street, and shared spaces were included in the rebuild of Christchurch following the 2011 earthquake.[2]

While Campbell-Reid credited the shared-space initiative to new overseas developments, the concept was actually a return to a state that had existed in New Zealand's cities before. The photograph on page 108 shows Dunedin's Princes Street was a shared space in the 1860s, with people travelling along its middle. Similarly, a photograph of Christchurch's Colombo Street in the 1910s shows pedestrians sharing the carriageway with cyclists and trams. In colonial cities pedestrians had the right of way and all street traffic was required to travel at walking pace; streets were as much social spaces as they were thoroughfares. Here people congregated, gossiped, protested, brawled, preached, shopped, worked, celebrated or watched the world go by. The street was indeed a theatre for public life.

OPPOSITE In recent times cities have converted some streets to shared spaces, where traffic and pedestrians share the carriageway. The premise is that in slowing traffic it will make streets safer and more pleasant. It has been represented as a new initiative, but as this detail from a photograph of central Christchurch in the 1910s shows, it was a return to how cities were in the past. Here pedestrians, cyclists and trams share the space along Colombo Street. Frederick George Radcliffe, Alexander Turnbull Library, 1/2-006524-G

Urban historians have shown that until the twentieth century, city streets had three main purposes: circulation, trade and sociability. Streets provided for the passage of people and goods through the city; street traders plied wares and fresh produce from carts and baskets there; and people gathered on streets to fraternise and entertain.[3] The street was a pluralistic and democratic space in which all townspeople had equal rights of access and use. As Peter Andersson has written, 'the public nature of the street was defined by the fact that everybody had access to it, making it a symbol of democratic spirit'.[4] However, at the turn of the twentieth century, the street underwent a fundamental social transformation. In North America, Europe and Australia, city authorities and urban reformers began to argue there was too much life on streets: that street life was anarchic and chaotic, and the production of modern city space required street activities to be functionally separated to impose a sense of spatial order and make streets easier to traverse. The new civic project was to 'civilise' or improve streets. Some people formerly accepted as integral to city life – street vendors, street prostitutes, street performers – were recast as obstacles or nuisances and subjected to strict regulation. Further encouraging the change was new technology like the electric tram and motorcar. These modern marvels competed for space with, and posed a hazard to, other street users, providing support for the idea of separating people and vehicular traffic. This process of spatial rationalisation diminished the diversity and sociability of street life.[5] In the words of one historian, it led to 'the effective "death" of the street as an area of social interaction'; in the words of another, it 'deliberately neutralised the street as the fundamental democratic forum'.[6] In sum, between 1880 and 1920, the city street moved from being a pluralistic space, encompassing many functions and activities, to one that privileged traffic.

This chapter considers how these modernising forces impacted on New Zealand cities. It focuses on a number of social groups who became targets of reformers' zeal. These include both those who did and those who did not make their living on streets: hawkers, coffee-stall operators, street prostitutes, larrikins, street orators and general pedestrians.[7] Like their overseas counterparts, local urban authorities and reformers were to assert that the production of modern city space required these groups to be regulated, or even banished from streets. Yet as we will see, all these groups resisted being brought into line, and they fought for their right to have continued access to the street. Employing Lefebvrian theory,

OPPOSITE Hawkers needed to be licensed to trade on city streets. To gain one they had to pass an annual good character test and pay a license fee to the local municipality. In August 1910 Aucklander Thomas Hennessy applied to renew his hawkers' license in the city, but the town clerk turned him down because he was deemed morally unfit to hold one. Auckland Council Archives, ACC 285 Item 186

Application for a Hawker's License.

To the Town Clerk, Auckland.

I *Thomas Hennessy*

residing in *Auckland* do hereby request that a Hawker's

License may be granted to me within the precincts of the City of

Auckland.

Dated **22 August** 1910

DECLINED.

SEP. 22. 1910

H.W.W. Town Clerk.

Thomas Hennessy Applicant.

We Certify that this Applicant is of good character.

Name *W Bell*   Address *Hayden St*

J. B. Dickson J P   *Auckland*

In the case of this License being granted to me I undertake not

to hawk in Queen Street, Karangahape Road, or Symond Street.

Thomas Hennessy Applicant.

Colonial streets were the site of trade as much as traffic. A familiar site was the 'rabbit man', with his crop of freshly killed rabbits strung up by their hind legs on the back of a cart. These men are inspecting his wares on an Auckland street in 1903. Sir George Grey Special Collections, Auckland Libraries, NZG-19030711-114-1

it was an argument between representations of space (of plans and conceptualisations) and representational spaces (of struggle and resistance). The resulting spatial practices were to highlight this tension.

Hawkers

In reminiscing in old age about his 1880s boyhood, Charles Arnold recalled the hawkers or street vendors who used to ply his North Dunedin neighbourhood.

> Bad boys of these times were warned they would be given to the sweep, and when he came around the corner with all his brushes in a bag over his shoulder and calling 'Swee-eep!', all the urchins made for the their gates like rabbits into a burrow. Speaking of rabbits, there was the rabbit man with their hind legs threaded in pairs on a bar across the cart. 'Rabbits, eight pence a pair!' There was Mr Old from across King street with his cry, 'All hot!' at supper time, with tasty hot rolls pushed around the street in a hand cart like

These boy hawkers are selling fresh produce in Dunedin's Princes Street in 1863. Doing business from the carts parked in the gutter, the boys would have been on their feet all day. Toitū Otago Settlers Museum, Mundy Album, Album 54, No 13

a warming oven. Then there was 'Black Joe' with his fish in a kerosene box on wheels.[8]

The booming cry of the hawker brought people out of their homes (or led scared children to seek refuge within them) and onto the street to buy goods and chat with neighbours. That such items as rabbits and hot rolls were regularly hawked in neighbourhoods might surprise twenty-first-century townspeople more attuned to street food being sold at night markets and festivals, but Arnold's image helps to underscore the reality that the colonial street was as much a channel for trade as it was for traffic.

Hawkers and street traders had been a feature of European urban life since medieval times. By the mid-1850s, Henry Mayhew calculated tens of thousands of Londoners – the likes of costermongers, piemen and flower sellers – made their living from the streets.[9] As an occupation, hawking attracted working people and others with limited means: it required only a small capital investment (a barrow or basket) and avoided the overhead costs (rents and rates) of shop-keepers. For new immigrants, hawking was often a short stepping stone to new lines of work; for others, it kept them from penury. The public generally welcomed hawkers because they could buy in small measure and prices were lower than in shops. Shopkeepers were less enthusiastic, resenting hawkers' competition, lack of overheads and incursion into the contiguous space outside their businesses.[10]

Almost as soon as streets were formed in New Zealand's nascent cities, there were reports of itinerant traders, Māori and settlers, using them to sell various wares and produce.[11] Hawkers feature in early photographs of city streets. For instance, an 1863 image shows two fruit and vegetable barrows lodged in the gutter outside the Bank of New Zealand's gold office in Dunedin's Princes Street. Both are manned by boys of about twelve years of age. Similarly, an 1864 view of Auckland shows hawkers' barrows, plump with fruit, at the corner of Queen and Victoria Streets.[12] Licensing of hawkers was suggested as early as 1845, and in 1854 Auckland Provincial Council led the way by requiring hawkers to be of good character and to take out a licence at the rate of 30 shilling per annum.[13] This was aimed at keeping disreputable characters from the trade and mediating shopkeepers' concerns that hawkers avoided overheads. During the 1890s, Premier Richard Seddon sought to introduce a national licensing system under his Undesirable Hawkers' Prevention Bill. It included a provision that all hawkers had to be British subjects or naturalised citizens. This, he said, was to 'check the influx of Assyrians [Lebanese] and other aliens' into the country.[14] Tom Brooking explains that this was among a number of racial-purity initiatives aimed at maintaining a white New Zealand, of which the 1896 Asiatic Restriction Act was the most infamous – it placed a £100 poll tax on Chinese immigrants. To Parliament's credit, the Hawkers' Bill was defeated in 1901.[15] Lebanese continued to settle in the colony, particularly in Dunedin, where many made a living hawking in and about the city.[16]

Hawkers maintained their trade with few complaints into the early twentieth century. This all changed in December 1907 when five Auckland fruiterers petitioned the Auckland City Council to restrict the number of hawkers along Queen Street. Hawkers were meant to keep moving under bylaws, but many stood outside the petitioners' 'shop doors for long periods bawling out their wares to our great annoyance'. In reporting the issue, the city's Traffic Inspector told city councillors that: 'The general public patronised hawking most extensively, and would object to the barrows being done away with.'[17] The Auckland Trades and

OPPOSITE In 1909 the Auckland city council tried, but failed, to ban hawking in the central city. This *Observer* cartoon satirised the outcome. National Library, Papers Past, *Observer*, 16 Oct 1909, p.12

The Observer

Saturday, October 16, 1909.

The City Council : *Aye there, you hawker, clear out of the road with that barrow, or we'll bust you to smithereens !*

The Hawker : *Seems to me you're in a bit of a mess.   Who's on top now ?*

LOOK BEFORE YOU LEAP.
Our City Fathers Come to Grief Over a Coster's Barrow.

Shoppers, mostly women, are clustered around a flower stall on the corner of Queen and Victoria streets in Auckland around 1916. A large dog is taking in the scene. Sir George Grey Special Collections, Auckland Libraries, 7-A13261

Labour Council said hawkers provided a valuable public service in supplying cheap and good-quality fish and fruit to the city's workers and ought to be supported.[18] In early 1909, the council compromised by banning hawking along Queen Street and creating 20 balloted, fixed produce stalls on side streets.[19] The measure failed to placate the shopkeepers. In August, the 90-strong Auckland Fruiterers' Protective Association called for the municipality to either abolish the stands or increase licensing fees to make it harder for hawkers to operate, as the present situation was ruining the retail trade.[20]

The following month the council adopted a resolution to close all but four central-city hawking stalls. Several fruit hawkers responded by returning to Queen Street to sell their produce. One told a reporter they had taken legal advice and were satisfied the council could not stop them from plying their trade so long as they kept moving. This proved correct and the council was forced to back down.[21] The reversal was pilloried in a two-framed *Observer* cartoon. In the first frame, a scrawny hawker (representing tradition and working people) stands with his overloaded barrow on the street as a billowing tractor carrying the mayor and councillors (representing modernity and shopkeepers' interests) bears

By 1925, when this fruit stand was photographed on Auckland's Wyndham Street, hawkers were becoming a less common sight in the city. Increases in license fees and the closure of stalls to improve traffic flows made hawking uneconomic and the trade petered out the following decade. Henry Winkelmann, Sir George Grey Special Collections, Auckland Libraries, 1-W625, (detail)

down on him. The hawker is warned to make way or face obliteration. The second frame shows the tractor upturned and its passengers in disarray after learning the council had no power to displace hawkers. The same paper ridiculed councillors' lack of backbone on the issue. Too many were unprepared to criticise hawkers for fear of being cast as an enemy of the working man. But, the paper went on:

> the rights and wrongs of the working man have nothing to do with the case. The question is whether we are to permit our leading thoroughfares to be made hideous by the raucous howl of the hawker, or whether these gentry are to be relegated to positions where they can ply their lawful calling without being unduly obtrusive.[22]

The solution lay in the establishment of a municipal market where hawkers could be centralised in one place, the newspaper concluded.

In Wellington, public debate over hawking took on a racial bent. In 1908, Wellington City Council responded to calls to curb hawker activity by installing

It is possible to make out three street traders' stands in this 1910s view along Wellington's Customhouse Quay. A fruit barrow is beside the turning motorcar; a news stand is sited outside the building, and further down the street another trader's barrow can be seen. The building is the city's busy Chief Post Office, so these would have been sought after stands. Sydney Charles Smith, Alexander Turnbull Library, 1/1-019843-G

fixed stands (as stalls were called in Wellington) in the central city and banning them from main streets. Some saw this a victory for the Chinese storekeepers who dominated the city's fruit and vegetable trade.[23] For instance, a press cartoon titled 'The Yellow Evil' depicts a Chinese greengrocer watching a council official boot away a hawker from his doorstep. The shopkeeper laughs and declares, 'me sellie fluit at any plice now'.[24] The cartoon played to hackneyed stereotypes of 'shifty' Chinese, but also exposed anxieties about white hegemony. Shopkeepers carried higher social status than hawkers in society. That whites were negotiating streets to trade while Chinese merchants owned shops subverted notions of European superiority, furthering white hostility toward Chinese and generating sympathy for hawkers.[25] *Truth* argued that hawkers should be encouraged, 'particularly as they bring fruit within the reach of all, and counteract the influence of the Chinamen'.[26] Such prejudice was by no means universal. Several Wellington women told a journalist that the quality and quantity of street produce often failed to meet the hawkers' promises and so they preferred dealing with the Chinese. 'They state that the yellow peril is not nearly so annoying as the white peril.'[27]

Hawking was a popular occupation for people from ethnic minorities. This Chinese man was photographed in 1903 as he trudged around Auckland with his baskets full of vegetables. Sir George Grey Special Collections, Auckland Libraries, NZG-19030912-743-1

In 1913, the race question took a different turn. By now the hawking community was becoming more ethnically diverse. Whereas race had once united hawkers against Chinese storekeepers, it now became a cause of internal strife, with white hawkers opposing the entry of non-whites into the trade. In May, the *Evening Post* reported that of the 25 licensed hawkers in the city, eleven were Indian, seven were European, and the rest were from Greece and elsewhere. The Indian hawkers had arrived in Wellington earlier in the year and their growing presence in streets led to an accusation the council was favouring foreigners over 'Britons'. The city's Chief Inspector vehemently denied this, stating the ballot for stands was fair and witnessed by journalists.[28]

The issue was not confined to Wellington. In October, Auckland's white hawkers complained to the city council about the number of licences being issued to 'Hindoos' (Fijian Indians) and called for them to be removed from the central city. Responding to the complaint, the city's Traffic Inspector reported that Indians held 19 of the 53 hawking licences in the city and whites held the rest.[29] By early 1914, the matter had escalated. The inspector told the council there was 'considerable discontent among the other Street Traders concerning the new arrivals from Fiji cutting them out of a living'.[30] The council was sympathetic. It introduced an unofficial policy whereby Indians were declined hawking licenses without reason. After lawyers acting for the affected Indian traders threatened to take the matter to the Supreme Court, the council identified twelve new stands suitable for Indian hawkers in suburban Newton and Freeman's Bay.[31] The inspector admitted the new policy 'will require careful handling, at the same time Blacks are gradually taking the place of the white men on the streets, in fact they are starving them out'.[32] In placing the Indian stands in less populous city-edge areas and reserving the busier central-city stands for whites, the council could follow the letter of the law while practising structural racism.

At the heart of the matter was patch protection. White hawkers saw the Indian hawkers as unwanted competition and used the issue of race to try to exclude them from the trade – echoing Māori experience in the 1870s. In pursuit of this goal, they relied on the popularity of racial purity discourse to gain public sympathy. However, the Indians were British subjects, so unlike the Chinese could not be openly discriminated against. In Wellington, the council resisted efforts to move against the Indians, and during the 1920s this group came to dominate the city's fruit hawking trade.[33] Conversely, the Auckland policy of informal discrimination was still in place in 1930.[34] The whole issue highlighted two further points: that hawking was often an important line of work for new immigrants from ethnic minorities; and, that despite the populist white New Zealand rhetoric, colonial cities were sites of cultural diversity. There can be no doubt that in the early twentieth century most townspeople were of European origin, but alongside them were growing enclaves of Chinese, Greek, Indian, Italian and Lebanese townspeople. In selling goods from shops, barrows and baskets, these communities provided a cosmopolitan edge to city life.[35]

The issue of race did not enter public debate over produce hawking in Christchurch or Dunedin. Instead, it traversed familiar ground. In 1912 a deputation of retail fruiterers went to the Christchurch City Council and repeated the refrain that because hawkers did not pay rents or rates, competition between them was unfair. Some councillors defended hawkers for providing good fruit at cheap prices, but in 1915 the council stopped issuing fruit-hawking licences on the basis the hawkers' fruit was 'neither cheaper nor better than that sold in shops'.[36] In Dunedin, fruit hawkers had already vanished from the city's streets. In September 1918, the city's Trades and Labour Council visited the mayor, James Clark, asking the council to rescind the bylaw preventing fruit hawking so 'fruit grown in Otago should be available for the people at as cheap a price as possible'. Clark replied there was no bylaw preventing fruit hawking and he suggested the group get someone to apply for a licence to test the council response.[37] In October, Edwin Ormrod from St Kilda applied for and was granted a licence. On hearing

This Chinese family ran a greengrocer shop in the early 1900s. Shops like these often sent hawkers, typically family members, out onto city streets to sell produce. Alexander Turnbull Library, 1/2-037502-G

this news, the Otago Retail Fruiterers Association sought a meeting with the council 'to place the true position' before it.[38] A week later, Ormrod wrote back to the Town Clerk saying that as the only licence-holder, and having learned the Fruiterers Association would work to defeat his enterprise, he had decided not to proceed. He had recently finished fighting the Germans and felt unable to take on the retail fruiterers, even though his venture 'would have been a good thing for the people'.[39]

Produce hawkers continued to work the streets of Wellington and Auckland into the 1930s, but they too came under sustained attack from critics. In January 1932, Wellington's fruiterers' association stepped up its campaign against hawking.[40] It found an ally in the local councillor and shopkeeper, W. Duncan, who put a motion to council to eliminate produce stands. As others had before him, he exploited anti-Asian sentiment: '[A] white fruit shopkeeper cannot hope to make his business pay if Asiatics are permitted to cut prices at their stands a few yards away.' The stands were an 'eyesore' whose time was up, he argued. His motion passed and the stands went.[41] In Auckland, the city council withstood similar lobbying. However, it noted that increases in licence fees and the closure of some stalls to improve traffic flows had seen their numbers dwindle from 25 in

1921 to only seven in 1934. With a sinking-lid policy in place, it was only a matter of time before there were none.[42]

The disappearance of produce hawkers' barrows from New Zealand city streets in the early twentieth century mirrors the experience of others from Melbourne to New York during this time. A New Zealand point of difference was that efficiency arguments about improving circulation by easing congestion did not loom as large. More important was the power of retailers to manipulate urban space. City authorities increasingly accepted their assertion that, as petty capitalists and ratepayers, they had a property right to the contiguous spaces beyond their shops. That this stance eroded traditional notions of the street as a democratic commercial space and ignored the reality that hawkers also paid rates through licensing fees failed to curb its influence. Initially, municipalities recognised hawkers provided a valuable service in making available fresh produce to working people and so resisted retailers' calls to ban them. In trying to meet shopkeepers' competition concerns, they circumscribed hawkers' movement in city space by introducing stands, confining them to side streets and compelling them to moderate their cries. As one newspaper said of Wellington in 1913, the days when hawkers 'looked no better than their distressing voices sounded' had gone.[43] Still, the containment and silencing of hawkers was not enough for the retailers. Having occupied its edge, the shopkeepers made a successful pitch for the whole street and eliminated their competition. Interestingly, in the overseas context the demise of hawking was often offset by the opening of produce markets, ensuring the public still had access to cheap produce.[44] Similar proposals for New Zealand cities were realised only with the creation of open-air markets in cities from the late 1970s.[45]

Coffee stalls

The coffee stall stood out from other street enterprises in being a nocturnal venture. It provided warming beverages and tasty snack food for late-goers and shift workers and a place to stop and chat with fellow midnight wayfarers. The coffee stall began as a barrow on which was placed a large board covered by an oilcloth and protected by an awning. On the board sat a large polished metal coffee urn that was heated by a charcoal burner. Cups and food like saveloys, meat pies, sandwiches, cakes and tarts covered the rest. A lamp broke the darkness and, alongside the fire, worked as a beacon.[46] By the early twentieth century, the coffee stall more often resembled a caravan, with a side that opened to reveal a counter behind which were a kitchen and the proprietor. Patrons gathered under an awning and stood or sat along the counter to consume their fare.

The coffee stall had become a fixture in London during the 1830s. In 1851, Henry Mayhew estimated there were upwards of 300 on the city's streets, mainly run by women. He split them into two types: those that opened at midnight catered to 'night walkers', 'fast gentlemen' and 'loose girls', while those that opened at three or four in the morning served 'working men'. The institution reached Australia in the 1850s and New Zealand in the 1860s.[47] By the 1880s, there were at least two or three in each of the main cities. They generally opened mid-evening and were closed by eight in the morning. Almost all were run and patronised by men; respectable women were home by midnight.[48]

Coffee stalls attracted a mixed crowd: 'homeless, shivering tatterdemalions rub shoulders with festive, dandified bucks and paunchy, bibulous old baldheads,' wrote one observer.[49] Another writer, drawn to a Christchurch stall by its lantern, wrote of:

> a collection of habitués who were simply delightful. The late eater is an unconscious humorist. He talks about anything and everything under the sun, and he talks with his mouth full of hot potato. There were three young men who had been to see 'Brewster's Millions,' one elderly philosopher who struggled valiantly with a meat pie, and a sleepy gent who was mostly feeding his whiskers.[50]

This writer was a coffee-stall enthusiast. Yet the stalls' existence in urban public space was contentious and, like the Māori market, occupied a liminal space. Some people saw them as offering a respectable service and some saw them as places of criminality. Critics considered their association with the night unsavoury, and there were business owners who argued coffee stalls obstructed their trade. In 1878, a Mr Hiorns complained to the Christchurch City Council about a coffee stall outside his Gloucester Street hotel. Despite the Town Clerk reporting there had never been any complaints about the stall and it did not obstruct traffic, the council ordered the stall owner to 'move on' so as to avoid being a nuisance to a ratepayer.[51] One affected customer protested to the local newspaper:

> Coffee stalls, Sir, and perapatetic [sic] institutions for the sale of trotters and such cheap delicacies to those whose business or pleasure might require them to be on the streets at night, are common enough in London and all large cities in England and the Colonies, and their establishment should be encouraged rather than regarded as a nuisance. Probably Christchurch is the only city in the world where such a thing as a coffee stall would be so regarded.[52]

Auckland City Council took a different approach. In 1880, the city's Police Inspector warned against granting an application for a coffee stall in Victoria Street East (stallholders had to pass good character tests) on the grounds that

THE COFFEE STAND—EARLY DAWN.

In the past cities closed down overnight, but as modern street lighting made them safer, more cities worked through the night. The nocturnal coffee stall originated in London during the 1830s to provide shift workers and midnight wayfarers with warming coffee and snack food. Coffee stalls arrived in Australasian cities during the 1850s. Early images of the fixture in New Zealand are elusive; this engraving depicts one in central Melbourne in 1863. Ebenezer and David Syme, State Library of Victoria, IAN24/12/63/13

those who patronised them were not well behaved or respectable. But councillors challenged the characterisation of stalls as disreputable, with two of them admitting they were regular patrons. Another thought coffee stalls 'were a real benefit as affording a counter-attraction to the public-houses' and to those 'obliged to labour at night'. The licence was granted.[53]

Nonetheless, police followed the line that coffee stalls were magnets for public disorder and illicit activity. There was some truth to this. Coffee-stall operators were periodically arrested for selling spirits, and altercations at or near stalls were not uncommon.[54] This included a dispute between the Mahurangi chief Te Hemara Tauhia and Auckland coffee-stall proprietor Thomas Brister in 1884. The

This 1922 view looking down Dunedin's Rattray Street, at its intersection with Princes Street, includes the thoroughfare's infamous coffee stall. Every evening dozens of men gathered beneath the soft glow of the gas streetlight to chat, sup coffee and eat the likes of saveloys or pies. Police argued the nocturnal fixture attracted semi-licit behaviour and worked hard to shut it down, but the city council believed it provided a valuable service and allowed it to remain. Dunedin City Archives, Photo 330/34

latter asserted that Te Hemara had paid only half the two-shilling charge for his meal; Te Hemara was adamant he had paid in full: a 'wordy warfare raged for some time' before Te Hemara's friends moved him on.[55] Police maintained coffee stalls attracted 'midnight prowlers' who befriended the unwary to rob them.[56] For instance, in 1906 Wellingtonians John Davey and William Kay were imprisoned for stealing £31 (the equivalent of about $5,000 in today's currency) from Wairarapa farm labourer Thomas Hanlon. Hanlon had found his way to Kay's coffee stall during his first night in the Big Smoke after he was locked out of his lodgings. Kay plied him with coffee laced with whisky and Hanlon spent freely, shouting his fellow patrons to the tune of £2. The next day, Kay invited Hanlon to his place for another drink, after which he and Davey stole his money. Hanlon, however, proved clear-headed enough to report his assailants to the police.[57]

It was the association with criminality that distinguished the Australasian coffee stall from those of Mayhew's London. The latter were under the policeman's eye, so few criminals frequented them. As Andrew Brown-May points out, the Melbourne coffee stalls in fact enhanced the police's surveillance power by providing a nightlight and valuable knowledge about local goings-on. Yet police continued to see them as a 'nocturnal pathology' and worked to remove them from the city's streets. From the eight or nine that had existed in Melbourne in the 1870s, only two survived the turn of the century.[58] New Zealand police saw coffee stalls the same way and succeeded in persuading municipalities to limit street-stall licences or/and reduce their hours.[59]

By 1910 Dunedin only had one coffee stall left, on the corner of Rattray and Princes streets. But this was one too many for the city's police. In early August, Police Inspector O'Brien wrote to the Town Clerk saying the presence of the institution in such a public space was a 'smudge on the fame of this fair City'. He said it was the rendezvous for loiterers and the semi-drunk, and that the behaviours enacted there were far from edifying. Shouting and yelling was common; some people urinated and expectorated on the footpath; and it was sometimes impossible to get through the crowd. He argued there was no need for the stall because the neighbourhood abounded with restaurants and tearooms that stayed open until after 11.30 p.m. O'Brien proposed using a bylaw prohibiting the obstruction of footpaths to close it down.[60]

The stall's proprietor, a Mr Docherty, vehemently denied the assertion that he catered to semi-drunkards and loiterers, saying that if this were the case then he would lose his best customers: 'the sober man who comes along regularly and likes to have his coffee and pie in peace'. He was sure any disreputable characters would soon move on if the police maintained a higher profile at his stall.[61] The council sent its Inspector of Nuisances (an official who enforced bylaws) to observe goings-on at the stall. On three different evenings he found no evidence of the scenes described by the police. Neither did he see or hear anything that would inconvenience the public. In fact, 'this institution seems to me to be catering for a very respectable section of the community viz: members of the Otago Daily Times Staff, Post and Telegraph men, Tramway men, Railway men, Wharf labourers, Cabmen & others whose duties are confined to night labour, about 50 men in all'.[62] The stall should therefore be allowed to stay.

O'Brien was undeterred. At the beginning of October, he wrote to the council concerning an alleged breach of the peace at the stall. According to a report by a Constable Sweeney, this occurred at 10.50 p.m. on 30 September. Sweeney had been on duty in Princes Street when he saw a number of young men by the coffee stall. They got into a fight and one of them was knocked to the ground. 'As I crossed the Street one of them said to the man that the other knocked down "I'll break your fucking jaw for that you fucking cunt".' When they saw Sweeney they all bolted down Rattray Street. The constable, who claimed obscene language was often heard at the stall, then approached Docherty to see if he knew where they were, but the stallholder replied that he hadn't seen or heard anything. Docherty's silence, Sweeney said, made it impossible for the police to identify the perpetrators.[63] O'Brien forwarded the constable's report to the council, along with a memo asserting such conduct would continue so long as the stall remained.[64] Again, the Inspector of Nuisances was sent to investigate. He spoke to Docherty, who said the disturbance took place not at his stall but in a lane behind the Bank of New Zealand; he also denied that Sweeney or any other policeman had spoken to him on the night in question. He further said that nothing exceptional had happened at his stall over the previous two months and expressed a wish that the police might be solicited to help keep it that way. The council inspector concluded the police had treated Docherty unfairly. 'Since my last report on this subject I have paid several visits to the above institution & have on each occasion found the same well conducted & orderly. I am at a loss in attempting to suggest a reason for the stand adopted by the police in this matter.'[65] The council considered the issue and concluded that action against the stallholder was both unnecessary and unjustified.[66]

If we take the council's view and accept that Docherty's coffee stall was a respectable enterprise, why did the police think otherwise and become so exercised about closing it down? It is quite likely there were occasional disturbances at or near the stall, but then why didn't O'Brien take up the stallholder's offer to work with him to maintain public order? One explanation lies in the way the meanings and functions of the night were changed by modernity. In the pre-modern city, people retreated indoors with the arrival of dusk, keeping themselves safe from the temporal and supernatural perils of the night. After dark, the city closed down. Those who went out without reason or carrying a light were seen by the night watchmen to be up to no good. These men were an authoritative presence in nocturnal urban space; their regular cries throughout the night reassured townspeople that 'all was well'.[67] The advent of gas street lighting in cities like London and Berlin from the 1820s – from the 1860s in New Zealand – modified townspeople's relationship with the night. As people found it possible to venture out without encountering danger, the idea it was full of menace became less believable. Artificial light and industrialisation also facilitated the growth of nightlife (restaurants, public houses, theatres) and night shift work (newspaper printing, freight forwarding, post and telegraph), making the city a site of continuous activity. The city itself no longer slept.[68]

These developments created a public debate about to whom the night belonged. Some continued to see the night as a closed-off time of retreat, while others wanted to open it up for life. As Joachim Schlör explains, the European street became a 'site of confrontation between the different social groups in the city, and between these groups on the one hand and the forces of order on the other. From the point of view of the custodians of the law there is always *trop de vie*, too much life on the street.'[69] Inspector O'Brien's actions can be located within this discourse. He wanted to curb nocturnal street life and restore the police ideal of a night-sleeping city. In representing Docherty's coffee stall as a place of public disorder and a moral pollutant, he was constructing a case for its removal. That he failed in this aim shows the very idea of a closed-down city had become an anachronism; it no longer suited the changed conditions of work and life in modern cities.[70] The survival of Dunedin's coffee stall was emblematic of this change.

Street prostitution

Another nocturnal trade that resisted reining in was street prostitution. While walking down Auckland's Queen Street in 1869, 'New Chum' noticed among the Saturday night crowd 'showily-dressed young women, some with pretty faces, which yet have that hard, bold look that tells of no true, sweet womanhood. These are "soiled doves."'[71] Two decades later, Revd G. B. Munro declared that prostitution in the city was rife: one could not 'walk from the top to the bottom of Queen-street on Saturday evening without meeting at least 50 young girls who are living a life of vice'. He then claimed the number of professional prostitutes in the city had skyrocketed from 75 in the mid-1880s to 400 now.[72] In 1895, the parliamentarian John Rigg maintained 'there was more prostitution in Wellington to-day than had ever been known in its history'.[73] At the same time, Revd Frank Isitt asserted there were 700 prostitutes working in Christchurch – a staggering 1.4 prostitutes per 100 residents.[74] Similarly, 'Paterfamilias' of Dunedin complained the spaces outside certain Princes Street hotels were 'constantly occupied by poor unfortunate girls, plying for hire from all and sundry'.[75] The clear message from these guardians of public morality was that prostitution was rampant and cities were entering a downward spiral of decadence.

British historian Elizabeth Wilson has characterised prostitution as the great social evil of the Victorian age. From the 1830s, British evangelicals labelled it a

OPPOSITE In 1879 William Smith of Haining Street in central Wellington wrote to local politician George Hunter, who was campaigning for re-election to the city council, about brothels in his street. He wanted Hunter to introduce a bylaw forcing brothel-keepers to hang a coloured lamp at their doors at night so patrons would know where to go. The respectable Mr Smith was bothered by men knocking on his door in the mistaken belief his house was a brothel. Wellington City Archives, AM002:1:5

To George Hunter, Esqr

1879
27-8-79

Sir – As i do not Care for asking
Questions from Amongst a crowd and
as i am living in a Street Where that
there is a great Number of prostitus
Women and are much annoied at
night by men Knocking at my door
through mistake Would you if re elected
try and bring in a Bill to Enable
Municipal Councils to pass a by law
Compelling these Women Keeping Brothels
and who are Known to the police to Keep
a Coloured lamp burning over there
doors from Sun set to Sun rise So
that respectable people would not
be desturbed during the night if
you Should please State So tonight
at the Adelaide Road and as
a man i will record my Vote
for you –

William Smith
Haining Street

i do not Want my name Called out
i am an Elector

moral miasma that spread depravity along city streets and polluted the unwary or weak; it was impossible to walk London streets without being physically and visually accosted by public women, they bemoaned.[76] The growth in street prostitution corresponded with London's rise as a metropolis. Rapid population growth fostered the sex trade, attracting ever more women who, through choice or necessity, became prostitutes to make a living. Their visibility in public space was enhanced by modern infrastructure like street lighting, heightening the magnetism and adventure of the nocturnal city for many men, but narrowing (middle-class) women's ability to negotiate the same space without being cast as a whore.[77] British moralists recognised they had no chance of eliminating prostitution, but through regulation they hoped to contain it. The Metropolitan Police Act 1839 forbade prostitutes from loitering in public spaces; the Contagious Diseases Act 1864 allowed police to submit suspected prostitutes to a genital examination and detain those who had venereal disease. Critics condemned the latter Act for creating a double standard of sexual morality whereby prostitutes were punished but not their male clients – a flaw that saw its repeal in 1886.[78] Another response was the creation of evangelical missions to 'rescue' prostitutes from the streets and 'reform' them in refuges. This strategy involved middle-class women going onto streets and into brothels to persuade 'fallen women' to leave their trade. Law courts could also place convicted prostitutes in refuges as an alternative to prison.[79]

New Zealand followed a similar path. Until the late nineteenth century, males far outnumbered females in colonial society, so there was some acceptance of prostitution as an inevitable consequence of demographic imbalance.[80] Moralists bristled, however, when it was revealed in the 1860s that some single women brought out to the colony to redress the disparity were working the streets.[81] As Charlotte Macdonald has shown, the matter came to a head in Christchurch in 1867. The point of contention was less the existence of the trade and more its blatant street presence.[82] In addressing a public meeting to debate the issue, the Dean of Christchurch, the Very Revd Henry Jacobs, declared the 'general impression' that:

> the great evil of prostitution – the great 'social evil' as it has commonly been called – was very largely on the increase in this place, both as regarded the numbers of abandoned women, and the boldness, openness, and defiance of the law and decency with which their iniquitous trade was carried on.[83]

The meeting called for central government to introduce measures to contain the trade and curb its offensive public display.[84] In 1869, the government moved in this direction. First, it amended the Vagrant Act 1866 so prostitutes could be charged with loitering and soliciting in public places.[85] The measure augmented the Act's existing provisions under which prostitutes could be charged with being an idle and disorderly person if they had no lawful means of support, and a rogue and vagabond if they engaged in obscene behaviour. Secondly, it passed the Contagious Diseases Act 1869. This was modelled on the British Act and became subject to the same public criticism. It was enacted only in the provinces of Canterbury and Auckland, and both revoked the measure in the mid-1880s, so police mainly relied on the Vagrant Act to control the problem.[86]

Generally, the police moved against prostitutes only when the public peace was disturbed.[87] In 1881, for example, six Wellington women came before the Magistrates Court charged with having no visible lawful means of support. The court heard they were often seen at the Thorndon Club (a brothel), where 'scenes of debauchery were of daily, if not hourly occurrence'. The women were said to be 'a source of great annoyance to the neighbourhood. They were addicted to looking out windows, and insulting ladies and coughing significantly to men as they passed by.' The judge accepted defence arguments that there was no proof the women had no means of support, but commented that while prostitution was not illegal, soliciting and riotous behaviour in public was. He delayed sentencing for a fortnight to see if the women's behaviour improved.[88]

As in Britain, New Zealand evangelicals formed rescue missions and refuges to save fallen women, and prostitutes who were convicted were often sent there to be reformed. The Salvation Army became a leading supplier of such services.[89] Not all 'soiled doves' were considered redeemable. In 1899, two sisters, Louie and Bella Steel, and Maggie Corbett, all aged 16 and 17, were convicted of being idle and disorderly persons. The girls worked in a brothel run by 'Chinaman' George Howe in Wellington's Haining Street. The court heard the sisters were orphans; Louie had previously spent time in a Salvation Army refuge; Howe lived off the girls' earnings; Louie and Maggie had been seen soliciting in the street; and Louie was incorrigible but Bella might be redeemed if separated from her sister. Bella was therefore offered a place in the Salvation Army refuge; the institution refused to take the other girls. The judge sentenced Louie and Maggie to three months in prison with the view to placing them in a state-run industrial school until they were 21. The two girls asked the judge if they could serve three months and not be sent to the school, known to be severe and grim. Their plea was dismissed.[90]

How far street prostitution was a real social problem in cities and how far it was imagined is uncertain. As Leif Jerram has noted in respect of nineteenth-century European cities, 'it is hard to tell from accounts whether one is dealing with a street full of hookers, or a street full of women out for a good time that an outraged bourgeois moralist is labelling as hookers'.[91] The Revd Munro might have vehemently believed he had seen 50 girls on the game in Queen Street, but the girls

The Door of Hope in Auckland was one of a number of charitable institutions dedicated to the reformation of prostitutes that opened in the late 19th century. Prostitutes were encouraged to leave the streets and live in the refuges, where they would be reformed into model citizens. This is the Door of Hope in 1900. The pram outside the gate is intriguing, perhaps suggesting some of the inmates had dependents. Sir George Grey Special Collections, Auckland Libraries, AWNS-19000921-3-3

he saw might simply have been enjoying the Saturday night crowd. Government occupational statistics did not categorise prostitution, so quantitative data on the trade is patchy and unsystematic.[92] Some insights can be garnered from court records – falling conviction rates for female vagrancy between 1872 and 1915 might signal a decline in prostitution – but the total number of people working in the trade across our period is elusive.[93] Still, qualitative evidence would suggest moralists exaggerated the social evil. For example, Pastor William Birch refuted Frank Isitt's claim of 700 prostitutes in Christchurch and said the true number was 129. Birch was in a good position to know. His evangelical Central Mission church ran the Avon Refuge and he was well acquainted with the seamier side of the city's life.[94] He conceded street prostitutes could be seen in the neighbourhood of George Street (off Manchester Street), 'but to say that every woman who goes to George-street for a jug of beer, or who walks through the street, or who is seen to stand and talk to anyone – that all these are prostitutes, is an invention that springs from the "father of lies" [the Devil]'.[95] Isitt, on the other hand, was a prominent prohibitionist who believed drinking and prostitution were invariably

LEFT Sister Laura Francis of the Door of Hope walked the streets of central Auckland at night in an attempt to 'rescue' prostitutes from a life of iniquity. Giving evidence before a royal commission into policing in 1898, Sister Francis claimed many prostitutes worked in factories during the day, angering both factory workers and their bosses. Sir George Grey Special Collections, Auckland Libraries, AWNS-19000921-3-1

RIGHT Like Sister Francis, Ada Wells was an active urban community worker. Living in Christchurch, she campaigned for the repeal of the Contagious Diseases Act 1869 and reform of prisons, local government and the charitable aid system. Alexander Turnbull Library, 1/2-C-016534-F

linked – some publicans owned brothels.[96] He probably overstated the number of prostitutes to generate public support for the prohibitionist cause.[97]

If moralists exaggerated the extent of the social evil of the sex trade, there were aspects of it that were undoubtedly disturbing – most notably the existence of juvenile prostitution. While juvenile prostitution was usually associated with girls, some newspaper and telegraph boys provided sexual services to men – Dunedin's Queen's Garden was one popular rendezvous. The difference was that if these liaisons were discovered and taken to court, it was typically the client rather than the child who faced charges.[98] In 1893, the female age of sexual consent was raised from 12 to 14, and then to 16 in 1896.[99] In the same year, Mary Davis (aged 14), Margaret Beat (14), Sarah Lucas (13) and Mary Boyd (11) all appeared in the Dunedin City Police Court charged with associating with prostitutes. Due to their age this was the only charge they could face, but the police declared them to be 'professional prostitutes'. Evidence was given of the girls tempting 'Chinamen' and soliciting in theatres; they did this in a daring and bold manner, and had no sense of right and wrong. 'They were not only going down themselves, but were drawing other young girls into the whirlpool.' Like Louie and Maggie in Wellington, the Dunedin girls were sent to an industrial school.[100]

The 1898 Royal Commission on the Police Force provided some insight into the extent of juvenile prostitution in Auckland.[101] One of its aims was to probe allegations that police were turning a blind eye to licensing breaches and were too familiar with prostitutes and bookmakers.[102] Among those firing the charges was Isitt, a prosecutor during the Auckland sitting. A specific complaint concerned under-age girls soliciting in the Devonport ferry waiting room and having sex with clients outside the Railway Wharf freezing works. Detective William Bailey opened the evidence from police. He admitted there were young girls aged 14 to 18 wearing short frocks (a code for a prostitute) on the streets at night, but he could not say if they were prostitutes, nor did he know of girls frequenting the ferry room or freezing works.[103] Another witness was cabbie Abraham Bowden. From his Queen Street stand he saw many prostitutes soliciting, some of whom were ten or eleven years of age. They picked up sailors and took them behind shops, or to the Market buildings or a green on Elliot Street for sex. If the girls saw the police, they vanished. He told Isitt, 'If you stood at my stand some nights your hair would drop off.'[104]

William Napier, former chairman of the Harbour Board, spoke next. He had frequently asked police to clear juvenile prostitutes from the ferry waiting room. Asked if he was certain they were there for immoral purposes, he replied: 'I do not know if they were there for immoral purposes, but from their appearance and language and other indications they appeared to be prostitutes, and they were with young men – with oyster-boys, and fishermen, and deck-hands: ladies would not go into the waiting room because of these circumstances.'[105] The chairman of the Auckland Freezing Company, Samuel Hanna, was also uncertain whether the girls he saw on city streets were prostitutes, but did acknowledge prostitutes and their clients frequented the reclamation area beside his freezing works. Asked by Isitt if any girls were involved, Hanna said no; the women were in their twenties and older.[106]

Someone with a more detailed knowledge of the scene than most was Sister Laura Francis of the Door of Hope Rescue in Cook Street. Francis was a street missionary who went onto the streets at night to reclaim fallen women. She believed there were between 12 and 20 child prostitutes working in the city, many living in brothels run by their parents. Francis told the commission about a mother who had sent a daughter out onto the streets from the age of nine; the girl was thrashed if she did not bring home sufficient money. Two other daughters and three other girls lived with this woman; all were prostitutes. The eldest daughter, aged 16, had recently finished a three-month prison term for public drunkenness and was now back on the street. The police had tried three times to have the girls taken from the mother, but each time she claimed she was kept by a man and so was not a prostitute under the law, meaning police were powerless to intervene.[107] The commission chairman Herbert Wardell then inquired if the city's prostitutes came from one social class. Francis explained the trade had two classes. The better class worked from 'respectable' brothels (often under the guise of boarding houses) and were not found on the street. The lower class worked the streets: 'to see them,' Sister Francis said, 'you would only say they were well-dressed girls, but I know their homes'.[108] She denied Wardell's proposition that the trade was a response to poverty, because many of the girls worked in factories during the day.[109] Francis's evidence received support from Mrs Charlotte Sparks, who managed the Salvation Army's Rescue Home in Grey Street (now Grey's Avenue). She said there were between 20 and 30 brothels in the city, and knew of child prostitutes as young as twelve who dared not go home without money. She thought the police were doing as much as they could under the circumstances.[110]

The commission evidence was extensively reported in the press.[111] Sister Francis's allegation that many juvenile prostitutes were factory girls generated a flurry of letters refuting the charge. The clothing manufacturer John Morran said it was as 'cruel as it is mischievous' because it contaminated a whole group by association. His own Lorne Street factory employed up to 150 girls and they struck him as highly principled. Workers in a Victoria Street clothing factory also took strong exception to Francis's statement, calling it a 'wanton and unwarranted misrepresentation'. Their letter continued:

> The workers in factories can be favourably compared with any other class of female workers in the city, who for the most part are honestly assisting their parents in the battle of life. Sister Francis; by making a statement like this, has thrown a stigma upon the character of every factory worker in the city, as it makes it appear to the public that in every factory there are prostitutes, which is a flagrant misrepresentation.

The workers called on Sister Francis to make reparation 'to rectify so gross an injustice'.[112]

We have seen how working-class women and prostitutes lived outside the separate spheres paradigm and occupied city space as public women. The factory girls' protest shows that many working-class girls and women resisted being identified with prostitutes in public space, and feared being typecast as or mistaken for a prostitute as much as their middle-class sisters did. The group saw themselves as above prostitutes in the colony's social order and were offended to have the taint of the sex trade ascribed to their own; in refuting the charge, the factory girls were defending their collective honour. In reply, Sister Francis said she regretted giving offence, but she stood by her comment that some prostitutes worked in factories.[113]

The commission's report concluded that police were not overly familiar with prostitutes and managed street prostitution the best they could within powers given to them.[114] While evidence presented to it confirmed juvenile prostitution existed in Auckland, the scale of the problem remained ambiguous. If Bowden believed many of the girls he saw on the streets at night were prostitutes, other witnesses could not say for sure. We can probably accept that Sister Francis's figure of a dozen or so juvenile prostitutes working in the city is correct. This is well short of the 50 whom Revd Munro supposedly encountered on Queen Street a few years earlier: these girls were more probably flamboyantly dressed factory workers. Yet it speaks volumes for the strength of the separate-spheres paradigm that moralists were quick to label any unchaperoned girl or woman in city public space at night as a prostitute. This certainly accounted for Isitt's 700 Christchurch figure but, as William Birch pointed out, it was an absurd calculation to make.

It is perhaps no coincidence that the 1890s debate over prostitution arose at the same time as women of all social classes were gaining greater access to city public space: as shoppers, factory and office workers (considered further in Chapter Eight), and participants in 'the crowd'. This growth in public women subverted the patriarchal and conservative precept that a respectable woman's place was in the home. We might surmise that in exaggerating the scale of the social evil on city streets and emphasising its further defiling links to drink, the moralists were seeking to circumscribe women's gains in the public sphere and lead them back to the sanctity of the private sphere. Their alarm over prostitution can therefore be seen as a veil that screened a deeper anxiety about the shaping of more gender-inclusive city spaces that eroded the traditional male dominance of public space. In any case, the moralists' fears of a *fin de siècle* fall into decadence proved unfounded. By the early 1900s, the issue had faded from public discourse, bar the odd salacious story in newspapers like *Truth*.[115] One historian has argued that by the 1910s prostitution was actually declining because the gender ratio had reached equilibrium and most men were finding sexual fulfilment in marital and/ or extra-marital relationships. By 1922, the police reportedly knew of only 104 professional prostitutes in the whole country.[116]

Larrikinism

Hawkers, coffee-stall operators and street prostitutes were all street traders, and strongly identified with the life of colonial city streets. But there were other groups who did not make their living on streets but were also widely regarded as street people. These included larrikins, vagrants and street orators. Like the street traders, these social groups had their origins in European city life and their emergence in New Zealand cities emphasised the mirroring of metropolitan life in the colonial context. Yet as the tradition of the street as a socially pluralistic space began to wane in the late nineteenth century, reformers recast these groups as public nuisances who obstructed the production of modern city space and so required greater regulation. Vagrants had been subject to restrictions since the 1860s. From the 1890s, city authorities also sought to better control larrikins, street performers and even pedestrians, spurring these groups to defend their customary rights to the street and creating new sites of resistance.

Larrikinism described children and adolescents who engaged in anti-social behaviour and was strongly identified with city life. Smaller local communities and towns were better able to keep children's behaviour in check through constant social surveillance, but such close policing was harder in cities. Larrikinism came to prominence during the last quarter of the nineteenth century.[117] One observer commented in 1883 that although everybody was speaking and writing about larrikins, the phenomenon was ill-defined. The writer then proceeded to fill the void, asserting that a larrikin was a male aged between and 12 and 21; lived in a town; liked to be on streets and about theatres; smoked; and fell into one of two main groups: the mischievous larrikin or the criminal larrikin.[118] (While it is true that most larrikins were boys, some girls also engaged in larrikin behaviour.) Another commentator noted how the larrikins underwent a nocturnal transmogrification.

> During the day he is a school-boy, errand boy, office-boy, factory-boy, or butcher-boy, and maintains this disguise with tolerable success until the shades of night have fallen. Beneath their friendly covert he goes in quest of his fellows. A boy is merely a boy until he meets another. Then he becomes a larrikin.[119]

That larrikins entered the street under the cover of darkness – with its cultural association with fear, danger and horror – increased their threat in the public mind.[120] But as the first writer observed, larrikin behaviour ranged from the merely mischievous to the deeply criminal. Most pursuits can be characterised as boisterous and harmless, such as playing street cricket, often accompanied by loud swearing and howling.[121] Knocking at doors, tampering with street fire alarms, and stone and egg throwing were also popular larks.[122] A more dangerous activity was placing obstructions on streets to cause collisions with traffic and unwary pedestrians.[123] Standing on street corners and/or harassing passers-by was perhaps the most characteristic larrikin behaviour. In 1876, a Wellingtonian declared that Willis Street larrikins 'have become so daring that it is dangerous for women to go out after dark. They even go so far as to call after gentlemen, and to address them in the most filthy language.' Shamefully, the ringleader was the son of a leading citizen.[124] In Dunedin, the *Otago Daily Times* said it was impossible for any respectable woman to go through the cricket oval without being insulted by hoodlums; the paper called for two or three constables to be spared from the vicinity of the Rattray Street coffee stall to sort them out.[125] In 1893, another Wellington resident pleaded something be done to stop a group of boys and girls, aged about 14, who gathered in Molesworth Street on Tuesday and Friday nights to smoke and hoot at respectable women heading to the opera.[126]

Criminal activity usually involved vandalising property or petty theft.[127] For instance, four boys appeared before the Auckland Police Court in 1889 charged with breaking into a shop and stealing jam, condensed milk and lollies. One boy was discharged, but the other three were fined 20 shillings and ordered to receive six strokes of the birch rod.[128] Occasionally, larrikins pursued physical violence. In 1882, a youth gang created fear on Christchurch streets by randomly attacking people at night. Victims included a woman who was savagely beaten when she went to the aid of a man being assaulted by the group.[129] By the early 1890s, the larrikin problem was worsening. In sentencing twelve boys for engaging in a stone, brick and mud battle that left Dunedin's Walker Street covered in rubbish, the judge commented on the growing tendency of New Zealand youth to fall into larrikinism.[130] The Commissioner of Police supported the view, asserting in 1892 that this was among the police's most pressing problems. He attributed its growth to a lack of legislation and bylaws for its suppression. It was difficult to get sufficient evidence to obtain a conviction for conduct like collecting on street corners or obstructing footpaths, so police were often powerless to move against it, he said.[131]

It can be argued that larrikin behaviours differed little from those of previous generations of colonial youth.[132] After all, we know that gangs of boys fought each other in 1840s Wellington, and that following the 1842 arrival of the 92 Parkhurst Boys (former juvenile inmates of England's Parkhurst Prison) Auckland experienced a spike in petty theft and lawless behaviour.[133] What did change between early and late colonial society was the cultural milieu. The rise of the middle-class nuclear family and separate spheres ideology in western societies led to the belief that childhood was a time of innocence and vulnerability; the parents' role was therefore to protect their progeny from defiling city influences until they were of age to manage them themselves.[134] This modern paradigm led to the creation of child-saving movements, such as the Society for the Protection of Women and Children (1893), to avert neglect and abuse and secure children's wellbeing. As Bronwyn Dalley points out, the flipside of the helpless child protected by parents from adult society was the potentially dangerous child living

THE LARRIKIN.

This 1895 sketch presents the hallmarks of the larrikin. The young man is standing idly about, slacked-lipped and smoking, with a slouched posture and insouciant look on his face. J. Stuart Allan, National Library of Australia, nla.pic-an3337493-s2

outside parental control: the juvenile delinquent.[135] 'Actions previously tolerated or accepted as youthful high spirits became redefined as delinquencies in most Western societies, and institutions established to protect children embodied a reformative, punitive function as well.'[136] In New Zealand this included refuges and industrial schools. In sum, children's behaviours were not necessarily worse than in the past, but changing middle-class views of childhood had made society less forgiving of children's more anti-social pursuits. Youth who continued with such behaviours were seen as troubled delinquents who needed saving from themselves.

The issue of larrikinism was not confined to New Zealand. Groups of boys gathering on streets and street corners to fraternise and loaf about were fixtures in many British cities.[137] The term actually originated in Melbourne in the 1860s when bands of young factory and street workers adopted it to express their social identity in city space.[138] But the proclivity of these groups to engage in anti-social behaviours meant that by the 1880s wider society had come to see larrikins as out-of-control adolescents who posed a risk to social stability.[139] As Martin Crotty has written, 'Larrikins, standing on street corners and abusing "respectable" members of society, offended middle-class sensibilities and at

Playgrounds appeared in town and cities from the 1910s, partly as a way of bringing children's play under adult supervision and control. These Auckland children are enjoying themselves at the Victoria Park playground in 1919. Henry Winkelmann, Sir George Grey Special Collections, Auckland Libraries, 1-W1657

the same time represented a threatening inversion of the correct social order.' Larrikins personified a middle-class fear that working-class interests and values were 'directly opposed to those of bourgeois society'. Their growth, says Crotty, was blamed on irreligious education and declining moral standards in Australian urban working-class communities.[140] Such anxieties did not loom as large in New Zealand larrikin discourse. Larrikinism was similarly rooted in urban working-class culture, but as the well-connected Willis Street ringleader showed, it had some crossover appeal to middle-class children too. In New Zealand, larrikinism was seen less as a symptom of latent class conflict and more a consequence of permissive parenting: too many parents were allowing their children to roam city streets unconstrained.

Such was the government's concern over the issue that in 1896 it introduced the Juvenile Depravity Suppression Bill into Parliament. Premier Seddon argued the measure was needed because some parents of city children were failing in their moral duty of care.[141] He had observed boys of 'tender years about our streets at nine, ten or eleven o'clock at night, congregating at the street-corners'.

While this began innocently enough, they soon joined the larrikin class. Through association with 'evil companions, along with the opportunities given by these late hours', many children of respectable but neglectful parents ended up before the judicial bench.[142] Despite larrikinism being largely a male problem, the proposed law focused on females. It gave police the power to apprehend girls under the age of 16 who were on city streets after ten o'clock at night if they believed them to be there for immoral purposes, and to take them home to their legal guardian. Repeat offenders could be committed to an industrial school. Police could also enter premises occupied by Chinese or prostitutes and remove all girls suspected of immorality. They could remove boys under age 17 from premises occupied by gamblers or prostitutes too.[143] In allowing boys to remain on streets, the measure appeared to target juvenile prostitution rather than larrikinism. Speaking for the influential Women's Christian Temperance Union (WCTU), Kate Sheppard proclaimed that unless the provision 'applies to boys as well as girls it will be pernicious'.[144] Dunedin MHR William Hutchison agreed, and said the large number of uncontrolled boys and girls on Auckland's streets at night was the strongest argument in the proposition's favour. His colleague, Robert Thompson, thought most members would have seen groups of young boys in city streets smoking cigarettes at all hours of the night, blocking footpaths and being a regular nuisance to other townspeople.[145]

For the Bill's supporters, the existence of children on city streets at night contravened the ideal of the nuclear family. While children could venture into the public sphere during the day – for school, work and play – the expectation was they would return to the purifying bosom of family life at night. As Hutchison noted: 'Children up to ten years of age living in all our towns should be under the shelter of the household roof after nightfall; and the parents and guardians of these children should be responsible that it was so, under a penalty.'[146] There was implicit acknowledgement that many working-class children had freer rein of public city space than other children. What particularly worried the reformers was the extent to which middle-class children from respectable families were being drawn into the larrikin sub-culture. Seddon blamed their parents for being too easy on them: 'If parents were more strict they would probably not require the State to interfere.'[147]

Despite the perceived crisis, the Bill failed to gain traction. Two parliamentarians suggested the number of boys and girls on city streets at night was exaggerated. Auckland MHR William Crother said he had lived in the city for 30 years and had not seen the scenes described.[148] Then there were the measure's severe powers. One commentator commended the Bill as an attempt to address an admitted evil but thought it was too great a threat to individual liberty to be palatable; the ills of the Contagious Diseases Act that unnecessarily humiliated girls would only be repeated.[149] Recognising the Bill was indeed a step too far, Seddon discharged it in October.[150] The *Press* applauded the move, placing it among its 'crank' legislation of the parliamentary session. 'It is not necessary to point out what an instrument of terror and oppression this Act might have become in the hands of muddle-headed or unscrupulous policemen, especially in dealing with children of the working classes.'[151]

If such legislation was the wrong way to get larrikins off streets, other measures proved more successful. These included the creation of organisations that provided adult supervision of children's activities and play. The rationale lay in the biblical axiom that 'the Devil makes work for idle hands': if boys and girls were occupied in moral-improving pursuits, there was less chance of them engaging in immoral ones. One organisation set up to afford 'a practical remedy for larrikinism' was the Wellington Boys' Institute, formed in 1892.[152] A building was soon erected, and classes offered in drawing, reading and arithmetic. A Bible Class was run on Sunday evenings and a Boys' Brigade with 120 members maintained. It outgrew its building within a year and so launched a public appeal for funds to expand.[153]

The early-twentieth-century growth of organised sports – football, cricket, basketball and tennis – as well as military drill in schools offered further avenues to keep larrikins off street corners.[154] From 1908, Boy Scouts and Girl Guides, with their focus on morally improving outdoor games, camping and survival skills, soon drew thousands of children to their ranks. After 1910, cinema-going became a further diversion from the street.[155] A new emphasis on the educational importance of play during the 1910s also saw the formation of municipal playgrounds featuring swings, roundabouts and seesaws. Playgrounds, playing fields and parks were important additions to cityscapes in that for the first time spaces within cities were purposely set aside for children's play.[156] With children better directed toward the straight and narrow, public anxiety about larrikins diminished. But this was not New Zealand's last moral panic over a city youth sub-culture. In the early 1950s, evidence of alleged immorality and delinquency among Hutt Valley teenagers created a similar furore, with blame once again pointing at lax parenting.[157]

A striking aspect of New Zealand colonial cities was the visibility of youth. In central-city neighbourhoods there were few other immediate places to play and socialise, so children and adolescents made the street and other city public spaces their own, a place where they could be with others their own age away from direct adult supervision. We saw in Chapter Five how children were also strongly represented in street crowds, even late-night ones; the twentieth-century conviction that children belonged in the suburbs and ought to be in bed by mid-evening was still to take root. Larrikinism illustrates how some city youth further exercised their social identities and agency in city space by shaping a street culture that was raucous and set them against their elders. The street corner became an emblematic site of youth resistance to the adult world.[158]

Street orators

With complaints of larrikinism becoming muted, those concerning other perceived nuisances like street orators became shrill. The main grievance was that they obstructed streets and created an irritating din. As early as 1895, a Wellington citizen declared it was time the police took steps to remove Saturday night 'temperance spouters and religious fanatics' from outside the Bank of New Zealand (Lambton Quay). Their oratory drew crowds that blocked footpaths and carriageways and prevented vehicles from passing safely.[159] By the early 1900s, street orators had joined street hawkers as targets for civic reform. As it had with the anti-street hawker campaign, one of those leading the charge was Auckland's *Observer* newspaper. In 1910 it proclaimed street orators to be a 'dangerous and intolerable nuisance'. Every Sunday evening between seven and eight o'clock Queen Street was handed over to 'screeching individuals':

> each one intent on ramming his own particular creed or opinion down the throat of the ignorant public. At one place the Salvation Army's particular champion is making the welkin ring with 'blood and fire' preaching; at another some self-constituted missionary is hold forth; in yet another the cold-water prophet is to heard propounding his peculiar doctrine; and besides these, all kinds of faddists, from Socialists to Shakers, make night hideous with their frenzied yells.

Although hawkers were regularly fined for crying their wares too loudly, seemingly nothing could be done 'to prevent any person from mounting a soap-box and firing off volleys of abuse and obscenity in the main street of the city'.[160] Shopkeepers further complained that street orators blocked shop fronts and made it difficult for them to hear their customers.[161] In December 1910, Christchurch City Council moved against the daily cacophony by passing a bylaw prohibiting meetings and busking in Cathedral Square without council permission.[162] The measure particularly affected the Salvation Army and Socialists, both of which held regular meetings in the space. In April 1911, the two groups tested the bylaw's legality by holding meetings without the required permit. The police took them to court, where the magistrate upheld the bylaw. Speaking after the verdict, the Socialist Frederick Cooke said his group was determined to insist on their right to free speech in the square and would continue to hold gatherings there, going to gaol if necessary.[163]

An Auckland street orator draws a crowd during the 1902 general election – he is probably the hatless man to the sign's right. Orators enlivened streets with their homilies or harangues on religion, politics and other vital matters of the moment. A skilled orator could attract large crowds that spilled across streets, getting them offside with reformers who saw them as a nuisance and wanted to keep streets clear for traffic. Sir George Grey Special Collections, Auckland Libraries, AWNS-19021204-1-4

The *Observer* applauded Christchurch's example and the judge's ruling and hoped Auckland would emulate the initiative. The issue came to a head in that city in late 1913, when Mayor Christopher Parr urged an end to public meetings in the main streets. Large crowds listening to numerous street orators blocked Quay and Queen streets beside the waterfront on Sunday afternoons; it was, he said, time for places like halls and parks to be set apart for holding such meetings.[164] This possibility led to a large deputation, representing the Prohibition League, WCTU, Good Templars, Peace Association, Ministers' Association and the Central Mission, to the council to protest the measure. W. Tuck of the Prohibition League conceded traffic should not be impeded; however, in the interests of informed debate and free speech street meetings must continue. Parks were unsuitable because they were away from where people gathered. Parr told the delegation an existing bylaw prohibited crowds from blocking traffic, although it had rarely been enforced. He was not against certain public places and streets being used for open-air meetings, but recent 'poisonous utterances' that 'were not conducive to the preservation of the King's peace' should be given 'short shrift' – a reference to the soapbox 'agitators' of the 1913 Great Strike. Henceforth, Queen and Quay streets would be kept clear, but a council committee would have the power to permit meetings in other streets.[165]

In this Auckland followed the permit system introduced in Christchurch, a gate-keeping measure Wellington and Dunedin municipalities also adopted. At the same time, Auckland introduced a licensing system for buskers.[166] Police already had the power to move buskers on if they were blocking streets, but this measure gave municipalities control over who could play. One commentator applauded the change: 'The new regulation will tend to the improvement and purification of street music, and Auckland deserves credit for its adoption of a modern and rational by-law.'[167]

The move to regulate the 'aural city' undermined the notion of the street as a democratic space where all and sundry were free to speak their mind – the Socialists certainly saw permits as a first step to excluding them entirely from Cathedral Square.[168] Implicit in the reform was the premise that that the hawker's call, orator's rant and the busker's ditty were anachronistic irritants in modern cities and so needed to be muffled or, better, silenced. The regulation of street orators was another victory in the civic project to civilise the streets and was indicative of growing middle-class power and control over city space. It was working people like hawkers, prostitutes and buskers who were most affected by the changes: a triumph of bourgeois over plebeian values. This was further underscored during the early twentieth century when the entry of motorised traffic continued the social transformation of the street.

The death of street life?

The arrival of electric trams, motorbikes and motorcars challenged the convention of streets as public space open to all people and activities as long as others were not endangered or annoyed. The motorcar's capacity for speed and manoeuvrability made it both inherently dangerous and a nuisance to other street users.[169] In the North American context, Peter Norton identifies three main, broadly chronological responses to the arrival of motorcars in city streets. The first was to compel motorists to conform to street custom by limiting speeds; the second was to make pedestrians take more responsibility for their own safety; and the third was to socially reconstruct the street as a motor thoroughfare and to confine pedestrians to crossings and footpaths.[170] The twentieth-century transition from pedestrian (or walking) to automotive cities necessitated the defeat of the first perspective and the triumph of the third.

Early on, pedestrians had the upper hand. As Norton explains, custom and Anglo-American legal tradition confirmed pedestrians' inalienable right to the street, which they could occupy, cross and, in the case of children, play on wherever they liked. Conversely, there was no inherent right of the motorcar to the street and pedestrians were quick to express indignation when motorists intruded on theirs.[171] When motorists and pedestrians were involved in accidents, the prevailing public view was the motorist was invariably at fault; the moral assumption was that a motorcar was not essential and there were few grounds for tolerating injury or death.[172] A dramatic rise in motoring accidents in city streets during the 1910s created fear among motorists that continuing bad publicity would lead authorities to restrict their movement in city space. To avoid such a fate, townspeople had to be convinced that city streets belonged to traffic and that motor vehicles were not a nuisance but a necessity.[173]

New Zealand followed a similar course. Wealthy enthusiasts began importing motor vehicles from 1898, and by the early 1900s motorcars were a familiar sight on city streets.[174] Initially municipalities reacted to motorised traffic by making it conform to existing city speed limits of about 8 to 10 miles per hour (13–16 kph) to protect pedestrians and not startle horses. Motorists who sped and/or hurt pedestrians usually faced unsympathetic judges. For instance, in 1904 Thomas Stone was charged with furiously riding a motorcycle down Dunedin's George Street. The prosecution alleged Stone was riding between 15 and 20 miles per hour – so fast 'that people were turning around to look at him' – before knocking down a boy standing on the street. The defence argued he was going only half

In 1907 Christchurch became the first place in New Zealand to get a dedicated traffic constable, who was stationed at the busy intersection between High, Hereford and Colombo streets. Pedestrians and motorists alike had to obey the constable's direction. This is the constable at work on a wet day in 1923. Robert Percy Moore, Alexander Turnbull Library, Pan-0463-F

that speed. The judge was unconvinced and fined Stone 50 shillings (equivalent to around $450 in today's currency) and court costs.[175] Of course, going fast was central to motoring's appeal. The motorcar followed the steam train and steam ship as the latest mechanical wonder that confirmed the modern age as one of speed. As Peter Conrad explains, 'Travellers addicted to motion wanted more than merely to reach their destination; they demanded the thrill of acceleration.'[176] Popular opinion initially pilloried this goal. In 1909, after the latest motoring death of a Christchurch pedestrian, the *Free Lance* launched an acerbic attack on the 'speed fiend' motorist. In an article titled 'Honk! Honk!! And Then the Inquest', the newspaper asked, 'Is there no law to determine just how fast the goggled maniac, who has succumbed to the speed craze, shall drive his machine through the thoroughfares of our towns to the terror of wayfarers?' Too often motorists raced through streets at 20 to 30mph as if 'the maximum speed of the car, and nothing short of it, were a matter of life or death to them'. The writer called on the police to 'arrest these reckless enemies of public safety'.[177]

The perception that motorists were becoming a law unto themselves saw the police increasingly drawn into traffic management. In 1907, the first full-time constable was assigned to point duty at Christchurch's bustling High, Hereford and Colombo street intersection. The initiative's success led other cities to follow suit.[178] But such measures did not stop motorists killing or injuring pedestrians. In 1913, for example, a car driven by George Hopkins in Auckland fatally struck Thomas Thorp, aged 19. The motorist had sounded his horn but too late for Thorp to get out of the way. During the coronial inquiry into the death, the judge, F. V. Frazer, commented that '[m]otorists ought to know – although some of them apparently did not – that they had no right to frighten a pedestrian off. The pedestrian had a perfect right to use the road. He had just as good a right as the motorist.'[179] Hopkins was found guilty of careless driving.

Yet only a few years later the convention that all users had equal rights to the street was being openly questioned. As in North America, transport reformers began arguing pedestrians were best removed from carriageways. They asserted that a modern and efficient transportation system demanded that competing activities should be assigned to lesser streets or new spaces altogether: hawkers to side streets or markets, for instance, or children to playgrounds. Such thinking was part of a wider discourse promoting the rationalisation of city space into specific functional zones.[180] More is said about this in the following chapter, but we can say for now that within this paradigm city streets were designated for vehicular traffic. Inspector Ellison of Wellington Police had first raised this prospect in 1904. In response to the introduction of electric trams in the city, he devised a traffic-management plan that necessitated removing people from their path. As he told the press:

> All street musicians, and particularly the German bands, were … an annoyance and a nuisance in a city like Wellington, and they should be by-lawed out of the tramway thoroughfares. No open-air meetings should be allowed either along or near the tramway route, and coffee-stalls, street vendors, and everything which tended to lead to a block of the streets should be prohibited.[181]

Ellison's call was far too radical for the time, but the conviction that people obstructed the efficient flow of city traffic gradually gained support. Ignoring the long history of the street as a social and trading space, the *Star* proclaimed in 1913 it would be 'no curtailment of the public liberty to keep streets free for traffic'.[182] As the number of motorists continued to grow (during the 1910s middle-class buyers entered the market), so did their power to claim the carriageway for traffic.[183] A motoring lobby, comprising civic officials, police and motoring clubs, emerged to pursue this goal.[184] It copied strategies of the American motor lobby, arguing that if pedestrians were removed from carriageways motorists could travel at higher speeds; speedier trips through city streets would increase business efficiency; and faster traffic would make pedestrians more alert to their own safety. In other words, sacrificing pedestrians' rights to the street was for their own good.[185] To advance their case, the lobby adopted the American term 'jaywalker' (a derogatory term used to describe pedestrians who crossed streets without regard to other traffic) and succeeded in making it part of popular parlance. For instance, Stuart Wilson of the Wellington Automobile Club argued that 'jaywalkers who foolishly allow themselves to be knocked down by moving vehicles should be liable to be summoned by a magistrate to explain their negligence'.[186] Other motorists agreed, with one asserting that if pedestrians and vehicle drivers were both summoned it would eliminate most road accidents.[187] With no lobby group to defend pedestrian rights, the debate shifted in motorists' favour. In 1919, the formerly hostile *Free Lance* conceded that motor vehicles had come to stay and pedestrians must adapt to modern conditions and 'keep to the footpaths as much as possible'.[188] In only a few years, the motor lobby had successfully replaced the speeding motorist with the jaywalking pedestrian as the public nuisance.

Thereafter, the transition of New Zealand cities from walking to automotive cities continued apace.[189] During the 1920s, the motoring lobby began calling for pedestrian crossings to be instituted in cities to discourage jaywalking.[190] In 1925, Wellington's Traffic Inspector suggested constables on point duty be given the power to direct pedestrians as well as motorists; pedestrians were blithely walking in front of motorcars that had been given the go-ahead from constables.[191] And motorists complained about pedestrians holding 'social gatherings' or loitering in the middle of streets.[192] In 1929, the first pedestrian crossings were introduced, but many people continued cross streets where and when they liked. It wasn't until after the Second World War that most pedestrians accepted the primacy of motor traffic on major city streets, if only as a matter of practical necessity to keep themselves safe. The motorcar's 'conquest' of the pedestrian was complete. As American historian Peter Baldwin comments, '[t]he change amounted to the monopolization of public space by a new form of transport technology, but also, more subtly, by a social class.'[193] While middle-class motorists continued to enjoy unfettered access to carriageways, the entry of working people and others unable to afford motorcars was circumscribed. Only with the mass ownership of automobiles in the late twentieth century was a degree of democracy restored.

As we have seen, the takeover of major streets by motor vehicles was only the latest in a long line of changes to detrimentally affect street life. With hawkers pushed off the main streets before disappearing altogether; with declining numbers of nocturnal coffee stalls; with fewer street prostitutes; with the suppression of larrikinism; with street orators muffled if not silenced; and with pedestrians prevented from lingering and socialising on carriageways, street life became less vibrant and diverse. While traffic engineers later held up central-city streets as exemplars of twentieth-century modernity – rational, ordered and efficient – these attributes also made them dull, insecure and uninviting places to be in. That early-twenty-first-century planners sought to bring back street life to central cities through measures like shared spaces were belated recognition that automotive cities deaden city life. Their idea of shifting the power balance in city space from vehicles to people may have seemed new, but it was a return to the colonial practice of the street as a theatre for public life.

Conclusion

The modernising forces that saw the 'death' of the street as a social and democratic space in overseas cities also blew through New Zealand. City authorities believed that street life was disordered and these spaces needed bringing into line. Within this paradigm, the likes of hawkers, street performers and pedestrians were viewed as obstacles that should be cleared from streets to make circulation through cities more efficient. Hawkers were the greatest casualties of this civic project. From crying their wares along main streets, they were removed to side streets, their calls silenced and then banished altogether. The free rein of street orators and buskers was also curbed, with only approved performers allowed to raise their voices. And whereas pedestrians had traditionally colonised the full expanse of the street, the arrival of motor vehicles saw them pushed out to its narrow edge. Although such measures brought about the desired functional specialisation of city space, it also exposed the reformers' inability to differentiate between disorder and diversity.[194] The mixing and mingling of multiple activities in colonial streets might have appeared chaotic but it gave these spaces a vital edge that the automotive city sought to extinguish.

The production of modern space also created sites of contestation and resistance. The advent of gas lighting allowed streets to remain open at night, and coffee carts became their controversial emblem. Midnight wayfarers and shift workers welcomed their warming fare and convivial sociability. The police saw them as a malady and pushed to close them down, failing in this aim because the notion of a night-sleeping city had passed. Similarly, morals campaigners might have hoped that in escalating the problem of street prostitution in cities they would encourage respectable women to stay at home, but their separate-spheres strategy clashed with the modern reality that middle-class women were taking to the streets with the same enthusiasm as their working-class sisters. Instrumental in the whole process was the exercise of power. Despite widespread popular support for the hawkers' services, retailers proved to have greater influence with city authorities and used it to close them down. When transport reformers challenged pedestrians' spatial rights to the full breadth of the street, pedestrians were forced to surrender their claim because they lacked the collective muscle to defeat the motoring lobby. Sometimes the less powerful were able to maintain their agency in city space. Prostitutes survived moralists' attempts to drive them from streets, probably because reformers overstated the social evil and regulators recognised a legislative response was futile. Larrikins were also able to colonise city streets with near impunity, to the chagrin of the respectable classes and authorities. Attempts to manage their movements proved ineffectual until diversions that appealed to the group were put in place.

There can be no doubt that street life diminished dramatically over our period, but urban historians' notion that modernity caused its death has perhaps been exaggerated. In the New Zealand context, the coffee cart survived as the pie cart and remained a nocturnal beacon for night owls in all cities; late shopping night (usually Fridays) regularly drew thousands of suburbanites to town, creating an atmosphere evocative of the Saturday night crowd; every now and then, throngs occupied streets to celebrate an event or protest a grievance; and street orators periodically mounted soapboxes and cut through the din of traffic. Such activities offered little in the way of theatre compared with what had existed before, but they were enough to keep streets alive.

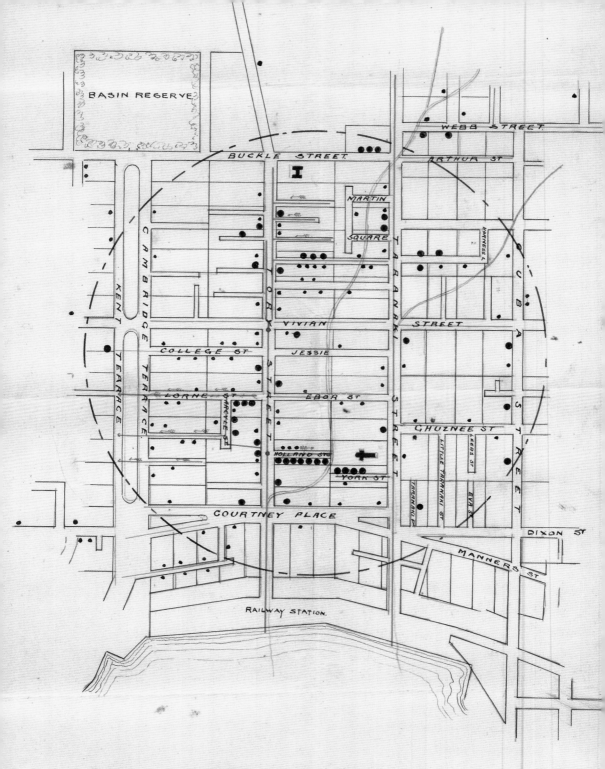

— TYPHOID AREA. —

● DENOTES TYPHOID CASES 1892.
  "   "   "   1890-1.

Chapter Seven

Creating Healthy Cities

In a letter to his parents in October 1863, Auckland labourer Samuel Harris revealed his wife Elizabeth had spent the previous ten weeks in bed with a fever at their Freeman's Bay cottage and that she had feared she might die. He too became sick and had to take weeks off work because of weakness and fatigue. Their four children remained healthy throughout, suggesting the two had caught a bacterial disease like typhoid after drinking contaminated water. Samuel was nonetheless pleased his family had their own home to live in. 'Our next neighbour was very kind to us but in cases of fever no one likes to go near.' He was happy to report that he was now 'as stout as ever I was in my life and Elizabeth is coming round very well'.[1] Samuel saw his and his wife's recovery as a near-run thing and thanked divine providence for their survival. The risk of catching a deadly contagious disease had been an accepted hazard of European city life since classical times and was reinforced by the onset of the devastating plague pandemics from the fourteenth century. Most townspeople expected periodic exposure to disease and, while taking precautions like avoiding sick households, put it down to fate as to whether they were affected. Settlers like Samuel Harris carried this mentality to New Zealand.

This chapter explores how public-health concerns shaped colonial city life. For as much as boosters represented colonial New Zealand as a healthy country in which settlers would live long and vigorous lives, within a very short time its cities were experiencing high mortality rates from infectious diseases. Reformers made various attempts to reduce disease outbreaks and improve urban public health, but such interventions could not fully protect cities from infectious diseases, and raised questions about the correlation between public health and

OPPOSITE This map of central Wellington drawn up by the city's medical officer William Chapple locates cases of the water-borne disease typhoid between 1890 and 1892. The clustering of the dots highlights the infectious nature of this disease. Wellington City Archives, 00233:34:1892/740 overcrowded housing. Reformers' continual calls to raze congested inner-city slums expressed their desire to build modern city space and restore the healthy-country ideal.

The public health of colonial cities has received more historiographical attention than any other topic considered in this book. One reason is the strong tradition of civic history in New Zealand: an improved sanitary infrastructure – principally water and sewerage pipes – usually rates highly among municipal achievements. Another explanation lies in the relative strength of health history, and the fact historians' topics often have an urban context or dimension. A leader in the field has been Geoffrey Rice. His 1980s research on late-colonial Christchurch showed how sanitation improvements – the laying of sewerage pipes and better public hygiene practices – contributed to a lowering of the city's mortality rate. His study of the 1918 influenza pandemic in New Zealand also had a strong city focus, including the finding that (along with rural Māori) city dwellers were badly affected by disease.[2] Alistair Woodward and Tony Blakely's 2014 history of life and death in New Zealand considers why Pākehā from 1860 to 1940 had the highest life expectancy in the world. They attribute this to, among other things, the high number of rural immigrants from Britain's healthier regions; a plentiful, protein-rich diet; the scarcity of health-damaging heavy industry; reduced fertility rates; and improved maternal health.

Another important work is Pamela Wood's 2005 cultural history of dirt in colonial Dunedin. By the early 1860s that city was defying the healthy-country image, with high rates of contagious disease caused by polluted water, dirt and other filth. Crowded dwellings compounded the problem. Wood charts how better sanitation and housing improved both the city's public health and its quality of life.[3] Wood's findings echo those of historians elsewhere who have shown how public-health interventions – from smallpox vaccination to government investments in urban cleanliness, to improved home hygiene – contributed to a decline in European mortality rates after 1850. As Peter Clark writes: 'For the first time since the Middle Ages, urban mortality rates fell below the countryside, while acute infectious diseases as the leading cause of death began to give way to the role of chronic and degenerative diseases.'[4] Wood's arguments remain cogent, and the purpose of this chapter is to consider the extent to which the Dunedin experience was replicated in other cities. An essential contention of the chapter is that improvements in the public-health and built environment of cities help to explain New Zealand's rapid urbanisation.

A salubrious climate

Among the selling points used by boosters to market colonial New Zealand to emigrants was the country's health-inducing properties. In leaving the

ABSTRACT of a JOURNAL of the WEATHER, kept daily at the residence of his Honour Mr. Justice CHAPMAN, at Karori, Wellington, 1847.

MONTHS.	THERMOMETER.				WEATHER.				PHENOMENA.			
	Lowest at 9 A.M.	Mean at 9 A.M.	Mean at 2 P.M.	Highest at 2 P.M.	Fine.	Cloudy.	Showery	Rainy.	Gales.	Night Frosts.	Thunder	Shocks of Earthquakes.
January...........	52°	61°5	67°8	80	19	4	6	2	7	..	1	..
February	54	60 9	68 4	78	20	1	4	3	4	..	2	2
March	54	59	66	78	17	1	11	2	5	..	1	1
April	44	52 5	60 9	69	20	6	8	2	5	..	..	1
May	40	50	54 3	64	15	1	7	8	6	1	..	..
June	34	47 5	54	58	17	2	3	8	3	3	..	1
July	40	47 1	51 5	57	14	2	9	6	5	3	1	1
August	40	46 4	54	62	21	0	6	4	6	6	..	2
September...........	38	47 4	53 5	64	19	2	5	4	11	3	..	2
October	42	52 3	58 5	68	20	2	5	4	10	1	..	3
November...........	44	57 2	60 8	68	17	2	9	2	9	..	1	1
December	45	64	67 2	80	23	3	3	2	6	..	..	2
1847..............	34	53 8	59 7	80	222	26	76	47	77	17	6	16
1846..............	31	52 5	59 7	78	213	24	82	46	49	21	13	24

NOTE.—The temperature is that during the day. The Thermometer is in the shade; aspect S.S.E., exposed to a free current of air. Nine o'clock is chosen, because it is believed to indicate pretty nearly the mean temperature of the twenty-four hours. The fine sunny days this year have exceeded those in 1846, but the wind has been greater. Besides strong winds, which just stopped short of being gales, we have had no less than thirty-six gales in four months, whereas last year we had only sixteen in the same time. But for eight shocks in one day last year, the numbers would have been equal. The early frosts marked are such as show at 9 A.M.: a self-registering Thermometer would, no doubt, have indicated a few more.

Early guidebooks extolled New Zealand's healthy climate and often included meteorological tables so prospective migrants could compare conditions in their current and intended homes. This table of weather measurements (which included earthquakes) by Judge Henry Chapman was published in a guidebook of 1849. G.B. Earp, *Handbook for Intending Emigrants to the Southern Settlements of New Zealand*, W.S. Orr, London, 1849, p.66

overcrowded smokestack cities of Britain for the spacious and bucolic climes of Otago or Auckland, settlers were promised both higher material rewards and better health. Pamela Wood has shown that health concerns indeed ranked highly among the reasons given in British immigration literature to entice settlers to Dunedin.[5] Otago settler James Barr, for example, left 'quill-driving in Glasgow' for the 'vigorous plying of the grub-hoe and axe' on a small farm he worked with his brother in Halfway Bush. 'We were in the pursuit of health,' he later wrote.[6]

It was both a medical and popular belief in Victorian society that climate affected wellbeing and health. Sudden changes in weather, and weather extremes, could bring sickness and disease. As Vladimir Jankovic has written: 'Climate health and society were interlocked in a way that made any suffering part of the natural course of things: People were sick because they inhaled miasmas or were exposed to unhealthy vapors, smells and winds. Bad air and rough weather were natural; sickness was, too.'[7] Neo-Hippocratic interest in climate and its effects on health spread as the reach of empire expanded.[8] Instruments for atmospheric measurement were taken by settlers to colonies like New Zealand and used to collate meteorological tables that were often included in immigration literature to support their claims of a salubrious climate.[9] George Butler Earp argued in his 1849 immigrant handbook that the first consideration of all intending emigrants should be to ascertain the nature of the climate of the country they were contemplating going to. The family man 'has no right to expose his dependents to excesses of climate unsuited to their constitutions' that could result in 'miseries far worse than those from which he is endeavouring to escape'.[10] Independence in a colony was reliant on good health, he continued, and climate determined the number of days a man could work remuneratively. The astute emigrant therefore chose the colony where the climate offered both the greatest certainty of health and the highest chances for remuneration. Using comparative meteorological data, he then proceeded to wax lyrical about the salubriousness of New Zealand's climate compared to that of its North American competitors.[11] Within this frame, even Wellington's notorious wind could be made into a boon. Earp quotes Bishop Selwyn of New Zealand, who broadcast:

[N]o one can speak of the healthfulness of New Zealand till he has been ventilated by restless breezes of Port Nicholson, where malaria is no more to be feared than on the top of Chimborazo [Ecuador], and where active habits of industry and enterprise are evidently favoured by the elastic tone of perpetual motion of the atmosphere. If I am not mistaken, no fog can ever linger long over Wellington, to deaden the intellectual faculties of its inhabitants.[12]

Others also emphasised the beneficial effects of the antipodean air. In 1845, one Wellingtonian claimed the town's children were 'the largest and finest of their age I ever saw. It is quite a common remark, that *the children born here, and now growing up, will be a race of giants.*'[13] Still others emphasised the climate's recuperative and regenerative effects. Samuel Grimstone asserted in 1847 that many Wellington settlers who had suffered from chest infections in England had now recovered.[14] A year after Dunedin's founding, William Cargill noted that of the settlers who had come out because a change in climate had been prescribed for their health, all but one was now in stout condition.[15] When Edward Gibbon Wakefield arrived in Christchurch in 1853 he expressed astonishment at the difference in the wellbeing and ruddiness of colonists compared to how they had been at home. 'It was very marked in some ladies who appeared ten years younger than when I parted from them in London,' he said.[16] While Wakefield rarely missed an opportunity to engage in puffery, the claims for a healthy climate had a tentative scientific basis. Using data collected as surgeon to Auckland's 58th Regiment between 1848 and 1853, Arthur S. Thomson found New Zealand soldiers had half the hospital-admission rates and a third the mortality from disease rates of soldiers stationed in Britain. He ascribed the lower rates among the New Zealand troops to the small number of deaths from fevers and diseases of the lungs (infectious diseases). Whereas 10 in every 1,000 soldiers died of fevers and diseases at home, the rate in the colony was only 2.5 per 1,000. He attributed the differences to New Zealand's climate, in particular the evenness of temperature and the encircling moist ocean air.[17]

The perceived salubriousness of the climate contributed to the collective perception of New Zealand as a healthy country.[18] The physician Alfred Newman helped to cement the view. In an 1882 paper to the Wellington Philosophical Society, he argued the colony's low mortality rate made it the healthiest country on the globe. He put this down to a number of causes, including the robustness of immigrants; warm clothing and wholesome food; and a less anxious lifestyle. Environmental factors were equally important. The high proportion of the population engaged in agriculture meant many New Zealanders lived outdoors and benefited from health-inducing fresh air and sunshine. Moreover, towns and cities were small, with scattered populations; there were 'no dark dens, no life-destroying alleys'. They were also free from 'that constant over-crowding so fatal among older civilizations, which leads to chronic ill health of the poor in large European cities and to the rapid spread of all infectious and contagious diseases,' he said. The paucity of large-scale manufacturing industries further lessened the death rate; the feeble and wan factory hands who filled Britain's cities were missing from colonial streets. Others parroted Newman's case, further entrenching the healthy-country view.[19] And many new immigrants embraced the line. A week after arriving in Auckland with his family in the early 1880s, John Smith declared:

> One thing is certain, it is a grand climate and I have no doubt that we will have better health. We are all picking up fast from our confinement on board ship and Ernest, who thought he would never see land, is already getting fat. Adam is losing his round shoulders and Jeannie [his wife] has not been so well for years.[20]

Healthy country, diseased cities

Not everyone was convinced. Since the late 1840s, a dissenting and urban-centred discourse had been aired. This asserted that even though New Zealand's cities started out as healthy environments, the advantage was slipping away because settlers were allowing cities to deteriorate and become hotbeds of infectious disease. The generator of this pestilence was said to be the unceasing accumulation of foul water and filth that littered properties and streets and

New Zealand may have been a clean, healthy country when the first European settlers arrived, but it didn't take long for the filth of the old world to appear in the new. A stream that ran along Auckland's Queen Street was soon fouled with human and industrial waste and animal carcasses, becoming an open sewer dubbed the 'Ligar Canal'. As shown in this 1860s photograph, rickety wooden bridges were tacked over the canal so pedestrians could cross the street. Sir George Grey Special Collections, Auckland Libraries, 4-400

released poisonous miasmas or vapours that sickened and killed people.[21] As one Aucklander complained in 1854:

> The stagnant waters and pools where the worst of the exhalations from the putrid matter, and green waters is to be found in every inhabited part of this City, dung is suffered to lay in the streets; greens, potatoe [sic] peelings, and all other offal thrown in the back lanes is permitted to lay and rot; and as a matter of course, fever in all directions is the natural consequence.[22]

The critic went on to denounce the lack of drainage in the settlement: the swamp in Vulcan Lane was putrid; effluent pooled under houses; and there were no channels to take away liquid waste from the numerous animal enclosures and manure heaps in the settlement. Too many townspeople were falling ill from these uncivilised conditions, and he called on authorities to charge a cleanliness

During epidemics, sick people were sometimes sent out of cities to make-shift hospitals in rural areas. In 1913 smallpox victims were treated at this camp near Kaikohe in Northland. Sir George Grey Special Collections, Auckland Libraries, AWNS-19130918-45-2

tax on all households and businesses so improvements could be made. 'Nature made this a healthy place, it is a disgrace that Europeans have reversed it, but it is an undeniable fact.'[23]

The idea that filth was responsible for infectious diseases was informed by Western knowledge of disease causation. Before the ascendency of germ theory in the late nineteenth century, opinion broadly fell into one of two camps: environmentalist and contagionist. The first argued that miasmas (bad air) rising from stagnant water and other putrefying matter infected people with diseases – the miasma was the agent of the disease. This made infectious diseases a geographical phenomenon, with some landscapes being conducive to illness.[24] The second postulated that contagion was the method of transmission: people caught diseases from each other or by contact with infected articles like clothing and furniture. This meant contagious diseases were capable of being carried between localities. Initially, contagion theory held sway.[25] The virulence of the plague in 1347–48 led northern Italian cities to institute public-health measures – inspection of travellers, quarantine of ships and the creation of lazarettos (isolation hospitals) – to contain its spread. Other European countries adopted the same strategies.[26]

During the eighteenth century, a decline in plague epidemics, together with improved diet, living conditions and public health infrastructure, reduced European mortality rates. New ideas about the body and disease also emerged. These included the Neo-Hippocratic notion that changing environmental conditions could prevent illness. In France, the Royal Society of Medicine made special studies of public health and proposed interventions to remove bad air by, for example, draining marshes and bodies of stagnant water to reduce transmission of the likes of dysentery and typhoid. As one historian has written: 'By the 1780s the unhealthy stenches of modern, especially urban, life – the odors of cemeteries, rubbish, cesspools and sewers – were under attack. Air had become the health issue, the nose was the diagnostic tool, and clean water was the solution to filthy atmosphere that bred disease.'[27] With inoculation against smallpox becoming more common, there was some optimism that Europe might become free from contagious disease.[28] The 1829–32 European cholera pandemic defeated that hope and created renewed debate as to cholera's cause. Those who believed in contagion argued the danger arose from people and goods moving around and transmitting illness; believers in environmental conditions pointed to miasmas and local environmental conditions as the culprit.[29]

Environmentalism was given a further boost during the 1830s by English sanitary reformers like Edwin Chadwick. Whereas Louis-René Villermé had found a strong spatial correlation between high rates of cholera and poverty in industrialising Paris (the remedy for which was to help the poor into better circumstances), Chadwick proffered a single causal explanation for the persistence of contagious diseases in modern cities: filth. Standing wastewater and piles of uncollected garbage were at fault. Filth in rivers, streets and buildings was dangerous because it affected the surrounding air. Chadwick called for the construction of massive new infrastructure that would bring clean water to every household and move polluted water out. The sanitary movement's main message was that flushing away filth would create a more healthy and civilised society. The construction of London's articulated water and sewerage network began after the 1853–54 cholera outbreak and became a model for other cities to follow.[30]

It was Chadwick's environmentalist view that the first settlers took to New Zealand. In decrying the degraded state of Auckland in the mid-1850s, the *Daily Southern Cross* declared the link between filth and disease was well understood. 'Is there any wonder, therefore, that there should exist here so much disease, where there has never been any attempt to drain the town, or see to its cleanliness in any way.' Cesspools, rubbish and house refuse were everywhere, and releasing poisonous and fatal exhalations. Although no official disease statistics were kept, anecdotal reports suggested the West Ward (the town west of Queen Street) had the highest fatality rate.[31] The newspaper credited this not to the area being dirtier than elsewhere, but to the clay soils that prevented filth from permeating the earth as it did in the other wards; all the poisons therefore evaporated into the air, 'to the greater destruction of the inhabitants'. It called for drainage and sewerage systems to be instituted in the city and for a proper supply of water to flush them

As this circa 1850s painting by James Edward Fitzgerald shows, Christchurch was built on a swamp. It was plagued with drainage problems and the health of residents suffered until cesspits were banned in 1878 and a public sewerage system built early the following decade. James Edward Fitzgerald, Canterbury Museum, 1938.238.36

to be obtained from the Government Domain. At the same time it conceded that it had raised the same issues two years before to no material effect.[32]

Auckland was not alone in being awash with filth. In spring 1854, the Wellingtonian James May reported the city's Te Aro district had experienced a fearful amount of sickness over the winter, a consequence, he said, of its lack of drainage and squalid environment. 'In my immediate neighbourhood there is an accumulation of filth, permitted and undisturbed by the authorities, sufficient to produce typhus or any other malignant fever.' There were no drains to take the effluent away. May urged the government to institute a programme of public works to relieve the situation.[33] In 1856, the *Otago Witness* complained that Dunedin's Rattray and Manse streets were becoming 'receptacles for stagnant water and filth, sufficient to breed pestilence'.[34] The town was hardly a decade old.

If the situation had become so dire so quickly, why didn't authorities move rapidly to improve it? One reason was expense. Drainage and water-supply infrastructure was costly to build and, as we saw in Chapter Two, government finances were already stretched by building and maintaining streets. Proper drains and pipes would have to wait their turn. Then there was the laissez-faire political economy in which calls for the likes of cleanliness taxes would have faced resistance.[35] A third factor was a cultural acceptance of dirt and filth in urban contexts. Most townspeople had recent experience of the muck of British cities. The piles of rubbish, evil smells and associated vermin that characterised colonial-city life might have been a nuisance but they were nothing out of the ordinary; creating colonial cities in the image of those back home included replicating their refuse and dirt. Exposure to deadly diseases was an accepted hazard of living in cities.[36]

Edwin Chadwick and other sanitary reformers changed this fatalistic mindset by demonising filth and showing how its removal could benefit both the quality of the urban environment and the health of people living within it. This meant successfully challenging laissez-faireism by arguing that the goal of healthier cities demanded collective action – an approach that culminated in the vast articulated water and sewerage systems of London and other cities.[37] In this light, the dissenting discourse can be seen as a reforming one. It agreed with the booster-driven view that New Zealand was blessed with a salubrious natural environment, but asserted that human-made cities had been sullied and made sick by settler complacency and neglect. What was needed were judicious sanitary improvements that would restore their vigour and so realise the healthy-country promise. Leading the charge were city newspaper editors, physicians, engineers, officials and concerned citizens who, in the manner of Chadwick, worked to raise public awareness of the dangers of urban filth and have it removed. Getting townspeople and governments to adopt their message, however, was easier said than done.

Sanitary commissions

Christchurch led the way on sanitation. Among the first acts of its new municipal council in 1862 was the appointment of a sanitary commission to report on the problem of drainage and waste disposal in the city. Christchurch had been built on low-lying and swampy land, and the poor drainage was not only a nuisance but also thought to be contributing to an increase in fever deaths.[38] The seven-member commission comprised councillors, officials and physicians, and heard evidence from a range of experts and lay people. Witnesses reported numerous clusters of contagious diseases – diarrhoea, dysentery and Asiatic cholera – in Durham, St Asaph and Cashel streets as well as Wilson's Triangle (High, Colombo and Cashel streets). The immigration barracks in Market Place (Victoria Square) was a further hotbed of disease. In common with the prevailing miasmic theory, experts blamed the outbreak on bad air and the accumulation of filth. According to a Dr Parkerson, the general cause of the fevers was undrained swamps and basins of stagnant water. The areas where the fevers prevailed 'were those which had been thoroughly filthy from the long residence of dirty people', he asserted.[39] Another local doctor, Alfred Barker (of Chapter Two), attributed the fevers to the city being on a delta and its subterranean blue silt; the state of decomposition of the silt meant it was able to generate a 'virulent miasma'. Conversely, he did not consider the impurities carried in the Avon River (and sewer) to have had any 'serious influence on the health of the town'.[40] Barker thought the immigration barracks was poorly sited, serving to increase its residents' risk of disease. A neighbour of the barracks, Mr Morley, described it as being in an unfit state: the ground was badly drained and forever damp, and the stench from the privies was 'very bad'.[41]

The commission reported in June. It ascribed Christchurch's unhealthy state to the filling of natural gullies. Rainwater that had formerly drained into streams became trapped on low-lying lands, creating putrefying ponds that generated bad air and miasmic fevers. Polluted water was only a secondary cause, it said. It pointed out that the city's river was purer than its well water, which was sunk into decaying vegetable matter and in close proximity to cesspools, the contents of which contaminated the surrounding soil and formed 'centres of disease by their noxious exhalations'.[42] As the cesspools polluted the earth beneath the ground, household slops and other refuse poisoned the surface:

> What the one leaves undone the other perfects; and thus, around a very large portion of dwellings, scattered through a town of considerable extent, the soil becomes a reeking, pestiferous mass, such as could hardly be improved upon if the object aimed at were the destruction, rather than the preservation of human life.'[43]

The report then listed a series of recommendations. Concerning drainage, the commission thought that once the city was more populous, an underground sewer system would be constructed, but in the meantime ponds should be filled and new stone channels be built to carry away wastewater. New artesian wells must be sunk about the city to improve water supply and quality. It also called for the replacement of cesspools with night-soil boxes that would be collected weekly or fortnightly on a cost-recovery basis. The dumping of slops and refuse on streets must also be prohibited, and each dwelling be required to provide a watertight receptacle for ashes and other rubbish for regular removal. As for the immigration barracks, the commission recommended they be demolished.[44]

In 1864, Dunedin established its own sanitary commission. As in Christchurch, a catalyst was the city's rising mortality rate. In August, the *Otago Daily Times* reported Dunedin had recorded a death rate of 34.4 per 1,000 people for the first half of the year, much higher than London's 20 and Liverpool's 28. Surely a 'community like ours, composed of men and women in the prime of life, among whom grey hairs are rarely to be met with ... should be exceptionally healthy, and any but the lowest death-rate can only be the result of exceptional folly'.[45] The commission shared the sentiment. It calculated nearly half of all deaths between 1861 and 1864 were of children under age five, and half of all the 1863–64 deaths were from contagious diseases. The city's defective drainage and water-supply system was to blame, it charged. It urged Dunedin to follow the example of some British cities, where improved sanitation measures had lowered mortality rates. The city adopted the advice, establishing a town water supply in 1867 and completing a central-city sewerage system a decade later.[46] Dunedin and the other cities also introduced initiatives to raise public awareness of the links between filth and disease.

Inspectors of nuisances

A pivotal measure was the employment of inspectors of nuisances (made compulsory in London from 1855) to enforce sanitary bylaws. Dunedin appointed the policeman James Nimmon to the role in 1861, and by 1864 he had served 870 notices and summoned 962 people for regulation breaches.[47] Christchurch chose William Pearce in 1863. His regular reports to council between 1863 and 1868 offer interesting insights into the extent to which city life was a daily assault on residents' olfactory senses. Urban space in settler societies was characterised by mixed land uses: breweries and brickworks were sited among colonial cottages; pigstys and slaughterhouses fell between shops, stables and offices. Animal odours were ubiquitous. Smells from the brewing of hops, the boiling of tallow or the baking of bread pervaded streets and entered buildings.[48] While such odours were sometimes pungent and offensive, most were usually fleeting and innocuous. Of greater concern were the dumping of 'miasma-causing' refuse in streets, leaching cesspits and overflowing privies. Pearce's job was to locate and remove such hazards.

His work mainly involved issuing compliance notices to do with issues like removing fetid water from properties or cleaning out stables. He also investigated townspeople's complaints of nuisances, and, as cesspits were phased out in favour of pans, collected their removal fee. Some problems were readily addressed. A complaint of an odious smell arising from a fishmonger's property was tracked to some bad cheese that had been placed on stable manure.[49] Other matters took longer to resolve. In December 1863, Pearce received a complaint from a Mr Dry

Open drains like this one in Dunedin's Walker Street (now Carroll Street), an area of run-down housing just south of the Octagon, were a common sight in cities. These children, out for a walk with their father in 1904, are peering at the drain. Their smocks, worn to protect the clothes underneath, are doing good service. Photograph courtesy of *Otago Daily Times, Otago Witness,* 10 February 1904, p.40

of Manchester Street who protested that he was unable to build on his property due to the 'noxious effluvia' arising from the adjoining property belonging to the butcher, Mr Cook. Pearce had received many complaints about the place and questioned whether Cook should be allowed to keep pigs there. A week later, he served Cook with two weeks' notice to remove the pigs. Cook replied he had no intention of observing the notice, so Pearce was obliged to seek police support in the matter. The next day, Sergeant Major Pender accompanied him to Cook's place and served the butcher with a court notice to remove the pigs within 36 hours. The following week, Pearce confirmed the pigs had gone.[50] (He conceded that the issue of pigs in cities wasn't straightforward. Despite the generation of foul odours, the porkers consumed high quantities of household refuse that might otherwise be dumped in streets.)[51]

A seemingly intractable problem was the accumulation of slops and other rubbish in the lane that ran behind the shops in Wilson's Triangle. Pearce first visited the site in June 1863 and found it blocked by piles of rubbish; inhabitants, he said, were willing to contribute to its cleansing if the council also assisted. The following month he went back and found the 'accumulation of rubbish and refuse of every description' was increasing daily. In August, he arranged a council contractor to cleanse the right-of-way and lay shingle, with costs to be collected from residents. The improvement was short-lived. By November, the lane was again blocked by a large quantity of refuse and Pearce was unable to raise money from the inhabitants to keep it clear.[52] The council then decided to take the owner of the lane, William Barbour Wilson, a prominent city businessman and landowner, to court on a charge of failing to remove the refuse. But Wilson denied all liability for the filth, stating he had leased the lane to his tenants for 21 years and was therefore not responsible. The judge concurred and ruled the tenants were answerable for the mess. In early 1864, the tenants presented a petition to the council, agreeing to submit to a local rate if the council metalled and kept the thoroughfare clean.[53] The council decided against the rate, but agreed to maintain the lane on a cost-recovery basis. In November, it laid a stone channel and organised for a contractor to regularly sweep it. A few months later, Pearce arranged with Wilson to relocate ash boxes (for solid waste) in the right-of-way because children and others were removing the contents and throwing it everywhere.[54] The space caused Pearce no further complaint until November 1866, when he reported the cleansing of the lane had ceased because a minority of tenants were refusing to pay their weekly share of the contractor's cost. As Pearce pointed out, '[a]s there is greater need for sanitary precaution in this locality from its central position and consequently it being more thickly inhabited, I beg to suggest the necessity for adopting some measures for ensuring its regularly cleansed'. He thought the only enduring solution was for council to charge a special local rate on all tenants.[55]

The Triangle saga highlighted how the laissez-faire political economy of colonial cities hindered the implementation of collective public health measures. A striking aspect of Pearce's reports is the constant buck-passing over who was liable for the accumulation of rubbish in common space. A general response was for inhabitants to deny individual responsibility altogether by claiming refuse and other filth was placed there by others. Responding to a complaint of a dirty cob house in Hereford Street, the inspector found five families living in separate rooms. The whole property was covered in rubbish. When he asked the lodgers why they refused to remove the mess, they replied it was already there when they moved in.[56] Their stance underlines not only their individualism but also their cultural acceptance of urban filth. Yet figures like Pearce were able to challenge this mentality by working with tenants, the landlord and the council to arrive at a common agreement for maintaining the lane. When a small minority reneged on the deal and the agreement collapsed, Pearce was forced to conclude the council must intervene and levy a compulsory rate to protect the public health of the wider community.[57] Such thinking eventually led municipalities to take full control of refuse collection.

Wellington and Auckland also appointed inspectors of nuisances. Some proved more effectual than others. Graham Bush suggests Auckland's long-serving inspector, George Goldie, was the wrong man for the job; he was loath 'to admit any connection between infant mortality and contagious disease on the one hand and primitive sewerage and the dumping of night soil within the city watershed on the other'.[58] For instance, in April 1875 he reported a great amount of sickness in the city – chiefly measles, diarrhoea and dysentery – and that 62 people, particularly children, had died from those causes in the previous month alone. But he then asserted the sanitary condition of the city was good because the streets were regularly swept.[59] The city council was similarly indifferent. In 1872, it ordained all cesspools be closed and replaced with earth closets but was then lax in enforcing the change. In 1873, it finally moved to pipe Queen Street's open and reeking sewer (Ligar Canal/Te Wai Horotiu) yet still allowed it to discharge into the harbour at the foot of the street. Only in the face of an impending epidemic did the council take vigorous action on public-health matters, argues Bush.[60]

Cesspits, epidemics and pipes

Auckland's experience underscores the importance of reform-driven individuals and authorities to developing a favourable public-health culture in cities. Again, Christchurch is a good example of this. The 1876 abolition of provincial government led to the replacement of the Public Health Act 1872 with new legislation based on the 1875 British Act. Under the new 1876 Act, local boards of health were placed under a national board of health (though, unlike the British measure, the appointment of medical officers was voluntary). Christchurch took up the option. This was because its newly formed Drainage Board – created to institute a city-wide wastewater and sewerage system – offered to take on the health board role and fund a full-time medical officer.[61] Geoffrey Rice has argued that despite the efforts of people like William Pearce to improve Christchurch's public health, it was New Zealand's unhealthiest city during the 1870s – a third of all deaths between 1874 and 1876 were caused by filth diseases like dysentery and typhoid.[62] Although these were bacterial diseases spread through contaminated water and human faeces, they were still understood as miasmatic diseases caused by infected effluvia. Repeating the view of the sanitary commission, the city's medical officer, Courtney Nedwill, argued that 'impure air from foul cesspits, and exhalations from a subsoil saturated with filth' was at the root of the problem.[63] Such reasoning led the city to ban cesspits in 1878. This was followed by a strong compliance campaign, and in 1881 Nedwill reported there were no cesspits remaining in the central city. The following year, the Drainage Board finished the initial stage of the city's sewerage network.[64] Rice has shown that deaths in Christchurch from zymotic (contagious) diseases fell sharply after the cesspit ban, and credits the fall to Nedwill and others' public health advocacy and the completion of the sewerage network.[65]

Wellington too benefited from a tenacious medical officer: William Chapple. In 1871, the eminent scientist James Hector analysed the city's drinking water and found all the samples collected from streams and wells in the inner city were unfit for human consumption. A safe water supply was urgently needed, he pleaded. This was achieved in 1874, when pipes were laid from a new reservoir in Karori to the city. However, plans for an extensive reticulated sewerage scheme were abandoned owing to its £150,000 cost (the equivalent of $20.7 million in today's currency). The city's waste continued to fester and ooze through a rudimentary system of pipes, drains and streams that eventually discharged into the harbour beside where children played. The capital was only woken from its sanitary slumber by a typhoid epidemic that killed 142 residents between 1889 and 1900.[66] Among the first to be infected was the son of the new Governor, Lord Onslow; the boy survived, but the vice-regal family fled to the safety of Nelson.[67] It became Wellington's turn to be nationally shamed as an unhealthy city.[68] The city council responded by abolishing cesspits and the backyard burial of night soil, as well as appointing two eminent engineers, Mr Ferguson and Mr Climie (of the Christchurch Drainage Board), to advise on a new city-wide sewerage scheme.[69]

The area most affected by the epidemic was Te Aro. In March 1892, William Chapple began an investigation into the causes of typhoid in the neighbourhood. He identified all cases in the area between 1890 and 1892, and plotted them on a street and drainage plan (see page 304). The map shows a cluster of cases along Holland Street, a short lane made up of 21 cottages housing 90 people. It was Chapple's first call. He soon came across a foul-smelling gully trap that was used by two houses to dispose of human and other household waste. This was a common practice, he conceded. Until recently, two families had occupied these dwellings. The first, a family of ten, had slept in two upstairs bedrooms; six of the occupants and one person from the other family were now in hospital with typhoid. He learned that even after the inception of typhoid the families continued to dispose of their dejecta (faeces) down sinks or into privies, increasing the risk of infection. In the neighbouring house, the gully trap was blocked by faecal matter, with the semi-liquid overflow trickling under the floorboards: the stench was 'abominably foul'. There were only two water closets in the whole street; the other houses had privies but these were badly managed: night soil was being buried in yards or piled against fences.[70]

On examining the drainage in Holland Street, Chapple found a large amount of contaminated water had leaked from the sewer and percolated into the surrounding soil. It was his view that this deposit accounted for the epidemic in the street:

> The putrefying deposit gave out volumes of gas whose line of least resistance was along the house drain inside it and outside it and under the houses. The other insanitary surroundings were the worst possible, and no doubt predisposed the victims to infection, while the neglected privies receiving typhoid dejecta played their part in the propagation of the disease.[71]

He then looked at the Tory Street sewer and discovered it was obstructed in many places by large filth deposits. Moreover, there were no ventilating grids along its course. Numerous house traps and syphons (barriers on drainage pipes to stop sewer gases reaching the surface) were broken, unconnected or defective. He saw many Bell trap (barrier) tops lying in the yards, 'very few people seeming to understand their function'.[72] That the sewers were also stormwater drains exacerbated the hazard. Using hospital records, he found a strong correlation between high typhoid admission rates and heavy rainstorms 10 to 14 days earlier (the typhoid incubation period). In heavy rain the sewers quickly filled with water, forcing the typhoid-infected sewer gases up into the houses. After rain everyone noticed the foul odours arising from the gully traps and water closets. Because there was no safe system for the disposal of typhoid dejecta in the area, most of it going into the drains (presumably because tenants with privies could not afford regular night-soil collection), Chapple thought it was to be expected that an epidemic would follow the displacement of sewer gas in the district.

The medical officer concluded that the primary course of typhoid in Te Aro was defective drainage and a secondary cause was irregular disposal of night soil – he was certain the reticulated water supply in the area was safe.[73] The danger arising from the district's insanitary state called for an immediate remedy, he urged: specifically, the installation of sewer ventilating shafts and regular flushing of sewers to minimise deposits.[74] 'Many people are panic-stricken. Some were fleeing the district, while others are sending their families to more healthy situations while they themselves attend their businesses.'[75] Chapple called for the inspection of all typhoid-affected houses and for the repair of all defective drains. Several houses in which typhoid had once been rife had become free of the disease following the adoption of remedial sanitation measures, he said, but 'nothing short of a complete system of sewerage on modern principles will make

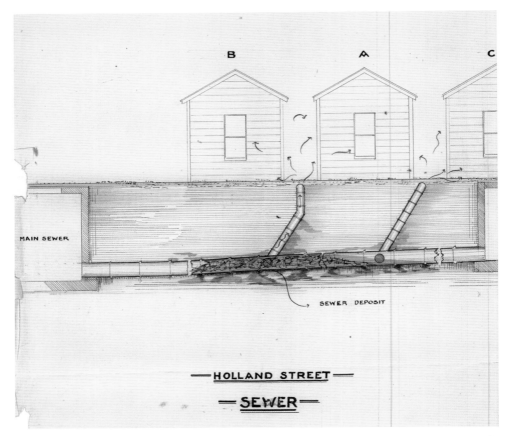

Wellington's Holland Street was badly affected by typhoid in the early 1890s. In 1892 Medical officer William Chapple discovered the street's sewer had leaked and contaminated the surrounding soil. His sketch shows the leaking sewer and unwholesome gas rising up from the soil. Wellington City Archives, 00233:34:1892/740

the City as free as it ought to be from preventable diseases'.[76] The city council agreed. A few months later, it proposed taking out a £165,000 loan to construct such a scheme. On the advice of its expert panel, sewage and stormwater would be carried in separate pipes, with all sewage being pumped into Cook Strait rather draining into the harbour. The initiative was put to a public meeting at the Opera House for approval. After a long and fiery debate, it was passed 113 votes to 65.[77] The scheme went ahead and was completed in 1899.

With his use of cartographic techniques and empirical fieldwork, Chapple's investigation was a pioneering epidemiological study in New Zealand. Although he was wrong in ascribing the epidemic to miasmatic causes (the Koch and Pasteur-associated bacteriological revolution was slow to be accepted in New

Zealand), he was correct in attributing its spread to an insanitary environment.[78] Poor disposal of night soil and unsafe hygiene practices among Te Aro residents made the district an ideal breeding ground for the typhoid bacillus. The spike in cases that arose after heavy rainfall was therefore probably due to contact with faecal-contaminated water in saturated yards. Similarly, as Rice identified, Christchurch's high contagious death rate in the 1870s was not caused by Nedwill's noxious effluvia but chiefly by bacterial cross-infection from cesspits into the city's well water.[79]

Declining city mortality rates

As Rice has shown for Christchurch, the proportion of people dying from zymotic or contagious diseases declined in the late nineteenth and early twentieth centuries, significantly improving the city's public health. But what happened in the other cities? The accompanying graphs chart contagious deaths as a proportion of total deaths in the each of the four cities; the combined city contagious rate against the national rate; and the national male and female rate.[80] In the official death returns, most contagious deaths came under the heading 'miasmatic diseases' and comprised a mixture of bacterial and viral contagious diseases, including scarlet fever, typhoid, diarrhoea, measles, whooping cough and influenza. This category remained largely unchanged until 1908 when the Bertillon classification of causes of death was adopted.[81] Between 1879 and 1882, the city-based data was not published, but we still have sufficient information to show long-term trends.

The pattern for the four cities (Figure 7.1) is a sliding tangle of peaks and troughs. Beginning with a rate hovering in the thirties in the 1870s, by the early 1900s the proportion of townspeople dying from contagious causes had fallen to single figures. The peaks signal specific epidemics in each city. For example, Auckland's high death rate in 1875 was chiefly attributable to a measles epidemic that killed 69 people. In the same year, a typhoid epidemic accounted for 25 deaths in Auckland, 27 in Wellington and 49 in Christchurch. A spike in Dunedin in 1877 included 52 deaths from scarlet fever; an 1889 peak in Wellington signalled the beginning of its typhoid epidemic; and a spike in Christchurch in 1899 was attributable to a diarrhoea epidemic that killed 52 children. (Diarrhoea was the single biggest cause of death from contagious diseases among young children over this period.) Finally, peaks in Auckland and Wellington in 1903 were caused by a measles epidemic that caused 49 and 40 deaths respectively.

Of the four cities, Auckland had the highest average contagious death rate, possibly reflecting its lax attitude to public health. Conversely, Dunedin had the lowest, suggesting its efforts to cleanse itself of filth were paying off. Figure 7.2 shows that the contagious disease death rate as a proportion of all deaths was

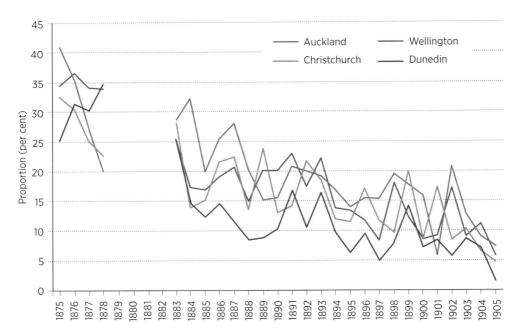

Figure 7.1 Proportion of deaths in the four main cities caused by infectious diseases, 1875–1905

Note: The data is the proportion of deaths attributed to 'zymotic' or infectious diseases and excludes Māori. Data was not published for the cities between 1879 and 1882. The peaks indicate epidemics. Notwithstanding these, infectious diseases became a less significant cause of death in Auckland, Wellington, Christchurch and Dunedin between 1875 and 1905.

Source: *Statistics of the Colony of New Zealand*, Government Printer, Wellington, 1875–1905.

generally higher in the four cities than in New Zealand as a whole, although by the end of the period there is concordance between the two. The difference was due to the higher population densities and pollutants in cities, making townspeople more susceptible to contagious diseases than country people. Harder to explain is the gender difference (Figure 7.3). Over the entire period, proportionately more females than males died from contagious causes. The reasons for this are uncertain. It might be that because more women lived in urban than in rural New Zealand (see Chapter Eight) they were more exposed to contagious diseases. It could be too that women provided more nursing care to patients, again increasing their exposure to infection. What is certain is the proportion of all New Zealanders dying from contagious diseases fell significantly over the period, from 33 per cent in 1875 to 5 per cent in 1905.[82] The fall also helped to lower mortality rates overall. The mean mortality rate of the four cities dropped from 27.9 deaths per 1,000 people in 1875 to 9.5 per 1,000 people by 1905 (Figure 7.4), while the national figure also declined, from 15.9 to 9.3 deaths per 1,000 people.[83] Whereas in 1875 city dwellers had died at almost twice the rate of other New Zealanders, by 1905

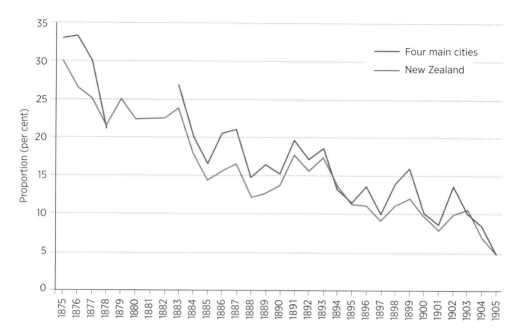

Figure 7.2 Proportion of deaths in the four main cities and New Zealand caused by infectious diseases, 1875–1905

Note: The data is the proportion of deaths attributed to 'zymotic' or infectious diseases and excludes Māori. Data was not published for the cities between 1879 and 1882. These diseases were a more significant cause of death in the four main cities (Auckland, Wellington, Christchurch and Dunedin) because of high population densities and pollution.

Source: *Statistics of the Colony of New Zealand*, Government Printer, Wellington, 1875–1905.

the odds were near even. The steep decline meant the gap between the ideal of New Zealand as a healthy country and the reality on the ground had narrowed considerably.

How far the fall in the contagious diseases and general mortality rates can be credited to public-health improvements like water and sewerage pipes is a moot point in historiography. Patrice Bourdelais asserts that in Europe there is a chronological concordance between cities adopting public health measures and a decline in contagious diseases. He argues that in Paris, Lyon and Marseilles, a fall in mortality between 1850 and 1900 coincided very closely with government water and sewer improvements.[84] Other historians believe the connection between the provision of pipes and improved mortality is relatively weak, and that social factors like improved diet, smaller family size, reduced crowding and better housing conditions were more significant.[85] In New Zealand, Alistair Woodward and Tony Blakely agree pipes were important, 'but they were not the only vehicles to improve better hygiene'. They suggest social factors 'may have overshadowed

Figure 7.3 Proportion of male and female deaths caused by infectious diseases, 1875–1905

Note: The data is the proportion of deaths attributed to 'zymotic' or infectious diseases and excludes Māori. Infectious diseases killed proportionally more women than men. This may be because more women than men lived in cities or because women were more likely to care for sick people.
Source: *Statistics of the Colony of New Zealand*, Government Printer, Wellington, 1875–1905.

the impact of public health engineering'.[86] Certainly, if we place contagious disease mortality rates against the completion dates for municipal water and sewer schemes, evidence for a strong correlation between their commissioning and a reduced mortality rate is ambiguous. For instance, Auckland got a reticulated water supply in 1877. The following year there was steep reduction in contagious disease deaths, possibly attributable to uncontaminated water. The completion of Christchurch's sewer network in 1882 saw a significant fall in contagious disease deaths thereafter – bar periodic epidemics. Conversely, the drop in contagious disease deaths to single figures in Auckland and Dunedin occurred before these cities completed their city-wide sewerage networks, in 1908 and 1914 respectively.[87] In short, it is hard to establish a clear link between the provision of pipes and lower mortality in the four cities. Clean drinking water must have reduced the risk of water-borne diseases like cholera and typhoid, but so did other sanitary measures. These included cesspit bans and a transition to water closets, better handling and collection of night soil and other rubbish, and safer hygiene behaviours and practices in domestic space. These and the aforementioned social factors convincingly explain the reduced mortality rate.

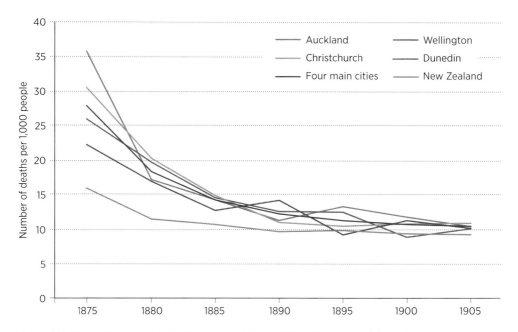

Figure 7.4 Mortality rates in the four main cities and New Zealand, 1875–1905

Note: The data excludes Māori. All-causes mortality rates dropped sharply in Auckland, Wellington, Christchurch and Dunedin between 1875 and 1905 as cities became healthier places to live. By 1905 they were not much higher than the New Zealand-wide rate.

Source: *Statistics of the Colony of New Zealand*, Government Printer, Wellington, 1875–1905.

If pipes had a limited impact on reducing deaths in cities, their role in improving the urban environment was palpable. In the early 1880s, a visitor to Wellington wrote that his first impression of the town had been unfavourable because he had arrived at low tide and been greeted by a 'nasty smell' arising from the polluted foreshore.[88] Just under two decades later, an *Otago Witness* correspondent wrote:

> The drainage system of Wellington has driven the stinks from the city, and purer air and cleaner water of the harbour delight the citizens. Time was when the sicklied atmosphere, begotten of the filth ever floating about the very pier piles, pervaded the whole air with poisons of any deadly plague, and no living thing could exist for long in the harbour waters, and when every sojourner in the city took days and weeks to overcome that terrible effort for an acquired taste enforced by the foul pervadence everywhere. Now the fishes have returned in shoals to the harbour … and Wellington and its atmosphere are healthy once more, after a lapse of over a quarter of a century of filth and deadly poison.[89]

It was a similar story in the other cities. With pipes carrying effluent beyond city peripheries and other waste being regularly taken from streets and properties, the maleficent odours and pollutants that had characterised city life for decades diminished, improving not only townspeople's health but also that of the natural environment. The clearing of filth and the reduction of the mortality rate from contagious diseases removed what had long been detrimental aspects of city life. As the nineteenth century gave way to the twentieth, the four cities had become as salubrious places in which to live as most other parts of New Zealand.

The 1913 smallpox epidemic

The success in reducing deaths from contagious diseases generated a level of complacency among townspeople about the risks of disease to health. Many believed that New Zealand's island situation and distance from metropolitan society offered some protection from overseas pandemics. This confidence was shaken during the bubonic plague scare of 1900, when an epidemic in Sydney appeared set to cross the Tasman Sea. Central and local governments responded by increasing inspections and quarantine of overseas shipping, fumigating cargo and placing a bounty of one penny or more on rats (which carried the plague bacillus) killed in city space. Such measures, or luck, kept the plague at bay, and by August the scare was over.[90] The episode resulted in the Public Health Act 1900, which gave birth to a Department of Public Health in place of the local boards of health.

The first Chief Health Officer was Dr James Mason. He stressed the need for continued vigilance against contagious diseases and promoted public vaccination against smallpox.[91] The Vaccination Act 1863 had made it compulsory for every infant to be vaccinated, but it was resisted by anti-vaccinationists and not widely enforced. Minor periodic outbreaks saw renewed flurries of vaccination, but as the perceived threat of smallpox receded so did vaccination rates. An opt-out clause in the 1900 and 1908 Public Health Acts further reduced rates so that by 1911 only 1.6 per cent of all children born in 1911 were vaccinated. Māori vaccination rates were also low: about 15 per cent for the total Māori population in 1912.[92] Both Māori and Pākehā were therefore ill-equipped to resist the disease when it arrived in the country the following year.

The carrier was the Mormon missionary, Richard Shumway, who arrived in Auckland from Vancouver on the SS *Zealandia* on 8 April 1913. After disembarking, he travelled north to Mangakāhia, near Whāngārei, to attend a hui (meeting). Shumway had caught the virus from a ship steward, but the twelve-day incubation period meant he sickened only after arriving at the hui, from where the disease became an epidemic. The Health Department responded slowly to the outbreak, initially believing it to be chickenpox: the symptoms appeared atypical of smallpox.[93] The prominent rugby league player James Rukutai of Auckland

Plague reached New Zealand in 1900 after an epidemic in Sydney. Run-down cottages like these in Auckland's Swanson Street were demolished in case they harboured the disease.
Sir George Grey Special Collections, Auckland Libraries, AWNS-19000511-10-2

personified the uncertainty.[94] In late May he fell ill at his Onehunga home. The local general practitioner, J. L. Harke, visited him in early June and diagnosed smallpox. Auckland's Assistant District Health Officer, Dr H. G. H. Monk, hurried to Onehunga and had Rukutai placed in the Point Chevalier isolation hospital – on a site that became Coyle Park. However, the medical superintendent at Auckland Hospital, Dr Charles Maguire, believed Rukutai had an acute case of chickenpox. It was 'extremely difficult to distinguish one of these diseases from the other in coloured people,' he claimed.[95] The following week, Maguire (erroneously) confirmed that Rukutai had caught chickenpox and suggested he would be well enough to be released in about ten days. Rukutai was fortunate – he recovered, and continued his sporting career.[96]

On hearing that ever more Aucklanders and Sydneysiders (the *Zealandia* had continued to Sydney) were suffering pustular rashes, the Health Department decided in early July to treat the disease as smallpox.[97] By 12 July, there were 14 patients in the Point Chevalier hospital: twelve men and two women, all but

Department of Public Health, New Zealand.

This is to Certify

that ....
has complied with the requirements of the Department
of Public Health ....

....

and may, on presentation of this certificate, be permitted
to travel from ....
to ....
Date: ....

....
District Health Officer.

2,000/8/13—13666]

one of whom were Māori. The escalating epidemic led to vigorous attempts to contain the disease. Public health officials inspected all Māori settlements in and about Auckland; residents showing rashes were sent to the isolation hospital and all others were vaccinated. In Monk's words, he was 'seeking to throw a protective barrier around Auckland'. Henceforth, no Māori would be allowed to travel in or out of the city without a vaccination certificate; Monk argued this 'ring of vaccinated natives' would stay the disease's advance.[98] Fearful this was no guarantee, Aucklanders rushed to be vaccinated. Lymph was manufactured in government laboratories in Wellington, which worked overtime to meet demand. By mid-July, some 15,000 Aucklanders had been vaccinated. Wellingtonians too clamoured to be protected. To shield the South Island, all passengers on the Wellington–Lyttelton ferry were vaccinated as well.[99] The government's Chief Health Officer, Dr Thomas Valintine, found the whole situation vexing: 'The public is now in a state of panic, and having ignored for years the representations of the Department with regard to vaccination, now expects the whole Dominion to be vaccinated in a week.'[100] By 19 July, the Point Chevalier hospital had 30 patients, some of whom were housed in tents. The most recent two arrivals were Europeans who lived in the central city. Three other Europeans were under observation in their homes in nearby suburbs.[101]

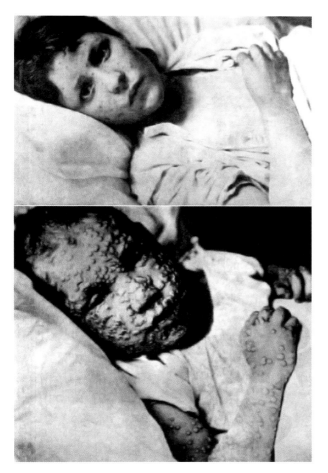

LEFT These children caught smallpox in the early 1900s. The child at the top had been vaccinated but the other had not and was much more severely affected. *Appendix to the Journals of the House of Representatives, 1902, H-31*

OPPOSITE During the 1913 smallpox epidemic Māori were not allowed to travel in or out of Auckland unless they produced a certificate proving they had been vaccinated. Māori were targeted because the epidemic started at a hui in Northland before spreading to Auckland. Archives New Zealand, Te Rua Mahara o te Kāwanatanga, ADQD 17422 W2334 R3W2334 13 1913/3819 (R13258162)

Despite the reality that Pākehā were succumbing to smallpox, in public discourse the epidemic was represented as a 'Maori disease', generating anxiety about and antipathy toward Māori in Auckland. Māori comprised only 1 per cent of Auckland's resident population but, as we saw in Chapter Four, many out-of-town Māori frequently visited the city.[102] Some blamed these visitors for the disease's spread, and the *New Zealand Herald* referred to it only as 'the Maori epidemic'.[103] On 23 July it claimed the epidemic was 'wholly and solely Maori':

None but Maoris or Europeans who have come into immediate and close contact with Maoris have as yet been infected yet while the Health officers denounce unvaccinated Europeans as 'a danger to community' they take no steps to prevent Maoris from travelling in trains, trams, steamers and taxi-cabs, excepting the farcical step of requiring these Maoris to be possessed of a vaccination certificate.[104]

The newspaper charged that there had been no attempt to isolate 'diseased Maoris and their infected districts' and alleged Auckland's reputation was suffering because the Health Department was unwilling to 'admit that the root of the evil is in the filthy Maori environment and that until every infected Maori is quarantined and his kainga tabooed and cleaned we can expect no relief from the epidemic'.[105] That James Rukutai had resided with his wife and child in a suburban cottage showed that living like a European was no protection from viral diseases like smallpox.[106] Yet the *Herald*'s stance reflected the environmentalist belief that insanitary habitations facilitated the spread of all contagious diseases.[107]

At the end of July there were 58 patients in the isolation hospital; 45 of them were Māori. Of the hospital's 66 cases to date, 18 had come from the central city and inner suburbs, and 39 from the outer suburbs, including 19 from Māngere.[108] Fearful the epidemic would keep people from the forthcoming Auckland Exhibition, its organiser, George Elliot, proposed Māori patients at the hospital to be relocated outside the city and the hospital be kept for white patients only. Valintine responded by saying this was impossible, because it would mean duplicating hospital staff. He asserted that all 'the loafing class of Maoris' had left Auckland and those who remained were working in the city before the epidemic, had been successfully vaccinated, and were living in boarding houses that had been inspected and cleansed where necessary. He was certain the epidemic would be over by the time of the exhibition.[109] Such assurances failed to allay critics. The city's mayor, Christopher Parr, saw the epidemic as a crisis and developed a six-point plan to fix it. First, all Māori boarding houses would be registered and inspected every other day to check and vaccinate new arrivals; Māori residing in the inner city would also have to report daily to a health officer or be quarantined. Second, if these precautions failed, all Māori should be removed from the city until the epidemic was over. Third, the Point Chevalier hospital was hopelessly inadequate and new buildings were required immediately; a separate Māori isolation hospital should also be built in the country. Fourth, all smallpox patients must go to the isolation hospital, as keeping them in their homes was insufficient protection. Fifth, Dr Valintine should be headquartered in Auckland for the duration of the epidemic. Last, everyone should be vaccinated. Doctors still saying the disease was not smallpox were mistaken.[110] Parr sent his plan to Health Minister Heaton Rhodes for approval.

OPPOSITE People clamoured to get vaccinated against smallpox during the 1913 epidemic. Staff at government laboratories in Wellington worked overtime to meet demand. This montage shows the cultivation of the vaccine, including the calves from which the lymph was extracted. Sir George Grey Special Collections, Auckland Libraries, AWNS-19130724-43-1

Parr's plan centred on restricting the movement of Māori. Europeans faced no such sanctions despite also being carriers of the disease, suggesting his stance was informed less by science and more by prejudice.[111] In this he appeared to be reflecting the view of many of his constituents. Such was the fear of Māori in city space that some Māori children selling ferns door-to-door in the city's suburbs were 'regarded with alarm in a community anxious to be rid of a serious menace to the public health'.[112] Discrimination towards marginalised groups has long characterised epidemics and pandemics worldwide. During European plague pandemics some cities sought to protect themselves by forcibly expelling the poor, lepers and Jews.[113] For Parr and others it was politically expedient to blame or scapegoat Māori because they were readily identifiable among an overwhelmingly white populace. That removing all Māori from Auckland would be draconian was less of a concern for Parr than his interest in being seen to be doing something tangible to protect the city.

In reply, Rhodes systematically rebutted Parr's main points. While accepting that the epidemic principally affected Māori, he pointed out that 'the disease did not originate spontaneously amongst the Maoris, that it was unwittingly conveyed to them, and that, in contrast with the European, unprotected by an ancestral acquired immunity, they have suffered most and fatally from the disease'. He noted that Māori had responded enthusiastically to vaccination calls, 'without any of the cavilling spirit so manifest among Europeans', and that this had helped contain the epidemic. He could see little value in compiling a register of Māori boarding houses because steps were well in train to ensure all Māori were vaccinated. Neither could he see any point in making all Māori report daily to health officials, as the proclamations restricting Māori travel had largely halted new arrivals to the city. As for the isolation hospital, it was in the nature of epidemics that hospital accommodation was hastily provided and less comfortable than permanent buildings. Still, no patient had complained about the facility. Rhodes did agree with Parr that Valintine be headquartered in Auckland. Finally, he said, smallpox vaccination had been made available to all city dwellers but demand was falling among Europeans.[114]

By the third week of August, there were 66 patients in the Point Chevalier hospital but all were recovering and the epidemic appeared to be waning. In Auckland no new cases had been reported for eleven days.[115] Sporadic cases continued to surface until December, when Rhodes was able to announce that Auckland was now free of the disease. He said that during the epidemic an estimated 1,884 cases were notified across New Zealand; of them, 113 patients were European. Forty-two deaths had been verified among Māori; there had been no European deaths.[116] A Health Department report the following September revised the figures slightly upward and revealed none of the affected Europeans had been vaccinated. It also

LEFT Auckland Mayor Christopher Parr's plan for containing the smallpox epidemic focused on restricting the movements of Māori, even though Europeans also carried the disease. His widely shared view stigmatised an already marginalised section of Auckland's population. Herman John Schmidt, Alexander Turnbull Library, 1/1-001604-G

RIGHT Minister of Health Heaton Rhodes did not share Mayor Parr's view that Māori were responsible for the smallpox epidemic. He accurately identified a European visitor to New Zealand as the original carrier of the disease, also noting that Māori had lower natural immunity and were thus more likely to catch it. William Henshaw Clarke, Alexander Turnbull Library, 35mm-00171-f-F

made the point that the 'sanitary state of the surroundings did not appear to affect the severity of the epidemic'. Māori living like Europeans suffered as much as those living traditionally.[117]

The smallpox epidemic underscored that in an age of speed, distance from metropolitan society offered New Zealand little protection from overseas-sourced diseases. It also showed that complacent attitudes towards such diseases could have serious consequences: if more people had been vaccinated against smallpox, the impact would have been less severe. And it further highlighted how epidemics could lead to the scapegoating of marginalised communities. The public framing of the outbreak as a Māori epidemic exposed latent Pākehā racism, fuelling the longstanding perception that Māori were outsiders in city space. Nonetheless, the experience also showed that control instruments like vaccination and isolating patients were effective in containing the disease. Without such measures, the outbreak could have been much worse.

Housing and health

If more could have been done to prevent the smallpox epidemic, this was hardly the case with the 1918 influenza pandemic. This particular strain of influenza proved particularly virulent and killed millions globally – nearly 8,600 of them New Zealanders.[118] Geoffrey Rice's book on the pandemic is a definitive account of its New Zealand impact, including in cities, so there is no need to reprise the story in depth here. What is important to note is that Europeans in large towns and cities experienced higher mortality rates than those in rural districts, particularly in Auckland (1,128 deaths; 7.6 per 1,000 people) and Wellington (757 deaths; 7.9 per 1,000 people).[119] In a study examining the pandemic in Auckland, Linda Bryder noted that despite evidence showing the virus struck rich and poor neighbourhoods alike, debate during and after the pandemic focused on the public-health risk of inner-city slum housing. Visitors to inner-city suburbs like Ponsonby and Freeman's Bay found evidence of overcrowding of families, dilapidated dwellings infested with vermin, and insanitary and damp conditions.[120] The *Observer* newspaper took the opportunity to inflame existing prejudice against the city's Fijian-Indian hawkers:

> The present epidemic has proved that our peaceful brethren, the Hindoo hawkers, even when suffering from the disease, live in pestilent filth and under conditions shocking in the extreme. These people are licensed by the City Council to sell fruit, and therefore to disseminate disease, for they take their stock of fruit to their awful dens every day, where they fester in darkness and vileness, and sell them to the citizens of Auckland next day.[121]

That the hawkers rented their 'awful dens' from negligent and profit-driven landlords was not considered. An official enquiry into the pandemic, the Influenza Epidemic Commission, subsequently visited inner-city areas and argued that:

> the bad conditions existing were due to an inheritance of wrong division of land; the continued habitation of old, dilapidated, worm-eaten, vermin-infested, and in some instances really rotten structures; the economic factors of short supply of decent houses and excessively high rents, and the personal habits of uncleanliness of a proportion of tenants … [T]here is no doubt that in all the centres groups of houses, and in some places nearly whole streets, stand as a constant menace to public health.[122]

The commission asserted that the health of the people was New Zealand's greatest asset, and called for municipalities to demolish and rebuild the areas with modern

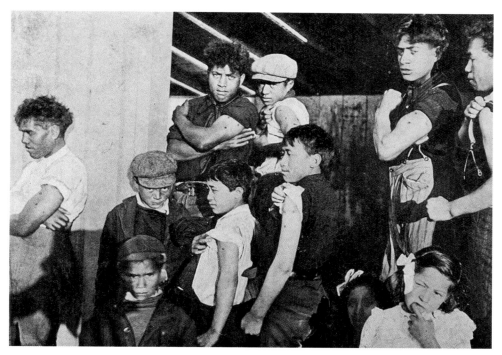

These children in the Māori settlement of Maketū in the Bay of Plenty were vaccinated against smallpox in 1913. The triangle of dots of their arms shows where the needle went in. Sir George Grey Special Collections, Auckland Libraries, AWNS-19130821-48-8

worker housing. Although the process would be expensive, the 'added efficiency of a completely healthy people' would ultimately defray the upfront costs.[123]

The commission's comments highlight how discourse about healthy cities had shifted from being focused on filth as an incubator of contagious disease to overcrowding as a principal cause. The initial emphasis of public-health reformers like Pearce and Chapple had been to raise public awareness of the dangers of filth, encourage more hygienic behaviours and practices, and deliver improved sanitary infrastructure. Reformers recognised that congested and poor housing conditions were detrimental to public health – Chapple mentioned the typhoid-stricken family of ten living in two bedrooms – but the strength of laissez-faireism made it hard to convince authorities to intervene. While the municipal provision of pipes and drains showed the benefits to be derived from doing so, it took the threat of bubonic plague to persuade authorities to move on housing.

The issues about worker housing raised by the Influenza Epidemic Commission had been talked about for decades – wrong land division, lack of supply, high rents, shoddy fabric and dirty tenants. Debate went back to the 1860s when gold seekers swamped Dunedin's housing market, forcing people to cram into boarding houses, makeshift cottages and even tents. In other cities, too, districts of tightly packed and densely settled housing emerged in their centres, defying the otherwise sprawling suburban pattern. In bourgeois society such overcrowding presented both a physical and moral danger, increasing occupants' exposure to filth and disease as well as to depravity and crime, as happened in British slums.

These slums had arisen from the 1820s as the rapid urbanisation experienced under industrial capitalism saw ever more workers crowd into city centres. In London, developers erected new housing, but much of it was shoddily built and quickly deteriorated. When charitable housing trusts and others built dwellings to a higher standard, they were forced to set rents at levels the poor could not afford to pay. Matters were made worse by the loss of dwellings during mid-nineteenth-century slum-clearance schemes for new streets, railways and docks. Such creative destruction was based on the premise that the evicted slum dwellers would move to the suburbs, but most of these people were tied a locality by work, long hours and high transport fares, so were forced to move into already congested tenements. Overcrowding and filth generated high morbidity and mortality rates from contagious diseases. The government intervened with legislation to remove and rebuild slum dwellings, and housing trusts were formed to rehouse 'deserving' workers, but these measures were insufficient to solve the growing problem. It was not until slum reformers like Andrew Mearns, author of the 1883 pamphlet *The Bitter Cry of Outcast London*, awakened the middle class to slum dwellers' plight that measures were introduced on the scale needed to tackle the crisis.[124]

As early as 1842 critics were warning that the practice of sub-dividing inner-city land into tiny allotments would give rise to Old World-like slums in the New (see Chapter Two). In 1859, William Swainson said of Auckland that '[n]o provision has been made to prevent the crowding together of miserable hovels in close and confined back streets'.[125] Other cities also worried about the emergence of slums. Commenting on Dunedin's situation in 1864, an incredulous *Otago Daily Times* said: 'It is a singular and almost unaccountable thing that even in infant cities in a young colony are to be found reproduced with faithful accuracy the wretched tenements, and filthy back slums of a crowded English town.' It complained that so-called cottages sat cheek by jowl, with no regard to comfort, ventilation and sanitation. Such conditions led to ill health, filth, immorality and crime, but nothing was being done to address the evil. The newspaper also railed against the high rents charged for the hovels: 'Wretched paling-built huts, which perhaps cost thirty or forty pounds, if so much, are rented at ten, fifteen, and even twenty shillings a week. And even at this exorbitant charge they are eagerly taken up, for they are the only alternative to living in a thin calico tent.'[126]

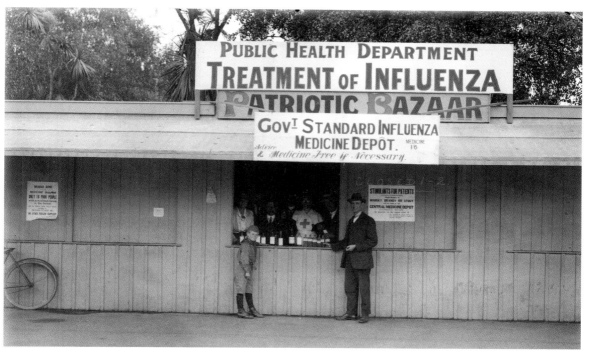

This boy and man are visiting an influenza medicine depot in Christchurch during the epidemic of 1918. *The Press* Collection, Alexander Turnbull Library, 1/1-008542-G

The *New Zealand Herald* attributed Auckland's worsening slum problem to individualism. While the axiom 'Every man has a right to do what he likes with his own' generally held true, it stated, there were times when he was bound to 'place the benefit of the commonwealth above that of his own'. Yet this notion had been spasmodically applied in the city. Authorities made residents with cesspools in crowded neighbourhoods regularly cleanse them, but turned a blind eye to those who 'for the sake of money-making' permitted 'abominable nests of squalid filth, the rookeries of small houses' in the city's back lanes. The underlying issue was not the supposed depravity of the working people living in the hovels but the avaricious behaviour of the middle-class landlords renting them out. Perhaps realising such an argument might alienate its readership, the paper backtracked by concluding that most blame rested not with individuals but with land sub-division practices that encouraged overcrowding, facilitating the spread of miasmas and disease. It called for authorities to intervene to raze the rookeries and rebuild the area with proper regard to ventilation, drainage and a clean water supply.[127]

This and subsequent pleas to demolish slum housing in Auckland (and in other cities) went largely unheeded; the laissez-faire attitude prevailed. Moreover, municipal elections were gerrymandered in favour of property owners; councils were therefore reluctant to move against such a pivotal constituency.[128] As in London, there was also the reality that city workers had to live within walking distance of workplaces because of the casual nature of their work. City population growth therefore tended to occur within existing limits, increasing the density of settlement and leading to overcrowding. Rather than rebuild their properties to accommodate the growth, landlords squeezed more and more people into the existing spaces and upped the rent.[129]

Occasionally, journalists would try to puncture the bubble of middle-class indifference by venturing into the slum district and reporting on the immoral and insanitary conditions therein. Their accounts usually employed the style of journalese pioneered by London's Henry Mayhew that represented slum life as 'a world apart' and slum residents as outsiders (from bourgeois society).[130] A local example of the genre concerns an unnamed Te Aro street in 1878:

> In a narrow street a few yards in length are some twenty dens, overcrowded with Maoris, half-castes, vagrants, boys, prostitutes, and the scum of society. There crime and drunkenness breed, and festive orgies of a most disgraceful character take place. At night the dens are filled with a mixture of tipsy Maoris, superannuated old prostitutes, and squalling children. The huts are filthy in the extreme, overrun with vermin, and reeking with various abominations. Here drunken men are decoyed and robbed; here all the abominations of Sodom and Gomorrah are perpetrated ... The police have done all in their power to cleanse these dens, but until the houses are razed, and the locality swept of its abominations; all efforts to eradicate existing evils must be fruitless.[131]

A primary purpose of these reports was to promote the reform of such districts but, as urban historians remind us, the representations were also often contrived for readers' entertainment, to astonish and titillate – that the above example was carried in a South Island newspaper supports this argument.[132] Whatever the motive, such accounts helped to deliver legislative change. The Public Health Act 1876 empowered boards of health to force owners of filthy buildings to cleanse them, and the Municipal Corporations Act 1886 enabled councils to demolish buildings that were unfit for occupation or dangerous to public health.[133] Yet city councils remained reluctant to employ these provisions, using demolition orders sparingly and avoiding wholesale slum clearance.

The 1900 plague scare changed this position. Authorities soon recognised that cramped and decadent inner-city housing was highly conducive to the plague's spread, and for everyone's sake the time had arrived to address the issue. As

Pamela Wood says of Dunedin, '[t]he plague threat provided both the motivation and legitimation for the bold move to demolish insanitary slums'.[134] In April, a team of sanitary inspectors and doctors examined 3,000 dwellings in the city and found 131 were in an insanitary condition. Of these 37 were condemned. Even then, some owners avoided the demolition of their buildings by making hasty repairs or forcing the council to take them to court.[135] In Auckland, sanitary inspections of inner-city housing areas were also increased, and many dwellings were condemned as plague threats and demolished.[136] This included a tenement of four dwellings in Auckland's Swanson Street (see page 329), occupied by old-age pensioners but deemed 'unfit for occupation and injurious to the public health'.[137] A similar house-to-house check in Wellington led to the demolition of numerous insanitary buildings in Mount Cook and Te Aro.[138] And an inspection of 4,116 houses in Christchurch found one-fifth required sanitary improvement.[139]

With Auckland and Wellington in particular experiencing rapid growth, the shortage of decent and affordable housing became acute. In 1903, a Wellington City Council committee inspected 303 houses in the central city and inner suburbs. Over half of them were in 'bad condition'; 60 houses were said to be 'unfit for habitation under conditions of cleanliness, decency, and health', and in 74 houses 'the rents charged are in excess of what the tenants are in a position to pay'.[140] Such conditions endangered residents' health, charged the *Evening Post*. It said the excessive rents were due to the laws of supply and demand; increasing the supply of workers' homes would force rents down. The newspaper argued this could best be done by opening up new suburban districts and linking them to the city's heart with cheap and modern public transport: 'Improved means of transport is the most valuable weapon for destroying slums.' A better rail line to the Hutt Valley and a new electric tramline to Miramar would be a good start. In short, as city workers boarded trams and trains for new lives in the suburbs, the slums would diminish.[141]

In the same year, the *New Zealand Herald* ran a series of articles on housing conditions in central Auckland written by their 'Special Lady Commissioner'. In the manner of an explorer entering a jungle:

[I] walked very gingerly down a very steep clay path into a gully, in which was a cluster of six cottages. On the way I passed the site of a demolished house, a result of the plague scare; but now that it was cleared I could scarcely believe that so small a place had ever held a dwelling. This was my introduction to some of the most unlovely and most neglected abodes that ever man built for housing his fellow creatures. But it was in and about these abodes that I found women working, and scores of children sitting. Wonderfully brave or resigned the women, strangely wide-eyed and unmerry the children! This is Auckland,

Grainger Street in central Wellington was a typical working-class street, closely packed with humble wooden cottages on narrow plots of land. In 1899 the whole street was compulsorily acquired by the Wellington Harbour Board and later cleared to make way for the extension of Allen Street and the creation of Blair Street. The case attracted some controversy, with the Premier Richard John Seddon accusing the harbour board of using its powers to remove poor people from their homes. Wellington City Archives, AC026:1:2

which sixty years ago was a scattered settlement! I could never have believed that in such a town as ours such circumstances as I saw existed.[142]

The writer's disbelief suggests she was somewhat out of touch, but then taking readers on a 'voyage of discovery' into an unknown world was a well-worn literary device. Her images of the slum dwellers were similarly hackneyed, focusing on their hospitality, bleak and acrid-smelling environs, high fecundity, respectability or disrespectability, and spendthrift habits. A new issue was their racial fitness. As she complained, Auckland's crowded inner-city districts were 'an unsightly mass of small cottages … [with] small backyards and narrow, dusty streets! And this where we are trying to rear what we call the bone and sinew of the race!' She doubted whether children raised in such environments could ever be perfectly healthy.[143]

Her interest in racial fitness reflected growing middle-class concern with eugenics and the belief that city life was debilitating. The perspective had gained currency with the rise of hereditary urban degeneration theory in

Young residents of the Grainger Street cottages pose for a photograph in 1898. By the time this photograph was taken the cottages were run-down and the area was seen as a slum, but for these children it was home. Wellington City Archives, AC026:1:25

Britain during the 1890s. This argued that every generation raised in crowded cities was successively more mentally and physically stunted. Cities therefore needed regular replenishment and revitalisation from hardy country stock, but a declining rural population made this vital function harder to fulfil. This in turn had ramifications for national efficiency: an enfeebled population might struggle to meet external threats. The theory gained credence during the Boer War when a very high proportion of volunteers from cities were rejected as unfit.[144] These ideas were widely reported in New Zealand, as were proposed solutions to the perceived problem.[145] Foremost among these was the creation of garden cities in the countryside. In proposing to move weakened city dwellers from the likes of London and resettle them in a network of small and bucolic garden cities, the British garden-city movement hoped both to meet townspeople's desire for urban amenities and improve their robustness.[146]

Town planning and the elimination of slums

Aside from raising the fecklessness of the poor, the Special Lady Commissioner failed to address the structural forces that had made the slums. One person who did so was the Premier, Richard Seddon. Frustrated that a continued lack of

Four Picture Proofs of "SLUMDOM" in Auckland

Three houses under one roof. In one house two families live, comprising 4 adults and 6 children. There is no water inside the houses. The yards are damp, narrow and dirty. The conveniences are of the usual antiquated type that need no description. One of the cellars when occupied held a separate family—father, mother, three children and a young girl boarder. They all slept in one room, the condition of which was filthy.

MONDAY NEXT, AUGUST 7th.

Total yard space of a four roomed house off a blind lane. There is only one outside tap and the convenience is of the usual antiquated type. This is one of a block of four houses.

'Four houses 'built under one roof, two up-stairs, two down. The combined rents yield the owner £2 1s. 6d. per week when let. The premises are in a wretched state.

Children playing at the back of old, condemned houses. The younger child has not been washed all day. The lecture will give instances of child-ren having been in the hospital as the direct result of the filthy conditions in which they are being brought up in.

The remainder to be shown at the Lecture are WORSE

Journalist Charles Reade was a pioneer of town planning in New Zealand. In 1911 he gave lectures in Auckland and Wellington, denouncing the slums he argued were the result of a laissez-faire approach to housing. This illustrated promotional flyer promised even more shocking images at the lecture. Special Collections, University of Auckland Libraries and Learning Service, Sir George Fowlds Papers, MSS & Archives A-17, item 3/65

This workers' dwelling in Sydenham, Christchurch, was built in 1907 as part of the government's first foray into state housing. The scheme aimed to entice workers out of dirty central cities and into clean suburbs, but high rents and commuting costs put the houses out of reach of most workers. Christchurch City Libraries, CCL KPCD09 IMG0097

affordable and good-quality worker housing in cities was threatening his Liberal government's economic policies – high city rents were leading to higher wage demands and creating an inflationary wages/prices spiral – Seddon first gave municipalities power to build worker housing. When that did not happen, he decided the state would instead.[147] Inspired by Britain's municipal housing schemes, in 1905 his government passed the Workers' Dwellings Act, whereby the state would build 5,000 rental houses for city workers. It was an unprecedented intervention in the New Zealand housing market, aimed at lowering market rents and improving housing quality. An important feature of the scheme was its salubrious suburban aspect. Land on the edge of cities was not only cheaper to purchase but was also well away from the inner city's physical and moral pollutants. Pockets of workers' dwellings were erected in suburban Ellerslie (Auckland), Petone and Newtown (Wellington), Sydenham (Christchurch) and Belleknowes (Dunedin). But higher than expected rents and the added time and expense of commuting to city workplaces meant that most workers preferred to remain in town, and the scheme never realised its initial promise.[148] Still, it was important in breaking the laissez-faire stranglehold in the housing market. Thereafter, governments accepted, to a greater or lesser extent, a role in housing provision.

The scheme's failure created a policy vacuum over what to do about the slum problem. The void was filled in the early 1910s by the formation of a New Zealand garden-city and town-planning movement. The starting point for the association in Britain and elsewhere was the contention that laissez-faireism had made cities disordered, congested and debased, and that the creation of more rational and artistic urban environments could remedy these faults. It called for the spatial division of cities into functional zones where particular activities – residential, industrial and commercial – had their own districts. It also promoted the creation of artistically designed and low-density built environments in salubrious parkland settings. These ideas found tangible expression in the building of Letchworth garden city in Hertfordshire in 1903 and London's Hampstead garden suburb in 1907. The first showed what could be achieved with a clean slate; the second showed how cities might be remade from within. Reformers saw the settlements as templates for production of modern city space.[149]

Among them was the Auckland journalist Charles Reade. His 1909 publication *The Revelation of Britain: A Book for Colonials* brought town planning into the New Zealand public realm. It attacked individualism for creating Britain's appalling slums, and promoted municipal socialism and garden cities as solutions.[150] Another town-planning advocate was the Auckland parliamentarian and former mayor, Arthur Myers. In 1911, he convened a municipal conference to consider a Town Planning Bill for the city 'to make provision for the growth of town life on lines of health and beauty.' Myers dropped his Bill in July when the government minister George Fowlds promised to sponsor a national measure.[151] The next month, Reade raised the movement's profile by giving talks in Auckland and Wellington on each city's slums. A promotional flyer for the event featured three photographs showing ramshackle dwellings in central Auckland. A fourth photo depicted two barefoot children, and carried the caption: 'Children playing at the back of old, condemned houses. The younger child has not been washed all day. The lecture will give instances of children having been in the hospital as the direct result of the filthy conditions in which they are being brought up in.'[152] Public interest was so high that hundreds were turned away from the venues where he spoke.[153] Reade's talk focused on overcrowding: Wellington's population density was 6.7 persons per acre, but in parts of Te Aro it reached 127 and in Auckland's Freeman's Bay it got up to 150 – densities that were not conducive to public health. Reade urged councils in both cities to intervene, level the slums and rebuild with garden suburb-like settlements.[154]

Municipalities again failed to act. The Wellington City Council believed reports of slums in the city were grossly exaggerated. In 1912, the City Engineer conceded the city had many derelict dwellings that should be demolished, but this was true of any city. He blamed the situation not on landlords failing to maintain their properties but on their tenants; there was, he said, a strong correlation between the shabbiest houses and those living in them. Although great improvements could be made, the cost of doing so would be considerable. It would require the 'wholesale clearance' and 'consequent remodelling' of slum areas and the introduction of new bylaws to prohibit intensive settlement.[155] In claiming the situation was not so bad, that dirty tenants were at fault and rebuilding would be horribly expensive, the council was supporting the status quo of removing the worst buildings but avoiding comprehensive reform.[156] For the garden-city movement, the status quo was unsustainable, preventing the creation of healthy and modern city space. In 1914, Reade toured New Zealand with the British town planer William Davidge to drum up more support. Reade stressed that town planning was not merely a 'synonym for beautification … its main purpose was the creation of healthy towns'.[157] The tour energised middle-class urban communities and led to the formation of local garden city associations to promote the cause to governments and the wider public.[158] With the end of the First World War in 1918, the movement seized the opportunity to push their case, organising New Zealand's first town-planning conference in Wellington in May 1919.

The event attracted over 200 delegates – government officials, architects and engineers, and enthusiasts – and was organised by the Christchurch architect (Samuel) Hurst Seager (a descendent of Edward Seager of Chapter One). The Governor-General, Lord Liverpool, opened the conference. He said that while there were not 'the same squalid areas in the Dominion as in the Mother-land, the late [influenza] epidemic has demonstrated there is considerable room for betterment in many of the localities of our larger centres of population.'[159] The Minister of Internal Affairs, George Russell, then stated that the conference's objective was to avoid Britain's mistakes, primarily population decline in the countryside and the rise of sordid slums in large cities where 'a healthy race cannot be reared.'[160] Concerns about racial fitness had also exercised the Influenza Epidemic Commission. Its recently completed report had argued that too little had been done to raze slum housing and the dithering over the issue had to stop. Unhealthy environments caused the degeneration of those living in them – evidenced by the high number of balloted war recruits who had failed fitness tests – so a national strategy was urgently needed to improve conditions.[161]

In advocating the building of new garden cities, the town-planning conference delivered such a plan. As Customs Minister Arthur Myers proposed, the 'State should acquire land in places designed by natural surroundings to give the greatest health and happiness, and where may be put up factories and garden cities'. Similarly, Hurst Seager proposed the resettlement of returned servicemen in sociable 'garden villages' rather than on isolated farms. These were scaled-down garden cities: small towns providing urban and rural work opportunities

and social amenities.[162] Both schemes were in the tradition of go-to-the-land solutions to reverse urban drift (considered in the next chapter). Rather than reforming cities from within to create modern and healthy spaces, as Reade had suggested with his garden suburb proposal, both Myers and Seager adopted the fresh-start approach. Russell alluded to another reason to leave town: fear of the mob. The 1913 waterfront dispute had led to violent clashes between inner-city workers and the authorities, and contemporary industrial unrest in the country's mines suggested worker militancy was returning. The Minister of Mines, William Macdonald, attributed the miners' bolshie behaviour to the 'sordidness' of their housing and the 'monotony of their home life'.[163] Russell picked up the theme and argued for a massive housing programme:

> I am satisfied that this country must embark upon a great housing scheme for the people, and that we must 'talk in millions' [of pounds] on this subject if we are to have a happy and contented people. Revolution and anarchy are not bred in the houses of men who have happy homes and delightful gardens. Its spawn comes from the crowded tenement, the squalid environment, and the slum.[164]

The belief that an improved physical environment could positively modify human behaviours and vice versa was a cornerstone of garden city thought. For most conference delegates the case for new garden cities was overwhelming. Even if slum districts were rebuilt, the high cost of inner-city land was such that garden suburbs were out of the question; workers would have to be rehoused in blocks of flats devoid of space and delightful gardens. These were slums in the making; the problems of overcrowding, poor health and worker militancy would continue. A dissident voice was the Labour Party delegate Robert Semple. He

These people attended the country's first town planning conference in 1919. Hosted at Wellington's town hall, the conference attracted over 200 delegates, including a small group of women who had their own sessions. Alexander Turnbull Library, PA6-298

suggested that the conference had failed to address the root causes of hovel life, which were landlordism and the government's failure to regulate capitalism for the welfare of all.[165] His lone critique fell on deaf ears, and the conference ended with an overwhelming call for the construction of a model garden city.

However, their garden-city vision remained unrealised – at least until the construction of the first Labour government's state-housing scheme in the late 1930s.[166] Instead, the government decided that a better approach was to build new suburbs for inner-city residents alongside tram and train lines, in the manner outlined by the *Evening Post* two decades before. Russell's proposal for a great housing scheme for the people came to fruition with the State Advances Amendment Act 1923, which allowed workers to borrow from the state up to 95 per cent of the cost of new suburban homes. It was principally about promoting a property-owning democracy. But it was also based on the premise that suburban life was not only healthier – it was more spacious and better ventilated – but that a large mortgage debt would secure worker loyalty to the establishment. Effectively, it was a return to the sprawling urbanism that New Zealand cities had begun with. For reformers, the tightly packed inner-city slum districts were an aberration, their very existence confirming the detrimental impact on city space and public health of unfettered laissez-faireism. In intervening in the market and promoting suburban life, the government was seeking to put New Zealand cities back on track and so restore the healthy-country ideal.

The housing subsidy created a building boom in the four cities, with new suburbs leapfrogging city limits, setting the pattern for the rest of the century.[167] As for the slums, they remained largely extant until the 1950s when urban renewal

Despite criticism of inner-city slums occurring from the late 19th century, most survived until the 1950s, when they were cleared for urban renewal schemes and industrial developments. These houses in central Auckland's Howe Street were just a few of the many hundreds demolished in this period. Sir George Grey Special Collections, Auckland Libraries, 589-21

schemes and industrial encroachment saw hundreds of houses demolished.[168] Gentrification from the 1970s saved many of the others: the former working-class slums began transitioning into fashionable middle-class neighbourhoods. The bourgeoisie, once the most vehement critics of inner-city housing, became its fiercest champions.

Conclusion

Claims of a salubrious climate were pivotal to selling colonial New Zealand as a destination for British emigrants. Boosters asserted those moving to the colony could better their health, and glowing testimonials from settlers seemingly backed them up. The idea of New Zealand as a healthy country took root. Despite Alfred Newman's assertions that the colony's cities were free from Old World ills, the evidence had for some time suggested something far less rosy. Cities had started off as healthy environments but they soon became corrupted and disease-ridden. Sanitary commissions and urban reformers pointed to poisonous miasmas generated by swampy, ill-drained ground and human filth as causes. The appointment of public health officials to enforce sanitary bylaws and educate people to the dangers of filth, together with the building of new sanitary infrastructure, cleansed cities and helped to reduce mortality rates from contagious diseases. By the early twentieth century, city dwellers had little more chance of dying from a contagious disease than other New Zealanders. But this did not cocoon them from epidemics. The smallpox epidemic showed how complacency about the threat of disease could have severe consequences. It also demonstrated that epidemics could generate discrimination toward marginalised groups. The protective cordon thrown around Auckland was ostensibly to safeguard public health, but it was also about confirming the Pākehā view that Māori did not belong in city space.

The smallpox epidemic and the influenza pandemic that followed refocused reformers' attention on the correlation between housing and public health. Since the 1860s, reformers had represented inner-city slum districts as endangering middle-class society: their presence undermined the belief in the superiority of New Zealand cities; their inhabitants were seen as outsiders and a moral hazard, and housing conditions within them were detrimental to public health. Initially, the threat to public health was contagious diseases: overcrowding and poor sanitation made the slums hotbeds of fever. As sanitary and other improvements reduced this risk, the threat became one of racial degeneration. Slum life was thought to enfeeble residents, necessitating their rehousing in more spacious and salubrious surroundings. Reformers argued that this required government intervention because the market had been unable or unwilling to deliver decent and affordable housing to the workers who lived in the slums. The failure of a government-sponsored housing scheme led garden city advocates to promote the building of new garden cities in the countryside. In the end, the belief that cities could be restored to health by returning to the low-density sprawling urbanism of the past won the day. The idea that the suburbs offered city dwellers the best experience of a healthy life became a twentieth-century truism.

European city life had long been associated with higher rates of contagious diseases and mortality than country life so, even accounting for the perceived salubriousness of the colony's climate, the emergence of a similar situation in New Zealand cities could not have been totally unexpected. More remarkable was how public health interventions were able to close the mortality gap between city and country, an achievement that significantly improved the quality and attractiveness of city life. While questions about racial fitness continued to dog city dwellers until eugenics was discredited in the 1940s, the perceived health deficit of city living had largely disappeared by the 1910s. It was perhaps no wonder then that ever more New Zealanders were flocking to live in the Big Smoke.

Chapter Eight

Backlash against the City

The year 1911 is not one that springs from New Zealand history books in the way 1840 (the signing of the Treaty of Waitangi) or 1893 (when women gained the vote) usually do. Yet a seminal event did take place that year, arousing much attention at the time but barely exciting historians thereafter. The Census of 1911 showed a higher proportion of people living in (urban) cities and boroughs than in (rural) counties. It marked the official transition of New Zealand from a rural to an urban society.

In making the transition, the country was following the course of Western modernity towards the concentration of populations in cities.[1] However, it alarmed those who believed that New Zealand should remain a rural society. If people were flocking to cities, how could the image of a nation of farmers and small-town dwellers be maintained? If farming was New Zealand's economic lifeblood, what would happen if there were insufficient farm workers to ensure it continued to flow? Such questions had been exercising New Zealand's most influential minds since the late 1870s, when urbanisation first emerged as a public issue. Most saw the movement of country dwellers to cities as detrimental and promoted policies to encourage people to go onto the land. Their reaction revealed a strong anti-city mentality in colonial society that had not been there at its beginning. Whereas the likes of Wakefield had promoted cities as beacons of civilisation in the wilderness, five decades later the wilderness was significantly cultivated and the city's civilising beam had dimmed. How do we account for such a fundamental shift in attitude toward the city? This final chapter examines the rise and influence of anti-city sentiment – better known as anti-urbanism – in New Zealand society and culture.

OPPOSITE In 1889 Belgian artist Jacques Carabain painted Queen Street in Auckland, which he probably visited during a trip to Australia. The painting is based on a photograph by George Valentine. Few artists painted New Zealand cityscapes in this period, instead focusing on bucolic landscapes, making Carabain's work comparatively rare. Jacques Carabain, *Queen Street, Auckland* (detail), Auckland Art Gallery Toi o Tāmaki, gift of the P. A. Edmiston Trust, 1986

The origins of anti-urbanism

Although anti-urbanism has been an important theme in political, social and cultural history, as the American political scientist Michael J. Thompson noted in 2009, it 'has received scant attention in the social scientific and historical literature'.[2] He sees anti-urbanism as a conservative reaction to the modernity of city life. It gained traction with the rise of eighteenth-century industrial capitalism, and was regarded as a means for restoring the traditional social relations and moral values that were disintegrating under the onslaught of modern city life. This situation was far removed from that of classical Greece, where the city was regarded as the highest form of social organisation and 'the realm of human fulfilment and happiness'.[3] The Puritans of early modern Britain took another view, aligning city life with idleness, corruption and debauchery. For the Enlightenment philosopher Jean-Jacques Rousseau, anti-urbanism was a response not only to economic change but to the ways cities were transforming social relations. Whereas country life was known for tight community bonds and primary social relations – the local community debate of Chapter Three – city life was thought to destroy these bonds and create mediated social relations. Critics therefore viewed cities 'as collections of rootless individuals characterized by competition, the impersonal, and conflict'. Rather than developing people, city life debased them.[4] Romanticism increased opposition to cities, as famously expressed in the poet William Cowper's maxim: 'God made the country, and man made the town.' This adage cuts to the essence of anti-urbanism: the distinction between what is perceived as 'natural' and what is 'artificial'.[5]

Anti-urbanism was carried to the New World. Robert Beauregard argues that its American variant arose as America's economy shifted from an agricultural to an industrial base. Since the eighteenth century, an agrarian myth had championed the moral superiority of the countryside. As Steven Conn points out, anti-urbanism was built into the structure of the Republic by guaranteeing two senators for every state regardless of their population, meaning that lightly populated rural states had and continue to have proportionately greater power than heavily populated metropolitan states – 'the tyranny of Wyoming', Conn calls it.[6] During the nineteenth century, American anti-urbanism expressed growing anxieties about the commercialisation of farming and a corresponding retreat of the small and independent (yeoman) farmer. After the Civil War (1861–1865), further farm mechanisation led rural youth to seek economic opportunities in cities, their exodus breaking up families and signalling the end of independent farming.[7] As a result, '[r]esentment on the part of those still clinging to rural life fed both a growing antiurbanism and a romantic rural nostalgia.'[8] Beauregard suggests that this bitterness was intensified by the perceived moral and physical

This Christmas card from the early 1900s celebrates rural New Zealand, linking the countryside with progress. Untamed nature, represented by the two Māori figures in the waka, has been superseded by the orderly farming scene. Kennett Watkins, Museum of New Zealand Te Papa Tongarewa, GH004845

dangers of the city: alcohol, prostitution, gambling, poor working conditions and unscrupulous landlords. Middle-class social reformers sought to alleviate these dangers by calling for the moral order of the countryside to be brought to the city. The temperance movement, anti-prostitution crusades and housing improvements tempered anti-urbanism by showing reform was possible. But as the economic power of the country waned and urbanisation increased, the rural romantics' ability to assert their moral power over cities diminished. By the 1920s, few still believed the moral and social order would collapse under the city's rise; instead, cities were being celebrated in American social thought for their diversity and openness. Only in the suburban 'middle realm' (between city and country) did fragments of the agrarian myth survive.[9]

Research on New Zealand anti-urbanism is slight.[10] The most important consideration of the issue is still Miles Fairburn's 1975 article, 'The Rural Myth and the New Urban Frontier'. He argued New Zealand anti-urbanism was grounded in the premise that, in a primary-producing country, the city was an 'artificial excrescence' because it had no productive base of its own.[11] Country folk were accordingly superior to townspeople because they worked the land and generated the colony's wealth. Such thinking gave birth to New Zealand's own agrarian or rural myth which, like its American counterpart, idealised the small farmer and country moral values.[12] Fairburn showed how this informed successive governments' schemes to get city dwellers to settle on the land – the new urban frontier – before linking the schemes' failure to urbanisation and the reality that some farms were uneconomic. For Fairburn, urbanisation presented the New Zealander with a dilemma:

> [H]is ethos was rigidly rural while his social structure became urban. Although he believed everything connected to the city was bad, it was there increasingly that he searched for security and opportunities. Urban employment fulfilled his material aspirations while rural life was the fulcrum of his values. His spiritual home was in the country whereas his physical nourishment came from the city.[13]

Twentieth-century suburbia offered a resolution to this tension. The single-unit dwelling on its own suburban section confirmed the family as a 'self-contained soil-rooted institution'. Suburbia was a compromise on the smallholding ideal, but if there was room for a garden and a few chickens it was the next best thing. 'Rejecting city culture, it strove to create a family centred Garden of Eden for the city worker.'[14] Here was a place that could meet the New Zealander's moral and material needs.

Go to the land

As we saw in Chapter One, the economic basis of New Zealand cities was trade. Commodities grown in, or extracted from, urban hinterlands would be shipped through their ports, and exported to London and other imperial nodes in exchange for manufactured goods and investment capital. It was the blueprint of all settler societies, based on the expectation that most settlers would work on the land; a smaller urban population would provide support services and a local market for perishable goods. The premise of the model was labour intensive: as the agricultural sector expanded, so would the demand for rural labour. Thus, while 1840s immigration literature had tried to attract settler capitalists with promises of city life and civilisation, that from the 1850s was aimed at enticing farmers and rural workers to settle and develop the barbaric wilderness – a process requiring

OPPOSITE Young Edgar and Owen Williams are watering their garden in the Dunedin suburb of Kew in the 1890s. Suburban living was an acceptable alternative to rural smallholdings because there was enough space for productive gardens and chicken coops. William Williams, Alexander Turnbull Library, 1/4-054947-G

OPPOSITE Rural life was celebrated, but life was often hard in the backblocks. Angela Jacob of Āpiti in Manawatū is doing the family washing in grim outdoor surroundings in the 1890s. Joseph F. Macedo, Museum of New Zealand Te Papa Tongarewa, O.030734

RIGHT Swaggers were men who walked around the country in search of work and if lucky, a free meal from a sympathetic farmer. They typified the Pākehā male stereotype of the rural drifter, independent and hardy. This swagger was photographed in Mākikihi, Canterbury, in 1905.
South Canterbury Museum, 2841

the alienation of Māori land. The initial prominence given to cities was replaced by an emphasis on the countryside.

The Aucklander Archibald Clark expressed the prevailing sentiment in 1866. New Zealand, he said, was 'well adapted for all kinds of workmen, it is indeed the place for the stout agricultural labourer, for the industrious artizan, the domestic servant, the small hardworking farmer, with a thrifty wife, and stalwart sons and daughters'.[15] Absent from the list are urban occupations like tailors, printers and clerks; Clark was targeting those who could live on the land. Within this model, the best settlers were those who arrived at a port city; spent a short time at an immigration barracks to acclimatise themselves and find a position; headed out onto the land to labour for their employer; saved until they could secure their own land; and then became independent farmers.[16] Conversely, the worst settlers were people like Edward Seager (of Chapter One), who settled in the city and failed to take the next step onto the land – a clear moral failing.

Here was an evocation of the rural myth. The notion that landless British work-ers could cross the globe and, through diligence and fortitude, become farm own-ers became a defining colonial narrative.[17] Historians have also contended that experience on the land shaped Pākehā masculinity. Jock Phillips argues that the surplus of single men who drifted between jobs in the countryside shaped colo-nial male culture.[18] Their work was strongly physical, and a respect for 'strenuous muscular performance' and an ability to endure hardship were essential charac-teristics. The men's distance from cities and its cerebral culture meant they 'held intellectual skill and bookmaking in low regard'.[19] Other attributes of male culture included loyal but fleeting friendships; an egalitarian ethos; and a proclivity to gamble, drink and fight.[20] Within this world, respectable women were outsiders. In their presence men had to restrain their bawdy behaviours; scorn of women therefore cemented male group identities, states Phillips.[21]

Out of these social beliefs and behaviours emerged a masculine stereotype. The archetypal Pākehā male was a rural drifter; muscular and stoic; anti-intellectual; a boozer and fighter; and wary of women. Phillips contends that the image arose because it was the most distinctive aspect of Pākehā society: 'the frontier experience was universalised and the urban experience ignored'.[22] He further explains how nostalgia for the frontier period led writers and others to romanticise rural life. Memoirs like Lady Barker's *Station Life in New Zealand* (1872) lyrically described life on a North Canterbury pastoral estate in the 1860s. Novels such as George Chamier's *Philosopher Dick: Adventures and Contemplations of a New Zealand Shepherd* (1891) examined the 'crude world' of single male rural labourers: 'They worked hard, played hard and fought hard.' Phillips notes that some poetry also mythologised frontier masculinity. David McKee Wright's *Station Ballads and Other Verses* (1897) celebrated backblocks swaggers, shearers and boundary riders: 'men who went on drunken sprees and told yarns in "the rude talk of rough men"'.[23] The 'helpmeet wife' is the closest New Zealand came to an equivalent feminine stereotype. In their role as wives, mothers, homemakers, housekeepers and guardians of society's morals, they enabled their husbands to focus on working the land. From the early twentieth century, the exemplary rugged smallholder and his helpmeet wife were increasingly celebrated for shaping dairy farms from dense forest and grain fields from stony river plains.[24] Their pluck and resolve were represented as qualities that helped to define Pākehā New Zealanders.[25]

Subsequent historians have noted that this experience was common to other settler societies too.[26] The Australian selectors (smallholders) who carved out farms from the bush and the American homesteaders who settled the western frontier similarly gained mythical status; the frontier experience in these societies was also seen as formative in the creation of white social identities. The problem with such universalising models is their exclusivity. What of those who do not fit the mould? Even after the colony moved from an urban to a rural society in the 1850s, a significant proportion of New Zealand settlers remained in town. For instance, the 1861 Census showed that 31 per cent of the Pākehā population lived in the main cities or towns.[27] This is a significant minority and worthy of consideration, but historians have instead concentrated on the (diminishing) majority on the land. If, however, we focus on the city-dwelling population, a counterweight to the strongly masculine reading of colonial society emerges.[28]

Excluding townspeople

A central strategy in marketing New Zealand as a land of beefy rural labourers and plucky smallholders was to belittle city dwellers. Increasingly, they were represented in immigration literature as constitutionally ill-suited to being successful farmers and therefore were poor emigrants. The cerebral and sedentary nature of urban middle-class work was said to make men weak and effeminate, whereas the physicality of farming increased their strength and masculinity. Such thinking had its immediate roots in the British eighteenth-century agricultural moralists, who had emphasised the purity of the countryside over the decadence of the city. Physicians like William Falconer had argued that outdoor (country) life was fortifying and indoor (city) life was enervating. Being indoors made people slothful, indolent and hypersensitive. As Vladimir Jankovic writes: 'The medical picture of a delicate *homme du monde* was one of a sedentary creature immersed in the phlogisticated [airless] atmosphere of the cardroom, in which his moral and physical faculties sank to stupor or sin.'[29]

Initially, immigration writers believed the city effete might be remade into burly types by heading to the colonies. Among these was Charles Hursthouse. In his 1852 book on Australasian emigration, he addressed a passage to his '"brotherhood of bachelors" (we veritable pariahs, who have been too busy, too bashful or too fastidious, to achieve wives)'.[30] This group was known as the afflicted surplus of the middle class who, denied a place in the establishment owing to intense competition, were forced to take up petty commercial positions instead. Hursthouse argued that emigration provided the group with an opportunity to secure their independence and manhood. Rather than remain in the metropolis, 'with only the choice evils between emasculating themselves in some draper's shop (selling pins to children and tape to mincing milliners) or of sinking into the engrossing or calculating mummy of the lawyer', he advised them to escape 'grinding serfdom' and hurry to the Australian goldfields or New Zealand grain fields.[31] By the 1880s, however, the notion that the effete might be redeemed in the colonies had passed. In the words of the emigration agent Arthur Clayden:

> I need not stop to indicate the utter ludicrousness of the bare idea of a Pall Mall exquisite finding himself in a colonial town. However desirable it might be for such idlers to quit their country for their country's good, they must not go to New Zealand. The paradise of the toiler would prove the purgatory of the self-indulgent idler.[32]

It was his view that such people had neither the temperament nor constitution to succeed in New Zealand, so should remain at home.

It is true that some settlers did not have what it took to realise the smallholding ideal. One of these was the merchant George Owen. In May 1859, he and his wife Annabel and two boys, Tom and Charlie, arrived in Auckland from Charlottetown, Prince Edward Island.[33] George soon opened a shop selling goods he had brought with him. But business proved slow. George believed the city had more shops than its population warranted, attributing this to the inaccessibility of the city's hinterland. In 1858, the Auckland provincial government had introduced a rural settlement scheme granting 40-acre rural allotments to adult settlers.[34] The problem was that speculators held much of the accessible land, and the lack of roads to the rest made cultivation difficult. Consequently, many settlers remained in town and opened shops to earn a living.

OPPOSITE City shops like James Smith of Wellington provided employment opportunities for people who had no interest in the rural life. These smartly dressed men, photographed in 1880, are likely employees of the well-known Wellington drapery shop. Alexander Turnbull Library, PAColl-3332-17-2

RIGHT This is Auckland Merchant George Owen pictured in the 1890s. George had an unhappy time cultivating his rural smallholding in the early 1860s and found success in the city instead. Sir George Grey Special Collections, Auckland Libraries, 4-JDR6626

Spotting what he thought was a gap in the market, George ordered a large consignment of stationery. But others had seen it earlier and by the time his stock arrived the market was flooded. Struggling to meet his expenses, George went to cultivate his smallholding. 'There I found the reason why so many who came here to farm were compelled to abandon that intention.'[35] To produce grain the soil needed to be worked for two or three seasons and only a few could afford to do this. He thought of farming cattle. However, he worried the beasts would stray, and with settlers 'nearly all a mile apart' his wife would be 'frightened to stay in a house a moment alone with the chance of Maori visitors'. Owen did not think he could manage a farm single-handedly, but he couldn't afford to employ a hand, so like others before him he returned to Auckland.

George and Annabel Owen defied the smallholding stereotype of the rugged farmer and helpmeet wife – Annabel had stayed in Auckland. When circumstances forced George to go onto the land, the experience was so repellent he soon returned to town. As he wrote, he discovered 'the land & everything so different from my anticipations, everything so rude & settlers so distant from each other'. George knew he did not have the constitution to live out the smallholding ideal. He was unwilling to spend countless backbreaking hours taming his land or to allow his family to live in isolation from neighbours: 'This place has brought persons like

myself very unsuitable to the country,' he freely admitted.[36] George and Annabel then resolved to return to Prince Edward Island. Annabel was deeply homesick. In a letter to her sister-in-law in May 1860, she revealed: 'you can have no idea of the feeling one has towards home where all my dear family are. I did not know how to value it until I left it. Everything is so different here.' She felt indignant that George had to work so hard to make a living; conceded she had not made any friends and was frightened by the imminent fighting. 'George has been called into the Militia. The next thing he will be called to fight them in the bush. Just fancy George fighting the Maoris with his spectacles on.' By this time, Annabel was pregnant, so the couple delayed their departure: 'We will come home very poor, but am quite content to put up with that.' But two months later, aged 33, she died in childbirth.[37]

It is evident that George and Annabel's temperaments were urban, not rural. But even if George was ill-suited to farming, this did not stop him making a mark on colonial society. Annabel's death would have been a setback for him, but it led him to stay in Auckland and build a substantial mercantile business. He became a self-made man. He later married his housekeeper, Annie Dewar, living in a large house in Ponsonby until his death in 1906.[38] Pluck and fortitude were qualities that were not unique to those who settled on the land.

Nonetheless, governments continued to believe that New Zealand's future rested on developing the land rather than cities. Under the 1870s assisted immigration schemes initiated by Julius Vogel, renewed emphasis was placed on attracting agricultural labourers, builders, artisans, young married couples and single women (as domestic servants) who would settle in the country. By 1872, there were scores of agents scattered throughout Britain who were promoting New Zealand as an emigration field at public meetings and selecting immigrants.[39] Among them was the London-based Charles Carter.[40] In an 1873 report, he gave an account of his work. It had included holding a meeting in a back street near Drury Lane for about 200 formerly intemperate workers who were willing to emigrate. After interviewing each applicant, Carter 'found their previous habits and present physical appearance precluded me from accepting them'. Three whom he thought might be eligible he later declined because they resided in 'dirty narrow lanes of this densely populated neighbourhood'. He also rejected a group of Birmingham factory labourers on the basis that indoor workers were unsuitable for outdoor work and they seemed unruly. The class of men he found most appropriate came from the counties of Berkshire, Wiltshire, Oxfordshire, Buckinghamshire and Warwickshire, and it was from these agricultural districts that he selected most of the 1,298 emigrants. Of these, 444 were farm labourers; 339 were labourers who could do farm work; 284 were navvies; 49 were general labourers; and 49 were miners. Also in the mix were 22 gardeners, 20 carpenters and seven sawyers. Just 36 of the contingent came from London.[41]

Despite the preference for country folk, many townspeople still got through screening processes. In 1878, the Otago politician James Macandrew complained to the Agent General that of the recent immigrants arriving in Otago most were neither Scottish nor farmers. 'So far as nationality is concerned that is of little moment; but it is unadvisable to forward to the colony persons only acquainted with life in large cities,' he wrote. Macandrew declared more effort should be made to get small farmers, agricultural labourers, dairymaids and domestic female servants from rural Scotland. He claimed that with the gradual extension of the railway bringing new lands within reach of settlement, the opportunities for small farmers and other rural workers had never been more favourable.[42] An official labour-market report backed Macandrew up, stating the province needed more skilled ploughmen, shepherds and farm couples. It noted that '[m]ost of our late arrivals are more suited for city life than country; this is a mistake.'[43] Auckland too wanted more rural workers. In the mid-1870s, the problem identified by George Owen of settlers staying in town rather than developing their land remained. In correspondence with the Immigration Minister, Auckland's Super-intendent, John Williamson, stated every effort was being made to discourage settlers from staying in towns but the province needed many more emigrants of

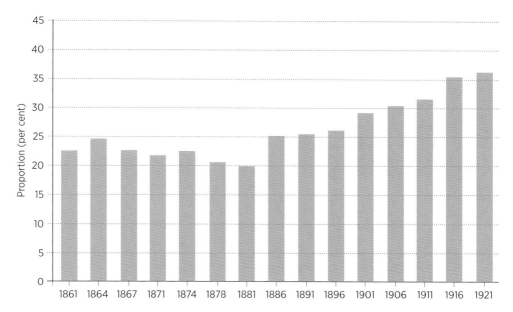

Figure 8.1 Proportion of the population in the four main cities, 1861–1921

Note: Population figures exclude Māori. The proportion of the population living in Auckland, Wellington, Christchurch and Dunedin dropped in the 1870s as immigration schemes pushed people into rural areas. The pattern changed from the 1880s and by 1921, over one-third of New Zealanders lived in these cities. *Source*: New Zealand Census, 1861–1921

the small farming class who could cultivate the land.[44] In other cities there were also reports of new settlers avoiding moving on. The cities were seeing an 'increase of idlers while the country districts are crying out for labor [*sic*],' slammed one newspaper.[45]

If most immigration agents followed their official brief and focused on promoting the land, at least one acknowledged there were opportunities in the cities. In his 1879 emigration book, Revd Joseph Berry described the colonial city economy: 'All the ordinary professions, as lawyers, doctors, &c. are there, and mechanics of every kind as busy.' City industries comprised a mixture of rural-processing and import-substitution enterprises: engineering firms, agricultural implement works, brickyards, cabinet making, tanneries, glue and soaps works, bootmaking, clothing and carriage factories, woollen mills, biscuit and flour mills, and cheese and meat curing. Berry proclaimed no trade or profession needed to fear unemployment in the colony. He recounted the story of a British butcher who had queried whether there were any openings in his trade because he had been told New Zealanders killed all their own meat. Dentists, drapers, clerks and grocers had also asked him if going to New Zealand necessitated becoming a farmer. Such perceptions were wrong, asserted Berry. 'As a rule, farmers might as

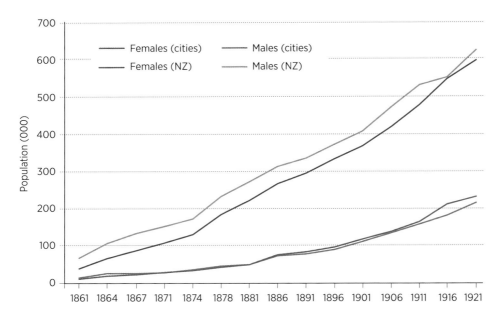

Figure 8.2 Male and female population of the four main cities and New Zealand, 1861–1921

Note: Population figures exclude Māori. Fewer females than males lived in colonial New Zealand, but this pattern was not repeated in the four main cities (Auckland, Wellington, Christchurch and Dunedin), which had very similar male and female populations.

Source: New Zealand Census, 1861–1921

well try and make false teeth as dentists attempt to follow the plough and attend to cattle.' In short, New Zealand could accommodate a full range of people and skills.[46] Perhaps realising his enthusiasm for city life had taken him too far off message, he later warned emigrants not to remain in town after landing but to move quickly to the countryside.[47]

Yet it was advice that ever more settlers were choosing to ignore. By the mid-1880s, official statistics were beginning to reveal a concentration of the population in urban New Zealand and especially in Auckland, Wellington, Christchurch and Dunedin. Figure 8.1 highlights the trend. It shows the proportion of the Pākehā population (Māori were excluded from the count) living in the four cities fell from 25 per cent in 1864 to 20 per cent in 1881. This coincided with the Vogel-era push to get fewer people staying in cities and more people settling on the land. However, the spurning of the Big Smoke was short-lived. By 1886, the cities had recaptured their 25 per cent ratio and their share of the total population continued to increase, reaching 36 per cent in 1921.

Perhaps the most fascinating aspect of the data is that a significantly higher proportion of females than males lived in the cities. In 1861, nearly 28 per cent of all Pākehā females resided in the cities as against just under 20 per cent of Pākehā

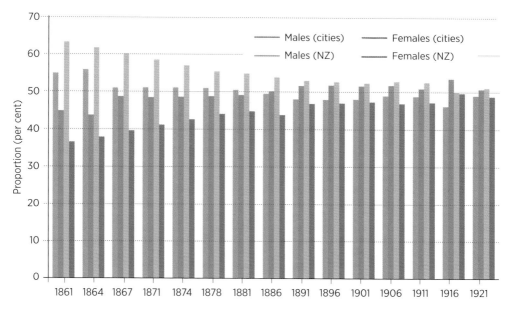

Figure 8.3 Proportion of the population in the four main cities and New Zealand by sex, 1861–1921

Note: Population figures exclude Māori. The gender gap in the four main cities was much narrower than in New Zealand as a whole and from the 1880s, city females outnumbered males.
Source: New Zealand Census, 1861–1921

males. The ratio narrowed a little thereafter, but a gap of about 5 per cent between the sexes remained throughout our period.

Because fewer females than males lived in the colony, this difference was not expressed numerically. Figures 8.2 and 8.3 show the total number and proportion of each sex living in the cities were very similar, with the female population only slightly outnumbering the male one from 1886. This was not the case for New Zealand as a whole, where males continued to outnumber females.[48] This was especially true in rural districts, where from 1878 to 1906 males hovered at around 60 per cent of the population. Over the same period, females increased their proportion of the urban population (towns and cities) from 40 to over 50 per cent. In summary, the statistics reveal three main points: the four cities continued to increase their share of the total population; a higher proportion of the colony's females than males lived in the cities; and the sex ratio was nearly even in cities but weighted towards males outside of them.[49]

Man's country, women's city?

If males demographically dominated rural districts and women urban ones, can we characterise colonial society as a man's country and a woman's city?[50]

To some extent we can. That women were strongly attracted to city life was a phenomenon not unique to New Zealand. Urban historians have shown that during the nineteenth century most European cities had more women than men. This is usually explained in terms of labour-market opportunities widening for women in industrialising cities while they were narrowing in the country because of mechanisation and land enclosures. Young working-class women in particular moved to cities in large numbers due to the high demand for the likes of textile workers, seamstresses, domestic servants and prostitutes.[51] Yet work was not the only magnet. Urbanisation freed these women from the traditional and sometimes repressive social relations of rural life. According to Leif Jerram:

> For some women, urbanization was profoundly liberating in a positive sense, freeing them *to* earn their own money, *to* go where they pleased, and *to* live how they liked. For other women, the move to the city was liberating in a negative sense, freeing them *from* constant observation, *from* oppression, *from* starvation, and *from* generations of grinding poverty.[52]

ABOVE These young housemaids are preparing food in the kitchen of a large Christchurch home in the 1910s, watched over by an older woman servant. *The Press* Collection, Alexander Turnbull Library, 1/1-017705-G

OPPOSITE In an attempt to encourage British women to work as domestic servants in New Zealand, this 1912 pamphlet produced by the High Commissioner in London presented a highly idealised version of this often onerous job. Local women preferred to work in factories or offices. Alexander Turnbull Library, Eph-A-IMMIGRATION-1912-cover

This is not to say that city life was substantially easier for many of these women – some continued to live hard and destitute lives – but its greater freedom and myriad opportunities could be reward enough. This further explains New Zealand immigration agents' emphasis on securing country-bred girls as emigrants. As two acknowledged in 1862: 'Town-bred girls … are on the whole unsuitable; they do not take kindly to the country, they cannot look out onto the street, or chat with a friend next door, or admire the milliner's shops, and they are dull and therefore dissatisfied.'[53]

During the 1870s, 60 per cent of the female wageworkers were domestic servants, but the demand for servants perennially outstripped the supply. The 'servant problem' was particularly acute in country areas.[54] In 1897, the *New Zealand Herald* reported that after 'some diplomacy and wire-drawn negotiations', Auckland's Labour Bureau had managed to persuade two girls to go to the country as cooks at £1 per week – a reasonable wage. Still, the newspaper noted the aversion to domestic service among young working-class women was growing, crediting the trend to inconsiderate treatment from employers and a desire for the independent life of a factory girl.[55]

The chance to become a factory girl was increasing. Secondary industries like those identified by Joseph Berry expanded rapidly from the 1870s as population growth and urbanisation created an expanding domestic market for manufactured goods.[56] Ian Hunter has shown that even in the Long Depression of the 1880s and early 1890s, the number of factories and workers engaged in manufacturing increased by a half and two-thirds respectively.[57] The physicality of manufacturing

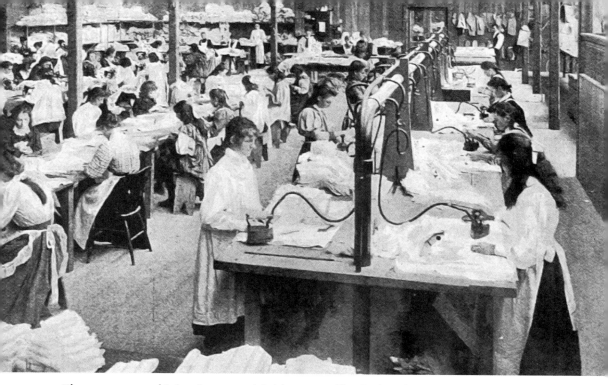

These women machinists, ironers and finishers are toiling in the white shirt department of the A. Clark and Sons clothing factory in Auckland in 1900. Women preferred factory work over domestic service because the pay and conditions were better. Sir George Grey Special Collections, Auckland Libraries, AWNS-19000406-11-2

work ensured that factories were male dominated until the 1870s, when mechanisation and the sub-division of labour provided new openings for girls and women, especially in clothing factories and woollen mills. To protect female workers from exploitation, the government limited working hours and ensured good working conditions.[58] Conversely, there was no equivalent protection for domestic servants: wages were low; working days could last 16 hours; there was a lack of freedom; and loneliness was a common affliction, especially in country districts. Historians have painted a similar picture in other countries. Sarah Deutsch has argued that 'servants are psychologically positioned in a way similar to prostitutes by having their bodies at the beck and call of others'.[59] This helps to explain why working women in late-nineteenth-century Boston would 'if at all possible … choose any occupation before they would choose domestic service'.[60] Daphne Spain makes the further point that factory work exposed girls and women to the discipline, skills and scheduling that were increasingly required to succeed in modern workplaces. Because domestic work did not provide the skills needed in the wider labour market, it 'did not prepare women to join modern society', she asserts.[61] It was therefore unsurprising that ever more of them spurned domestic service for the better pay, shorter hours, sociability, independence and modernity of factory work.[62]

White collar jobs grew in number as the tertiary sector expanded from the late 19th century. These men worked in Dunedin's telegraph office in 1893. William Williams, Alexander Turnbull Library, 1/1-025835-G

Illustrative of this mind-set was a 14-year-old girl whom the *Herald*'s 'Special Lady Commissioner' (of Chapter Seven) met on her 1903 tour of Auckland's inner-city slum. The commissioner asked her why she didn't find a job:

> She said there was no room for her at the factory. 'I've got my name down at Clark's and me name down at Brown's.' I suggested domestic service. She actually yelled at the idea, and glared so that I wondered how I was to escape. But I averted the storm somehow, and elicited the fact that if she could get a 'place wur they treat yer well, and let yer come 'ome at night,' she might go, 'but no country for me!'[63]

Alongside factory work, there were new opportunities for women in the expanding tertiary or service sector of city economies, particularly in the clerical and retail industries.[64] The rise of the service sector was aligned with the modernisation of Western commerce. Industrial capitalism increased the demand for capital and led to the creation of joint-stock banks (public companies with shares owned by investors) to speed up capital flows, which in turn saw a proliferation of insurance services because so much commerce became dependent on credit.

Herbert Spackman was employed as a clerk in the Government Life Insurance office in the 1890s. On his desk sits the emblem of modern office work: the typewriter. Alexander Turnbull Library, PA1-o-465-14

Ancillary businesses – accountancy, legal, advertising, printing and telegraph – also developed. All this increased the need for functionaries who could process, manage, implement and record information flows to local and global markets.[65] The expansion of government meant it too required a growing contingent of bureaucrats to administer its affairs. Between 1886 and 1911, New Zealand's white-collar workforce tripled from 5.2 to 14.4 per cent of the total.[66] Unlike workshops and factories, which could be located in country districts, clerical work was strongly city based. As with manufacturing, it was initially dominated by men, but as it too became more specialised and mechanised (famously symbolised by the typewriter) the sector opened to women.[67]

Service or white-collar employment was widely perceived as middle-class work. Clerical workers had to be proficient in writing and able to comport themselves in a respectable manner, and private commercial colleges soon opened in cities to train them.[68] The higher status of service work meant it was keenly sought by those seeking upward social mobility. But, as with all work, the wages and salaries paid to women were much less than those paid to men on the basis that men needed to support a family – the breadwinner wage.[69] For most young women work was seen as an interlude between leaving school and marrying.

Women clerical workers first moved into the public service during the 1890s. The Wellington clerk Herbert Spackman (of Chapter Three) was among those who applauded their arrival. In April 1895 he recorded: 'The Commissioner informed me that a Miss Diamond had been appointed as a shorthand-writer, but he added, "It won't make any difference to you Spackman." Two girl cadets also appointed. Women have at last made their entrance into Government Insurance.'[70]

Spackman might have welcomed women in his office but their appearance generated a crisis among middle-class men. George Chauncey argues American middle-class men's sense of self was rooted in their ability to support families from their productive work and, above all, in their skill as entrepreneurs and independence from other men. With the rise of the service sector and the growth of salaried work, many men lost this independence because they had to submit to another man – the boss. Further, the growing presence of women in offices was seen to feminise workplace culture and diminish its status as a masculine domain. Women also threatened other masculine realms. The suffrage movement

ABOVE By the time these Railways Department typists were photographed at work in 1931, women were well established in the clerical professions. Women clerks first moved into the public service in the 1890s. Archives New Zealand, Te Rua Mahara o te Kāwanatanga, AAVK W3493 DRAW 37 C654

OPPOSITE This 1904 cartoon subverts the usual social order, with women occupying roles traditionally held by men. It was inspired by reports attributing the shortage of domestic servants to growing demand for female clerks. National Library, Papers Past, *New Zealand Free Lance*, 28 May 1904, p.7

Saturday, May 28, 1904. THE FREE LANCE. 7

One of the numerous reasons put forward to explain the shortage of domestic servants has been the increasing demand for female clerks and the opening of the door of the merchant's office to the trip of feminine feet.—N.Z. Times.

THE REIGN OF WOMAN—"See the Conquering Angel Comes."

challenged men's prerogative to represent the women and their families in the public sphere, while the campaign by the Women's Christian Temperance Union (WCTU) to restrict or ban alcohol suggested to some that women were trying to control men's lives.[71] Threats to middle-class masculinity also came from other men. If middle-class men exerted power over working men in factories, the very physicality of manual work afforded working men a stronger basis for asserting their manhood.[72] Politicians like Theodore Roosevelt warned of the risk of 'over-civilisation' to American manhood and culture. As Chauncey notes, this was 'a not very oblique reference to the dangers of women's civilizing influence and the effeminization of men'. It was a fear that led men to create numerous social groups, like Boy Scouts, aimed at restoring the role of men in the socialisation of boys.[73]

Evidence suggests New Zealand middle-class men faced a similar crisis. Many men resented women's entry into office work and some clerks' unions excluded women members.[74] The success of the women's suffrage movement in 1893 and the growing strength of the WCTU showed that, even more than in the United States, New Zealand women (and male supporters) were beginning to move into masculine domains. That city women were at the forefront of these reform movements – the WCTU leader Kate Sheppard lived in Christchurch – reinforced the impression of the city as a woman's space.[75]

The perception was lampooned in a 1904 *New Zealand Free Lance* cartoon (see page 375). Responding to reports suggesting the shortage of domestic servants was due to increasing demand for female clerks in merchants' offices, the cartoonist imagined a time when women dominated city life. Titled 'The Reign of Women – See the Conquering Angel Comes', the cartoon comprises a series of vignettes in which contemporary gender roles are reversed. One of these is a scene headed 'The Male Pram Nuisance'. It depicts harried men in dresses and frilly trousers pushing prams along a city street. Two masculine-looking women, one a city merchant and the other a constable, step onto the street. The merchant calls the men a 'positive nuisance' and demands the constable remove them. Another scene depicts the feminisation of the Premier's office. As female clerks type in the background, pretty young women pamper Premier Seddon. At the doorway is a startled Opposition leader, William Massey, who apologises for his incursion; Seddon tells him not to be bashful and, like him, he will get used to the feminine attention. There is a degree of male fantasy to this vignette, but some of the others are more confronting. They include a marriage ceremony in which the husband promises to 'obey' his wife (subverting patriarchal custom); a job interview at which an employer replaces a 'mere man' with a woman on a lower salary (threatening male job security); and a depiction of a female mayor and council (challenging traditional leadership roles). Many early-twentieth-

EDUCATION A FAILURE.
Farm labourers and navvies are at a premium this Christmas, and some big cheques have come to town. Clerks are at a big discount, and numbers are eagerly seeking employment.—*Labour report.*
Unemployed Bank Clerk: Isn't this sickening—that great hulking, uneducated crew living on the fat of the land this Christmas, while I'm starving? There's no room for brains here. Why wasn't I brought up a navvy?

A CLAIM FOR OVERTIME.
Boss: You claim two hours overtime this week; pray when did that happen? *Member of Clerks' Union:* I woke up at five yesterday morning, and thought of my work until seven.

LEFT Clerks were a favourite target of newspaper cartoonists. In this 1907 sketch, a weedy-looking unemployed clerk thinks uneducated agricultural workers have it easy while his intellect goes unappreciated. National Library, Papers Past, *Observer*, 5 Jan 1907, p.16

RIGHT In this cartoon of 1911, clerks are characterised as foppish and entitled. A slouching, dandified clerk is demanding over-time wages for merely thinking about his work. National Library, Papers Past, *Observer*, 28 Oct 1911, p.17

century readers would have laughed at the seeming absurdity of the scenes; the astonishing thing from our perspective 100 years later is how much of it has come to pass (excepting the harem around the Premier).[76]

The emasculated clerk

Until the 1870s, the personification of widespread anxiety about the emasculating nature of city life had been the before-mentioned Pall Mall exquisite. This type, however, was discouraged from emigrating, so a new target emerged: the city clerk. He became a figure of both fun and vitriol in colonial society. He was invariably represented as a wasp-wasted effete who, in sporting stiff shirt collars, not a simple neckband, and holding a pen, rather than axe, failed miserably to live up to the colonial masculine ideal. Immigration agents were in broad agreement that clerks were not wanted in the colony. Writing in the early 1870s, Alexander Bathgate asserted: 'It may be laid down as a general principle that any man who likes to work and can use his hands will succeed, but I cannot advise clerks and shopmen and men of that stamp to come here.'[77] At the end of the decade, Arthur

In 1888 Dr Hutchinson of Wellington gave up his city medical practice and made a new life at this farm in Taranaki. His story was published in a number of newspapers as an example of a new pioneering spirit that young urban folk should emulate. Puke Ariki, A64.087

Clayden reinforced the message. He recounted being accosted by a smartly dressed man and asked what the prospects for clerks were in New Zealand. 'Utter ruin and self-destruction,' Clayden advised, before explaining the 'peculiarities of colonial life are wholly unsuited to that artificial existence' in which clerks resided.[78] It was a recitation of the Romantic idea that cities were artificial and 'real' people lived on the land. In 1886, Frederick Pennefather also advised against clerks emigrating, explaining that new countries had to be agricultural rather than mercantile communities, so vacancies in commerce were necessarily rare.[79] These writers therefore found it puzzling that increasing numbers of young men were favouring city over country work. Clayden blamed their mothers:

> The suicidal vanity of bringing up children with a view to them wearing broadcloth and idling away their time behind bank counters or at lawyers' desks, is not confined to the mother country. The Mrs Brown of a New Zealand city has much in common with her namesake at home. She is very apt to think

This group of Māori workers were part of a gang that constructed the road to Lake Waikaremoana in the 1890s. Their lives were a world away from those of the much-maligned city clerk. Alexander Turnbull Library, PAColl-7273-01

her Frederick, dressed like a gentleman and sporting a lot of jewellery, is a much finer sight than the same unique being would be at work behind his father's bench or guiding his father's plough.[80]

Equally perplexed by the phenomenon of the over-civilised city male was a Dr Hutchinson. In early 1888, Hutchinson gave up his Wellington medical practice for a Taranaki farm. He had grown tired of professional life and saw it as his duty to begin again on the land. There was 'no life so independent as that of the pushing, successful farmer', he affirmed. Hutchinson believed young men should settle on farms and realise their independence instead of entering the civil service or banks, where they lived in fear of being dismissed and had to fawn over their managers. He declared:

There is no independence to be secured in the Civil Service, or in many of the occupations of city life, and I cannot understand how the young men of the colony prefer a dependent, miserable sort of life when, if they only showed energy and manliness, they would enter upon the healthy and active life on a farm.[81]

In other words, farming allowed men to regain their independence and manhood that was lost by having to succumb to other men in city workplaces.[82] But if Hutchinson was happily living out the rural myth, he also acknowledged it was losing its appeal among the upcoming generation. As Pennefather too conceded: 'That young men should prefer the routine drudgery of a desk to the free life on a farm is a mystery to me; I believe it chiefly comes from a false notion of gentility; but it is a fact that must be recognised.'[83]

Among the young men who chose city over country life was 17-year-old William Derry. His mother had died and his father laboured on the land, so he had been living with his older sister Sarah, a teacher in rural Springston, Canterbury.[84] Knowing she was finding it hard to manage on her salary, William reluctantly left school in 1880 to make his own way in life. Rather than finding work on nearby farms, he headed for Christchurch, where he secured a clerical position in the property firm of Lewis & Gould, and accommodation in a Conference Street boarding house. In a letter to his English cousin Harry, he said he was taking advantage of the city's amenities: taking out a subscription to the public library, visiting the Industrial Exhibition and boating on the Avon River. Although he was in work, he noted the city was in such a depressed state that a soup kitchen had opened to feed the poor. 'There is such a number of unemployed here, loafing at every corner of the Street.'[85] (Canterbury was especially affected by the 1880s depression, leading many agricultural workers to move to Christchurch.)[86] In William's next letter to Harry, in 1883, he told his cousin he shared his preference for vivacious young women who could carry a conversation. 'I agree with you in liking girls with some life in them and I always steer clear of those lifeless ones of which you only get "yes" or "no" and a sickly smile sometimes. There are a few of them knocking about in N.Z.,' he said. He also revealed he had been promoted and now had control of the life assurance part of the office.[87]

Due to the desire of AMP to create a branch-office network, Lewis & Gould lost the life-assurance agency the following year. William accepted a transfer to AMP's Wellington head office. It was among the largest in the city, with 16 clerks, nine of whom were beneath him. 'I feel satisfied at this change, because I think there is more chance of a fellow getting on in an office like this.' But he detested Wellington and its climate: it was 'always blowing most terrifically'. He also disliked the wooden buildings and narrow streets.[88] A few months later, William admitted he had become 'much more reconciled to this place'. He had found it easy to make friends – they were 'one of the greatest boons of my life' – and the city provided 'plenty of enjoyment'. He had just received an invitation to a fancy-dress ball and had decided to go as a Spanish Count.[89] In an April 1885 letter to Harry, he attached a photograph of himself and expressed doubts over his masculinity. 'You see I am beardless boy still, although I have reached my 21st Birthday. Of course I envy all fellows who possess a moustache and growl at my misfortune in being so smooth.' The Russian scare was in full flight – Anglo–Russian rivalry in Afghanistan had created fear of a Russian invasion – and William also worried about being called up to fight. 'I wonder what sort of soldier yours truly will make, up to the present time I have never ever fired a gun off, so will require a deal of practice.' On a more uplifting note, he announced his sister Sarah had given birth to a girl; he was 'awfully mashed on the child' and relished being an uncle.[90]

William was the inverse image of the colonial masculine stereotype. He had a steady and stimulating city job, was interested in ideas, had a stable group of friends, enjoyed the company of women, and relished the social and cultural life of cities. His correspondence also reveals no interest in gambling, fighting or drinking. Although he worried about appearing and being unmanly, cursing his lack of facial hair and questioning his soldiering ability, he seemed more than content with his lot. His existence was far from the diminished life caricatured by Hutchinson. Hursthouse and Pennefather, however, would have labelled William effeminate. William continued to advance in AMP. In 1897 he married Edith Dyer in a choral service at St Mary's church, Karori; among the bridesmaids were Kathleen Beauchamp, later the writer Katherine Mansfield.[91] The couple had one son. In 1905, William was appointed the AMP branch manager in Auckland and in 1917 was promoted to head the West Australian office in Perth, where he died in 1931.[92]

Anxiety over the emasculating effects of city life meant the colonial masculine stereotype continued to influence male middle-class culture even as the life of the rural drifter became the experience of fewer and fewer men. This deep unease made people blind to the reality that such a figure was in fact a poor role model to champion in a rapidly urbanising society. The skills and attributes that made men successful in the countryside were not necessarily those that commanded success in the city. A sharpness of mind, a willingness to settle and stable social relationships were more likely to generate achievement in cities than brute strength, a transitory lifestyle and fleeting social relationships. (Acumen aided the success of an enterprise; a firm location helped an enterprise to grow; and stable social relations encouraged customer loyalty). In William Derry, George Owen and Herbert Spackman we can see a less muscular and more emotive expression of masculinity than the colonial stereotype. If this form was poorly suited to life on the land, it was eminently suited to life in cities.

Muscular masculinity

Nonetheless, such was the alarm over the feminisation of cities that a new muscular expression of masculinity – sometimes called the 'cult of muscularity' – emerged within middle-class society in New Zealand and overseas. (Its ascent was also associated with growing concern about the degenerative effects of city environments on racial fitness and national efficiency, discussed in Chapter Seven.) From the late nineteenth century, growing numbers of city men and boys engaged in strenuous recreation as a means of proving their manliness.[93] Rough sports like rugby union were made compulsory in boys' secondary schools, both to control their games in a civilised setting and improve boys' moral character and virility. Boxing also became popular and was praised for fostering strength and stoicism (against pain).[94] Bodybuilding took off in New Zealand following a 1902 visit by the famous strongman Eugen Sandow, who became an object of adulation for both sexes. He and his acolytes showed how even the puniest townsmen could become strapping exemplars of manhood using the Sandow exercise system.[95] George Chauncey's point that 'building manly bodies and focusing on the physical basis of manliness allowed men to emphasize their difference from women at a time when women seemed to be insisting on the similarity of the sexes' holds true for New Zealand.[96] A toned physique also made it possible for men to reconcile city life with the rural masculine stereotype. In a similar vein to how the suburb combined the space of the country with the amenities of the city, the cult of muscularity united the 'brawn' of the rural stereotype with the 'brains' of its urban counterpart. In identifying with this hybrid expression of masculinity, white-collar men could feel at ease with the sedentary and cerebral nature of their productive work so long as they remained strong and physically active outside of it.[97]

An early promoter of muscular masculinity was George Thomson, whose wife Emma wrote the diary quoted in Chapter Three. Born in Calcutta and educated in Edinburgh, George immigrated with his family to New Zealand in 1868. The family farmed unsuccessfully in Southland for three years before moving to Dunedin, where George became a tutor at Otago Boys' High School in 1871 and science master in 1877. He was instrumental in organising cadet corps and rugby at the school, arranging the first public rugby game between the university and the school in 1871. He subsequently founded the Dunedin and University rugby clubs. Attending rugby games was a regular leisure activity for the Thomson family, and no doubt George and Emma's sons were encouraged to play the game. Certainly their children were physically active and robust. George was less so after being accidentally shot in the foot during a cadets' corps practice – it was later amputated. If this proved a physical restraint it did not hinder his productive work. He became a leader in Dunedin's educational and scientific circles, founding

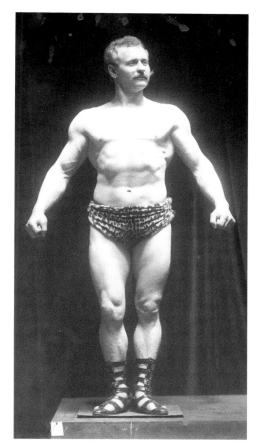

LEFT City men flocked to demonstrations by the Prussian bodybuilder Eugen Sandow, who toured New Zealand in 1902 and 1903. White-collar workers could emulate Sandow's impressive physique by signing up for mail-order exercise programmes and joining gymnasiums. Herman John Schmidt, Alexander Turnbull Library, 1/1-001833-G

RIGHT Gyms opened throughout the country in the wake of Eugen Sandow's tour. Exercising at gyms allowed city men to feel more robust and manly, and dispel the stereotype that they were effeminate and weedy. J. W. Harrison's Gymnasium and School of Physical Culture used Sandow's name as a selling point. Alexander Turnbull Library, Eph-B-VARIETY-1902-01-013

technical education in the city in 1888 and the Portobello marine research station in 1902. Over his long career he published 375 papers in the biological sciences. He entered Parliament in 1908 as a supporter of William Massey and later served on the Legislative Council. He died in 1933.[98] George's experience with farming failed but, like George Owen, he achieved considerable success in the city. It is indicative of the strength of anti-urbanism in colonial society that no myth arose to celebrate townspeople's pioneering achievements in shaping New Zealand society. This is in stark contrast with the United States, where city-based figures like John D. Rockefeller, Andrew Carnegie, Thomas Edison, Jane Addams and Henry Ford became heroic figures in late-nineteenth- and early-twentieth-century American society.

Politicising anti-urbanism

We have seen how anti-urbanism was expressed both in immigration policy that discriminated against townspeople and in a cultural anxiety that city life was emasculating and feminising. A third manifestation was that identified by Miles Fairburn: cities were seen as inessential in an agricultural-based economy like New Zealand's. Townspeople were therefore represented as less important than farmers, who were championed as the (economic) backbone of the country.[99]

This expression of anti-urbanism officially emerged with the Representation Act 1881, which introduced the 'country quota' that gave a 25 per cent weighting to rural electorates. (The gerrymander made rural electorates 25 per cent smaller, meaning fewer people were required to create a rural than an urban electorate.) Supporters had argued the quota was necessary because townspeople had easier access to polling booths and to parliamentarians than country folk and so were better able to exert political influence. They also believed urban plural voters exercised a disproportionate influence in country electorates (urban-domiciled voters could vote in country constituencies if they held land there and vice versa).[100] As Neill Atkinson points out, 'this was as much an argument for abolishing plural voting as for adopting a country quota'. He also notes the practical difficulties of rural voting could have been alleviated by providing more polling booths. Neither idea was considered, and the measure became law.[101]

In 1889, a government Bill proposing to increase the weighting to 33 per cent met with outrage from city members, one of whom suggested it be named 'A Bill to give a Large Increase of Representation to Land, to Cattle and to Sheep'.[102] Opponents managed to reduce the figure to 28 per cent and exclude provincial towns from its realm. The quota was applied to all electorates except those containing urban settlements with populations over 2,000.[103] In 1889, the urban population comprised 43 per cent of the total population; by excluding centres with populations under 2,000, the proportion was even less.[104] So the notion that the 'country' was under imminent threat from the 'city' was fantastical. The quota's purpose was ostensibly to strike a power balance between urban and rural electorates, but it was really about making sure country political factions maintained their political dominance. This was underlined when the Labour government moved to abolish the quota in 1945. The Farmers' Union mounted a virulent campaign against the change, threatening to cut town milk supplies and even seeking the intervention of the King. Prime Minister Peter Fraser was unrepentant. He was determined to uphold the principle of one vote, one value. Anything else, he said, 'was hopelessly reactionary and a negation of democracy'.[105] He got his way. After 64 years of being treated as lesser citizens within the body politic, townspeople gained equality with their country brethren.

The subservient place of townspeople in public discourse came to the fore during the Liberal era of the late nineteenth and early twentieth centuries. David Hamer's research on the Liberal Party revealed deep-seated tension over the importance of cities in New Zealand life. He showed, for example, how in 1896 Walter Symes summed up the views of country members by asserting 'if it were not for people going on the land there would be no cities at all. Their very existence depended on the settlement on the land.'[106] Symes's colleague Andrew Rutherford further charged that it was only Customs duties and protected industry that allowed cities to survive; if free trade was introduced, farmers could get their supplies more cheaply and cities could be done away with altogether. Country members continually reiterated that farmers were the colony's backbone; if their interests came first, then all of New Zealand benefited went the refrain.[107]

City members tried to repudiate the dependence argument by stressing the interdependence between town and country. Not least, towns and cities provided a local market for farm-sourced goods and so helped to relieve farmers' reliance on export markets and their inherent boom/bust cycles. William Hutchison believed a nation comprising only of farmers would be lacklustre and inert: 'A country of shepherds and herdsmen may be a Lotos-land [a place of languid contentment] where it is always afternoon, but it will never be a land of great achievement or heroic deeds.'[108] For Hutchison, it was the energy and commotion of city life that generated success. Yet other city members supported the 'Farmer Backbone mantra', as James Belich aptly called it.[109] In 1909, Frederick Baume declared that farmers could survive without lawyers and shopkeepers but townspeople could not survive without farmers.[110] Hamer believed they took this stance because they 'valued the "country" as a resource that would prevent towns in New Zealand – which they themselves wished to continue to live in – from coming to resemble the congested, crime-ridden cities of the Old World'.[111] They wanted to check urbanisation and encourage townspeople onto the land.

An agrarian cult

Concern about the detrimental effects of city growth united country and city Liberals over the necessity of land reform. The 'bursting-up' of the large pastoral estates into smaller family farms was one aspect of this policy; the provision of salubrious suburban allotments on the edge of cities and towns was another. City Liberals argued that the suburban scheme was required because few city workers were interested in conventional farming but might be tempted by a smallholding in a hamlet within commuting distance of town – the ideal was 3 acres and a cow. Suburban homes would also reduce competition for scarce inner-city properties and ease overcrowding. Under the 1897 Workmen's Homes policy, city workers would be provided with state leasehold land on which to build homes and meet their subsistence needs when work was scarce. There were other perceived advantages: in making workers more self-reliant, the drain on hospitals and charities during slumps would be reduced; in decreasing competition for central-city rental properties, overcrowding would be eased; and in giving city workers a chance to secure an affordable home, social mobility would be advanced.[112] Hamlets of workers' homes were founded in places like Riccarton (Christchurch) and Henderson (Auckland). However, the scheme failed. The government's refusal to provide sufficient credit to erect homes or offer the right of freehold reduced its appeal.[113] There were also practical difficulties. As one critic put it: '[A] man who has been engaged during the day at hard manual labour does not wish to live far from his work. Physical exercise and country homes would suit the clerical and ordinary business men in this respect, but the labourer has had his exercise in his work.'[114]

Opposition among city workers to suburban living was another deterrent. According to the Dunedin lawyer, A. R. Barclay, 'a great many of the workers do not like to go outside; they like to live in the towns'.[115] Even if they did want to go, the expense and time of commuting to city workplaces could be unassailable.[116] On the government's side, the rising cost of purchasing peri-urban land was making the whole scheme uneconomic. In 1903, Premier Seddon admitted the initiative was dead. The government moved in a new direction with the Workers' Dwelling Act 1905, which provided for the erection of suburban state-rental housing within city boundaries.[117] As we saw in the previous chapter, it struck similar problems to this scheme, as workers clung to central-city homes.

City workers were not the only ones resisting the call to the land. In 1902, the public intellectual and former Liberal politician, William Pember Reeves, labelled New Zealand's back-to-the-land culture an 'agrarian cult' and expressed exasperation at the anti-urbanism underpinning it.

'Go to the land!' has been the doctrine preached to the hesitating, the enterprising, or the unemployed, by newspapers, orators, writers of books, by globe-trotters without any knowledge, and by old colonists speaking from the fulness [sic] of experience. In this cry, at any rate, Progressives and Conservatives have joined. So fashionable had the agrarian cult been, that, at times, to be a townsman has almost been to wear a badge of inferiority, and large towns have been denounced as blots on the landscape. Manufactures have been classed as artificialities, professional men as parasites, and artisans

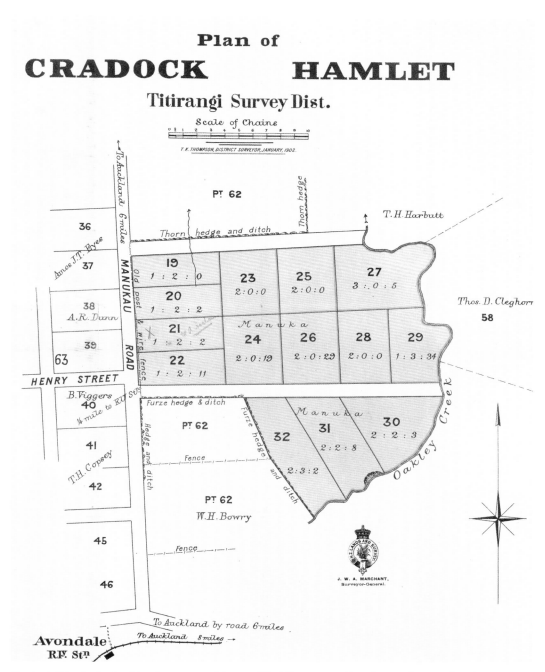

Cradock Hamlet in Auckland was one of the smallholding areas offered to workers under the 1897 Workmen's Homes policy. Located on the corner of present-day Blockhouse Bay Road and Cradock Street, the plots were between 1 and 3 acres. Robert C Airey, Auckland War Memorial Museum Tāmaki Paenga Hira, G9081.G46A8 roundly termed a race of loafers. Even to-day numbers of intelligent colonists look upon the growth of their cities with mixed feelings – healthy, wealthy and orderly as these cities are.[118]

Reeves's rant exposed the deep-seated ambivalence about cities and city life that had arisen in middle-class society. Since the 1880s, townspeople had been told their vote was worth less than country people's, their men folk were less manly than rural men, and their part in the colony's prosperity was nothing compared to that of farmers'.[119] It was a huge fall from grace for the colony's cities of the 1860s and 1870s that had been championed as symbols of British civilisation and material progress. In pointing out that New Zealand's cities were 'healthy, wealthy, and orderly', Reeves sought to reassert the importance of cities in colonial life. Reeves's passage can be located in a wider public debate over the merits of city versus country life. A catalyst for the discussion was the gathering of the unemployed in cities during the Long Depression, such as the one William Derry saw in Christchurch. The *Southland Times* insisted there was ample work for the unemployed in the country, but the attractions of city life were keeping them from leaving. As well as the diversions of the theatre, concert hall and lecture room, 'there is all the pleasure and excitement arising from the gossip and scandal and even the improving conversation of people living in large masses together'. Yet the country offered its own attractions, claimed the newspaper: fresh air free from the pestilential odours, a higher standard of health and a simpler lifestyle. While the *Times* admitted the clerk and shopkeeper were 'perhaps' as useful as the bushman or ploughman, it thought 'going out to reclaim the wilderness from waste' was a nobler pursuit. Such workers were more directly contributing to the colony's wealth than those doing 'mere copying work or selling cotton or calicoes'. The development of the soil 'is a man's work' whereas the work of the shop or office could be 'done by weak women'. The newspaper therefore declared for the country: 'Just as the advice to young men in the United States is – "Go West," so we say to our young men – Go to the country.'[120] The *Waikato Times* agreed. It published a list of aphorisms juxtaposing the country's 'naturalness' against the city's 'artificiality'. Among others, these included: 'in the country you make friends, in the city acquaintances … in the country flowers, in the city dresses … in the country stars, in the city, gas-lights'. While conceding the 'rush of the age' was towards the towns, it proclaimed the 'country is the place to live in'.[121]

In 1890, the *Otago Witness* columnist 'Cigarette' made a fervent case for the city. He began with Cowper's maxim:

'God made the country, man made the town'; but for all that the town is nicer to live in. The country is all very well for lovers to spoon in, for artists to

This 1886 painting of Milford Sound by John Gibb captures two images central to New Zealand's rural mythology: the majestic natural landscape and the man-alone rural figure represented by the swaggers. Landscape painters of the period preferred wilderness settings over urban views. John Gibb, Museum of New Zealand Te Papa Tongarewa, 2002-0027-1

paint, and for poets to rave about, but as a place of residence for an ordinary nineteenth century mortal it is monotonous in the extreme.

He proceeded to question the reputed advantages of country living, asking whether fresh eggs, milk and butter atoned for the lack of newspapers, letters and sociability. He also noted many country youth were leaving for the cities. This was not surprising:

for there is a fascination in cities that is not to be found in the fields. And where does that fascination lie? Not in the cities themselves, but in the human beings, whose habitations they are. The life and stir and noise and excitement going on in cities have a charm of their own; there are living, breathing souls on all sides; the air is alive with the thoughts and speech of thousands; every minute brings fresh faces into view; there is action going on all round; and thus in the crowded streets, rubbing shoulders with our fellowmen, life seems more real than when it creeps slowly by through fields and country roads, where the days are filled with ever-recurring duties, and the weeks and months marked only by seed time and harvest.

Here was a testimonial for the mutability and verve of city life, the existential thrill of being surrounded by others in a city crowd. Cigarette claimed country life was not as poetical as people imagined. Growing your own strawberries and cream sounded very nice until your back ached from weeding strawberry beds and keeping the dairy clean. He further disputed the notion that country living delivered peace and contentment: 'as for "profiting by Nature's teachings," and being "elevated by her moods," that is all nonsense, for if you want to find a good specimen of an idiot you must seek it in the country.' He stated that 'most of the lunatics' who filled New Zealand's asylums came from the country, and cited the lonely shepherd who loses his mind because for months on end he hears no voice other than his own. Finally, Cigarette asserted it was townspeople who 'rave most' about the country but 'very few' were prepared to live there.[122]

At the end of the decade, the same newspaper brought a feminine perspective to the debate. Each month, the women readers who constituted its 'Cosy Corner Club' submitted their views on a chosen topic to a moderator called 'Emmeline', and when the subject was the advantages and disadvantages of town and country life, ten responses were published. 'Fidelas' preferred the city because it 'has the advantage of intelligence'. It was the abode of philosophy and science, whose discoveries and inventions improved life. 'Inconnue' also valued the cerebral nature of cities. 'First of all you are in the thick of life. There is so much of interest to hear and see going on around you. You are in the midst of books, lectures, and friction with other minds more cultivated than your own.' Most correspondents, however, favoured the country; even the Dunedin-domiciled Emmeline professed a strong preference for it. 'Gnib' contended family life was richer because there were fewer evening diversions to take people from the home. 'Ted' thought she could appreciate a month of two in the city but would soon tire of its pretence: 'The society side of town life seems to me a most unenviable thing. Its claims are almost overwhelming, and it is simply painful to have to dress in one's best and go to a crowded "at home," where you don't want to see anyone.' Sitting on the proverbial fence was 'Interested': 'I prefer neither the town nor the country, but somewhere about the suburbs, where I could enjoy a little of what I like of both town and country.'[123] This preference for the middle realm became ascendant in the twentieth century.[124]

The debate essentially concerned individual and collective social identities:

were Pākehā a rural or an urban people? The *Southland Times* and *Waikato Times* both argued New Zealanders were fundamentally country folk, and it was their destiny to settle and exploit the wealth of the land. The barb that shop or office work was best suited to weak women underscored the notion that townspeople were effete and inferior to the rugged souls who worked the soil. Conversely, 'Cigarette' believed that ever more Pākehā were identifying as city people. He asserted the country was monotonous compared to the city and this was why its youth were leaving it. Some in the Cosy Corner Club relished the sophistication of the city too, but most preferred the simplicity of the country. Interestingly, Emmeline's pro-country stance supported Cigarette's point that it was townspeople who most idealised country life. This probably explains why the debate remains unresolved. Nearly a century later, a study on cities by the Parliamentary Commissioner for the Environment found that submitters to its research 'were divided on whether urban New Zealanders see themselves as a rural or urban people … Some thought New Zealanders see themselves as a suburban or even a frontier people and this, in part, accounts for the neglect of urban [environmental] issues.'[125] By then about 85 per cent of New Zealanders lived in towns or cities, but evidently some still imagined themselves as people of the land, underscoring how social identities are flexible and multi-faceted.[126]

Urban drift

Whether or not New Zealanders identified with country or city life, the fact remained that, at the turn of the twentieth century, most people knew it was only a matter of time before the colony became an urban society. The 1896 Census had shown that 44 per cent of the total (Pākehā) population was now living in cities and boroughs. By 1906, the figure had climbed to 48 per cent (see Figure 8.4). The cities too were taking off. As we can see in Figure 8.5, between 1891 and 1906 all but Dunedin more or less doubled their populations – Dunedin's gold-driven growth was over and it was now experiencing relative decline. The realisation that New Zealand was transitioning from a rural to an urban society created alarm among those who believed prosperity rested on keeping people on the land. Why was urban drift (as urbanisation was called) happening and what could be done to check it before the point of no return was reached, they asked?

Unlike twentieth-century Māori urbanisation, which is relatively well documented in historiography (although there is plenty of scope for further research), Pākehā urbanisation has been barely considered.[127] There is little research besides Miles Fairburn's 'Rural Myth' article; general New Zealand histories treat it as given.[128] The demographer Ian Pool is among the few others to consider the question. In line with overseas research, he attributes Pākehā urbanisation to labour-market changes: the rise in urban manufacturing and

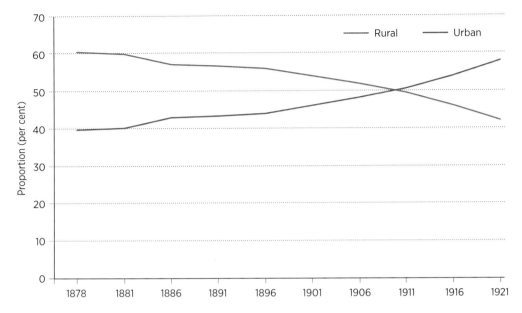

Figure 8.4 Urban and rural population, 1878–1921

Note: Population figures exclude Māori. In the last quarter of the 19th century, the urban share of New Zealand's population grew and the rural share correspondingly declined. By the 1911 Census, New Zealand's population was more urban than rural.

Source: New Zealand Census, 1861–1921

service employment coincided with a decline in rural farming, mining and forestry employment.[129] This creates the impression that country dwellers were forced to move to towns and cities to secure work. There is no doubt that growing employment opportunities in cities were important drivers of urbanisation, but the country versus city discourse showed the social and cultural allure of cities was important too. As Peter Andersson has written in relation to Europe: 'It is easy to concentrate on factors of economy or employment when looking for reasons for urbanisation, but the attraction of entertainment and leisure pursuits should not be underestimated.'[130] Certainly if we look at Pākehā urbanisation these latter aspects loom large in explanations for the phenomenon.

As early as 1879, a provincial Otago newspaper declared urban drift 'A Foolish and Dangerous Movement' and asked how it could be prevented. It claimed: 'Large cities are large fires, to which human moths, whose native sphere is the country, flock in their blind ignorance, their incapacity to distinguish between what is beneficent and what is baleful'. The solution, it said, was to raise the standard of life in the country through the provision of urban amenities like small libraries and encouraging pastimes like cricket.[131] Some newspapers placed New Zealand's experience within a global context. The population of France was static, said

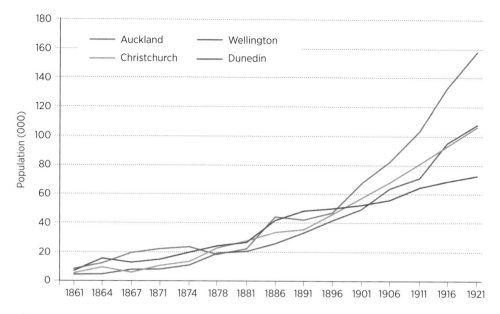

Figure 8.5 Population of the four main cities, 1861–1921

Note: Population figures exclude Māori. The populations of Auckland, Wellington, Christchurch and Dunedin grew throughout the 19th century and into the early 20th. Auckland, Wellington and Christchurch nearly doubled in size between 1891 and 1906 but Dunedin's growth was much slower. *Source*: New Zealand Census, 1861–1921

the Christchurch *Star* in 1896, but Paris was growing rapidly. Even in the great agricultural states of Ohio, Indiana and Illinois in the United States, people were abandoning farming and moving to the cities. Yet in pursuing city lives, people lost contact with nature. The *Star* reported a survey of Boston six-year-olds that found that 70 per cent had never seen a cornfield, 60 per cent had never seen a robin, and some thought a cow was as big as their thumb.

The proximity of the countryside and cheap railway excursions to it meant New Zealand's town-bred children were spared such ignorance, but the newspaper worried that, in exposing country children 'to the allurements of town life', these trips would exacerbate urbanisation. In 1907, Wellington's *Evening Post* reported on the growing concentration of Australia's population in its state capitals. Whereas in 1871 Sydney held 27 per cent of New South Wales' population, in 1901 it was 35 per cent. Over the same time, the share of Victoria's population in Melbourne and Queensland's in Brisbane climbed from 28 to 41 per cent and 12 to 23 per cent respectively. By comparison, New Zealand's biggest city, Auckland, held only 8 per cent of the total population. The *Post* reassured readers that in having comparatively few of its people penned in cities, New Zealand was much better off.[132]

This Dunedin street is sprayed with water to keep the dust down. By the time this photograph was taken around 1924, city streets were being covered with asphalt. This eliminated dust in the summer and mud in the winter, making cities more pleasant places to live in. Dunedin City Archives, Photo 150/10a

This was cold comfort to the government. It was increasingly concerned about the reluctance of new immigrants to take up country work. As a Wellington Labour Department official observed in 1908: '[The] complaint is not a new one, nor is it peculiar to the Englishmen. The young New Zealander has similar desires. He dislikes country life, and sighs for the city, with its attractions and distractions, its gaiety, and its variety.' The official told of receiving a telegram earlier that day requesting 30 'pick and shovel men' for work in a small Taranaki township; despite the good wages on offer, he was unable to meet the request because there were insufficient men willing to go. Even men who were 'used to farm work in England seem to have a dislike to country life as soon as they arrive in New Zealand,' he lamented.[133]

The following year, Agriculture Minister Thomas Mackenzie proclaimed the country was not fulfilling its potential because too many people were staying in towns. Such concentration might be justified in cities that were large manufacturing centres, but this was not the case in New Zealand. He cited Census data showing that between 1901 and 1906 the urban population had risen by 75,000 as against 41,000 for the rural population. 'These figures are certainly surprising,' he said, 'and in an agricultural and pastoral country like New Zealand should without doubt be reversed.' If the nation was to prosper more effort was needed to 'increase our backbone industries': wool, mutton and dairy produce, as well as mining. Much had been done in recent years, he said, to improve conditions on farms, so it was difficult to understand why the unemployed continued to gather in cities when the country cried out for workers. He returned to Clayden's earlier point as way of explanation: that parents encouraged their sons to pursue city occupations rather than sending them off to labour on the land.[134] Yet such labour developed both the mind and the body and offered young men the best 'chance of improving their positions in life', insisted Mackenzie.[135]

For the *Evening Post* the explanation lay elsewhere. It noted that over the last decade there had been 'a wonderful improvement in the attractiveness of towns and cities'.

> Founded in wood, they are rapidly being rebuilt in brick and stone. Water supply, drainage, and lighting have been perfected. In the great centres the streets have been wood-blocked, and electric cars [trams] have superseded the old horse vehicles. Everything has been done to make life in towns pleasanter, richer, fuller, both for residents and for visitors, and withal more seductive to the country folk. The towns of New Zealand are year by year becoming better places to live in, and the better they become the stronger their influence of their magnetism on the rural population.[136]

The passage provided some more compelling answers to the puzzle of urban drift. As we have seen, for much of the nineteenth century living conditions in cities were primitive, with muddy streets, rickety buildings, bad drainage, mounds of filth and high rates of infectious disease. For some settlers this was encouragement enough to go onto the land. As city streets were paved, eliminating putrid mud and blinding dust; pipes put down, delivering clean water and removing disease-causing waste; and frontier-era buildings demolished, making room for more permanent and elegant piles, cities became more modern and alluring. This was enhanced by their richer and more diverse cultural and social life, and the wider work opportunities available in the cities' secondary and tertiary industries. The perennial cry that work was going begging in the country belies any assumption that country dwellers were flocking to cities because there was no work on the land. It was more the case that the attractions of city life meant that, for some workers at least, it was better to be out of work in the city than in work in the country and removed from civilisation. The ethos for these people was less 'rigidly rural' (after Fairburn) and more obstinately urban.

In a last-minute effort to hold back the tide, the Attorney General, Dr John Findlay, warned in 1911 of 'national decay' if urbanisation continued. Enlisting the urban degeneration theory, he proclaimed not only that country folk were stronger and healthier than townspeople, but that city life made women both unfit for and disinclined towards motherhood. He asserted the birth rate in rural districts was a third higher than in cities – official statistics show otherwise – and that much more should be done to 'draw people to the land'.[137] It was to no avail. The April Census showed two demographic milestones had been reached: New Zealand's population had passed the one million mark, and a few more Pākehā lived in urban than rural areas.[138] (If the Māori population had been included in the count, New Zealand became an urban society in 1916, but the official transition date has remained 1911.)

Urbanise the country

There were two main responses to the news. The first was denial: as late as 1921, the government statisticians argued that a population of 2,500 should be used to define an urban area, in which case New Zealand would still be a rural society. The second and larger response was a call to urbanise the country by stepping up efforts to make it more attractive and reduce, if not stem, the urbanising flow.[139] As we have seen, the provision of urban amenities like libraries in rural districts had been suggested as far back as 1879. Findlay had resurrected the issue in his national decay speech, arguing the task at hand was to 'urbanise the country' through more schools, telephones and public halls.[140] Thomas Mackenzie picked up the theme in 1912. The solution to urban drift was to reduce social isolation by improving rural communications, he said. To this end the government was improving roads (farmers were early adopters of the motorcar), had introduced daily rural mail delivery, and was extending the telephone network.[141] Of these, the telephone was possibly the most anticipated improvement. As the *Auckland Star* enthused, 'The telephone annihilates distance, and brings these little island communities in touch with the main lands of civilisation.'[142]

By 1917, some commentators were suggesting the drift might be countered by encouraging soldiers to settle on the land after their return from the First World War. This is where the garden-city advocates' proposals for groupings of returned soldiers' farms around garden-city-inspired villages gained significant traction.[143] In promoting such a scheme, Hurst Seager argued that having seen the 'extreme beauty of English and Continental villages … [the repatriated men] will not be content with the collection of rough stores and shanties which are huddled together to form the majority of New Zealand townships, nor will they be content to settle down in a shack in the middle of a 50-acre paddock'.[144] But as we saw in Chapter Seven, the garden-city-inspired rural settlement schemes went nowhere. Rather than urbanising the country, the government chose to ruralise the city. As Miles Fairburn long ago identified, suburbia enabled New Zealanders to feel rooted in the soil, and it was to the suburbs they increasingly flocked. But if Fairburn thought suburbia was a rejection of city culture, those who lived there more often saw it as a hybrid culture, fusing the best of city and country – the middle realm or landscape. In the morning they could be digging their gardens in shirtsleeves; in the evening they could be out on the town dressed to the nines. As in Britain, the United States, Australia and similar countries, modern city life in New Zealand became equated with suburban life.

Anti-urbanism sustained

By the 1920s it was evident to all but the most avid rural romantics that New Zealand society would continue to urbanise and ever more New Zealanders would call the city home. Yet unlike in the United States, where rising urbanisation curbed anti-urbanism and the city became celebrated in American social thought, New Zealand anti-urbanism failed to temper. One reason is that city-based manufacturing never grew to rival the land-based primary industries, meaning that the countryside retained its economic and political power. During the 1920s and 1930s, the Farmer Backbone mantra remained entrenched in New Zealand society and culture. In 1938, the economist William Sutch made the following observation:

> The tradition of regarding the farmers as the 'backbone of the country' has become firmly established not only in the minds of rural dwellers but in the estimation of most of the townsfolk also. The farmers contend that the urban industries are parasitical in that they depend for their very existence on the lifeblood of the farmer.[145]

It was a recitation of the city as an artificial excrescence argument. The counter-argument that farmers' livelihoods were equally reliant on city-based processing industries, services and markets was rarely made, let alone heard.[146]

Anti-urbanism was also sustained in the arts. Novels like Jane Mander's *The Story of a New Zealand River* (1920) and John Mulgan's *Man Alone* (1939) reinforced the idea of the country being at the heart of Pākehā culture – there is no comparable city-based novel from the period.[147] As Francis Pound has shown, anti-urbanism reached its zenith in the nationalist art of the 1930s and 1940s. The fantasy of living in the backblocks 'impelled an endless writing and painting of the landscape, and an endless refusal of the city,' he wrote. 'Everywhere in Nationalist art is the desire (to regress) into a pastoral passivity.'[148] Accordingly, when protagonists such as *Man Alone*'s Johnson visit the city, it is often only to confirm they don't belong:

> He meant to stay in Auckland and see city life, but when he got there he couldn't like it. It was too noisy after the country, and the summer was coming in and the air smelt good from the hills west of the city and the sunlight splendid on the blue Coromandel range across the gulf.[149]

Johnson was the modern incarnation of the colonial male drifter who valued the country's naturalness over the city's artificiality. Nationalist writers like A. R. D. Fairburn promoted the same view. In 1932 he wrote:

> I see myself as sitting down somewhere and tilling the soil. I'm coming to think it's the only worthy and satisfactory method of earning a living. I refuse to be a suburbanite, or an office-worker, or any of the other by-products of life. I'm going to be a *peasant*, if necessary in order to keep in touch with life.[150]

The passage recalls Dr Hutchinson, whose motivations for leaving the city for the land were similar. Fairburn, however, remained fixed in the middle realm of suburban Auckland.[151] Of particular concern to him were the city's emasculating effects. He complained that city life enervated men who, exhausted by the age of 30, were 'easy prey' for their more robust women. He called for the 'masculine' to be revived by decentralising cities and forming 'a closer link with agriculture and the more stable life of the countryside'.[152] It was a cry Hutchinson and others had made some 60 years before.

While this is but a brief glance at the issue, it is enough to show that anti-urbanism was an important influence in nationalist art.[153] And it has remained a theme in popular culture. Barry Crump's *Good Keen Men* books in the 1960s and the Speight's beer 'Southern Man' advertising campaign (1987–2012) both celebrated the rural male drifter, and reinforced the message that 'real' men lived in the country and avoided the effeminate city.

OPPOSITE Writers of the 1920s and 1930s upheld anti-urban feeling by locating New Zealand's culture in the country. A. R. D Fairburn (pictured at left with F. H. Worsfold and Eric Lee-Johnson around 1944) championed the virtues of a rural life, despite living in suburban Auckland. Sir George Grey Special Collections, Auckland Libraries, 1360-Album-251-15-8

Reacting against modernity

So how far was New Zealand anti-urbanism a conservative reaction to the modernity of city life? Whereas overseas anti-urbanism expressed anxiety about how urbanisation was changing traditional social relations and moral values, this was of lesser concern in New Zealand. It may have been that New Zealand cities were too small to create the level of mediated or impersonal social relations that characterised much bigger cities; the strength of the rural myth also meant that the moral superiority of the countryside went largely unquestioned. Instead, anti-urbanism was expressed in other ways. Foremost among these was the contention that urbanisation threatened New Zealand's rural-based economy. Although the city never posed a threat to the country's economic dominance, its pulling power with rural workers was thought to be holding the country back. The government's go-to-the-land policies were therefore designed to ensure there was sufficient labour on the land to mine and grow export commodities. Despite the use of moral suasion – primarily the puffery of independence and manliness embodied in the rural myth – these policies did not check urbanisation. The attractions of city life were too great.

Efforts to turn the urbanisation tide were both a reaction against the city's modernity and the consequence of a failure to see that rural New Zealand was modernising too. Many settler farmers brought machinery with them to New Zealand or imported it after their arrival. The mechanisation of labour-intensive tasks like sowing, reaping and binding reduced the need for labour at peak times and instead spread it throughout the year. Labour-market shortages saw farmers further invest in labour-saving technology like milking machines and tractors to increase productivity.[154] Anti-urbanism presumed that farming would remain labour intensive – hence the go-to-the-land call – but agriculture was rapidly becoming capital intensive and did not need large labour pools. Meanwhile, the contention that city life was emasculating was a regressive response to the growing presence and influence of women in city life. As modernising forces opened up new opportunities for women in city workplaces and elsewhere, the production of more gender-inclusive spaces in cities showed men's traditional domination of the public realm was weakening.

If not much could be done about the first development, this strain of anti-urbanism proffered city men two solutions for the second: embrace muscular masculinity or, better still, head for the male bastion of the land. In seeking to halt urbanisation, in wanting to check women's advance into city public spaces and in calling for city men to go to the country, anti-urbanism was clearly a conservative reaction to the city's modernity. That urbanisation continued apace, that women continued to claim city public space, and most city men remained in town, shows anti-urbanism was ineffectual in turning back the modernising forces at play.

Conclusion

Whereas in the 1840s settlers had been lured to New Zealand by the prospect of splendid cities to come, it was the promise of life on the land that became the main selling point thereafter. The change in emphasis brought a change in attitude. The formerly positive views of towns and cities were overtaken by representations that were dismissive of their role in New Zealand life. By the 1870s, anti-urbanism had become a pivotal mentality in colonial society. It had three main expressions: an immigration policy that discriminated against townspeople; an anxiety that city life was emasculating and feminising; and a belief that cities threatened economic prosperity. The discrimination against townspeople was based on the premise that New Zealand needed people who could work the land. This required those who were physically and mentally strong enough to ensure the hardships of the natural environment. Townspeople, of whom the city clerk was the derided emblem, were not wanted because the artificial existence of city life was believed to be enfeebling. The idea that cities were becoming feminised spaces gathered strength as the female population in cities drew equal to and then surpassed the male population; girls and women moving into city workplaces that were once the domain of men gave further weight to this view. Many middle-class city men responded by joining the cult of masculinity which enabled them to feel more secure in their manhood while reconciling them to living in cities. But this did not stop wider society from viewing townspeople as morally inferior to country folk, not least because the farmer was considered the backbone of the economy. As urban drift increased, so did the concern it would lead to ruin. Numerous go-to-the-land schemes failed to reverse the tide, and in 1911 New Zealand officially became an urban society. Despite the doomsday scenarios, the country continued to prosper.

Of the three expressions, only the discriminatory immigration policy was justified. With the Vogel-era push to open up more land, New Zealand required immigrants who were willing to settle and develop it. And as we saw with George Owen, not all townspeople were up to the task. The notion that city life was emasculating was true insofar as desk-bound city workers were often physically weaker than manual country (and city) workers. It was also true that city spaces were more feminised than country spaces, not least because there were proportionately more women living in cities. But the perception that the presence of women in work and other places somehow effeminised men was far-fetched and exposed a deeper cultural anxiety about the growing power of women in city space. At a wider level, the issue highlighted how city life could accommodate difference. This included diverse expressions of masculinity, among them the rugged drifter, the sensitive clerk and the muscular professional. Meanwhile, the

city as an artificial excrescence was based on the premise that it had no productive base independent of the primary sector, creating the image of the townsperson as a parasite who sucked the lifeblood of farmers to survive. This ignored both the co-dependence argument that without townspeople farmers would also perish and the reality that, with the rise of the secondary and tertiary sectors, cities were building a productive base independent of farming. Even so, the Farmer Backbone mantra could still be heard in the 2010s, making it the most enduring and virulent strain of New Zealand anti-urbanism.

The transition of New Zealand from a rural to an urban society was not only a demographic milestone but a cultural one too. Since urban drift had first become evident in the 1880s, its critics had looked at ways to check its advance. As some city dwellers followed the go-to-the-land call and became farmers, ever more rural youth headed the other way and became factory girls, shop assistants and junior clerks. They recognised, even if their elders did not, that New Zealand was irrevocably changing and their own future rested not on the land but in the Big Smoke. The year 1911 represents the moment when it became evident that for most New Zealanders the pursuit of modern life was to be had in cities.

OPPOSITE Owen and Edgar Williams sit on the doorstep of their house in Royal Terrace, Dunedin, in the late 1890s. Both are clutching toy guns. The central city and harbour are visible through the open door. William Williams, Alexander Turnbull Library, 1/2-140929-G

Conclusion

Alongside the familiar New Zealand story of colonial settlers taming the land, building farms and shaping hamlet-like communities in pastoral places, there is a less known, but parallel, story of others who settled in cities, erected buildings, factories and dwellings, and created communities centred more in common interests than place. An aim of this book has been to take this latter story out of the shadows and into the light.

From the beginning of New Zealand's colonisation, a significant proportion of its settler population were townspeople. Many had come from large towns and cities back in Britain, and had urban sensibilities that had been generations in the making. These settlers liked the sociability, diversity and the vivacity of city life, and wanted to shape a new urban society that both reflected and improved upon the one they had left behind. To a large extent they succeeded. This is perhaps best shown by the tide of people who flocked to towns and cities to live. It took only seven decades for New Zealand to move from a rural to an urban society – among the fastest transitions of all New World settler colonies.[1]

It therefore remains a paradox that some 100 years after the change New Zealand sees and represents itself as a society rooted in the land. This is evident in the marketing of New Zealand as a green and pure land, in public discourse that emphasises the rural economy, and in the bucolic images that dominate the nation's cultural production. One reason for the rural emphasis is that the structure of Māori society is based on tribal homelands or tūrangawaewae and these are usually in rural areas: although many Māori live in towns and cities, most still identify, first, with an ancestral homeland. It is less immediately apparent why Pākehā social identities have been fixed in the soil. Relatively few have places on the land that they return to regularly and identify as home, although it could be argued beach houses, baches or cribs fulfil this purpose for some. And while pursuits like hunting, tramping and fishing in the 'great outdoors' provide many with a periodic connection to the land, most Pākehā spend most of their time in cities. Why then are there so few cultural representations of them as a city people?

OPPOSITE This Roland Hipkins' painting, executed around 1930, records the city's suburban sprawl. The area is Wadestown in the northern suburbs. Roland Hipkins, *A Wellington Suburb* (detail), Sarjeant Gallery Te Whare o Rehua Whanganui, 1931/3/1

A key explanation was explored in Chapter Eight: anti-urbanism. Its vice-like hold on New Zealand society and culture has extended to historians, who have generally championed the idea that cities were handmaidens to the shaping of a strongly ruralised society. But it was only when I began questioning the relevance of this story to my own family's experience of living in New Zealand that the wider significance of its bias became clear. Few have explored the reasons why people were attracted to live in cities, what those cities looked like and how they changed over time, and the ways townspeople experienced everyday city life.

The greatest attraction of city life was other people. Settlers liked living in cities because their larger populations meant it was easier to find like-minded others with whom they could forge friendships and social groups. Social class or gender often framed these horizontal social relations, but sometimes groups transcended these boundaries, perhaps no more so than when townspeople came together as imagined communities in a crowd, to promenade, spectate and protest. Alongside this social capital, cities also produced cultural capital. From the beginning of settlements, townspeople gathered together to foster associational culture – mechanics' institutes, horticultural societies and gentlemen's clubs. From the 1870s, new institutions like museums, theatres and art galleries further raised the cultural capital of cities. These sites signified growing middle-class power in urban space and provided new sites of sociability, especially for women.

City life appealed more to women than to men. The social and cultural capital of cities was important to women, and so were the greater employment opportunities, especially in modern factory and service industries. But men also valued the broader range of city work. Many men did not like or were not cut out to labour on the land, preferring the cerebral nature of office work or the physicality of manufacturing work. Māori too were attracted to cities. With the exception of early Wellington, relatively few Māori lived in them, but many frequently visited to trade foodstuffs for European goods. When this trade dried up, Māori continued to exercise agency in city space, coming to cities on business, to work and to showcase their culture. There were also myriad personal reasons why settlers chose to live in cities. For instance, Edward Seager had lived in London and was a townsperson at heart; Emma Thomson had kith and kin in the city or nearby; and George Owen saw the city as the best place to start a business. A final and implicit attraction was that cities offered escape from the close social surveillance and strictures that characterised village and rural life; in cities people were more anonymous and so better able to shape and reshape their sense of self or social identities. This was a liberating aspect of city life for many.

New Zealand's cities were founded as speculative enterprises, and the exercise of capitalist social relations largely continued to determine their look or form over successive waves of rebuilding – the process of creative destruction. Beginning as collections of utilitarian canvas tents, wooden prefabricated cottages and raupō houses, the cities grew upwards and outwards, and featured CBDs of brick, stone and wooden edifices that sported the latest Neo-classical and Neo-Gothic architectural styles from Europe. Such structures expressed not only the cities' material progress but also the architecture of British colonialism, confirming their location within imperial economic and cultural networks. Outside city centres, suburbs of stand-alone cottages and villas, many owner-occupied, sprawled over hill and vale into the countryside. It was the sprawling or suburban urbanism that most distinguished New Zealand from British cities, the chance to pursue suburban home ownership influencing many settlers' decisions to immigrate. However, pretty cottages and verdant gardens belied the primitive environmental conditions that characterised cities until the late nineteenth century. Muddy or dusty streets strewn with festering rubbish, blocked or non-existent drains, and polluted drinking water not only assaulted townspeople's senses but were also vectors for deadly filth diseases like typhoid. In seeking to improve the public health of cities, reformers like William Pearce and William Chapple promoted modern sanitary practices and persuaded local governments to intervene and construct water and sewerage networks. The success in cleansing cities and reducing mortality rates made cities more salubrious and pleasant, drawing ever more people to live in them.

The experiences and spatial practices of everyday city life became richer and more diverse over our period. Initially townspeople's lived experience was limited by the small size of cities. Middle-class sociability was characterised by informality and spontaneity. Mary Petre spent her days meeting friends, going walking or riding, or playing music and singing. An after-work pursuit for many townspeople was going to the public house, which continued to serve as a vital social centre for men especially. For those who did not integrate into existing social networks, city life could be alienating and lonely. Still, most townspeople's social worlds extended beyond local ties to those back 'home', and letter writing and reading were common pursuits. When ships from overseas arrived in port, expectant queues would form at post offices to collect prized mail.

As cities grew and developed, new diversions and more formalised spatial practices emerged. With the construction of modern performance venues, cities became more integrated into global networks of cultural exchange, with visits from leading public intellectuals and performers that drew large audiences. The rise of organised sport created new public spectacles and encouraged collective social identities; going to the game or match became a regular activity for townspeople of all social classes. A centre of daily life for middle-class women like Emma Thomson was the home. Routines of cooking and housework were one aspect of this; visiting or hosting other women at home was another. Yet these women did not confine their lives to domestic space, regularly entering the public sphere to shop, attend events and participate in associational culture, with or without men.

The street was the 'living room' of everyday city life. It was a democratic and pluralistic space where people gathered to socialise and perform specific spatial practices. These ranged from promenades like 'doing the block' and joining the Saturday night crowd, to watching or participating in processions for Royal visits and other civic ceremonies, to protest marches to publicise grievances. Such crowds served to raise the (often multiple) social identities of participants and gave them fleeting opportunities to manipulate urban space for their own purposes. Young people also occupied streets as playgrounds, with larrikins indulging in behaviours the adult world labelled anti-social. Māori too made claims on city streets, making footpaths and street edges a vital site of sociability. The diversity of street life was enhanced by the conduct of trade: hawkers sold fruit and other wares; coffee-stall proprietors sold warming beverages; and prostitutes sold sexual services. The new twentieth-century idea that streets should privilege motorised traffic led middle-class reformers to mount campaigns against working-class street traders and street people. These succeeded in severely curbing social activity on streets, but they did not kill off street life altogether. Townspeople continued to periodically take to the streets to trade, celebrate and protest.

Providing a lens for understanding what attracted people to cities, how they changed and the lived experience within them has been the concept of modernity. I adopted an experiential definition of modernity that sought to explore the relationship between modernisation of the environment and society, new ways of making sense of a changing world, and the emergence of new forms of self and group consciousness. This was evident in the constant rebuilding of cities, in the provision of bourgeois cultural capital and in the promotion of suburbia as a modern mode of living. It was also evident in the airing and debating of new ideas about race and racial difference, disease causation and public health, and the gendering of public and private city space. It was further evident in the construction of individual and collective identities: social and domestic feminists, rural and urban masculinities, and Māori and Pākehā, among others. The incessant intercourse of these conceptualisations and spatial practices made city life modern life. Modernity was not confined to cities, but it was in cities that it was most discernible.

The framing of the book as an intra-national or trans-local history was done to move on from the insularity of the city biography genre and to enable us to explore shared ties and common features between cities. It also had the advantage of bringing greater clarity to points of difference. In weighing up between what was shared and what was variant, it seems to me New Zealand's colonial cities had more in common with one another than they had apart, despite longstanding claims of regional exceptionalism and the current enthusiasm for difference. That cities shared ties and common features was manifest in their founding as capitalist speculations and use of the grid plan; their social institutions and associational culture; their built environment and sprawling morphology; their representations of and social relations with Māori; their experience of city crowds and city rituals; their treatment of street traders and people; and their approach to public health and worker housing. This is not to deny there were also significant points of difference. For example, Auckland was more cosmopolitan; Wellington was a city of timber; Nelson was confined by its hinterland; Christchurch's street culture was less diverse; Dunedin was more parochial. There were other differences too, and those who go looking will find them, but one should also be alert to commonalities where they existed. It could well be argued the similarities between the cities, rather than their differences, help to explain the regular movement between them. In leaving one city for another, townspeople found a welcome sense of the familiar. In illuminating both shared and distinguishing ties and features, future research might benefit from adopting this intra-national approach.

So where might future research be best directed? As noted in the introduction, New Zealand's colonial cities were part of an urban system of regional and district towns and townships, a network that this book deliberately ignores. There is much scope for exploring the importance of these linkages in facilitating economic growth and enabling cities and towns to dominate their regions and districts, while also explaining why some towns failed to prosper or disappeared altogether. Important too are the function of towns in Māori land alienation and the creation of settled landscapes. Wairarapa comes to mind here: during the 1850s, inland towns like Greytown and Masterton became vital service centres to pastoralists and smallholders farming recently alienated Māori land. To what extent was this true of other regions as well? The role of modern transport technologies – coastal shipping, road and rail – in shaping towns and regional economies is also ripe for further investigation. New research in these areas would help to ascertain the importance of urban-based networks in the country's development and perhaps finally put to rest the idea that towns and cities were handmaidens to the process.

Another fruitful area of research would be the ways in which urbanisation has shaped New Zealand culture and social identities. Although New Zealand still represents itself as rooted in the land, it's a moot point how long this self-representation can be sustained. There is increasing evidence in the 2010s that the hackneyed images of taciturn and rugged outdoors men, the mustering and shearing of sheep, and romantic backblocks sheds no longer resonate with how most New Zealander see themselves – if they ever did. Symptomatic of this shift, in popular culture at least, was the ending of the long-running Speight's 'Southern Man' advertising campaign in 2012. As a Speight's beer executive explained at the time, 'the urbanisation of New Zealand meant the relevance of the outdoor life has changed'. Future campaigns would be city-based, he said.[2] The rise of Auckland to become New Zealand's only metropolis has much to do with the change. The notion that shepherds, sheep and sheds somehow go to the heart of what it is to be a New Zealander must seem incongruous when one is living in a sprawling city alongside 1.5 million others. Important too have been waves of Pasifika and Asian immigrants from the 1950s onwards. While many Pasifika people came from villages, most settled in cities, primarily Auckland, but also Wellington and Christchurch. Most recent Asian immigrants have come from large cities like Seoul and Beijing, and have settled in New Zealand's metropolis. In other words, the precept that New Zealanders primarily identify with the land is increasingly anachronistic and so is the imagery that goes with it. What is needed is a new matrix of images that better represents what it is to be a New Zealander in a city-based and multi-cultural society.

Historians can help in this process by ensuring the images that emerge are historically grounded. For instance, this book highlights how there were other expressions of colonial masculinity than the lackadaisical, stoic and reserved rural drifter. The likes of George Owen, Herbert Spackman and William Derry expressed a city-based version of masculinity that emphasised enterprise, cultural engagement and self-expression. These are attributes that still define, and better represent, many more New Zealand men than the Southern Man stereotype. Further, if historians are to help explain New Zealand's modern transition to a multi-cultural society, then they need to consider the urbanising experiences of not just Europeans and Māori, but Samoans, Tongans, Cook Islanders, Vietnamese and Koreans as well. What can their experiences reveal about the toleration of difference in late twentieth-century cities as compared to the prevailing attitudes towards the Chinese, Indian and Lebanese urban communities at the century's start? Can we say that acceptance of multi-culturalism is now a national trait? Of course there are myriad other avenues of inquiry that could and should be made. The main point to be taken is that historians can no longer ignore New Zealand's urban history, especially in an age of mega-cities and in a world that is becoming ever more urban. If we are to better understand what is happening in New Zealand society in the present, then historians need to enter the city streets, lanes and cul-de-sacs of its past.

This call for further New Zealand urban history research will, I hope, not be lost in the ether in the same way the Americans Clyde and Sally Griffen's call was. This book certainly provides a starting point for better understanding why between 1840 and 1920 hundreds of thousands of New Zealanders chose to live in cities rather than the countryside. If there was ever a single explanation for this, it would surely come down to the inherent fascination of city life: the exhilaration of being a crowd, laughing or crying at a cultural performance, buying fresh fruit from a hawker or a new dress in a splendid department store, chatting with work colleagues or next-door neighbours, or simply watching others going about their business from a street kerb or doorway. It was the sociability and diversity of these daily experiences that led people like Edward Seager, Mary Swainson, Emma Thomson, Herbert Spackman, Eliza Collier, William Pember Reeves and James Schrader to call the Big Smoke home.

Notes

Introduction

1   Schrader is a common German family name, but I don't know when or why my ancestors left Germany for England. I'd like to thank my sister Jan Schrader, who researched much of the genealogical evidence in this chapter.

2   'Bermondsey History', Southwark Council, www.southwark.gov.uk/info/200159/history_of_southwark/1009/bermondsey_history (accessed 21 Mar 2016).

3   Francis stayed in Liverpool, became a shopkeeper and baker, married in 1887 and had six children.

4   *Star*, 23 Nov 1868, p.1.

5   Ibid., 26 Oct 1871, p.1.

6   *Wellington Independen*t, 1 May 1874, p.3.

7   *Star*, 10 Apr 1876, p.3; 28 Oct 1879, p.3; 29 Jan 1880, p.3.

8   In a collection of essays on Pākehā identities, Michael King speaks of growing up in a culture that had 'an attachment to the land'. Other contributors to the volume also stressed their identification with the land. Michael King, 'Being Pakeha', in Michael King (ed.), *Pakeha: The Quest for Identity in New Zealand*, Penguin, Auckland, 1991, p.13.

9   'Estimated Resident Population: New Zealand: Urban/Rural Profile Areas at 30 June 2001–14', Statistics New Zealand, www.stats.govt.nz/~/media/Statistics/browse-categories/maps-and-geography/geographic-areas/urban-rural-profile-update/population-estimates.xls (accessed 21 Mar 2016).

10   Russell Stone's seminal study of the Auckland business community rates as New Zealand's first urban history. R.C.J. Stone, *Makers of Fortune: A Colonial Business Community and its Fall*, Auckland University Press, Auckland, 1973. More recent business histories include: Ian Hunter and Diana Morrow (eds), *City of Enterprise: Perspectives on Auckland Business History*, Auckland University Press, Auckland, 2006; and Ian Hunter, *Age of Enterprise: Rediscovering the New Zealand Entrepreneur 1880–1910*, Auckland University Press, Auckland, 2007.

11   Keith Sinclair and Wendy Harrex, *Looking Back: A Photographic History of New Zealand*, Oxford University Press, Wellington, 1978, p.134.

12   The absence of cities in the new edition is an extraordinary omission. Cities don't even make it into the index! W.H. Oliver with B.R. Williams (eds), *The Oxford History of New Zealand*, Oxford University Press, Wellington, 1981; Geoffrey W. Rice (ed.), *The Oxford History of New Zealand: Second Edition*, Oxford University Press, Auckland, 1992; and Giselle Byrnes (ed.), *The New Oxford History of New Zealand*, Oxford University Press, South Melbourne, 2009.

13   Atholl Anderson, Judith Binney and Aroha Harris, *Tangata Whenua: An Illustrated History*, Bridget Williams Books, Wellington, 2014; Barbara Brookes, *A History of New Zealand Women*, Bridget Williams Books, Wellington, 2016.

14   James Belich, *Making Peoples: A History of the New Zealanders From Polynesian Settlement to the End of the Nineteenth Century*, Allen Lane, Auckland, 1996; and *Paradise Reforged: A History of the New Zealanders From the 1880s to the Year 2000*, Allen Lane, Auckland, 2001.

15   Malcolm McKinnon (ed.), *Bateman New Zealand Historical Atlas: Visualising New Zealand: Ko Papatuanuku e Takoto Nei*, Bateman, Auckland, 1997.

16 Bronwyn Dalley and Gavin McLean, *Frontier of Dreams: The Story of New Zealand*, Hodder Moa, Auckland, 2005. The URL for the city-based *Te Ara* theme is: www.teara.govt.nz/en/economy-and-the-city.

17 Graeme Wynn, 'Reflections on the Writing of New Zealand History', *New Zealand Journal of History* (*NZJH*), 18, 2 (1984), pp.115–16.

18 Clyde and Sally Griffen, 'Towards an Urban Social History for New Zealand', *NZJH*, 20, 2 (1986), p.116.

19 Geoffrey W. Rice also produced an illustrated history of Christchurch. David Hamer and Roberta Nicholls (eds), *The Making of Wellington, 1800–1914: 11 Essays*, Victoria University Press, Wellington, 1990; John Cookson and Graeme Dunstall (eds), *Southern Capital: Christchurch: Towards a City Biography, 1850–2000*, Canterbury University Press, Christchurch, 2000; Geoffrey W. Rice, *Christchurch Changing: An Illustrated History*, Canterbury University Press, Christchurch, 1999.

20 Redmer Yska's compelling civic history of Wellington partly addressed this lack. Redmer Yska, *Wellington: Biography of a City*, Reed, Auckland, 2006.

21 Caroline Daley, *Girls and Women, Men and Boys: Gender in Taradale, 1886–1930*, Auckland University Press, Auckland, 1999. Other notable town and city biographies include P.J. Gibbons, *Astride the River: A History of Hamilton*, Whitcoulls, Christchurch, 1977; David Pearson, *Johnsonville: Continuity and Change in a New Zealand Township*, George Allen & Unwin, Auckland, 1980; Mary Boyd, *City of the Plains: A History of Hastings*, Victoria University Press, Wellington, 1984.

22 To a large extent suburban history has been a surrogate for urban history in New Zealand. There are too many suburban biographies to list here. Among the best are: Jenny Carlyon and Diana Morrow, *Urban Village: The Story of Ponsonby, Freemans Bay and St Mary's Bay*, Random House, Auckland, 2008; W.J. Gardner, 'New Zealand Regional History and its Place in Schools', *NZJH*, 13, 2 (1979), pp.182–93; Tony Ballantyne, *Webs of Empire: Locating New Zealand's Colonial Past*, Bridget Williams Books, Wellington, 2012, pp.268, 275.

23 Peter Clark, *European Cities and Towns: 400–2000*, Oxford University Press, Oxford, 2009, p.9.

24 'Overview: Background', The Caversham Project, University of Otago, http://caversham.otago.ac.nz/resource/background/index.html (accessed 15 Nov 2015).

25 Erik Olssen, 'The Shaping of a Field', in Tony Ballantyne and Brian Moloughney (eds), *Disputed Histories: Imagining New Zealand's Pasts*, University of Otago Press, Dunedin, 2006, p.217; Robert Harrison, 'The "New" Social History in America', in Peter Lambert and Phillip Schofield (eds), *Making History: An Introduction to the History and Practices of a Discipline*, Routledge, London, 2004, pp.114–15.

26 Olssen, 'The Shaping of a Field', p.218; Timothy J. Gilfoyle, 'Michael Katz on Place and Space in Urban History', *Journal of Urban History* (*JUH*), 41, 4 (2015), p.573.

27 A list of theses, academic journal articles and monographs up to 2001 is available on the Caversham Project website. 'Academic Resources', The Caversham Project, University of Otago, http://caversham.otago.ac.nz/resource/teacher/academic.html (accessed 15 Nov 2015).

28 The priority given to abstract ideas like social class and gender is highlighted in the titles of the monographs generated from the project, such as: Barbara Brookes, Annabel Cooper and Robin Law (eds), *Sites of Gender: Women, Men and Modernity in Southern Dunedin, 1890–1939*, Auckland University Press, Auckland, 2003.

29 Michael B. Katz, 'Urban as Site to Urban as Place: Reflections on (Almost) a Half-Century of U.S. Urban History', *JUH*, 41, 4 (2015), p.561.

30 Gilfoyle, 'Michael Katz on Place and Space in Urban History', pp.574–75.

31 David Hamer, 'Towns in Nineteenth-Century New Zealand', *NZJH*, 13, 1 (1979), pp.5–24.

32 David Hamer, *New Towns in the New World: Images and Perceptions of the Nineteenth-Century Urban Frontier*, Columbia University Press, New York, 1990.

33 In 2016 it survives only as an undergraduate Christchurch History course taught by Katie Pickles at the University of Canterbury.

34 See, for example, Julia Gatley and Paul Walker, *Vertical Living: The Architectural Centre and the Remaking of Wellington*, Auckland University Press, Auckland, 2014; Garth Falconer, *Living in Paradox: A History of Urban Design Across Kainga, Towns and Cities in New Zealand*, Blue Acres Press, Matakana, 2015.

35 See, for example, Ben Schrader, *We Call It Home: A History of State Housing in New Zealand*, Reed, Auckland, 2005; Geoffrey W. Rice, *Victoria Square: Cradle of Christchurch*, Canterbury University Press, Christchurch, 2014.

36 Jock Phillips, *A Man's Country? The Image of the Pakeha Male: A History*, Penguin, Auckland, 1987; Miles Fairburn, *The Ideal Society and its Enemies: The Foundations of Modern New Zealand Society, 1850–1900*, Auckland University Press, Auckland, 1989.

37 William Cronon, *Nature's Metropolis, Chicago and the Great West*, W.W. Norton & Co., New York, 1991.

38 The two articles are by Katie Pickles and Eric Pawson. As Pawson acknowledges, the 'writing of [New Zealand] environmental history has been heavily ruralised'. Eric Pawson, 'On the Edge: Making Urban Places', in Eric Pawson and Tom Brooking (eds) *Making a New Land: Environmental Histories of New Zealand*, Otago University Press, Dunedin, 2013, p.226.

39 See, for example, Harvey S. Franklin, 'The Village and the Bush: The Evolution of Village Community', in J. Foster (ed.), *Social Process in New Zealand*, Longman Paul, Auckland, 1969, pp.102–43; Kenneth Cumberland, *Landmarks*, Reader's Digest, Surry Hills, 1981; M.K. Watson and B.R. Patterson, 'The Growth and Subordination of the Maori Economy in the Wellington Region of New Zealand, 1840–52', *Pacific Viewpoint*, 26, 3 (1985), pp.521–45; Pawson, 'On the Edge', pp.226–40.

40 Ballantyne, *Webs of Empire*, pp.277, 279. The article first appeared in the *New Zealand Journal of History* in April 2011.

41 See, for example, Peter J. Rimmer, 'The Changing Status of New Zealand Seaports, 1853–1968', in Ron J. Johnston (ed.), *Urbanisation in New Zealand: Geographical Essays*, Reed, Wellington, 1973, pp.15–40.

42 Melissa Matutina Williams, *Panguru and the City: Kāinga Tahi, Kāinga Rua*, Bridget Williams Books, Wellington, 2014; Erin Keenan, 'Māori Urban Migrations and Identities: Ko Ngā Iwi Nuku Whenua: A Study of Urbanisation in the Wellington Region during the Twentieth Century', PhD thesis, Victoria University of Wellington, 2014. Pioneer works in this area include: Joan Metge, *A New Maori Migration: Rural and Urban Relations in Northern New Zealand*, Athlone Press, London, 1964, and Patricia Grace, Irihapeti Ramsden and Jonathan Dennis, *The Silent Migration: Ngāti Pōneke Young Māori Club 1937–1948*, Huia, Wellington, 2001.

43 Belich, *Making Peoples*, p.370.

44 This arrangement survived until the late 20th century, when Auckland brought the whole country into its orbit, becoming the Big One (a primate city) and reducing the other three cities to regional players only – another story.

45 An overview of New Zealand's urban history is given in David Thorns and Ben Schrader, 'City History and People', *Te Ara*, www.teara.govt.nz/en/city-history-and-people (accessed 3 May 2016).

46 I examined New Zealand's urban system in plates 65 and 90 of the *New Zealand Historical Atlas* (1997), but it warrants deeper research and analysis.

47 I accept the precept of post-colonial scholarship that colonisation is an ongoing process. The basis of the statement is the historiographical notion that New Zealand emerged from the First World War with a stronger sense of a collective social identity that was distinct from Britain's.

48 See, for example, Erik Olssen and Maureen Hickey, *Class and Occupation: The New Zealand Reality*, University of Otago Press, Dunedin, 2005; Erik Olssen, *Building the New World: Work, Politics and Society in Caversham 1880s–1920s*, Auckland University Press, Auckland, 1995.

49 Chris Brickell's history of gay New Zealand has strong coverage of city-based gay communities and urban culture. See Chris Brickell, *Mates and Lovers: A History of Gay New Zealand*,

Godwit, Auckland, 2008.

50 Timothy J. Gilfoyle, 'White Cities, Linguistic Turns, and Disneylands: The New Paradigms of Urban History', c. 1998, www.luc.edu/history.whitecitieslinguisticturnsandthe newparadigmsofurbanhistory (accessed 15 Nov 2015).

51 Giselle Byrnes, 'Introduction: Reframing New Zealand History', in Byrnes (ed.), *The New Oxford History*, pp.7–8, 14.

52 A practical reason for this is that as an independent historian I lacked the financial resources to engage in overseas research. But I also wanted to pursue the intra-national approach in part so there could be a small body of work on which to base further transnational research.

53 R.C.J. Stone, *Logan Campbell's Auckland: Tales from the Early Years*, Auckland University Press, Auckland, 2007, p.vii.

54 Malcolm McKinnon, 'Colonial and Provincial Government – War, Debt and the Provinces, 1863 to 1870', *Te Ara*, www.teara.govt.nz/en/colonial-and-provincial-government/page-3 (accessed 21 Mar 2016); Erik Olssen, *A History of Otago*, John McIndoe, Dunedin, 1984, pp.46, 96.

55 If we accept that mobility and circulation characterised colonial society, then this is to be expected; people moving between places meant social practices and behaviours could be quickly adopted.

56 The sociologist Georg Simmel argued in the early 20th century that the 'the city is both the location and embodiment of modernity'. James Donald, *Imagining the Modern City*, University of Minnesota Press, Minneapolis, 1999, p.10; John Jervis, *Exploring the Modern: Patterns of Western Culture and Civilization*, Blackwell, Maldon, 1998, p.65.

57 Jill Julius Matthews, *Dance Hall and Picture Palace: Sydney's Romance with Modernity*, Currency Press, Sydney, 2005, p.13. A good overview of the concept of modernity within cultural theory is given in Peter Wagner, *Modernity: Understanding the Present*, Polity Press, Cambridge, 2012, especially pp.19–21.

58 In this definition Berman and Harvey built on foundations laid by Charles Baudelaire, Walter Benjamin, Sigmund Freud, Karl Marx and Georg Simmel. Richard Dennis, 'Urban Modernity, Networks and Places', Institute of Historical Research, 2008, www.history.ac.uk/ihr/Focus/City/articles/dennis.html (accessed 15 Nov 2015).

59 Richard Dennis, *Cities in Modernity: Representations and Productions of Metropolitan Space, 1840–1930*, Cambridge University Press, Cambridge, 2008, p.1.

60 Nicolas Kenny, 'Making Sense of Modernity', H-Net Review, Feb 2010, www.h-net.org/reviews/showrev.php?id=25393 (accessed 21 Mar 2016).

61 Dennis, 'Urban Modernity', and *Cities in Modernity*, pp.2, 135; Malcolm Miles, *Cities and Cultures*, Routledge, Abingdon, 2007, pp.26–27.

62 Michel de Certeau, *The Practice of Everyday Life*, University of California Press, Berkeley, 1984, p.117, cited in Dennis, *Cities in Modernity*, p.105.

63 It should be acknowledged the Māori history of Tāmaki is contested and other interpretations of it exist. Margaret McClure, 'Auckland Region – Māori History', *Te Ara*, www.teara.govt.nz/en/auckland-region/page-6 (accessed 21 Mar 2016). A fuller portrait of Māori occupation of Tāmaki is given in Russell Stone, *From Tamaki-Makau-Rau to Auckland*, Auckland University Press, Auckland, 2001.

64 Neither would have thought the transaction would cause the permanent alienation of their land. Angela Ballara, 'Te Whanganui-a-Tara: Phases of Maori Occupation of Wellington Harbour c. 1800–1840', in Hamer and Nicholls (eds), *The Making of Wellington*, pp.18–21, 25, 30–33; Chris McLean, 'Wellington Region – Early Māori History', *Te Ara*, www.teara.govt.nz/en/wellington-region.page-5 (accessed 21 Mar 2016).

65 Jim McAloon, *Nelson: A Regional History*, Cape Catley, Queen Charlotte Sound, 1997, pp.12–14; Carl Walrond, 'Nelson Region – Māori History', *Te Ara*, www.teara.govt.nz/en/nelson-region/page-4 (accessed 21 Mar 2016).

66 Te Maire Tau, 'Ngai Tahu', *Te Ara*, www.teara.govt.nz/nem/ngai-tahu (accessed 21 Mar 2016).

67 'The Okatou Purchase Summary' and 'The Kemp Purchase Summary', Waitangi Tribunal, *Ngai Tahu Land Report*, Department of Justice, Wellington 1991, pp.30–43, 51–83; Te Maire Tau, 'Ngāi Tahu – the Ngāi Tahu Claim', *Te Ara*, www.teara.govt.nz/nem/ngai-tahu/page-8 (accessed 21 Mar 2016).

68 On very windy days as a boy I sometimes walked up Te Ahumairangi with others to be buffeted by the wind. *Dominion Post*, 15 Sept 2012, www.stuff.co.nz/dominion-post/capital-life/7677963/The-king-of-Wellington-hills (accessed 15 Nov 2015).

69 The lexicologist Harry Orsman says the term gained particular parlance with rural dwellers, for whom it had a favourable connotation. Harry Orsman, *The Dictionary of New Zealand English: A Dictionary of New Zealandisms on Historical Principles*, Oxford University Press, Auckland, 1997, p.50.

70 By the early 20th century, Auckland and Wellington were popularly referred to as New Zealand's 'big smoke'. See, for example, *New Zealand Free Lance*, 20 Feb 1904, p.22, and *Observer*, 13 Feb 1904, p.7.

Chapter One

1 *Star*, 13 Jun 1903, p.4.

2 Ibid., and *Star*, 20 June 1903, p.4; Sherwood Young, 'Seager, Edward William', *Te Ara*, www.teara.govt.nz/en/biographies/1s3/seager-edward-william (accessed 21 Mar 2016).

3 *Star*, 13 June 1903, p.4.

4 Jeffrey C. Alexander, *The Dark Side of Modernity*, Polity Press, Cambridge, 2013, p.130.

5 These histories include: Lowther Broad, *The Jubilee History of Nelson from 1842 to 1892*, Bond Finney & Co, Nelson, 1892; Alan Mulgan, *The City of the Strait: Wellington and its Province: A Centennial History*, A.H. & A.W. Reed, Wellington, 1939; Department of Internal Affairs, *Making New Zealand: Pictorial Surveys of a Century: Missionaries and Settlers*, Vol. 1, No. 5, Wilson & Horton, Auckland, 1939; J.P. Morrison, *The Evolution of a City: Christchurch and its Suburbs*, Christchurch City Council, Christchurch, 1948.

6 Auckland's commercial standing was underscored in the title of a 2006 business history of the city: *City of Enterprise*. Ian Hunter and Diana Morrow, *City of Enterprise: Perspectives on Auckland Business History*, Auckland University Press, Auckland, 2006.

7 Geoffrey W. Rice, *Christchurch Changing: An Illustrated History*, Canterbury University Press, Christchurch, 1999, p.15.

8 Edward Gibbon Wakefield's bust was placed in the elegant Centennial Memorial on the crest of Mt Victoria in 1939. No equivalent monument was erected to Auckland's founder, Governor William Hobson, perhaps reflecting the ambivalence with which he was regarded in the city. H. Dean Bamford, 'Edward Gibbon Wakefield', *New Zealand Illustrated Magazine*, 1 Jan 1903, p.313.

9 In 1898, William Pember Reeves wrote: 'The character of the settlers which it [the New Zealand Company] then afterwards gave New Zealand may well be held to cover a multitude of the Company's sins.' Similarly, in 1930, J.B. Condliffe wrote that the New Zealand Company scheme 'was an outstanding experiment in the economics of group settlement … Its mistakes and weaknesses were those of pioneer venture.' William Pember Reeves, *The Long White Cloud: Ao Tea Roa*, George Allen & Unwin, London, 1898 (1956 edn), p.143; J.B. Condliffe, *New Zealand in the Making: A Survey of Economic and Social Development*, George Allen & Unwin, London, 1930, p.95.

10 John Miller, *Early Victorian New Zealand: A Study of Racial Tension and Social Attitudes 1839–1852*, Oxford University Press, London, 1958, pp.192–93.

11 Michael Turnbull, *The New Zealand Bubble: The Wakefield Theory in Practice*, Price Milburn & Co., Wellington, 1959.

12 Broad, *The Jubilee History of Nelson*, p.3.

13 Robert D. Grant, *Representations of British Emigration, Colonisation and Settlement: Imagining Empire*, Palgrave Macmillan, Basingstoke, 2005, p.61.

14 Turnbull, *The New Zealand Bubble*, p.18.

15 Ibid., p.16.

16 Patricia Burns, *Fatal Success: A History of the New Zealand Company*, Heinemann Reed, Auckland, 1989, pp.106–7.

17 Russell Stone, *From Tamaki-Makau-Rau to Auckland*, Auckland University Press, Auckland, 2001, p.210; David Hamer, 'The Making of Urban New Zealand', *Journal of Urban History*, 22, 1 (1995), p.17.

18 Turnbull, *The New Zealand Bubble*, p.31.

19 Charles Terry, *New Zealand: Its Advantages and Prospects as a British Colony*, T. & W. Boone, London, 1843, p.131.

20 Ibid., p.139.

21 Ibid., p.135. Terry lists the highest price was £1,605 per acre; the lowest was £235 per acre. Stone, *From Tamaki-Makau-Rau to Auckland*, p.297.

22 Miles Fairburn, *The Ideal Society and its Enemies: The Foundations of Modern New Zealand Society, 1850–1900*, Auckland University Press, Auckland, 1989, p.15.

23 This undoubtedly helped to advance his strongly rural-centric argument, but it also means he missed the ways in which cities shaped and continued to shape colonial society.

24 This heightened political aspect came to the fore in the mid-1980s when debate raged over whether Pākehā historians should write Māori history. Charges by some Māori activists of Pākehā historians being 'academic raiders' increased sensitivities about the writing of colonial history generally. See Robert Mannion, 'Michael King: A Pakeha Writer Meets the Maori Renaissance', *Auckland Metro*, 40 (1984), pp.100–6.

25 There are some exceptions. Philip Temple's history of the Wakefield family has good coverage of the founding of the Wakefield settlements. Paul Moon gives some consideration of Auckland and Wellington in his history of the decade, although it covers familiar ground. Other recent works are the sesqui-centennial city biographies. These adopt a less progressive, more nuanced view of town founding than the centennial versions. Philip Temple, *A Sort of Conscience: The Wakefields*, Auckland University Press,

Auckland, 2002; Paul Moon, *The Newest Country in the World: A History of New Zealand in the Decade of the Treaty*, Penguin, Auckland, 2007; David Hamer and Roberta Nicholls (eds), *The Making of Wellington, 1800–1914: 11 Essays*, Victoria University Press, Wellington, 1990; Jim McAloon, *Nelson: A Regional History*, Cape Catley, Queen Charlotte Sound, 1997; John Cookson and Graeme Dunstall (eds), *Southern Capital: Christchurch: Towards a City Biography, 1850–2000*, Canterbury University Press, Christchurch, 2000.

26 Jim McAloon, 'New Zealand Economy, 1792–1914', in Giselle Byrnes (ed.), *The New Oxford History of New Zealand*, Oxford University Press, South Melbourne, 2009, p.205: Philippa Mein Smith, *A Concise History of New Zealand*, Cambridge University Press, Melbourne, 2005, p.54.

27 Peter Clark, *European Cities and Towns: 400–2000*, Oxford University Press, Oxford, 2009, pp.45, 86.

28 Ibid., pp.49–50.

29 Ibid., p.54.

30 Ibid., pp.52–54.

31 Ibid., p.55.

32 Ibid., p.121.

33 Ibid., pp.151–55, 188–90, 191–92.

34 Ibid., p.192.

35 Ibid., p.194.

36 Erik Olssen, 'Wakefield and the Scottish Enlightenment, with Particular Reference to Adam Smith and his *Wealth of Nations*', in Friends of the Turnbull Library, *Edward Gibbon Wakefield and the Colonial Dream: A Reconsideration*, GP Publications, Wellington, 1997, p.60; David Hamer, *New Towns in the New World: Images and Perceptions of the Nineteenth-Century Urban Frontier*, Columbia University Press, New York, 1990, p.93.

37 Olssen, 'Wakefield and the Scottish Enlightenment', p.59.

38 Peter Wagner, *Modernity: Understanding the Present*, Polity Press, Cambridge, 2012, p.88.

39 An historian who has recognised the importance of towns to Wakefield's scheme is Trevor Burnard. In an essay for Christchurch's

sesqui-centenary history he argued early Canterbury settlers saw city life as morally superior to country life. 'Unlike historians and nostalgists, who have championed the pioneering rural frontiersman, miner or farmer as the emblematic New Zealand nineteenth-century hero, the founders of Canterbury saw moral virtue not in the "barbaric" countryside but in the "civilised" town.' Trevor Burnard, 'An Artisanal Town – The Economic Sinews of Christchurch', in Cookson and Dunstall (eds), *Southern Capital*, p.117.

40 Robert Gouger (ed.), *A Letter from Sydney; the Principal Town of Australasia*, Joseph Cross, London, 1829, p.53.

41 Hamer, *New Towns in the New World*, pp.104, 111.

42 John Stuart Mill, *The Principles of Political Economy*, 1900 edn, London, p.75, cited in Temple, *A Sort of Conscience*, p.131.

43 Civil society comprises civic sociability and associational life and the practices and habits that guide civic behaviour. Daniel J. Monti, 'Civil Society', in Roger W. Caves (ed.), *Encyclopedia of the City*, Routledge, London, 2005, p.74.

44 As Jane M. Jacobs writes, 'The city is also an important component in the spatiality of imperialism. It was in outpost cities that the spatial order of imperial imaginings was rapidly and deftly realised. And it was through these cities that the resources of colonised lands were harnessed and reconnected to cities in imperial heartlands.' John Darwin, *Unfinished Empire: The Global Expansion of Britain*, Allen Lane, London, 2012, p.101; Jane M. Jacobs, *Edge of Empire: Postcolonialism and the City*, Routledge, London, 1996, p.4.

45 Ian Hunter, *Age of Enterprise: Rediscovering the New Zealand Entrepreneur 1880–1910*, Auckland University Press, Auckland, 2007, p.30.

46 Ibid., p.28; Janice C. Mogford, 'Nathan, David', *Te Ara*, www.teara.govt.nz/en/biographies/1n1/nathan-david (accessed 21 Mar 2016).

47 *New Zealand Gazette and Wellington Spectator* (*NZG&WS*), 18 Apr 1840, p.1.

48 Ibid., 23 May 1840, p.2.

49 Ibid., 12 Nov 1842, p.2.

50 *Nelson Examiner*, 17 May 1851, p.51.

51 *NZG&WS*, 8 Jan 1842, p.3; 7 Mar 1846, p.4.

52 William Dew to his brother James Dew, 2 Oct 1842, in *Letters from Settlers and Labouring Emigrants in the New Zealand Company's Settlements of Wellington, Nelson and New Plymouth: from February, 1842 to January 1843*, Smith, Elder & Co., London, 1843, p.37 [*emphasis in original*].

53 Settler in Wellington to Unidentified, 5 Sep 1842, *Letters from Settlers*, p.31.

54 J.D. Greenwood to Mr Miller, 7 Jun 1843, 'Greenwood. 1842–1870. Letters', The Nelson Provincial Museum, Archives Collection: NPM2004.161.2.

55 *NZG&WS*, 28 Nov 1840, p.2.

56 'Imports and Exports in Detail', New Zealand Government, *Statistics of New Zealand for 1853, 1854, 1855, and 1856*, W.C. Wilson, Auckland, 1856, Tables 7–8, 24–25, 28–29, 30–31, 34–35.

57 This is not to say that Māori did not dispute or contest sales of land in Auckland, as Russell Stone's examination of the issue in the 1840s testifies. See Stone, *Tamaki-Makau-Rau*, pp.306–13.

58 John Singleton, 'Auckland Business: the National and International Context', in Hunter and Morrow (eds), *City of Enterprise*, p.13; *Daily Southern Cross*, 3 Feb 1844, p.2.

59 *New Zealander*, 11 Feb 1852, p.3.

60 Jim McAloon, 'The Christchurch Elite', in Cookson and Dunstall (eds), *Southern Capital*, pp.195–98; Roberta Nicholls, 'Elite Society in Victorian and Edwardian Wellington', in Hamer and Nicholls (eds), *The Making of Wellington*, pp.196–97.

61 Clark, *European Cities*, p.314.

62 As James Belich writes, 'Instant civilization, with cathedrals and libraries planned in Britain or on the voyage out, was an integral part of the Wakefield prospectus.' James Belich, *Making Peoples: A History of the New Zealanders From Polynesian Settlement to the End of the Nineteenth Century*, Allen Lane, Auckland, 1996, p.305.

63 John Ward, *Information Relative to New Zealand, Compiled for the Use of Colonists*, John W. Parker, London, 1842, p.137.

64 *NZG&WS*, 19 Dec 1840, p.3. A second society called the Wellington Exchange was founded in early 1841. In April it erected a wooden hall, known as 'The Exchange', for its own and wider use on the Te Aro foreshore. Ibid., 3 Apr 1841, p.1; 10 Apr 1841, p.1.

65 Andrew Lees and Lynn Hollen Lees, *Cities and the Making of Modern Europe, 1750–1914*, Cambridge University Press, Cambridge, 2007, p.90.

66 *NZG&WS*, 19 Dec 1840, p.3.

67 *NZG&WS*, 26 Dec 1840, p.2; 9 Jan 1841, p.4.

68 Lees and Hollen Lees, *Cities and the Making of Modern Europe*, p.92.

69 *NZG&WS*, 26 Dec 1840, p.2; 'Report from S. Woodward of establishment of Wellington Working Men's Association', *New Zealand Journal*, 37 (1841), p.152.

70 *NZG&WS*, 20 Feb 1841, p.2.

71 Ibid., 24 May 1842, p.2; *Nelson Examiner and New Zealand Chronicle*, 21 May 1842, p.43.

72 The Port Nicholson Exchange and Public Library wound up in April 1842 due to insufficient support from its members. *NZG&WS*, 16 Apr 1842, p.1.

73 *Nelson Examiner and New Zealand Chronicle*, 17 Dec 1842, p.163.

74 *NZG&WS*, 10 Nov 1841, p.2; *New Zealand Journal*, 60 (1842), p.101.

75 *NZG&WS*, 10 Nov 1841, p.2.

76 Ibid., 8 Apr 1843, p.3.

77 The society's annual reports provide total memberships but not by gender. One account of the January 1842 Exhibition reported 'many lady visitors' and a 'show of vegetables [that] would have done honour to the London show'. See 'J.M. Taylor to sister, 10 Feb, 1842', in *Letters from Settlers*, p.5.

78 *NZG&WS*, 2 Aug 1843, p.2.

79 Ibid., 13 Sep 1843, p.2.

80 Peter Downes, *Shadows on the Stage: Theatre in New Zealand: The First 70 Years*, John McIndoe, Dunedin, 1975, p.18.

81 Ernst Dieffenbach, *Travels in New Zealand with Contributions to the Geography, Botany and Natural History of that Country*, John Murray, London, 1843, p.67.

82 *New Zealand Colonist and Port Nicholson Advertiser (NZC&PNA)*, 12 May 1843, p.2.

83 Ibid., 23 May 1843, p.2; *New Zealand Spectator and Cook's Strait Guardian*, 13 Apr 1850, p.2.

84 John Wood, *Twelve Months in Port Nicholson: or Notes for the Public and the New Zealand Company*, Pelham Richardson, London, 1843, p.31.

85 Tony Ballantyne has argued in relation to Gore that conflict was an integral element in community formation and that community itself was often produced out of contestation. Similarly, Caroline Daley found in her study of Taradale that even if social institutions like lodges and churches did not survive, other similar institutions replaced them. See Tony Ballantyne, 'Thinking Local: Knowledge, Sociability and Community in Gore's Intellectual Life, 1875–1914', *NZJH*, 44, 2 (Oct 2010), p.151; Caroline Daley, 'Taradale Meets the Ideal Society', in Judith Binney (ed.), *The Shaping of History: Essays from the New Zealand Journal of History*, Bridget Williams Books, Wellington, 2001, p.281.

86 *Wellington Independent*, 13 Apr 1850, p.2.

87 *Daily Southern Cross*, 10 Jun 1843, p.2; *NZG&WS*, 2 Nov 1842, p.3; *Nelson Examiner and New Zealand Chronicle*, 21 Jan 1843, p.183.

88 Broad, *The Jubilee History of Nelson*, pp.19, 83.

89 *NZG&WS*, 28 May 1842, p.2. Revd Thomas Nicholson arrived in Nelson in June 1848 after travelling with the first Dunedin settlers on the ship *John Wickcliffe*, 'Rev T.D. Nicholson', www.theprow.org.nz/yourstory/rev-t-d-nicholson/#.UmH8hCiCjnY (accessed 22 Mar 2016).

90 Erik Olssen, *A History of Otago*, John McIndoe, Dunedin, 1984, pp.41–42.

91 Dunedin's Mechanics' Institute was founded in July 1851 and shortly afterwards erected a hall on the Princes and Rattray Street (seaward) corner. *Otago Witness*, 5 July 1851, p.2. As Tony Ballantyne has convincingly argued, the colonial emphasis on mutual and

self-improvement meant 'mechanics institutes, literary and debating societies, and mutual improvement societies were vitally important social and intellectual spaces' in New Zealand between 1850 and 1900. Tony Ballantyne, *Webs of Empire: Locating New Zealand's Colonial Past*, Bridget Williams Books, Wellington, 2012, p.241.

92 *Nelson Examiner*, 17 May 1851, p.51.

93 Ballantyne, *Webs of Empire*, pp.239–41.

94 Belich, *Making Peoples*, p.281. It should be noted all three crops can be grown in Wellington, but the climate is far from ideal.

95 For example, its *Letters From Settlers* (1843) carried many glowing reports of colonial life, but some also acknowledged it was not a bed of roses, one letter conceding the first cohort of Wellington settlers had fared relatively badly compared to subsequent ones. 'From a Gentleman at Wellington, to Friend in England, February 14, 1842', *Letters from Settlers*, p.7; Lydia Wevers, *Country of Writing: Travel Writing and New Zealand*, Auckland University Press, Auckland, 2002, pp.127–28; Belich, *Making Peoples*, pp.281–82; Grant, *Representations of British Emigration*, p.104.

96 John Wood, *Twelve Months in Port Nicholson; or Notes for the Public and the New Zealand Company*, Pelham Richardson, London, 1843, pp.16, 28, 50.

97 Ibid., pp.15, 51.

98 Carl Abbott, *Boosters and Businessmen: Popular Economic Thought and Urban Growth in the Antebellum Middle West*, Greenwood Press, Westport, 1981, p.4; Hamer, *New Towns in the New World*, pp.85–87.

99 Felicity Barnes, *New Zealand's London: A Colony and its Metropolis*, Auckland University Press, Auckland, 2012, p.126.

100 The first to quote Wood was John Miller in *Early Victorian New Zealand* (p.42). Subsequent historians have repeated the passage, including: Belich, *Making Peoples*, p.338; Gavin McLean, *Wellington: The First Years of European Settlement 1840–1850*, Penguin, Auckland, 2000, p.18; Redmer Yska, *Wellington: Biography of a City*, Reed, Auckland, 2006, p.20.

101 Wood, *Twelve Months in Port Nicholson*, p.9.

102 Melanie Lovell-Smith, 'Early mapping – Mapping for settlement', *Te Ara*, www.teara. govt.nz/en/interactive/10790/proposed-plan-of-wellington-1840 (accessed 22 Mar 2016).

103 Hamer, *New Towns in the New World*, pp.174–75.

104 The area is now part of the Southern Cemetery. It was named after a group of immigrant weavers who had emigrated from Paisley after their craft was industrialised.

105 Grant, *Representations of British Emigration*, p.4.

106 Robin Skinner, '"Doing More to Promote Emigration than a Thousand Speeches and Resolutions": Brees's Panorama of New Zealand', *Proceedings of the XXIVth International Conference of the Society of Architectural Historians, Australia and New Zealand*, Adelaide, Australia, 21–24 Sept 2007, p.824.

107 Marion Minson, 'Brees, Samuel Charles', *Te Ara*, www.teara.govt.nz/en/biographies/1b31/brees-samuel-charles (accessed 22 Mar 2016).

108 Mimi Colligan states that of the 164 panoramas shown in Leicester Square and the Strand between 1793 and 1863, 112 were of cities. Mimi Colligan, *Canvas Documentaries: Panoramic Entertainments in Nineteenth Century Australia and New Zealand*, Melbourne University Press, Melbourne, 2002, p.15.

109 'Trip from Leicester Square and Back', advertising poster, 1849, Ephemera collection, Eph-C-Graphic-Arts-1849-01, ATL.

110 'Trip from Leicester Square and Back'; Grant, *Representations of British Emigration*, p.3; Leonard Bell, *Colonial Constructs: European Images of Maori 1840–1914*, Auckland University Press, Auckland, 1992, p.29.

111 S.C. Brees, *Guide and Description of the Panorama of New Zealand … Colony and the Bush*, Savill & Edwards, London, 1849.

112 Ibid., p.13.

113 Ibid., pp.16–17.

114 Ibid., pp.18, 22.

115 Ibid., pp.20–21.

116 Ibid., p.22.

117 Ibid., pp.24–25.

118 Ibid., pp.30–32. It is probable that Brees was referring to Te Kaeaea's attack on the Ngāti Kahungunu pā of Pehikatea in 1830, during which many defenders were killed or taken captive. Whether cannibalism took place is unrecorded in his official biography. Angela Ballara, 'Te Kaeaea', *Te Ara*, www.teara.govt. nz/en/biographies/1t38/te-kaeaea (accessed 22 Mar 2016).

119 'Brees's Colonial Panorama of New Zealand', advertising flyer, 1849, B-031-034-1, ATL. Robin Skinner notes that Brees quoted this phrase so often it became his personal motto. Skinner, 'Doing More', p.822.

120 'Bree's Colonial Panorama of New Zealand', advertising flyer; 'Trip from Leicester Square and Back', advertising poster.

121 *The Times*, 20 May 1851, cited in Ewan Johnston, '"A valuable and tolerably extensive collection of native and other products": New Zealand at the Crystal Palace', in Jeffrey A. Auerbach and Peter H. Hoffenberg (eds), *Britain, the Empire, and the World at the Great Exhibition of 1851*, Ashgate, Aldershot, 2008, p.84.

122 Skinner, 'Doing More', p.284.

123 *Star*, 13 Jun 1903, p.4. Charlotte Godley mentions that her mother saw the panorama. Charlotte Godley, *Letters from Early New Zealand*, 1936, NZETC edn, p.60, http://nzetc. victoria.ac.nz/tm/scholarly/tei-GodLett.html (accessed 29 Mar 2016).

124 *Star*, 13 Jun 1903, p.4.

125 Turnbull, *The New Zealand Bubble*, pp.44, 64.

126 Despite Dunedin's Scottish foundations, historian Erik Olssen notes that '[d]uring the 1840s and 1850s a surprising number of Caversham's [in South Dunedin] citizens had lived in London'. Erik Olssen, *Building the New World: Work, Politics and Society in Caversham 1880s–1920s*, Auckland University Press, Auckland, 1995, p.232.

127 Jock Phillips and Terry Hearn, *Settlers: New Zealand Immigrants from England, Ireland and Scotland, 1800–1945*, Auckland University Press, Auckland, 2008, p.78.

128 Ibid., pp.110, 120.

129 Ibid., p.74.

130 Ibid., p.84. An 1845 demographic survey of Wellington gave a similar result. It found that 295 (18.2 per cent) of the working population of 1,620 were employed in white-collar occupations, including 99 storekeepers, 29 government officials, 13 doctors, 9 lawyers and 6 clergymen. S.E. Grimstone, *The Southern Settlements of New Zealand*, R. Stokes, Wellington, 1847, p.40.

131 Phillips and Hearn, *Settlers*, p.81.

132 John Wilson, 'Australians – Early Arrivals', *Te Ara*, www.teara.govt.nz.en/australians/page-2 (accessed 22 Mar 2016); William Fox, *The Six Colonies of New Zealand*, John W. Parker & Son, London, 1851, p.40.

133 Robert Home, *Of Planting and Planning: The Making of British Colonial Cities*, E. & F.N. Spon, London, 1997, p.21; Darwin, *Unfinished Empire*, p.67.

134 Clark, *European Cities and Towns*, p.32.

135 Lees and Hollen Lees, *Cities and the Making of Modern Europe*, p.20.

136 Ibid., pp.262–65; Penelope Edmonds, *Urbanizing Frontiers: Indigenous Peoples and Settlers in 19th-Century Pacific Rim Cities*, UBC Press, Vancouver, 2010, pp.56, 64–65.

137 Sandip Hazareesingh, 'Colonial Modernism and the Flawed Paradigms of Urban Renewal: Uneven Development in Bombay, 1900–25', *Urban History*, 28, 2 (2001), pp.236–37.

138 Letter from Captain W. Hobson to His Excellency Lieutenant General Sir Richard Bourke, 8 Aug 1837, Enclosure A, FO 58/1, National Archives, London; Tony Ballantyne, 'The State, Politics and Power, 1769–1893', in Byrnes (ed.), *The New Oxford History*, p.103.

139 Edmonds, *Urbanizing Frontiers*, p.33.

140 The Wairau confrontation happened after the leader of the Nelson settlement Arthur Wakefield led an armed party to arrest the chiefs Te Rauparaha and Te Rangihaeata for evicting a survey party from disputed Wairau Valley land. An altercation ensued and people on both sides were killed, including Te Rangihaeata's wife, Te Rongo. Wakefield and

his party then surrendered, but Te Rangihaeata killed them as utu (revenge) for the death of his wife. Settlers called it a massacre. The destruction of Kororāreka happened in March 1845 after the Ngāpuhi chief Hone Heke led an assault on the town to reassert his authority in the region. About 33 people were killed, most of the town was destroyed, and many settlers subsequently sought refuge in Auckland. Burns, *Fatal Success*, pp.227–38; McAloon, *Nelson: A Regional History*, pp.32–35; 'The Sacking of Kororāreka', Ministry for Culture and Heritage, www.nzhistory.net.nz/war/sacking-kororareka (accessed 22 Mar 2016).

141 Darwin, *Unfinished Empire*, p.46.

142 David Hamer, 'Wellington on the Urban Frontier', in Hamer and Nicholls (eds), *The Making of Wellington*, p.228.

143 Richard Wade, *The Urban Frontier: Pioneer Life in Early Pittsburgh, Cincinnati, Lexington, Louisville, and St. Louis*, University of Chicago Press, Chicago, 1959, p.1.

Chapter Two

1 The point is reinforced in the 2013 edition of New Zealand environmental histories, in which most of the essays consider the modification of rural natural landscapes. Eric Pawson and Tom Brooking (eds), *Making a New Land: Environmental Histories of New Zealand*, Otago University Press, Dunedin, 2013.

2 As the researcher Paul Star writes: 'The acclimatisation of some birds was justified by their being insectivorous, and game and fish had nutritional value, but the prime motivation was sentiment. Many settlers lamented the absence of English birds and opportunities to shoot and fish.' Paul Star, 'Humans and the Environment in New Zealand', in Giselle Byrnes (ed.), *The New Oxford History of New Zealand*, Oxford University Press, South Melbourne, 2009, pp.50–53. See also 'The Introduction of Species: Faunal and Floral Colonisation', in Malcolm McKinnon (ed.), *Bateman New Zealand Historical Atlas: Visualising New Zealand: Ko Papatuanuku e Takoto Nei*, Bateman, Auckland, 1997, plate 42; Janet Wilmshurst, 'Human Effects on the

Environment – European Impact', *Te Ara*, www.teara.govt.nz/en/human-effects-on-the-environment/3 (accessed 24 Mar 2016).

3 Chris Otter, 'Locating Matter: The Place of Materiality in Urban History', in Tony Bennet and Patrick Joyce (eds), *Material Powers: Cultural Studies, History and the Material Turn*, Routledge, London, 2010, p.39; Malcolm Miles, *Cities and Culture*, Routledge, London, 2007, pp.12–13.

4 Peter Wagner, *Modernity: Understanding the Present*, Polity Press, Cambridge, 2012, p.92.

5 Otter, 'Locating Matter', pp.39, 43; James Donald, *Imagining the Modern City*, University of Minnesota Press, Minneapolis, 1999, pp.10–11.

6 Marx famously coined the phrase 'All that is solid melts into air' to describe this paradoxical process. Max Page, *The Creative Destruction of New York*, University of Chicago Press, Chicago, 1999, p.2.

7 Otter, 'Locating Matter', p.40.

8 Ibid., pp.41–43; Graeme Davison, 'Reading a Building', in Graeme Davison and Chris McConville (eds), *A Heritage Handbook*, Allen & Unwin, St Leonards, 1991, p.180.

9 Mona Domosh, *Invented Cities: The Creation of Landscape in Nineteenth-Century New York and Boston*, Yale University Press, New Haven, 1996, p.6.

10 Gail Fenske, *The Skyscraper and the City: The Woolworth Building and the Making of Modern New York*, University of Chicago Press, Chicago, 2008.

11 As well as Julia Gatley's work mentioned in the introduction, Adrian Humphris and Geoff Mew's history of suburban Wellington is perhaps the best example of 'site and place' urban history. Adrian Humphris and Geoff Mews, *Ring Around the City: Wellington's New Suburbs 1900–1930*, Steele Roberts, Wellington, 2009.

12 Alan Mulgan, *City of the Strait: A Centennial History, Wellington and its Province*, A.H. & A.W. Reed, Wellington, 1939, p.94.

13 Cadastral reasons largely account for the survival of the plan. Reshaping the plan

would have raised too many issues about land ownership.

14 The historical geographer Robert Home has identified eight main constituents of the 'Grand Model': 1) a policy of deliberate urbanisation; 2) land is allocated in packages of urban, suburban and country lots; 3) town is laid out in advance of settlement; 4) streets are laid out on grid plans; 5) public squares; 6) spacious rectangular plots; 7) some plots reserved for public purposes; and 8) a physical distinction between town and country, often a green belt. Robert Home, *Of Planting and Planning: The Making of British Colonial Cities*, E. & F.N. Spon, London, 1997, pp.9, 22.

15 John Rennie Short, *Urban Theory: A Critical Assessment*, Palgrave Macmillan, Houndsmill, 2006, p.10; Andrew Brown-May, *Melbourne Street Life*, Australian Scholarly Publishing, Melbourne, 1998, pp.7–12; Giselle Byrnes, *Boundary Markers: Land Surveying and the Colonisation of New Zealand*, Bridget Williams Books, Wellington, 2001, p.56.

16 Penelope Edmonds, *Urbanizing Frontiers: Indigenous Peoples and Settlers in 19th-Century Pacific Rim Cities*, UBC Press, Vancouver, 2010, p.84. On the other hand, the grid was criticised for its monotonous form and ignoring the contours of the land; survey lines ran over hills rather than around them, making for some very steep streets.

17 Brad Patterson, '"A Queer Cantankerous Lot …": The Human Factor in the Conduct of the New Zealand Company's Wellington Surveys', in David Hamer and Roberta Nicholls (eds), *The Making of Wellington, 1800–1914: 11 Essays*, Victoria University Press, Wellington, 1990, pp.67–68.

18 *New Zealand Gazette and Wellington Spectator* (*NZG&WS*), 21 Aug 1839, p.3.

19 Although some new towns such as colonial Philadelphia had featured common lands, the provision of reserve lands separating town and country was new. Home, *Of Planning and Planning*, p.14.

20 Such thinking led to the rise of large urban parks, such as New York's Central Park, often represented as the (purifying) 'lungs' of cities.

21 Edward Jerningham Wakefield, *Adventure in New Zealand*, abridged edn, Whitcombe & Tombs, Christchurch, 1955, p.149.

22 The number one landholder was a Duncan Dunbar. Number two was Colonel Robert Torrens, an absentee who had been instrumental in founding Adelaide. Louis Ward, *Early Wellington*, Whitcombe & Tombs, Wellington, 1928, p.194; Ben Schrader, 'City Planning', *Te Ara*, www.teara.govt.nz/en/city-planning/1/5/2 (accessed 24 Mar 2016).

23 Brown-May, *Melbourne Street Life,* p.12; Spiro Kostof, *The City Shaped: Urban Patterns and Meanings Through History*, Bulfinch, Boston, 1991, p.121.

24 Wakefield, *Adventure in New Zealand*, p.149.

25 The provision of Native reserves happened only in Wellington and Nelson. The practice had been discontinued by the time Dunedin and Christchurch were founded, largely on the basis of troubled social relations with Māori in the former settlements.

26 New Zealand Company, *Instructions from the New Zealand Land Company to Colonel Wakefield, Principal Agent of the Company*, John W. Parker, London, 1839, p.23.

27 Patricia Burns, *Fatal Success: A History of the New Zealand Company*, Heinemann Reed, Auckland, 1989, p.161.

28 Waitangi Tribunal, *Te Whanganui a Tara: Me Ona Takiwa: Report on the Wellington District, Wai 145*, Waitangi Tribunal, Wellington, 2003, p.87.

29 Kostof, *The City Shaped*, p.72, and Spiro Kostof, *The City Assembled: The Elements of Urban Form Through History*, Thames & Hudson, London, 1992, p.151.

30 J. Rutherford (ed.), *The Founding of New Zealand: The Journals of Felton Mathew, First Surveyor of New Zealand and his Wife, 1840–1847*, A.H. & A.W. Reed, Wellington, 1940, p.197.

31 Alexander Marjoribanks, *Travels in New Zealand with a Map of the Country*, Smith, Elder & Co., London, 1846, p.41.

32 S.M.D. Martin, *New Zealand: In a Series of Letters*, Simmonds & Ward, London, 1845, p.132.

33 In the end, 100 acres of town and suburban land was 'given' to Māori, but no rural land. Nearly half of it was subsequently alienated and most of the rest became tied up in perpetual leases. Hillary and John Mitchell, 'The Native Tenths Reserves', www.theprow.org.nz/the-native-tenths-reserves/#.UJQqyY6Cjny (accessed 24 Mar 2016); Carl Walrond, 'Nelson Region', *Te Ara*, www.teara.govt.nz/en/nelson-region/5/2/1 (accessed 24 Mar 2016).

34 Pamela Wood, *Dirt: Filth and Decay in a New World Arcadia*, Auckland University Press, Auckland, 2005, p.12.

35 Schrader, 'City Planning'.

36 W. David McIntyre, 'Outwards and Upwards', in John Cookson and Graeme Dunstall (eds), *Southern Capital: Christchurch: Towards a City Biography, 1850–2000*, Canterbury University Press, Christchurch, 2000, pp.88–89.

37 Another reason might be that because land orders were under-subscribed there was less pressure to give public land over to commerce.

38 *Lyttelton Times*, 11 Nov 1854, p.2.

39 Most of it was to go in one fell swoop in 1855, when some 400 acres was sold to pay off the Association's liabilities. The land was sold in 5-acre blocks or less for £50 per acre. Ibid., 26 Feb 1853, p.10; J.P. Morrison, *The Evolution of a City*, Christchurch City Council, Christchurch, 1948, pp.13–14.

40 Interestingly, Christchurch's 2012 central-city earthquake recovery plan included two tracts of open land on the eastern and southern edges. Called 'The Frame', it was designed to 1) solve a central-city land glut by reducing its size, and 2) provide a land bank for future development – in the manner of the original 1850 town reserves. Christchurch Earthquake Recovery Authority (CERA), *Christchurch Central Recovery Plan Summary*, CERA, Christchurch, 2012, p.5.

41 Barry Bergdoll, Peter Christensen and Ron Broadhurst (eds), *Home Delivery: Fabricating the Modern Dwelling*, Museum of Modern Art, New York, 2008, p.40.

42 G.B. Earp, *Hand-book for Intending Immigrants to the Southern Settlements of New Zealand*, W.S. Orr, London, 1849, p.46.

43 J.C. Loudon, *An Encyclopaedia of Cottage, Farm, and Villa Architecture and Furniture*, Longman, London, 1833, pp.251–56.

44 Bergdoll, Christensen and Broadhurst (eds), *Home Delivery*, p.40.

45 *NZG&WS*, 21 Aug 1839, p.1; 18 Apr 1840, p.4.

46 Ibid., 21 Aug 1839, p.1.

47 Jenny Gregory, 'Journeying Across Colonial Landscapes: Portable Housing in Nineteenth Century Australia', in Alan Mayne (ed.), *Beyond the Black Stump: Histories of Outback Australia*, Wakefield Press, Kent Town, 2008, p.214.

48 *NZG&WS*, 18 April 1840, p.4.

49 Louis Ward, *Early Wellington*, Whitcombe & Tombs, Wellington, 1928, pp.45, 47; *NZG&WS*, 21 Aug 1839, p.1.

50 Julie Bremner, 'Barrett's Hotel: The Victorian Rendezvous', in Hamer and Nicholls (eds), *The Making of Wellington*, p.151; Ward, *Early Wellington*, p.250.

51 John Wood, *Twelve Months in Port Nicholson: or Notes for the Public and the New Zealand Company*, Pelham Richardson, London, 1843, p.10.

52 'Mary to Grandparents', 21 Aug 1842, 'Letters of Mary Frederica Swainson to her grandparents in England, 1841–1854', QMS-1337-1339, ATL, p.34.

53 'Greenwood to Daw', June 1844, cited in Ruth Allan, *Nelson: A History of Early Settlement*, Reed, Wellington, 1965, p.138.

54 Jeremy Salmond, *Old New Zealand Houses*, Heinemann Reed, Auckland, 1986, pp.31–32.

55 *New Zealand Illustrated Magazine*, 1 Jul 1900, p.5.

56 'Extract of letter from Dr Evans', 9 July 1840, *New Zealand Journal*, 23 (1840), pp.292–93.

57 Mathew, Sarah Louisa, 1805–1890: Extracts from diary, qMS-1350, ATL.

58 William Toomath, *Built in New Zealand: The Houses We Live In*, Harper Collins, Auckland, 1996, p.25.

59 *New Zealand Journal*, 1841, p.311, cited in Ward, *Early Wellington*, p.25.

60 For example, in Māori society notions of tapu and noa meant cooking and sleeping functions were undertaken in different structures: kāuta and whare puni respectively. Deidre Brown, *Māori Architecture: From Fale to Wharenui and Beyond*, Reed, Auckland, 2009, p.30.

61 Sydney Evelyn Liardet Wright, 1825–1897, Journal extract, MS-Papers-4282, ATL.

62 *NZS&WS*, 12 Nov 1842, p.2.

63 'Joseph White to his mother', 24 Dec 1842, in *Letters from Settlers and Labouring Emigrants in the New Zealand Company's Settlements of Wellington, Nelson and New Plymouth: from February 1842 to January 1843*, Smith, Elder & Co., London, 1843, p.57.

64 Cyclopedia Company Limited, *Cyclopedia of New Zealand* [Wellington Provincial District], Wellington, 1897, pp.245–46.

65 *NZS&WS*, 12 Nov 1842, p.2.

66 A meeting was held on 11 November in the Exchange, where £400 was subscribed for the relief of victims. Ibid. White recorded that local Māori collected £5 'for the sufferers'. White, in *Letters from Settlers*, p.57.

67 *NZG&WS*, 12 Nov 1842, p.2.

68 The Governor could apply the ordinance by proclamation if petitioned by a town. Nigel Isaacs, 'Early Building Legislation', *Build*, 122 (2011), p.90.

69 *New Zealand Colonist and Port Nicholson Advertiser* (*NZC&PNA*), 5 Aug 1842, p.2.

70 The 1843 survey counted 621 houses in the town, of which 315 were of native (raupō) construction. It also identified 11 public buildings: a church (also used as a courthouse), two chapels, an exchange, a customhouse, a post office, a clubhouse, a theatre and an immigration depot. There were 22 warehouses and stores, five forges and workshops, and two mills in the town. *NZG&WS*, 9 Dec 1843, p.2. An 1844 New Zealand Company report calculated that 56 per cent of Wellington dwellings were of raupō construction. See M.K. Watson and B.R. Patterson, 'The Growth and Subordination of the Maori Economy in the Wellington Region of New Zealand, 1840–52', *Pacific Viewpoint*, 26, 3 (1985), p.527.

71 *NZG&WS*, 16 Sept 1843, p.2.

72 Joseph Newman to Rev E. Prout, 20 Jul 1841, Letters 1841–1857, NZMS 1199, Auckland City Library.

73 Nigel Isaacs, 'Going Back in Time – Raupo Houses', *Build*, 90 (2005), p.103.

74 *New Zealand Spectator and Cook's Strait Guardian* (*NZS&CSG*), 13 Apr 1850, p.2.

75 Christine McCarthy 'Ground Floor Attics: Canterbury's V Huts', in Christine McCarthy (ed.), *'A Distressing Lack of Regularity': New Zealand Architecture in the 1850s: A One Day Symposium*, Faculty of Architecture and Design, Victoria University of Wellington, Wellington, 2012, pp.41–42.

76 Johannes Anderson, *Old Christchurch in Picture and Story*, Simpson & Williams, Christchurch, 1949, pp.61–63; Anna Peterson, *New Zealanders at Home: A Cultural History of Domestic Interiors 1814–1914*, University of Otago Press, Dunedin, 2001, p.42.

77 Anderson, *Old Christchurch*, p.66.

78 Ibid., p.64.

79 Ibid., pp.65–66.

80 Jeremy Salmond, *Old New Zealand Houses, 1840–1940*, Heinemann Reed, Auckland, 1986, p.154.

81 The use of a rural building type underscored the pastoral character of New Zealand towns. Toomath, *Built in New Zealand*, pp.28–29; Tony Dingle, 'Necessity the Mother of Invention', in Patrick Troy (ed.), *European Housing in Australia*, Cambridge University of Press, Cambridge, p.60.

82 Julius Vogel, *The Official Handbook of New Zealand*, Wyman & Sons, London, 1875, pp.214, 240, cited in Salmond, *New Zealand Houses*, p.61.

83 Salmond, *New Zealand Houses*, pp.60–63, 73–75.

84 Charlotte Godley, *Letters from Early New Zealand*, 1936, NZETC edn, p.48, http://nzetc.victoria.ac.nz/tm/scholarly/tei-GodLett.html (accessed 24 Mar 2016).

85 Annabel Owen to her sister, 25 May 1860, 'Letters and papers relating to the Owen and Hazard families', MS 1164, 82/37, Auckland Museum.

86 Emma Thomson Diary, 7 June 1888, Diary of Emma Thomson/transcribed by Sheila Irwin, 1887, MS-2076/001, Hocken Library.

87 It was not until 1978 that insulation in new houses was made mandatory and the idea of heating the whole house gained ground. 'Energy at Local NZ', Physics Department, University of Otago, www.physics.otago.ac.nz/eman/hew/elocal/enzhousing.html# (accessed 15 Nov 2015).

88 The influx of Australian emigrants to Auckland in the 1840s and the region's sultry climes probably explains why it caught on there before being adopted elsewhere.

89 Toomath, *Built in New Zealand*, p.43.

90 11 Jan 1858, Crump John A, Rev, 1828–1912, Diary of a Voyage to New Zealand, MS-Papers-7337, ATL.

91 'William Parr to parents', 26 Aug 1859, Journal of James Parr and Letters of Mary, James and William Parr, 1857–1869, qMS-1628, ATL.

92 Salmond, *New Zealand Houses*, p.154; Toomath, *Built in New Zealand*, pp.124–25.

93 *Sydney Gazette and New South Wales Advertiser*, 12 Jul 1842, p.2.

94 Cyclopedia Company Limited, *Cyclopedia of New Zealand* [Canterbury Provincial District], Christchurch, 1903, p.69.

95 'Letter from a settler', 13 Sept 1849, *Otago Journal*, 4 (1850), p.89, cited in Pamela Wood, *Dirt: Filth and Decay in a New World Arcadia*, Auckland University Press, Auckland, 2005, p.48.

96 Wood, *Dirt*, p.49.

97 *Nelson Examiner and New Zealand Chronicle* (*NE&NZC*), 14 Oct 1848, p.132.

98 *Daily Southern Cross*, 3 Jun 1843, p.3.

99 Joseph Blades, 'A Retrospective View of Auckland from 1859', MS 29, Auckland War Memorial Museum, p.44; Adrian Humphris, 'Streets and Lighting – Street Lighting', *Te Ara*, www.teara.govt.nz/en/streets-and-lighting (accessed 24 Mar 2016).

100 *NZG&WS*, 13 Jul 1842, p.2; 'Private Letter from Wellington', 28 April 1845, *New Zealand Journal*, 11 (1845), p.261. In Wellington, absentees owned 60 per cent of allotments. Burns, *Fatal Success*, p.161.

101 'From a Resident in Wellington, to a New Zealand Land Proprietor in England', 20 June 1842, *Letters from Settlers*, pp.23–24.

102 *NE&NZC*, 7 May 1842, p.34.

103 G.W.A. Bush, *Decently and in Order: The Centennial History of the Auckland City Council*, Collins, Auckland 1971, p.65; Redmer Yska, *Wellington: Biography of a City*, Reed, Auckland, 2006, p.34; J.P. Morrison, *The Evolution of a City: Christchurch and its Suburbs*, Christchurch City Council, Christchurch, 1948, p.37.

104 *Wellington Independent*, 2 Aug 1861, p.5; Bush, *Decently and in Order*, p.63; Yska, *Wellington*, p.31.

105 Yska, *Wellington*, p.31.

106 Henry Lawson, 'New Zealand from an Australian's Point of View', *Fair Play*, 1, 9 (1893), p.22.

107 *Lyttelton Times*, 11 Oct 1862, p.3; Morrison, *The Evolution of a City*, p.42.

108 Charmian Smith, 'The Anatomy of a City', 4 Apr 2009, www.odt.co.nz/news/dunedin/83598/the-anatomy-a-city (accessed 24 Mar 2016).

109 Graeme Wynn provides a good explanation of the doctrine in an examination of colonial forest clearance. Graeme Wynn, 'Destruction Under the Guise of Improvement: The Forest, 1840–1920', in Pawson and Brooking (eds), *Making a New Land*, pp.122, 134.

110 *The Cyclopedia of New Zealand* [Canterbury Provincial District], p.72.

111 Urbanism is defined as the spatial organisation of urban settlements.

112 *The Cyclopedia of New Zealand* [Canterbury Provincial District], p.142; 'Land in Auckland', *New Zealand Journal*, 59 (1842), p.1.

113 C. Warren Adams, *A Spring in the Canterbury Settlement*, Brown Green & Longmans, London, 1853, p.33.

114 'William Parr to E. Parr', 1 Feb 1859, Journal

of James Parr and letters of Mary, James and William Parr, 1857–1868, qMS-1628, ATL.

115 The 1860s New Zealand wars were occurring. Auckland was an exception because it had a capacious military fort. 'Further Papers on the Subject of Colonial Responsibility in Native Affairs', *Appendices to the Journals of the House of Representatives*, 1863, E-7A, p.8.

116 Graeme Davison, 'Australia: First Suburban Nation?', *Journal of Urban History*, 22, 1 (1995), p.43.

117 'G. Fellingham to his parents', 12 Mar 1842, in *Letters from Settlers*, p.8.

118 'Mary Ann Eleanor Petre, 1825–1885, Diary', 31 Jan 1843, MS-1772, ATL.

119 Erik Olssen, Clyde Griffen and Frank Jones, *An Accidental Utopia?: Social Mobility and the Foundation of an Egalitarian Society, 1880–1940*, Otago University Press, Dunedin, 2011, p.253.

120 Toomath, *Built in New Zealand*, p.73.

121 Erik Olssen notes that a handful of two-storeyed tenements were built in suburban southern Dunedin, but they were so unpopular that they were demolished by 1940. Olssen, *An Accidental Utopia*, p.40. Surviving examples of terrace housing in 2013 included the Dundas Street and Stuart Street terraces in Dunedin. See Heritage New Zealand List: www.historic.org.nz.

122 Graeme Davison, 'Colonial Origins of the Australian Home', in Troy (ed.), *European Housing in Australia*, p.9.

123 Olssen, *An Accidental Utopia*, p.253.

124 Using 1892 Department of Labour data, Miles Fairburn has estimated that one-third of working-class households were homeowners. If we add in other social classes, the total figure would have been higher. Miles Fairburn, *The Ideal Society and its Enemies: The Foundations of Modern New Zealand Society, 1850–1900*, Auckland University Press, Auckland, 1989, p.93; Lionel Frost, *The New Urban Frontier: Urbanisation and City Building in Australasia and the American West*, New South Wales University Press, Kensington, 1991, p.124; Ben Schrader, 'Housing and Government – A Property-owning

Democracy', *Te Ara*, www.teara.govt.nz/en/graph/32431/housing-tenure (accessed 24 Mar 2016).

125 Richard Dennis, *English Industrial Cities of the Nineteenth Century: A Social Geography*, Cambridge University Press, Cambridge, 1986, p.142.

126 John Darwin, *Unfinished Empire: The Global Expansion of Britain*, Allen Lane, London, 2012, p.96.

127 Davison, 'Colonial Origins of the Australian Home', p.11.

128 J.F. Blackwood to Andrew Blackwood, 24 Feb 1861, Blackwood, Andrew: Letters, 1857–1863, Misc-MS-0389, Hocken Library.

129 Alexander Bathgate, *Colonial Experience, or Sketches of People and Places in the Province of Otago*, Glasgow, 1874, pp.44–45, cited in Fairburn, *An Ideal Society*, p.43.

130 David Hamer, 'Centralization and Nationalism', in Keith Sinclair (ed.), *The Oxford Illustrated History of New Zealand*, Oxford University Press, Auckland, 1990, p.142; Ben Schrader, 'Suburban Streets: Social Differentiation in Auckland, 1890–1950s', in McKinnon (ed.), *Bateman New Zealand Historical Atlas*, plate 73.

131 As Miles Fairburn notes, 'the roomy house' was an 'effective medium for advertising superior status'. Fairburn, 'Local Community or Atomised Society?', in Judith Binney (ed.), *The Shaping of History: Essays from the New Zealand Journal of History*, Bridget Williams Books, Wellington, 2001, p.233.

132 *Sydney Gazette and New South Wales Advertiser*, 12 Jul 1842, p.2.

133 George Butler Earp, *New Zealand: Its Emigration and Gold Fields*, George Routledge & Co., London, 1853, p.48.

134 Similarly, in 1885, the Australian James Hingston wrote: 'Auckland has grown, in some forty-five years or so, since its settlement, house by house at a time, and presents, like to Sydney, the singularity of such gradual growth, in no two houses scarcely looking alike in architecture or in age.' William Swainson, *Auckland, The Capital of New Zealand and the Country Adjacent*, Smith, Elder & Son, 1853,

p.29; James Hingston, *The Australian Abroad: On Branches From the Main Routes Around the World*, William Inglis & Co., Melbourne, 1886, p.192.

135 Mona Domosh, *Invented Cities: The Creation of Landscape in Nineteenth Century New York and Boston*, Yale University Press, New Haven, 1996, p.22.

136 Ben Schrader, 'Paris or New York? Contesting Melbourne's Skyline 1880–1958', *Journal of Urban History*, 36, 6 (2010), p.818.

137 Ernst Plishke, *Design and Living*, Department of Internal Affairs, Wellington, 1947, p.52.

138 Ben Schrader, 'City Planning – From Motorways to the Resource Management Act', *Te Ara*, www.teara.govt.nz/en/city-planning/5 (accessed 24 Mar 2016).

139 David Thorns and Ben Schrader, 'City History and People – Towns to Cities', *Te Ara*, www.teara.govt.nz/en/city-history-and-people/page-3 (accessed 24 Mar 2016).

140 Ben Schrader and Paul Husbands, 'Colonial Auckland: Boom and Bust, 1850s to 1890s', in McKinnon (ed.), *Bateman New Zealand Historical Atlas*, plate 57; John Barr, *The Ports of Auckland and Manukau*, Unity, Auckland, 1926, p.147.

141 *Daily Southern Cross*, 9 Nov 1864, p.4.

142 'Lewis to Sister', 3 Apr 1865, Letters from Lewis Haslam to Members of his Family in England, MS-Papers-3895-07, ATL.

143 *Daily Southern Cross*, 30 Apr 1863, p.3; 5 Oct 1863, p.3.

144 Tristram Hunt, *Building Jerusalem: The Rise and Fall of the Victorian City*, Phoenix, London, 2004, p.233.

145 *Daily Southern Cross*, 11 May 1864, p.3.

146 John Stacpoole, *Colonial Architecture in New Zealand*, A.H. & A.W. Reed, Wellington, 1976, pp.119–20.

147 Jon Stobart, 'Identity, Competition and Place Promotion in the Five Towns', *Urban History*, 30, 2 (2003), p.168.

148 John Stacpoole, *Colonial Architecture in New Zealand*, p.119; Bank of New Zealand Building, Heritage New Zealand List, www.heritage.org.nz/the-list/details/95 (accessed 24 Mar 2016).

149 Geoffrey W. Rice, *Christchurch Changing: An Illustrated History*, Canterbury University Press, Christchurch, 1999, p.32.

150 Hunt, *Building Jerusalem*, pp.105–7.

151 Ian Lochhead, 'Canterbury Provincial Council Buildings', paper presented to one-day symposium: '"A Distressing Lack of Regularity": New Zealand Architecture in the 1850s', Faculty of Architecture and Design, Victoria University of Wellington, 7 Dec 2012.

152 *Daily Southern Cross*, 19 Feb 1858, p.4.

153 Stacpoole, *Colonial Architecture*, pp.108–9.

154 Erik Olssen, *A History of Otago*, John McIndoe, Dunedin, 1984, pp.56, 69.

155 John Stacpoole, *William Mason: The First New Zealand Architect*, Auckland University Press, Auckland, 1971, p.85. Mason had been a member of Auckland's founding party. He practised architecture in the town – most notably designing the second Government House in 1856 – before moving to Dunedin in 1862.

156 *Otago Daily Times (ODT)*, 3 Feb 1868, p.4.

157 Stacpoole, *William Mason*, p.85.

158 Stacpoole, *Colonial Architecture*, p.98.

159 *ODT*, 9 Jun 1868, p.4. The councillor was a Mr Main.

160 Ibid., 16 Nov 1867, p.5; 9 Jun 1868, p.5; *Otago Witness*, 13 Jun 1868, p.12.

161 Stacpoole has argued the building's generous size and magnificence 'shocked' post office officials and the provincial council, and this led to the acquisition proposal. As both sides had signed off on the plans this seems implausible, but it might have been a rationale after the fact. Stacpoole, *Colonial Architecture*, p.98, and *William Mason*, p.85.

162 Melbourne's General Post Office well illustrates this point. Miles Lewis, *Melbourne: The City's History and Development*, City of Melbourne, Melbourne, 1995, p.52.

163 Erik Olssen, 'Macandrew, James', *Te Ara*, www.teara.govt.nz/en/biographies/1m1/macandrew-james (accessed 29 Mar 2016).

164 The dominance of provincial over central government in Otago was reinforced when the province reneged on building a new post office

and housed it instead in the north-west corner of the Provincial Council Building. *ODT*, 7 July 1869, p.3.

165 The university occupied the building from 1871 to 1877, when it moved to its existing site. The Colonial Bank bought it before it became a 'temple of commerce' as the city's stock exchange in 1900. Stacpoole, *William Mason*, p.85.

166 Jo Galer, 'City Has No Difficulty in Ignoring its History', *ODT*, 10 Sep 2009, www.odt.co.nz/opinion/opinion/73321/city-has-no-difficulty-ignoring-its-history (accessed 29 Mar 2016).

167 Ward, *Early Wellington*, pp.144–46, 160–62.

168 Edwin Hodder, *Memories of New Zealand Life*, George Unwin, Gresham Steam Press, London, 1863, p.122.

169 David Kennedy, *Kennedy's Colonial Travel: A Narrative of a Four Years' Tour Through Australia, New Zealand, Canada, &c*, Simpkin, Marshall & Co., London, 1876, p.209.

170 David Hamer, 'Wellington on the Urban Frontier', in Hamer and Nicholls (eds), *The Making of Wellington*, p.248.

171 'Government Buildings', Heritage New Zealand List, www.heritage.org.nz/the-list/details/37 (accessed 29 Mar 2016); Martin Hill, *New Zealand Architecture*, Government Printer, Wellington, 1976, pp.16–17; *Evening Post*, 9 Dec 1907, p.7.

172 Ibid., 1 Dec 1897, p.2.

173 To ensure the new building was as safe as possible, concrete piles were driven below sea level into the bedrock. Stacpoole, *Colonial Architecture*, pp.136–37; Chris Cochran, 'Supreme Court, 42 Stout Street, Wellington, Conservation Report', unpublished report for Ministry for Justice, Wellington, 2006, p.25.

174 *Evening Post*, 4 Dec 1879, p.2.

175 Ibid.; *Bay of Plenty Times*, 2 Dec 1879, p.3.

176 *Evening Post*, 4 Dec 1879, p.2.

177 *Bay of Plenty Times*, 2 Dec 1879, p.3.

178 Jim McAloon, *Nelson: A Regional History*, Cape Catley, Queen Charlotte Sound, 1997, pp.85, 93, 103.

179 Felicity Barnes, *New Zealand's London: A Colony and its Metropolis*, Auckland University Press, Auckland, 2012, p.126.

Chapter Three

1 'Swainson, William, 1789–1855', *Te Ara*, www.teara.govt.nz/en/1966/swainson-william-1789-1855 (accessed 29 Mar 2016).

2 Here we see the settler impulse to counter metropolitan society's wilderness image of colonial life with one that stressed its civilisation. 'Mary to her grandparents', 3 Jun 1841, Letters of Mary Frederica Swainson to her grandparents in England, 1841–1854, QMS-1337-1339, ATL, p.17.

3 Ibid.

4 As Robert Harrison further explains: 'cultural historians moved beyond group behaviour to examine the cultural conventions that informed it'. Robert Harrison, 'The New Social History in America', in Peter Lambert and Phillip Schofield (eds), *Making History: An Introduction to the History and Practices of a Discipline*, Routledge, London, 2004, p.116.

5 Among the most influential late-20th-century works on colonial Pākehā society are: David Pearson, *Johnsonville: Continuity and Change in a New Zealand Township*, George Allen & Unwin, Sydney, 1979; Jock Phillips, *A Man's Country? The Image of the Pakeha Male: A History*, Penguin, Auckland, 1987; Miles Fairburn, *The Ideal Society and its Enemies: The Foundations of Modern New Zealand Society, 1850–1900*, Auckland University Press, Auckland, 1989; Erik Olssen, *Building the New World: Work, Politics and Society in Caversham 1880s–1920s*, Auckland University Press, Auckland, 1995; Rollo Arnold, *Settler Kaponga 1881–1914: A Frontier Fragment of the Western World*, Victoria University Press, Wellington, 1997; Caroline Daley, *Girls and Women, Men and Boys: Gender in Taradale, 1886–1930*, Auckland University Press, Auckland, 1999.

6 Tony Ballantyne, 'Thinking Local Knowledge, Sociability and Community in Gore's Intellectual Life, 1875–1914', *New Zealand Journal of History*, 44, 2 (2010), pp.138–56.

7 Stuart C. Aitkin, 'Gemeinshaft' and 'Gesellshaft', in Roger W. Caves (ed.), *Encyclopedia of the City*, Routledge, London,

2005, pp.194, 204; Malcolm Miles, *Cities and Cultures*, Routledge, Abingdon, 2007, p.12; James Donald, *Imagining the Modern City*, University of Minnesota Press, Minneapolis, 1999, p.11.

8   In this usage, as cultural geographer Doreen J. Mattingly writes, 'the term "community" appeals to a sort of shared identity that transcends geography and a common experience that unites strangers'. Doreen J. Mattingly, 'Community', in Caves (ed.), *Encyclopedia of the City*, p.83.

9   Fairburn, *The Ideal Society*, pp.158–59.

10 W.J. Gardner, 'Grass Roots and Dredge Tailings', *Landfall*, 11 (1957), p.225, cited in Miles Fairburn, 'Local Community or Atomised Society? The Social Structure of Nineteenth Century New Zealand', in Judith Binney (ed.), *The Shaping of History: Essays from the New Zealand Journal of History*, Bridget Williams Books, Wellington, 2001, p.229.

11 Olssen, *Building the New World*, pp.9, 227–30; Fairburn, 'Local Community or Atomised Society?', pp.229–30.

12 Erik Olssen, 'Towards a New Society', in W.H. Oliver with B.R. Williams (eds), *The Oxford History of New Zealand*, Oxford University Press, Wellington, 1981, p.257.

13 Fairburn, *The Ideal Society*, p.11.

14 Ibid., p.165.

15 Ibid., pp.137–43, 155.

16 'New Zealand localities were more like transit camps than island communities,' wrote Fairburn. Even where groups of people resided in particular districts, poor roads kept them out of easy reach and inhibited associational culture. Fairburn, 'Local Community or Atomised Society?', pp.167, 239.

17 Ibid., pp.234–35.

18 Fairburn, *The Ideal Society*, pp.196, 202.

19 This sub-culture comprised young, single, manual-working men whose work encouraged transiency. Caroline Daley, 'Taradale Meets the Ideal Society and its Enemies', in Binney (ed.), *The Shaping of History*, pp.273, 277.

20 Ibid., pp.272, 274.

21 Dean Wilson, 'Community and Gender in Victorian Auckland', in Binney (ed.), *The Shaping of History*, pp.216–26.

22 Jock Phillips, 'Of Verandahs and Fish and Chips and Footie on Saturday Afternoon: Reflections on 100 Years of New Zealand Historiography', in Binney (ed.), *The Shaping of History*, p.334; Daley, 'Taradale Meets the Ideal Society and its Enemies', p.270.

23 Fairburn, *The Ideal Society*, pp.127–32, 177–81, 225–28.

24 'Hopeful', *'Taken In': A Sketch of New Zealand Life*, W.H. Allen & Co., London, 1888 (Capper Press edn, 1974), p.147.

25 Fairburn cites the same passage on two different occasions. Fairburn, *The Ideal Society*, pp.169, 217.

26 She even thought it a pity there were not more such institutions like it at home. 'Hopeful', *'Taken In'*, pp.80–81.

27 Ibid., pp.83, 147–48.

28 Ibid., p.83.

29 Interestingly, he obliquely acknowledges that cities were more socially vital than country districts when discussing loneliness, citing this example: 'Captain and Mrs Ferguson, who occupied the Ōpouriao Valley near Whakatāne in 1875, soon returned to Auckland after "Tiring of the solitude."' Fairburn, *The Ideal Society*, p.196.

30 This study adopts Erik Olssen, Clyde Griffen and Frank Jones's occupational-based definition of social class. Their classification used nine strata: 1) large employers and higher managers; 2) professionals; 3) semi-professionals; 4) self-employed and small employers; 5) petty officials and supervisors; 6) white collar (sales and clerical); 7) skilled manual; 8) semi-skilled manual; and 9) unskilled manual. These could be collapsed into three main classes: upper-middle, middle and working classes. Erik Olssen, Clyde Griffen and Frank Jones, *An Accidental Utopia?: Social Mobility and the Foundation of an Egalitarian Society, 1880–1940*, Otago University Press, Dunedin, 2011, pp.27–29.

31 In 2005, historian Sven Beckett argued 'that if we want to understand the politics, economics,

culture, and ideas of nineteenth century, we better come to terms with this group of people [the middle class]'. Sven Beckett, 'Comments on "Studying the Middle Class in the Modern City"', *Journal of Urban History*, 31, 3 (2005), p.394. See also Marshall Berman, *All that is Solid Melts into Air: The Experience of Modernity*, Penguin, New York, 1988.

32 'Webber, Edmund, 1817–1860, Transcript of Journal', MS-Papers-10957, ATL, pp.35–36, 39.

33 Ibid., pp.36, 54.

34 Ibid., p.52.

35 Ibid.

36 Ibid., p.59.

37 Edmund's journal ends soon after the termination of his employment. It appears that with few immediate prospects in New Zealand, he left the colony. His journal was deposited in the William Cocksworthy Museum, Kingsbridge, Devon.

38 Sarah's biographer says that she and Felton were 'at the centre of social life' in Auckland. Hilary F. Reid, 'Mathew, Sarah Louise', *Te Ara*, www.teara.govt.nz/en/biographies/1m25/ mathew-sarah-louise (accessed 29 Mar 2016).

39 'Mathew, Sarah Louise, 1805–1890, Extracts from diary (autobiography) of Mrs Felton Mathew', qMS-1350, ATL, p.18.

40 On another occasion she described Mary as 'very lively and good natured'. Charlotte Godley, *Letters from Early New Zealand*, 1936, NZETC edn, pp.41, 68, http://nzetc. victoria.ac.nz/tm/scholarly/tei-GodLett.html (accessed 29 Mar 2016).

41 Eliza's husband was the doctor John Fitzgerald. 'Petre, Mary Ann Eleanor, 1825–1885, Diary', MS-1772, ATL, 26 Mar 1843.

42 Ibid., 8 May 1843.

43 Ibid., 9 Mar 1843; Georgina White, *Light Fantastic: Dance Floor Courtship in New Zealand*, Harper Collins, Auckland, 2007, p.23.

44 Ibid., 16 May 1843.

45 Ibid., 17 Sept 1843.

46 Margaret Marsh, *Suburban Lives*, Rutgers University Press, New Brunswick, 1990, p.36.

47 Ian J. Lochhead, 'Petre, Francis William', *Te Ara*, www.teara.govt.nz/en/biographies/2p13/ petre-francis-william (accessed 29 Mar 2016).

48 'Copy of Letter from Joseph Hudgell to his Parents in London', *New Zealand Journal*, 4 Sep 1841, p.225.

49 S.M.D. Martin, *New Zealand in a Series of Letters*, Simmonds & Ward, London, 1845, p.94.

50 As Catharine Coleborne writes, 'Loneliness … shaped experiences for wealthy settlers and poor immigrants alike.' Catharine Coleborne, 'Health and Illness, 1840–1990s', in Giselle Byrnes (ed.), *The New Oxford History of New Zealand*, Oxford University Press, South Melbourne, 2009, p.495.

51 John to Charlotte, 2 Oct 1842, 'John Henry Wilson, Letters to his Wife', MS-Papers-3356, ATL.

52 Ibid., 25 Sept 1842.

53 Charlotte Godley stated that Eliza was 'little liked' in colonial society due to her 'satirical expression', and this could explain her predicament. Godley, *Letters from Early New Zealand*, p.165. Keith Sinclair, 'Grey, George', *Te Ara*, www.teara.govt.nz/en/biographies/1g21/ grey-george (accessed 29 Mar 2016).

54 'Eliza Grey to Maggie Watts', 21 Jun 1846, Grey, Eliza Lucy, Lady, 1823–1898, MS-Papers-0860, ATL.

55 Miles, *Cities and Cultures*, pp.12–13.

56 'Rose to Grace', 30 Mar 1862, cited in Jean Garner and Kate Foster (eds), *Letters to Grace: Writing Home from Colonial New Zealand*, Canterbury University Press, Christchurch, 2011, p.14.

57 'Diary, 12 Aug 1843', Petre, Mary Ann Eleanor, 1825–1885, Diary, MS-1772, ATL.

58 Godley, *Letters from Early New Zealand*, pp.77–78.

59 Edwin Hodder, *Memories of New Zealand Life*, 2nd edn, Jackson, Walford & Hodder, London, 1863, p.92.

60 Godley, *Letters from Early New Zealand*, p.193.

61 Ibid., p.93.

62 'Samuel Harris to Parents', 6 Aug 1861, Harris Family Letters, MS-Papers-6987, ATL.

63 Mary Anne Hunter to 'Friend', April 1867,

Hunter, Mary Anne, fl 1867, MS-Papers-1279, ATL.

64 'Eliza Collier to Jane', 6 Oct 1865, Collier Family Papers, MS-Papers-3946, ATL.

65 Fairburn, 'Local Community of Atomised Society', p.402, fn 47.

66 Fairburn, *The Ideal Society*, pp.201–2.

67 Garner and Foster (eds), *Letters to Grace*, p.14.

68 John A. Askew, *A Voyage to Australia and New Zealand*, Simpkin, Marshall & Co., London, 1857, p.343.

69 'John to Brother', 6 Feb 1862, Kirkwood, John fl 1862–1906, Letter, MS-Papers-1044, ATL.

70 'Lewis to Sister', 6 Jul 1865, Letters from Lewis Haslam to Members of his Family, MS-Papers-3895-07, ATL. John Askew made a similar point in his 1857 book, noting that drinking was 'carried on to an alarming extent' among working people. 'This state of things is much to be lamented, as most working-men might soon be independent if they were careful and sober.' Whether drinking was a means to escape loneliness (after Fairburn) or a response to a lack of other urban amusements is uncertain. Askew, *A Voyage*, p.356.

71 '7 January 1858', Crump, John A. Rev, 1828–1912, Diary of a Voyage of New Zealand, MS-Papers-7337, ATL.

72 Hodder, *Memories of New Zealand Life*, p.49.

73 Ibid., p.50.

74 Ibid., pp.49–50.

75 Ibid., pp.50–51.

76 Ibid., pp.124–25.

77 Campbell, Daniel, fl 1851, Letter, MS-Papers-2333, ATL.

78 'Agnes to Auntie', 27 Sept 1868, in Garner and Foster (eds), *Letters to Grace*, p.159.

79 'Eliza to Jane', 6 Oct 1865, and Eliza to Jessie, 7 Jan 1866, Collier Family Papers, MS-Papers-3946, ATL.

80 Mary Anne Hunter to 'Friend', April 1867, Hunter, Mary Anne, fl 1867, MS-Papers-1279, ATL.

81 The data comes from: 'Population General Summary', 'Cities and Towns' and 'Four Chief Cities and Suburbs' tables in the 'Population and Dwellings' section of the New Zealand Census, 1861–1921. New Zealand Government, *Census of New Zealand*, Government Printer, Wellington (Auckland 1861 and 1864), 1867–1886.

82 James Belich, 'European Ideas About Māori – The Dying Māori and Social Darwinism', *Te Ara*, www.teara.govt.nz/en/interactive/29882/maori-population-1840-2009 (accessed 29 Mar 2016).

83 Peter Clark, *European Cities and Towns: 400–2000*, Oxford University Press, Oxford, 2009, p.310.

84 As Jon Stobart has written: 'Investment in cultural capital was vital in bourgeois attempts to (re)construct the city in their own image.' Jon Stobart, 'Identity, Competition and Place Promotion in the Five Towns', *Urban History*, 30, 2 (2003), p.182.

85 Judith R. Walkowitz, *City of Dreadful Delight: Narratives of Sexual Desire in Late-Victorian London*, University of Chicago Press, Chicago, 1992, p.45.

86 Andrew Lees and Lynn Hollen Lees, *Cities and the Making of Modern Europe, 1750–1914*, Cambridge University Press, Cambridge, 2007, pp.208–9.

87 *Daily Southern Cross*, 5 Jun 1876, p.2. Arguably the colony's first museum was that attached to the Nelson Institute, which moved into its own building in 1842. It was primarily a library but had a museum storehouse. Whether this can be classified as a public space is a moot point. 'Our Museum History', The Nelson Provincial Museum, www.museumnp.org.nz/about/history.htm (accessed 15 Apr 2014).

88 *Daily Southern Cross*, 5 Jun 1876, p.2.; Ben Schrader, 'Public Buildings – Civic and Cultural Buildings', *Te Ara*, www.teara.govt.nz/en/public-buildings/page-3 (accessed 24 Mar 2016).

89 *Press*, 13 Mar 1872, p.3; 12 Jul 1883, p.5.

90 Clark, *European Cities and Towns*, p.312.

91 *New Zealand Herald*, 15 Jul 1879, p.6.

92 'A Brief History of Christchurch Libraries', http://christchurchcitylibraries.com/Heritage/LocalHistory/ChristchurchCityLibraries/

(accessed 20 Mar 2016); 'History of Wellington City Libraries', www.wcl.govt.nz/about/branches/history.html (accessed 30 Apr 2014).

93 Roger Blackley, 'Art Galleries and Collections', *Te Ara*, www.teara.govt.nz/en/art-galleries-and-collections (accessed 29 Mar 2016).

94 Some of these paintings were hung in a gallery at the Auckland Museum. Two of the works were by the Italian Renaissance painter Guido Reni. When Mackelvie died in 1885, he left a bequest of £40,000 (the equivalent of $7.45 million in today's currency) for a new art gallery. With the construction of the Auckland gallery already underway this was deemed unnecessary, and in 1893 a room in the new gallery was made available for his collection instead. *New Zealand Herald*, 9 Sept 1882, p.4; 15 Nov 1882, p.5.

95 *New Zealand Herald*, 5 Jun 1885, p.6: G.W.A. Bush, *Decently and in Order: The Centennial History of the Auckland City Council*, Collins, Auckland, 1971, pp.172–73.

96 Ibid.

97 Blackley, 'Art Galleries and Collections'.

98 Adrienne Simpson, *Opera's Farthest Frontier: A History of Professional Opera in New Zealand*, Reed, Auckland, 1996, pp.25, 47; Lindis Taylor, 'Opera and Musical Theatre – Light Opera and Musical Theatre', *Te Ara*, www.teara.govt.nz/en/opera-and-musical-theatre/page-2 (accessed 29 Mar 2016).

99 Jock Phillips, 'Culture and Recreation in the City – Organised Culture Before 1900', *Te Ara*, www.teara.govt.nz/en/culture-and-recreation-in-the-city/page-3 (accessed 29 Mar 2016).

100 Peter Downes, *Shadows on the Stage: Theatre in New Zealand: The First 70 Years*, John McIndoe, Dunedin, 1975, p.71.

101 Leif Jerram, *Streetlife: The Untold Story of Europe's Twentieth Century*, Oxford University Press, Oxford, 2011, p.180.

102 Ben Schrader, 'Theatres, Cinemas and Halls – Colonial Period', *Te Ara*, www.teara.govt.nz/en/theatres-cinemas-and-halls/page-1 (accessed 29 Mar 2016); Jonathan Mane-Wheoki, 'The High Arts in a Regional Culture – From Englishness to Self-Reliance', in John Cookson and Graeme Dunstall (eds),

Southern Capital: Christchurch: Towards a City Biography, 1850–2000, Canterbury University Press, Christchurch, 2000, p.303.

103 'William to Harry', 16 Jun 1883, Derry Family Letters, MS-Papers-1043, ATL.

104 Keith Sinclair and Wendy Harrex, *Looking Back: A Photographic History of New Zealand*, Oxford University Press, Wellington, 1978, p.135; *Colonist*, 12 Jan 1889, p.4.

105 *Wairarapa Daily Times*, 21 Sept 1894, p.2.

106 Herbert Spackman Diary, 1 Oct 1894, Spackman, Herbert, 1891–1900, MS-Papers-1788, ATL. The Governor's stage fright was ignored by most press reports but recorded by the *Nelson Evening Mail*, 20 Oct 1894, p.2.

107 *Marlborough Express*, 9 Apr 1894, p.3.

108 *Evening Post*, 8 Oct 1894, p.2; 16 Oct 1894, p.3.

109 Charlotte Macdonald, 'Ways of Belonging: Sporting Spaces in New Zealand History', in Byrnes (ed.), *New Oxford History*, p.270; Greg Ryan, 'Sport and Society – Sport Comes to New Zealand', *Te Ara*, www.teara.govt.nz/en/sport-and-society/page-2 (accessed 29 Mar 2016).

110 Macdonald, 'Ways of Belonging', p.270.

111 Clark, *European Cities and Towns*, p.315.

112 Greg Ryan, 'Sport and Society – Growth, 1860s and 1870s', *Te Ara*, www.teara.govt.nz/en/sport-and-society/page-3 (accessed 29 Mar 2016).

113 Jerram, *Streetlife*, p.192.

114 Until the opening of Eden Park, the Domain was Auckland's main sportsground. Jock Phillips, 'Sports Venues – The First City Sportsground, 1850–1914', *Te Ara*, www.teara.govt.nz/en/sports-venues/page-1 (accessed 29 Mar 2016).

115 Macdonald, 'Ways of Belonging', p.275.

116 Ben Schrader, 'Children and Sport – Early Sport, 1860 to 1919', *Te Ara*, www.teara.govt.nz/en/children-and-sport/page-1 (accessed 29 Mar 2016).

117 Macdonald, 'Ways of Belonging', p.275.

118 Lees and Hollen Lees, *Cities and the Making of Modern Europe*, p.231.

119 Miles Fairburn estimated only about 2 per cent

of city dwellers played organised sport in the early 1890s. Fairburn, *The Ideal Society*, pp.181, 186.

120 *Otago Daily Times*, 20 Aug 1891, p.2.

121 Jock Phillips, 'Culture and Recreation in the City – Sport in Colonial Cities', *Te Ara*, www.teara.govt.nz/en/culture-and-recreation-in-the-city/page-4 (accessed 29 Mar 2016); Cricket Archives, http://cricketarchive.com/Archive/Scorecards/131/131956.html (accessed 30 Apr 2014).

122 Kennett Brothers, *Ride: A History of Cycling in New Zealand*, Kennett Bros, Wellington, 2004, pp.88–92.

123 Diary of Emma Thomson, transcribed by Sheila Irwin, 1887, MS-2076/001, Hocken Library. I would like to thank Ali Clarke of the Hocken Library for alerting me to this diary.

124 Ross Galbreath, *Scholars and Gentlemen Both: G.M. & Allan Thomson in New Zealand Science and Education*, Royal Society of New Zealand, Wellington, 2002, pp.41–44.

125 Erik Olssen, *A History of Otago*, John McIndoe, Dunedin, 1984, p.75.

126 Clark, *European Cities and Towns*, p.306.

127 For some of the period covered in the diary, the Thomsons lived in the rectory of Otago Boys' High School, where they looked after the school's boarders. E. Yvonne Speirs, 'Thomson, George Malcolm', *Te Ara*, www.teara.govt.nz/en/biographies/2t40/Thomson-george-malcolm (accessed 29 Mar 2016).

128 Delores Hayden, *Building Suburbia: Greenfields and Urban Growth, 1820–2000*, Pantheon Books, New York, 2003, p.35.

129 Timothy R. Mahoney, 'Middle-class Experience in the United States in the Gilded Age, 1865–1900', *Journal of Urban History*, 31, 3 (2005), p.356.

130 Emma Thomson Diary, 16 Nov 1888.

131 Emma sometimes bought the cakes in town. Ibid., 5 Apr 1887; 20 Nov 1888.

132 Ibid., 21 Feb 1887.

133 Ibid., 20 Nov 1888.

134 Ibid., 29 Mar 1887.

135 Helen B. Laurenson, *Going Up, Going Down:* *The Rise and Fall of the Department Store*, Auckland University Press, Auckland, 2006, p.10; Richard Dennis, *Cities in Modernity: Representations and Productions of Metropolitan Space, 1840–1930*, Cambridge University Press, Cambridge, 2008, p.312; Jessica Ellen Sewell, *Women and the Everyday City: Public Space in San Francisco, 1890–1915*, University of Minnesota Press, Minneapolis, 2011, p.xxi.

136 Dennis, *Cities in Modernity*, pp.312–13; Walkowitz, *City of Dreadful Delight*, pp.46–49.

137 Walkowitz, *City of Dreadful Delight*, p.49.

138 Emma Thomson Diary, 30 Mar 1887; 16 Feb 1889; 15 May 1890; Lees and Hollen Lees, *Cities and the Making of Modern Europe*, p.226.

139 Emma Thomson Diary, 5 Oct 1891.

140 The Choral Hall (previously the Temperance Hall) is now (in 2016) Oxford Buildings.

141 Emma Thomson Diary, 8 Sept 1891; *ODT*, 9 Sept 1891, p.2.

142 Ibid., 12 Oct 1887; *ODT*, 10 Oct 1887, p.2.

143 Belcher, wife of the Boys' High School rector, acknowledged the University of New Zealand was among the first to admit women but argued more could be done to ease their entry. Her talk was one in a series in aid of funds for a Boys' High football ground on the flat. *ODT*, 21 Sept 1888, p.2; 22 Sept 1888, p.2; 24 Sept 1888, p.4; 25 Sept 1888, p.4.

144 Emma Thomson Diary, 21 Sept 1888.

145 Hayden, *Building Suburbia*, p.38.

146 Annabel Cooper, Erik Olssen, Kirsten Thomlinson and Robin Law, 'The Landscape of Gender Politics: Place, People and Two Mobilisations', in Barbara Brookes, Annabel Cooper and Robin Law (eds), *Sites of Gender: Women, Men and Modernity in Southern Dunedin, 1890–1939*, Auckland University Press, Auckland, 2003, pp.44, 47–48.

147 Emma Thomson Diary, 4 Sep 1890.

148 Ibid., 19 Jun 1887.

149 Hayden, *Building Suburbia*, p.42.

150 Emma Thomson Diary, 27 Sep 1889; 25 Apr 1890.

151 Ibid., 7 Jun and 25 Jul 1890.

152 Ibid., 7 June 1888.

153 Ibid., 11 Jan 1888.

154 Ibid., 30 Mar 1887; 17 Feb 1889; 15 May 1890.

155 Ibid., 21 Nov 1888; 24 Jul 1891.

156 Ibid., 5 Sep 1891; *ODT*, 7 Sept 1891, p.3.

157 Emma Thomson Diary, 9 Mar 1889.

158 Ibid., 24 Nov 1888.

159 Ibid., 20 Dec 1889.

160 *ODT*, 11 Apr 1887, p.3.

161 Māori culture does not rate a mention in Emma's diary. Emma Thomson Diary, 9 Apr 1887.

162 Clark, *European Cities and Towns*, p.320.

163 Jock Phillips, 'Exhibitions and World's Fairs – The Purpose of Exhibitions and the Great Exhibition, 1851', *Te Ara*, www.teara.govt.nz/en/exhibitions-and-worlds-fairs/page-1 (accessed 30 Mar 2016).

164 Emma Thomson Diary, 23 Dec 1889.

165 Ibid., 19 Apr 1890.

166 Ibid., 28 May 1894; *ODT*, 24 Jul 1894, p.2.

167 Herbert Spackman Diary, 3 Sep 1892.

168 Ibid., 10 Nov 1892.

169 Ibid., 16 Dec 1892.

170 Ibid., 3 and 6 May 1893.

171 *Christchurch Star*, 9 May 1893, p.4.

172 O'Rell was famous in the English-speaking world for his caricatures of national stereotypes and knowledge of cross-cultural morals and manners. Jana Verhoeven, 'The Biggest Thing in Years: Max O'Rell's Lecture Tour in Australasia', *Explorations*, 44 (2008), pp.7–8.

173 Ibid., p.7.

174 Herbert Spackman Diary, 1 Feb 1893.

175 It was one of three lectures on women's health and relationships she presented during a national tour, and the only one open to men. Herbert Spackman Diary, 16 Feb 1893; *Evening Post*, 14 Feb 1893, p.2; 16 Feb 1893, p.2.

176 Ibid., 17 Feb 1893, p.2. The advice about waistlines probably related to the wearing of stays (corsets) to gain the fashionable hourglass shape, but this could cause (as Potts pointed out in another lecture) disfigurement and health complications. Potts was among the first woman gynaecologists and in her women-only lectures she encouraged women to seek medical treatment for disease. She toured with Dr Charles Harrison, who gave men-only lectures on male health and venereal disease.

177 Marsh, *Suburban Lives*, pp.35–36.

178 Ibid.; Herbert Spackman Diary, 16 Feb 1893.

179 Ibid., 21 Jan 1894.

180 Ibid., 26 Dec 1894; 24 Dec 1896; 28 Dec 1895; 3 Jan 1898.

181 Ibid., 2 Oct 1894.

182 Ibid., 10 Dec 1894.

183 Ibid., 31 Jan 1895.

184 *Evening Post*, 28 Jan 1895; *Nelson Evening Mail*, 22 Jan 1895, p.2.

185 Herbert Spackman Diary, 8 Oct and 11 Dec 1895.

186 Ibid., 22 Feb 1893.

187 Ibid., 23 Oct 1897.

188 Ibid., 29 Jun 1896.

189 Ibid., 18 Jan 1897.

190 This may have been William Chapple, a prominent Wellington physician, who is a subject in Chapter Seven.

191 Herbert Spackman Diary, 3 Apr 1897.

192 Ibid., 5 and 6 Apr 1897.

193 Ibid., 2 Feb 1898.

194 Ibid., 26 Feb 1898.

Chapter Four

1 Spiro Kostof, *The City Assembled: The Elements of Urban Form Through History*, Thames & Hudson, London, 1992, pp.26–27.

2 The penal colony of Sydney began as a settlement where settlers and Aboriginals people lived alongside each other. However, within the first decades of its founding, the settler population had become dominant and the Aboriginal community had either perished from introduced diseases or been confined to particular districts like Woolloomooloo. Grace Karskens, *The Rocks: Life in Early Sydney*, Melbourne University Press, Carlton, 1997,

pp.16–17; John Darwin, *Unfinished Empire: The Global Expansion of Britain*, Allen Lane, London, 2012, pp.44–47.

3   Patricia Burns, *Fatal Success: A History of the New Zealand Company*, Heinemann Reed, Auckland, 1989, pp.56–60; Catherine Hall, *Civilising Subjects: Metropole and Colony in the English Imagination, 1830–1867*, Polity Press, Cambridge, 2002, pp.43–44.

4   The British believed that colonies could be lawfully established on indigenous people's lands if they were not occupied or cultivated. Māori had permanent settlements, so were deemed to be land occupiers; Aboriginals were a nomadic people and so were deemed not to be. Giselle Byrnes, *Boundary Markers: Land Surveying and the Colonisation of New Zealand*, Bridget William Books, Wellington, 2001, p.17; Patricia Grimshaw, Marilyn Lake, Ann McGrath and Marian Quartly, *Creating a Nation, 1788–1900*, McPhee Gribble, Ringwood, 1994, pp.133–34.

5   New Zealand Company, *Instructions From the New Zealand Land Company to Colonel Wakefield, Principal Agent of the Company*, John W. Parker, London, 1839, p.23.

6   William Cronon, *Nature's Metropolis: Chicago and the Great West*, W.W. Norton, New York, 1992, p.26.

7   Ibid., pp.27–29; Jacqueline Peterson, 'The Founding Fathers: The Absorption of French-Indian Chicago, 1816–1837', in Terry Straus (ed.), *Native Chicago*, Albatross Press, 2nd edn, New York, 2002, pp.58–60.

8   Penelope Edmonds, *Urbanizing Frontiers: Indigenous Peoples and Settlers in 19th-Century Pacific Rim Cities*, UBC Press, Vancouver, 2010, pp.74–75, 80.

9   Ibid., pp.125–30. For more on these representations, see Andrew Brown-May, *Melbourne Street Life*, Australian Scholarly Publishing, Melbourne 1998, pp.68–69.

10 Edmonds, *Urbanizing Frontiers*, pp.138–40.

11 Ibid., p.97.

12 Ibid., pp.97–99.

13 Erin Keenan, 'Māori Urban Migrations and Identities: Ko Ngā Iwi Nuku Whenua: A Study of Urbanisation in the Wellington Region during the Twentieth Century', PhD thesis, Victoria University of Wellington, 2014, p.77.

14 It needs to be stated that this chapter concerns Pākehā representations of Māori drawn from European sources. It is therefore unable to provide a Māori perspective on the events described, a weakness I hope subsequent researchers might be motivated to correct.

15 Kurt M. Peters, 'Indians on the Chicago Landscape 1870', in Straus, *Native Chicago*, p.111; Terry Straus, 'Founding Mothers: Indian Women in Early Chicago', in Straus, *Native Chicago*, p.76.

16 I would like to thank Peter Clayworth and Ewan Lincoln for their help in the construction of a theoretical framework for this chapter.

17 As Jane M. Jacobs points out, 'Such metropolitan constructs of Self and Other were integral to the territorial, military, political, and economic extensions of European power across the globe.' Jane M. Jacobs, *Edge of Empire: Postcolonialism and the City*, Routledge, London, 1996, p.13.

18 Robert D. Grant, *Representations of British Emigration, Colonisation and Settlement: Imagining Empire, 1800–1860*, Palgrave Macmillan, Basingstoke, 2005, p.177.

19 Ibid., pp.175–76; James Belich, 'Myth, Race and Identity in New Zealand', in Judith Binney (ed.), *The Shaping of History: Essays from the New Zealand Journal of History*, Bridget Williams Books, Wellington, 2001, pp.356–59; Angela Ballara, *Proud to be White: A Survey of Pakeha Prejudice in New Zealand*, Heinemann, Auckland, 1986, pp.8–9.

20 M.K.P. Sorrenson, 'How to Civilise the Savages: Some "Answers" from Nineteenth-century New Zealand', in M.P.K. Sorrenson, *Ko Te Whenua Te Utu: Land is the Price: Essays on Māori History, Land and Politics*, Auckland University Press, Auckland, 2014, pp.65–66.

21 James Belich, 'European Ideas About Māori – The Aryan Māori and other Stereotypes', *Te Ara*, www.teara.govt.nz/en/european-ideas-about-maori/page-5 (accessed 31 Mar 2016).

22 Sorrenson, 'How to Civilise the Savages', p.62;

Tony Ballantyne, *Webs of Empire: Locating New Zealand's Colonial Past*, Bridget Williams Books, Wellington, 2012, p.241.

23 John Miller, *Early Victorian New Zealand: A Study of Racial Tension and Social Attitudes 1839–1852*, Oxford University Press, London, 1958, pp.9–10. See also Ballara, *Proud to be White*, pp.16–17.

24 Erik Olssen, 'Mr Wakefield and New Zealand as a Social Experiment', *New Zealand Journal of History*, 31, 2 (1997), p.212. As Keith Sorrenson points out, the amalgamation project became state policy when settlers realised self-government. Sorrenson, 'How to Civilise the Savages', p.62.

25 In 1844, William Spain found the population of different kāinga about Wellington ranged between 10 and 200. M.K. Watson and B.R. Patterson, 'The Growth and Subordination of the Maori Economy in the Wellington Region of New Zealand, 1840–52', *Pacific Viewpoint*, 26, 3 (1985), p.540; Russell Stone, *From Tamaki-Makau-Rau to Auckland*, Auckland University Press, Auckland, 2001, pp.28, 36–38; Atholl Anderson, 'Origins, Settlement and Society of Pre-European South Polynesia', in Giselle Byrnes (ed.), *The New Oxford History of New Zealand*, Oxford University Press, South Melbourne, 2009, p.41.

26 E. Jerningham Wakefield, *Adventure in New Zealand* (abridged version), Whitcombe & Tombs, Christchurch, 1955, p.87.

27 Henry William Petre, *An Account of the Settlements of the New Zealand Company: From Personal Observation During a Residence There*, Smith, Elder & Co., 2nd edn, London, 1841, p.16.

28 Conversely, Campbell described Māori women as 'ugly wretches, coarse and haggard in the extreme'. Others shared his view, but certainly not all. Fellow Wellington settler J.M. Taylor thought some Māori women were 'very pretty – rather thick lips & flat noses, but well formed in other respects; fine eyes, and very soft feminine manner of address'. *New Zealand Journal*, 25 (1841), p.311; 60 (1842), p.103.

29 Ibid., 27 (1841), p.33.

30 Petre, *An Account of the Settlements*, p.16.

31 *New Zealand Journal*, 24 (1840), p.303.

32 Donald Gollan to John Grieve, Aug–Nov 1841, Gollan, Donald, 1811–1887, FMS-Papers-7990, ATL.

33 'Petre, Mary Ann Eleanor, 1825–1885, Diary', MS-1772, ATL.

34 *New Zealand Journal*, 23 (1840), p.293.

35 'From an Officer of the Surveying Staff, 16 Jan 1843', in *Letters from Settlers and Labouring Emigrants in the New Zealand Company's Settlements of Wellington, Nelson and New Plymouth: from February 1842 to January 1843*, Smith, Elder & Co., London, 1843, p.63.

36 His view is at odds with recent historical research arguing Company settlers rarely entered inter-racial marriages because 60 per cent of adults arriving in 1840s New Zealand were married, but the existence of at least some inter-racial unions in Wellington adds weight to the notion that the Company's racial amalgamation policy was not all words. Angela Wanhalla, *Matters of the Heart: A History of Interracial Marriage in New Zealand*, Auckland University Press, Auckland, 2013, p.77.

37 Concerning Auckland, William Swainson wrote: 'the two races have continued to appreciate the advantage to be derived from the presence of each other. Useful neighbours, good-humoured, ever ready to enjoy a joke, self satisfied and contended, the presence of natives, instead of being regarded a drawback, has always given life and animation to the Northern Province.' William Swainson, *New Zealand and its Colonization*, Smith, Elder & Co., London, 1859, p.226.

38 'Webber, Edmund, 1817–1860, Transcript of Journal', MS-Papers-10957, ATL, p.36.

39 After she arrived back north, her brother told her to return to Montefiore. Ibid., pp.51–52.

40 James Belich makes the point that writers and settlers could accept contradictory racial theories. James Belich, 'European Ideas about Māori – The Dying Māori and Social Darwinism', *Te Ara*, www.teara.govt.nz/en/european-ideas-about-maori/page-4 (accessed 31 Mar 2016).

41 Edmund Webber Journal, p.52.

42 As Angela Wanhalla notes, it was not uncommon for soldiers, surveyors and government officials to have Māori 'mistresses'. Wanhalla, *Matters of the Heart*, p.84.

43 Edmund Webber Journal, p.52.

44 James Belich, *Making Peoples: A History of the New Zealanders From Polynesian Settlement to the End of the Nineteenth Century*, Allen Lane, Auckland, 1996, p.215; Hazel Petrie, 'Māori Enterprise: Ships and Flourmills', in Ian Hunter and Diana Morrow (eds), *City of Enterprise: Perspectives on Auckland Business History*, Auckland University Press, Auckland, 2006, p.43.

45 Auckland Point Market, TheProw.org.nz, www.theprow.org.nz/maori/auckland-point-market/#.U6-FgSjN_nZ (accessed 31 Mar 2016).

46 Māori produce accounted for 5–10 per cent of Wellington's exports by value between 1843 and 1847. Watson and Patterson, 'The Growth and Subordination of the Maori Economy', pp.525, 529.

47 *The Australian*, 17 May 1842, p.3.

48 *The New Zealander*, 13 Feb 1847, p.3.

49 William Swainson, *Auckland: The Capital of New Zealand and the Country Adjacent*, Smith, Elder & Son, London, 1853, pp.28, 34; J.A. Askew, *A Voyage to Australia and New Zealand*, Simpkin, Marshall & Co., London, 1857, p.346.

50 Alexander Marjoribanks, *Travels in New Zealand with a Map of the Country*, Smith, Elder & Co., London, 1846, p.65.

51 William Fox, *Report on the Settlement of Nelson in New Zealand*, Smith, Elder & Co., London, 1849, p.21.

52 George Butler Earp, *New Zealand: Its Emigration and Gold Fields*, George Routledge & Co., London, 1853, p.100.

53 Swainson, *New Zealand and its Colonization*, p.226; Petrie, 'Maori Enterprise: Ships and Flourmills', p.38.

54 Askew, *A Voyage to Australia and New Zealand*, p.334.

55 Gavin McLean, *Wellington: The First Years of European Settlement 1840–1850*, Penguin, Auckland, 2000, p.34; A.G. Bagnall, *Wairarapa: An Historical Excursion*, Hedley's Bookshop Ltd, Masterton, 1976, p.120; I. Rhodes Cooper, *The New Zealand Settler's Guide*, Edward Stanford, London, 1857, p.95.

56 That Māori built roads designed to aid the alienation of their lands is bitterly ironic.

57 *Wellington Independent*, 25 Sep 1847, p.2.

58 Ibid., p.3.

59 Ibid., 29 Sept 1847, p.3. The spokesman took the pseudonym RASP.

60 *Daily Southern Cross*, 30 Sept 1848, p.2.

61 Edwin G. Burrows and Mike Wallace, *Gotham: A History of New York City to 1898*, Oxford University Press, New York, 1999, p.744.

62 Hazel Petrie, *Chiefs of Industry: Māori Tribal Enterprise in Early Colonial New Zealand*, Auckland University Press, Auckland, 2006, pp.238–39.

63 In 1856, the Māori population stood at 56,000 and the settler population at 59,000. Ian Pool, 'Population change – Key population trends', *Te Ara*, www.teara.govt.nz/en/graph/28720/new-zealand-population-by-ethnicity-1840-2006 (accessed 1 Apr 2016).

64 The introduction of modern steam ships to coastal trade furthered this aim because such vessels were beyond the reach of Māori and other smaller traders. Petrie, 'Māori Enterprise: Ships and Flourmills', p.45, and *Chiefs of Industry*, pp.256–60; Belich, *Making Peoples*, p.250.

65 The Wairau confrontation is discussed in note 140 of Chapter One.

66 The redoubts and stockades were Fort Arthur in Nelson, and Thorndon and Clay Point (Te Aro) in Wellington. A. Walton, *New Zealand Redoubts, Stockades and Blockhouses, 1840–1848*, Department of Conservation, Wellington, 2003, p.6.

67 'Extract from Sarah Greenwood', 4 Oct 1843, Greenwood, 1842–1870, Letters, NPM2004.161, Archives Collection, Nelson Provincial Museum, p.31.

68 Mary Petre Diary, 20 Jun 1843.

69 Ibid., 2 Jul 1843.

70 McLean, *Wellington*, pp.75–79.

71 Built on a prominent headland above the town, it comprised stone barracks with loopholes and blockhouses. Walton, *New Zealand Redoubts*, p.10.

72 Various sources show reassurances from local Māori regarding invasion fears. For example when Ngāpuhi came south to urge Te Wherowhero of Waikato-Tainui to join them in an attack on Auckland, he told them, 'you must fight me if come on to Auckland; for these Europeans are under my protection' (C.O. Davis, *The Life and Times of Patuone, The Celebrated Ngapuhi Chief*, J.H. Field, Auckland, 1876, p.88). Another source had Te Wherowhero warning Hone Heke, 'kia tupato ki te remu o taku kakahu (beware the hem of my cloak)' (cited in Waitangi Tribunal, *Report of the Waitangi Tribunal on the Manukau Claim*, Waitangi Tribunal, Wellington, 1985, sec. 3.5). The point was made even clearer when Governor FitzRoy had a house built for Te Wherowhero within the Auckland Domain, in which he lived intermittently until returning to the Waikato in 1858 (*Nelson Examiner* and *New Zealand Chronicle*, 9 August 1845; 'Tree Memorial', *New Zealand Herald*, 8 August 1940). I am grateful to Bruce Stirling for his assistance with this note.

73 'Albert Barracks Wall', Heritage New Zealand List, www.heritage.org.nz/the-list/details/12 (accessed 12 Jul 2014).

74 Rahui Papa and Paul Meredith, 'Kīngitanga – the Māori King Movement', *Te Ara*, www.teara.govt.nz/en/kingitanga-the-maori-king-movement (accessed 1 Apr 2016).

75 Danny Keenan, 'New Zealand Wars – North Taranaki War, 1860–1861', *Te Ara*, www.teara.govt.nz/en/new-zealand-wars/page-4 (accessed 5 May 2016); 'Taranaki and Waikato Wars', Ministry for Culture and Heritage, www.nzhistory.net.nz/war/the-new-zealand-wars (accessed 5 May 2016).

76 'Invasion Plans', Ministry for Culture and Heritage, www.nzhistory.net.nz/war/war-in-waikato/invasion-plans (accessed 1 Apr 2016).

77 The press had printed the Māori newspaper *Te Pihoihoi* under the editorship of the resident magistrate John Gorst. The paper's trenchant criticism of the Kīngitanga led Rewi Maniapoto and Aporo to remove both Gorst and his press. *Daily Southern Cross*, 6 Apr 1863, p.3; *Otago Daily Times* (*ODT*), 7 Jul 1863, p.5; Steven Oliver, 'Te Tuhi, Wiremu Patara', *Te Ara*, www.teara.govt.nz/en/biographies/1t78/te-tuhi-wiremu-patara (accessed 1 Apr 2016).

78 'Fred to Papa', 21 June 1863, Haslam Family, MS-Papers-3895-4, ATL. James Belich explains the colonial forces fell into three categories: 1) A regular force comprising the Colonial Defence Force and Forest Rangers; 2) the Waikato Militia or 'Military Settlers', recruited largely from the Otago and Australian goldfields; and 3) the Auckland Militia and Volunteers. Fred Haslam was in the third group. James Belich, *The New Zealand Wars and the Victorian Interpretation of Racial Conflict*, Penguin, Auckland, 1986, p.126.

79 'Fred to Emily', 8 Jul 1863, Haslam Family.

80 Ibid.

81 Belich, *The New Zealand Wars*, p.133.

82 *New Zealander*, 10 July 1863; John Gorst, *The Maori King*, 1864, p.376; *Daily Southern Cross*, 18 August 1863; *ODT*, 18 September 1863.

83 *Wellington Independent*, 21 July 1863, p.3; *Daily Southern Cross*, 11 Jul 1863, p.3; *ODT*, 27 Jul 1863, p.3.

84 'Fred to Emily', 8 Jul 1863, Haslam Family.

85 Ibid.

86 'Fred to his parents', 5 Nov 1863, Haslam Family. Five hundred imperial troops arrived from Australia in October 1863 to fight in the Waikato campaign. Belich, *The New Zealand Wars*, p.139.

87 Ibid.

88 The date of his return is given in the biographical information for the Haslam manuscript, ATL.

89 According to historian Ian Hunter, Māori entrepreneurship went into abeyance following the conflict, re-emerging only in the late 20th century. Ian Hunter, *Age of Enterprise: Rediscovering the New Zealand Entrepreneur, 1880–1910*, Auckland University Press, Auckland, 2007, p.32.

90 The section of wall runs through Auckland University grounds by the main library

building. 'Albert Barracks Wall', Heritage New Zealand, www.heritage.org.nz/the-list/details/12 (accessed 12 Jul 2014).

91 Jeffrey C. Alexander, *The Dark Side of Modernity*, Polity Press, Cambridge, 2013, pp.125–26.

92 Editor of the Australian and New Zealand Gazette, *Hand-book to the Province of Wellington, New Zealand*, Algar & Street, London, 1858, p.5.

93 Ferdinand von Hochstetter, *New Zealand: Its Physical Geography, Geology and Natural History with Special Reference to Results of Government Expeditions in the Provinces of Auckland and Nelson*, J.G. Cotta, Stuttgart, 1867, p.220.

94 David Hamer, *New Towns in the New World: Images and Perceptions of the Nineteenth-Century Urban Frontier*, Columbia University Press, New York, 1990, p.217.

95 *The Australian*, 27 Dec 1838, cited in Edmonds, *Urbanizing Frontiers*, p.122.

96 Hamer, *New Towns*, pp.219–20.

97 Alexander, *The Dark Side of Modernity*, pp.78–79.

98 Edmonds, *Urbanizing Frontiers*, p.17.

99 Hamer, *New Towns*, pp.221–23.

100 Edmonds, *Urbanizing Frontiers*, p.36.

101 James Hingston, *The Australian Abroad: On Branches from the Main Routes Around the World*, William Inglis & Co., Melbourne, 1886, p.203.

102 Arthur Clayden, *The England of the Pacific: Or New Zealand as an English Middle-Class Emigration-Field: A Lecture*, Wyman & Sons, London, 1879, p.32.

103 The 'fatal impact' proposition that Māori were doomed to extinction in the face of European civilisation had gained currency from the 1850s as Māori succumbed to European diseases and experienced lower life expectancy and fertility rates. Ian Pool and Tahu Kukutai, 'Taupori Māori – Māori population change – Decades of despair, 1840–1900', *Te Ara*, www.teara.govt.nz/en/taupori-maori-maori-population-change/page-2 (accessed 6 Apr 2016).

104 *Daily Southern Cross*, 19 Feb 1866, p.3; 15 Jan 1870, p.5. The Pākehā market was located in the Old Supreme Court Building on Queen Street (long demolished).

105 *Daily Southern Cross*, 26 Nov 1869, p.3.

106 *Hawke's Bay Herald*, 25 Mar 1870, p.3.

107 Ibid.; *Daily Southern Cross*, 21 Mar 1868, p.3; *West Coast Times*, 26 May 1869, p.3.

108 A half-caste Māori was one with a Pākehā and a Māori parent. Within colonial society they carried higher social status than full-blooded Māori. The writer implies the half-caste women bought their modern clothing and accessories with earnings from prostitution. *Hawke's Bay Herald*, 25 Mar 1870, p.3.

109 Ibid.

110 *ODT*, 13 Apr 1871, p.3.

111 *Otago Witness*, 5 Aug 1871, p.6; *Hawke's Bay Herald*, 25 Mar 1870, p.3.

112 *Daily Southern Cross*, 9 Jun 1871, p.3; 12 July 1871, p.5; *ODT*, 13 Apr 1871, p.3.

113 *Auckland Star*, 15 Jul 1871, p.2.

114 Ibid., 19 Aug 1871, p.2.

115 Merchants and shopkeepers dominated the city council. Graham Bush, *Decently and in Order: The Centennial History of the Auckland City Council*, Collins, Auckland, 1971, p.99.

116 *Tuapeka Times*, 13 Aug 1884, p.5.

117 *Auckland Star*, 1 Dec 1898, p.9.

118 Stevan Eldred-Grigg with Zen Dazheng, *White Ghost, Yellow Peril: China and New Zealand, 1790–1950*, Otago University Press, Dunedin, 2014, p.104.

119 Waitangi Tribunal, *Te Whanganui a Tara Me Ona Takiwa: Report on the Wellington District*, Waitangi Tribunal, Wellington, 2003, p.339.

120 H. Tracy Kemp, 'Notes, Taken Under the Direction of Government, Embracing Statistical Returns in connection with the Native Population … Report No.1, Port Nicolson District, 1 January 1850', *Government Gazette*, 21 Aug 1850, republished in *Wellington Independent*, 31 Aug 1850, p.5.

121 *Wellington Independent*, 12 Sept 1865, p.7.

122 The perceived insanitary nature of the pā had been a cause for periodic settler complaint

for decades. In 1848, a settler described them as 'filthy kennels'. In 1871, a newspaper said Te Aro pā needed a visit from the Inspector of Nuisances on sanitary grounds. Conditions might not have been ideal in the pā but, as we will see in Chapter Seven, nor were they elsewhere in the city. *Wellington Independent*, 6 Dec 1848, p.3; *Evening Post*, 19 Aug 1871, p.2.

123 Waitangi Tribunal, *Te Whanganui a Tara*, pp.341–42.

124 *Evening Post*, 19 Aug 1871, p.2.

125 *Wellington Independent*, 11 Jul 1873, p.2.

126 The 1891 Thomas Ward (fire) maps show large pockets of vacant or unimproved land in Te Aro Flat within the built-up areas. Local or absentee Pākehā investors held these properties but, in contrast to Pipitea and Te Aro pā landowners, they were neither viewed as anti-modern nor pressured to sell up. 'Historic Thomas Ward Maps', Wellington City Council, http://wellington.govt.nz/your-council/archives/whats-in-the-archives/historic-thomas-ward-maps (accessed 30 Jul 2014).

127 New Zealand Government, 'Census of the Maori Population, 1881, G-03', *Appendices to the Journals of House of Representatives (AJHR)*, 1881, p.26.

128 Waitangi Tribunal, *Te Whanganui a Tara*, p.342; Atholl Anderson, Judith Binney, Aroha Harris, *Tangata Whenua: An Illustrated History*, Bridget Williams Books, Wellington, 2014, pp.218–19.

129 Edmonds, *Urbanizing Frontiers*, p.197.

130 Ibid., pp.196–201.

131 There were exceptions to this contention, particularly during the New Zealand wars.

132 Such was the universality of the practice that its rationale appears not to have been questioned. None of the scores of primary documents about Native hostelries examined explicitly reveals why Māori could not be accommodated in existing hotels and boarding houses.

133 Angela Wanhalla, *In/visible Sight: The Mixed Descent Families of Southern New Zealand*, Bridget Williams Books, Wellington, 2008,

p.88. As late as 1938, a survey of Hamilton hoteliers and boarding-house keepers found 26 out of 27 of them refused to accommodate Māori. *Auckland Star*, 23 Sept 1935, p.8.

134 Paul Groth, *Living Downtown: The History of Residential Hotels in the United States*, University of California Press, Berkeley, 1994, pp.22–23.

135 There is some evidence that by the early 20th century restrictions on Māori staying in boarding houses and hotels were easing, but prejudice still existed. See, for example, *New Zealand Herald*, 29 Jul 1916, p.1.

136 Edwin Hodder, *Memories of New Zealand Life*, 2nd edn, Jackson, Walford & Hodder, London, 1863, p.31.

137 The hostelry was replaced in 1899 and a new one built, for which visiting Māori could obtain a key. Hilary and John Mitchell, 'Auckland Point Market', theProw.org.nz, www.theprow.org.nz/auckland-point-market/#.Ua_P6-CCjnY (accessed 15 Nov 2015); *Nelson Evening Mail*, 19 Jun 1899, p.3; A.F.G., 'Historic Maori Hostelry Pulled Down', *Journal of the Auckland Historical Society*, 9 (1966), p.12.

138 *New Zealander*, 27 Feb 1850, p.2. This abject state of affairs later featured in William Satchell's novel *The Greenstone Door*. In his trip to Auckland, the protagonist Trevarthen recalls seeing Māori 'men and women lying wrapped in blankets, asleep in the doorways and at corners of streets, the winter rain falling on them. Yet they must have known that no white had ever so lain within reach of the shelter of Maori whare.' William Satchell, *The Greenstone Door*, Auckland, Whitcombe & Tombs, 1914, p.156.

139 *New Zealander*, 27 Feb 1850, p.2.

140 *Daily Southern Cross*, 9 Sept 1848, p.3.

141 The site was near the intersection of Parnell Rise and Stanley Street. 'Endowment for Native Hostelry, Auckland', Colonial Secretary's Office, Auckland, 12 May 1851, *New Zealand Gazette*, NZETC.

142 *The New Zealander*, 27 Feb 1850, p.2.

143 Ibid.

144 *Daily Southern Cross*, 9 March 1852, p.2.

145 *Auckland Star*, 29 Sept 1944, p.3.

146 Petrie, 'Māori Enterprise', p.35.

147 Askew, *A Voyage to Australia and New Zealand*, p.339.

148 Ibid., pp.353–54.

149 Nugent to Colonial Secretary, 18 Aug 1852, Maori Affairs Department, series 4, Outward Letterbooks, 1840–1916, Micro R6541, ANZ.

150 The land was set aside by the New Zealand Company as Tenths reserve, but was taken for public reserve by McCleverty agreements in 1847.

151 *Evening Post*, 28 Jul 1928, p.17.

152 *New Zealand Parliamentary Debates*, 25 July 1856, p.306.

153 A well-known boarder in the hostel was Ngatau Omahuru, the son of Hinewai and Te Karere of Ngā Ruahine in Taranaki, who was kidnapped by colonial forces in 1868 at age six. He lived at the hostel before being adopted by its harshest critic, William Fox. Ngatau later returned to his Taranaki family. Basil Keane, 'Whāngai – customary fostering and adoption – the custom of whāngai', *Te Ara*, www.teara. govt.nz/en/whangai-customary-fostering-and-adoption/page-1 (accessed 2 Apr 2016).

154 'Potiki, et al. to Superintendent – Petition from Natives of Otago for Erection of Hostelry for their Accommodation in Dunedin', 6 Nov 1854, AAAC 707 D500 126/B No137, ANZ.

155 *Otago Colonist*, 1857 (no date other than year), cited in Marie Goodall and George Griffiths, *Maori Dunedin*, Otago Heritage Books, Dunedin, 1980, p.24.

156 'C. W. Richmond, Colonial Treasurer to Superintendent – As to Erecting a Hostelry for Natives at Dunedin', 22 Nov 1858, AAAC 706 D500 124/B No58, ANZ; Waitangi Tribunal, 'Princes Street Reserve', *The Ngai Tahu Report*, Waitangi Tribunal, Wellington, 1991, sections 7.3.1–7.3.7; *ODT*, 15 Nov 1882, p.2.

157 'Certificate by Mr Thomson that Maori Hostelry Completed', Archives 2/2/2/7/B, and 'Specification of Work to be Executed in Building Maori Hostelry Dunedin', 8 Dec 1858, Archives 2/2/2/2/A, Toitū Otago Settlers Museum.

158 Goodall and Griffiths, *Maori Dunedin*, p.26; Waitangi Tribunal, *The Ngai Tahu Report*, 7.3.7.

159 William A. Taylor, *Lore and History of the South Island Maori*, Bascands, Christchurch, 1952, p.51. The petition is held in Archives New Zealand's Christchurch office, which was closed due to the Canterbury earthquakes during the research of this book. New Plymouth, Whanganui, Tauranga, Napier and Bluff also built Māori hostelries.

160 The Native hostelry was built at Dampier Bay in Lyttelton. *Press*, 13 Mar 1865, p.2; 27 Apr 1878, p.3.

161 In 1908, the Waitōtara chief Wiremu Kaiuki complained that having arrived in Wellington for a Native Land Court sitting, he was offered a hotel room (due to his high social status) but his party had to sleep in Lambton railway station. Considering the great number of Māori who came to Wellington on government-related business – visitors who spent up large in the city – Kaiuki said it was high time the state provided somewhere for them to stay. *Wanganui Herald*, 17 Mar 1908, p.4.

162 *Evening Post*, 12 Sept 1935.

163 The body of Hone Heke was en route to his birthplace at Kaikohe and the Auckland tangi provided an opportunity for local Māori to pay their respects. *Star*, 16 Feb 1909, p.2.

164 *New Zealand Herald*, 29 Jul 1916, p.1. Te Kooti Arikirangi Te Turuki also stayed at the hostel in 1889, recuperating from a bout of bronchitis. *Auckland Star*, 24 Sep 1889, p.1.

165 *Observer*, 12 Sept 1903, p.7; *New Zealand Herald*, 10 Sept 1938, p.10.

166 *Auckland Star*, 29 Sept 1944, p.3.

167 The route wasn't needed and in 2016 the site was a carpark. A.F.G., 'Historic Maori Hostelry Pulled Down', *Journal of the Auckland Historical Society*, 9 (1966), p.12.

168 John Rennie Short, *Urban Theory: A Critical Assessment*, Palgrave McMillan, Houndsmill, 2006, p.3.

169 The 1878 city figure could arguably be augmented by 12 prisoners in Mt Eden gaol, four hospital patients, 6 lunatic asylum patients and 60 boarding students at St

Stephen's School (Parnell) and Three Kings School. F.D. Fenton, *Observations on the State of the Aboriginal Inhabitants of New Zealand*, W.C. Wilson, Auckland 1859, pp.iv–vii; New Zealand Government, 'Census of the Maori Population, 1878, G-2', *AJHR*, 1878, pp.14, 25–26.

170 S.E. Grimstone, *The Southern Settlements of New Zealand*, R. Stokes, Wellington, 1847, p.44.

171 The environs comprised Hutt Valley, Upper Hutt and Porirua.

172 In Christchurch the environs comprised Kaiapoi, Rāpaki and Koukourarata (Port Levy); in Dunedin they comprised Waikouaiti and Ōtākou (Otago Heads).

173 The Fenton census did not include a spatial breakdown of Canterbury's Māori population, but this was later included in Appendix H of the 1861 Census and its figures are used here.

174 The total Māori population in 1858 was 56,049 and in 1878 it was 42,819.

175 An 1898 newspaper included the following section on contemporary Māori social conditions: 'In their own settlements the social life of the Maori people is to a considerable extent unchanged by the encroachments of civilisation … The primitive "whare" roofed with raupo, nikau or toetoe, and floor covered with native mats ("takapau" or "whariki") is still the usual dwelling place of the people.' *Auckland Star*, 1 Dec 1898, p.9; Ben Schrader, 'Māori housing – te noho whare – Wharepuni to European house', *Te Ara*, www.teara.govt. nz/en/maori-housing-te-noho-whare/page-1 (accessed 2 Apr 2016).

176 For instance, with the founding of Auckland, Māori from outside the district gained rights from local iwi to settle and cultivate land to produce food for the Auckland market. Petrie, 'Maori Enterprise', p.35.

177 Ngata, Apirana Turupa (Sir), 1874–1950: Where Do the Maoris Come In?, 27 Aug 1928, MS-Papers-8068, ATL.

178 William Swainson, *New Zealand and its Colonization*, Smith, Elder & Co., London 1859, p.225.

179 'William to Harry', 14 Aug 1880, Derry Family Letters, MS-Papers-1043, ATL.

180 *Daily Southern Cross*, 20 Aug 1868, p.3.

181 Hingston, *The Australian Abroad*, p.204.

182 Similarly, in 1913, the *New Zealand Herald* reported the corner of Queen and Customs streets (then the foot of Queens Wharf) was a common gathering place for Māori visiting the city. It suggested a hall be built for them to socialise in. Patrick Joseph Hogan, 'No 4, Auckland, 1852, New Zealand', Ref C-010-020, ATL; J. Blades, 'A Retrospective Review of Auckland from 1859–1863', qMS-0240, ATL; *New Zealand Herald*, 12 May 1913, p.4.

183 Edmonds, *Urbanizing Frontiers*, p.47.

184 A good New Zealand example of this motif is Edward Ashworth's 1843 painting of Auckland, in which three Māori are placed outside the growing town. 'Ashworth, Edward, Auckland Looking North West, 1843?', A-275-007, ATL.

185 In the early 1880s, the travel writer James Partington recorded that it was 'a curious sight' in towns to see Māori 'loafing about in all directions, dressed in the most outrageous costume, especially the women, who sit outside shops smoking and chattering'. James E. Partington, *Random Rot: A Journal of Three Years Wandering About the World*, Guardian Office, Altrimcham, 1883, p.352.

186 *Observer*, 1 Apr 1911, p.3.

187 G.L. Meredith, *Adventuring in Maoriland in the Seventies*, Angus & Robertson, Sydney, 1935, p.18.

188 David Kennedy, *Kennedy's Colonial Travel: A Narrative of a Four Year's Tour Through Australia, New Zealand, Canada, &c*, Simpkin, Marshall & Co., London, 1876, p.211.

189 Ibid., p.231.

190 Interestingly, American historian Dell Upton has shown how American Indians visiting 19th-century New Orleans 'adopted a carefully composed, conspicuous self-presentation', which included wearing an ensemble of indigenous and European dress. Dell Upton, *Another City: Urban Life and Urban Spaces in the New American Republic*, Yale University Press, New Haven, 2008, pp.100–1.

191 In 1884, a Dunedin visitor to Auckland reported that '[s]pecimens of the noble savage,

got up in a variety of ways, may be seen about the streets of the city. Some rangatiras [chiefs], with bell-hoppers and gold ornaments, strut about with an air of superlative importance.' *Tuapeka Times*, 13 Aug 1884, p.5.

192 Kennedy, *Kennedy's Colonial Travel*, p.232.

193 Ibid.

194 James Winter, *London's Teeming Streets 1830–1910*, Routledge, London, 1993, p.178.

195 Lydia Wevers, *Country of Writing: Travel Writing and New Zealand, 1809–1900*, Auckland University Press, Auckland, 2002, pp.174–86; Margaret McClure, *The Wonder Country: Making New Zealand Tourism*, Auckland University Press, Auckland, 2004, pp.15, 57.

196 *Auckland Star*, 1 Dec 1898, p.9.

197 Ibid., 9 Jan 1895, p.5.

198 Ibid., 10 Jan 1898, p.5.

199 Ibid., 11 Jan 1895, p.3.

200 *ODT*, 17 Oct 1885, p.3; *Star*, 26 Sept 1885, p.2.

201 Ashley Gould, 'Maori and the Boer War', in Ian McGibbon (ed.), *The Oxford Companion to New Zealand Military History*, Oxford University Press, Auckland, 2000, p.296.

202 Tare was from Waikouaiti. His father, Tame Haereroa Parata, was MHR for Southern Maori, a seat Tare won in 1911. Te Rongokahira was from Tauranga. Angela Ballara, 'Parata, Katherine Te Rongokahira – Biography', *Te Ara*, www.teara.govt.nz/en/biographies/3p6/parata-katherine-te-rongokahira (accessed 2 Apr 2016).

203 *Evening Post*, 28 Mar 1900, p.6. Represented iwi were Ngāti Kahungunu (Hawke's Bay/Wairarapa), Rangitāne (Manawatū/Wairarapa), Ngāti Raukawa (Ōtaki) and Ngāti Toa (Porirua). Interestingly, there appears to have been no representation from Wellington-based mana whenua, Te Āti Awa.

204 Ibid., 12 Mar 1900, p.6; 24 Mar 1900, p.5.

205 Ibid., 27 Mar 1900, p.6.

206 Ibid., 29 Mar 1900, p.5.

207 Ibid., 7 April 1900, p.1.

208 *Colonist*, 30 Mar 1900, p.4.

209 *Evening Post*, 29 Mar 1900, p.5.

210 Ibid., 30 Aug 1900, p.6.

211 Ballantyne, *Webs of Empire*, pp.27–36.

212 *Otago Witness*, 26 Apr 1900, p.35.

213 Parata subsequently helped to organise a Māori carnival at Lancaster Park in December 1900 for Christchurch's jubilee celebrations. Māori carnivals were also staged in Dunedin in June 1902 and Invercargill in April 1903. *Star*, 6 Nov 1900, p.1; *Otago Witness*, 2 Jul 1902, p.65; *Southland Times*, 14 Apr 1903, p.2.

214 *Evening Post*, 8 Sept 1915, p.3.

215 Ibid., 16 Sept 1915, p.3.

216 Ibid., 11 Sept 1915, p.2.

217 *Truth*, 18 Sept 1915, p.2.

218 *Evening Post*, 17 Sept 1915, p.8.

219 'Table 4: Maoris and Maori Europeans – Counties, Boroughs, and Town Districts, 1936 and 1926', Māori Census, *New Zealand Census*, Government Printer, Wellington, 1936, pp.3–9.

220 Ian Pool, Arunachalam Dharmalingam and Janet Sceats, *The New Zealand Family from 1840: A Demographic History*, Auckland University Press, Auckland, 2007, p.203; James Belich, *Paradise Reforged: A History of the New Zealanders: From the 1880s to the Year 2000*, Allen Lane, Auckland, 2001, pp.472–73; Philippa Mein Smith, *A Concise History of New Zealand*, Cambridge University Press, Melbourne, 2005, p.186.

Chapter Five

1   Notable exceptions are Jacques Carabain's topographical view of Auckland's Queen Street in 1886, and the Impressionist painter Girolami Nerli's *Dunedin Street Scene* of 1893. See Peter Shaw, *Rainbow Over Mount Eden: Images of Auckland*, Godwit, Auckland, 2002, p.52; Hamish Keith, *The Big Picture: A History of New Zealand Art From 1642*, Godwit, Auckland, 2007, p.99.

2   Peter Andersson, *Streetlife in Late Victorian London: The Constable and the Crowd*, Palgrave Macmillan, Houndsmill, 2013, p.3.

3   A 2005 collection of essays on the 1913 Great Strike exemplifies this lack. Some of the writers mention street protests and conflicts but not how streets framed the protests. See

Melanie Nolan (ed.), *Revolution: The 1913 Great Strike in New Zealand*, Canterbury University Press, Christchurch, 2005.

4   Robin Law, 'On the Streets of Southern Dunedin: Gender in Transport', in Barbara Brookes, Annabel Cooper and Robin Law (eds), *Sites of Gender: Women, Men and Modernity in Southern Dunedin, 1890–1939*, Auckland University Press, Auckland, 2003, pp.265, 277, 280; Alison Clarke, 'Feasts and Fasts: Holidays, Religion and Ethnicity in Nineteenth-Century Otago', PhD thesis, University of Otago, 2003, pp.253–87.

5   *Daily Southern Cross*, 30 Oct 1869, p.7.

6   *Otago Witness*, 22 Apr 1871, p.6.

7   *Wanganui Chronicle*, 24 Jan 1885, p.2.

8   Ibid., 8 Sept 1885, p.2.

9   Deborah L. Parsons, *Streetwalking the Metropolis: Women, the City, and Modernity*, Oxford University Press, Oxford, 2003, p.45.

10 Lynda Nead, *Victorian Babylon: People, Streets and Images in Nineteenth Century London*, Yale University Press, New Haven, 2000 (2011 edn), p.67.

11 Andersson, *Streetlife in Late Victorian London*, p.218.

12 Lisa Keller, *Triumph of Order: Democracy and Public Space in New York and London*, Columbia University Press, New York, 2009, p.44.

13 Stephen Reicher and Clifford Stott, 'Becoming the Subjects of History: An Outline of the Psychology of Crowds', in Matthias Reiss (ed.), *The Street as Stage: Protest Marches and Public Rallies since the Nineteenth Century*, Oxford University Press, Oxford, 2007, pp.26–29.

14 Ibid., p.35.

15 Ibid., pp.35–36.

16 The concept of 'imagined community' arises when many categories or groups (gender, class, nation) have to be imagined because they are too large for members to know all other members personally. It was forged by Benedict Anderson to explain the development of the nation state. He examined how European print languages laid the basis for national consciousness and set the stage for the imagined community of the nation state. See Benedict Anderson, *Imagined Communities*, Verso, London, 1991, pp.36–46.

17 Reicher and Stott, 'Becoming the Subjects of History', p.38.

18 Jessica Ellen Sewell, *Women and the Everyday City: Public Space in San Francisco, 1890–1915*, University of Minnesota Press, Minneapolis, 2011, p.4; Dean Wilson's examination of a 19th-century working-class community in central Auckland emphasised the street as a social space for women but revealed little about particular street practices or behaviours. Dean Wilson, 'Community and Gender in Victorian Auckland', in Judith Binney (ed.), *The Shaping of History: Essays from the New Zealand Journal of History*, Bridget Williams Books, Wellington, 2001, pp.218–19.

19 Sarah Deutsch, *Women and the City: Gender, Space and Power in Boston, 1870–1940*, Oxford University Press, Oxford, 2000, p.12.

20 Sewell, *Women and the Everyday City*, p.xxiii.

21 Nead, *Victorian Babylon*, pp.63–66; Jill Julius Matthews, *Dance Hall and Picture Palace: Sydney's Romance with Modernity*, Currency Press, Sydney, 2005, p.28.

22 Sewell, *Women and the Everyday City*, pp.3–4.

23 Ibid., p.5.

24 Nead, *Victorian Babylon*, pp.72–73; Sewell, *Women and the Everyday City*, p.6; Deutsch, *Women and the City*, p.4.

25 Andrew Brown-May, *Melbourne Street Life*, Australian Scholarly Publishing, Melbourne 1998, p.59; Parsons, *Streetwalking the Metropolis*, p.45.

26 Andersson, *Streetlife in Late Victorian London*, p.8.

27 Ibid., pp.7–9.

28 Nead, *Victorian Babylon*, p.66.

29 Lynda Nead has described the 'cut' as 'the respectable lady's heavy artillery in her social weaponry'. It ranged from a stiff bow without a smile to letting a man see his approach was noticed and then turning away. A gentleman was never allowed to cut a lady. Emily observed this happening: a man seeing an older woman approach turned his back at

the last moment. The woman turned red and her eyes swelled, leading Emily to imagine running a 'darning needle into his great broad contemptible back'. Nead, *Victorian Babylon*, p.73; *Otago Witness*, 13 Sept 1873, p.8.

30 Ibid.

31 Ibid., 20 Sept 1873, p.5.

32 As Peter Andersson explains, the flâneur functions in historical research 'as a symbol of the specifically urban way of life which turns the individual into a spectator rather an actor, the anonymous consumer of mass culture'. Andersson, *Streetlife in Late Victorian London*, p.4.

33 Richard Dennis argues that while middle-class women traversed city streets, it was always for a reason and with a fixed destination in mind. Female flâneurs were not as free to negotiate city space as male flâneurs were. Richard Dennis, *Cities in Modernity: Representations and Productions of Metropolitan Space, 1840–1930*, Cambridge University Press, Cambridge, 2008, p.152.

34 *New Zealand Free Lance*, 19 Dec 1908, p.4.

35 Andersson, *Streetlife in Late Victorian London*, pp.31, 146.

36 Charlotte Macdonald, *The Vote, the Pill and the Demon Drink: A History of Feminist Writing in New Zealand*, Bridget Williams Books, Wellington, 1993, p.34; Fiona McKergow, 'Clothes – Women's Clothes', *Te Ara*, www.teara.govt.nz/en/clothes/page-1 (accessed 5 Apr 2016).

37 *Press*, 16 Jan 1897, p.8. The phenomenon appears to have been unique to Wellington. I haven't found evidence of it happening in other cities.

38 Barbara Brookes notes this included the right to be educated and live independent lives unsupported by men. Barbara Brookes, *A History of New Zealand Women*, Bridget Williams Books, Wellington, 2016, p.145. Caroline Daley, *Leisure and Pleasure: Reshaping and Revealing the New Zealand Body 1900–1960*, Auckland University Press, Auckland, 2003, p.7; Judith R. Walkowitz, *City of Dreadful Delight: Narratives of Sexual Desire in Late-Victorian London*, University of

Chicago Press, Chicago, 1992, pp.72–73.

39 *Press*, 30 Mar 1901, p.6.

40 In this it resembled the modern Italian *passeggiata*, where young women of marriageable age promenade in streets after work, and flirt with and court young men. Giovanna P. Del Negro, *The Passeggiata and Popular Culture in an Italian Town: Folklore and the Performance of Modernity*, McGill-Queens University Press, Quebec, 2004, p.16.

41 *Otago Witness*, 4 Dec 1890, p.38.

42 Nead, *Victorian Babylon*, p.71. Of women promenading on Broadway, Richard Dennis has written: 'Women were certainly the objects of the male gaze, but they were also expected to do their share of looking at others of both sexes.' Dennis, *Cities in Modernity*, p.155.

43 Newspaper references to the ritual peter out in the early 1910s and disappear following the implementation of six o'clock closing. Newspaper reports in the months following the measure's introduction identified a sharp decline of people and drunkenness on city streets and the emergence of a 'stay-at-home habit' among suburbanites. *Dominion*, 1 Jan 1918, p.6; *Evening Post*, 1 Jan 1918, p.4.

44 During the 1910s, Friday night became late shopping night in many cities after trade unions argued it was unfair that shop workers had only one-day weekends; the Saturday night crowd became the Friday night crowd. Ben Schrader, 'Street Life – Street Life Declines', *Te Ara*, www.teara.govt.nz/en/street-life/page-4 (accessed 5 Apr 2016).

45 *Daily Southern Cross*, 30 Oct 1869, p.7.

46 *Otago Witness*, 14 Jun 1900, p.64.

47 *Wanganui Chronicle*, 8 Sept 1885, p.2.

48 The 'melting wells of electricity suspended in echoing mid-air' presumably refers to the overhead electricity cables that spark on the points and carry the sound of an approaching tram. *Evening Post*, 17 Nov 1906, p.10.

49 Ibid.

50 Andersson, *Streetlife in Late Victorian London*, p.214.

51 Parsons, *Streetwalking the Metropolis*, p.43.

52 Her diary does not record a time when she

ventured onto streets alone or participated in the 'doing the block' ritual.

53 The electoral system in 19th-century New Zealand comprised single- and multi-member electorates. The multi-member electorates were mainly in cities. In both instances, the candidates with the most votes won. Nigel S. Roberts, 'Electoral Systems – Turning Votes into Seats', *Te Ara*, www.teara.govt.nz/en/electoral-systems/page-1 (accessed 5 Apr 2016).

54 Herbert Spackman Diary, 28 Nov 1893, Spackman, Herbert, 1891–1900, MS-Papers-1788, ATL.

55 *Evening Post*, 29 Nov 1893, p.2.

56 Herbert Spackman Diary, 28 Nov 1893.

57 *Evening Post*, 29 Nov 1893, p.2.

58 Tom Brooking, *Richard Seddon: King of God's Own: The Life and Times of New Zealand's Longest-serving Prime Minister*, Penguin, Auckland, 2014, p.133.

59 *Evening Post*, 29 Nov 1893, p.2.

60 Ibid.

61 *Otago Daily Times (ODT)*, 29 Nov 1893, p.2. Pinkerton was also the top-polling national candidate.

62 *Evening Post*, 29 Nov 1893, p.2.

63 *Star*, 29 Nov 1893, p.1.

64 Two out of three adult women voted in the election. Brookes, *A History of New Zealand Women*, p.132; *Auckland Star*, 29 Nov 1893, p.4.

65 Ibid.

66 Ibid.

67 *Evening Post*, 29 Nov 1893, p.2.

68 The agora was a central open space in classical Greek cities where citizens convened to make democratic decisions.

69 Tony Ballantyne, *Webs of Empire: Locating New Zealand's Colonial Past*, Bridget Williams Books, Wellington, 2012, p.273.

70 George Earp was in Auckland at the time and argued that Māori tikanga justified the killing of Bull because he had offended Maketu's mana, but in killing the others he had exceeded his chiefly authority and so was delivered up to Crown authorities. Earp

provides a personal and detailed account of the events leading to the execution. George Butler Earp, *New Zealand: Its Emigration and Gold Fields*, George Routledge & Co., London, 1853, pp.50–55.

71 Steven Oliver, 'Maketu, Wiremu Kingi', *Te Ara*, www.teara.govt.nz/en/biographies/1m5/maketu-wiremu-kingi (accessed 5 Apr 2016); Richard S. Hill, *Policing the Colonial Frontier: Part 1*, Government Printer, Wellington, 1986, pp.214–16.

72 'Webber, Edmund, 1817–1860, Transcript of Journal', MS-Papers-10957, ATL, p.45.

73 Oliver, 'Maketu, Wiremu Kingi'.

74 The gaol was a few metres along from the south-west intersection of Victoria and Queen streets. *New Zealand Spectator and Wellington Gazette*, 26 Mar 1842, p.2.

75 Webber, 'Transcript of Journal', pp.46–47.

76 Earp, *New Zealand*, p.52.

77 Ibid., p.55.

78 Auckland's settler population at the end of 1841 was 1,835. G.W.A. Bush, *Decently and in Order: The Centennial History of the Auckland City Council*, Collins, Auckland, 1971, p.22.

79 Webber, 'Transcript of Journal', p.47.

80 Oliver, 'Maketu, Wiremu Kingi'.

81 Interestingly, two months before, two Aboriginals, Timme and Tunnerminnerwait, were hanged on Melbourne's Eastern Hill for their part in the killing of four whites. It was the town's first public hanging and attracted a crowd of 6,000, both settlers and Kulin people. Penelope Edmonds argues the hanging was 'an object lesson in British justice', aimed at deterring Aboriginal attacks on the town. Penelope Edmonds, *Urbanizing Frontiers: Indigenous Peoples and Settlers in 19th-Century Pacific Rim Cities*, UBC Press, Vancouver, 2010, p.152.

82 Some Pākehā agreed. In 1858, a correspondent to a newspaper described hanging as torture and suggested the colonial government should follow Māori practice and end a condemned prisoner's life with a quick blow to the head using a mere or axe. Oliver, 'Maketu, Wiremu Kingi'; *New Zealander*, 22 May 1858, p.1.

83 Sherwood Young, *Guilty on the Gallows: Famous Capital Crimes in New Zealand*, Grantham House, Wellington, 1998, p.1; 'List of Executions', Ministry for Culture and Heritage, www.nzhistory.net.nz/culture/the-death-penalty/notable-executions (accessed 7 Apr 2016).

84 *Daily Southern Cross*, 3 Jun 1848, p.3; *New Zealander*, 7 Jun 1848, p.3; Janice C. Mogford, 'Burns, Joseph', *Te Ara*, www.teara.govt.nz/en/biographies/1b51/burns-joseph (accessed 7 Apr 2016).

85 *New Zealander*, 21 Jun 1848, p.2.

86 Ibid.; *Daily Southern Cross*, 16 Jun 1848, p.2.

87 *Nelson Examiner and New Zealand Chronicle (NE&NZC)*, 28 Apr 1849, p.33.

88 *New Zealand Spectator and Cook's Strait Guardian*, 19 Jun 1850, p.2; *NE&NZC*, 7 Apr 1849, p.22.

89 *Daily Southern Cross*, 4 Dec 1855, p.3.

90 Ibid., 15 Feb 1856, p.3.

91 *New Zealander*, 9 Jul 1856, p.3.

92 *NE&NZC*, 26 Jun 1858, p.3; Execution of Criminals Act (1858), sec. 1, www.nzlii.org/nz/legis/hist_act/eoca185821a22v1858n10372 (accessed 7 Apr 2016).

93 Matthias Reiss, 'Introduction', in Reiss, *The Street as a Stage*, p.2.

94 Brown-May, *Melbourne Street Life*, p.197.

95 Ibid., pp.197, 200; Keller, *Triumph of Order*, p.46; Dennis, *Cities in Modernity*, p.166.

96 Reiss, 'Introduction', p.12.

97 Ibid., p.4.

98 Ibid., p.3.

99 Ibid., p.10.

100 Gavin McLean, *Wellington: The First Years of European Settlement 1840–1850*, Penguin, Auckland, 2000, p.43. We saw in Chapter Four how such shows of force were also used to try to intimidate Wellington-based Māori in the wake of the 1843 Wairau confrontation.

101 *Daily Southern Cross*, 12 May 1870, p.3.

102 J. Blades, fl 1859–1963, A Retrospective Review of Auckland from 1859–1863, qMS-0240, ATL.

103 'George to Lizzie', 20 May 1900, Dutton, George William, 1829–1904, MS-Papers-10976, ATL; *Evening Post*, 19 May 1900, p.6.

104 *Evening Post*, 21 May 1900, p.2.

105 The market was located on the platform to the right of the wharf entrance, but the space is clear in the photograph.

106 *Evening Post*, 16 May 1901, p.5.

107 The moniker was coined after Wellington secured the imperial Panama mail route in 1866. Redmer Yska, *Wellington: Biography of a City*, Reed, Auckland, 2006, p.35.

108 *Hawera and Normanby Star*, 18 Jun 1901, p.2.

109 *Evening Post*, 18 Jun 1901, p.5.

110 *Daily Southern Cross*, 19 Feb 1858, p.4; *Lyttelton Times*, 6 Jan 1858, p.4.

111 Clarke, 'Feasts and Fasts', p.255.

112 Ibid., pp.256, 260.

113 Ibid., p.267.

114 Ibid., p.272.

115 Ibid.

116 Ibid., p.253.

117 Ibid., pp.255, 277.

118 'Labour Day', Ministry of Culture and Heritage, www.nzhistory.net.nz/politics/labour-day (accessed 13 Apr 2016); *Evening Post*, 8 Oct 1901, p.5.

119 *Wanganui Herald*, 11 Oct 1905, p.5.

120 *Daily Southern Cross*, 9 Sept 1843, p.3. Shortland's perceived pomposity and lack of tact alienated settlers.

121 *New Zealand Spectator and Cook's Strait Guardian*, 11 Oct 1845, p.2. That Māori had carried the effigy led to claims that FitzRoy's opponents had hired them for the purpose with the aim of disparaging Māori in the eyes of the new Governor, George Grey. A newspaper correspondent denied this. Māori had been caught up in the frolic and did not know 'the meaning of the fun'. Ibid., 13 Oct 1843, p.3.

122 *Otago Witness*, 23 Feb 1861, p.4.

123 Jim McAloon, *Nelson: A Regional History*, Cape Catley, Queen Charlotte Sound, 1997, pp.28–29.

124 *Press*, 8 Aug 1877, p.3.

125 *Auckland Star*, 21 July 1886, p.3.

126 Ibid., 6 Aug 1877, p.3.

127 *ODT*, 6 Aug 1877, p.3.

128 Ibid.

129 *ODT*, 6 Aug 1877, p.3; *Auckland Star*, 6 Aug 1877, p.3.

130 Neill Atkinson, *Trainland: How Railways Made New Zealand*, Random House, Auckland, 2007, pp.36–37.

131 Dennis, *Cities in Modernity*, p.166.

132 *Star*, 27 May 1879, p.2.

133 See, for example, Erik Olssen, *Red Feds: Revolutionary Industrial Unionism and the New Zealand Federation of Labour*, Auckland University Press, Auckland, 1988; Melanie Nolan (ed.), *Revolution: The 1913 Great Strike in New Zealand*, Canterbury University Press, Christchurch, 2005; 'The 1913 Great Strike', Ministry for Culture and Heritage, www.nzhistory.net.nz/politics/1913-great-strike (accessed 7 Apr 2016).

134 Peter Franks, 'Chronology of Events', in Nolan (ed.), *Revolution*, pp.10–11; 'The 1913 Strike in Wellington', Ministry for Culture and Heritage, www.nzhistory.net.nz/politics/1913-great-strike/wellington (accessed 7 Apr 2016).

135 Erik Olssen, 'The Lessons of 1913', in Nolan (ed.), *Revolution*, p.45; Ben Schrader, 'City Images – City Versus Country, 20th Century', *Te Ara*, www.teara.govt.nz/en/city-images/page-2 (accessed 7 Apr 2016).

136 John Crawford, 'A Tale of Two Cities: Military Involvement in the 1913 Strike', in Nolan (ed.), *Revolution*, p.128.

137 Marjorie Lees, 'Two Wellington Childhoods', 1972 *Spectrum* documentary. The section runs from 23:56 to 28:26, www.radionz.co.nz/national/programmes/spectrum/library?utf8=%E2%9C%93&q=two+wellington+childhoods.

138 E.S. Heard, Waterside Workers Strike – October, November, December 1913, in 'Aid to the Civil Power', R3885678 AAYS 8648, AD11 1/2/1, Archives New Zealand, p.9.

139 Peter Franks, 'Chronology of Events', in Nolan (ed.), *Revolution*, p.12.

140 Lees, 'Two Wellington Childhoods'.

141 Ibid.

142 Ibid.

143 It is very likely Smith took the images minutes apart. A man in a boater, possibly a journalist, appears in both of them.

144 *Dominion*, 4 Nov 1913, p.6.

145 This chronology was gained from three different newspaper reports. They largely agree on the sequence of events, except on whether Cullen turned the hoses on before or after the two mounted constables tried to push the crowd back. *Dominion*, 4 Nov 1913, p.6; *Evening Post*, 4 Nov 1913, p.7; *Truth*, 8 Nov 1913, p.5.

146 Davis, 'Two Wellington Childhoods'.

147 Pat Lawlor later wrote that Commissioner Cullen asked the editor to remove suggestions that the specials had used firearms. However, both the *Evening Post* and *Truth* spoke to reliable witnesses who said the specials fired into the crowd. *Evening Post*, 4 Nov 1913, p.7; *Truth*, 8 Nov 1913, p.5; Pat Lawlor, *Confessions of a Journalist: With Observations on Some Australian and New Zealand Writers*, Whitcombe & Tombs, Wellington, 1935, pp.20–21.

148 *Evening Post*, 4 Nov 1913, p.7.

149 Heard, Waterside Workers Strike, pp.14–15.

150 *Dominion*, 4 Nov 1913, p.6. Under the Riot Act, people gathered in assemblies had to peaceably disperse immediately or face the possibility of imprisonment with hard labour for life. *Dominion*, 5 Nov 1913, p.4.

151 *Truth*, 8 Nov 1913, p.5. The allegation the specials were drunk was supported by George Farland of the Watersiders' Union, who had evidence the specials bought £40 (the equivalent of more than $6,000 in today's currency) of liquor in two hours that morning. *Dominion*, 5 Nov 1913, p.7.

152 *Truth*, 8 Nov 1913, p.5.

153 *Evening Post*, 4 Nov 1913, p.4.

154 *Dominion*, 5 Nov 1913, p.7.

155 *Truth*, 8 Nov 1913, p.6.

156 *Evening Post*, 4 Nov 1913, p.8.

157 Ibid., p.5.

158 'The 1913 Strike in Wellington', Ministry for Culture and Heritage.

159 *Evening Post*, 6 Nov 1913, p.3.

160 The 1981 tour of the apartheid-era South African Springbok rugby team largely pitted anti-tour city dwellers against pro-tour country dwellers, and led to violent confrontations between both sides and with the police in city streets. Street violence erupted during the 1932 Depression 'riots', but it was between one social group (the unemployed) and the police.

161 Docherty was on his way home from work and had nothing to do with the strike. *Evening Post*, 4 Nov 1913, p.7; *Truth*, 8 Nov 1913, p.5.

Chapter Six

1 'How Shared Spaces are Transforming Auckland's CBD', 20 Nov 2012, *3 News*, www.newshub.co.nz/Tabld/1741/AuthorID/12/ImogenCrispe/Author.aspx (accessed 18 Aug 2014).

2 'Section 3: Sharing the Streets and Spaces Differently', Christchurch Central Development Unit, https://ccdu.govt.nz/the-plan/an-accessible-city/questions-and-answers-accessible-city (accessed 30 Aug 2014).

3 Concerning late-19th-century London, Peter Andersson described the street 'as much a place of congregating and fraternising' as it was 'a place to which to move about'. Peter Andersson, *Streetlife in Late Victorian London: The Constable and the Crowd*, Palgrave Macmillan, Houndsmill, 2013, p.112.

4 Ibid., p.36.

5 Perry Duis, *Challenging Chicago: Coping with Everyday Life, 1837–1920*, University of Illinois Press, Urbana, 1998, pp.49–58; Spiro Kostof, *The City Assembled: The Elements of Urban Form Through History*, Thames & Hudson, London, 1992, pp.189, 234; James Winter, *London's Teeming Streets 1830–1910*, Routledge, London, 1993, pp.101–2.

6 Andersson, *Streetlife in Late Victorian London*, p.31; Andrew Brown-May, *Melbourne Street Life*, Australian Scholarly Publishing, Melbourne 1998, p.206.

7 Other social groups who were also 'street people' – beggars, bootblacks, flower sellers, newsboys, vagrants, buskers – are not, or only briefly, considered here for brevity's sake.

8 T.J. Arnold, 'Reminiscences of a Dunedin Boy of the 1880s', Misc-MS-0154, Hocken Library, p.6. It is feasible that 'Black Joe' was a Māori hawker. This cannot be certain, but in 1884 the artist William Barraud drew caricatures of numerous Dunedin traders. Among them was a Māori fishmonger. Barraud, William Francis. 'Dunedin tradesmen', 1884, E-310-q-010, ATL.

9 Brown-May, *Melbourne Street Life*, p.143; Peter Quennell (ed.), *Mayhew's London: Being Selections from 'London Labour and the London Poor' by Henry Mayhew*, Spring Books, London, 1969, p.30; Andersson, *Streetlife in Late Victorian London*, p.183.

10 Brown-May, *Melbourne Street Life*, p.143; Peter C. Baldwin, *Domesticating the Street: The Reform of Public Space in Hartford, 1850–1930*, Ohio State University Press, Ohio, 1999, pp.185–87; Daniel Bluestone, 'The Pushcart Evil', in David Ward and Oliver Zunz (eds), *The Landscape of Modernity: New York City 1900–1940*, John Hopkins University Press, Baltimore, 1992, p.292; Winter, *London's Teeming Streets*, pp.109–10.

11 See, for example, *New Zealand Spectator and Wellington Guardian (NZS&WG)*, 4 Jan 1845, p.3; *Daily Southern Cross*, 9 Mar 1852, p.3; *Lyttelton Times*, 29 Jan 1853, p.10.

12 Hardwicke Knight, *Princes Street By Gaslight*, John McIndoe, Dunedin, 1976, p.36.

13 *NZS&WG*, 22 Mar 1845, p.3; *Daily Southern Cross*, 28 Mar 1854, p.3.

14 *Press*, 29 Jul 1896, p.6. From 1893, some of the Australian colonies placed restrictions on Assyrian immigration and labour-market participation. Seddon's 'fear' was they would come to New Zealand instead. See *Otago Daily Times (ODT)*, 15 May 1893, p.3; *Observer*, 16 Feb 1895, p.2.

15 Tom Brooking, *Richard Seddon: King of God's Own: The Life and Times of New Zealand's Longest-serving Prime Minister*, Penguin, Auckland, 2014, pp.163–64; James Veitch and Dalia Tinawi, 'Middle Eastern Peoples – The

Lebanese', *Te Ara*, www.teara.govt.nz/en/ middle-eastern-peoples/page-1 (accessed 8 Apr 2016); *ODT*, 19 Jul 1901, p.5.

16 A 1911 *Truth* article said that in Dunedin it was common to see Syrian women and girls traversing streets with an old pram laden with bric-a-brac for sale. Men tended to trade in the countryside. *Truth*, 6 May 1911, p.5.

17 'To Mayor and Councillors from J.D. Webster', 18 Dec 1907, ACC 285,186, Box 33 Hawkers, A–Z, Auckland City Archives; *Evening Post*, 21 Dec 1907, p.3.

18 'Auckland Trades and Labour Council to Mayor and Councillors', 7 Jun 1909, ACC 285,186, Box 33 Hawkers, A–Z, Auckland City Archives.

19 'Town Clerk to Mr W. Carter', 1 Feb 1909 and 4 Mar 1909, Ibid.

20 'Auckland Fruiterers Protective Association to Auckland City Council', 1 Aug 1909, Ibid.

21 *Otago Witness*, 29 Sept 1909, p.10; 13 Oct 1909, p.29. The regulation was based on the British Police Act 1839, whereby so long as street vendors kept moving they stayed within the law. Winter, *London's Teeming Streets*, p.106.

22 *Observer*, 9 Oct 1909, p.2.

23 *Evening Post*, 12 Mar 1909, p.8; *Truth*, 3 Jan 1910, p.6.

24 *New Zealand Free Lance*, 8 Feb 1908, p.12.

25 According to historian Stevan Eldred-Grigg, hostility toward Chinese greengrocers began in the 1890s when an alliance between the Master Grocers' Association and the Trades and Labour Council (unsuccessfully) tried to get working men to boycott Chinese shops. Stevan Eldred-Grigg with Zen Dazheng, *White Ghost, Yellow Peril: China and New Zealand 1790–1950*, Otago University Press, Dunedin, 2014, p.156; Redmer Yska, *Truth: The Rise and Fall of the People's Paper*, Craig Potton Publishing, Nelson, 2010, pp.32–33.

26 *Truth*, 3 Dec 1910, p.6.

27 *Evening Post*, 21 Jul 1909, p.8.

28 Ibid., 24 May 1913, p.3; 28 May 1913, p.8.

29 'Gustave H. Solomon to Town Clerk', 28 Oct 1913; 'Traffic Inspector to Town Clerk', 29 Oct 1913, ACC 275,13-159, 2 Hindu Hawkers, Auckland City Archives.

30 'Town Clerk to Traffic Inspector', 18 Jan 1914, Ibid.

31 'Traffic Inspector to Town Clerk', 18 Jan 1914; 'Devore, Martin and Prendergast to Town Clerk', 19 Oct 1914, Ibid.

32 'Traffic Inspector to Mayor, Councillors and Town Clerk', 19 Nov 1911, Ibid.

33 A 1931 report showed Indians held all but one of the 14 stands in the central city. *Dominion*, 8 Jan 1931, p.8.

34 *Auckland Star*, 21 Dec 1920, p.5; 14 Mar 1930, p.8.

35 *Te Ara*'s New Zealand peoples theme shows that in 1900 Chinese and Greek communities existed in Auckland, Wellington and Dunedin; Indian communities existed in Auckland, Wellington and Christchurch; Italian communities existed in Wellington and Nelson; and Lebanese communities existed in Auckland and Dunedin. See www.teara.govt. nz/en/new-zealand-peoples.

36 *Evening Post*, 30 Mar 1915, p.8.

37 'Mayor's Minute: Fruit Hawking', 23 Sept 1918, Gen H/2 6210, Dunedin City Archives.

38 'Otago Retail Fruiterers Association to Town Clerk', 17 Oct 1918, Gen H/2 6195, Dunedin City Archives.

39 'E. Ormrod to Town Clerk', 28 Oct 1918, Gen H/2 5698, Dunedin City Archives.

40 *Dominion*, 28 Jan 1932, p.8.

41 Ibid., 1 Feb 1932, p.8; 6 Sept 1932, p.10. During the 1910s, white storekeepers had eroded the Chinese hold on the retail fruit and vegetable trade, especially in the central city. *Press*, 22 May 1913, p.10. While the street stands went, peripatetic hawking continued in the central city until 1939 when it too was banned for all except flower sellers. 'City Engineer to Town Clerk', 31 Jan 1939, 1/984:25/35 part 2, Wellington City Archives.

42 *Auckland Star*, 22 Jun 1934, p.14 and 13 Jul 1934, p.11. It is unclear exactly when the last street fruit stall closed in central Auckland.

43 The city's Chief Inspector had weeded out the rowdy and 'now has an orderly team which does not make the day or night hideous with raucous cries'. *Evening Post*, 24 May 1913, p.3.

44 Bluestone, 'The Pushcart Evil', p.300; Baldwin, *Domesticating the Street*, p.188.

45 Perrin Rowland, 'Markets – Open Air Markets', *Te Ara*, www.teara.govt.nz/en/markets/page-4 (accessed 8 Apr 2016).

46 The description is based on a Melbourne source because I have been unable to find a New Zealand description of a coffee stall. They are very unlikely to have differed substantially. Brown-May, *Melbourne Street Life*, p.135.

47 Quennell (ed.), *Mayhew's London*, p.129; Andrew Brown-May, *Espresso: Melbourne Coffee Stories*, Arcadia, Melbourne, 2001, p.10; Brown-May, *Melbourne Street Life*, p.138.

48 By 1864 there was one on the corner of Dunedin's Princes and Rattray streets and another at the foot of Auckland's Queens Wharf. *ODT*, 8 Aug 1863, p.3; *Daily Southern Cross*, 9 May 1864, p.3; *Evening Post*, 3 Feb 1877, p.2; *Star*, 4 Dec 1874, p.2.

49 *Truth*, 9 Oct 1909, p.7.

50 *Brewster's Millions* was the Broadway play of George Barr McCutcheon's 1902 novel. *Star*, 18 Jan 1908, p.4.

51 *Star*, 26 Feb 1878, p.3. A few years later the same council revoked the licence of another Gloucester Street coffee-stall owner on the basis of a complaint from a businessman wanting to open a coffee palace nearby. This suggested a Christchurch bias toward fixed businesses as against peripatetic ones. *Press*, 24 May 1881, p.3.

52 *Star*, 27 Feb 1878, p.3.

53 *Auckland Star*, 10 Jun 1880, p.3. In providing a counter-attraction to pubs, coffee stalls gained the support of temperance advocates. In 1877, the Nelson Anglican Synod called for more of them in city streets. *Tuapeka Times*, 28 Feb 1877, p.2.

54 For example, in 1876, the Dunedin coffee-stall operator, William Davis, was convicted of selling spirits at his stall. Three years later a Dunedin ratepayer complained to the city council of being unable to sleep due to the 'fighting and vicious Billingsgate' [swearing] coming from a coffee stall beside his house. *Otago Witness*, 20 May 1876, p.5; *West Coast Times*, 24 Jan 1879, p.2; *Hawera and Normanby Star*, 30 Oct 1906, p.8.

55 Ibid., 4 Mar 1884, p.2.

56 'Inspector of Police to Town Clerk', 10 Dec 1906, 00233:136:1906/1968, Wellington City Archives.

57 *Evening Post*, 27 Oct 1906, p.5; 23 Nov 1906, pp.2, 5.

58 Brown-May, *Melbourne Street Life*, pp.136–38.

59 For example, Joseph Healey wrote to the Wellington City Council in 1906 asking that his coffee-stall hours be extended from midnight to 3 a.m. as he could not otherwise make a living. Police opposed the extension. 'Joseph Healey to Town Clerk', 6 Dec 1906, and 'Inspector of Police to Town Clerk', 10 Dec 1906, 00233:136:1906/1968, Wellington City Archives.

60 'Inspector of Police to Town Clerk', 8 Aug 1910, C1 3250, Dunedin City Archives.

61 *ODT*, 18 Aug 1910, p.4.

62 'Inspector of Nuisances to Town Clerk', 29 Aug 1910, M/1 3260, Dunedin City Archives.

63 'Report of Constable Sweeney Relative to Breach of the Peace and Obscene Language at the Coffee Stall', 1 Oct 1910, C/6 4108, Dunedin City Archives.

64 'Inspector of Police to Town Clerk', 13 Oct 1910, C/6 4108, Dunedin City Archives.

65 'Inspector of Nuisances to Town Clerk', 7 Nov 1910, C/6 4108, Dunedin City Archives.

66 'Town Clerk to Inspector of Police', 10 Nov 1910, C/6 4108, Dunedin City Archives.

67 Joachim Schlör, *Nights in the Big City*, Reaktion Books, London, 1998, p.35.

68 Ibid., pp.21, 35, 59–58, 83, 93.

69 Ibid., p.33.

70 Ibid., p.119.

71 *Daily Southern Cross*, 30 Oct 1869, p.7.

72 *Evening Post*, 24 Sept 1889, p.3.

73 John Rigg, 30 Jul 1895, *New Zealand Parliamentary Debates* (*NZPD*), Vol. 88, p.273.

74 *Taranaki Herald*, 17 Aug 1895, p.2. The population of Christchurch in 1896 was just over 50,000.

75 *ODT*, 21 Feb 1895, p.5.

76   Elizabeth Wilson, *The Sphinx in the City: Urban Life, the Control of Disorder, and Women*, University of California Press, Berkeley, 1991, pp.38–40.

77   Schlör, *Nights in the Big City*, pp.171–72.

78   Ibid., pp.191–93; Judith R. Walkowitz, *City of Dreadful Delight: Narratives of Sexual Desire in Late-Victorian London*, University of Chicago Press, Chicago, 1992, p.23.

79   Lynda Nead, *Victorian Babylon: People, Streets and Images in Nineteenth-Century London*, Yale University Press, New Haven, 2000, pp.103–4; Schlör, *Nights in the Big City*, pp.218–22; Winter, *London's Teeming Streets*, pp.135–36.

80   In 1864 males comprised 61.9 per cent of the population (excluding Māori); by 1891 the figure was down to 53.1 per cent. 'Results of a Census of the Colony of New Zealand, 5th April, 1891', Statistics New Zealand, www3.stats.govt.nz/historic_publications//1891-census/1891-results-census/1891-results-census.html#d50e870 (accessed 9 June 2016).

81   Charlotte Macdonald, *A Woman of Good Character: Single Women as Immigrant Settlers in Nineteenth Century New Zealand*, Bridget Williams Books, Wellington, 1990, pp.173–74, 181; Charlotte Macdonald, 'The Social Evil: Prostitution and the Passage of the 1869 Contagious Diseases Act', in Barbara Brookes, Charlotte Macdonald and Margaret Tennant (eds), *Women in History: Essays on European Women in New Zealand*, Allen & Unwin, Wellington, 1986, pp.19–20.

82   Macdonald, *A Woman of Good Character*, p.180.

83   *Lyttelton Times*, 22 Nov 1867, p.2, cited in Macdonald, *A Woman of Good Character*, p.179.

84   Macdonald, *A Woman of Good Character*, pp.180–81.

85   'The Vagrant Act 1866 Amendment Act 1869', cl. 2, New Zealand Legal Information Institute, www.nzlii.org/nz/legis/hist_act/tva1866aa186932a33v1869n53364 and 'The Vagrant Act 1866', sec. 2, cl. 1 and sec. 4, cl. 5, www.nzlii.org/nz/legis/hist_act/va186630v1866n10217 (both accessed 1 Sep 2014).

86   Macdonald. *A Woman of Good Character*, p.187.

87   Stevan Eldred-Grigg, *Pleasures of the Flesh: Sex and Drugs in Colonial New Zealand 1840–1915*, A.H. & A.W. Reed, Wellington, 1984, pp.35–36.

88   *Evening Post*, 26 Apr 1881, p.2. I was unable to ascertain the sentence of the women.

89   Eldred-Grigg, *Pleasures of the Flesh*, pp.155–57.

90   *Evening Post*, 25 Mar 1899, p.5. Howe was also charged with being an idle and disorderly person and jailed for twelve months.

91   Leif Jerram, *Streetlife: The Untold Story of Europe's Twentieth Century*, Oxford University Press, Oxford, 2011, p.181.

92   The 1869 Select Committee on Social Evil included a survey of the number of prostitutes in Dunedin and Christchurch brothels, but as Charlotte Macdonald notes, prostitution is a 'very sparsely documented area of nineteenth-century life'. Macdonald, *A Woman of Good Character*, p.186.

93   According to Stevan Eldred-Grigg, the female vagrancy rate fell from 33.4 per 10,000 women in the early 1870s to 4.9 in the early 1910s. See Eldred-Grigg, *Pleasures of the Flesh*, p.276.

94   Birch had been the pastor of Auckland's Baptist Tabernacle, but in 1890 fell out with his congregation and set up a new Union church. He was a staunch social gospel advocate, believing the church should engage in political and social issues. He left for Christchurch in 1892 and set up the Central Mission church, which in 1894 opened the Avon Refuge for homeless unemployed men. The church developed a strong ministry with the city's 'down and out'. *Auckland Star*, 28 Apr 1891, p.5; *Star*, 1 Mar 1892, p.3; *New Zealand Herald*, 12 May 1894, p.5.

95   *Taranaki Herald*, 17 Aug 1895, p.2.

96   Eldred-Grigg, *Pleasures of the Flesh*, pp.43, 48.

97   A correspondent to the *Press* provides some support for this conclusion. 'Old Colonist' condemned Isitt's figures and supported Birch's before stating: 'It is about time that the public of Christchurch … should take exception to the maligning and foul traducing of this city by a few rabid advocates for prohibition.' *Press*, 2 Aug 1895, p.9.

98   Homosexual sex was illegal in New Zealand

until 1986, which may be why male clients rather than the boy prostitutes were prosecuted. Chris Brickell, *Mates and Lovers: A History of Gay New Zealand*, Godwit, Auckland, 2008, pp.123–24.

99 Sandra Coney, *Standing in the Sunshine: A History of New Zealand Women Since They Won the Vote*, Viking, Auckland, 1993, p.127.

100 *Otago Witness*, 25 Jun 1896, p.12.

101 It was set up to inquire into the organisation and management, remuneration and general conduct of the force. New Zealand Government, 'Report and Evidence of the Royal Commission on the Police Force of New Zealand', *Appendices to the Journals of the House of Representatives (AJHR)*, 1898, H-02, p.iii.

102 Richard S. Hill, *The Iron Hand in the Velvet Glove: The Modernisation of Policing in New Zealand, 1886–1917*, Dunmore Press, Palmerston North, 1995, pp.96–97.

103 New Zealand Government, 'Report and Evidence', p.1053.

104 Ibid., pp.1062–63. His stand was outside Milne & Choyce's department store, corner of Queen and Victoria streets. Questioned over girls' ages, he said he had asked their ages and this was their reply.

105 Ibid., p.1064.

106 Ibid., pp.1066–67.

107 Ibid., pp.1068–70.

108 Ibid., p.1069.

109 Ibid., p.1070.

110 Ibid., pp.1071–72.

111 See, for example, *Auckland Star*, 16 Jun 1898, p.5 and 17 Jun 1898, p.2; *Evening Post*, 17 Jun 1898, p.6; *ODT*, 18 Jun 1898, p.6.

112 *Auckland Star*, 20 Jun 1898, p.2.

113 Ibid. For more on the public debate see *Auckland Star*, 21 Jun 1898, p.2; *Observer* 25 Jun 1898, p.3.

114 As the commissioners wrote: 'The class of prostitutes found in the streets, as long as they conduct themselves with decency and do not "solicit," do not come within the power of the police, however offensive their presence may

be to the public.' New Zealand Government, 'Report and Evidence', p.xxvi.

115 See, for example, *Truth*, 25 Aug 1906, p.6; 8 Sept 1906, p.6.

116 Eldred-Grigg, *Pleasures of the Flesh*, p.164.

117 Bronwyn Dalley, *Family Matters: Child Welfare in Twentieth Century*, Auckland University Press, Auckland, 1998, p.17.

118 *Education Monthly*, 4 Aug 1883, p.7, cited in Harry Orsman, *The Dictionary of New Zealand English: A Dictionary of New Zealandisms on Historical Principles*, Oxford University Press, Auckland, 1997, p.438. Historian Simon Sleight defines a larrikin in the Australian context as someone aged 11 to 21. Simon Sleight, *Young People and the Shaping of Public Space in Melbourne, 1870–1914*, Ashgate, Farnham, 2013, p.132.

119 *Evening Post*, 28 Feb 1880, p.1.

120 Schlör, *Nights in the Big City*, p.120.

121 *Evening Post*, 12 Nov 1892, p.4; 29 Jan 1898, p.2.

122 *New Zealand Free Lance*, 6 Aug 1904, p.13; *Evening Post*, 19 Aug 1890, p.4.

123 *ODT*, 14 Jan 1879, p.2; *Evening Post*, 19 May 1890, p.4.

124 *Evening Post*, 24 Oct 1876, p.2.

125 *ODT*, 14 Jan 1879, p.2.

126 *Evening Post*, 23 Aug 1893, p.3.

127 Vandalism included smashing the seats at Dunedin's cricket oval. *North Otago Times*, 2 Oct 1877, p.2.

128 *Evening Post*, 19 Dec 1889, p.2.

129 Police eventually caught most of the offenders, who were sentenced to gaol or heavily fined. *West Coast Times*, 11 Mar 1882, p.2. Similarly, a Dunedin larrikin ringleader was fined £3.10s in 1885 for assaulting a Chinese man 'for the fun of the thing'. *North Otago Times*, 31 Jul 1885, p.2.

130 *Evening Post*, 15 Aug 1890, p.3.

131 'The Police Force of the Colony (Annual Report on)', *AJHR*, H-21, Wellington, 1892, p.2.

132 Simon Sleight considers larrikin was a new term for a pre-existing condition, noting that youth gangs had existed in 1820s Sydney and 1850s Melbourne. Sleight, *Young People and the*

Shaping of Public Space, p.133.

133 Brian Sutton-Smith, *A History of Children's Play: The New Zealand Playground, 1840–1950*, University of Pennsylvania Press, Philadelphia, 1981, p.10; R.C.J. Stone, *Logan Campbell's Auckland: Tales from the Early Years*, Auckland University Press, Auckland, 2007, pp.124–28.

134 The change signalled the beginning of a transition from what James Belich has called the Chattel Child model to the Cherished Child model. The childhood of the former is characterised by work and obedience and emotional distance from parents; that of the latter by emotional attachment to parents, a result of growing societal recognition of children's social capital. For the New Zealand colonial context, Belich replaces the Chattel Child with his own Wild Child model, arguing that factors such as larger families and a less built-up living environment made local children wilder and more autonomous than those of Britain. While larrikins could certainly be situated within such a model, their behaviours might be considered tame compared to those of London street boys. See James Belich, *Paradise Reforged: A History of the New Zealanders from the 1880s to the Year 2000*, Allen Lane, Auckland, 2001, pp.357–63.

135 Dalley, *Family Matters*, pp.14–15; Barbara Brookes, *A History of New Zealand Women*, Bridget Williams Books, Wellington, 2016, p.149.

136 Ibid., p.15.

137 Groups of boys also gathered on streets to fraternise and loaf about in British cities. Andersson, *Streetlife in Late Victorian London*, p.162; Winter, *London's Teeming Streets*, p.69.

138 Melissa Bellanta, *Larrikins: A History*, University of Queensland Press, St Lucia, 2012, p.10. Bellanta's and Simon Sleight's research on Australian larrikinism emphasises how larrikin social identities were semiotically expressed through language and dress. This could also be a rich vein of inquiry in the New Zealand context, but one with insufficient space to consider here.

139 Ibid., p.4.

140 Martin Crotty, *Making the Australian Male: Middle-class Masculinity 1870–1920*, Melbourne University Press, Carlton, 2001, pp.15–16.

141 This belief adds weight to James Belich's claim there was less parental control of children's play and socialisation in 19th- and 20th-century New Zealand. Belich, *Paradise Reforged*, p.359.

142 Richard Seddon, 13 Aug 1896, *NZPD*, Vol. 94, p.319.

143 Ibid., pp.320–21; *Christchurch Star*, 7 Aug 1896, p.2.

144 *Oamaru Mail*, 24 Aug 1896, p.4.

145 Robert Thompson, 13 Aug 1996, *NZPD*, Vol. 94, p.326.

146 William Hutchison, Ibid., p.324.

147 Richard Seddon, Ibid., p.331.

148 The other sceptical parliamentarian was Auckland MHR Charles Button. Ibid., p.326.

149 *Manawatu Herald*, 15 Aug 1896, p.2.

150 *NZPD*, 16 Oct 1896, Vol. 94, p.876.

151 *Press*, 14 Dec 1896, p.4. Many of the same measures were placed in the following year's Young Person's Protection Bill, but it too failed to pass. *Star*, 2 Oct 1897, p.6; Jeanine Graham, 'Child Employment in New Zealand', *New Zealand Journal of History*, 21, 1 (1987), pp.72–73.

152 *Evening Post*, 19 Jun 1893, p.2.

153 Ibid.

154 Barbara Brookes, Erik Olssen and Emma Beer, 'Six Spare Time? Leisure, Gender and Modernity', in Barbara Brookes, Annabel Cooper and Robin Law (eds), *Sites of Gender: Women, Men and Modernity in Southern Dunedin, 1890–1939*, Auckland University Press, Auckland, 2003, p.175; Belich, *Paradise Reforged*, p.365.

155 Andrew Lees and Lynn Hollen Lees, *Cities and the Making of Modern Europe, 1750–1914*, Cambridge University Press, Cambridge, 2007, p.177; Belich, *Paradise Reforged*, p.367.

156 Brookes, Olssen and Beer, 'Six Spare Time', p.175; Baldwin, *Domesticating the Street*, p.149.

157 Chris Brickell, 'Sexuality, Morality and Society', in Giselle Byrnes (ed.), *The New*

Oxford History of New Zealand, Oxford University Press, South Melbourne, 2009, p.474. The inclination to blame delinquent behaviour on poor parenting was reinforced in March 2015, when nine children (aged between 10 and 16) were arrested for violently attacking a couple in central Auckland. One child advocate suggested police would be 'looking hard' at their parents. *New Zealand Herald*, 10 Mar 2015, www.nzherald.co.nz/news/print.cfm?objectid=11414528 (accessed 13 Mar 2015).

158 Baldwin, *Domesticating the Street*, p.147.

159 *Evening Post*, 26 Feb 1895, p.3.

160 *Observer*, 12 Mar 1910, p.3. See also *Observer*, 26 Jun 1909, p.3.

161 *New Zealand Herald*, 22 Oct 1909, p.6.

162 *Press*, 23 Dec 1910, p.7.

163 *New Zealand Herald*, 11 Apr 1911, p.5.

164 *Auckland Star*, 28 Nov 1913, p.4.

165 *New Zealand Herald,* 12 Dec 1913, p.8.

166 *New Zealand Free Lance*, 1 Nov 1913, p.7.

167 Ibid.

168 *New Zealand Herald*, 11 Apr 1911, p.5.

169 Historian Perry Duis calls the motorcar 'the most dangerous form of transport ever introduced to the street'. Perry R. Duis, *Challenging Chicago: Coping with Everyday Life*, University of Illinois Press, Urbana, 1998, p.49.

170 Peter D. Norton, *Fighting Traffic: The Dawn of the Motor Age in the American City*, MIT Press, Cambridge, 2011, p.65.

171 Ibid., pp.66–70; Baldwin, *Domesticating the Street*, pp.215–18.

172 Ibid., pp.30–31.

173 Ibid., p.66.

174 Municipalities registered motor vehicles until the institution of a national system in 1925. James Watson, *Links: A History of Transport and New Zealand Society*, GP Publications, Wellington, 1996, p.17.

175 The injured boy recovered. *ODT*, 19 Jan 1904, p.7.

176 Peter Conrad, *Modern Times; Modern Places:* *Life and Art in the 20th Century*, Thames & Hudson, London, 1999, p.92. This was underscored by a motorist who appeared on a furious driving charge in a Christchurch court in 1916. Asked by the judge why he sped, the defendant replied: 'Well … the road was very clear and there were no pedestrians about, and I let her go.' The judge fined him 60 shillings (the equivalent of about $400 in today's currency). *Auckland Star*, 19 Dec 1916, p.4.

177 *New Zealand Free Lance*, 23 Oct 1909, p.6.

178 Hill, *The Iron Hand in the Velvet Glove*, pp.373–74.

179 *Auckland Star*, 22 Oct 1913, p.8.

180 Baldwin, *Domesticating the Street*, p.5.

181 *New Zealand Herald*, 21 Apr 1904, p.5.

182 *Star*, 1 Apr 1913, p.2.

183 The following figures indicate the growth of motor vehicles in city space. Between 1910 and 1917 the number of registered vehicles in Auckland City grew from 147 to 841. In Wellington City, registrations rose from 1,000 in 1916 to 3,740 in 1920. G. W. A. Bush, *Decently and in Order: The Centennial History of the Auckland City Council*, Collins, Auckland, 1971, pp.160–61; Redmer Yska, *Wellington: Biography of a City*, Reed, Auckland, 2006, pp.96, 134.

184 'History of the AA', www.aa.co.nz/about/the-aa/history-of-the-aa (accessed 13 Mar 2015).

185 Baldwin, *Domesticating the Street*, pp.6, 214–16.

186 *Evening Post*, 23 Jan 1920, p.10.

187 Ibid., 21 Jan 1920, p.8.

188 *New Zealand Free Lance*, 21 May 1919, p.10. Similarly, a pedestrian who, after being 'nearly bowled over' by a motorist, called for motorcars to be limited to 3 miles per hour in city streets was labelled mad and ignorant by a motorist. '[W]hether you like it or not,' said the motorist, 'motors have come to stay.' *Evening Post*, 17 Nov 1919, p.8.

189 Because the story falls outside our period only a brief outline is given here. Further information can be found on the *Te Ara* 'Street Life' entry, www.teara.govt.nz/en/street-life.

190 'Secretary of Wellington Automobile Club to Town Clerk', 23 Jun 1925, 00001:1524:38/8 part 1, Wellington City Council Archives.

191 'Traffic Inspector to City Engineer', 30 Oct 1926, 00001:1524:38/8 part 1, Wellington City Council Archives.

192 *Evening Post*, 19 Aug 1924, p.3.

193 Baldwin, *Domesticating the Street*, p.224.

194 Richard Dennis, *Cities in Modernity: Representations and Productions of Metropolitan Space, 1840–1930*, Cambridge University Press, Cambridge, 2008, p.146.

Chapter Seven

1 The long duration of the disease was unusual for a bacterial disease, so she might have had a weak immune system. 'Samuel Harris to Parents', 4 Oct 1863, Harris Family Letters, MS-Papers-6987, ATL.

2 Geoffrey W. Rice, 'Public Health in Christchurch, 1875–1910: Mortality and Sanitation', in Linda Bryder (ed.), *A Healthy Country: Essays on the Social History of Medicine in New Zealand*, Bridget Williams Books, Wellington, 1991, pp.85–108, and *Black November: The 1918 Influenza Pandemic in New Zealand*, Canterbury University Press, Christchurch, 2005 edn, p.202. Linda Bryder's contemporaneous work on tuberculosis and Derek Dow's history of New Zealand public health also touch upon city life. Linda Bryder, '"Lessons" of the 1918 Influenza Epidemic in Auckland', *New Zealand Journal of History (NZJH)*, 16, 2 (1982), pp.97–121; Derek A. Dow, *Safeguarding the Public Health: A History of the New Zealand Department of Health*, Victoria University Press, Wellington, 1995.

3 Pamela Wood, *Dirt: Filth and Decay in a New World Arcadia*, Auckland University Press, Auckland, 2005.

4 Patrice Bourdelais, *Epidemics Laid Low: A History of What Happened in Rich Countries*, John Hopkins University Press, Baltimore, 2006, p.98; Peter Clark, *European Cities and Towns: 400–2000*, Oxford University Press, Oxford, 2009, pp.283–84.

5 Wood, *Dirt*, p.20. This section is strongly informed by Wood's first chapter.

6 James Barr, *The Old Identities: Being Sketches and Reminiscences During the First Decade of the Province of Otago, NZ*, Mills, Dick & Co., Dunedin, 1879, pp.15, 50, cited in Wood, *Dirt*, p.20.

7 Vladimir Jankovic, *Confronting the Climate: British Airs and the Making of Environmental Medicine*, Palgrave McMillan, New York, 2010, p.16.

8 Ibid., pp.15–16; Alister Woodward and Tony Blakely, *The Healthy Country?: A History of Life and Death in New Zealand*, Auckland University Press, Auckland, 2014, p.101; Wood, *Dirt*, p.21.

9 For example, Samuel Grimstone's 1847 monograph on Wellington and William Fox's 1849 report on Nelson included meteorological tables showing temperature ranges and the number of fine, rainy, cloudy and windy days per month. The number of earthquakes was also recorded. S.E. Grimstone, *Southern Settlements of New Zealand*, R. Stokes, Wellington, 1847, p.101; William Fox, *Report on the Settlement of Nelson in New Zealand*, Smith, Elder and Co., London, 1849, pp.26–28.

10 G.B. Earp, *Handbook for Intending Immigrants to the Southern Settlements of New Zealand*, W.S. Orr, London, 1849, p.60.

11 Ibid., pp.60–64.

12 Ibid., p.65.

13 'Private Letter from Wellington', 28 Apr 1845, *New Zealand Journal*, 151 (1845), p.261.

14 Grimstone, *Southern Settlements*, p.97.

15 Wood, *Dirt*, p.23.

16 It was believed that London's bad air made Londoners languid and sallow-looking in comparison to ruddy country dwellers. 'Letter to Robert Rintoul from Edward Gibbon Wakefield', 17 Apr 1853, Copies of Letters from Edward Gibbon Wakefield, Paper; ff. 75. A.D. 1897–8, Folio, British Library; Jankovic, *Confronting the Climate*, p.44.

17 Thomson argued that soldiers were the best standard for measuring the salubriousness of the climate of any colony because soldiers in all British regiments were of about the same age, were fed a similar diet, and generally performed the same amount of labour wherever they were stationed in the Empire. Arthur S. Thomson, *The Story of New Zealand:*

Past and Present – Savage and Civilised, Vol. 1, John Murray, London, 1859, pp.45–50.

18 Derek A. Dow, *Safeguarding the Public Health: A History of the New Zealand Department of Health*, Victoria University Press, Wellington, 1995, p.16; Wood, *Dirt*, p.23; Woodward and Blakely, *The Healthy Country?*, p.72.

19 Interestingly, his explanation shares much with that advanced by Woodwood and Blakely. A.K. Newman, 'Is New Zealand a Healthy Country?', *Proceedings of the Royal Society of New Zealand*, 15 (1882), pp.506–8; Dow, *Safeguarding the Public Health*, p.16; John Stenhouse, '"A Disappearing Race Before We Came Here": Dr Alfred Kingcome Newman, the Dying Maori, and Victorian Scientific Racism', *NZJH*, 30, 2 (1996), pp.132, 137.

20 'Notes on my Voyage to Auckland', John Smith, fl 1880–1881, MS-1958, ATL.

21 As early as 1847, an Auckland newspaper declared the town already had 'enough filthy lanes and dirty drains to keep a perpetual plague' had it been situated in less breezy climes. By 1851, a critic described the town's working-class Chancery district as unfit for habitation. *New Zealander*, 11 Dec 1847, p.2; *Daily Southern Cross*, 7 Jan 1851, p.3.

22 Ibid., 24 Oct 1854, p.3.

23 Ibid.

24 As Dell Upton puts it: 'Miasma caused disease, while the qualities of the landscape – the *topographe physio-médicale* – generated miasma.' Dell Upton, *Another City: Urban Life and Urban Spaces in the New American Republic*, Yale University Press, New Haven, 2008, p.56.

25 While miasmatic theorists dismissed the contagion theory, they did vaguely acknowledge 'formite' agents that could cling to the clothing and furniture of contagious disease victims. Ibid., p.57.

26 Patrice Bourdelais, *Epidemics Laid Low: A History of What Happened in Rich Countries*, The John Hopkins University Press, Baltimore, 2006, pp.14–15, 25–26.

27 J.N. Hays, *The Burdens of Disease: Epidemics and the Human Response in Western History*, Rutgers University Press, New Brunswick, 2009, p.110.

28 Bourdelais, *Epidemics Laid Low*, p.47.

29 Ibid., p.54.

30 Ibid., pp.146–49.

31 The absence of such statistics means claims of high rates of infectious diseases in Auckland are impressionistic and should be treated with some caution. As other historians have noted, New Zealand generally lacks reliable mortality and morbidity statistics for the early colonial period. Nonetheless, data from Wellington death registers between 1840 and 1847 could suggest that infectious diseases were an important cause of death from the beginning of urban colonial settlement. The leading causes of deaths recorded in the register were: 1) Decline – an undiagnosed slow death; 2) Drowning; 3) Inflammation – mainly of the lung; 4) Consumption – Phthisis (tuberculosis); and 5) Fevers. Consumption and fevers were infectious diseases. The reliability of the data is uncertain but they appear as an appendix in Louis Ward, *Early Wellington*, Whitcombe & Tombs, Wellington, 1928, pp.459–61. On the dearth of statistics, see Woodward and Blakely, *The Healthy Country?*, p.78.

32 *Daily Southern Cross*, 24 Oct 1854, p.3.

33 *Wellington Independent*, 16 Sept 1854, p.4.

34 *Otago Witness*, 11 Oct 1856, p.3.

35 G.W.A. Bush, *Decently and in Order: The Centennial History of the Auckland City Council*, Collins, Auckland, 1971, pp.41, 64, 68; Wood, *Dirt*, p.96.

36 As Jankovic has written, 'city people generally suspended environmental expectations they would otherwise maintain in the country: the city was *meant* to be polluted and urban dwellers were *meant* to adjust to it'. Jankovic, *Confronting the Climate*, p.88.

37 Roy Porter, *London: A Social History*, Harvard University Press, Cambridge, 1998, pp.260–65.

38 Statistics compiled by the Registrar of Deaths, Dr Alfred Barker, and presented to the commission showed that between 1851 and 1859 fever-attributed deaths in Christchurch had averaged 9 per cent of all deaths (24 out of 267 recorded deaths), but from 1860 to early 1862 the figure had been running at

15 per cent (35 out of 230 recorded deaths). Barker conceded the statistics were imperfect but thought fever data was relatively reliable. 'Minutes of Sanitary Commission', 6 May 1862, CCC/ARC/343/78/4, Christchurch City Archives (CCA); John Wilson, *Christchurch: Swamp to City: A Short History of the Christchurch Drainage Board 1875–1898*, Te Waihora Press, Lincoln, 1989, p.9.

39 'Minutes of Sanitary Commission', 2 May 1862, CCC/ARC/343/78/4, CCA.

40 Ibid., 6 May 1862, CCC/ARC/343/78/5, CCA.

41 Ibid., 9 May 1862, CCC/ARC/343/78/5, CCA.

42 *Lyttelton Times*, 5 Jul 1862, p.4.

43 'Report of the Sanitary Commission', 27 Jun 1862, CCA.

44 A new immigration barracks was constructed in Addington in 1864. Ibid.; *Press*, 30 Aug 1862, p.4.

45 *Otago Daily Times*, 10 Aug 1864, p.4.

46 Wood, *Dirt*, pp.72, 102–03, 159–64. It was not until the creation of a Dunedin drainage board in 1900 that a city-wide sewerage scheme was able to be realised in 1908 – the Lawyer's Head scheme. See K.C. McDonald, *City of Dunedin: A Century of Civic Enterprise*, Dunedin City Corporation, Dunedin, 1965, pp.239–44, 294.

47 Wood, *Dirt*, pp.144, 148.

48 Upton, *Another City*, pp.41–42.

49 'Inspector of Nuisances Reports, 1863–1868', 5 Mar 1866, CCC/ARC/343/80/38, CCA.

50 Ibid., 7, 14 and 21 Dec 1863, CCC/ARC/343/78/50, CCC/ARC/343/78/51 and CCC/ARC/343/78/51, CCA.

51 Ibid., 19 Oct 1863, CCC/ARC/343/78/43, CCA.

52 Ibid., 22 Jun, 13 Jul, 31 Aug, 9 Nov 1863, CCC/ARC/343/78/26, CCC/ARC/343/78/28, CCC/ARC/343/78/36 and CCC/ARC/343/78/46, CCA.

53 Ibid., 30 Nov and 21 Dec 1863, CCC/ARC/343/78/49 and CCC/ARC/343/78/52, CCA; *Press*, 22 Dec 1863, p.2; *Lyttelton Times*, 18 Feb 1864, p.5.

54 Ibid., 7 Nov 1864 and 6 Feb 1865, CCC/ARC/343/79/3 and CCC/ARC/343/80/1, CCA.

55 Ibid., 26 Nov 1866, CCC/ARC/343/80/61, CCA.

56 Ibid., 27 May 1863, CCC/ARC/343/78/22, CCA.

57 Others shared this view. For example, in wondering why Aucklanders tolerated an open sewer running down their main street (Queen Street), the *New Zealand Herald* suggested that 'to the majority of people, dirt and filth were not the abomination they should be to a civilised people, and that cleanliness like education must be made compulsory to become generally enjoyed'. *New Zealand Herald*, 31 Mar 1870, p.3.

58 Bush, *Decently and in Order*, p.120.

59 'Mr Goldie to the Secretary, Central Board of Health', *Appendices of the Journals of the House of Representatives (AJHR)*, 1875, Session I, H-22, p.3.

60 Bush, *Decently and in Order*, pp.118–24.

61 Geoffrey W. Rice, 'Public Health in Christchurch, 1875–1910: Mortality and Sanitation', in Linda Bryder (ed.), *A Healthy Country: Essays on the Social History of Medicine in New Zealand*, Bridget Williams Books, Wellington, 1991, p.95; Wilson, *Christchurch: Swamp to City*, p.22.

62 Rice, 'Public Health in Christchurch', pp.88–89.

63 *Star*, 18 May 1880, p.4.

64 Rice, 'Public Health in Christchurch', pp.100–2.

65 Ibid., p.107.

66 Auckland also experienced a typhoid epidemic over this period, with 139 deaths. By comparison, 40 died from typhoid in Christchurch and 39 in Dunedin. New Zealand Government, 'Vital Statistics: Boroughs – Causes of Death – Class, Orders and Diseases', *Statistics of the Colony of New Zealand*, Wellington, Government Print, 1889–1900.

67 Redmer Yska, *Wellington: Biography of a City*, Reed, Auckland, 2006, pp.51–53, 55, 76–78.

68 In 1890 the local Board of Health received reports of 194 cases of scarlet fever, 71 of typhoid and 8 of diphtheria, a substantial increase over previous years. *Evening Post*, 16 Sept 1892, p.4.

69 I am grateful to Redmer Yska for alerting me to Chapple's report.

70 William Chapple, 'To the Mayor and City

Councillors of the City of Wellington', unpublished report, 1892, WCA, 00233:34:1892/740, pp.2–4.

71 Ibid., p.7.

72 Ibid., p.8.

73 Ibid., p.4.

74 Ibid., pp.13–14.

75 Ibid., p.12.

76 Ibid., p.14.

77 *Evening Post*, 16 Sept 1892, p.4.

78 Rice, 'Public Health in Christchurch', p.89.

79 Ibid., p.90.

80 The data excludes Māori and comes from the 'Ages of Death From Each Cause' and the 'Boroughs – Causes of Death – Classes Orders and Diseases' tables in the 'Vital Statistics' section of the annual *Statistics of New Zealand*. New Zealand Government, *Statistics of the Colony of New Zealand*, Government Printer, Wellington, 1875–1905.

81 Parasitic diseases were included in the zymotic category until 1885, when they were removed.

82 In numerical terms: of the 1,520 deaths recorded in 1875, 501 were from zymotic causes; of the 2,388 deaths recorded in 1905, just 115 were from zymotic causes. In reporting the 1875 figure, the *Evening Post* called it 'a deplorable fact' that a third of all deaths in the colony 'resulted from zymotic diseases, or in other words, from disease preventable by observance of the simplest and most ordinary precautions'. *Evening Post*, 25 Feb 1876, p.2.

83 Most of the data comes from 'Chief Towns – Births and Deaths' and 'Proportion of Births, Marriages and Deaths to the Living Population – Decennial Return' tables in the 'Vital Statistics' section of New Zealand Government, *Statistics of the Colony of New Zealand*, 1875–1905. The city mortality rates for 1875 and 1880 were not given in *Statistics of New Zealand* and were gained from collating monthly vital statistics reports published in newspapers.

84 Similarly, Roy Porter has attributed a declining contagious death rate over the same period to improved sanitary infrastructure. Bourdelais, *Epidemics Laid Low*, p.98; Porter, *London*,

p.274.

85 A leading proponent of this view was Thomas McKeown of the University of Birmingham, who in the 1970s argued improved diet was the most important factor in reducing Victorian mortality rates because it increased a population's resistance to disease. Bourdelais, *Epidemics Laid Low*, p.94; Woodward and Blakely, *The Healthy Country?*, pp.108–9; Rice, 'Public Health in Christchurch', pp.86–87.

86 Woodward and Blakely, *The Healthy Country?*, p.109.

87 Ben Schrader, 'Drains and Plagues: Making Christchurch Healthy, 1860s to 1910s', in Malcolm McKinnon (ed.), *Bateman New Zealand Historical Atlas*, Bateman, Auckland, 1997, plate 55.

88 James E. Partington, *Random Rot: A Journal of Three Year's Wanderings About the World*, Guardian Office, Atrincham, 1883, p.343.

89 *Otago Witness*, 26 Jan 1899, p.21.

90 Yska, *Wellington*, p.102; *Auckland Star*, 19 Apr 1900, p.8; 23 Apr 1900, p.5; 28 Apr 1900, p.6.

91 Smallpox was the first disease that biomedical science had shown could be checked through inoculation. In 1740s England, tens of thousands of people were inoculated. Following Edward Jenner's experiments with cowpox, vaccination became the favoured preventative measure. Bourdelais, *Epidemics Laid Low*, pp.40–42.

92 Dow, *Safeguarding the Public Health*, pp.29–30, 49–53; Alison Day, '"Chastising Its People With Scorpions": Maori and the 1913 Smallpox Epidemic', *NZJH*, 33, 2 (1999), pp.181, 184.

93 There were two strains of smallpox: *variola major* and *variola minor*. The former was characterised by a severe body rash that appeared within 24 hours of infection and was better known to New Zealand health professionals. The latter strain was milder and typified by successive crops of rash over a few days, symptomatically resembling chickenpox. *Kai Tiaki: The Journal of the Nurses of New Zealand*, 2 (1914), p.82; *Singleton Argus* (New South Wales), 5 Aug 1913, p.2; Day, '"Chastising Its People"', p.185.

94 John Oliver and Bernie Wood, *100 Years:*

Māori Rugby League, 1908–2008, Huia, Wellington, 2008, pp.55–58.

95   Subsequent investigations revealed that Rukutai had caught it from Māori who had been at the Northland hui. *Auckland Star*, 5 Jun 1913, p.5. Maguire did not provide a rationale for this assertion.

96   *New Zealand Herald*, 11 Jun 1913, p.8.

97   Day, '"Chastising Its People"', p.186.

98   *New Zealand Herald*, 12 July 1913, p.8.

99   Ibid.; *Auckland Star*, 15 July 1913, p.5.

100 *Dominion*, 22 Jul 1913, p.5.

101 *New Zealand Herald*, 19 Jul 1913, p.8.

102 The 1911 Māori Census identified 714 resident Māori living about Auckland. At the same time the city's total population was 103,000. 'Census of the Maori Population', *AJHR*, 1911, H-14A, p.20.

103 Conversely, the *Auckland Star* generally referred to it as 'the epidemic'.

104 *New Zealand Herald*, 23 Jul 1913, p.6.

105 Ibid.

106 *Auckland Star*, 5 Jun 1913, p.5.

107 From a European perspective, Māori settlements, with their traditional whare and communal living arrangements, were hothouses for the propagation and spread of disease. Only by adopting European housing and sanitary arrangements would Māori reduce their risk of contracting contagious diseases. Ben Schrader, 'Māori Housing – Te Noho Whare', *Te Ara*, www.teara.govt.nz/en/maori-housing-te-noho-whare/page-2 (accessed 11 Apr 2016); Day, '"Chastising its People"', p.197.

108 *New Zealand Herald*, 30 Jul 1913, p.8.

109 Ibid., 9 Aug 1913, p.8.

110 Ibid., 12 Aug 1913, p.8.

111 As Day has written: '[a]ccepted smallpox procedures were distorted by racial prejudice and resulted in discriminatory application'. Day, '"Chastising its People"', p.198.

112 *New Zealand Herald*, 12 Aug 1913, p.8.

113 Bourdelais, *Epidemics Laid Low*, p.20.

114 *New Zealand Herald*, 18 Aug 1913, p.8.

115 *Auckland Star*, 21 Aug 1913, p.5.

116 *New Zealand Herald*, 15 Dec 1913, p.8.

117 The final estimates for the epidemic were: 1,978 cases, of which 116 were Europeans. There were 55 fatalities, all of whom were Māori. 'Particulars Relative to the Smallpox Epidemic', *AJHR*, 1914, H-33, p.2.

118 Rice, *Black November*, p.221.

119 The mortality rate in Christchurch was 4.9 per 1,000, and 3.9 per 1,000 in Dunedin. Rice, *Black November*, pp.115, 202–3. Health researchers have suggested that the remoteness and greater social distancing in rural areas may have provided some protection from mortality. Kirsten McSweeny, Atalie Colman, Nick Fancourt et al., 'Was Rurality Protective in the 1918 Influenza Pandemic in New Zealand?', *New Zealand Medical Journal*, 120, 1256, (2007), p.1.

120 Linda Bryder, '"Lessons" of the 1918 Influenza Epidemic in Auckland', *NZJH*, 16, 2 (1982), pp.97, 104–5.

121 *Observer*, 23 Nov 1918, p.16.

122 'Report of the Influenza Epidemic Commission', Session 1, *AJHR*, 1919, H-31A, p.31.

123 Ibid., p.32.

124 The main measure was the Housing of the Working Classes Act 1890, which focused on municipal housing provision. Stephen Inwood, *A History of London*, Carroll & Graf, New York, 2000, pp.529–38; Porter, *London*, pp.268–71.

125 William Swainson, *New Zealand and its Colonization*, Smith, Elder & Co., London 1859, p.225.

126 *Otago Daily Times*, 28 Jan 1864, p.4.

127 *New Zealand Herald*, 7 Apr 1864, p.3.

128 The gerrymandering was inherited from Britain. The Municipal Corporations Act 1867 introduced a sliding scale of plural voting based on rateable value; property owners were able to exercise up to five votes depending on the total rateable value of their property. Between 1901 and 1913, the franchise was extended to all adults with three months' residence in a municipality. Leif Jerram, *Streetlife: The Untold Story of Europe's*

Twentieth Century, Oxford University Press, Oxford, 2011, p.332; Bush, *Decently and in Order*, pp.86, 488; Yska, *Wellington*, p.99.

129 Inwood, *A History of London*, p.518.

130 Graeme Davison, '"This Moral Pandemonium": Images of Low Life', in Graeme Davison and Chris McConville (eds), *The Outcasts of Melbourne*, Allen & Unwin, Sydney, 1985, p.29.

131 *Clutha Leader*, 11 Oct 1878, p.6.

132 Alan Mayne, *Representing the Slum: Popular Journalism in a Late 19th Century City*, University of Melbourne, Melbourne, 1990, p.6. See also, for example, *New Zealand Herald*, 22 Apr 1873, p.2; *Truth*, 31 Aug 1907, p.6.

133 Public Health Act 1876, sec. 51, www.nzlii.org/nz/legis/hist_act/pha187640v1876n60246; Municipal Corporations Act 1886, secs 302, 303, www.nzlii.org/nz/legis/hist_act/mca188650v1886n50338 (accessed 11 Apr 2016).

134 Wood, *Dirt*, p.194.

135 Ibid., pp.195–96.

136 *Auckland Star*, 17 Jan 1900, p.5; 19 Apr 1900, p.8; 23 Apr 1900, p.5; Yska, *Wellington*, pp.99, 102.

137 *Auckland Star*, 2 May 1900, p.5.

138 Yska, *Wellington*, p.102.

139 *Press*, 7 Nov 1900, p.9.

140 Wellington City Council Minute Book, 30 Mar 1903, Vol. 16, p.65, WCC Archives; *Evening Post*, 31 Mar 1903, p.2.

141 *Evening Post*, 1 Apr 1903, p.1.

142 *New Zealand Herald Supplement*, 3 Oct 1903, p.1.

143 Ibid., 26 Sep 1903, p.1. The series ran on successive weeks from this date.

144 Leif Jerram notes that only 10 per cent of volunteers from Manchester made it into the army. Jerram, *Streetlife*, pp.327–28. Stanley Buder, *Visionaries and Planners: The Garden City Movement and the Modern Community*, Oxford University Press, Oxford, 1990, pp.71–72.

145 In 1891 the New Zealand press carried articles on Englishman Dr James Cantlie's discovery of a degenerative disease called *urbo-morbus*.

It was caused by breathing bad city air and could be cured by exercising in country air. Local reports about urban degeneration and solutions to it picked up again in the wake of the Boer War. *Bay of Plenty Times*, 11 Dec 1891, p.2; *Hawke's Bay Herald*, 2 Jan 1892, p.4; *Oamaru Mail*, 10 Oct 1903, p.2; *Wanganui Herald*, 31 Dec 1903, p.5.

146 Jerram, *Streetlife*, p.332.

147 Ben Schrader, *We Call It Home: A History of State Housing in New Zealand*, Reed, Auckland, 2005, pp.22–23.

148 Ibid., pp.24–30.

149 I recognise that alongside spatial planning, the garden city model had a strong social component, the crux of which was that spaces could be so planned to promote sociability and local community. This is discussed further in Schrader, *We Call it Home*, pp.167–68, and Ben Schrader, 'Planning Happy Families: A History of the Naenae Idea', MA thesis, Victoria University of Wellington, 1993, pp.19–24; Jerram, *Streetlife*, pp.332–35.

150 Charles Reade, *The Revelation of Britain: A Book for Colonials*, Gordon & Gotch, Auckland, 1909, pp.10–12, 62–63; Ben Schrader, 'Avoiding the Mistakes of the "Mother Country": The New Zealand Garden City Movement 1900–1926', *Planning Perspectives*, 14 (1999), pp.397–98.

151 The Bill was modelled on the 1909 British Town Planning Act but did not pass until 1926. Arthur Myers, 'Paper on Town-Planning', in *Official Volume of Proceedings of the New Zealand Town-Planning Conference and Exhibition*, Government Printer, Wellington, 1919, p.46.

152 Sir George Fowlds Papers, MSS & Archives A-17 3/65, Special Collections, University of Auckland Library – Te Tumu Herenga.

153 *Evening Post*, 7 Aug 1911, p.7.

154 Ibid., 8 Aug 1911, p.3; *Dominion*, 8 Aug 1911, p.9.

155 'Report on Statement Made by NZ Times Concerning Slums, 1912', 00233:230:1912/2163, and Re: Slums – Town Clerk, 1907, 00233:145:1907/1542, Wellington City Archives.

156 Blaming tenants for poor housing conditions was not unique to Wellington. Linda Bryder shows this happened in Auckland following the 1918 influenza pandemic, citing the city's Chief Sanitary Inspector, C.T. Haynes, who stated, 'One of the phases of the housing question which has been mainly responsible for the scathing remarks regarding insanitary condition … is that of the dirty, destructive, careless, workshy, and artless tenant. A bad tenant can soon transform a good house into a slum.' 'Influenza Epidemic, Report by C.T. Haynes, Chief Sanitary Inspector', p.2, cited in Bryder, '"Lessons" of the 1918 Epidemic', p.111.

157 *Wanganui Herald*, 14 Jul 1914, p.5.

158 Schrader, 'Avoiding the Mistakes', p.400.

159 'His Excellency's Address', *Official Volume of Proceedings*, p.27.

160 G.W. Russell, 'Address by the Hon G.W. Russell', *Official Volume of Proceedings*, p.33.

161 'Report of the Influenza Epidemic Commission', p.32.

162 S. Hurst Seager, 'The Garden City in Relation to the Reconstruction and Repatriation Problems', *Official Volume of Proceedings*, pp.119–20; A.M. Myers, 'Paper on Town Planning', *Official Volume of Proceedings*, p.47.

163 W.D.S. Macdonald, 'Address', in *Official Volume of Proceedings*, p.126.

164 'Russell Address', *Official Volume of Proceedings*, p.38.

165 *Official Volume of Proceedings*, p.229.

166 Schrader, *We Call it Home*, pp.166–86.

167 Ibid., p.30.

168 The Housing Improvement Act 1945 gave local authorities the power to redevelop decadent areas, a measure municipalities increasingly used from the 1950s. Ben Schrader, 'Modernising Wellington', in John Wilson (ed.), *Zeal and Crusade: The Modern Movement in Wellington*, Te Waihora Press, Christchurch, 1996, p.19.

Chapter Eight

1 Lionel Frost, *The New Urban Frontier: Urbanisation and the City Building in Australasia and the American West*, New South Wales University Press, Kensington, 1991, p.38.

2 Michael, J. Thompson (ed.), *Fleeing the City: Studies in the Culture and Politics of Antiurbanism*, Palgrave McMillan, New York, 2009, p.1.

3 Ibid., p.2.

4 Ibid., p.3.

5 Ibid., p.1.

6 Steven Conn, *Americans Against the City: Anti-urbanism in the Twentieth Century*, Oxford University Press, New York, 2014, p.13.

7 Robert A. Beauregard, 'Antiurbanism in the United States, England, and China', in Thompson (ed.), *Fleeing the City*, pp.37–38.

8 Ibid., p.38.

9 Ibid., pp.39–40.

10 David Hamer touched upon it in his 1988 study of the New Zealand Liberals; more recently, Francis Pound considered its role in the production of Nationalist art. David Hamer, *The New Zealand Liberals: The Years in Power, 1891–1912*, Auckland University Press, Auckland, 1988; Francis Pound, *The Invention of New Zealand: Art and National Identity, 1930–1970*, Auckland University Press, Auckland, 2009.

11 The city survived by processing rural-sourced commodities and providing rural services, creating the image of the city as a parasite that lived off the country. Miles Fairburn, 'The Rural Myth and the New Urban Frontier: An Approach to New Zealand Social History, 1870–1940', *New Zealand Journal of History* (*NZJH*), 9, 1 (1975), p.4.

12 Ibid., p.8.

13 Ibid., pp.9–10.

14 Ibid., p.15.

15 Archibald Clark, *A Sketch of the Colony of New Zealand*, James Gibb & Co., Glasgow, 1866, p.38.

16 The process was akin to an apprenticeship. As C. Holloway explained in 1875, the New Zealand system was for farm labourers to 'work their way upward; say, work for a some employer for a year or two, thus acquiring a knowledge of colonial life … and when they

are in a position to take up land they will find no difficulty in suiting themselves in the Colony of New Zealand.' Miles Fairburn charts this process of upward social mobility, from newly arrived wage worker to independent landholder. 'Reports of Mr. C. Holloway to the Agricultural Labourers' Union', *Appendices to the Journals of the House of Representatives (AJHR)*, 1875, D-6, p.4; Miles Fairburn, *The Ideal Society and its Enemies: The Foundations of Modern New Zealand Society, 1850–1900*, Auckland University Press, Auckland, 1989, p.57.

17   Jock Phillips, 'Rural Mythologies – Immigrant Hopes', *Te Ara*, www.teara.govt.nz/en/rural-mythologies/page-2 (accessed 11 Apr 2016); Fairburn, *The Ideal Society*, pp.42–43; James Belich, *Paradise Reforged: A History of the New Zealanders From the 1880s to the Year 2000*, Allen Lane, Auckland, 2001, p.153.

18   Jock Phillips, *A Man's Country? The Image of the Pakeha Male: A History*, Penguin, Auckland, 1987, p.11.

19   Ibid., pp.23–25.

20   Ibid., pp.26–35.

21   Marriage was therefore viewed as a betrayal of the group and those who left for it were ridiculed by those left behind. Ibid., pp.36–37.

22   Ibid., p.39.

23   Jock Phillips, 'Rural Mythologies – Colonial Myth Making', *Te Ara*, www.teara.govt.nz/en/rural-mythologies/page-3 (accessed 11 Apr 2016).

24   Raewyn Dalziel, 'The Colonial Helpmeet: Women's Role in the Vote in Nineteenth Century New Zealand', in Judith Binney (ed.), *The Shaping of History: Essays from the New Zealand Journal of History*, Bridget Williams Books, Wellington, 2001, p.191.

25   Phillips, *A Man's Country*, pp.38–40.

26   Charlotte Macdonald, 'Too Many Men and Too Few Women: Gender's Fatal Impact in Nineteenth Century Colonies', in Caroline Daley and Deborah Montgomery (eds), *The Gendered Kiwi*, Auckland University Press, Auckland, 1999, pp.21–22.

27   The towns were: Auckland, New Plymouth, Wanganui, Wellington, Nelson, Christchurch,

Dunedin and Invercargill. 'Population of Chief Cities or Towns', *Census of New Zealand 1861*, Government Printer, Auckland, 1861, p.5.

28   Although Charlotte Macdonald has noted the colonial masculine stereotype was not the only expression of colonial masculinity, excepting Chris Brickell's work on male homosexuality, there has been surprisingly little research on the other expressions. Macdonald, 'Too Many Men', p.20.

29   Jankovic points out such images tended to come from vigorous Scots, offended at the way 'continental effeminacy' had taken hold of metropolitan life. Vladimir Jankovic, *Confronting the Climate: British Airs and the Making of Environmental Medicine*, Palgrave Macmillan, New York, 2010, p.47.

30   Charles Hursthouse, *Emigration: Where to Go and Who Should Go: Australia and New Zealand as Emigration Fields*, Trelawny Saunders, London, 1852, p.93.

31   Ibid., pp.93–94.

32   Arthur Clayden, *The England of the Pacific: or New Zealand as an English Middle-Class Emigration-Field*, Wyman & Sons, London, 1879, p.10.

33   The Owens were one of twelve families who emigrated from Prince Edward Island, in the Gulf of St Lawrence, to Auckland in December 1858. An Owen descendent cited the lack of economic opportunities for growing families and the short summer season as the main motivation for the move. Beryl M. Jones, 'Foreword', Letters and papers relating to the Owen and Haszard families (Owen papers), MS 1164, 82/37, Auckland Museum.

34   Jock Phillips and Terry Hearn, *Settlers: New Zealand Immigrants from England, Ireland and Scotland, 1800–1945*, Auckland University Press, Auckland, 2008, p.36.

35   Letter, George Owen to his father, 26 Mar 1860, Owen papers.

36   Ibid.

37   Letter, Annabel Owen to her Sister-in-law, 25 May 1860, Owen papers; *Daily Southern Cross*, 31 July 1860, p.4.

38   The business was called G. W. Owen and

Company. Letter extracts 1861–1872, Owen papers; *New Zealand Herald*, 10 May 1906, p.4.

39 Phillips and Hearn, *Settlers*, pp.42–43.

40 Carter had been an early settler in Wellington, where he created a thriving building business – the Wairarapa town of Carterton was named for him. He returned to England in the 1860s, where he acted as an immigration agent. G.H. Sutherland, 'Carter, Charles Rooking', *Te Ara*, www.teara.govt.nz/en/biographies/1c8/carter-charles-rooking (accessed 11 Apr 2016).

41 Ibid., p.30.

42 'The Hon. The Minister for Immigration to the Agent General', *AJHR*, 1878, D-1, p.3.

43 *Otago Witness*, 20 Jul 1878, p.11. The point had been made the previous year, when the same Labour official stated that '[m]any come here trained only for city life.' *Bruce Herald*, 27 Nov 1877, p.4.

44 'Correspondence between His Honour the Superintendent, Auckland, and the Hon, the Minister for Immigration', *AJHR*, 1875, D-1, p.4.

45 *West Coast Times*, 5 Jan 1875, p.2.

46 Rev. J. Berry, *New Zealand as a Field for Emigration*, London, James Clark & Co., 1879, p.11.

47 Ibid., p.36.

48 Demographers argue the closing of the sex-ratio gap signals a population's maturation. Macdonald, 'Too Many Men', p.23; Ian Pool, *The New Zealand Family From 1840: A Demographic History*, Auckland University Press, Auckland, 2007, p.70.

49 The data come from: 'Population General Summary', 'Cities and Towns' and 'Four Chief Cities and Suburbs' tables in the 'Population and Dwellings' section of the New Zealand Census, 1861–1921. New Zealand Government, *Census of New Zealand*, Government Printer, Wellington (Auckland 1861 and 1864), 1861–1921. The five-yearly period of the Census was introduced in 1881. Before then it was generally conducted every three years, hence the lack of standardisation in the dates.

50 Historian Caroline Daley employed the phrase 'man's country, women's city?' for a *Te Ara*

entry on men and women in the city.

51 Andrew Lees and Lynn Hollen Lees, *Cities and the Making of Modern Europe, 1750–1914*, Cambridge University Press, Cambridge, 2007, p.52; Frost, *The New Urban Frontier*, pp.2–3.

52 Leif Jerram, *Streetlife: The Untold Story of Europe's Twentieth Century*, Oxford University Press, Oxford, 2011, p.103.

53 Henry Selfe and John Marshman, *Canterbury, New Zealand, in 1862*, G. Street, London, 1862, pp.42–43.

54 Raewyn Dalziel, 'Railways and Relief Centres (1870–1890)', in Keith Sinclair (ed.), *The Oxford Illustrated History of New Zealand*, Oxford University Press, Auckland, 1990, p.115; Jane Tolerton, 'Household Services – The Servant Problem', *Te Ara*, www.teara.govt.nz/en/household-services/page-2 (accessed 11 Apr 2016).

55 *New Zealand Herald*, 13 Feb 1897, p.4.

56 Ian Hunter, *Age of Enterprise: Rediscovering the New Zealand Entrepreneur, 1880–1910*, Auckland University Press, Auckland, 2007, p.63.

57 Hunter argues the Long Depression is misnamed and 'the dominant characteristic of the colonial colony between 1878 and 1896 was expansion not retrenchment'. Ibid., p.67, and 'Manufacturing – An Overview – Manufacturing Boom, 1880s–1890s', *Te Ara*, www.teara.govt.nz/en/manufacturing-an-overview/page-2 (accessed 11 Apr 2016).

58 Erik Olssen, 'Working Gender, Gendering Work: Occupation Change and Continuity in Southern Dunedin', in Barbara Brookes, Annabel Cooper and Robin Law (eds), *Sites of Gender: Women, Men and Modernity in Southern Dunedin, 1890–1939*, Auckland University Press, Auckland, 2003, p.70.

59 Sarah Deutsch, *Women in the City: Gender, Space, and Power in Boston, 1870–1940,* Oxford University Press, Oxford, 2000, p.61.

60 Ibid., p.56.

61 Daphne Spain, *Gendered Spaces*, University of North Carolina Press, Chapel Hill, 1992, p.178.

62 Ibid., pp.172–77; Tolerton, 'Household Services – The Servant Problem'; Barbara Brookes,

A History of New Zealand Women, Bridget Williams Books, Wellington, 2016, p.162.

63 *New Zealand Herald Supplement*, 3 Oct 1903, p.1.

64 Brookes, *New Zealand Women*, p.166.

65 Richard Dennis, *Cities in Modernity: Representations and Productions of Metropolitan Space, 1840–1930*, Cambridge University Press, Cambridge, 2008, pp.271–73.

66 Belich, *Paradise Reforged*, p.140.

67 Melanie Nolan, 'Constantly on the Move, But Going Nowhere? Work, Community and Social Mobility', in Giselle Byrnes (ed.), *The New Oxford History of New Zealand*, Oxford University Press, South Melbourne, 2009, p.360.

68 Oliver Zunz, *Making America Corporate 1870–1920*, University of Chicago Press, Chicago, 1990, p.127; Belich, *Paradise Reforged*, p.187.

69 Olssen, 'Working Gender, Gendering Work', pp.72, 78.

70 Herbert Spackman Diary, 22 Apr 1895, Spackman, Herbert, 1891–1900, MS-Papers-1788, ATL.

71 George Chauncey, *Gay New York: Gender, Urban Culture, and the Making of the Gay Urban World 1890–1940*, Basic Books, New York, 1994, pp.111–12.

72 As such, working-class men and boys often challenged the authority of middle-class men by questioning their supervisors' manliness and physically attacking middle-class boys. Ibid., p.112.

73 Ibid., p.113.

74 *New Zealand Herald*, 10 Nov 1909, p.7; Brookes, *A History of New Zealand Women*, p.163.

75 Phillips, *A Man's Country*, p.98.

76 *New Zealand Free Lance*, 28 May 1904, p.7.

77 Even the pro-city Joseph Berry made an exception for clerks. Alexander Bathgate, *Colonial Experiences*, James Maclehose, Glasgow, 1874, p.45; Berry, *New Zealand as a Field for Emigration*, p.12.

78 Clayden, *England of the Pacific*, p.9.

79 Frederick W. Pennefather, *New Zealand: A Field for Emigration*, William Clowes & Son, London, 1886, pp.5, 7.

80 Clayden, *England of the Pacific*, p.10.

81 *Evening Post*, 14 Jan 1888, p.2; 30 Oct 1889, p.4.

82 As Miles Fairburn points out, there was a perception that the city's artificial economic base was incapable of generating sufficient opportunities for one to become, through hard work, an independent or self-made man. Fairburn, 'The Rural Myth', p.5.

83 Pennefather, *New Zealand*, p.8.

84 William mentions his father in a couple of early letters, but doesn't explain why he was not living with the family. It seems he was a drunkard. In an 1880 letter, he speaks of his father spending all his wages on a bender in a rural pub, forcing him to ask Sarah for money to buy new clothes. 'William to Uncle', 28 Feb 1880, Derry Family Letters, MS-Papers-1043, ATL.

85 'William to Harry', 14 Aug 1880, Derry Family Letters.

86 This report and the unemployment demonstrations mentioned in Chapter Five suggest that even if Ian Hunter's argument is correct and expansion characterised the 1880s, there were still many people who struggled during the period. John E. Martin, *The Forgotten Worker: The Rural Wage Earner in Nineteenth-Century New Zealand*, Allen & Unwin/Trade Union History Project, Wellington, 1990, pp.26–27.

87 'William to Harry', 16 Jun 1883, Derry Family Letters.

88 'William to Harry', 13 Apr 1884, Derry Family Letters.

89 'William to Harry', 4 Dec 1884, Derry Family Letters.

90 'William to Harry', 8 Apr 1885, Derry Family Letters. The surviving correspondence ends there.

91 Kathleen's father Harold Beauchamp was married to Edith's sister Annie. The reception was held at the Beauchamps' Karori residence, Chesney Wold. *Evening Post*, 28 Oct 1897, p.5.

92 *Auckland Star*, 23 Apr 1931, p.3. My thanks

to Elizabeth Cox for alerting me to these later details of William's life.

93 Chauncey, *Gay New York*, p.113.

94 Phillips, *A Man's Country*, p.98; Ben Schrader, 'Children and Sport – Early Sport', *Te Ara*, www.teara.govt.nz/en/children-and-sport/page-1 (accessed 11 Apr 2016).

95 Caroline Daley, *Leisure and Pleasure: Reshaping and Revealing the New Zealand Body 1900–1960*, Auckland University Press, Auckland, 2003, pp.21–23, 42–54.

96 Chauncey, *Gay New York*, p.114.

97 The 21st-century city professionals who lift weights in gymnasiums at lunchtimes or enter half marathons are the modern inheritors of the cult.

98 His biographer wrote that 'Through his public spirit and diverse talents he had contributed greatly to Dunedin and New Zealand.' E. Yvonne Speirs, 'Thomson, George Malcolm', *Te Ara*, www.teara.govt.nz/en/biographies/2t40/thomson-george-malcolm (accessed 11 Apr 2016).

99 As Miles Fairburn succinctly puts it: 'In a primary-producing country, town economies were artificial.' Fairburn, *The Ideal Society*, p.55.

100 Neill Atkinson, *Adventures in Democracy: A History of the Vote in New Zealand*, University of Otago Press, Dunedin, 2003, p.73.

101 Plural voting was abolished in 1889. Each country member now represented, on average, a population of 4,903, compared to 6,537 in urban electorates. Ibid., p.74.

102 Richard Taylor, 16 Jul 1889, *New Zealand Parliamentary Debates (NZPD)*, Vol. 64, p.455.

103 Atkinson, *Adventures in Democracy*, p.76.

104 See Fig 8.4.

105 Atkinson, *Adventures in Democracy*, p.158.

106 Walter Symes, 2 Jun 1903, *NZPD*, Vol. 123, p.94.

107 Hamer, *The New Zealand Liberals*, p.169.

108 William Hutchison, 20 Jul 1892, *NZPD*, Vol. 75, p.606.

109 Belich, *Paradise Reforged*, p.152.

110 Frederick Baume, 27 Oct 1909, *NZPD*, Vol. 147, p.630. The sentiment echoed the American politician William Jennings Bryan's famous 'Cross of Gold' speech of 1893. It included this famous passage: 'I tell you that the great cities rest upon the broad and fertile prairie. Burn down your cities and leave our farms, and your cities will spring up again as if by magic. But destroy our farms and grass will grow in the streets of every city in the country.' Conn, *Americans Against the City*, p.18.

111 Hamer, *The New Zealand Liberals*, p.171.

112 Ibid., pp.177–80.

113 Gael Ferguson, *Building the New Zealand Dream*, Dunmore Press, Palmerston North, 1994, pp.42–44.

114 *Supplement to the New Zealand Herald*, 26 Sept 1903, p.1.

115 A. R. Barclay, 'Evidence to Land Commission', *AJHR*, 1905, C-4, p.326, cited in Ferguson, *Building the New Zealand Dream*, p.43.

116 *Supplement to the New Zealand Herald*, 26 Sept 1903, p.1.

117 Hamer, The *New Zealand Liberals*, p.181.

118 William Pember Reeves, *State Experiments in Australia and New Zealand, Vol. 1*, Macmillan of Australia, South Melbourne, 1969 edn, pp.360–61.

119 In 1910 the Christchurch MP, George Russell, expressed exasperation at this representation, stating townspeople 'were constantly being told it was people living in the country districts that made New Zealand, and that the city population … were a kind of parasite living on people who were on the soil. It was quite time they [the critics] realized that the men in the cities had their activities in connection with the Dominion as well as the men who lived in the soil … it was the people in the cities who manufactured the raw material, who acted as bankers and financed the country people, and without them the country people would have a very bad time.' George Russell, 17 Aug 1910, *NZPD*, Vol. 150, p.671.

120 *Southland Times*, 12 Feb 1885, p.2.

121 *Waikato Times*, 28 Mar 1885, p.2.

122 *Otago Witness*, 24 Jul 1890, p.38.

123 *Otago Witness*, 9 Feb 1899, pp.51–52.

124 The debate continued into the 20th century.

Some of the more strident views were carried in *Star*, 18 May 1901, p.3, and *Hawera & Normanby Star*, 16 Sep 1907, p.5.

125 Office of the Parliamentary Commissioner for the Environment, *The Cities and their People: New Zealand's Urban Environment*, Wellington, 1998, p.11.

126 James H. Liu, Tim McCreanor, Tracey McIntosh and Teresia Teaiwa, 'Introduction: Constructing New Zealand Identities', in James H. Liu, Tim McCreanor, Tracey McIntosh, Teresia Teaiwa (eds), *New Zealand Identities: Departures and Destinations*, Victoria University Press, Wellington, 2005, pp.14, 19.

127 Māori urbanisation is habitually considered in general histories. Two important monographs on the topic are: Patricia Grace, Irihapeti Ramsden and Jonathan Dennis, *The Silent Migration, Ngāti Poneke Young Māori Club 1927–1948*, Huia, Wellington, 2001, and Melissa Matutina Williams, *Panguru and the City: Kāinga Tahi, Kāinga Rua: An Urban Migration History*, Bridget Williams Books, Wellington, 2015. The study of New Zealand urbanisation has been largely the domain of geographers, particularly in the 1960s and 70s, when a major output was R.J. Johnston, *Urbanisation in New Zealand: Geographical Essays*, Reed Education, Wellington, 1973.

128 Of the general histories, Erik Olssen in the first volume of the first *Oxford* history and Paul Star and Angela Wanhalla in the *New Oxford* history mention urbanisation only in passing. Similarly, Philippa Mein Smith confines the topic to one sentence: 'New Zealanders were more urban than rural by the 1920s.' Erik Olssen, 'Towards a New Society', in W.H. Oliver with B.R. Williams (eds), *The Oxford History of New Zealand*, Oxford University Press, Wellington, 1981, p.251; Paul Star, 'Human and the Environment in New Zealand, c. 1800 to 2000', and Angela Wanhalla, 'Family, Community and Gender', in Byrnes (ed), *The New Oxford History*, pp.60, 461; Philippa Mein Smith, *A Concise History of New Zealand*, Cambridge University Press, Melbourne, 2005, p.141.

129 Ian Pool, 'Population Change – Key Population Trends', *Te Ara*, www.teara.govt.nz/en/population-change/page-1 (accessed 11 Apr 2016).

130 Peter Andersson, *Streetlife in Late Victorian London: The Constable and the Crowd*, Palgrave Macmillan, London, 2015, p.25.

131 *North Otago Times*, 6 Jun 1879, p.1.

132 The claim is a bit misleading. If the population of the four cities is combined, then the proportion of New Zealanders living in cities climbs to 29 per cent in 1901, behind Sydney but ahead of Brisbane. *Evening Post*, 30 Mar 1907, p.9.

133 One reason for this might have been that country life was more socially isolating than in Britain, where farm workers often lived in or near to villages, making it easier for them to socialise with neighbours. In New Zealand, the closest neighbour could be miles away. *Evening Post*, 3 Jan 1908, p.7.

134 Miles Fairburn noted that from the 1890s parents gradually recognised that white-collar occupations were 'sources of material security and social prestige', leading them to push their children into academic school streams that would be a meal ticket to entering the service sector. Fairburn, 'The Rural Myth', p.9.

135 *Otago Witness*, 7 Jul 1909, p.6.

136 *Evening Post*, 17 Jul 1909, p.9.

137 Official statistics showed that in 1909 the New Zealand birth rate was 27.3 per 1,000 people and in the four cities the rate was 27.0 per 1,000 people. Four years earlier the birth rate had actually been higher in cities. *Press*, 5 Sep 1910, p.7; *Evening Post*, 2 Mar 1906, p.5; 25 Jan 1911, p.3; 31 Jan 1911, p.11.

138 People who lived in cities and boroughs were classed as urban and those who lived in counties were rural. It was officially acknowledged that some counties had pockets of urban population, and vice versa, but it was thought these divergent elements balanced each other out. From 1926, urban was officially defined as a settlement with a population of 1,000 or more. The United States adopted 2,500 as its urban threshold in 1910 and some urban historians use this as the standard definition, in which case New Zealand would

not have become an urban society until 1926. Because this is not how urban was understood in colonial New Zealand, I have used the contemporary counties/boroughs distinction. 'Population and Dwellings', *New Zealand Census*, Government Printer, Wellington, 1921, p.54; Frost, *The New Urban Frontier*, p.38.

139 'Population and Dwellings', *New Zealand Census*, 1921, p.55.

140 *Evening Post*, 31 Jan 1911, p.11.

141 *Wanganui Herald*, 31 May 1912, p.4.

142 *Auckland Star*, 14 Apr 1919, p.4.

143 *New Zealand Herald*, 26 Aug 1916, p.1; Ben Schrader, 'A Peaceful Path to Reform: The Garden City/Suburb Movement in New Zealand/Aotearoa, 1900–1930', History 489 Research Essay, Victoria University Wellington, 1991, pp.30–31.

144 *Press*, 6 Sep 1917, p.9.

145 New Zealand Institute of International Affairs, *Contemporary New Zealand: A Survey of Domestic and Foreign Policy*, Whitcombe & Tombs, Wellington, 1938, p.63. The publication was a collection of essays from Sutch and other authors.

146 In September 2015, the Stuff website delivered over 200 hits with the search phrase: 'farmer backbone of country'.

147 John A. Lee's semi-autobiographical *Children of the Poor* (1934) and Robin Hyde's *The Godwits Fly* (1937) have Dunedin and Wellington settings respectively, but whether they have the commanding presence in New Zealand literature as Mander's and Mulgan's books is a moot point.

148 Pound, *The Invention of New Zealand*, p.179.

149 John Mulgan, *Man Alone*, Paul's Book Arcade, Hamilton, 1960 edn, p.30.

150 Lauris Edmond (ed.), *The Letters of A.R.D. Fairburn*, Oxford University Press, Auckland, 1981, pp.62–63, cited in Pound, *The Invention of New Zealand*, p.179.

151 He lived in suburban New Lynn and then Devonport, supporting the point that it was townspeople who most idealised rural life. Denys Trussell, 'Fairburn, Arthur Rex Dugard', *Te Ara*, www.teara.govt.nz/en/ biographies/4fn/fairburn-arthur-rex-dugard (accessed 11 Apr 2016).

152 A.R.D. Fairburn, 'The Women Problem', in Denis Glover and Geoffrey Fairburn (eds), *The Woman Problem and Other Prose*, Blackwood & Janet Paul, Auckland, 1967, p.24, cited in Pound, *The Invention of New Zealand*, p.180.

153 The topic is considered further in my *Te Ara* entry on city images, www.teara.govt.nz/ en/city-images, but it is worthy of further research.

154 Martin, *The Forgotten Worker*, pp.197–98; James Watson, 'Farm Mechanisation', *Te Ara*, www.teara.govt.nz/en/farm-mechanisation (accessed 11 Apr 2016).

Conclusion

1 The historian Lionel Frost has shown that between 1871 and 1911, only Argentina's urban population grew at a greater rate than New Zealand's. Lionel Frost, *The New Urban Frontier: Urbanisation and City Building in Australasia and the American West*, New South Wales University Press, Kensington, 1991, p.38.

2 *National Business Review*, 2 Nov 2012, www.nbr.co.nz/article/kiwi-ad-icon-axed-vy-p-131741 (accessed 20 Sep 2015).

Index